NEW PERSPECTIVES ON POLISH CULTURE

New Perspectives on Polish Culture

Personal Encounters, Public Affairs

Edited by

Tamara Trojanowska,
Artur Płaczkiewicz,
Agnieszka Polakowska,
and Olga Ponichtera

PIASA BOOKS
New York

Published by PIASA Books
The Polish Institute of Arts and Sciences of America
208 East 30th St., New York, NY 10016

Library of Congress Cataloging-in-Publication Data

New perspectives on Polish culture : personal encounters, public affairs / edited by Tamara Trojanowska ... [et al.].
p. cm.
ISBN 978-0-940962-73-6
1. Poland—Civilization—20th century.
2. Poland—Intellectual life.
3. Polish literature—History and criticism.
4. Arts and society—Poland.
I. Trojanowska, Tamara.
DK4115.N49 2012
943.805–dc23 2012000908

www.piasa.org/pb.html
Printed in the United States of America

Contents

CONTENTS

CONTENTS

Acknowledgments

The incentive to collate this volume of essays was born out of the success of an international conference, "In Search of (Creative) Diversity: New Perspectives in Polish Literary and Cultural Studies Abroad," which was held at the University of Toronto in February 2006. This conference was organized and hosted by the editors of this volume, and has since become an important biannual event for Polish Studies in North America. Its two further renderings found their home at Indiana University in 2008, and the University of Michigan at Ann Arbor in 2010. The conference also initiated a few collaborative projects—a forthcoming book, *A History of Polish Culture: New Perspectives on the Twentieth and Twenty-First Centuries*, and a translation series—strengthening and creating new links among specialists in Polish literature and culture in North America and trans-continentally. Given its success, the idea to publish the conference proceedings quickly turned into a much more focused and problem-specific project, with the present collection being its final result. The articles gathered herein include extended versions of selected works presented at the conference, as well as a few additional, invited articles: together, they all contribute to the discussion of the changing dynamics of Polish culture in the context of European modernity, especially as it pertains to the relationship between private and public realms of human experience.

This volume would not have come to be without the financial cooperation of the main organizers of the conference: the University of Toronto (including the Department of Slavic Languages and Literatures, the Faculty of Arts and Science, the School of Graduate Studies, and the Centre for European, Russian, and Eurasian Studies), Ohio State University (the Center for Slavic and East European Studies, the Polish Studies Center and Russian and East European Institute, and the Office of International Programs), and Jagiellonian University (Katedra Międzynarodowych Studiów Polonistycznych and Wydział Polonistyki). We also want to gratefully acknowledge the support of various Polish organizations in Toronto, including the Council of Canadian Polish Congress for the Support of Polish Studies, the Mickiewicz Foundation, the Reymont Foundation, the Polish Institute of Arts and Sciences in Canada, and the Polish Students' Association at the University of Toronto. A number of Polish businesses in Toronto also extended their financial assistance for the event, among them Artus Polish Bookstore, Master Printing, Pegaz For You, punkt.ca, and Queen Syrena Travel. Finally, two renowned Toronto artists, Daria Beer and the late Jerzy Kołacz, contributed both time and imagination to create the visual face of the 2006 conference.

Our gratitude extends also to our many colleagues who helped both with the conceptualization and the organization of the conference: Professor Halina Stephan of Ohio State University, with whom Professor Tamara Trojanowska first discussed her idea of the conference, and from whom she received (as always) strong words of support and encouragement; Professors Michał Paweł Markowski of the Jagiellonian University (now of the University of Illinois in Chicago), and Bill Johnston of Indiana University–Bloomington; Professor Christina Kramer, the steadfast Chair of the Department of Slavic Languages and Literatures at the University of Toronto, as well as the supporting staff at the time, in particular Toni Eyer and Tomasz Bednarczyk; Professors Justyna Beinek, who was at the time a Mellon Foundation postdoctoral student at our Slavic Department, and Agnieszka Karolczuk of the Catholic University in Lublin, who was a Visiting Lecturer in the Polish Language and Literature Program during 2006; and last but not least, Professor Artur Grabowski of Jagiellonian University, for his generous discussion of the initial concept of this volume during the conference in 2006. Finally, we would like to thank each other and our families for unending support in the long, but fruitful process of getting this manuscript ready for publication.

New Perspectives on Polish Culture

Introduction

Tamara Trojanowska

The importance of the relationship between the public and the private, the shared and the intimate—or in different configurations, between the national, collective, or social and individual—to the dominating strands, strategies, and conflicts of modernity goes without saying. This relationship shapes political systems in their understanding of individualism, freedom, justice, rights, social relations, institutions, and obligations. It has also informed diverse, if often closely related, studies, from the philosophy of human subjectivity and discussions about the place of the self in the world, through the ever-growing interest in identity politics, to the explorations of temporal and spatial relations and their impact on individual perception of the world, social issues, and economic justice.

On the one hand, the tensions inherent in this relationship give rise to the quintessentially modern conviction of the oppressive nature of social structures and institutions in relation to individual freedom, and of the unquestionable need for ceaseless emancipatory actions.[1] On the other, they incite arguments in favor of necessary renegotiations of individual freedom and social responsibility, self-reliance and engagement, and autonomy and dependency in the relationship between individuals and modern society.[2]

The frictions between private and public realms relate directly to discourses and politics of identity, both collective and individual.[3] In his discussion of community, Zygmunt Bauman recalls the remarks of Eric Hobsbawm and Jock Young concerning the correlation between the disappearing community and the invention of identity.[4] Conversely, in his magisterial study *Sources of the Self: The Making of the Modern Identity*, Charles Taylor points out the links between the community and the making of modern identity in the notions of human good and ordinary life. The tensions between public, collective identifications (whether they are linked to religion, nationality, ethnicity, race, culture, class, gender, or sexual orientation), and private, individual identities are of fundamental importance to the process of identity formation, to liberal social ontology, and to the practices of identity politics, including the inherent frictions over its essentialism and separatism. So are the tensions between sameness and difference, homogeneity, heterogeneity, and multiculturalism.[5]

Finally, the intellectual scrutiny of the fluidity of the public-private divide reflects on the changing dynamics of these two aspects of our temporal and spatial interactions with and understanding of the world and other human beings.[6] Such scrutiny sheds light, for example, on the transformations of modern cities and our interactions with their modern architecture, streets, neighborhoods, and transportation systems. It probes the changing possibilities for our participation in public life, and the consequences of our new relationship with our own bodies, technology, and virtual worlds, to mention just a few aspects associated with our temporal and spatial existence.

INTRODUCTION

The greatest strength of the essays presented in this volume is their commitment to critical reinterpretations of the public-private dynamic in the context of interaction between Polish culture and the tensions, ambiguities, and idiosyncrasies of European modernity. The centrality of this dynamic to contemporary Polish culture should come as no surprise. Robbed by the eighteenth-century partitions of the typical nineteenth-century European modernity, and ruined by its twentieth-century totalitarian experiments—Nazism and Communism—Poland emerged twenty years ago free, but deeply scarred. Marred by the discontinuities of its social, political, cultural, and economic structures and networks, and struggling with the neglected, contentious, and deeply divisive narratives of its immediate past, the country remains unsure of its role in the current phase of the European identity-building project and ambivalent in attitudes to its own conflicting traditions. The century-long debates and hostilities between tradition and modernization, and much more important tensions imbedded in different modernizing projects became prominent once Poland gained its historic chance to define itself anew. These tensions now return (with a bite) in daily political commentaries, and are problematized in the context of European and Polish modernity in the crucial works of sociologists and historians of ideas, particularly those of Marek Cichocki, Zdzisław Krasnodębski, Marcin Król, Ryszard Legutko, Andrzej Mencwel, Jadwiga Staniszkis, Paweł Śpiewak, and Andrzej Walicki.[7]

Poland's chance to revisit these issues happens to coincide with major shifts in global postmodern culture, including rapid changes in technology, politics, and the economy, as well as the current project of New Europe. That is to say, the West is no longer the same construct as Poland imagined it to be during its decades-long efforts to be once again embraced by it. It has been remapping itself, literally and metaphorically, under the impact of new cultural, political, and economic concepts and ideas, along with the fluctuations in European (and American) international interests and the discourses that rationalize them. European modernity has entered a new, "liquid," for a lack of a better term, phase.[8] To put it differently, Poland's chance to reclaim its place in the democratic world comes together with the need to comprehend and also actively co-shape the changing cultural, political, and economic landscapes in Europe. This task goes hand in hand with the necessity for Poland to rethink its own identity, traditions, and ambitions for the future, its relation to and problems with modernity, in the context of this changing world—a daunting task, indeed, even if many of the responsibilities that come with it have already been met successfully. The revaluation of the public-private dynamic, which has often been imagined as a dichotomy and as such had a particularly strong footing in Polish culture, is at the very core of such rethinking.

It has been a long-standing—and one may also add, justified—practice in literary criticism and the history of ideas to attribute this unusually deep rift between the public and the private to Romanticism, even though the anti-individualistic democracy of the gentry already played its role in an unusually strong validation of the national and communal ethos.[9] However, it was Romanticism, and later the nineteenth-century novel that in other modern cultures established the importance of the private and confirmed its cultural rights. Maria Janion puts it bluntly: "'The system' of Polish literature was created by Romanticism, which—particularly after the fall of the November Uprising—imposed on Polish culture a certain antinomy, unknown in such an intensity to other modern cultures, and a univocal resolution to it. This antinomy comprised the individual/private and the social/collective. And all the highest grounds were granted solely to the latter side of it."[10] In the same short text, Janion points to Mickiewicz's *Forefathers' Eve, Part IV* as "one of the lost, vanished links of Polish Romanticism" to privacy in need of rehabilitation.[11] It is thus not a coincidence that this volume on the private-public dynamic starts with an analysis of this missing link.

For decades, the Romantic paradigm (in its many variants) has been exercising its grip on the Polish imagination. Those who felt this grip to be crippling have tried to exorcise it repeatedly.[12] However, such exorcisms have encountered paradoxical obstacles for, as Teresa Walas usefully explains, the Romantico-symbolic paradigm managed to embrace all those idealistic national and patriotic discourses that call for the individuals to sacrifice themselves for the benefit of the collective, and thus it effectively disarmed otherwise conflicting ideological projects, as was the case with Polish Positivism and much, though not all, of Polish modernism.[13] Indeed, many of the nineteenth-century thinkers who waged war with the Romantic paradigm, and made the positioning of individual existence in the national and social frameworks one of their battles, fell into this embrace.[14] "Our duels for Romanticism," to quote the title of a 1993 Warsaw conference and its published proceedings, continued in the interwar period under the shared (though applied differently in different corners) banner of the modernization of Polish culture.[15] In the postwar era, such duels first aided the anti-Romantic ideological agenda of the communists, then reflected the westernizing aspirations of the new intelligentsia,[16] and finally proposed philosophically sophisticated and wide-ranging alternatives to the Polish Romatic paradigm and the public-private antagonism generated by it.[17]

Many of the writers who dared such duels figure prominently in this volume. Their uniqueness is found not only in how expertly they problematized the public-private dynamic and its cultural consequences in their works, but also in how courageously they personalized it, made it their own. Such was the case with Jan Lechoń (1899–1956), who in his famous 1920 poem, "Herostrates," asked to see spring in spring (rather than Poland), and who in the end shared the exilic fate and much of his imagination with the Polish Romantics, but under the watchful eyes of the FBI, who by scrutinizing his private life affected the public one as well. Such was also the case with Gombrowicz (1904–1969), another émigré, whose assault on national usurpations and social impositions went hand in hand with his own emancipatory life project; or with

Miron Białoszewski (1922–1983), another great "Other" of Polish literature and a discoverer of the everyday and the ordinary. Finally, Tadeusz Różewicz (b. 1921) can be easily put in this category as a paradoxical keeper of public and private memories, in contrast to Sławomir Mrożek (b. 1930), a successful discoverer of the constructivist concepts of identity in his personal exilic experiment.

Contrary to some expectations, the Romantic paradigm survived Maria Janion's 1996 declaration of its most probable demise in post-1989 Polish culture.[18] In her reply, Teresa Walas thoughtfully traces contemporary continuities of the once lively model so uncompromisingly rejected by most of young Polish culture.[19] However, notwithstanding such continuities (whether with or without difference), one thing remains certain: the strength and the appeal of the universal, idealist imaginarium, and those grand narratives that organize it, has lessened considerably. Our skeptical, mistrustful attitude to them, including history, nation, identity, and communication, and the growing liquidity of such discourses, raise new questions about the relationship between the public and the private, national or social and individual, and finally, between what is shared and what remains intimate. It also seriously challenges the established ways of maintaining cultural continuity and links to the past, while creating new concepts of selfhood, both collective and individual, and reclaiming the gaps, silences, concealments, and erasures in Polish culture.[20] In this volume much attention has been devoted to these current and pressing issues.

II

The volume is divided into five parts, each of which addresses a different set of problems related to the public-private dynamic and their relevance to the main conflicts of modernity in Polish culture. The first three parts propose new theoretical approaches to and interpretations of these dynamics, with a marked focus on tensions between communal, societal, and individualistic understanding of dominant Polish cultural traditions. "Paradigmatic Shifts" concentrates on the dominance of collective paradigms throughout Polish history, and creative ways of either overcoming or subverting their cultural authority. "Experiences of the Self" places emphasis on individual struggles against various pressures generated by the collective,, w whereas "New Dynamics" proposes theoretically informed readings of new cultural phenomena in post-1989 Poland, pointing to new ways in which Polish culture transgresses the private-public divide.

The last two parts refer to the extreme historical experiences of European twentieth-century modernity: World War II and the Holocaust, Communism, and exile— all of which affected Polish culture in especially traumatic ways. They redefined the relationships between the individual and the collective, the communal and the societal, the intimate and the shared, often in a most radical manner. Part 4, entitled "Memory, Trauma, Mourning," discusses these relationships within the well-fitting frameworks of memory and trauma discourses, while part 5, "Transatlantic Connections," incorporates the exilic into the picture, and closes the volume with a text that traces the obliteration of borders in the cross-cultural art of translation. It is best to read these two parts in the context of current discussions about European identity, which apparently requires historical amnesia to free itself from the demonic past of the twentieth century.[21] The focus on memory and mourning, on the ways in which the past is remembered and worked through while remaining an integral part of how we define our own world, counteracts the utopian project of historical amnesia in the name of a conflict-free future, but also defines Polish specificity in the context of European forgetting.

When considered from the point of view of its opening and closing arguments, the volume bridges the nineteenth, twentieth, and twenty-first centuries in Polish culture—from an original reading of its canonical writer, Adam Mickiewicz, and his no-less-canonical work *The Forefathers' Eve*, to a consideration of the poets of the "bruLion" generation, who were the young rebels of the first years of Poland's independence in the 1990s; from the decentering of the prevailing focus on our national bard's collective concerns, to the affirmation of the everyday, the ordinary, and the personal in the young poetry of the 1990s; from a critique of the seemingly untranslatable specificity of Polish problems and the literary works that epitomize them, to a critical reading of cultural osmosis.

When viewed from the perspective of its internal dynamics, this volume offers a broad spectrum of theoretical and philosophical positions, including performance, gender, and postcolonial theories, pragmatism, and recent trauma and memory discourses. It revisits Polish canonical works from both the nineteenth and the twentieth centuries (Mickiewicz and Gombrowicz), and reinterprets their impact on the private-public relationship. With the help of new concepts and approaches, it reads anew the works of such contemporaries as Białoszewski, Mrożek, and Różewicz, authors who have shaped Polish postwar culture, and reimagined public-private tensions. It systematizes public-private dynamics in post-1989 literature within an impressive scope of cultural and political debates about modernization. Finally, it consults archival documents to put under analytical scrutiny marginalized works that can shed a new light on exilic experiences—both public and private.

The essays presented in "Paradigmatic Shifts" analyze the increasingly problematic relationship between individualism and collectivism in Polish culture, and approach its ambiguities primarily in terms of the contentious dominance of collectivism. They challenge such dominance in various ways: Filipowicz through a novel reading of a canonical text against its long-established interpretations; Iłłakowicz by analyzing a potentially subversive use of the dominant Polish cultural model in the discussion of European modernity; Gasyna by comparing early and late modernist visions of a national collective; and Płaczkiewicz by proposing a new reading of an alternative artistic and philosophical attitude to private-public dualism. In all four articles, their authors reinterpret the dynamics between individualism and collectivism in Polish literature by employing new theoretical and philosophical frameworks in the task. These frameworks emphasize both the complexity of the discussed dynamics and the possibilities offered by present-day methodologies to finesse our understanding of it. In consequence, the analyses of shifting paradigms in Polish culture also shift the interpretative potential of the paradigms themselves.

The essential concepts underlying the four essays presented in the next part of the volume, "Experiences of the Self," are human subjectivity, in its relation to body, space, time, and other human beings, and potential ways of transgressing the confines of its relationship with the world. The authors of these articles are concerned primarily with the positioning of the individual vis-à-vis some of the most important challenges of the modern world: be it problematic corporeality and its experiences of the changing notions of space and time, modern reevaluations of spatial and temporal relationships, or the intricate interaction between the self and the other, whether that other is an individual human being, or the social and national collective. The authors privilege instances of transgression in their analyses; they all use relational, intercultural frameworks of comparison, starting from one's own positioning, which is nonetheless constantly directed towards the Other. Tomasz Bilczewski perceives literary and cultural comparison as fundamentally transgressive; Benjamin Paloff builds his comparative case about shame and doubling in Central European prose on the human need and inability to transgress his or her being; Artur Grabowski traces the transgressive potential of individual self-awareness and self-creation in relation to dominant paradigms; and Joanna Niżyńska probes the artistic and philosophical consequences of transgressing temporal dualisms.

The five articles that follow in the next part, "New Dynamics," all share a common goal: to identify and map out the various factors involved in shaping the culture of present-day Poland. The analytical spotlight of each essay falls on a different issue, of course. Przemysław Czapliński focuses on literary representations of "Solidarity" in the last three decades of Polish prose; Tamara Trojanowska looks at the social and cultural contexts of the spectacular successes of young drama; Jerzy Jarzębski's attention is directed toward the formation and function of a literary canon; and Magdalena Kay explores the potential of applying postcolonial theory in a Polish context, while Dariusz Skórczewski uses that framework in his reading of a particular novel. Despite these overt differences, both the manner in which each author approaches his or her chosen subject matter and the conclusions that they draw from their analyses reveal a number of parallels that merit critical attention. While individually the articles presented herein offer new and worthwhile insights into specific aspects of Polish cultural life, linking the points at which they overlap and intersect serves as a useful, albeit incomplete outline of the prevalent frameworks in which Polish culture is currently conceptualized.

The essays collected under the heading "Memory, Trauma, Mourning" use testimonies and memory of life in extremis during the Second World War and the Holocaust as the main frame of reference for their reflections on ways in which traumatic personal and collective historical experiences are processed and reconciled. Central to these essays are the ethical and aesthetic problems connected with artistic renderings of these experiences. The relationship between the private and the public, the individual and the collective, and the personal and the historical proves to be particularly relevant in this context, since traumas lived through and experienced individually often need collective processing to attain psychological, cultural, or historical closure. The conditions necessary for such closure are discussed in a broad—national and postcolonial—context (Thompson), in light of the unavoidable tensions between commemoration and remembering (Ponichtera), with the help of current memory theory and psychoanalysis (Gluhovic), and finally with reference to modernist aporias (Shallcross).

The last part of this volume, "Transatlantic Connections," explores the exilic dimension of the private-public dynamic and the intercultural options of cultural exchange. As earlier essays by George Gasyna, Krystyna Iłłakowicz, and Artur Grabowski contend, exile may provide an individual with a welcome refuge or liberation from collective and communal expectations and pressures. Such was clearly the case with the exilic experience of both Gombrowicz and Mrożek. However, exile may also have a reverse effect, for frequently the resulting exilic communities act to strengthen their grip on the individual by way of fortifying the collective ethos in the face of the "otherness" of the host society, in defense of its imagined identity. Such a preservationist mode of collective existence can lead to many tensions between generations, genders, ethnicities, and cultures, particularly with regard to the official institutions, laws, and politics of the host country. Such tensions complicate relationships within the community, while intensifying the potential conflicts between an individual and the collective.

III

To anyone following public discourse in Poland, it is clear that Polish culture has already successfully engaged in the intellectual ferments of late modernity, such as poststructuralism, deconstruction, gender and postcolonial studies, and feminism (to name a few of the usual suspects), making their main theoreticians and ideas a regular presence in academic writing and education, literary, theatre, and art criticism, and ideological debates. As the present volume attests, the exchange between intellectuals working abroad and in Poland in the field of Polish Studies is fruitful for both parties, for their interpretive perspectives and the contexts in which they apply the aforementioned tools differ from those commonly encountered in the Western world, opening a new, third space for intellectual cross-fertilization. It is the hope that the essays collected here will contribute further to this process, which has sustained the editors of this volume during the sometimes difficult, but always stimulating task of putting it together.

Notes

1. Thinkers such as Friedrich Nietzsche, Sigmund Freud, and Michel Foucault all propose distinct ways of overcoming such oppression, while noticing different limitations to the prospects of full emancipation. Gilles Deleuze and Félix Guattari complicate the matter further with such concepts as schizoanalysis, rhizomatics, and nomadism in their analysis of the relationship between the modern individual, nation-state, and capitalism.

2. This point is argued by such diverse communitarians (who are often uncomfortable with this label) as Alasdair MacIntyre, Robert Putnam, Michael Sandel, Charles Taylor, or Michael Walzer. Andrzej Szahaj summarizes the debate between liberalism and communitarianizm in Poland in his book, *Jednostka czy wspólnota? Spór liberałów z komunitarystami a "sprawa polska."*

3. Collective identity has an overwhelming bibliography that encompasses nation, religion, ethnicity, gender, and sexual orientation, among many other group and collective designations. Anthony D. Smith's *National Identity* is a particularly useful introduction to the problem. For a unique take on the issue of national character that links public and private, see Antoni Kępiński (1918–1972), a practicing psychiatrist and philosopher, who developed a concept of "energetic informational metabolism" that connected human subjectivity to social experiences, consciousness to biology, and allowed him to use individual psychopathology to make claims about national character. Kępiński's axiological psychiatry influenced Józef Tischner (1931–2000), another important force in Polish discussion about the self-world dynamic, and his philosophy of dialogue, meeting, and drama.

4. Bauman, *Community*, 15.

5. These tensions have been scrutinized in the works of some of the most influential European theorists, such as Michel Foucault in his *History of Sexuality*; Deleuze, whose concept of difference developed in *Difference and Repetition*; and the poststructuralists, with their insistence on the subject being the product of discourse (for example in Judith Butler's *Gender Trouble: Feminism and the Subversion of Identity*). They have been envisioned as a confrontation between two strong human desires, one for individual uniqueness, the other for mimetic imitation in René Girard's *Violence and the Sacred*, have been analyzed in Taylor's *Multiculturalism and the Politics of Recognition*, or by the complex and diversified postcolonial discourse of the same/other binary that informs Edward Said's seminal *Orientalism* or Gayatri Spivak's *The Postcolonial Critic*.

6. The reading list for this aspect of modernity could start with Walter Benjamin's essay on Baudelaire and his masterly analysis of the concept of

the *flâneur*, as well as with his *Arcades Project*, which analyzes the relationship between the outside and the inside in the context of the process of commodification and its impact on our experience of history, and it could close with Peter Sloterdijk's *Spheres*.

7. The most interesting works in this debate include: Cichocki, *Pamięć i władza*; Krasnodębski, *Demokracja peryferii* and *Drzemka rozsądnych*; Król, *Patriotyzm przyszłości* and *Romantyzm: piekło i niebo Polaków*; Legutko, *Esej o duszy polskiej*; Mencwel, *Przedwośnie czy potop*; Staniszkis, *Postkomunizm: próba opisu*; Śpiewak, *Spór o Polskę 1989–99* and *Polska jedna czy wiele?*; and Walicki, *Polskie zmagania z wolnością*.

8. See Bauman, *Liquid Modernity*.

9. Discussions about the strengths and weaknesses of the gentry paradigm shaped Polish political thought from the Renaissance on, to recall Karol Frycz Modrzewski's (1503–72) *On the Reform of the Commonwealth* (1551) and Piotr Skarga's (1536–1612) *Sermons to the Diet* (1597). For the outline of the three traditions in Polish patriotism, see Walicki, *Three Traditions*.

10. Janion, *Tragizm, historia, prywatność*, 446; my translation.

11. Ibid., 448.

12. See, for example, Piwińska; Bieńczyk and Siwicka; Łukaszuk and Seweryn; and an excellent essay by Walas.

13. See Walas, and also Rymkiewicz, "Hodujmy róże!" (particularly for his views on Polish modernism).

14. Whether they proposed alternative visions of work, art, and history, like Cyprian Kamil Norwid (1821–83), the closest of kin to the Romantics, or Stanisław Wyspiański (1869–1907), the most versatile of Polish modernists; or formulated a new ethos of social engagement, like Aleksander Świętochowski (1849–1938), Wacław Nałkowski (1851–1911), Ludwik Krzywicki (1859–1941), Stefan Żeromski (1864–1925), and Stanisław Brzozowski (1878–1911)–all so compellingly presented by Bohdan Cywiński in *Rodowody niepokornych*, the once most influential book about Polish nineteenth-century intellectual traditions.

15. The need to finally dispose of national obligations of literature, for example, afflicted such diverse poetic groups as Skamander, the Cracow avantgarde, and the futurists. Boy-Żeleński (1874–1941) promoted social and cultural liberalism, while Witold Gombrowicz (1904–69) combated the crippling effect of national and social forms (both traditional and modern) on individual existence.

16. Writers like Stanisław Grochowiak (1934–76) or Sławomir Mrożek.

17. In the works of Gombrowicz (particularly in his *Diary*), Miron Białoszewski, and Tadeusz Różewicz, for example.

18. See Janion, "Zmierzch paradygmatu." Janion herself is a scholar whose research "on the 'internal man' (e.g., in *Transgressions* published in Gdańsk) could go only so far because it was countering a 'historical man'; it was responding to one extreme with another and it was rescuing what was then endangered." Bieńczyk, my translation.

19. See Walas. For the analysis of Polish contemporary prose, see Czapliński's *Polska do wymiany* and his text in this volume.
20. See, for example, Gosk and Karwowska.
21. See, for example, Sloterdijk and Staniszkis.

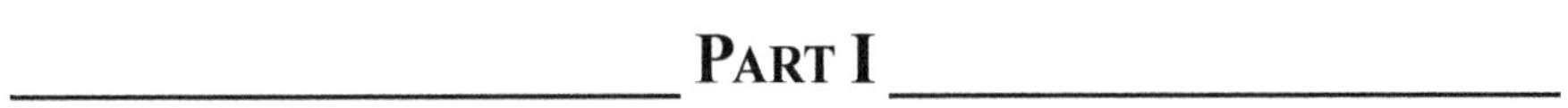

Part I

Paradigmatic Shifts

What's Love Got to Do with It?

Adam Mickiewicz's *Forefathers' Eve, Part 4* and the Art of Transgressing the Private/Public Divide

Halina Filipowicz

For well over a century, the image of Adam Mickiewicz has been so closely intertwined in Polish culture with a certain idea of masterful authorship and authority that the phrase "Mickiewiczean authority" is nearly a redundancy. What does *Mickiewiczean* mean if not *authoritative*? But what, in the context of a discussion of public and private spheres in this volume, does the persistence of Mickiewicz's authoritativeness mean?

At first glance, the answer is obvious. It is a commonplace of Polish literary studies that Mickiewicz, in his canonical drama *Forefathers' Eve* (*Dziady*), has authorized a paradigm of the private/public divide for modern Polish culture.[1] Part 4 of *Forefathers' Eve* insistently focuses on the private at the expense of, and in opposition to, any notion of the community or collective life. It shows a young man named Gustaw who at some previous time fell completely—perhaps the right word is "irretrievably"—in love, but the object of his love, Maryla, soon afterward entered a marriage of convenience with another man.[2] Emotionally wounded and ambivalent, Gustaw pours out his sorrows to his interlocutor, the Priest, who suspects his sanity. In part 3, which in Mickiewicz's ordering of the play comes after part 4, Gustaw metamorphoses thoroughly, if somewhat miraculously, into Konrad: a self-proclaimed leader of patriotic resistance to foreign occupation, who shuns private concerns in favor of political aspirations. While lovesick Gustaw seems to be speaking from a position of powerlessness, Konrad's empowering authority makes sure that history does not appear as a process entirely beyond the control of its victims.[3]

Intriguingly, the patriotic mandate to put the public good before private concerns and, if need be, to risk one's life for one's homeland receives a curious twist in *Forefathers' Eve*. That is to say, the issue here is not the familiar gap between the private man and his public role. Rather, *Forefathers' Eve* sets the stakes higher by insisting on the "originary" act of the protagonist's symbolic suicide: in the prologue to part 3, the private man, Gustaw, must die so that the public man, Konrad, may be born. It is not enough, in other words, to give up private life temporarily, or to serve the public cause only part-time. In the world of the play, finding a balance between the private and public modes of existence does not seem to be an option. Instead, the protagonist must forfeit his private self because the public good requires his undivided attention. It is difficult to avoid the conclusion that the play deems political activism necessarily superior to personal, intimate concerns; therefore it draws an impassable boundary line between the private and public spheres.[4]

It would be reasonable, if a little glib, to suggest that Mickiewicz's protagonist moves from obsessive self-absorption and introspection to public engagement, from melancholy to politics, from the passive to the active precisely because Maryla's betrayal opens a deep wound, a wound that never heals properly. At first, Gustaw can be seen as a melancholic who is talking to drown his pain and to come to terms with the loss of a woman he loves. As he is talking, however, the loss of his lover, of access to love, activates and is contiguous with a sense of his other losses—of his parents, of his childhood home, of the world he remembers, and, ultimately, of cultural stability. There is perhaps a concatenation of traumatic experiences, of literal and figurative deaths, in part 4. But the argument that the agony of unrequited love produces a sense of loss greater, or at least other, than the one caused by the initial trauma can go only so far. It certainly would be naive to invoke a common didactic embellishment of classroom commentary on *Forefathers' Eve*, which claims that the lovelorn protagonist of part 4 grows in the course of his private ordeal, and learns to channel his energies into political action.

Obsessive, driven, wilfully enigmatic, Gustaw is difficult to grasp. Given the strains and stresses of Poland's political circumstances in the nineteenth and twentieth centuries, however, it is hardly surprising that Polish readers and playgoers have accepted Gustaw's transformation into Konrad as inevitable, and that part 3 of *Forefathers' Eve* has come to be considered the definitive Polish embodiment of the Ciceronian imperative of country before self, along with its moral calculus that determines the relation of events to an individual's actions and failures to act.[5] Admittedly, Konrad's patriotic engagement is not without problems, which scholars typically attribute to his hubris.[6] But they are willing to overlook his imperfections precisely because they regard him as a brilliant individual stretched on the rack of his powerful imagination, and goaded to high heaven by the trials of being a full-time patriot. Theatre artists concur with this opinion. Consequently, Konrad is still the ultimate "personality role" in Polish theatre. While such Romantic dramas as Byron's *Manfred* and *Cain* and Shelley's *The Cenci* and *Prometheus Unbound* are perceived as dated and dispensable, part 3 of *Forefathers' Eve* shows no signs of vanishing into historical inertia.[7]

Commentators find it more difficult to ignore Gustaw's perceived shortcomings. As Kazimierz Mężyński points out, several generations of scholars have pursued with energy an interpretive approach that presents Gustaw as a character myopically focused on the private mode of existence, as if an essential part of his identity was to be entirely unconcerned with any collective identity.[8] In a magisterial study that has had a far-reaching impact on Mickiewicz scholarship, Juliusz Kleiner argues that part 4 ultimately exposes "Gustaw's antisocial egotism."[9] Zofia Szmydtowa goes even further. She contrasts Gustaw's sentimental self-absorption with the traditional social emphasis on active virtue. An enormously gifted man, he has "wasted" his talents and therefore has failed society. Gustaw's life, Szmydtowa concludes, is "a failure."[10] But the harshest verdict comes from Konrad Górski. In a richly historicized analysis of the ethical framework of part 4, he contends that Mickiewicz "condemns" those who "lock themselves in a realm of individual experience, to the detriment of society."[11] Part 4 thus depends not only on a representation of Gustaw's psychic trauma, but also on the idea that Gustaw's pain is a form of "punishment for his transgression against society."[12]

It goes almost without saying, then, that part 4 has not received the same attention in scholarship as part 3. Though such oversights may be innocent, they signal the hermeneutical difficulty of recognizing concerns that fall outside the purview of prevalent cultural and critical paradigms. Granted, we have important studies on selected aspects of part 4, chief among them its much-vaunted lyrical poetry. But the point of such commentary is usually to reassert the superiority of the political part 3 over the notoriously personal part 4, which conveys Gustaw's most intimate thoughts and feelings, his morbid, sometimes masochistic preoccupations with lovesickness and despair, and his misanthropic sentiments and necrophiliac urges.

For the most part, as I have been arguing here, scholars have accepted the private/public divide as the defining, central feature of *Forefathers' Eve*. A notable exception to this general tendency is an article by Irena Grudzińska Gross, "Adam Mickiewicz: A European from Nowogródek." She questions the axiomatic disjunction between the private and public realms in *Forefathers' Eve* by contending that the causes of Gustaw's trauma are political as well as personal. In her interpretation, "the fundamental quality" that defines Gustaw is "the loss of historical continuity," brought about by the political ravages of the late eighteenth century, particularly the French Revolution and the partitioning of the Polish-Lithuanian Commonwealth.[13] Having witnessed the dissolution of his homeland, metonymically represented by the ruins of his ancestral home, he is doomed to live "in a suspended state, as though he had emerged from a cataclysm."[14] In other words, he is an unwilling participant in a European spectacle for which history wrote the script. Read in this light, part 4 of *Forefathers' Eve* demonstrates Mickiewicz's art of transforming historical crisis into the troubled experience of an individual caught between past and future.

Grudzińska Gross's article goes a long way toward calling into question the familiar bifurcation in *Forefathers' Eve* scholarship, which claims that Gustaw is haunted by personal history, Konrad by Polish history, and which, accordingly, casts parts 4 and 3 as two contrary sets of events: psychic events in part 4, and political events in part 3. To complicate matters even further, it should be noted that Gustaw is not only a victim of the revolutionary changes that swept across Europe in the late eighteenth century, but also a potential revolutionary. His attitude toward the Priest in particular, and the Catholic clergy in general, is by turns aloof, contemptuous, sarcastic and plainly rude, rather than deferential—in short, insistently antiauthoritarian.[15] Moreover, cross-dressed across class lines in a peasant coat (*sukmana*), Gustaw vents his rage against the rich and their insidious power; brandishing a dagger, he threatens to overturn the hierarchies of status, authority, and economic privilege.

In a much longer study, it would be possible to examine the entire text of *Forefathers' Eve* in order to argue that the private/public divide, or the distinction between the personal and the sociopolitical, is ultimately unsatisfactory as an explanatory model for *Forefathers' Eve* because it is simply too crude an instrument—too rigid and totalizing—for understanding the complicated ways in which the play engages with the concepts of the private and the public.[16] To offer an alternative, nonbinary reading of the shape-shifting, threshold-crossing, and boundary-violating figure of Gustaw/Konrad, for example, it would be necessary to consider the full implications of the fact that, in part 4, Gustaw insinuates himself into another person's home. The visit is frustrating for both guest and host, and yet it suggests that Gustaw is determined to stop seeking silence and isolation. And to stop avoiding the acknowledgment of human interaction is to recognize the solidarity and burden of action in such a way as to end one's separateness.

In lieu of an extended investigation that would encompass all of Mickiewicz's drama, I will concentrate on part 4. I hope to shed new light on this section of *Forefathers' Eve* by approaching the vexing problem of the relation between the private and the public from a different perspective. Rather than focusing on the political circumstances that affect, tacitly or directly, Gustaw/Konrad, I propose to detour along roads less traveled to look for new insights. Accordingly, it is the Priest, rather than Gustaw, who provides a point of departure for my analysis and interpretation. In a much-reprinted study, Józef Kallenbach asks: "Why does the Hermit [Gustaw] choose the home of the Priest, rather than that of, say, an older lay teacher, to reveal his thoughts and feelings?"[17] One of the main points of Grudzińska Gross's article is that Gustaw turns to the Priest in order to reconstruct, if only imaginatively, "the continuity of tradition whose severing undermines the existence of our hero."[18] She emphasizes that the Priest represents not only a broader continuity of cultural tradition, but also "(though only to a limited degree) a continuity of institutional tradition," that is, the tradition of the Catholic Church.[19] By contrast, Kallenbach views the Priest as a spokesman for an institution that has interrupted the continuity of cultural tradition by banning old folk customs and beliefs, such as the ritual of invoking the spirits of the dead (*dziady*). Kallenbach's answer to his own question, then, may be summed up as follows: Gustaw visits the Priest, rather than one of his lay teachers, to demand on behalf of the dead that the Catholic Church restore the ritual of *dziady*.[20]

To develop a fuller and more complex understanding of the relation between the private and the public in part 4, I want to extend Kallenbach's question by asking: what is the significance (if any) of the fact that Gustaw visits the home of a man who is not only a clergyman, but also a recent widower?[21]

Perhaps the most fruitful strategy to broach this question is to posit a double set of negotiations, involving theatre and performance art.

When I first started working on this project, I assumed that I would be following in the footsteps of Mickiewicz scholars. This study does aim at picking up where these scholars have left off by drawing on an immense trove of accumulated knowledge in Mickiewicz studies. Yet the more I studied part 4, the more convinced I became that to take full advantage of the available knowledge requires that we interrogate some earlier assumptions, and raise questions about what others may have taken for granted. For instance, what is it that still gives part 4 its innovative distinctiveness, a source of continuing interpretive difficulties? Is there anything to be found beneath the familiar excesses of this playtext, its torrential outpouring of speech, coupled with its relative unconcern with plot?

An obvious place to begin examining these questions is the subtitle of *Forefathers' Eve, A Poema*. In modern Polish usage, the term *poema* is typically understood to mean a long poem (*poemat*). Given that *Forefathers' Eve* is a drama in verse, the subtitle makes sense. It is worth remembering, however, that opera reviewers in the early nineteenth century used *poema* as a synonym for libretto.[22] Mickiewicz's teasing designation of *Forefathers' Eve* as a libretto can be seen as an invitation to move away from the strictly literary sense of dramatic writing, but also away from definitions of performance that depend on an artificially narrow sense of the relation between the page and the stage.

This essay challenges at least two major premises of *Forefathers' Eve* scholarship: first, that the study of part 4 can contribute much less than part 3 to how we understand *Forefathers' Eve* and its cultural contents; and second, that part 4 is not a fully developed play but a variation of the lyrical genre, subject to the same rules of interpretation as poetry.[23] I argue not only that closer attention to part 4 might provide for a reappraisal of those aspects of *Forefathers' Eve* and, more broadly, Polish Romantic drama, that remain insufficiently understood, but also that part 4 marks a site of an early exploration of concerns and techniques that are today associated with currents within performance art, as opposed to the traditional art of theatre.

My approach is threefold. I begin by considering the interpretive implications of a recently discovered playbill for a stage production of part 4, which toured the southeastern region of the former Polish-Lithuanian Commonwealth in 1832. Then, drawing on the double sense of the word *performance* (both its narrow sense as theatrical enactment, and its broader sense as behavior), I examine Gustaw's performative activity. I want to argue that part 4 may be understood not only as a work in the tradition of scripted dramatic theatre, but also as a quasi-Austinian "act" that constructs the "reality" of Gustaw through his own (nontheatrical) performance.[24] To be sure, Gustaw's performance art is available to us only in the form of a play. Therefore, I introduce the paradoxical concept of the textual "production" of performance or, more succinctly, textual performance. The paradox here is that the reader's experience of the physical event encoded in a play is at the mercy of the script, yet no readerly attention or critical commentary is able to capture the grain of the performer's voice, the inflections of his/her speech, the grace of his/her body. The concept of textual performance freely acknowledges the perceived incompatibility between text and performance, while inviting us to rethink a simple opposition between the two, or between the paradigms we constitute to frame them.[25] Finally, I return to the problem of the private/public divide by bringing into my analysis the work of the French historian Philippe Ariès, whose rich discussion of a new response to death in European culture during the Romantic era—a response that is best described as an unprecedented, obsessional anxiety about death—relates in interesting ways to the concerns of the present essay.

II

If part 4 of *Forefathers' Eve* is judged to be nondramatic in a manner characteristic of the Romantic era, the judgment must be due to a perception that it fails to exploit the sine qua non of drama: dialogue. Of the 1,285 lines that make up part 4, more than 1,000 are spoken by Gustaw, while the remaining lines are allocated to the Priest and the Priest's children. However, it is more precise to say that part 4 does not simply lack dialogue, but rather declines to presuppose the possibility of communication. The coherent dialogue between Gustaw and the Priest does take place, paradoxically, despite a total absence of communication between the speakers. That said, the sheer weight of Gustaw's words can begin to seem oppressive. He articulates in rich, if circumlocutory detail what it is like to live on after going through a disastrous love affair. It is difficult to avoid the conclusion that part 4 is mainly a protracted monologue, and that, therefore, it was indifferent to the expectations of contemporary audiences. Since we know that this section of *Forefathers' Eve* was performed on the stage in the 1820s and 1830s, it is tempting to assume that it was poorly received by its first audiences.

The complaints about theatre audiences by Romantic playwrights seeking to develop new modes of dramatic writing make it clear that audiences fought back, resisting plays that tampered with their expectations. The distaste that the poets of the Romantic generation had for theatre is well known. For example, Byron was rather proud that he rendered *Manfred "quite impossible for the stage."* He continued: "[M]y intercourse with Drury Lane has given me the greatest contempt [for the stage]. . . . The thing . . . could never be attempted or thought of for the stage. . . . I composed it actually with a *horror* of the stage, and with a view to render the thought of it impracticable."[26]

To examine audience responses to part 4 in the Romantic era, I turn to the evidence discovered by Zbigniew Jędrychowski in a Kiev archive: a playbill for a performance that took place in Kamieniec Podolski on May 30, 1832.[27] The playbill is a major addition to the production history of *Forefathers' Eve*, correcting a widespread misconception that the play was not performed in the nineteenth century. Moreover, Jędrychowski's archival finding gives hope that a poster for an earlier production of part 4, believed to have premiered sometime between 1823 and 1830, will also turn up somewhere in a bundle of old papers.[28] But the issue, as I will argue, goes beyond setting the historical record straight.

As a preface to my discussion of the 1832 playbill, I want to point out that an earlier production of part 4 was staged as a solo performance under the title of *Gustaw*. It starred Seweryn Malinowski, one of the most talented and charismatic actors of his generation. It is Jędrychowski's argument that Malinowski's performances as Gustaw in the 1820s mark "the beginning of the Romantic era in Polish theatre."[29] In 1832, as the Kamieniec Podolski advertisement makes clear, part 4 was presented as a full-cast production. Entitled *Forefathers' Eve*, it featured Malinowski as Gustaw and a supporting cast of five.

What caught my attention in the 1832 playbill was the information that part 4 was performed at the request of audience members. It would be reasonable to assume that they wanted to see part 4 on the stage because they had admired it on the page. But the issue is not so simple. There is voluminous evidence documenting not only theatre audiences' praise for Malinowski's virtuoso acting, but also the powerful hold that his solo performances as Gustaw had on the imagination of his contemporaries. For example, in an age when actors, particularly actors working in the provinces, were typically treated as social outcasts, Malinowski's portraits graced the walls of countless upper-class homes in the southeast of the former Commonwealth.[30] So it is not too far-fetched to assume that those who wanted to see Malinowski play Gustaw again in 1832 had been deeply taken by his legendary solo performances in the 1820s.[31] The audiences' enthusiastic endorsement of Malinowski's *Gustaw*, in other words, was not a passing fancy.

That endorsement challenges the historian of drama and theatre to think creatively and humbly about the possibility of ever making sense of the past. Part 4, short on action but long on monologues, seems hardly a play at all. Gustaw tells his story in flashes—an action rapidly framed, a picture that creates a sudden insight. It is as if a door has been opened, then slammed shut again by an unseen hand. Not surprisingly, there is a general consensus in *Forefathers' Eve* scholarship that part 4 is "an impetuous torrent of poems."[32] In other words, the ostensible subject of the plot in part 4—Gustaw's loss of love and his lavish suffering—is only recounted rather than fully dramatized. And yet Malinowski's *Gustaw* held audiences in thrall, even though he acted solo, without a supporting cast. Later, he capitalized on his stock of experience with *Gustaw* to make a full-cast version of part 4 work on the stage.

How to account for the passionate intensity of the contemporary engagement with a play that is widely regarded today as the least stageable section of *Forefathers' Eve?* To ask this question is to train our attention on the rising cult of Mickiewicz in the wake of the publication of part 4 in 1823. Malinowski's solo performances, however, challenge those approaches to drama that give sovereignty to the playwright's text over performance. To perform *Gustaw*, Malinowski had to refashion Mickiewicz's text into a monodrama by eliminating the other roles in part 4. In short, Malinowski's production did not claim to sustain Mickiewicz's textual authority. "Yet when a production 'works,'" as Robert Hapgood argues, "it is in large part because text and performance have meshed, sometimes to the point where the two seem indistinguishable."[33] In his response to Hapgood, W. B. Worthen contends that while some productions "work" by "rendering a seamless sense of identity between play and performance . . . , there are other productions that 'work' by rendering their distance from conventional understandings of 'the play.'"[34]

Everything we know about Malinowski's *Gustaw* indicates that his solo presentations of part 4 did "work." One reviewer, writing in 1840, compared Malinowski's display of virtuosic performing skills in *Gustaw* to "Paganini's violin."[35] That is to say, text and performance meshed. Since Malinowski took considerable liberties with Mickiewicz's text, however, *Gustaw* worked not by being faithful to a conventional understanding of the play, but by replacing the play with Malinowski's own performance text within a historically particular theatrical and cultural space. In other words, *Gustaw* was more than simply fashionable; it encapsulated new structures of feeling, a new model of sensitivity, a new phenomenology of self and other. In so doing, it made a seminal contribution to what might be called "the fabrication of Romantic sensitivity."[36] This, I believe, is what Jędrychowski means when he says that Malinowski's *Gustaw* inaugurated the Romantic era in Polish theatre.

Closer attention to part 4, arguably the foundational text of Polish Romantic theatre and drama, provides an opportunity for accommodating phenomena that literary historians have found puzzling, such as the enigmatic and elusive figure of Gustaw. It also provides the occasion for the formulation of questions about those aspects of Polish Romantic drama and theatre that remain poorly understood. My interest, however, is not only historical. As Hapgood points out, "it is dramatists who have generally led the way" in inspiring innovations in performance "for their own times and those to come."[37] While recognizing Malinowski's path-breaking work on part 4 and the encompassing emotional power of his virtuoso performances as Gustaw, I now want to examine the remarkably generative playtext that inspired him to develop new modes of theatrical behavior.

III

Part 4 of *Forefathers' Eve* is both theatrical and antitheatrical. Its theatrically oriented design is not difficult to see: the ratio of visual information to spoken lines is surprisingly high for poetic drama.[38] Part 4, in other words, emphatically demonstrates that it exists within a genre framework that is sensitive to the requirements of the theatrical medium. Or, to be more precise, part 4 insistently reminds us that theatre is a physical rather than primarily verbal art; therefore it is not enough to engage literature as an interpretive institution for the recuperation of the meaning of drama.

To say that the fictional character of Gustaw is a role to be enacted by an actor on the stage is to suggest the obvious. However, Gustaw's character is not limited to the persona of a betrayed and discarded lover who spends his time mourning unrequited love. The sufferer who, within the illusion of the play, would seem to be the most "real" person on the stage begins to appear pale, superficial, even fussily garrulous, while Gustaw takes on the personae of an actor-manager who runs the show as well as an actor-spectator who admires his own power to hold center stage.[39] As a result, an actor cast as Gustaw must switch back and forth between at least three overlapping yet distinct roles. While part 4 may appear straightforward in literary terms, then, the acting talents required to carry it off are considerable. Because of the different levels of action, it demands both virtuoso role-playing and role-breaking, which go beyond the art of the actor who lives his character from within and conceals this duplicity while he is on the stage.

As a means of rounding out my theatre-centered approach, I want to take a closer look at how part 4 achieves its theatrical effects. When he insinuates himself into the Priest's modest household on a stormy evening, Gustaw could not have chosen a better moment. His unexpected arrival interrupts a comfortable domestic routine, and thus provides an understandable *frisson*. But it also creates enough apprehension to keep his audience—the Priest and the Priest's children—on edge. Moreover, in order to engage their attention, the intruder does not neglect the simple but direct visual impact that costume can make. He has bits of leaves and grass in his hair, and his clothing—a fantastic dress of rags, silk, ribbons, and beads—looks as if it has been lifted from an old farce. In short, Gustaw presents himself as a cross between a scarecrow and a monstrous apparition, even though one might expect a chronic melancholic to wear solemn black. As the action unfolds, he does odd things, baffling as well as amusing. At one point, for example, he brings in an evergreen branch and introduces it as if it were a person. Time and again, he bursts into song. Furthermore, he emerges as a master of theatrical contrivance, captivating his audience with his technical stunts, such as ventriloquizing voices and blowing out candles while standing several feet away. He is a kind of illusionist: his greatest feat is a conversation with a spirit that lives in a chest of drawers; his last trick is the classic one of vanishing. When the clock strikes midnight in the final scene, he disappears as mysteriously as he appeared.

Though weak, vulnerable, and prone to depression, then, Gustaw holds the stage. Against a world that has failed him, he deploys the powerful weapon of words. He also deploys the powerful weapon of theatrical performance.

With remarkable self-discipline and stamina, he stages a magnetic theatrical event that gives him authority and protection. It is he who frames the narrative, he who shapes the action, he, if you like, who midwives his own text. His is a very public persona: theatrical, self-consciously paradoxical, both naive and faux naive, seemingly spontaneous and confessional, but artfully prepared and always relishing attention and flourishing in the spotlight. In other words, to see Gustaw solely in terms of his distress and world-weary cynicism is to overlook his wavering between seriousness and play, as well as his gift for both overblown operatic passion and lightness of touch. It is precisely this constantly shifting stance that makes part 4 alternately comical, bitter, absurd, necessary, delightful, euphoric, and ironic, thus preventing Gustaw's speeches from sounding, to postromantic ears, like exercises in melodramatic excess.

The most complex, ambiguous, and metaphor-laden scene occurs toward the end of part 4, when Gustaw stabs himself with a dagger. The idea that this highly charged scene marks the crux of part 4 has become familiar to every Mickiewicz scholar. The problem, of course, is that Gustaw is not overcome by paroxysms of pain; instead, he calmly pulls the dagger out of his body and hides it under his shirt. This moment of theatrical surprise is breathtaking: we see Gustaw the actor admiring his own power to hold center stage. The fact that the Priest mistakes a blatant display of theatrical contrivance for an actual suicide attempt, the result of the young man's supercharged sensibility, is a good indicator of Gustaw's power. Even though he dismisses the Priest's insistent questions with a rather aloof line, "Sorcery, trickery, sleight-of-hand," the Priest nevertheless rushes to help: "Sit down, lie down, give me this murderous weapon, let me take care of your wounds."[40] The Priest's line of thinking is not without its sterling logic. He is well aware of Gustaw's distress, and he has seen him stab himself; therefore he concludes that the young man must be badly wounded. It takes the bewildered Priest several moments to realize that there are no wounds to dress.

The suicide scene demonstrates convincingly, and with panache, that Gustaw, despite his melancholic self-absorption and ferocious self-reflexivity, can be a Puckish trickster. He falls back on his arsenal of stage tricks to consolidate his intellectual advantage over his former mentor. It is not necessarily helpful, however, to say that Gustaw has played a practical joke on the gullible Priest; therefore the whole scene is an imposture, the arrogant delivery of a fraud. After all, the scene suggests the disturbing possibility that we can never be positively certain that the feeling elicited by theatrical artifice is less real than that solicited by actual events. Seen from this perspective, the scene is a tribute to the seductive, indeed hypnotic, powers of theatrical enactment in general, and to Gustaw's acting skills in particular.

A different way to approach this scene is to see it as a laboratory for studying the antitheatricality that provides a pattern for an alternative understanding of part 4. To begin with, the focus on deception obscures the fact that Gustaw lays bare the devices of his artifice. If he can stab his body without hurting himself, it is obvious that he uses either a fake dagger or a knife with a retractable blade. By demystifying theatrical sleight-of-hand, he exposes what might be called the lie at the heart of theatre. In so doing, he takes the risk of breaking the aesthetic illusion and fraying the spectator's emotional tie to the figure on the stage. Moreover, the scene enables us to focus on Gustaw's body apart from the social contexts assumed in any drama. More specifically, the stabbing actualizes his body, and thus makes us see his corporeality. That is to say, the stabbing makes it clear, for readers of drama as well as theatre audiences, that he speaks from, and is, a body. Not only does the scene dismantle Gustaw's theatrical make-believe, then, but it also disrupts the conventional iconicity that laminates body to character.

The suicide scene raises provocative questions about just what a Mickiewiczean playtext is. It invites us to probe beneath the familiar level of part 4 that offers a character in a dramatic action, to be embodied (through theatrical enactment) by an actor. To put this point more broadly, the suicide scene epitomizes a move from the world of theatrical reproduction to the realm of performance art, from the world of representing, impersonating, or acting to the realm of doing or performing, from the world of a character to be enacted by an actor on the stage to the realm of the performer. To cite Patrice Pavis's useful definition, "a performer is someone who speaks and acts on his own behalf (as an artist and as a person) . . ., while the actor represents his character and pretends not to know he is only a theatre actor. The performer stages his own self, while the actor plays the role of another."[41] It is my argument that part 4 marks a site of early experimentation with what is called today performance art. In fostering a zone of porousness between theatre and performance or, more specifically, between theatrical and nontheatrical performance, part 4 renounces character and puts the artist himself on the stage. By the artist, I do not mean Mickiewicz. Instead, I mean Gustaw, understood as a performer presenting himself ("playing the part" of himself) on the stage.

Of the many characteristic features of performance art, Josette Féral has identified the performer's use of his/her body to explore and manipulate its potential as one of "the essential foundations of all performance."[42] Marvin Carlson adds: "the typical performance artist uses little of the elaborate scenic surroundings of the traditional stage, but at most a few props, a bit of furniture, and whatever costume (sometimes even nudity) is most suitable to the performance situation."[43] His body, voice, a few props, and a makeshift costume are the only resources Gustaw has, but he uses them effectively to bring to light his emotional flows and fantasies, his desires and repressions. In particular, it is his body that serves as a focus of his performative self-expressivity. He makes no attempt to mask his own working body. From beginning to end, he directs our attention to his corporeal elasticity and expertise. His body is put on display, made visible through, and discernible as, the performer's, rather than the character's or actor's, labor. Most importantly, Gustaw's body becomes a tool of the anxious self-exploration that drives performance art. He uses his body to investigate the limits of himself. In this context, it is especially significant that he always carries a dagger attached to a string tied around his neck. And although (unlike some late-twentieth-century performance artists) he never actually cuts himself, he regularly displays the dagger as if he were ready to strike and mutilate his body at any moment. Such demonstrations turn Gustaw's performance into provocative body art, in which he manipulates the relation between his body and his dagger in ways that could put him at risk.[44]

In her study of the constitutive features of performance art, Féral also includes an exploration of "the relation that performance institutes between the artist and the spectators, between the spectators and the work of art, and between the work of art and the artist."[45] To examine this point in the context of part 4, I want first to detour through the realm of theatre and to consider how actors mine playtexts for cues, explicit or hidden, that help them find gestures and movements appropriate to a particular scene.

While many plays include few stage directions, they provide cues that are encoded in the spoken lines. Shakespeare's dramas fall into this category. As J. L. Styan argues, it is not possible for the actor playing Othello to say the words "cold, cold, my girl" without touching Desdemona's dead body, and "conveying how close to her he is. Another kiss perhaps? For the first kiss Desdemona was alive, for the second dead, but Othello's feeling for her was constant."[46] In short, actors rely not only on explicit stage directions for gesture and movement, but also on the signs and signals conveyed by the spoken lines, although some of the cues are buried more deeply than others. Styan's comment that every line in Shakespeare's dramas "carries within it some suggestion of how it is to be seen or heard, and therefore how it is to be spoken or matched with gesture and movement" can be extended to plays by other writers.[47] Part 4 of *Forefathers' Eve* is filled with lines that, to use Styan's phrase, "may be alive with gesture for the actor as well as rich in dramatic meaning for the spectator" and the reader.[48]

When Gustaw enters in the opening scene, he is mistaken by the Priest's children for an authentic corpse, or an equally authentic apparition. As a result, he evokes repulsion mixed with fear and fascination. But the Priest's response is different. He vaguely recognizes in Gustaw a young man whom he has met before. When Gustaw evades questions about his identity, the Priest does not pursue the matter further. Instead, he concentrates on Gustaw's corporeality: "You're soaking wet. You look pale. You are so cold that you're shivering."[49] It is difficult to imagine the actor playing the Priest saying these words without touching Gustaw's wet and cold body. Later, after Gustaw has stabbed himself, the Priest cries out: "Help! . . . Run to the vicar and wake him up. . . . Get the other people!"[50] This time, it is not possible for the actor to deliver these lines without gesturing to house servants to help him attend to Gustaw's wounds.

We know from the stage directions for the stabbing scene that the servants enter only moments before Gustaw stages his suicide. They are thus conveniently at hand when the Priest needs them. And since the initial stage directions for part 4 list only four characters—the Priest, the Priest's children, and the Hermit (i.e., Gustaw)—it is easy to assume that for most of the action, that is, until the suicide scene, Gustaw performs before an audience of three (the Priest and the children). However, the cues encoded in the spoken lines tell a different story. In the opening scene, when Gustaw displays his dagger for the first time, the Priest reacts nervously: "What's this? You must be crazy! . . . Take away his dagger, make him unclench his fists."[51] It is hard to imagine that the Priest is urging his small children to disarm and subdue an intruder. Rather, it is the servants' presence that is ghosted, so to speak, in the Priest's frantic commands.

The Priest's commands in the opening scene make it clear that the servants are present on the stage long before their entrance is announced in the stage directions for the suicide scene. It is likely that they come to clear the table after supper or, as yet another line by the Priest indicates, to stoke the fireplace. In short, the servants come and go throughout part 4, but the stage directions take no notice of their comings and goings. This puzzling oversight raises the question: why do the stage directions emphatically register the servants' presence on the stage just before the suicide scene? The second question predictably follows from the first: why is it important that Gustaw should stab himself before a larger audience that includes the servants? The intersection of the would-be suicide and the broadening of the audience suggests a deliberate textual effort to alert us that Gustaw's performance, seemingly a self-individuated, private project, is in fact a form of public exposure that is watched by others outside a family circle. To examine the implications of this emphasis on public display, and to consider the question about the significance (if any) of the Priest's widowerhood, I now want to turn to Philippe Ariès's study *The Hour of Our Death.*

IV

Time and again, *Forefathers' Eve* crosses the line that separates life and death. The dead (e.g., the spirits invoked in part 2) seem to "live" again, while conversely, the living (e.g., the absent Maryla in part 4) "haunt" the mind's eye in the manner of ghosts. This ambiguity is especially evident in the case of Gustaw. He is flesh and bone, yet he repeatedly alludes to his earlier, presumably successful, suicide attempt. To put it quite simply: is he a living man, possibly the "ghost" of an absent person, or, rather, the ghost of a dead person? Life and death have become peculiarly indistinguishable. Admittedly, such a fantasy—of a breakdown of the limit between life and death—lies at the heart of part 4 and underwrites an understanding of Gustaw's ambiguous thanatological status as an ontological transgressor. Yet it is precisely this essentially fantastic ambiguity that requires historical analysis.

Philippe Ariès's research offers a helpful guide. His book *The Hour of Our Death* originally published in French in 1977 as *L'Homme devant la mort,* is a study of changing attitudes toward death and dying in European culture since the Middle Ages. Ariès argues that new and increasingly repressive emotional attitudes toward death in the late eighteenth century constituted a major "revolution in feeling" with far-reaching consequences.[52] In contrast to earlier periods, when death was generally accepted as an organic, integral, and centrally meaningful facet of human existence, late-eighteenth-century culture was characterized by a growing dissociation from corporeal reality, and by a new and unprecedented antipathy toward death in all its aspects. A break with traditional patterns was first apparent, Ariès suggests, in the practical sphere, in the period's obsession with what he calls "the beautiful death"—its concern with hiding or denying the physical signs of mortality and decay.[53] Where death was once a public spectacle of considerable magnitude, it now became a primarily private event, witnessed only by one's closest relatives. Funerals were carried out more and more discreetly. Cemeteries were removed from their once central locations in cities and towns to outlying areas, and were designed as gardens of remembrance, with landscaped walks and prospects, to obscure their necrological function.

The nineteenth century, Ariès contends, inherited these new attitudes toward death. Through a complex process of displacement, European culture repressed the body and its exigencies; in the face of death, it retreated into anxious mystification and denial. But the most important sign of shifting sensibilities, according to Ariès, was the emergence of the Romantic cult of the dead, that is, a growing fascination with idealized images of the deceased and with the sentimental fantasy of meeting the dead. Folk beliefs regarding the eternal life of disembodied spirits, who continue to dwell in a nearby invisible realm and come to visit the living, only reinforced popular emotion. The underlying dream, however, was that the dead are not really dead because, after all, one can still "see" them in one's mind. Ariès calls this hope—a hope for an afterlife that "is not so much the heavenly home as the earthly home saved from the menace of time"—"the great religious fact of the whole contemporary era."[54] In other words, the new phenomenon, which emerged in the eighteenth and nineteenth centuries, was "the replacement of the ancient ideas about the beyond (the idea of repose, so general and so popular, and the later idea of the beatific vision, which was slow to gain acceptance and in fact never completely won over the masses) by a new and anthropomorphic image, a transference of emotional demands of earthly life."[55]

It is with these points in mind that I would like to resume my analysis of part 4 of *Forefathers' Eve*. Certainly, characters preoccupied with death had appeared in European Romantic literature before Mickiewicz's drama. It is hardly necessary to say that Goethe's *The Sorrows of Young Werther*, in particular, had a powerful shaping influence on contemporary psychic life (including the psychic life of Mickiewicz's Gustaw). What is striking in *Forefathers' Eve*, however, is the fervor with which the finality of death is negated over and over again, from the return of the dead in the prefatory ballad

"The Phantom" ("Upiór") and in part 2, through the arrival of the thanatologically ambiguous Gustaw in part 4, to the transmutation of Gustaw into Konrad in part 3. This is an appropriate point to return to the scene of Gustaw's would-be suicide. Reading this scene through Ariès, and in the context of the numerous denials of mortality in *Forefathers' Eve*, we sense both an unprecedented, obsessional anxiety about death and the accompanying desire to overcome or undo death. By staging a denial of physical death, Gustaw ironically plays into the expectations of those who want to see the boundary between life and death suspended and the dead brought back to life, because to "see" the dead live again is to know that one, too, will live forever.

Among those who witness the would-be suicide there is the perpetually mourning Priest, who, like Gustaw, has experienced the loss of a woman he loves. While Gustaw's loss of Maryla is figurative, the Priest's loss of his wife is not. Together, these losses—the Priest's and Gustaw's—locate part 4's center of interest in grieving. Folding the story of the Priest's loss within the story of Gustaw's loss, part 4 pitches itself against a conventional notion from the era prior to what Ariès calls "the revolution in feeling"—a notion that mourning must be worked through. Indeed, part 4 implicitly argues for—and persistently works to effect—a sustaining of grief. Grief involves remembering, and the devices of memory "create" presence out of absence.

However, it is precisely this process that, as Ariès suggests, led to an unprecedented collective flight into fantastic ideation, or a persistent preoccupation with nostalgic and idealizing images of the dead. This historic shift toward the phantasmic also fed the illusion that one's internalized images or mental "souvenirs" of other people were more real in some sense, and far more satisfying, than any direct interaction with them could ever be. It was tempting, in other words, to deny one's own corporeality and the corporeality of others, and to cherish the life of the mind over life itself because corporeality—always subject to change, death, and decay—was precisely what became so problematic. Gustaw as character demonstrates how easy it is to become absorbed in the increasingly vivid, if also hallucinatory contents of the mind itself. And his would-be suicide responds to his contemporaries' growing antipathy toward the body and its contingencies with the comforting final illusion that there is no such thing as a real corpse. By contrast, Gustaw as performer undermines the cultural reorientation toward the phantasmic by putting his corporeality in the public spotlight, before an audience onstage and, implicitly, offstage. Paradoxically, he makes sure that the direct experience of his corporeality is emotionally intolerable to members of his audience. His body is not idealized or beautified. And since it may be subjected to cutting or mutilation at any moment, his body is likely to reinforce his contemporaries' growing antipathy toward corporeality and its contingencies. Seen in broader terms, through Ariès's study, Gustaw's performance art nonetheless stands out as a rich experimental work shaped around an effort to counter the historic shift toward ideation with corporeal immediacy that ultimately always surrenders to change, decay, and dissolution.

While *Forefathers' Eve* appears to be divided absolutely, if schematically, between the private realm in part 4 and the public realm in part 3, closer attention to part 4 provides an opportunity for the reconsideration of the seemingly self-evident concept of the private/public divide in Mickiewicz's drama. By focusing less on the literary aspects of part 4 than on Gustaw's performance art, and by situating part 4 in a broader thanatological and affective context, it becomes possible to appreciate the significance of Gustaw's shifting and contradictory engagements with both private and public spheres. The scope of part 4, in other words, reaches beyond Gustaw's private concerns to encompass larger processes that, as Ariès reminds us, were taking place in European culture at the turn of the nineteenth century.

NOTES

I presented earlier versions of this essay at the conference "On the Brink of the Modern: In Commemoration of the 200th Anniversary of the Birth of Adam Mickiewicz," organized by Joanna Kurowska-Młynarczyk at the University of Chicago in 1999, and at a panel entitled "Love and Sex in Central and East European Theater," organized by Tamara Trojanowska for a convention of the American Association for the Advancement of Slavic Studies, which took place in Denver in 2000. I would like to thank both organizers for giving me the opportunity to discuss my work-in-progress. My thanks go as well to the members of the audiences in Chicago and Denver who asked questions that have repeatedly led me to rethink what I was doing.

1. The title of the play refers to a folk ritual that was celebrated in Belarus and Lithuania every year between mid-October and mid-November. Its purpose was to lure the dead to return briefly to this world and to convey to the living a direct message from beyond the grave. Mickiewicz began writing *Forefathers' Eve* in 1820, and published parts 2 and 4 in 1823. In 1832, he resumed his work on the play and wrote part 3, which came out in the same year. Part 1, begun some time between 1821 and 1823, but left unfinished, was published posthumously in 1860. According to a long-standing assumption, *Forefathers' Eve* was introduced to Polish theatre audiences only in 1901, because censorship restrictions and the limitations of theatre technology had made earlier productions impossible. In truth, part 4 and excerpts from part 3 were staged in Polish theatres in the nineteenth century, even during Mickiewicz's lifetime. See Ciechowicz, 52–57; Jędrychowski; *Pięć studiów*; Sivert et al.; Witkowski, 162–90.

2. Most commentators have been quick to interpret part 4 as a thinly disguised autobiographical account of a love affair between Mickiewicz and Maryla Puttkamer née Wereszczaka, but they have not looked in the opposite direction to register signs of theatre's influence on the way in which Mic-

kiewicz conducted the affair. By contrast, Marta Zielińska has explored the affair's theatrical dimension; without minimizing the reality of Mickiewicz's relationship with Maryla Puttkamer, she has made it clear how much of his creative power, including his histrionic flair, was invested in carefully staging the affair as if it were a public performance. See Zielińska.

3. The literature on *Forefathers' Eve* is too vast to be fully represented here. For bibliographies of indispensable studies in Polish through 1998, see Cieśla-Korytowska, "Introduction," 87–88; Dopart, *Romantyzm polski*, 199–207. For studies in Polish published after 1998, see, for example, Cieśla-Korytowska, *O Mickiewiczu i Słowackim*; Dopart, *"Dziady"*; Dopart, *Poemat profetyczny*; Dopart, *Romantyzm polski*, 42–85; Hetel; Kuczera-Chachulska and Prussak; Ursel; Ziołowicz. For recent studies published outside Poland, see especially Fieguth, 227–330; Goldberg; Grudzińska Gross; Koropeckyj, 35–92.

4. There is a general agreement in scholarship that a paradigm of the private/public divide, represented in *Forefathers' Eve*, correlates with the great divide in Polish Romanticism between its early manifestations and its later stages. For this argument see, for example, Pigoń, 6–7.

5. For the locus classicus on love of country, see Cicero.

6. For the most thorough and incisive version of this argument, see Przybylski.

7. Part 4, in contrast, is performed only rarely.

8. See Mężyński, 89–91.

9. Kleiner, 1: 435.

10. Szmydtowa, 119; see also 121–22.

11. Górski, 147.

12. Ibid.

13. Grudzińska Gross, 306.

14. Ibid., 307.

15. As Józef Kallenbach has aptly remarked, "Every time Gustaw addresses the Priest directly, he speaks with such forceful surety and intellectual aloofness that we feel sorry for the kind-hearted clergyman who, in return for his hospitality, must bear the brunt of his former pupil's bitterness." 1:298.

16. Although the dividing line between private and public spheres had always been contentious and unstable, it became more porous in late eighteenth century (see, for example, Barrell); this historical moment, which coincided with the rise of European Romanticism, is crucial to my discussion.

17. Kallenbach, 1:300.

18. Grudzińska Gross, 307.

19. Ibid., 308.

20. See Kallenbach, 1:299–301.

21. The Priest is a member of the Greek Catholic (rather than Roman Catholic) Church, in which celibacy is not a requirement for priesthood.

22. I owe this observation to Michał Witkowski's study, which cites an anonymous review published in 1816 and Mickiewicz's review written in 1820. See Witkowski, 145, 259 n. 22; see also Lipiński, 159.

23. For an overview of debates over the generic classification of part 4, see Zetowski; Ziołowicz, 63–99. For the argument about the supremacy of lyric poetry in part 4, see especially Kleiner, 1:406–45. For a recent example of legitimating poetry over drama as a means of critical access to part 4, see Kuczera-Chachulska. She goes as far as to assert that "the dramatic character" of part 4 is "an illusion" (8). For a dissenting view, see Cieśla-Korytowska, who points out that the stage directions in part 4 are so precise and detailed as if they were meant to substitute for a stage production of the play, "Introduction," 23–24. She does not, however, pursue the issue further.

24. For studies that reinterpret J. L. Austin's account of speech acts for the field of performance studies, see especially Parker and Sedgwick; Worthen, "Drama, Performativity, and Performance."

25. To develop a conceptual framework for my analysis and interpretation, I have adapted major strands in the scholarship of Barbara Hodgdon, Dobrochna Ratajczakowa, and William B. Worthen, who explore methodological alternatives to the prevailing interpretive norms of text-versus-performance and text-to-performance approaches.

26. Byron, 263; Byron's italics.

27. For a reproduction of the playbill, see Jędrychowski, 259. The date printed on the playbill, 19 May 1832, follows the Julian calendar.

28. See Witkowski, 169–71; see also Ciechowicz, 54–55; Jędrychowski, 262.

29. Jędrychowski, 262.

30. See Witkowski, 266 n. 12.

31. Circumstantial evidence suggests that Malinowski's *Gustaw* "most likely" had its première in Kamieniec Podolski. See Jędrychowski, 262.

32. Kleiner, 1:430.

33. Hapgood, 225.

34. Worthen, "Reply to letter of Robert Hapgood," 226.

35. Quoted in Jędrychowski, 252.

36. I have borrowed this phrase from the chapter "Readers Respond to Rousseau: The Fabrication of Romantic Sensitivity," in Darnton, 215–56.

37. Hapgood, 225. In addition, the influence of *Forefathers' Eve* on Jerzy Grotowski, for example, was powerful and lasting. Grotowski staged a revisionist production of *Forefathers' Eve* in 1961, but his dialogue with Mickiewicz was not confined to that production.

38. Mickiewicz, it is worth noting, was well steeped in the theatrical practice of his day. He caught stage fever while in high school, and learned the theatre trade from the bottom up, working as actor, acting coach, and stage manager. See Witkowski, 5–52.

39. See Ziołowicz, 95. Writing about part 4 in a different context and from a literature-centered perspective, she notes that at times Gustaw assumes the roles of an actor and a theatre director.

40. Mickiewicz, *Dzieła*, 90.

41. Pavis, 262.

42. Féral, 171.

43. Carlson, *Performance*, 6.

44. Today, aspects of part 4, such as the sustained emphasis on the individual body or the boundary crossings between theatrical simulation and performative antisimulation, which I have described in terms of performance art, may strike us as a legitimate part of present-day theatrical practice. This is not surprising. Over the past thirty years, many features of performance art have been appropriated by theatrical production, experimental as well as mainstream. For further discussion of the relationship between theatre and performance art, see, for example, Carlson, *Performance*, ix; Féral, 175–79.

45. Féral, 171.

46. Styan, 139.

47. Ibid.

48. Ibid.

49. Mickiewicz, *Dzieła*, 45.

50. Ibid., 89, 93.

51. Ibid., 48.

52. Ariès, 471.

53. Ibid., 409.

54. Ibid., 471.

55. Ibid., 449.

Flâneur Polonaise

Witold Gombrowicz and Slow Modalities

Krystyna Lipińska Iłłakowicz

> Above that scrap of land, narrow and forlorn, the skies opened once again deeper and vaster than anywhere else; enormous sky like a dome, tall and responsive, full of unfinished frescoes and improvisations, flying draperies and vehement ascensions.
>
> —Bruno Schulz, *The Republic of Dreams*

In opposition to the haste, vitality, and technological glitter of the modern metropolis, provincial culture has been traditionally associated with drowsiness, backwardness, and a slow pace of life. In a provincial town, time stands still and the landscape never changes. If, as Paul Virilio proposes, we describe culture using speed as a qualifier, and European modernity (or the West) as a culture of speed, then, as Milan Kundera implies in his novel *Slowness*, Eastern Europe can be perceived as a slow culture.[1] However, the use of a modality of slowness as a cultural metaphor inadvertently causes problems.

When, in the first chapter of his novel, Kundera resorts to slowness in order to criticize the commodification and instrumentalization of contemporary Western societies, he opens a Pandora's box full of stereotypical cultural classifications. He laments the disintegration of traditional slow temporalities, which in the past allowed us to appreciate and cherish every moment of life: "Why has the pleasure of slowness disappeared? Ah, where have they gone, the amblers of yesteryear."[2] Kundera's nostalgia for the "pleasure of slowness" necessarily brings speed to the fore as a ubiquitous, relentless denominator of modernity, together with its contingent categories of agency, technologization, efficiency, commitment, and universality. Similarly, the text juxtaposes the city space (with its infrastructure and network of speedy highways) and the country estate (with its winding paths), the former constituting a locus of modernity, and the latter representing the obsolete culture of the past. Slowness, in spite of its desirable ecological (antitechnological) and aesthetic connotations (in other places in the novel Kundera suggests that the real appreciation of pleasure can only happen slowly), necessarily resurfaces as the other, hidden side of the traditional speed/slowness binary, connoting the inaction, indolence, boredom, and parochialism that constitute a historically undesired backwardness. Slowness definitely does not occupy a privileged position in the modern world.

Retaining Kundera's insights about the cultural significance of slowness, but moving beyond his nostalgia, I propose to approach Polish culture's aspirations to participate in the discourse of modernity and its interactions with the West through the speed/slowness binary. Such an approach posits the very tempo of human action and the mode of unfolding of historical processes as a cultural signifier. Every culture situates itself in a specific performative space, and unfolds in that space and time as movement—its rhythms and the tempo of its unfolding carry meaning. Toward the end of Kundera's novel one of the protagonists, Vincent, hastily departs on his motorcycle, while another, the Chevalier who is the premodern alter ego of the modern Vincent, "walks slowly toward the chaise."[3] The slow, measured walk of the Chevalier makes the narrator ponder the meaning of this slow movement; he "want[s] to relish the rhythm of his steps: the farther he goes, the slower they are."[4] Aesthetic pleasure, or the pleasure of life in general, cannot be appreciated hastily because it is always connected with remembering and processing past experience. "In that slowness" the narrator ponders, "I seem to recognize a sign of happiness."[5] Without slow reflection happiness is not possible, and the modern Vincent on "his motorcycle . . . will forget everything . . . he will forget himself."[6] Kundera seems to suggest that in culture, as in dance, slow and fast rhythms are symptomatic; they imply specific aesthetics, politics, and a particular system of norms and values. They signal tensions and shifts occurring within cultures, and serve as a potent analytical instrument for the examination of cultural exchanges. It is implicit in Kundera's book that even though slow modalities were largely replaced in the West by the hegemonic narrative of speed, they still operate in an occluded way in the West itself and, we can add, subtend the traditional modalities in many Eastern European cultures, as well as in Asia, South America, and Africa.

The present discussion adopts this movement-related approach and investigates the question of Poland's participation in modernization through the writings of Witold Gombrowicz, who posits the slowness/speed binary as central to his own reflection on modernity. In various ways, Gombrowicz confronts and questions the validity of speed as a foundation for the modern structure of universality and the system of cultural valorizing by showing that both speed and slowness are ambivalent notions. The modality of slowness, also inflected as "weakness" and "softening" in Gombrowicz's texts, challenges the privileged position of speed. Yet slowness is figured not only as a countermodality to speed, but also and predominantly as ambivalent energy rupturing the system of binary cultural categorizations. Slowing down in Gombrowicz, similar to regression in Schulz, is central to the revision of epistemic and aesthetic systems. These modes question the irreversibility of change, positing change and movement not as linear but as circular, aleatory, and random. My readings of Gombrowicz's novels, his *Diary*, and his final statements in *A Kind of Testament* demonstrate that cultural meanings can be constructed through alternative modes that depart from the traditional notions of change.

The peripheral space sets the context for Gombrowicz's dialogues with modernity through which the received binaries of the provincial and the universal, and the high and the low are destabilized.

I suggest that slowness has been consistently perceived as a kind of "handicapped" modality, always presupposing incongruence and incompatibility with the spatial and temporal configurations of modernity. Such a perception implies the lack of historicity, and consequently brings about marginalization and/or "provincialization" of slower cultures. My conceptualization of slowness as a "handicapped" mode alludes to Ann McClintock's concept of an "anachronistic space"[7] encoding a practice of dehistoricization of the colonized territories by the colonizing narratives. Both the act of slowing down and the colonial context framing it are important for my discussion, and indeed any analysis of Polish modernity. "The term 'anachronistic space' suggests a conflation of time and space into a nondifferentiated temporality, in which cultural subjects"—most often colonized and women—"are deprived of the agency attributed to 'the historical time of modernity.'"[8] Similarly, the perception of slowness as a handicapped modality deprives cultural subjects of their agency and historic validity. As a result, cultures that display a different (slower) mode of development are often deemed unfit to join the properly developed part of the world.

Central to my concerns are Enlightenment constructions of speed as a carrier of civilization. These constructions informed Western Europeans' understanding of change, newness, and technological advancement; they also involved a desire for the rapid unfolding of those processes. Since the notion of progress structured the hierarchy of values, its corollary, speed, also became acclaimed as universally valid. In this regard, the speed-related binaries in Kant's system, such as movement/stasis or action/inaction, are essential for my discussion.[9] These binaries not only constitute Kant's notion of history and the development of mankind, but underlie his whole system of rationality figured in terms of purposeful and decisive, even aggressive progress. Consequently, for Kant, and later Hegel and his followers as well as Marx, speed-related modalities and temporalities associated with change, forms of strength and agency, and effectiveness of action acquire a universally valid status.

Modernity figured speed and its temporal and spatial modalities such as tempo, frequency, and change as indisputable attributes of progress, and as such they were accorded a universal value. Without speed neither progress nor cultural change was thought possible. Such a privileging of speed and its universalization had very important consequences, because speed became one of the constitutive elements in the knowledge-construction process. As Foucault observes in *The Order of Things*, real knowledge was supposed to induce unity in the world, and disclose "the universal possibility of tabulated order."[10] Since the classical period, any "real knowledge" (synonymous with philosophy) was supposed either "to provid[e] a foundation" or to be "capable of revealing" hidden laws that give meaning to the world.[11] Speed is universal in both senses.

It functions as an instrumental factor of change (and by extension, of progress), and it also orients and structures a series of contingencies that constitute a historical narrative, thus allowing for our understanding of the processes that contribute to the concept of civilization.

It is clear, then, that attributing power to speed necessitated that slow modalities associated with noncentral, distant localities and a slower tempo of life be denied value because they lacked universality. Not only non-Western cultures, such as those of most of African, South American, and Asian countries, but also peripheral European cultures, including that of Eastern Europe, were perceived as embodiments of such slow temporalities, and deemed secondary (or subaltern in Gramsci's terminology), acquiring in the eyes of the Western proponents of modernity all possible connotations of lagging behind and backwardness.[12] More important, such a negative cultural assessment penetrated into Eastern Europeans' perceptions of themselves, so that they began to think of their culture as backward and lacking. In eighteenth-century Poland, this tendency resurfaces in the writings of Enlightenment intellectuals, many of whom gathered around *Monitor* magazine, which translated the ideas presented in the English *Spectator* into the Polish context. These intellectuals propagated a wide range of political, social, educational, agrarian, and cultural reforms, but often added a critical element to these imported cultural models. Necessarily, such perceptions urged modernization and catching up with the "civilized" West, but they also created a counterreaction calling for the rethinking of indigenous traditions. In Russia, the monumental project of modernization initiated by Peter the Great continued into the nineteenth century, and often triggered heated and long-lasting debates between the *slavophiles* and the *westernizer*s. In the most general sense, Eastern European responses to the temporalities of cultural change unfold as two prevailing, although dissenting, tendencies. One highlights the modern imperative of dynamic change and the ethos of accomplishment, while the other counters it by propagating "indigenous" temporalities traditionally associated with provincial slowness unfavorable to change.

Such debates, initiated by Enlightenment intellectuals, continued through the turbulent period of romantic upheavals, and subtended the late-nineteenth-century positivistic disputes. I mention them briefly here in order to point out that they resurfaced in the interwar period between 1919 and 1939 (*dwudziestolecie międzywojenne*), once Poland regained its statehood and national entity after 130 years of colonial subjugation.[13] The recovery of national sovereignty allowed for the continuation of interrupted Enlightenment, romantic, and positivistic discussions about Polish cultural identity and traditions in the new political situation. Poland's aspirations to modernity were obviously at the core of these discussions. And indeed, almost all writers of that period—Stanisław Wyspiański, Stefan Żeromski, Władysław Reymont, Zofia Nałkowska, Stanisław Ignacy Witkiewicz, and Gombrowicz, to name only a few—contributed to the an ongoing reckoning with the old and new ways, and the revalorization of the entire national tradition.

Poland's cultural assessments and dilemmas from the beginning of the twentieth century converge in Gombrowicz's writing, which in turn not only absorbed the epistemic currents of its time but also significantly subverted them. Gombrowicz's metaphor of "slowing down" functions as a multidimensional trope that translates into alternative ways of seeing, thinking, and constructing meaning. The trope of slowness, reconfigured also as "weakness" or "softening," creates the possibility of reconstituting the function of difference in cultural discourse as an open and inclusive cognitive attitude. In Gombrowicz, the space of difference itself is affected by the process of "weakening" and "softening"; the difference triggers movement and stimulates the processes of signification, but at the same time the weakening mechanism suspends the apparatus of cultural valorization. Such a reconstitution of cultural difference enables the recovery of provincialism as a space in which cultural identity can develop as a process of ongoing questioning on two planes: the diachronic (including historic legacies and traditions) and the synchronic (including contemporary realities and trends).[14]

The Villager Enters the Scene

Gombrowicz's critique of the culture of modernity, or more strictly the processes of modernization (understood as colonization of the peripheral/local traditions by the dominating mainstream culture), can be traced practically in all of his works, starting from the collection of short stories *Memoir from a Time of Immaturity* (in English translated as *Bacacay*), *Ferdydurke, Ivona,Princess of Burgundia, Pornography*, and *Cosmos*. The concept of immaturity, fundamental to Gombrowicz's early work, always presupposes the confrontation of centrally established, traditional sets of norms with the discordant, opposing tendencies articulated from the off-center (lower, inferior, or not fully established) cultural position. Gombrowicz's cultural insights persistently question the idea of development, which, as a variable of progress, is at the core of all modern constructs. Resorting to his Polish and Argentinian experience, he challenges this dominant mode of modern cultural movement by pointing to various forms of countermodalities such as "slowing down," "weakness/softening," "imperfection," "inferiority," "provinciality," "rusticity," and many other inflections that all relate to the power/powerlessness binary, and that are always in relation to his concept of form. The dialogue between speed and slowness in Gombrowicz's novels often surfaces in the relationship between the intense city lifestyle and the "softened" and relaxed country habits and rituals. In *Ferdydurke*, these two spaces meet in the gesture of the fraternizing of a city student with a country boy. In *Pornography*, two city intellectuals invade the space of a quiet manor house, and in *Cosmos*, the events unfold in a space between the city and the village: on the periphery, so to speak, where the rules of reason slowly dissolve into the mode of uncertainty. This theme acquires overtly intercontinental/global dimensions in

Trans-Atlantyk when the space of the Argentinian *estanza* (reflecting estranged and mutated but at the same time blurred European traditions and customs) is invaded by the duelling city dwellers representing conservative European traditions of chivalry and war.[15]

In a discursive and more theoretical manner, the idea of slowness is articulated in Gombrowicz's *Diary* and *A Kind of Testament*, where it emerges as a central element of his reflection on the relationship between Polish and European culture. His concerns, as he comments in the latter work, expand into "an open criticism of modern culture" undertaken from a "villager['s]" perspective, which he defines as "a rustic *laisser-faire*" counterreaction "to the tensions which have accumulated in the metropolises of Europe and America."[16] This critique of the modality of speed not only subtends Gombrowicz's perceptions of metropolitan life, human relations, and the modern structure of power, but also informs his insights into the formation of knowledge. In *A Kind of Testament* his reflection about the *Diary* turns into a critique of the fast, superficial, and (we might say today, alluding to Slavoj Žižek or Jean Baudrillard) continuously "morphing"[17] modes of knowing. Reflecting on intellectuals' daily habits, Gombrowicz comments:

> In the morning, after breakfast, a cultural human being leafs through a cultural magazine and passionately reads an important polemic between a structuralist and an existentialist. This is so intelligent, that to say it bluntly, it is stupid . . . stupid because both thinkers pretend to be wiser than they really are. In fact they know something hastily, hurriedly, superficially (can we know in any other way these days?).[18]

By pointing to the hasty mode of reading and intellectual activity that masquerades as various, quickly changing fashionable trends, Gombrowicz not only points to the superficiality of modern culture, but makes a very important comment about the production of knowledge and, years before Žižek, Virilio, or Baudrillard, situates speed at the center of the modern cognitive process. The metaphor of the world as a fashion show from *Operetta*—which was finished in 1966, two years before the statements from *A Kind of Testament*—pointedly captures the speed-based nature of the self-propelling cultural mechanism that produces more and more just for the sake of mutability and changing political and economic trends. (Žižek refers to a similar syndrome using the term *morphing*, Virilio points to the *techniques of disappearance*, Baudrillard recasts it as *simulations* or *simulacra*.)

Speed, however, is not the only condition of cultural agency, and Gombrowicz proposes alternative modes that are pertinent for both Western and Eastern modernity, and ingrained in local traditions and indigenous rhythms. In the following passage from the *Diary*, he succinctly formulates his critique of the modern language of speed, and maps the historical, social, and aesthetic ramifications of his position.

> And I, my dear sir, vintage squire farmer, extend my hand and say: Slow down! This is not the way! What in the devil do you need this [Europeanism and modernity] for?

> First of all, you won't catch up, because forms of thinking and style take shape slowly. Second, it is not worth it, because it is not worth the trouble. Third, it would be great if you would consider the following: today you have the aces; your slowness is beginning to be on top. What has been your shame until now can be introduced to Europe as a starting point for a salutary revision.[19]

If, as Gombrowicz argues, slowness characterizes all processes of construction of meaning because "forms of thinking and style take shape slowly," then slowness must be ingrained, although occluded, in the structures of modernity. Thus "slowness" is figured not only as a property of the presumably low, village cultures, but also as an attribute of the supposedly superior city cultures of "Europeanism and modernity." On the other hand, through installing slowness's ascendancy ("beginning to be on top"), the text collapses the very notion of the top, and undermines the structure of cultural values predicated on the distinction between high and low. Such a positioning of slowness disrupts all other inflections of high and low, which are recast in Gombrowicz's writing as city/village, center/periphery, universality/provinciality, or modernity/belatedness, to which I will refer later in this discussion.

Thus, even if modernity does not want to recognize it, slowness—and not speed—facilitates the processes of thinking and as such allows a space for revisions, delaying the finality of those processes. In fact, Gombrowicz makes it very clear that such revision is a foundation of all thinking, and that no deep, valid philosophical analysis can ever take place within a mode of speed. By extension, the slowness that the vintage squire can retrieve and offer to "Europe" as a "starting point for a salutary revision" loses its "shame," because of its demonstrable validity as a mode of cultural development.

Gombrowicz pronounces the hierarchy of cultural valorizing grounded in speed defunct. He points out that adhering to speed is not only pointless but also self-defeating; if cultural development is a slow process, then speed is of little help in achieving it. For the same reasons he opposes the practice of cultural copying expressed by another speed-related metaphor, that of "catch[ing] up."

While speed, for Gombrowicz, remains a possible modality of cultural movement for the West, for small or marginalized cultures he still proposes "slow[ing] down" as a mode of bringing their inner rhythm and the indigenous value structure into the process of the production of meaning. Slowness, by permitting a disclosure of the suppressed, "forgotten" values and their reevaluation as culturally relevant—as "aces"—becomes for those cultures an accessible mode for experiencing cultural processes. Slowness effaces shame: in the absence of hasty judgments, all aspects of the culture—its peripherality, smallness, backwardness, and subsidiary status—can be confronted and reappraised, rather than dismissed as shameful. Thus, this space of slowness stimulates the construction of a more "realistic," or postcolonial cultural identity. The quoted passage clearly shows that while the culture retrieves its suppressed narrative and obtains a voice through the mode of slowing down, the "catching-up" attitude only discloses enslavement in the dominating modes of cultural production, and is therefore counterproductive. Catching up, then, is in a way coterminous with the state when the so-called belated, or slower cultures still have not fully accepted their own tempo of cultural production, and are stuck in their "colonized identity," unable to articulate their indigenous mode of being (this state of being in between Homi Bhabha calls *hybridization*). In this sense, they are still mute. Gombrowicz's reflection on the syndromes of catching up and cultural copying (both have a long tradition in Polish history) is reminiscent of Kundera's remarks about the speed-oriented protagonist from his novel *Slowness*, to whom I referred at the beginning of this essay. As a result of his dedication to speed, Vincent, who is preoccupied only with reaching his goal—be it a car in front of him or sexual intercourse—loses any meaningful contact with the surrounding reality, and is unable to fully experience and enjoy it.

Gombrowicz's critique addresses cultural structures of both the center and the periphery. By alerting the squire to the significance of slowing down, he questions the construction of change within the modern system of historicity; at the same time, his analysis challenges the peripheral cultures' mechanism of subjugation to such structures. Once a peripheral culture acknowledges speed as universally desirable, its own slower tempo of change becomes characterized as backward and lacking.

Against that sort of denigration of local cultural structures and values, Gombrowicz subversively calls for a rethinking of a premodern cultural mode known as the "Sarmatian style," which programmatically opposed modern ideas. Sarmatism (*sarmatyzm*) denotes the seventeenth-century Polish gentry culture that was traditionally associated with political anarchy, and an excessively rich and boisterous, conspicuous consumption.[20] By the time Gombrowicz enlists it, the term *sarmatism* had come to connote all possible vices of the Polish seventeenth-century squirearchy: obscurantism, national megalomania and xenophobia, lack of tolerance, and religious fanaticism, to name only a few. These stereotypical connotations coalesced around this term during the Enlightenment, and their pejorative meaning subsequently persisted among the cultural elite.

Two aspects of sarmatism, its political ideals and its cultural connection to the East, play an especially significant role in Gombrowicz's approach. As Ewa Płonowska Ziarek points out, in opposition to Western democratic systems grounded in dynamic structures of capitalism, the Polish seventeenth-century gentry constructed a democratic system grounded in the "agrarian ideal of the country."[21] This return to the "agrarian ideal" seems central for Gombrowicz. By retrieving the figure of the seventeenth-century squire for the purpose of his discussion of cultural identity, he refrains from historical evaluations of the Sarmatian culture and instead focuses solely on the unprecedented zeal of the Sarmatian enterprise to construct a political system grounded in indigenous cultural, economic, and political structures.[22]

That programmatic, anti-urban, and pro-rural stance of sarmatism, aimed against the imported "city" lifestyle, is also foundational for Gombrowicz's discussion of cultural identity. His "stroll" through culture subsumes this attitude. In *A Kind of Testament* he writes: "I walked through culture like a farmer through his orchard, biting into a pear here, a prune there, and saying: this is good, that one isn't."[23] His deployment of metaphors relating to rural culture, such as portraying himself as a villager, and reenacting the tempo of village life by strolling through the orchard of (Western) culture, recalls the Sarmatian will to rely on its own cultural values and its simultaneous resistance to Western cultural hegemony.[24]

Indeed, sarmatism's connection to the East seems to have been inflected by Polish Western-oriented eighteenth-century intellectuals, just as McClintock figures "anachronistic space" as atemporal and static, and therefore invalid for modernity. Eastern influences in the Sarmatian lifestyle must have promoted its perception as equally "anachronistic," and therefore an obstacle to more desirable Western models.[25] Thus, through textual references to sarmatism, Gombrowicz initiates the interrogation of Enlightenment intellectual practices that aimed at erasing Poland's median position between the East and the West, and at the same time reclaims sarmatism for the Polish cultural vocabulary not as a one-sided cultural blemish, but as a polyvalent term, providing insight into complex cultural processes of identity.

Most significantly, Gombrowicz's recourse to Sarmatian culture undermines the traditional opposition between the universal and the provincial that is foundational for modern European philosophy. He points out that the local, commonsense "peasant" philosophy may offer an equally wide, but more eclectic view than the perspective of universalism. Sarmatian culture's distrust of mainstream developments and its narrow provincial perspective paradoxically allow for distancing from the all-embracing, but center-oriented, and therefore restrictive, universalizing overview: "Instead of Poland, put Argentine, Canada, Romania and so on, and you'll see that my allusions (and my sufferings) can be applied to most of the globe. They concern all secondary European cultures."[26] With this statement Gombrowicz demonstrates that the "provincial" receives magnitude and relevance from alliance with other noncentral cultures and acquires its own kind of universalist attributes. At the same time, the global contextualization of a singular predicament achieves a refigured universality in which difference is retained not as a sign of separation but as an indication of shared experience. If, as Gombrowicz points out, "secondary cultures" constitute "most of the globe," then the primary space narrows and loses its traditional universality. Thus, he shows that the traditional criteria of universality encompassing range and distance also characterize the "provincial," and therefore cannot be appropriated exclusively in order to render the provincial and the universal as opposites.[27]

By deploying the metaphor of slowness, Gombrowicz destabilizes another Kantian opposition between stasis and movement, which posits progress as a linear succession of finalized, dynamic changes. Slowness permits Gombrowicz to negotiate and revise the notion of change and agency in order to consider a variety of modes of movement such as delay, lingering, circulation, and drifting, which also engender some action and contribute to change, but in a less strategically oriented manner. This slowness, represented for instance by the action of casual strolling through the orchard, presupposes a fluid, continuous movement, and suggests the conflation of stasis and movement that diffuses the binary. More importantly, since the slow mode blurs the division between stasis and movement, it also makes figuring the limits of change and distinguishing between the specific links within a chain of change impossible. Ultimately, through the mode of slowness, Gombrowicz's revisions contribute to challenging the value of the completion of cultural processes, and rupture all parameters codifying the idea of progress as a linear, goal-oriented, and structured succession of changes.

Thus, Gombrowicz's "salutary revision" suggests a call for an open-ended approach to cultural production and a nonevaluative notion of difference collapsing the established hierarchies and the strictly codified system of norms and values. While reclaiming slowness for the cultural discourse, Gombrowicz does not propose to obliterate the division between the specific cultures, nor does he abolish the concept of East and West. What he attempts to abolish is the system of cultural hierarchy predicated on the idea of development. In this sense, Gombrowicz's position is anti-Kantian and anti-Enlightenment, and his recourse to a Sarmatian, premodern model of society points to the arbitrariness of the universalist cultural classifications of the Enlightenment.

Weakening

Such classifications are also reflected in the structures of power underlying modern civil societies, which Gombrowicz's writing is especially keen on tracing and exposing. Through the metaphors of "weakening" and "softening," which are both variations of slowness, Gombrowicz collapses and confuses the traditional connotations of power in Western and Eastern European cultural discourse. He introduces the notion of weakening through references to Poland's geographical position "between the East and the West, where Europe starts to draw to an end,"[28] thus pointing to Poland's specific positioning (on the imaginary map of Europe) that was responsible for its belated, or partial participation in the processes of industrialization that were fundamental for the consolidation of Western modernity. Such a view figures Poland as an exhausted, partially articulated and ambivalent part of Europe, both geographically and historically, which in the time of technological, social, and political transformation was still dominated by old-fashioned values and obsolete social structures and economic models, thus inevitably losing political significance in the modern world. Gombrowicz draws a picture of such a weak, village culture:

> This was a culture of plains and villages, deprived of big cities and a strong bourgeoisie where life concentrates and complicates, raises and gains momentum due to a multiplicity of interhuman couplings. That was a culture of squire, peasant, and priest. The squire hustled the peasant to work, and the parish priest was the oracle.[29]

This account, which clearly echoes eighteenth-century Western descriptions, juxtaposes two cultures, one representing a "strong" and the other a "weak" cultural modality. The first characterizes modern social, civil, and urban constructs, and is expressed in the intense and energetic language of action embodied in "life" that "concentrates and complicates, raises and gains momentum." The second is figured through references to a rural landscape and obsolete social and political formations based on the domination of religion and superstition. Gombrowicz's rhetoric is very complex here. His binary mimics (and parodies) the Western system of cultural evaluations by assuming an authoritative position representative of one single perspective and system of values—that of modern urban culture. However, in order to understand better the binary rhetoric of Gombrowicz's description, one needs to look at another provocative statement, immediately preceding this one, relating to Polish history: "None of the great movements of European culture has ever really ploughed through Poland, not the Renaissance, not the religious wars, not the French revolution, not the industrial revolution. Here we only caught the softened echoes of these processes."[30] From the Western stereotypical perspective, Poland must really seem like a backward province where nothing ever happens, or if something happens, it is "softened" (*złagodzone*), always secondary, and never experienced directly (always mediated). It is not even a full echo, but a sort of reverberated echo, not a real historical process, but something that is only an imitation and a shadow of history. In certain ways, Gombrowicz's passage sounds like a parody of Hegel's famous (or rather infamous) classification of world cultures from the point of view of their participation in history (or European history, which for Hegel is the only history). Hegel's movement- and progress-based perspective makes him decree in one short paragraph that Poland, Russia, and all Slavic lands belong to history only tangentially because of their static, transitory, and partially visible position as a bridge between Asia and Europe.[31] By mimicking such a patronizing perspective (unfortunately, today's views about the West and the rest of the world are still deeply grounded in Hegel's categorizations),[32] Gombrowicz enhances the double-edged rhetoric of his critique. He counterbalances Western arrogance and ignorance not by adopting the typical defensive attitude (in most cases highlighting the Polish national ethos), but—on the contrary—by distancing himself from the Polish heroic tradition.[33] This way he avoids the trap of the catching-up/copying syndrome synonymous with following the dominant discursive paradigms. Even though Polish patriotism and devotion to the national cause, especially during the time of partitions, are claimed by many as indigenous Polish inventions, they are nevertheless derivative of the Western chivalric tradition (both are painfully ridiculed in *Trans-Atlantyk* in scenes of endless duels.) Instead, by resorting to the rural and slow ("softened") side of Polish culture, which I call a space of discursive dissolution, Gombrowicz reclaims the suppressed sphere of indigenous intensities and rhythms, and reinstates its potential for cultural discourse.

By associating Polish culture with rural structures of "plains and villages," and by highlighting a lack of the historical processes that characterize "great movements of European culture," Gombrowicz parodies stereotypical Western perceptions of the East of Europe. In fact, *A Kind of Testament* and the *Diary* abound in evaluative and deprecatory terms referring to Eastern European and other small countries as "secondary European cultures," or "minor, weaker countries." Similarly, Eastern Europeans are designated as "second-hand Europeans [who] could only try to equal Europe."[34] However, by echoing such popular stereotypical valorizations and making excessive use of the terms "Europe" and "European role," Gombrowicz ruptures the stereotypical notion of Europe and Europeanism and its construction in the Eastern and Western mind. Interestingly, by grouping together Poland, Argentina, and Bulgaria (as well as Norway and Holland, which appear only in the English version) as "minor, weaker countries," he simultaneously collapses the geographical configuration of marginalization.[35]

At the same time, Gombrowicz's passage implies that the narratives of heroism and national martyrdom, so conspicuous in Polish history, not only evolve as responses to Western marginalization of Polish culture, but also signal a deeply ingrained inferiority complex. The intertwining and refractions of these discourses crack the surface construction that mimics the Western narrative of cultural superiority. More important, the voices in this ongoing, subtle dialogue configure yet another narrative: a fragile, vacillating and intrinsically weak voice of identity that is constantly suppressed and never fully surfaces, but that undeniably underlies the dominant narrative traditions and rituals. In a sort of post-Freudian manner, the text suggests that what we perceive as ourselves is only a façade, but Gombrowicz finds nothing wrong in that, since "to be human is to be artificial."[36] Gombrowicz's addition to this well-established Freudian construct consists in highlighting that the façade is always in relation with the "weak," fading, imperfect, or "secondary" parts of ourselves (or cultures). In other words, no strong form exists by itself; it is necessarily contaminated, or "softened" (*osłabiana*) in Gombrowicz's language, by the weak (nondominant) forms. Thus, every seemingly monologic or strong form (including the concept of identity) must be intrinsically dialogic, and continuously disrupted by a variety of voices or narratives. Gombrowicz's concept of identity (he often refers to it as the *interhuman church* or as "interhuman couplings," as in the earlier quoted passage), which resembles Bakhtinian heteroglossia, emphasizes that in cultural or aesthetic practice one can deal only with continuous "weakening" (*osłabianie*), or the ongoing dialogue of the forms that are neither fully strong, nor completely fading. In fact, Gombrowicz is very close to Gianni Vattimo's rethinking of the Hegelian

Aufhebung—crucial to Hegel's structuring of movement/development—which Vattimo also frames in terms of weakening as *pensiero debole* (weak thought).[37] As Gombrowicz and later Vattimo (in a way countering Hegel) point out, the strong forms of discourse only freeze movement and are discursively counterproductive, whereas weakness, rephrased as ambivalence or malleability of forms, enriches human contacts and opens up the space for cultural exchange.

In Gombrowicz's writing, the structures of weakness disrupt binary oppositions and the univocal narrative of meaning; the "borrowed," parodic voice (which is always relational) not only ruptures the codified definitions of East and West, but, more importantly, points to their mutual interconnectedness—there is no West without East and vice versa. Similarly, within this construct of weakness, the question of Poland's historical identity, and more specifically the inability to achieve closure on that identity, is posited not as a negative tendency, but as a positive, or natural modality characterizing the processes of identity formation.

The space limitations of this essay do not allow me to expand on the complexities and intricacies of the relationship between Poland and Argentina in Gombrowicz's writing, to which I alluded earlier. Let me just reflect briefly on the way Argentina, although geographically positioned on the other side of the globe, far from Europe and Poland, continuously masquerades in Gombrowicz's writing as a refraction of both: there are obvious references to Argentina as a liberated Europe, but at the same time Argentina often becomes a reinvented, less constricted, open-ended version of Poland, and these two versions merge and overlap. Gonzalo's estate from *Trans-Atlantyk* displays the complexities of this important, yet never unambiguous relationship. Argentina continues European tradition, but contaminates it with its own cultural codes. Therefore, all the dogs at Gonzalo's estate are strangely muted and crossed not only with different kinds of their own species, but also with completely different species or, we can say, different orders of thinking. Similarly, the books in Gonzalo's library and the artifacts in the numerous salons of his opulent residence represent all possible, often very unusual creations of humanity, or combinations of thought, traditions, and cultures. This constructed cosmopolitanism, however, does not suggest a mutual acceptance and seamless blending of two cultural strands: the books, dogs, and art objects are in constant friction. They "bite" each other, as Gombrowicz's narrator comments, but they do not dominate one another; instead, they "get cheaper" (*tanieją*) and coexist because they literally melt into each other. Their individual value is destabilized in that space of dissolution: the discursive fabric loosens up and allows for the nondivisive and nonexclusionary conceptualization of the difference.[38] The weakened, and therefore more culturally receptive space of Argentina allows for the coexistence of various (even the most bizarre) forms, and permits the reinscription into its discursive fabric of a more open, less stereotypical Europe, and by extension a more open, less heroic or fundamentalist Poland. The last scene of *Trans-Atlantyk* ends the book with the image of overpowering, echoing laughter that only reconfirms the book's multiple contentions about the untenability and irrationality of the total domination of strong forms in any type of discourse—aesthetic, historical, social, or political. For Gombrowicz, modern intensities, grounded in strong paradigms of power, are stifling and oppressive, and therefore contradict the very movement of modernity.

Gombrowicz's conceptualization of form clearly demonstrates the exhaustion of the structures of meaning and communication grounded in the strong (or closed) paradigms of meaning. As the previously quoted passages show, his approach to form relies on the overlapping of two inseparable orders: one that connotes a codified system of organization, authority, normative coherence, and cognitive stability, and the other that manifests itself as disjunction, chaos, irregularity, incoherence, and cognitive fluctuation.[39] However, these two orders can be distinguished only in their mutual intertwining and interrelation; every attempt to separate them as "strong" and "weak" leads to arbitrariness that proves untenable and destroys both orders.[40] Instead, Gombrowicz proposes a system of mediation through weakening. When he asks rhetorically, "What is Poland?" and responds, "It is a country between the East and the West, where Europe starts to draw to an end, a border country where the East and the West soften into each other,"[41] he suggests not only that this part of Europe constitutes a middle ground between the two opposite points, or moments, on the East-West trajectory, but also that these points are arbitrary, unstable, and dependent on the observer's position. It is virtually impossible to dissociate one from the other or to draw a line between the two, since they "soften into each other" and form "a country of weakened forms."[42] The idea of softening or weakening, while blurring the contours of forms, also implies a less phallic and "centric" mode of being and communication,[43] and simultaneously signals an aesthetic attitude congenial to Bakhtin's concept of identity or Heideggerian *Mitsein*.

As I have already mentioned, Gombrowicz's notion of softening, as well as his concept of identity, implies the relational concept of form. Such an approach characterizes Jean Luc Nancy's notion of a community perceived as a "sharing, diffusion, or impregnation of an identity by a plurality."[44] Both Gombrowicz and Nancy pronounce the impossibility of drawing a stable boundary—be it East and West, or self and other. Yet, while Nancy collapses the notion of boundary, in Gombrowicz the boundaries as circumscriptive orders are not always already collapsed; he inscribes them in order to dislodge them. This preoccupation with framing and unframing, and perhaps more specifically with the locus and moment of breaking—when the crack is perceived, so to speak (as for instance in *Cosmos* when Witold and Fuchs observe the lines on the ceiling)—locates Gombrowicz closer to Bakhtin's position, which deems the process of framing and unframing necessary for true communication.[45] Softening, or slowing down, is synonymous with the moments of discursive dissolution, or "unknotting" (my paraphrase of Nancy's term)[46] of firmly coded structures of meaning. When the fabric of discourse loosens up, we begin to see the structure itself, with the intertwining of and frictions between various discursive strands. There are numerous examples of such moments even in Gombrowicz's early work. The beggar with the twig and the famous compote scene from *Ferdydurke*, or Ivona's choking on the bone and her persistent silence, indicate such moments of discursive ambiguity and transformation into another order of meaning. What we are witnessing in these scenes is the crumbling of the discourse of rationality and authority, and the transition to the postmodern mode of uncertainty.

"Intrusion," another of Gombrowicz's metaphors, demonstrates how softening operates: although intrusion is traditionally associated with strong modes of action, when situated within a context of the peasant metaphor it loses its semantic stability, or becomes dialogized in the Bakhtinian sense. Toward the end of A *Kind of Testament*, Gombrowicz invites his reader to "think of [his] *Diary* as such an *intrusion* into the European culture of a villager, of a Polish squire, with all the mistrust, the common sense, and the realism of a peasant."[47] On the surface, this intrusion seems like a classic, decisive intervention of one mode into another, in this case of a supposedly lower into a seemingly higher order. However, since in the whole text the meanings coalescing around the metaphors of the village tempo of life, "peasant" philosophy, and provincial values come to denote the undoing or blurring of what has previously been encoded, the notion of intrusion also becomes contaminated by these connotations.

Cultural critique, according to Gombrowicz, should operate as such softened intrusion, that is, as an order that opens itself up to be modified or diffused by other modalities of thinking (and since Gombrowicz maintains that modes of thinking are slow, he simultaneously implies modification by slow modes of agency). In *A Kind of Testament* he writes:

> I emphasize my rustic background because that seems to me the most creative element in my diary and that is where the criticism starts. Although this criticism . . . is not so simple. Indeed, my campaign against intensity couldn't itself be intense, my diary couldn't become what it wanted to put into question, it couldn't turn into all that it was fighting against. This critique had to be casual and relaxed . . . and it had to be relaxed even in its relaxation. . . . I don't want to be like a wave breaking against a cliff, but . . . I want to be like water that soaks, drenches, saturates.[48]

Thus, the criticism to which Gombrowicz alludes as "intensity," in order to become effective, needs to be modified by the "rustic background." Only then can it become "casual and relaxed." This softened or relaxed criticism does not need to "be like a wave breaking against a cliff"; it does not need to resort to categorizing and validating since, as Gombrowicz emphasizes, "its strength . . . lay in its weakness."[49] Softening and weakening turn into a self-aware critical strategy, which uses its own indigenous modes of agency in order to be effective. Intrusion, then, from the Eastern European perspective, suggests a critique by contamination and sharing instead of maintaining a distance, by admitting one's own insufficiencies rather than claiming one's superiority, by pointing to the variety of possible solutions instead of clinging to one "objective" critical strategy. Eventually, by aligning intrusion with "rustic background," Gombrowicz shrinks the universalist perspective of criticism to everyday, local dimensions.

Gombrowicz's rethinking of the mode of speed and his reevaluation of the slow, indigenous modalities of thinking and cultural development are his fundamental contribution to the discussion about the participation of Eastern Europe in the processes of modernization. This question was extremely pertinent in the 1920s, but it is still vital in the postcommunist (postcolonial) era, during the first years of Polish participation in the European Union. His consistent questioning of the stereotypical privileging of strong forms of discourse (authority, rationality) and fast modes of agency (speed), and his opposition to dismissing the slow and weakened local modes as obsolete prove vital not only for Eastern European countries like Poland, the Czech Republic, and Romania, but also for all other typically marginalized cultures. As I have pointed out, Gombrowicz's long-ranging Polish-European-Argentinian perspective is especially valuable in the present global world. His emphasis on the function of slowness and weakening as the intrinsic components of the paradigm of movement and cultural change proves that any discussion of modernity without this element is incomplete and lacking. Change solely grounded in speed, as Virilio observed years after Gombrowicz, can function only as a syndrome of disappearance and movement for its own sake. Together with his contemporaries, like Schulz or Jaroslav Hašek, as well as philosophers like Vattimo (who years after Gombrowicz framed the moment of Hegelian sublation in terms of weak thought), Gombrowicz, through his recourse to local rhythms and indigenous modes of cultural change, offers a more inclusive and more realistic view of the processes of modernization, and his insights seem equally pertinent to European and to global communities. The rustic *flâneur* strolling through the orchard of European culture reminds us that if we accept speed as the foundational construct of modern discourse, we must also accept slowness as its necessary counterpart.

NOTES

1. Virilio refers to speed as a "dynamic metaphor . . . transcribed in philosophical and political terms." *Speed and Politics*, 23.
2. Kundera, *Slowness*, 3.
3. Ibid., 155.
4. Ibid.
5. Ibid.

6. Ibid., 154.

7. McClintock points out that "[i]mperial progress across the space of empire is figured as a journey backwards in time to an anachronistic moment in prehistory. By extension, the return journey to Europe is seen as rehearsing the evolutionary logic of historical progress, forward and upward to the apogee of the Enlightenment in the European metropolis" (40). The journey to "anachronistic spaces always presupposes a modality of slowing down or a delay (both figuratively and physically) because of bad roads, bad services, the loss of direction, and many other obstacles that all travelers to the East have always encountered (be it in reality or in their imagination). Similarly, the journey back to the West is simultaneous with a quicker tempo, efficient services, better roads, and clear vision enabling fast completion of the journey." Ibid.

8. Ibid.

9. I refer to Kant's formulations expounded in his political and historical essays. See Kant, *Perpetual Peace and Other Essays*.

10. Foucault, 247.

11. Ibid., 248.

12. I refer here to the huge body of texts in cultural and literary studies that investigate the general strategies of modernity, including those by Michael Foucault, Fredric Jameson, Timothy Reiss, Paul de Man, and Benedict Anderson, to name a few. Others, like Edward Said, Homi Bhabha, Ngũgĩ Wa Thiongo, Gayatri Chakravorty Spivak, and Henry Louis Gates Jr., mark the main areas of investigation in colonial and postcolonial studies. The texts by Eric Hobsbawm, Gregory Jusdanis, Tomoslav Longinovich, and Larry Wolff focus on the tensions and frictions between the dominating strands of modernity and the subjugated indigenous traditions. I narrow my discussion to the space of Eastern Europe, and even more to Poland, but I situate it within the broader context of discussions about the implementation of the dominating discourse of modernity, and all countercurrents and reactions that such a process triggers. For compelling Western travelers' accounts of Eastern Europe in the eighteenth and nineteenth centuries, see Wolff.

13. I refer here to the partitions of Poland in 1772, 1793, and 1795 by Russia, Austria, and Prussia, which are examples of colonization within Europe. See, for instance, Davies, *Heart of Europe*, 306–11.

14. Such a discursive approach to identity construction reflects Gombrowicz's central notion of the "interhuman church" (*kościół międzyludzki*), which is grounded in the idea of dialogue and sharing with the other.

15. Like Max Horkheimer and Theodor Adorno, Gombrowicz approaches war as a continuation of Enlightenment formulations of modernity. He also anticipates Virilio's configurations of war (in *Speed and Politics*) as an embodiment of speed. See also Gombrowicz's reflections on the pre–World War II period in terms of increased dynamization of European production in the late 1930s in *A Kind of Testament*, 58–59.

16. Gombrowicz, *A Kind of Testament*, 118.

17. I refer here to Slavoj Žižek's article "The Ongoing 'Soft Revolution'" about the crisis of intellectualism in the twenty-first century, published in the winter 2004 *Critical Inquiry*, which was fully devoted to this problem. Žižek and other participants in the discussion, such as William J. Thomas Mitchell, Fredric Jameson, Homi Bhabha, Wayne Booth, and others, diagnosing the state of critical thinking in the postcapitalist/postmodern era, point to the disappearance of the mode of production itself, which is replaced by the flow of changing affects.

18. Gombrowicz and Roux, 103–4; my translation. Every time I highlight a specific meaning I use my own translation from the Polish version of *A Kind of Testament* (revised by Gombrowicz).

19. Gombrowicz, *Diary*, 46.

20. In popular perception, sarmatism was also encoded as orientalization of customs and aesthetic inclinations. A taste for oriental design influenced fashions and household decoration. Men's garments especially were modeled on an Eastern (mostly Turkish) fashion. Households dazzled visitors with the splendour of Eastern rugs and tapestries. See the entry for "Sarmatyzm" in Kopaliński, 1037. See also Płonowska Ziarek, 219–21, and Wandycz, *Price of Freedom*, 89–90.

21. Płonowska Ziarek, 219.

22. As Wandycz points out, historical evaluations of sarmatism and the political system of the Polish seventeenth-century commonwealth known as "Respublica" vary; some, like R. H. Lord, see in it "the largest and the most ambitious experiment with a republican form of government that the world had seen since the days of the Romans." (88). Others, like the Dutch lawyer Hugo Grotius, also quoted by Wandycz, perceive sarmatism as the embodiment of the Polish gentry's love for freedom. Wandycz situates the question of sarmatism within a broader context of political and economic crisis in seventeenth-century East Central Europe. In Poland, this crisis surfaced as the conflict between the centralizing, absolutist tendency represented by the magnates, and the decentralizing aim of the squirearchy. For a discussion of seventeenth-century East Central Europe, see Wandycz, *Price of Freedom*, chapter 3, and especially pp. 85–90 describing the situation in Poland.

23. Gombrowicz, *A Kind of Testament*, 118.

24. Wandycz points out the interconnectedness between rural, Eastern, and political aspects of sarmatism when he comments: "Sarmatism involved a view of Poland as a granary of Europe and a shield of Christendom against Turks and Tartars, but above all as the realization of a superior form of government inspired by the Roman republic and based on the 'golden freedom'" (*Price of Freedom*, 89). Orientalization (albeit involuntary) and recourse to Roman ideals seem to indicate ways for the Polish squirearchy to circumvent Western economic, political, and cultural modes. This is how Wandycz further comments on Sarmatian philosophy: "There was nothing the Poles could learn from the West, and the oriental dress they adopted from their Muslim foes was underlying their distinct and original identity." Ibid.

25. Stereotypical perceptions of the East (mostly Turkey and Tartary) permeate the critique of sarmatism in *Monitor* articles, as well as Ignacy Krasicki's satires and his *Adventures of Mr. Nicolas Wisdom*. The depictions of sarmatian vices such as a luxurious lifestyle, pomp, and wastefulness are obviously contaminated with the Enlightenment's perceptions of the East.

26. Gombrowicz, *A Kind of Testament*, 53.

27. In the context of the current discussion on globalization, Gombrowicz's problematizing of the opposition between the universal and the provincial, or the global and the provincial, strikes one as especially important. Marshall McLuhan's global village seemed to propagate an optimistic belief in the possibility of sharing the "provincial" within a broader global space. However, recent practices of globalization within the economic and political sphere contradict this optimism from the 1960s; rather than suggesting sharing in diversity, globalization implies operations of the subjugation of small provincial economies to the hegemonic "universal" powers.

28. Gombrowicz, *A Kind of Testament*, 53.

29. Gombrowicz and Roux, 36; my translation.

30. Ibid.

31. In the introduction to *The Philosophy of History*, Hegel presents his view of history as a constant progressive movement. The lack of movement is synonymous with the lack of historical identity and the state of nonbeing. By ascribing the unchanging and nonprogressive status of a "connection with Asia" to Poland, Russia, and Eastern Europe, Hegel excludes these countries from full participation in history. See Hegel, 102.

32. See, for instance, a recent collection of essays relating to the question of European identity, *Old Europe, New Europe, Core Europe: Transatlantic Relations after the Iraq War*, edited by Daniel Levy, Max Pensky, and John Torpey.

33. What I refer to as "heroic" is a tradition in Polish literature and historical discourse that exalts the Polish military and cultural mission, as for instance in messianism. In *Ferdydurke, Trans-Atlantyk*, and the *Diary*, Gombrowicz often parodies the idealization of Polish culture and its military and patriotic traditions. The passage in *Ferdydurke* describing a literature lesson, or a scene presenting the duelling Poles in *Trans-Atlantyk*, are good examples of Gombrowicz's critique.

34. Gombrowicz, *A Kind of Testament*, 55. See also 53–57.

35. Ibid., 57.

36. Gombrowicz and Roux, 40; my translation.

37. See Vattimo.

38. "These Masterpieces, Paintings, Statues, all of them closed here are melting into each other and getting cheaper, because of their own excess they have already become so cheap." Gombrowicz, *Dzieła*, 3:82; my translation.

39. Jerzy Jarzębski points to the epistemological antinomy in Gombrowicz that characterizes his concept of form and his whole philosophy. "One

can either *describe* life, the world, and oneself—but in order to do that, one needs to stand outside and relinquish the possibility of capturing reality directly, without resorting to abstract categories that falsify reality—or one can spontaneously and nonreflexively throw oneself into life. In the latter case, however, one deprives oneself of the possibility of rationalizing one's epistemological experience; one cuts oneself off from culture, which functions as a reservoir of forms and structures that we can utilize while comparing phenomena. That act of comparison also implies being dominated by categorization. We can either face the world through understanding, but then it needs to be falsified, or we can accept the world as a magma and as a flow of billions of individual beings and events, as a *tertium non datur*" ("Między kreacją," 179; my translation).

40. Gombrowicz's writing often uses the construct of a duel to demonstrate the untenability of rigid binaries. In *Ferdydurke* the duel between Filidor, Doctor of Synthesis, and anti-Filidor collapses the system of binary oppositions. See *Ferdydurke*, chap. 5, "The Child Runs Deep in Filidor," (87–101).

41. Gombrowicz, *A Kind of Testament*, 53.

42. Ibid.

43. The mode of dissolution clearly divulges Polish macho traditions of heroism and struggle—in *Trans-Atlantyk* we encounter them as *ojczyzna* (fatherland) and *synczyzna* (son-land)—and invites revisiting them from the less rigid feminine perspective. I discuss this problem more thoroughly in a forthcoming book, provisionally titled *Cultures of Slowness*.

44. Nancy, *Inoperative Community*, 9.

45. In spite of the stress on flexibility and flow contained in the concepts of heteroglossia and dialogism, Bakhtin's theory also points to moments of finalization or closure, no matter how temporary. For instance, in "From Notes Made in 1970–71," he stresses that the exchange between one and the other always entails breaking provisionally constructed boundaries. During the dialogic exchange those boundaries collapse and then get reshaped. The moment of provisional finalization of meaning represents something like a monologic strain in the dialogic infinite flow. Bakhtin believes that the struggle resulting from the constant crossing of the boundary between the monologic and the dialogic constitutes "the act of understanding, [and] . . . results in mutual change and enrichment." *Speech Genres and Other Late Essays,* 142.

46. I am referring to the metaphor of a discursive fabric with knots that Nancy uses in his essay "Exscription," which analyses the rigid hierarchies of power and meaning in Western meaning-bestowing practices. He writes that "the loose ends of something in our history have now been tied up [and] the West is knotted up with writer's cramp" (49).

47. Gombrowicz and Roux, 104–5; my translation and emphasis.

48. Gombrowicz, *A Kind of Testament*, 119.

49. Ibid.

THE NATION AS PATHOLOGY

Representations of Community in Joseph Conrad and Witold Gombrowicz

George Gasyna

I want to start with a problem of definition, actually several problems. How do we conceive of a nation? Can community be thought of as part of the natural order, or is it a social prosthesis or a form of affliction? Does such a thing as community actually exist, or, as Benedict Anderson proposes, is it ultimately an imagined construct?[1] I start with these queries because in various ways they all relate to my main question: Can a writer belong to a community? And the short answer, at least in the case of Joseph Conrad and Witold Gombrowicz, is no, not easily, not naturally. If we leave aside for a moment commonplace romantic (or romanticized) conceptualizations of what nations are and do, and consider instead the nation-construct as a kind of apotheosis of organized power, then the idea of community can be easily condensed to a technique of state coercion over the body politic. To be sure, any such—let us call it Foucauldian—definition of a nation will operate in a dialectic: it will require a collective counterforce such as religion or patriotism, or any number of other sustaining myths of commonality. In other words, the community structurally proposes—or even compels—a collective response to the use of power, and situates this entire process in opposition to the will of the individual. What should be clear by now about this series of abstractions about nation and community is that I am working toward a modern definition of the nation, one that was first introduced—as a discourse—during the French Revolution and that simultaneously gestures to the modalities of the contemporary state and to the emergence of autonomous subjectivity apart from the state and its heads.

As is well known, for all the insistence on the part of nationalist discourses on enforcing organic myths of community, nations and cultures do not arise spontaneously from some pure "essence." Far from representing natural or inevitable expressions of tradition, or even spontaneous inventions, they are elaborate *constructions* guided by what Homi Bhabha has termed a complex performative and enunciative rhetoric of "social reference," which directs the inscription of inclusion and exclusion within some universalist totality.[2] Or, as Ernesto Laclau puts it, the modern postrevolutionary nation-state is the *creation of its citizenry*, which in the name of the common myth of collective transcendence allows itself to be sublimated to a regulatory idea.[3] This is to say that the nation is really a technology of the subject, but one that, while aspiring to express collective/universalist will, often demotes the search for authentic autonomy into a transgressive act. Indeed, those subjects who attempt to assert individuality at all cost—for instance writers and other creative artists—will frequently find themselves ejected from the common space; in Giorgio Agamben's terms they are "banned" from the "sovereign order."[4] In Conrad's case, when such searches for autonomy collide with the discourses of nationalism, patriotism, and empire, for example, the *nation* as an object becomes theorized as a Sustaining Illusion, in other words, as a kind of conceptual pathology. For Gombrowicz, the Nation, particularly its public sphere, is more like a cancer—a soul-draining pathology that is reinforced by both domestic and émigré institutions, and thus all the more socially debilitating to the subject in his search for authenticity and, above all, autonomy.

Conrad's often-expressed identification with the seafaring community, imaginary or not, can be viewed as an antidote to overly deterministic rhetorics of nationalism, both Polish and British. We can see examples of this self-devised affiliation—in Edward Said's sense[5]—in the opening passages of *Heart of Darkness* and "Youth," where Conrad speaks eloquently about the bond of the sea that he shares with his crewmates, and their common fidelity to duty.[6] Besides providing a measure of comfort, the device also allows Conrad to float, as it were, in an ahistorical space, abstracted from the nation (although the ships that he commands sail out from British ports and are manned primarily by English sailors). This dynamic is well established in Conrad's memoirs, or more precisely his two works of strategic auto-fiction, *The Mirror of the Sea* and *A Personal Record*. The short passage cited below, from the last page of *A Personal Record*, attests to the sense of the symbolic power of community for Conrad. Sailing into a Malay harbor on the South China Sea, Conrad notices a departing British ship: "The Red Ensign! In the pellucid colourless atmosphere bathing the drab and grey masses of that southern land, it was as far as the eye could reach the only spot of ardent colour. . . . The Red Ensign—the protecting warm bit of bunting, destined for so many years to be the only roof over my head."[7] If nation can be thought of in some way as a sickness, then it is often—as it is here—a kind of homesickness. Like a mild case of the flu, it has many familiar nostalgic comforts and does not fully incapacitate or kill off the (in this case expatriated and culturally twice-displaced) subject.

For Gombrowicz, as I suggested, the nation stands as a pathology that blocks one's way to self-actualization. The ways in which this dialectic between nation and individual operates in his writing have been rehearsed on numerous occasions. Critics as varied as Jan Błoński, Hanjo Berressem, and Jerzy Jarzębski have attempted to disentangle the vectors of Gombrowicz's antinomian drives and his near-obsession with thinking about art and culture within this structuring system. To get a sense of these dynamics at work, all that the reader needs to do is open Gombrowicz's *Diary* at random: this three-volume exercise in self-making is a text in which the equation between nation and illness is unequivocally established and which represents Gombrowicz's ultimate attempt to work through the urgent problem of individual versus national form. Gombrowicz ultimately capitulates and concludes that "it is those that become most deformed and are made most ill by the forces of collectivity . . . that can best oppose the nation."[8] In other words, one must first accept one's illness—in his case an affliction that he terms "decadence" and "deformation"—in order to assert individuality without compromise. This essential relation would persist with only minor modifications for the rest of his writing life, as Gombrowicz proceeded with his diatribes against Polish culture and the common mantle of Western civilization in works like *A Kind of Testament* and *Wspomnienia polskie* (recently translated as *Polish Memories*), where refrains analogous to those found throughout *Diary* reoccur with frequency.

But let us return to the initial opposition stipulated in this essay, namely, the binary of home and elsewhere. Both Gombrowicz and Conrad are exilic Polish writers; this is how I read them for reasons that should be obvious and that will, in any case, become obvious shortly. Expatriation, or more specifically exilic displacement, is the star that guides their identity politics. While Conrad's voluminous correspondence is the main instrument for delineating his hybrid identity, a number of essays in volumes such as *Notes on Life and Letters* are also concerned with the construction of an ambivalent subject alternating between a politics of resistance and a pragmatics of belonging.

It is no secret that the idea of Poland formed a tropological backdrop for Conrad's polemics with a set of recurring bêtes noires. Central amongst these was the status of the two main partitioning powers, Russia and Germany, on the European stage. Germany's mounting international prestige in the last decades of the nineteenth century and the first decade of the twentieth rankled Conrad. One might even say that at times he textually negated the German nation, and in fact the whole Teutonic region, strategically repositioning it as a nulle place. This is symmetrical with his dismissal of "autocratic Russia" as "le néant"—a nothingness—but the likely motives were very different.[9] My sense is that Conrad's effacements of Germany and Russia reveal a symbolic symmetry with Poland's predicament as a country existing in the heart, but found on no map, for all but the last six years of his life. Thus, with no uncertain defiance, Conrad writes that Germany *scarcely* manages to draw his attention as he traverses it by train while on a journey to Poland in the summer of 1914.[10] It is admittedly a curious situation: this eminent traveler, who on several occasions sailed around the world spurred by nothing more than wanderlust, relinquishes any knowledge of Poland's direct neighbor to the west. In the magisterial essay "Poland Revisited," Conrad gives vent to the following solidly Germanophobe sentiment:

> Germany is that part of the earth's solid surface of which I know the least. And the very little I saw of it was through the window of a railway carriage at express speed. I was *so incurious* that I would have liked to have fallen asleep on the shores of England and opened my eyes, if it were possible, only on the other side of the Silesian frontier. I have never lingered in that land which, on the whole, is so singularly barren of memorable manifestations of generous sympathies and magnanimous impulses. I

> let myself be carried through Germany as if it were *pure space*, without sights, without sounds.[11]

Like the "dark" heart of Africa for the Western colonizers, Germany has been reduced here to a blank space on the map. In a patent transcription of imperialist dialectics, familiar to readers of Conrad in particular from *Heart of Darkness*, the geographically nameless becomes inconsequential *in itself*, and thus inferior. Moreover, by its effacement from Conrad's mental map, Germany is symbolically made to share Poland's unhappy fate. In the same work Russia is represented as a metaphysical blankness. The Russian empire's vast size and power are negated in strict proportion to what Conrad perceives as the tsardom's denials of basic liberties to its subjects. In the somewhat programmatic, some might say tendentious essay "Autocracy and War," the author even describes Russia as "a country held by an evil spell," with its ruling régime apparently reveling in "the ruthless destruction of innumerable minds and hopes."[12]

While Russia and Germany are represented by double inversion as "no-places" by a writer himself hailing from a "noncountry" that had once been located between them, Conrad's inscription of Poland, and Cracow in particular, belongs to an atemporal realm of nostalgia. Precisely because of their synchronous qualities, Conrad's "imaginary domestic topographies" work to counter the discourses of nation and empire. In "Poland Revisited," Conrad's final reunion with Cracow in 1914 with his son Borys is depicted as a kind of pilgrimage to a private identity long superseded by a series of public ones. The return here has all the hallmarks of the surreal. For instance, Conrad remarks that "I felt so much like a ghost that the discovery that I could remember such material things as which turn to take and the general direction of the street gave me a moment of wistful surprise."[13] Further, though he confides in the reader that he has changed in fundamental ways, the old royal capital and now Austrian colonial (and military) outpost remains locked in the chronotopes of his memory, curiously unchanged, as though "exterior" linear time has been suspended during his absence. Cracow thus emerges essentially as a realm of memory in Pierre Nora's sense.[14] This particular *lieu de mémoire* hovers in an interior tropological space:

> The [Market] Square, *immense in its solitude*, was full to the brim of moonlight. I noticed with infinite satisfaction that the unnecessary trees the Municipality insisted on sticking between the stones had been steadily refusing to grow. They were not a bit bigger than the *poor victims* that I could remember. Also, the paving operations seemed to be exactly at the same point at which I left them forty years before.[15]

I want to draw your attention to those two words *immense* and *solitude* in the depiction of the market square. Who is remembering thus? To whom would Cracow's Rynek Główny seem immense? Certainly to an orphaned boy, and this I think is the point, for while the Rynek constitutes a large medieval square, it is not particularly immense when compared with the public urban spaces of London or Paris. As for solitude, whose solitude can this symbolically invoke if not Conrad's own, a sense of his private isolation that constitutes a primary function of exilic displacement? In fact, the passage represents a remarkable piece of mnemotechnics: on one level Conrad is giving full expression to nostalgia, which, as Proust would remind us, has to do not so much with spatial as with temporal dislocation. On another level, especially in the context of the Russification and Germanization programs imposed on ethnically Polish regions during the Partitions, the reference to the trees as "poor victims" seems markedly cathected. No doubt these were *not* the same trees that Conrad remembers from forty years before. But that's almost immaterial; they are far more potent as signifiers of a certain kind of narratological focalization. What counts is their metonymic status as innocents subjected to coercion; they are pilloried between stones, an image of imprisonment par excellence. We might also note their tangible resistance to this force: the trees were "steadily refusing to grow" within the forms *imposed* on them from the outside. As embodiments of the particular Conradian set of Sustaining Illusions, then, these trees are both reassuring and distressing, a fitting metaphor for the author's ambivalence toward notions of affiliation and national belonging.

When Conrad inscribes such personally vital notions into his essays on Poland and memory, it may well be in an effort to work through their influence on his worldview. But such ideas and the ideologies backing them were largely foreign to his English readership, outside the usual scope of social experience of a metropolitan culture that was then the center of a worldwide empire. How, then, could Conrad connect to this readership? My view is that the two tropes that ended up displacing bona fide Polish thematics—with the exception of the tale "Prince Roman" and a handful of political essays—are those of the ship and the voyage, and the Homo Duplex persona. Each of these figures, or more precisely narratological modes of approach, represents a way of symbolically universalizing his experience.

Ships, as means of transport and as shelter, are microcosms of the ordinary world and its conflicts. More germane to Conrad's poetics, perhaps, their hermetic conditions are also to some degree variations on Noah's ark, with all the implicit potentialities of community building and the coercions of mutual interdependence to be textually exploited. On a banal—or bourgeois, Victorian—level, voyages constitute an important part of practical, and even sentimental, education. But they can also incorporate an epistemological prerogative, as is the case with voyages of "self-discovery," whose hoped-for trajectory is always oriented toward penetrating the mysteries of existence. The figure of the ship thus functions for Conrad as a kind of neuter, a zero point. Nominally ships belong to states or empires, of course; hence Conrad's attachment to them as symbolic shelters. At the same time, however, ships operate in free zones; moving in international waters, they proceed from contact point to contact point along seaboards. As synecdoches of nation they are thus far less inevitable or immutable than embassies, or even texts. In the novella "Youth," Conrad even suggests that one ship is like another, that they are all fundamentally the same:[16] in other words, for Conrad ships serve as backgrounds, platforms for setting into motion urgent private dramas of identity construction and public ones of community formation.

As far as is known, Conrad's first self-reference as a Double Man can be found in his 1903 letter to Kazimierz Waliszewski, a Polish historian then living in Paris.[17] Conrad was at the time in the midst of completing *Nostromo*, the first of his novels not to be set on the sea or to deal principally with marine themes and autobiographical motifs. Perhaps his confrontation with the problematics of writing about the full breadth of social issues is what prompted Conrad to face his own duality of career and language. The first intimation of the plurality of his life story, and of his view of himself as multiple, however, may have registered as early as 1890, while he was still at sea. While briefly on land in the exotic Canary Islands, Conrad wrote a letter to his aunt, Marguerite Poradowska, who was then living in Brussels, in which he reported: "[T]he screw turns, taking me into the unknown. Happily there is *another I* who roams all over Europe, who is *at this moment with you*, who will go before you to Poland. Another I who moves from one place to another with great ease, who can even be in two places at once."[18] As can be gleaned from that declaration, initially the Conradian self is split geographically, rather than intellectually, though some kind of disjunctive blueprint that cannot be ascribed to romantic transcendentalist notions of motion seemed in the offing. Conrad may not have been fully aware of its implications, but the fissure apparently represented a serious-enough matter: "Don't laugh!" he admonishes Poradowska before adding, "however, I permit you to say 'how foolish he is!'"[19] As he continued to rework the Homo Duplex identity, however, he found a kind of psychological compromise. The public figure of a Polish émigré who managed to liberate himself from both the national martyrology and the legendary figure of his insurrectionist father-martyr, Apollo, began increasingly to be coupled with an equally public and largely self-fashioned image of the provincial British novelist (in the sense of his chosen domestic situation, not choice of themes, of course).

Returning to Polish settings, Cracow as a locus of memory represented for Conrad the site of family rupture, the space of orphanage; only in 1914 would it become the site of an orchestrated reterritorialization, as Conrad showed his son Borys the metaphorical zone of his own father, the locus of his private tragedies and secrets. In fact, that nocturnal walk with Borys closely follows the path taken by Apollo Korzeniowski's funeral cortège and even coincides with it for several blocks.[20] This is not something that is volunteered by the text, of course. It remains up to the reader to piece together the two trajectories described, locate the sites mentioned, and realize that as Conrad retraces his steps in his Fathertown, he is triumphing—here and now, with his son, as an indisputably successful though "foreign" author—over the very sense of historical injustice that sent him into exile to be a wanderer. Conrad thus not only demarcates the imaginative space of his father and of their past perambulations but also symbolically reclaims the Fatherland as his own. He is gesturing both to a time long gone, when such perambulations with his father were possible, and to his present cultural hybridity as a *dual subject*. The passage, then, defuses and condenses to the level of anecdote the full emotional charge of what was, in fact, an exultant return of a former victim and orphan, but now unquestionably a survivor and *paterfamilias* with a legacy of his own in the making. Conrad thus metonymically completes the cycle of personal and paternal peregrinations—a history, as we know well, whose Polish chapter ended in tragedy, with his parents' premature deaths.

On the other hand, the Polish countryside, associated with the impoverished though dignified existence of the once-magnificent gentry—the *szlachta*—remained a positively charged space for Conrad (especially in his letters), even if brushes with the forces and whims of empire were inevitable there as well. This conceptual coupling of "land" ownership, that is, of living close to the land as a natural prerogative, with positive cultural value holds true for Conrad's memories of his childhood homes and the bucolic estate of his maternal uncle Tadeusz Bobrowski, where Conrad spent time as a youth and where he returned to stay for lengthy periods between his seafaring adventures. In contrast with the Arcadian purity of the countryside, in the Conradian narrative the City, with all its anonymity and multiplication of fates and aspirations, constitutes a locus of suspicion and anarchy (for example, in *The Secret Agent*) or of political foment and moral degeneracy (as in *Under Western Eyes* or *Nostromo*). The notion of land and landownership, then, provides a conceptual foothold for the author's resistance to new social ideologies such as imperialist nationalism or communitarian alternatives like socialism. It is ironic to see such a defense of old-school notions of the *Heimat* in a writer otherwise as peripatetic and cosmopolitan as Conrad, but it is unmistakably there. In fact, one of his closest friends and collaborators in England, Ford Madox Ford, wrote that Conrad, though "above all things, a Pole of the last century," actively sought to become and to be taken for a "country gentleman"—though Ford sees this as an assumption of an "English" identity.[21]

Considering the fact that country estates were something Conrad knew well and loved from his *Polish* youth, it seems to me that his decision to leave London for a series of residences in the Home Counties may have had more to do with being able to reproduce key tropes of *szlachta* existence in relative privacy and isolation. The *szlachcic* ideal is iconographically buttressed by a sizable portrait of Marshal Piłsudski, another larger-than-life Pole from the eastern borderlands or Kresy, displayed in a prominent place in Conrad's study at his home at Oswalds (near Canterbury) and spotted there by visitors as early as 1919.[22] And it is reinforced symbolically by his refusal, in 1924, of an offer of an English knighthood, based on the argument that as a Korzeniowski and as a Nałęcz, he was already a noble and had no use for a British peerage. This overall trajectory strikes me, in the last analysis, as an archetypally classist reaction—a kind of homing instinct, or a corrective to the narrative of recurrent deterritorializations that started when, at the age of six years, Conrad was carted off from Warsaw to Vologda for four years with his father and mother.

Conrad's dynamic scripting of class identity, then, forms the final counterindication to the pathology of nation. Conrad the double man, the Homo Duplex, charted his own middle way between the grand narratives of his time. And thus we end with another classically Conradian paradox, which could be expressed in the following formula: to the extent that Conrad retained an essential measure of hybrid vitality as he negotiated his exilic displacement, he succeeded in large part because he rejected nation while remaining faithful to the sustaining illusions of his class, not only the sailors but also, and principally, the landed gentry.

Out-of-the-way bucolic estates also figure in Gombrowicz's writing, not only in his prose and dramatic works, but also in his *Diary* and other memoir-type narratives. However, compared with Conrad's childhood recollections, which involve the psychological projection of otherness and nostalgia, Gombrowicz's memory writing is part of what I shall call his formal exilic imaginary. At the core, all of these texts revolve around problems of form, class, nation, and deviation from these communal markers, within a dialectic of orthodoxy versus alterity that Gombrowicz applies retroactively to his Polish years.

We see this antinome in anecdotes about such matters as the formality of his upbringing, the mannerisms of his social class, and the infrequency of his contacts with the outside world. In a number of emblematic passages in *A Kind of Testament* that deal with his domestic situation, one is immediately struck by the impact of the national form on the configurations of individual identity and by the correlation between class identity and the possibility of autonomous subjectivity. For example, the reader is told—in *A Kind of Testament* as well as the presumably more self-consciously confessional *Polish Memories*[23]—that the Gombrowicz clan's ancestral estate in Lithuania was confiscated after the uprising of 1863, as a result of which the family was forced to relocate, ending up at Małoszyce, a modest manor house in the part of eastern Poland then under Russian control (in Sandomierz province). However, rather than viewing this as a straightforward case of deterritorialization, Gombrowicz seizes the opportunity to decrypt the various social hierarchies of the Polish borderlands within the broader context of intersubjective identity formation. It was at Małoszyce that Gombrowicz caught glimpses of imperial Russian, German, and Austrian troop movements en route to World War I battlefields; this initial contact established a primary connection with the male homosocial world that would reappear in his novels. In *A Kind of Testament*, Gombrowicz reports the scene in the following way:

> The odor of brutality rose around us, invaded, excited us all—though by *virtue of my class* I was protected from any direct contact with the war effort. Nonetheless, the front passed our way four times, the far-off rumble of artillery at times growing louder; conflagrations, attacking battalions, battalions retreating, corpses lying there around the pond—and we local boys collected the spent shells, old bayonets, bits and pieces of materiel. . . . My sense of eroticism, fed by war, by stories of rape, by the smell of soldierly sweat, made me turn away from my salon upbringing, toward the lower depths, *away from the aristocrat within me and toward the slave*, toward bodies and toil. Oh, I became quite the Marxist in those early days.[24]

The passage is captivating and revealing not only because of its evocation of military aesthetics but specifically because the major questions animating Gombrowicz's writing are all present and accounted for here, albeit in embryo form. We can note his almost obsessive interest in class and status, the emergent homoerotic poetics, a fascination with the corporeal generally, and last but not least, his formal dialectics of the speaking subject positioned either as trapped within a national form or else as vacillating from one available or imagined form to another (e.g., serf vs. landowner).

For the most part, the life of the *ziemiaństwo* (landowners) as Gombrowicz knew them was isolated and artificial. Especially when contrasted with the professional and educated middle classes, whose daily work "brought them in confrontation with everyday realities," Gombrowicz's own small *szlachta* class was self-quarantined, had no authentic contact with life.[25] In his view, class echelons in the Polish provinces during the Partitions were very clearly demarcated. The working classes worked and served—simple enough. But the upper classes, while nominally free (though of course subject to a foreign empire), were actually far from liberated. Specifically, their self-imprisonment within a socially mannerist straitjacket is what made them seem "grotesque" and "idiotic" in the eyes of the "populace." For Gombrowicz, the upheaval of World War I and the sense of "emotional awakening" at its finale, apart from shaking him out of childhood self-absorption and a placid life with the various sickly "aunties" who doted on him (some of whom may have been countesses), irreversibly altered these social dynamics in Poland.[26]

Gombrowicz's second foundational drama vis-à-vis nation occurred when he was a student at a lycée in Warsaw, against the background of the 1920 Bolshevik invasion of Poland. Gombrowicz treats the event rather laconically in *Polish Memories*, written in Argentina during the late 1950s, likely because the subject matter would have been censored—and the eventual publisher censured—had the book ever reached communist Poland. Nevertheless, the personal pressure of this decisive confrontation between a classist instrument of domination (bolshevism) and a collective "national" resistance to it (Polish nationalism) would prove cathartic. Gombrowicz makes it clear that the prevailing sentiment in Poland during the fateful summer of 1920 was *fear of revolution*, though possibly this fear permeated mainly his own social sphere; some certainly welcomed the notion of social transformation, at least in theory. Specifically, the talk of general mobilization to repel the Soviet invaders compelled Gombrowicz to seek a way out of the confrontation of the great narratives of nation and class playing out before his eyes. The discourse of individualism offered just such a means of escape. The phenomenon of war generally, and the conflict of 1920 specifically, was what made him aware of the fundamental meaning of the "I" and of the inherent "value" of individual existence. In Gombrowicz's view, these matters had been traditionally discounted in Poland, especially in contrast with constructs of subjectivity in Western countries, as reflected by their respective literatures.[27]

To summarize, Gombrowicz is a priori unwilling to consider the "ultimate sacrifice" for any collective, or for any institution, no matter how seductive its agenda (or propaganda). Moreover, the account of his reactions to the wars waged during his youth is realized through the prism of individual sensibility; in other words, it is as far abstracted from the mythopoeic collective experience of those events as possible. Thus, ostentatiously sublimating the upheaval of an entire nation to a personal drama in *Polish Memories*, Gombrowicz is only being consistent when he concludes, "[T]he year of 1920 made me what I have remained to the present day—an individualist."[28]

In what follows, I examine the ways in which the opposition between the individual and the national form is configured in Gombrowicz's first exilic work, *Trans-Atlantyk*. Here, the identity drama evolves from an antinomian couplet of home and elsewhere to a set of triangulations between the language and culture of the displaced foreigner, those of the local South Americans, and those of the Polish diasporic communities. In their various interpenetrations we glimpse the possibility of a new autonomous hybrid identity. The novella begins with the promise of a transoceanic sea voyage, a journey through a smooth and deterritorialized space, which Zdravko Malić has referred to as the "zero-point" between "two force-fields" of the Fatherland and the land of expatriation.[29] Suspended between these totalities, Gombrowicz's narrator, much like the free-floating diarist Conrad of the merchant marine period, drifts in a "fluid" space where cultural and national affiliation can temporarily be forgotten. Speaking of this voyage, the textual "Gombrowicz" declares: "Exquisitely pleasurable the sail from Gdynia to Buenos Aires, and somewhat loathe was I to go ashore, for 20 days a man between Sky and water, nothing remembered, bathed in air, melted in wave, through-blown with wind."[30]

Departing from this undivided state of pleasurable liminary existence, the narrative's first discursive function is to outline the semiologies and iconographies of the various alternatives available to the suddenly exilic subject. As the Lacanian critic Hanjo Berressem has observed, the move from Poland to Argentina signifies a moment in the work when the stable patriarchal symbolic order is seemingly annulled, but a new one has not yet become assembled.[31] Yet while the author's real-life exile to Argentina structures the narration and imposes a strict linear chronology, the factor of geographical displacement in and of itself acts merely as a prompt, initiating the vastly more important metanarrative of expatriate becoming. This is why initially the notion of ambivalence inherent in expatriation becomes subsumed in the novel into an ethos of the individual: the individual who is thrust against a cultural dialectic and forced to commit to *certain* forms of exilic belonging but not others. Again, recall that Gombrowicz's artistic credo is that the individual must under no circumstances give up his autonomy—and certainly not his life—for any abstraction or ideal. The individual, he suggests in the second volume of the *Diary*, represents an essence more fundamental than the nation. He must therefore take precedence over the nation and all conceptualizations of the national idea or "national thought." Indeed, in order to begin to "exist in reality" (that is, in authentic form), the Polish individual must "liberate himself from the nation."[32] This position is dialectically reinforced by Gombrowicz's denunciation of collectivity and ideals of collective consciousness in statements that immediately follow this manifesto. There he elaborates a "simple law" by consequence of which the power of the collective can remain strong: "the power of the nation is always consolidated at the expense of the individual . . . everyone makes a kind of concession of his or her individuality and resistance."[33] Perhaps the best way to describe *Trans-Atlantyk* is that the work is intended as a willful transgression of that particular law at a time when its legislative power is strongest and most manifest, namely, during times of national crisis, specifically wartime.

Still, in spite of affirmations of individual autonomy with which the novel is punctuated, a crucial measure of ambivalence is strategically inscribed through the figure of Pan Cieciszowski. His is the kind of ambivalence that usually becomes sublimated into either homesickness and nostalgia, or else a drive toward acculturation and assimilation at the expense of one's former domestic self—though in this particular case his subjectivity has somehow not coagulated. The needed intertext here is the breakout of World War II just a few days earlier, which prompted many of those who found themselves abroad to desperately seek a passage home to join the fight against the Nazis. Herewith, a fragment of Cieciszowski's now-famous counseling session:

> "No Remedy! I understand your Sorrow, but you can't jump over the ocean, so I approve of your Resolution or disapprove and well you did to remain here, but perchance you did Not."
>
> "Is this your view?"
>
> "I'm not so mad as to have any views These Days or not to have them. But now that you have tarried here, get ye anon to the Legation or do not get ye there and Report your presence there or do not Report it, for if you Report your presence or you do not Report it, you may be in great trouble or you may not."[34]

What the heavy though bitter farce of the passage (which continues for another paragraph) makes clear is that the destruction of the old Polish order cannot be finalized in the place of exile precisely because, and so long as, patriotic agencies such as the Polish Legation continue to exert power over the diaspora. If the faithfully transplanted pre–World War II class distinctions and codes of decorum are anxiously reproduced in Argentina by the majority of the expatriates, it is not only in an attempt to reinforce a communal sense of identity but also as an exercise in power politics that figuratively extends the zone of the Fatherland beyond its legislated borders. In *Trans-Atlantyk* Gombrowicz is particularly merciless about exposing this underside of the émigré project, showing traditional Polish chivalry and grandiloquence to be anachronisms mobilized in support of a vocabulary of vacuous gestures, which are in turn exaggerated even further, having been removed from their cultural source and reconstituted in an opposition to the forms found in exile. Gombrowicz's depictions of "treasured" national institutions such as duels, folk dances, secret societies, and chivalric orders, once rhapsodized over by Polish Romantic poets and in Henryk Sienkiewicz's *Trilogy*, find themselves formally distended beyond endurance in *Trans-Atlantyk*. Transformed into parodies, they only underscore their ultimate emptiness as legitimate cultural signifiers.

But Gombrowicz is not content with just attacking convenient instantiations of static cultural forms. From the liminary space of *Trans-Atlantyk* he goes after their sources, the moments of their crystallization; through brutal deconstruction and refiguration, he parodies the enduring pathological myth of Polish messianism first disseminated by Romantics like Juliusz Słowacki and Adam Mickiewicz, and later by positivists such as Sienkiewicz.[35] To a reader aware of the iconic place that the works Gombrowicz attacks hold within the national cultural imagination, the cumulative effect is one of dismemberment of what the author's widow, Rita, once called the metaphorical zone of the Fatherland.[36] The immigrant's rejection of the diaspora in Gombrowicz is thus performed wholesale, beginning with specifics (the pitiless exposition of the formal rigor mortis of the legation's staff), and ending with the universal (Polish) myth of Romantic martyrology.

The second aspect of his discourse against nation in *Trans-Atlantyk* has to do with tracing the emergence of an exilic imagination on a formal register, within the idiom of narration itself. To this end, the traditional bastion of Romantic poetic language with its martyrological ethos, which Gombrowicz considered to be an artificial literary accretion (from English and German prototypes), is bypassed. Instead, he makes a strategic return to the Polish baroque, a cultural moment in which, according to Ewa Płonowska Ziarek, poetic language had not yet become irrevocably severed from the vernacular, and high literary forms commingled with vulgate speech.[37] The resultant narratological style, the Gombrowiczian *gawęda*, with its atmosphere of suspended ranks and toppled hierarchies reminiscent of a Rabelaisian carnival as theorized by Mikhail Bakhtin, constitutes an original assemblage, a neobaroque hybrid.[38] This linguistic platform of the *gawęda* becomes a forum for the creation of private exilic spaces and identities abstracted from nation. It announces that the zone of the autonomous subject, if it may be said to exist at all, defies spatiotemporal localization and will be accessed solely through language.

Similar to the kind of *skaz* narratives analyzed by Bakhtin, *gawęda* relies heavily on an impression of unmediated orality.[39] A major difference between *gawęda* and *skaz* is that the latter frequently employs a naïve or somehow transparent narrator or—alternatively—uneducated yet cunning rogues.[40] The speech of Gombrowicz's narrator in *Trans-Atlantyk*, on the other hand, with its profusion of Latinisms, extensive use of citation, and an ornate descriptive vocabulary, presumes a cultivated speaker belonging to the Polish squirearchy. The memoir form of the *gawęda* was especially popular among the seventeenth- and eighteenth-century *szlachta*.[41] Significantly, as Płonowska Ziarek observes, while *gawęda* was marked by a high degree of performativity and theatricality (and therefore inflected by a kind of hybridity), its earthiness and parochial "intimacy" were also consciously opposed to more urbane genres, such as poetry or philosophical tracts, and thus represents a kind of "fallen Baroque."[42] Perhaps the best-known and most influential of such accounts is Jan Chryzostom Pasek's memoir, *The Writings of Jan Chryzostom Pasek, A Squire of the Commonwealth of Poland and Lithuania*, compiled toward the end of the seventeenth century.[43] As a number of critics have remarked, Pasek's narrative derives its unusual emotive potency by engaging a number of genres that are not entirely compatible, including "elements of the picaresque novel; the chivalric romance, the campaign tale, the chronicle; and also aspects of the diary and the family album."[44] These tales of adventure and wisdom were usually not written down; often they were performed orally in front of small audiences, with repeated retellings of specific exciting passages guaranteeing the impression of a masterful and colorful delivery.[45] More important for our purposes here is the unassailable fact that the *gawęda* is specifically autochthonous; it is a discrete Polish literary form, a fact Gombrowicz would surely have appreciated. Moreover, with Pasek's *Memoirs*, the narrow-mindedness of the genre and its provincial resonance are transformed into a far more universal work, a text that holds some interest to a readership beyond the immediate circle of *szlachta* friends and well-wishers. In his *Historia literatury polskiej*, Julian Krzyżanowski ascribes this work's readability to Pasek's uncommon literary talent, his phantasmagoric yet historically accurate imagination, and his uncanny ear for language, among other laudable features,[46] all of which help mask the central problem of this work, and indeed the entire genre, namely, a lightness of being reflected by thematic superficiality and a reliance on mannerism.[47] In *The History of Polish Literature*, still the standard work in its field in the English language, Czesław Miłosz likewise focuses on the trademark orality and mannerisms of Pasek's style. However, he also argues that it is precisely by using "everyday language, its diction and its exclamations," and by treating what "to us" today may appear odd "as the most natural thing in the world," that Pasek's *Memoirs* not only replicated the "standards of the average gentry" of the day[48] but also created a charismatic, larger-than-life persona whose narratological thrust very nearly hijacks the reader's (and viewer's) sense of disbelief.

But where Pasek would have counted on a sympathetic ear—indeed, the formal structures of the narrative imply a group receptivity of the most accommodating kind, uninterrupted and essentially aural—Gombrowicz's dialectical strategies of parody/pastiche and provocation put the reader on notice, if not *en garde*, almost immediately. His recreation with a difference of a seventeenth-century *gawędziarz*-narrator in the manner of Pasek makes for a significant development for two reasons. First, in terms of Polish literary history, *Trans-Atlantyk* mimics Pasek's narrative mode even as it mocks the Sarmatian propensity for exaggeration and pretense. With the opening invocation, "Witold" the narrator immediately establishes a sense of urgency while inviting the reader to partake in the performance he is about to enact: "I feel a need to relate here for Family, kin, and friends of mine the beginning of these my adventures, now ten years old, in the Argentinean capital."[49] The narrator's insistence on such a large chronological disjunction, in my view, only amplifies the narratological thrust: *suddenly*, he tells us, he *feels the need* to tell a ten-year-old story. Of course we will listen, since this won't be just any story: how can it be, if the speaker has waited ten years to relate it! The mock urgency and the essential orality formally inscribed by this *gawęda* ("I feel the need to *tell*") fixes the plot within a carnivalesque chronotope, a unique conjunction of disrupted temporality and hybrid locus.

Second, in terms of stylistic correspondences, both Pasek's and Gombrowicz's accounts are infused with a sense of superabundance, or what Catherine Leach has termed the *silvae rerum*, "forests of things."[50] Given the formal rules governing this device, the coexistence of discrepant objects and textures is to be expected and to an extent even naturalized. The mere exposition of discordant things in Pasek, however, gives way in Gombrowicz's text to interbreeding and imbrication *among* the disparate orders of a possible other world. It is a world that coagulates in a phantasmagoric garden within a walled compound belonging to the narrator's friend Gonzalo, a homosexual Argentinean millionaire. In fact, it is a kind of *third zone* situated between the nation (or Fatherland) and exile (or Sonland) that serves up hybrids and suggests potentialities for new forms that to the narrator vacillating between forms are clearly compelling, on both physical and conceptual registers. For instance, when a group of quasi-canine but essentially hybrid creatures scurries through Gonzalo's garden and the narrator inquires as to their pedigree, it is not surprising that Gonzalo transforms his question about physical attributes into one about the essential taxonomy of things. He quips that he coupled a wolfhound bitch with a hamster,[51] a possible metaphor for the story of Latin American miscegenation that enthralled Gombrowicz because of the sheer potentiality of Mestizo culture (as opposed to calcified European forms and styles derided by the author in his *Diaries* and in *A Kind of Testament*).

For Gonzalo, the guardian of this heterodox domain, the hybrid structure has become normative. As in Foucault's famous enumeration of the "Emperor's animals" from Borges's fictive "Chinese Encyclopedia" in the preface to *The Order of Things*, where binding (epistemological) distinctions are made between animals that "belong to the Emperor," those that are "embalmed," and those that have just "broken the water pitcher,"[52] here, too, familiar modes of ontic classification have been supplanted. Or, more precisely, the world as we know it becomes interposed with a *new* "possible order."[53] In *Trans-Atlantyk* another, more properly postmodern phenomenon emerges as formerly stable ontological boundaries begin to dissolve. The readers are invited to immerse themselves in this discursive zone in the interstices of normalized orders, where language and form connect to produce unexpected new cultural essences and forms of being.

Finally, this specific exilic universe into which Gombrowicz "escapes" during his flight from nation is a world that self-consciously ignores the onerous expatriate prerogative, so frequently imposed by "Compatriots," to become mouthpieces for the interests of the lost Homeland or to sacrifice themselves to the demands of another collectivity. In the end, Gombrowicz's narrator chooses to respond to Gonzalo's call for autonomous exploration of the potentialities of expatriation by saying: "Don't you want to become something else, someone New? . . . Oh, let the Boys out of the paternal cage, Let them fly over the barrens, so that they may glimpse the Unknown." [54] This salvo, incidentally, constitutes the book's direct challenge to the reader as well. For his part, when Gombrowicz himself wanted to take a stand against the dominance of the communitarian-coercive essentialisms of nation and against the attendant erosion of the self, he did so unequivocally on his own terms and with incomparable originality, through writings such as *Trans-Atlantyk*, thus completing the discursive trajectory of the exilic subject.

In the end, whether expressed as a function of exilic hybridity or as part of a dissident philosophy of the self, resistance to nation in favor of producing private realms for the subject is immanent in both the Gombrowiczian and the Conradian text. But in both cases, as I have tried to show, their strategies of scripting the expatriate persona against the coercion of nationalist and communitarian discourses were complex and ambivalent. Fed by an essential iconoclasm, both authors worked against mainstream nationalist discourses in ways that announced the rise of independent subjectivity. The final paradox, then, is that both Conrad and Gombrowicz remained long dependent on the discourses of nation and the national imaginaries as the ideational frameworks for their own (exilic) narratives of subjective self-actualization. In Gombrowicz's case, the Polish cultural reality circa 1939—but also the more synchronous émigré spaces during and after World War II—was configured as an antagonistic "other" to be mastered and rejected immediately thereafter. This rejection, however, was incomplete: the locus classicus of his polemics, the novel *Trans-Atlantyk*, clearly demonstrates, on the level of both production and reception, that the "Polish question" in international affairs, and indeed the idea of "Polishness" as a viable cultural and social identity, remained as the two central sustaining metaphors. Moreover, because the parameters of Polish reality changed so drastically after 1945 in ways that Gombrowicz, in his status as an émigré, could not immediately apprehend, to sustain his crucial ipseity-alterity opposition the author *returns* to a Polish thematics on two more occasions, situating the plot of his final novels *Kosmos* and *Pornografia* respectively in the 1920s Poland of his youth and in a Nazi-occupied Poland of his imagination.[55]

For Conrad, affiliation meant becoming a ready victim of a particularly naturalizing sustaining illusion of comradeship and organic work toward a common—though occasionally romanticized and overdetermined—objective. In this possibly subconscious transcription of a broadly Positivist poetics into the minidrama of the (controlled environment of the) ship, Conrad in the last analysis envisions an idealized version of social existence. It remains, however, an oddly schematized vision, stripped of the ready flotsam and jetsam of "real" life—those spontaneous encounters and small quotidian accidents and incidents that so enrich our existence. That is to say, for all of Conrad's imaginative faculties, his version of reality—especially as elaborated in the seafaring novels—can appear close, even claustrophobic: this life feels impoverished to the extent that the range of available experiences is circumscribed, cut off from representation as a structural a priori. Though calamities may need to be overcome along the way, most ships reach their destinations on course; yet when the crew members finally disembark, the individuals who just a few minutes prior constituted a reliably self-sufficient unit merge again into the anonymous crowd, shedding their temporary imagined community, free—or rather condemned—to forge new sustaining illusions of their choice in the exile of reality. It is only when Conrad the novelist decided to follow his maritime heroes onto unstable lands (as in *Nostromo*), and trained his gaze on the antiheroes and rogues set loose amongst anonymous crowds (as in *The Secret Agent* and *Under Western Eyes*), that he produced his richest and most suggestive works.

Notes

1. See Anderson, introduction and first chapter, especially 18–47.
2. See Bhabha, "Dissemination," 296–302. The key argument of Bhabha's early writings, such as those included in *Nation and Narration*, is that a "People" does not come into being as simply a consequence of either common ethnicity or a sequence of historical events. To the contrary, like so many abstract constructs, the People, in order to become reified and naturalized amongst the people, has to be represented (in text, song, public performance).
3. By the term "regulatory idea" Laclau means the Law, broadly conceived. Paper delivered at the University at Buffalo Humanities Institute Inaugural Conference, SUNY–Buffalo, October 28, 2005.

4. Agamben, *Homo Sacer*, 15–17.
5. See Said, *The World, the Text*, 15–21.
6. Witness the following invocation of the sea in "Youth": "Between us there was . . . the strong bond of the sea, and also the fellowship of the craft, which no amount of enthusiasm for yachting, cruising, and so on can give, since one is only the amusement of life and the other is life itself" (9–10). Compare *Heart of Darkness:* "The minds [of most seamen] are of a stay-at-home order, and *their home is always with them*—the ship; and so is *their country*—the sea . . . there is nothing mysterious to a seaman unless it be the sea itself, which is the mistress of his existence" (5; my emphasis).
7. Conrad, *Personal Record*, 137–38.
8. Gombrowicz, *Dzieła*, 8:25–26; my translation.
9. Conrad, *Notes on Life and Letters*, 101.
10. Ibid., 164.
11. Ibid., 146–47; my emphasis.
12. Ibid., 102–5.
13. Ibid., 164.
14. In a preface to the second volume of his seven-volume collaborative study of French history and culture, *Lieux de mémoire*, Pierre Nora describes "a realm of memory" as any site or artifact whose cultural meaning—and thus its semiotic functioning as a symbol for a nation or a community—has been subjected to ideologically determined reifications (e.g., "the land" and its produce, the cathedral, national museums, memorials to a nation's dead). Certainly, this phenomenon can also be experienced on an individual register, as an individual mnemosyne. See the preface to the first volume, 7–10. See also Nora and Kritzman, xv–xxiv.
15. Conrad, *Notes on Life and Letters*, 165; my emphasis.
16. Conrad, *Youth*, 10.
17. Najder, 295.
18. Conrad, *Letters*, 10–11; my emphasis.
19. Ibid., 11.
20. See Najder, 398–99, 582.
21. Ford, 57, 55. According to Ford, Conrad desired this identity modification "with a passion" (55), not least because the Great Britain of Conrad's inner eye, admittedly a glorious if fictionalized, and at bottom *imaginary*, construct, could be emotionally employed to counter Russia, the depraved partitioning power held directly accountable for destroying the Korzeniowski family's life in Poland.
22. See Najder, 401.
23. Gombrowicz, *Polish Memories*, 3–4.
24. Gombrowicz and Roux, 12–13; my translation and emphasis.
25. Gombrowicz, *Polish Memories*, 7–11.
26. Ibid., 13–17.
27. See ibid., 21–22.

28. Ibid., 22.
29. Malić, 236.
30. Gombrowicz, *Trans-Atlantyk*, 3.
31. Berressem, "Laws of Deviation," 110–11.
32. Gombrowicz, *Dzieła*, 8:22; my translation.
33. Ibid., 23; my translation.
34. Gombrowicz, *Trans-Atlantyk*, 8.
35. Cf. Grzegorczyk, 146–47; Płonowska Ziarek, 222–26.
36. R. Gombrowicz, 88–90.
37. Płonowska Ziarek, 217–18.
38. The language of *Trans-Atlantyk* is a fitting example of the Bakhtinian concept of heteroglossia in its sourcing of new linguistic forms through the isolation of a multitude of distinct languages (not solely dialects) within each individual one, of which both the dominant mode and the subordinates are in all cases *zadan'* (posited) as such within a system by social convention, and are thus arbitrary in the end. For a detailed discussion of the concept of heteroglossia, see Morson and Emerson, 141–43.
39. In Bakhtin's theory of literary genre, *skaz* narration is characterized as a written, often parodic form, in which the narrator is not entirely "in control" of a work that is being created "without revisions." Its similarity with *gawęda* is reinforced in the stipulation that even though it is a written genre, *skaz* is nonetheless most often oriented toward the "idiosyncrasies" of orality, dialects, and stylization in particular (see Morson and Emerson, 153–54). Bakhtin himself expressly defines *skaz* as a discourse that is by nature oriented "toward oral speech and its corresponding language characteristics" and more specifically "towards *someone else's* speech," meaning that the actual storyteller "is not a literary person [but] belongs *in most cases* to the lower social strata, to the common people—and he brings with him oral speech" (Bakhtin, *Problems of Dostoevsky's Poetics*, 191–92; my emphasis).
40. These correspond to the *plut, shut,* and *durak* figures in Bakhtin's gallery of subaltern characters and translate roughly to knave, scoundrel, and fool.
41. On the baroque form of "świecka powieść," and the simultaneous rise of *pamiętniki* of *szlachta* life, see Krzyżanowski, 368–75. Cf. Miłosz, *History of Polish Literature*, 145–46; Thompson, *Witold Gombrowicz*, 80–82.
42. Płonowska Ziarek, 221. See also 219–22.
43. In fact, Pasek's narrative was not published in its entirety until much later, in fact 1836, when a run of 250 copies was commissioned by Count Edward Raczyński of Poznań and, writes Leach, caused a literary furor. See Leach, xvi.
44. Leach, lvii–lviii.
45. See Miłosz's *The History of Polish Literature*, where the author notes that Adam Mickiewicz in his lectures on the Polish baroque given at the College de France had remarked already in the 1840s that "Pasek's phrases should

be punctuated by special signs, denoting gestures" (146). Leach, following Miłosz and others (see note 49), situates the Sarmatian baroque memoir as distinct from the journal or the diary form. The latter two are concerned with "registering the present," while the former should be regarded as a literary work "of reminiscence about the past, based upon the author's direct or indirect experience," and hence allowing for "greater freedom in selecting material and constructing the narrative [and] for more refinement in constructing a central figure, [which also] presupposes a greater degree of self-consciousness and greater self-deception" (Leach, liv). Taken together, these devices load the narrative toward "a fictional treatment" of its subject matter by the reader.

46. Krzyżanowski, 369–70.

47. On the *gawęda* form and other aspects of Pasek's writing in the context of the Sarmatian baroque in Poland, see, for example, Rybicka-Nowacka, Rytel, Tazbir, and Wyrobisz. Krzysztof Kłosiński's recent book *W stronę inności: Rozbiory i debaty* reads the Gombrowiczian foray into sarmatism through the lens of poststructuralist discourses of alterity and difference. For further discussion of the influence of Sarmatian memoirist styles on Gombrowicz's émigré prose (and on his identity and textual politics), see Błoński, *Forma, śmiech i rzeczy ostateczne*; Jarzębski, *Gra w Gombrowicza* and *Podglądanie Gombrowicza.*

48. Miłosz, *History of Polish Literature*, 145–46.

49. Gombrowicz, *Trans-Atlantyk*, 3.

50. Leach, liii.

51. Gombrowicz, *Trans-Atlantyk*, 81–85.

52. Foucault, *Order of Things*, xv–xvi.

53. Ibid., xvii.

54. Gombrowicz, *Dzieła*, 3:60; my translation.

55. Gombrowicz openly acknowledges the imaginary dimension of Poland in his preface to *Pornografia*: "I do not know the Poland of wartime. I wasn't present there. . . . This is an imaginary Poland." *Dzieła*, 4:5; editors' translation.

CONSEQUENCES OF LIFE-WRITING PHILOSOPHY

The Case of Miron Białoszewski

Artur Płaczkiewicz

> [In Białoszewski's texts] there is a story for the story's sake. Not a text-narration, but a text-style. Between the speaker and his world there are other relations being created than mere reporting.[1]

> "This is what style is," write Deleuze and Guattari, "the moment when language is no longer defined by what it says, but by what causes it to move, to flow. . . . For literature is . . . a process and not a goal . . . a pure process that fulfills itself, and that never ceases to reach fulfillment as it proceeds—art as 'experimentation.'" Likewise, reading a text is never an act of interpretation, it "is never a scholarly exercise in search of what is signified, still a highly textual exercise in search of a signifier"; it too is an act of experimentation, "a productive use of the literary machine."[2]

Miron Białoszewski's originality and unpredictable consistency escape critical evaluations. His work always seems to extend beyond the explanations provided by his critics. In my view this is the case because all previous approaches to this artist's work are in some way reductive, or employ reductive methodologies. For Stanisław Barańczak, in Białoszewski's world everything is reduced to a fundamental dualism between the Self and the Other; for Anna Sobolewska, Białoszewski employs "phenomenological reduction" ("pure seeing") to describe reality as he perceives it. Both approaches also misinterpret Białoszewski's attitude toward language.

I argue that the poet's language is rooted in his life, in his specific life-writing philosophy. Zaworska, who is one of the most observant critics of Białoszewski, writes, "Sharpness and specificity in the reception of reality, and not reality-as-such, are at the basis of his poetry-prose."[3] The poet's interactions with reality consist in bi-directional relations that traverse essential dualisms: traverse rather than overcome, for there is no reconciliation, and no translation or explanation of one aspect of reality in terms of another. Białoszewski does not judge; there is no privileged partner in the dualisms he explores, and no hierarchy that would bring order to the participating elements, or give structure to an event.

Ryszard Nycz observes that "the uniqueness of Białoszewski's writings on the map of Polish literature is as undisputable as it is intriguing,"[4] while Stanisław Rosiek remarks that "perhaps nobody has made an attempt to describe the radical nature and courage of Białoszewski's project within the realm of literature and—simultaneously—within the realm of his own life."[5] This essay aims to remedy this situation by describing some of the main aspects of Białoszewski's radical project, a project that does not rely on the employment of some fixed methodology, but which consistently realizes and propagates a certain attitude toward life, language, and reality. The poet does not tear down the curtains of inauthentic appearances to reveal authentic essences, but rather discovers that artificiality is as authentic as naturalness. For Białoszewski, it is precisely the ordinary that is mysterious and unexplainable, manifesting itself in multiple and various interrelations and processes.

There is consistency in Białoszewski's artistic oeuvre. There is also a shift in his artistic career. This shift takes place sometime between 1965 and 1975, and although the change is not radical, but rather the result of continual growth, it brings about a qualitative rearrangement that becomes fully realized and noticeable in his poetry after 1975. "Starting with *The Heart Attack*, Białoszewski essentially enters into 'new worlds,' previously absent from his writings. . . . The saying 'to write from the beginning' meant something else—to write from a different perspective, to establish the relations between writing and being differently."[6] In this new perspective, essential dualisms and hierarchies between subject and object, the animate and the inanimate, the authentic and the inauthentic, the natural and the artificial, and especially between life and art are erased.

It is my contention that the philosophical project inscribed in Białoszewski's radical artistic praxis is closely connected with what Joanna Niżyńska described as his "shift from a teleological view of the everyday, in which meaning must be recovered, to the view of the everyday as a realm which needs no justification."[7] Still, there are no raptures within this radicalization, as it is rooted in a nonfoundationalist philosophy, without formal methodology, and without a preestablished goal to be reached. According to this philosophy, "The artist's duty is a similar one to the philosopher's, to bear witness in his or her own area of activity: 'We must find new paths in order to approach new artistic clouds and new clouds of thought.' Risk-taking, lightness, probity, touch, and svelteness become the order of the day, and art can be a prime means of developing these qualities and keeping phrase linkages open."[8] This philosophy values life simply for "being there." It teaches respect for the different and for the Other with a full realization that the Other cannot be known in its entirety. It is based in the total responsibility of the subject for his actions, since there are no privileged positions and no essences that have to prevail in the final consideration. This responsibility is cleared of pride and expectations, because it is based in the subject's awareness and alertness, and it places no demands on the Other (objects, reality, and/or people). This responsibility accepts everything as it is, for it has no intention to impose its own views on the Other, and no methodology to cope with the unknown, but only its vital and affirmative forces to rely on, and its curiosity, which is manifested through the author's openness and willingness to experiment with novel situations:

> Białoszewski will describe his maximal attitude for the reception of reality in more novel terms: "I, a guard, a lighthouse keeper, transmit from my 'ant-house.'" An antenna, a receiving or relaying station catching the waves of life present within its range. He does not attempt to order them into some fixed informational system, does not choose one interpretation. He has "multiple worldviews" not because of egocentrism or indifference, but because of his fascination with variety and the constant changeability of everything.[9]

The poet's radical philosophical positioning, although unique on the Polish literary scene, is not entirely foreign to Western tradition. It can be traced to Wittgenstein's later works, in which, as Susan B. Brill argues, the philosopher acknowledges that "any human judgment is necessarily constrained by the limitations of language and perception (understanding)."[10] Following Brill's argument further, according to Wittgenstein "our investigations must be descriptive rather than explanatory."[11] This radical realization is a consequence of the philosopher's view of language. According to Ilham Dilman, Wittgenstein displaces Platonic logocentrism by asserting that:

> our language is not founded on an empirical reality with which we are in contact through sense perception. Rather it is our language, conceived as part of our life and our life as a life of the language we speak, that determines the kind of contact we have with such a reality in our conception of it insofar as we live its life.[12]

In other words, for Białoszewski, as for Wittgenstein, language is rooted in life and not in reality. People are linguistic beings for whom thinking takes place in language, and there is, as Gilles Deleuze observes, a "unity of life and thought. It is a complex unity: one step for life, one step for thought. Modes of life inspire ways of thinking; modes of thinking create ways of living. Life *activates* thought, and thought in turn *affirms* life."[13]

Literature is no longer seen as mirroring reality, or reaching its essential attributes. It no longer has a mission of translating reality into language; thus it has no preestablished goal to reach. Białoszewski's "later books of poetry not only questioned the ability of literature to mirror reality and influence people's lives, but postulated that literature ought to 'adopt the life of its environment' and open itself in this way to other than traditionally literary forms of 'linguistic communication.'"[14] Białoszewski in his later writings approaches literature in Deleuzian terms, as "the passage of life within language that constitutes Ideas."[15] Moreover, since life is all-embracing and all-connecting, there are no strict divisions between various human activities.

> I want to go
> it's hard

my legs carry me
no, I carry my legs
I—an artificial product
sweat is leaking from me[16]

Białoszewski's "I" is "an artificial product," because it is a result of contextual interactions. He is not "natural" because he has no unchanging essence and is constantly being produced anew. Language is not a problem from this perspective, because it is not expected to produce a perfect transfer. Language stops being a problem for the poet, because he views it not as something that has to be dominated anymore, but rather as something that cannot be separated from either the subject or the object. Białoszewski gradually radicalizes his attitude toward language by seeing it as equally continuous with both the subject and reality as it is known. The separation and alienation of the subject from his language, and the detachment of language from reality, are rethought and redescribed by the artist. This process demystifies language by treating it not as a mystical medium, but as nothing more than a useful tool.

For Białoszewski, the Cartesian *cogito ergo sum* is not a given. He does not see himself as a man of science for whom the presentation of the true picture of reality is only a matter of time: instead, he recognizes the "unpresentness" of reality, and consequently uses his language as a tool, and not as a medium. When used in this way, language's purpose is not to represent the essence of reality or experience, but rather to give a useful description of it (in the sense of producing an awareness of the contingency of reality and producing possibilities to better cope with it, rather than of finding its underlying order). The poet states:

Artificial, artificially the same
artificially they are and are
and even this is good[17]

For Białoszewski's subject it makes no difference whether "nature" is natural or artificial; what remains important is that this nature is contextual and approached through descriptions. His demystifying consists in continually redescribing his copings with reality, and in providing descriptions of various causal relations and interactions. This is why "writing and life go hand in hand. And sometimes they are the same."[18] They causally influence each other, but without any metaphysical foundations. This is neither metaphysics nor logocentrism, because there is no search for the absolute to be revealed. It is not the case that something is explained in terms of something else, that language demystifies appearances while grasping the hidden essence of reality.

Metaphors are connected not with essences, but with practices of the subject. They acquire their meanings only after being produced, not before. Their "adequacy" is evaluated on the basis of their consequences and causal results, and not in universal terms. Instead of representing reality, language affects it in some way because "reasons can be causes" (Richard Rorty) and "words can be actions" (Białoszewski). Matter in this context is not so much absolute as it is relevant, because many different (hi)stories of the world are engraved in its descriptions. And descriptions are the result of causal interactions as well as being the causes for (inter)actions. Their consequences are influenced by the context in which they appear, rather than by the word's essential nature.

The causal effect of words can be seen in Białoszewski's frequent employment of minidialogues or "citations." For instance, the following fragment illustrates the causal (i.e., nonrepresentational) usage of words:

> they ask from my right hand
> "do you feel dizzy now?"
> "no . . . ah yes, I do now"
>
> and suddenly a noise of beds, shaking
> somebody moans, so I do too
> a voice from behind uncertainty
> "we've finished your surgery, sir"[19]

The poem is a description of a minor surgery. The first stanza describes the moment just before the operation, while the second stanza deals with the moment just after it. By the end of the first stanza, the subject falls asleep, and by the beginning of the second one, he is already in the moment of awakening. The words used in the poem do not signify any essence of the event, but rather are produced by the context. They are causally related to what is happening. They are caused by the "unfolding" of the event, and they have causal effects on other elements within the network of interrelations, the subject among others. In the first stanza, the question follows the administration of an anesthetic, and the response is connected with the answer that consists in describing the subject's state ("no . . . ah yes, I do now"). The second stanza starts with the very first perceptions of the subject as he wakes up after his minor surgery. The input from the environment in some way causes the subject to react by analogy (he moans because others do). This is causally related to the clarifying response ("we've finished your surgery").

In summary, the words are used not to signify some essential aspect of the situation, but to describe the causal interactions within the context. The words do not represent the context, but come from within it; they are causally determined by it. Each word is, in a sense, produced by the context, by the situation itself. The words themselves, however, cannot disclose this event; they can only signal its contingent interconnections. Finally, this nature is strictly relational and nonessential. Thus, both matter and words are contextually determined, albeit with no pretensions to ontology, metaphysics, or logocentrism.

Białoszewski distrusts all metanarratives, including the privileged status of matter, or the body. If he has any metaphysical tendencies, they would be toward metaphysical realism, which asserts that matter exists even when there are no observers around, meaning that the world does not disappear when we do not look at it. This is a metaphysical assumption, because it proposes a view that cannot be proved, since any observer would violate its premise. Białoszewski, however, is interested only in that which can be observed or experienced. Therefore, although he probably believes this assumption to be true, he is not very interested in reality without his participation. He is always, in some way or another, present in his texts, and his descriptions are never entirely imaginary productions.

Marian Stala interprets Białoszewski's conversations with his own body as proof that matter possesses some ontological status, since it "can take an active part in the dialogue of beings."[20]

so what if I've put on weight?
rheumatism
up and down the stairs
clicks
my skeleton
in its stiff bows
"Your Corporality's planning for long?"[21]

I disagree with Stala that the human body has some independent ontological status in this poem. Rather, I interpret this text as a humorous description of a belief in a post-Darwinian or Freudian—rather than Cartesian—model of the self. If we assume that Białoszewski views the self as a centerless web of beliefs and desires that is permanently being rewoven, and that he believes in the Freudian division between the conscious and the unconscious, then it is plausible to interpret this poem in mechanistic and physical terms without any references to metaphysics.

Białoszewski's subject treats the communication with his own body not as a conversation between two separate beings, but rather as a dialogue within one contingent self. In the poem, the subject first identifies the self with the body ("*I*'ve put on weight"), then as something that possesses or controls the body ("*my* skeleton"), and finally as something separate from the self ("*Your* Corporality"). These various identifications are different descriptions of his continual process of self-formation, which has no end because the subject views the self as inherently contingent and unstable. The self does not reside in the body, but is formed together with the body, from which it cannot be separated ("do not sever your legs from yourself," Białoszewski states in another text).[22] The poet's self is a tangle of associations, parts of an interactional network of beliefs and desires that have linguistic outcomes or manifestations. In Białoszewski's poem, "Your Corporality" is not given an absolute status; evidently, its status is relational, or causal. The poem is a redescription of the self as it gathers new data from its corporal parts ("rheumatism / up and down the stairs / clicks").

The poet's self is not the Cartesian one, strictly divided and hierarchically ordered between the mind with its reasons, and the body with its passions. Rather, it fits a Freudian model, in which the self is a centerless and dynamic network of beliefs and desires, and in which the subconscious is acknowledged as a semi-independent or alternate part of the self, a part that cannot be fully (i.e., consciously) controlled. At the same time, this recognition is merely one of many facts of life:

> **And if I come back**
> then as the other same
> artificially stable
> precisely so unclearly[23]

Białoszewski's philosophy is a philosophy of connections, of experimentation, of creating relations between—and forming insights into—yet unknown domains. This attitude toward reality, consisting in inclusiveness and openness toward various events and encounters with the Other, leads to a constant growth and enlargement of the subject, and results in the constant traversing of his limits. Simultaneously, since the subject is aware of his own limitations of understanding, he rejects stable, hierarchical, dualistic, and dialectic modes of thinking, and remains within nonreductive and nonnormative domains of endless processes and interactions. In his later writings, Białoszewski's ordinary reality is no longer raised to the level of the extraordinary, and neither is the extraordinary dragged down to the level of the ordinary. This reality does not need firm explanations, only approximate descriptions: "for to think is to experiment and not, in the first place, to judge," as John Rajchman points out.[24] At the same time, as convincingly argued by Deleuze, "judgment prevents the emergence of any new mode of existence."[25]

There can be no fixed method or theory that would stabilize the relations of encounters within the context of reality. Therefore, Białoszewski's subject does not hold any assumptions that would reach outside a particular context, and he does not have any preestablished method to approach new situations. Instead, he approaches reality according to neopragmatist postulates.[26] He relies entirely on three interrelated modes of coping in order to make changes in his belief system: perception ("unobviousness"), language, and inference ("conjectures"). The inherent instability of the constantly changing subject prevents him from articulating an objective truth about the world (hence curious and experimental "unobviousness"). Perception is able to influence the ways in which the subject conceptualizes reality, but it says nothing about reality-as-it-is. Language can produce statements about and descriptions of the environment, but language as such cannot reach (or transfer) reality and put it into its verbal equivalent. Inference helps the subject create new relations and interactions with his context, but it is unable to provide stable pieces of knowledge (hence "conjectures"), and the descriptions remain descriptions without ever reaching the level of representation (i.e., final description). Differently put, for Białoszewski's subject cognition is not always, and not only, recognition and/or analogy (representations), because it would not then result in the growth of his subject, since the underlying presumption of recognition is that there can be nothing new. Cognition must also take place through associations (which are nonrepresentational), for they force the subject to make new connections, to create new relations, and to constantly redescribe and recontextualize.

Białoszewski's life-writing philosophy is rooted in the full participation and exposure of the subject. It results in the traversal of any dualism that is commonly viewed as an essential or natural division of reality. Therefore, as noticed by Andrzej Tchórzewski, "Białoszewski treats the whole literary arsenal functionally, as something to be used. In this way he escapes ideological disputes ('romantics/classicists,' 'modernists/traditionalists'), . . . does not have to 'take sides.' He stands aside, and yet nevertheless in the center."[27] In this holist vision, life, art, and science cannot be approached independently. Moreover, in this contextual reality there is only the here and now, and nothing is privileged to reach outside the present context. There are only causal relations and influences in the context, but this causality differs from empirical minimalist approaches. It is rather in concord with Deleuze's view on causality, which "requires that I go from something that is given to me to the idea of something that has never been given to me, that isn't even giveable in experience. . . . In other words, causality is a relation according to which I go beyond the given; I say more than what is given or giveable—in short, *I infer and I believe*, I expect that. . . . [I]t puts belief at the basis and the origin of knowledge."[28]

The connections and relations created within a given context cause the event, and not its inherent structure or order. All elements present within a context are equally active participants, and the influences are bi-directional. Thus, it becomes impossible to separate the subject from the object, because the relations between them are multiple and dynamic. This dynamism, and the shift in focus from objects to relations and processes, are responsible for the inseparability of the subject from the object of his investigation, and testify to the "something more"—the unpresentable, the accidental and unexpected, the unknown—as an irreducible element of any event. At the same time, neither the subject nor the object is totalized or reconciled; they both preserve their singularities, remaining unique, although not in the sense of "extraordinary." As Nycz rightly observes, "it cannot be ruled out that we are dealing in this case with the most radical (and certainly the most artistically satisfying) attempt to articulate and report subjectivity in speech, a successful realization of a personal attitude toward language, which through the widening of its descriptive possibilities simultaneously gives a unique, personal mark to artistic statements."[29] Białoszewski refrains from articulating judgments and explanations, and his existence, although obviously a given, remains outside the subject-object dualism. Daniel W. Smith describes this process as follows for Deleuze's philosophy: "In a becoming, one term does not become another;

rather, each term encounters the other, and the becoming is something between the two, outside the two. This 'something' is what Deleuze calls a pure *affect* or *percept*, which is irreducible to the affections or perceptions of a subject."[30]

Nevertheless, this "something else" that is indefinably present in Białoszewski's texts cannot belong to the realm of metaphysics; it must belong to the here and now, since the poet's subject does not know any other time besides the present moment. The interrelations and processes taking place within an event are never external to that event. It seems, then, that Białoszewski's "transcendental field" is not Kantian, but rather Deleuzian: "it constitutes the conditions of real experience and not merely possible experience; and it is never larger than what it conditions, but is itself determined at the same time as it determines what it conditions."[31]

It is still realism, but it must be defined otherwise than in terms of stable relations. In this realism, different elements in a given context are treated like events in the sense that there is always "something more," something unexplainable about them, which is manifested through the manner in which the subject approaches them. The dynamism and multiplicity of interacting factors force the subject to remain "realistic" precisely during those moments in which he cannot decide or judge, but only experiment and create new interactions. His life must remain vague and indefinite in order to encompass this potential for new possibilities, and retain the ability to enter into complex relations with other beings, objects, or elements in a context that can never be entirely known or controlled. This contingency and vagueness of the subject's life are not seen as problematic, so they do not have to be corrected. Rather, they are viewed as a source of new possibilities, and it is exactly this contingency that makes the creation of new relations and connections possible. As Rajchman explains, "what is 'peculiar to us' without being 'particular about us' is then nothing personal or conscious, but on the contrary, something unattributable, unpredictable in our being and being together."[32] There is always "something else" within the realm of the here and now.

This "something else" displays the author's hope for, and amazement at life as he experiences it. It also manifests his belief in the possibilities latent in this world, as opposed to some other reality that is removed from the present context (be it a utopian past or future, or religion). Białoszewski does not attempt to change or revolutionize the world (an avant-gardist dream) because he is not sure what direction the change ought to take. At the same time, he constantly recontextualizes his position, undergoing permanent growth and enlargement. However, while doing all this, he always remains on the surface, and does not reach for essences hidden in the depths or heights, because for him a one-to-one correspondence between physical reality and its conceptualizations is an illusion, and cannot be proved based on experimental data. As a result, the Cartesian split between the subject and external objects should not be approached as an essential division:

> The assumption that a one-to-one correspondence exists between every element of physical reality and physical theory may serve to bridge the gap between mind and world for those who use physical theories. But it also suggests that the Cartesian division is real and insurmountable in constructions of physical reality based on ordinary language. This explains in no small part why the radical separation between mind and world sanctioned by classical physics and formalized by Descartes remains, as philosophical postmodernism attests, one of the most pervasive features of Western intellectual life.[33]

Białoszewski's late writings demonstrate his belief that the quest for certainty is not a valid option for literature. For Białoszewski, to write is to describe yet unknown feelings and desires, to entertain new relations and connections. As Andrzej Zieniewicz rightly observes, "the narrator is in the position of a scientist describing his experiment 'right on the spot.' He does not know 'what is going to happen next.'"[34] Białoszewski's philosophy rejects Platonic assumptions. According to Rorty, "Plato and Aristotle built what Dewey called 'the quest for certainty' into our sense of what thinking is for. They thought that unless we can make the object of inquiry *evident*—get it clear and distinct, directly present to the eye of the mind, and get agreement about it from all those qualified to discuss it—we are falling short of our goal."[35] Białoszewski's artistic praxis shows that he does not share in, or cherish the Platonic tradition, since it creates in the subject an overwhelming resentment for the lost absolute. His poetry does not aim at recovering an ideal, and so it refrains from normative assumptions. As Rajchman points out, "perhaps that is the secret—to practice aesthetics as the affirmative play of conceptual experimentation and novelty, and not as tribunal and judgment."[36] Białoszewski regards artistic action as the production of descriptions of something new and singular that can help the subject to recontextualize his position, and enlarge himself through constant growth and becoming, the permanent redescribing of his self, over and over again and always anew.

NOTES

1. Zieniewicz, 36. All translations are my own.
2. Smith in Deleuze, *Essays Critical and Clinical*, li.
3. Zaworska, 54.
4. Nycz, "'Szare eminencje zachwytu,'" 179.
5. Rosiek, 132.
6. Ibid., 139.
7. Niżyńska, 200.
8. Sim, 130.
9. Zaworska, 50.
10. Brill, 138.
11. Ibid.
12. Dilman, 10.

13. Deleuze, *Pure Immanence*, 66.
14. Wantuch, 157–58.
15. Lambert, 132.
16. Białoszewski, *Utwory zebrane*, 7:78.
17. Ibid., 188.
18. Białoszewski in Burkot, 143.
19. Białoszewski, *Utwory zebrane*, 10:147.
20. Stala, "Czy Białoszewski jest poetą metafizycznym?," 108.
21. Białoszewski, *Utwory zebrane*, 10:71.
22. Ibid., 8:236.
23. Ibid., 7:189.
24. Rajchman, 5.
25. Deleuze, *Essays Critical and Clinical*, 135.
26. According to Rorty, neopragmatists believe that "there are three ways in which a new belief can be added to our previous beliefs, thereby forcing us to reweave the fabric of our beliefs and desires—viz., perception, inference, and metaphor. Perception changes our beliefs by intruding a new belief into the network of previous beliefs. . . . Inference changes our beliefs by making us see that our previous beliefs commit us to a belief we had not previously held—thereby forcing us to decide whether to alter those previous beliefs, or instead to explore the consequences of the new one. . . . Both perception and interference leave our language, our way of dividing up the realm of possibility, unchanged. They alter the truth-value of sentences, but not our repertoire of sentences. . . . By contrast, to think of metaphor as a third source of beliefs, and thus a third motive for reweaving our networks of beliefs and desires, is to think of language, logical space, and the realm of possibility, as open-ended. It is to abandon the idea that the aim of thought is the attainment of a God's-eye view" (12).
27. Tchórzewski, 55.
28. Deleuze, *Pure Immanence*, 40.
29. Nycz, "'Szare eminencje zachwytu,'" 183.
30. Smith in Deleuze, *Essays Critical and Clinical*, xxx.
31. Ibid., xxiv.
32. Rajchman, 84.
33. Nadeau and Kafatos, 148.
34. Zieniewicz, 36.
35. Rorty, 29.
36. Rajchman, 119.

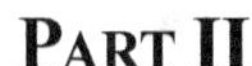

Part II

Experiences of the Self

Comparative Literature

Mental Cartography?

Tomasz Bilczewski

Drawn for the centuries
the space of comparison
has been well preserved.

That was the thing
that lured us out of the depths of our kind.
. . . .

That was the thing
that turned our head to a human one.
—Wisława Szymborska, "A Note"

Body, Movement, and Love

Among the numerous attempts to answer recent questions about the nature of comparative research in the age of multiculturalism and globalization, I find those referring to the poetics of autobiography to be particularly appealing.[1] In fact, they provide more profound insight into the character of the discipline than the already quite extensive collection of theoretical works on the subject. They often reveal the way in which abstract and institutionalized constructions are verified in individual professional and personal lives based on various cultural experiences. Even though I am not trying to follow this kind of rhetoric here, I would like to invoke a voice that incorporates autobiography. The oeuvre of Czesław Miłosz, who witnessed the changes of Polish history and culture for nearly the entire previous century, calls for a comparative perspective. His writing exists at the crossroads of different cultures and intellectual traditions, beliefs and values, languages and lifestyles, and mirrors an incessant—both literally and metaphorically—existence in translation.

On many occasions Czesław Miłosz himself commented on his continuously displaced location, searching for an intellectual frame of reference for his "ego." One of the most trusted companions in this journey was Oscar Miłosz, his distant relative and a somewhat forgotten poet of the French language. The author of *The Issa Valley* treated Oscar Miłosz's metaphysical poems as a school of thought about the relation between the body and space. Let me quote here some crucial phrases from Oscar Miłosz's "Letter to Storge":

> In truth, we do not bring either space or time into nature, but just the movement of our body and knowledge, or rather awareness and love of that movement, awareness and love which we call Thought and which is at the origin of our first and fundamental ability to situate all things, beginning with ourselves.[2]

In emphasizing the sensorimotor character of our interaction with the world, Oscar Miłosz follows his intuition, which perceives the awareness of space as the most elementary action of the human mind. The action is not a sheer work of *cogito* but rather is entangled in bodily meanderings, matching the dynamics of the human organism. This is how the author himself in his commentary to the first verse of "Les Arcanes" sheds more light on the nature of the above-mentioned dynamics:

> To the man who sees, space is revealed by the movement of light; to the blind man, by that of his arm, of any limb or of his whole body; to the blind man and to the man who sees, and also to the paralytic stricken with blindness, by the very notion of movement, their basic thought, point of departure of the most abstract operation, in short, *a spiritual principle linked . . . to the very flow of their blood.*[3]

Such terms as "basic thought," "the very notion of movement," "a spiritual principle"—expressions that seem to be borrowed from the Cartesian lexicon—are contrasted in these excerpts with very specific sensual vocabulary employing human physiology in search of "first and fundamental ability." Through poetic imagery, the somatic element confronts metaphysics; spiritual meets physical, and the mind pulsates with the rhythm of blood, with "its own flow." Intuitively equating the awareness of movement[4] and experience of the body with the process of thinking, Oscar Miłosz tries to bridge the gap that separates *res cogitans* from *res extensa.*[5] The elementary perception of space does not exist as the act of a pure mind but rather is a kind of desire that can be defined as an "obligation to place all things," involving even the space and time in which the very process of placing occurs.

The author of *The Land of Ulro* rightly points out that "the son of Descartes set out to revise the maxim 'I think, therefore I am' to read 'I move, therefore I am.'"[6] However, the awareness of this movement is not the result of reflection carefully separated from the senses. It is the result of love. If we consider love as a force that strives for connection, unity, and completion (one of the meanings of the Greek term *erasthai* refers to the feeling that something is lacking), then this movement can be understood as a reciprocated immersion of the mind in the space of the body; it is an inseparable entanglement of object and subject, reasoning and affect, that at the same time goes beyond the painful dilemma[7] inherited from the age of reason, which, as Jean-Luc Nancy writes, changed "body" into a word bringing to mind "some kind of pornoscope."[8]

For the postmodern subject, which differs from its Cartesian predecessor in that its body is an integral part of its identity, this heavy load of the Enlightenment period turned out to be too much to bear. This can be clearly observed in the 1960s and 1970s, especially in the art of interpretation, where dry analysis was replaced, as in Roland Barthes, by the sensual pleasure of reading. Aesthetics heads for eroticism, semiotics for the somatic, and hermeneutic explication becomes a way to touch the idiomatic character of a text, the living tissue of writing. Thus, an intelligent and living body becomes the focal point of the act of interpretation.[9]

This corporeal turn present in the works of Jacques Lacan, Michel Foucault, Jacques Derrida, and Philippe Lacoue-Labarthe was to some extent heralded and later "reinforced" by the phenomenological writings of Maurice Merleau-Ponty, who, like Oscar Miłosz, believed that the roots of thinking began in one's preconscious access to the world constructed through one's perception—a fountainhead-like experience that allows us a dialogue between the corporeal subject and object.[10] According to the author of *The Visible and the Invisible*, "être-au-monde" requires an intuitive opening of the self to reality, which determines all forms of conceptualization and pragmatic processing of one's experience. What Oscar Miłosz described as "the love of movement," Merleau-Ponty called "motor intentionality" or "experienced space." For Miłosz, this striving for placement is the basis of existence and stems directly from the structure of the organism; in Merleau-Ponty's approach placement comes from one's presence in a particular situation and the spreading of one's individual spatial net, which is the source of intellectual operations.

Placing: Space and Desire

Why do I bring up this poetic and philosophical chapter from the rich tradition of reflecting on the mind-body issue here? Precisely because what is defined in philosophy as "egocentric spatial perception"[11] seems to me to be of crucial importance, both to understanding the status of the interpreting subject and to defining my point of interest, since I perceive comparative literary studies as a unique act of interpretation originating in the experience of the body. The "nucleus" of this act is the very process of comparison. Let me quote Oscar Miłosz once again: "To think is first of all to situate and to compare: still, the two operations may be reduced to one, for the initial comparison is the relation of one place to another."[12] Placement and comparison thus viewed as two sides of a coin, defined by Miłosz as reasoning, are then deeply rooted in the elementary movement of the body. Comparison has its roots in a peculiar (to use Merleau-Ponty's language) spreading of the bodily spatial net. As one goes through this process, one becomes aware of being in a certain configuration. In order to describe the position, however, one has to find its relation to other places. Defining one's own location, which is subject to constant movement owing to its dependence on the position in which one finds oneself, gives us a reason for the act that we call comparison. Although this act is part of our consciousness, it originates in the prereflexive opening of our body to the world. It is then that the perceived reality imprints itself on the individual mental map of the "self," in this way allowing the subject to interact with the "outside world."

The act of reading performed by the corporeal subject can also be defined as the specific designation of place. But this time it is an encounter with the world of a text. As Paul Ricoeur claims, the extent to which we open ourselves to a text determines how the text will open to us. Following Hans-Georg Gadamer, the author of *Du texte à l'action* defines this double opening as a fusion of horizons.[13] The geographical character of this metaphor remarkably shows that reading is a unique mental cartography; it is an attempt to find the relation of the "self" to the proposed reality offered by the text. The effort of the imagination, moved by the act of reading, allows us to impose possible, prospective worlds on the space of our experience. It is clear that each text demands engagement on the part of the reader in a comparative act, an action poignantly defined by Oscar Miłosz with the use of the verb *situer*. However, in the field of *ars interpretandi*, there exists a domain that is particularly focused on the process of enlarging the scope of interpretation. Comparative studies formulate and emphasize their entrenchment and involvement in crossing cultural, linguistic, and semiotic boundaries, and this perspective clearly reveals the transterritorial, spatial, and transgressive aspects of the discipline. As such it meets the basic need to place all things; it meets the needs coming from the structure of the body that is part and parcel of the reasoning process.

I do not, therefore, regard the act of comparison as an operation connecting texts and cultural phenomena in the face of some sort of *tertium comparationis*, searching for invariants and universals governing the world of literature. Closer to my perspective is the belief that the discipline offers a set of mechanisms that allow one or more subjects to connect in a "single" act of reasoning. Those mechanisms break linguistic, cultural, and semiotic boundaries. Furthermore, one object is observed in relation to the other and, in the words of Condillac, we encounter "doubled or even multiplied attention."[14]

"Space" and "desire" are two key terms that encompass the perspective outlined above and give rise to two kinds of metaphors present in comparative methodological discourse. The first one is geographical and describes the drive to overcome the obstacles that limit the range of the comparative act. The inclination is to inhabit cross-border territories of other disciplines and to enter the realm of interaction between different theoretical schools. This predilection for occupying an "in-between" place is often emphasized by images of overcoming barriers and moving beyond rigid divisions. Elsewhere I have tried to demonstrate that this sort of language is a link connecting comparative studies and hermeneutics.[15] The use of this kind of metaphor has intensified over the history of the discipline, especially during the stage where we emphasized the need for reaction to multiculturalism and globalization. Nowadays comparative practices try even more deliberately to cross frontiers and demarcation lines, acting as a hermeneutical tool that accompanies our *ex*istence. Thus, in keeping with the etymology of the word, they go "beyond," to "the different," in order to endlessly enrich one's being in the world. We can say, therefore, that in the case of comparative analysis we also have to account for a particular drive for the fusion of horizons. To put it another way, there is an ongoing widening of the spectrum, in which the old look meets the new one and in this way results in a deepening of our understanding. It is also worth noting the tradition that treats literary comparative studies as an art of interpretation based on the spatial placement of elements separated from each other owing to language and cultural differences. I refer here to the concept of "placing" that came into being on British soil and was described in S. Prawer's *Comparative Literary Studies: An Introduction* published in 1973: "By 'placing,' then, I mean the mutual illumination of several texts, or series of texts, considered side by side; the greater understanding we derive from juxtaposing a number of (frequently very different) works, authors and literary traditions."[16]

The second metaphor in comparative methodological discourse makes use of various references to the body. It originated during the initial stage of the discipline's development in the very genesis of its name, which arose as an analogy to Georges Cuvier's "anatomie comparée."[17] In many respects, the first anthologies by François J. Noël and François G. de La Place, in which they contrasted and showed specimens that were supposed to stand as testimony to the excellence of human nature, resembled anatomical atlases.[18] In the nineteenth century, special attention was paid to the link between comparative studies and natural science. The concept of the evolutionary sequential character of literary forms, enforced by Darwin's theory, survived in the field until the twentieth century.[19] The most visible sign that it had realized its objectives was its formulation of a specific body of texts, similar to Goethe's idea of "world literature."[20] Favoring borderline territories led the comparative discourse to a position in which it constantly had to define its place on the academic map. As a consequence, the twentieth century saw the rise of a whole series of concepts used to diagnose the problems facing the weak organism of comparative studies, which heralded their fall, death, and annihilation. The coming demise was repeatedly invoked in the first half of the twentieth century and reinforced later by René Wellek and René Etiemble.[21] Paradoxically, however, the discipline has continually shown itself as a true Proteus able to face ever-new challenges and emerge victorious. The image of the discipline reminds us, therefore, less of an agonized body than of a Phoenix, which dies only to be reborn.

Embodied or Disembodied: Scandals of Comparisons

Images that present comparative studies either as an area of constant border crossings or as a body that dies only to be reborn have accompanied the ongoing debate on the discipline. This fact is reflected in Gayatri Spivak's *Death of a Discipline*.[22] The title alludes to the famous *Death of the Author* by Roland

Barthes, which paradoxically brought a spirit of revival into the ossified world of literary categories. Spivak, however, does not prognosticate the imminent death of comparative literary studies. Rather she claims that a particular institutionalized concept that tied them to certain mechanisms of political dependence is drawing to a close. Without going into the details of her diagnoses and prognoses, I would like to draw attention to the fact that she introduces a new geography of comparative studies, focused on the symbolic fall of the Berlin Wall. This particular event not only marks the end of cold war politics, whose impact was reflected in the institutional nature of American comparative studies, but also encourages new forms of cultural translation through openness to experience shared by the countries that not such a long time ago fell victim to Soviet domination and are only now finally able to contribute to the study of mechanisms of power and the way in which they affect culture. In this way, Spivak tries to bridge a gap in the map of postcolonial reflection, helping to include the cultural heritage of postcommunist countries in her vision of a new comparative perspective based on an ethically motivated category of "teleopoiesis."[23] Her efforts on behalf of areas newly opened thanks to the fall of the Iron Curtain are not isolated. Among the many responses to the recently published report on standards prepared by the committee chaired by Haunn Saussy, the voice representing "a kidnapped West" (to recall the title of Kundera's famous essay) was for the first time in the history of such documents resounding:

> The region is intuitively "comparative." In Eastern Europe, one town would commonly speak several native languages, belong to two or three empires in the course of a single generation, and assume most of its residents to be hybrids who carried the dividing-lines of nationality within themselves. (As the famous story goes, Franz Kafka and Jaroslav Hašek drank at the same Prague pub, Kafka his coffee upstairs and Hašek his beer downstairs, one writing in German, the other in Czech, both knowing both languages and greeting one another on the stairs). Exile, displacement, multilanguagedness, heteroglossia, outsideness to oneself and thus a taste for irony, the constant crossing of borders, and the absence of a tranquil, organic, homogenized center that belongs to you alone: all these Bakhtinian virtues and prerequisites for genuine dialogue have long been endemic to Central Europe.[24]

Unfortunately, Polish comparative studies still respond to this openness toward the East with "scandal." If we consider a scandal to be the grossly unfavorable conditions or circumstances accompanying certain phenomena, we can state that the outline of Polish comparative research, although becoming clearer and more visible, can still be described by this term. Comparative literature in Poland remains a nebulous phenomenon with dubious academic foundations. There is still no professional periodical specializing in this field, and even the most prominent libraries have an extremely limited selection of works indispensable for acquiring the rudiments of the discipline's metalanguage. All this seems to be a scandalous legacy of the communist regime and makes one acutely aware of the fact that comparative literature as an academic institution has to be rebuilt in Poland from the ground up. These grossly discreditable conditions are indeed irritating but are no longer a wall separating our professional life from that of our colleagues living in neighboring or more distant countries. How Polish comparative literature, without institutional foundations, can become involved in and contribute to significant ongoing discussions remains an open question. It is clear that the process of institutionalization equally preserves and binds. There is nothing worse than academic ossification and routine. But what is the alternative in which we could make our voice heard and recognized? I believe this is possible only by defining proper standards and submitting to their incessant questioning. Without such an initiative, a young Polish comparatist will be left alone and forced to search for inspiration more often abroad than in his home country. Such a situation could result in a kind of constant dismay.

One of the factors that could contribute to overcoming the ephemeral and "scandalous" nature of our local comparative studies—in their institutional dimension—is the possibility of closer and renewed contacts and relations with centers of Polish studies abroad. Any student interested in Polish literature in the context of foreign literatures has only a handful of opportunities within the five-year university period to meet a scholar visiting Cracow from abroad. If a jubilee occurs in that time, like the Witold Gombrowicz anniversary we celebrated in 2004, we rejoice at the opportunity to observe discussions in an extended, international circle. This joy, however, is short-lived and cannot sustain us until the next jubilee celebrations. A handful of books published from time to time examine the native Polish literary scene "from the outside"[25] but often do not bring many changes to this bleak picture. What happens in the area of Polish studies abroad is, to a great extent, a black hole, a distant terra incognita. On the other hand, Polish studies abroad, which enjoy cultural diversity, seem to be well equipped to offer a rejuvenating comparative "questioning spirit"[26] to our literary reflection and didactics. In order to evoke and implement such reflection, there is need for a space in which to meet, a need that Goethe referred to on many occasions and which, from the contemporary perspective, brings to mind the recent books of such authors as Pascal Casanova, David Damrosch, or Christopher Prendergast. Although we can see on the horizon a rough outline of comparative literature in Poland, much effort is still needed to help it gain weight and body, so that it can find its place within the geography drafted by Spivak and, most important, meet the elementary need for placement that Czesław and Oscar Miłosz wrote about. For the young generation living in a country liberated from the totalitarian power, adopting a comparative perspective is both a chance to question our existing mental cartography, which is influenced by the tumultuous past and constructed in confrontation with social and mental transformations in progress, and a way to perceive and create collectivities to which we can belong. But at this stage such hopes are unfortunately merely unfulfilled desires or, so to speak, hopes that bear Utopian traits—traits, finally, of "no place."

NOTES

1. See two important collections of essays: Gossman and Spariosu; and Bernheimer.

2. Miłosz, *The Land of Ulro*, 99. All quotations of the metaphysical poems by Oscar Miłosz ("Letter to Storge," "Les Arcanes") come from this collection of essays.

3. Ibid., 199. The relation between space and mind, which Oscar Miłosz presents by means of intuitive images of the paralytic and the blind man, is described in modern philosophy and psychology of mind through direct references to experiments conducted on patients with dysfunctional central nervous systems. Giving the example of a patient named Schneider, Merleau-Ponty introduces a distinction between understanding related to the prereflexive activity of the body and understanding connected with conscious intellectual activity (103). This distinction is confirmed and elaborated upon by the recent work of psychologists. Carnaham discusses the difference between "grasping" and "pointing" (188); Milner and Goodale mention essential bodily as well as cognitive-reflexive understandings of space (126–28).

4. On the elementary way of filling space through movement that is described as a "repulsive force" taken from Leibniz and treated by Kant as "the essence of matter" and on the category of "impenetrability," see Warren, 93–116.

5. On the Cartesian concept of the body, which at the same time belongs to the subject and is distinct from it, treated as an object among other objects; on the relation between the experience of the body and conceptual thinking; and on the criticism of Cartesian dualism and Merleau-Ponty's philosophy outlined in *The Visible and the Invisible* (1968), see Cassam, "Representing Bodies," and *Self and World.*

6. Miłosz, *The Land of Ulro*, 200.

7. See Leder.

8. Nancy, 11.

9. See Burzyńska.

10. Clearly, the above-mentioned names represent various ways of thinking about embodiment and corporeality. The relation between space and the body has been perceived very differently even on the phenomenological ground (Husserl, Heidegger, Patočka, et al.). See Buczyńska-Garewicz, 235–48. The work of Merleau-Ponty still remains the focal point of "the philosophy of body," which is even manifested by its increasing popularity in the area of analytical philosophy (see Proudfoot). For the reception of Merleau-Ponty's concepts, see Varela, Thompson, and Rosch; Sheets-Johnstone. For one of the most recent publications on Merleau-Ponty's thought, see Todes. The category of the "lived body" takes center stage in some influential works representing feminist criticism. See Moi; Kruks.

11. For commentary on the term, see Gaynesford, 22–24. For a survey of various approaches to the relation between perception and action in the con-

text of the philosophy of mind and psychology, see Hurley. On awareness of the body and self-awareness, consult Cassam, "Introspection and Bodily Self-Ascription," and Shoemaker.

12. Miłosz, *The Land of Ulro*, 209.

13. See Ricoeur, *Du texte à l'action*, 110.

14. See Lalande, 154.

15. See Bilczewski.

16. Prawer, 144.

17. See R. Bauer, 41–47. See the first works that try to incorporate comparative practices: M. l'abbé de Tressan, *Mythologie comparée avec l'histoire* (London: T. Cadell, Jr., and W. Davies, 1797); Joseph M. Degérando, *Histoire comparée des systèmes de philosophie* (Paris: Henrichs, 1804); Jean-François. Sobry, *Poétique des Arts, ou cours de peinture et de littérature comparées* (Paris: Delaunay, Brunot-Labbe, Colnet [etc.], 1810); François J. M. Raynouard, *Grammaire comparée des langues de l'Europe latine dans leurs rapports avec la langue des troubadours* (Paris: F. Didot, 1816).

18. See François J. Noël and François G. de La Place, *Leçons françaises de littérature et de morale*, 7th ed. (Paris: Le Normant, 1816).

19. The following texts, representing this kind of approach, were usually regarded as the most influential: Ferdinand Brunetière, *L'Évolution des genres dans l'histoire de la literature* (Paris: Hachette, 1890) and *L'Évolution de la poésie lyrique en France au dix-neuvième siècle* (Paris: Hachette, 1894).

20. See Pizer; Hoesel-Uhlig, 47.

21. See Routh; Chandler; S. Putnam; Wellek, "The Crisis of Comparative Literature"; Etiemble.

22. See Spivak, *Death of a Discipline*.

23. See Cavanagh.

24. Emerson, 204–5.

25. I think here especially about such projects as "Polish Studies Abroad," a collection of books published by the Institute of Literary Research of the Polish Academy of Sciences since 1997. So far fourteen volumes have come out. Some excellent comparative works have also been published independently. I would like to mention only one author, Arent van Nieukerken. On the originality of his book, see Mitosek.

26. See Sławek, 391; Pratt, 31.

Denatured Spirits

Shame and Doubling in Witold Gombrowicz and Richard Weiner

Benjamin Paloff

Shame is a psychometaphysical condition; doubling is its conditioned response. Witold Gombrowicz (1904–69) and Richard Weiner (1884–1937) were no strangers to these issues, and it is an accident of fate that they were strangers to each other. When a young Gombrowicz went to Paris in the late 1920s, he could have easily encountered Weiner, a Czech poet and journalist well integrated in the cultural life of the city, a cultural life from which Gombrowicz kept a cool distance.[1] But in the masterworks of both authors, produced within a few years of each other, we find a remarkably similar treatment of shame as a basic symptom of Being, as well as of the double as the consequence of shame in the literary text.

The plot of *Ferdydurke*, Gombrowicz's remarkable 1937 novel, is quite simple; its concatenated adventures remind one of Cervantes, or of the English sentimentalist novels so admired by Georg Lukács, Mikhail Bakhtin, and other literary theorists of Gombrowicz's day.[2] Józio, a writer and unmistakable stand-in for Gombrowicz himself, is abducted by Pimko, his old schoolmaster. Pimko drags Józio back to the schoolhouse, where he must then relive all the humiliations of adolescence. In each chapter, Józio has a chance to escape his captivity: first, however, he must endure some embarrassing crisis. And because he retreats from these crises, his adventures become a chain of repeated failures. Each time Józio approaches an uncomfortable boundary he withdraws back into his degrading imprisonment.

The novel's central question, to which Gombrowicz draws our attention time and again, concerns whether an individual can ever be completely self-contained or, on the other hand, utterly dispersed in the social collective. Józio's dilemma is not simply how to reclaim his mature existence, but how to reconcile his internal lack of definition—his immaturity—with his well-formed, adult exterior. That is, Józio's Being is an intermediate condition a priori, and in the opening pages of *Ferdydurke* Gombrowicz furnishes us with everything we need to understand the metaphysical construct of his narrative:

> On Tuesday I awoke at that soulless, dim hour when night has in fact already ended but dawn has not yet managed to begin in earnest. Suddenly awakened, I wanted to rush by taxi to the station, for it seemed to me that I was going away—at just the next minute I was heartbroken to realize there was no train awaiting me at the station, no hour had struck. I was lying in the murky light, and my body was unbearably afraid, oppressing my spirit with terror, my spirit oppressed my body, and the most minute

> fiber seized up in anticipation that nothing would happen, nothing would change, nothing would ever occur, and no matter what I undertook, nothing, nothing would come of it.[3]

Gombrowicz places Józio in a strangely open-ended temporal confinement: night has ended, but day has not yet begun, and our hero is in fact certain that nothing will ever happen. With no temporal boundary to cross, he is already a captive, and he feels his captivity as his body and spirit mutually oppressing one another. In a chapter appropriately called "Abduction" ("Porwanie"), he is stuck between times, though he will soon discover that his anxiety does not stem from a sense that time is not moving forward, but that it is, in effect, repeating itself. Józio's Being is essentially bifurcated into mature and immature essences bound together, so that everything that happens in his present adult life inscribes within itself the image of a shameful immaturity:

> The dream that vexed me in the night, the one that woke me, was an exponent of dread. Through a reversal of time that should be forbidden to nature, I saw myself as I had been when I was fifteen or sixteen—I had shifted into youth—and standing in the breeze, on a rock, right next to the mill by the river, I was saying something, I heard my own long-buried voice, chickenlike and squeaky, I saw a not-fully-grown nose on a not-fully-formed face and too-large hands—I felt the unpleasant consistency of that intermediate, transitory phase of development. I awoke in laughter and horror, because it seemed to me that the way I am today, in my thirties, is mimicking and making fun of the unfledged pipsqueak I had been, and then he is mimicking me—and by the same principle—that we are both being mimicked by ourselves.[4]

In the notion of self-mimicry *as* self-mockery, we already find the roots of doubling, of the expropriation of the Self. In his nightmare, Józio discovers a chain of mimetic activity within himself, with his youthful self-image comically, horribly mirroring his older self-image in a continuous, unbroken loop, a scene that will repeat itself in the novel's infamous third chapter, which represents a duel of youths making faces at each other. The circularity of this process provides an excellent figure for the function of one of the novel's richest motifs, the "tushy" or "bottom" (*pupa*). The "tushy" serves as the seat—if you will forgive the pun—of our hero's immaturity, an immaturity that is inextricable from him, and which plays two roles in the novel, of both enslaver and temporary liberator: as Józio is being dragged back to school, he declares "The idiotic, infantile tushy was paralyzing, removing any possibility of resistance."[5] At the same time, that dastardly "tushy," that pervasive immaturity, is the very thing that Józio reaches for when his humiliating circumstances precipitate a crisis, since it liberates him from society's demands for maturity and resolve.

I have already suggested, and many scholars have noted that, for Gombrowicz, immaturity is an inherent and inescapable condition of Being.[6] Immaturity helps us understand Józio's individuality as a compromise, the "intermediate, transitory phase" between the elusive freedom of formlessness and the solidity of form. Accordingly, the "tushy" as a figure for immaturity can neither be eliminated nor ignored, and this dooms Józio's struggle from the beginning. For Józio's ultimate goal, to keep his past from regurgitating itself into his present, is tantamount to a struggle to escape Being. And this struggle, while doomed to failure, necessitates the expropriation of the Self into a double, the exteriorization of the Self that, through mimicry and mockery, brings the thinking subject to a shameful awareness of his Being.

Emmanuel Lévinas describes this process in his essay "On Escape" ("De l'évasion," 1935). This text, contemporary with *Ferdydurke*, marks Lévinas's early departure from Heidegger:

> Existence is an absolute that is asserted without reference to anything else. It is identity. But in this reference to himself, man perceives a type of duality. His identity with himself loses the character of a logical or tautological form; it takes on a dramatic form. . . . In the identity of the I, the identity of being reveals its nature as enchainment, for it appears in the form of suffering and invites us to escape. Thus, escape is the need to get out of oneself, that is, *to break that most radical and unalterably binding of chains, the fact that the I is oneself.*[7]

The "duality" that Lévinas posits is precisely what we witness in Józio's repeated encounters with mimicry, instances of mimesis that take on the character of a confrontation with the Self. The most widely discussed instance of this kind, which has become common currency in Polish popular culture, comes in the scene in chapter 3, "Catching and Further Crushing" ("Przyłapanie i dalsze miętoszenie"), in which Józio and his classmates engage in a duel of face making, imitating one another for a kind of existential supremacy.[8] In his dream, however, Józio faces an image not of an immature Other, but of the immature component of his own Being, from which he cannot escape.

As though this manifestation of the Other were not clear enough, just before Pimko abducts Józio—for his rematuration by means of dematuration—Gombrowicz literalizes the immature double Józio has seen in his dream:

> I realized that I was not alone. There was someone other than me in the corner, next to the oven, where the light did not yet reach—another person was in the room. . . . And again the dryness in the mouth, the beating of the heart, the halting of the breath—that was me, myself, standing by the oven. This time it was no dream—there was actually a double standing by the oven.[9]

This moment serves as the linchpin to both the novel's plot and its philosophical structure. Gombrowicz tells us that the double in Józio's room is afraid, that it does not wish to return the protagonist's gaze, and this displacement from Self, in which the subject does *not* wish to look at his double, is characteristic of the shame of Being. Józio immediately recognizes the dual nature of this apparition, both himself and not, both present and absent, "something alien, imposed, a kind of compromise between the external world and the internal one."[10] Gombrowicz's formulation, which explicitly posits the intermediacy of the thinking subject, could not be more apt for what is about to transpire. For the protagonist, with a redoubled will toward escape into an existence that is both singular and whole, reaches for his writing instruments, his pen and blank paper, in order to invent a work that will define and distinguish him, that will in effect *be* him, and that will therefore abolish his compromised existence and secure his individuality: "I start to write the first pages of my very own work, just like me, identical with me, arising straight out of me."[11] But Józio never succeeds in composing a work coterminous with himself, because at the very moment he seizes this opportunity for self-definition, Pimko enters. Józio puts up no resistance. He is, after all, of a piece with his "tushy," which seeks only to preserve itself as immaturity.

In *Ferdydurke*, the immaturity of the thinking subject binds the impossibility of escape to memory and shame. Memory, because the hero is tormented by the recollection of his immaturity, of the disorderly, unruly, disobedient world of his youth, which makes him feel that his very existence is collapsing and that he must escape, though flight is impossible, since memory cannot be outrun. Shame, because according to Lévinas shame arises from our inability to escape our Being, and from the fact that this failure is obvious to all gazes directed toward us:

> Shame does not depend—as we might believe—on the limitation of our being, inasmuch as it is liable to sin, but rather on the very being of our being, on its incapacity to break with itself. Shame is founded upon the solidarity of our being, which obliges us to claim responsibility for ourselves. . . . It is therefore our intimacy, that is, our presence to ourselves that is shameful. It reveals not our nothingness but rather the totality of our existence. Nakedness is the need to excuse one's existence. Shame is, in the last analysis, an existence that seeks excuses. What shame discovers is the being who *uncovers* himself.[12]

Lévinas lays bare—or *uncovers*—the basic mechanism behind the appearance of the double. In the absence of an Other, Gombrowicz invents another in whose eyes the thinking subject's immaturity—that is, his disorder and excess—is shameful. As Bernard Williams notes in his study of shame in classical Greek culture, one of the paradoxes of shame in the Western imagination is its binding effect, at the same time linking one person to another and prompting an impulse to flee.[13] This effect can be seen even in the absence of the Other. After all, the thinking subject need only *imagine* the Other's gaze in order to posit a sense of shame.

That the Other may not exist at all, that he may be nothing more than a psycholinguistic function after the manner of Jacques Lacan, raises a fundamental ethical dilemma.[14] For if the otherness of the Other does not refer us to a real thinking subject, then no act can be ethically consequential; the Other is little more than a plaything of the Self. Gombrowicz was aware of this tension, and his work demonstrates a repetitive oscillation between the Other-as-Subject and the Other-as-Absence. Janusz Margański points this out in reference to

Gombrowicz's work before and after *Ferdydurke*: "It is true that even in his parodic revelations there appears a kind of absolute otherness. But it is also true that it arises in nothingness and through nothingness. It is, in a sense, negation confirming itself in negation, an ultimate lack. For conventional signs, by which we assimilate the Absolute, are first dodged and then sanctioned by custom, but then something arises that no one can name."[15] Margański describes the process by which "conventional signs," including those for Self and Other, define and delimit the thinking subject and his world, until he encounters something that *cannot* be named or defined. And that remainder, that indefinable quality or absolute otherness, arises from within—and is discovered by—the very process of defining and delimiting the world. In the absence of an indisputable authority—the Author or God—the thinking subject resorts to conventional definitions, but he eventually finds them too restrictive.

As Margański further suggests, the thinking subject must then waver between the ideal of an unknowable absolute and contact with ethically independent thinking subjects, a movement between Self and Other:

> In fact, Gombrowicz always confronts his heroes with this antinomy, which, we may add, keeps getting deeper, revealing its historical dimension. Man, wishing to extract himself from the oppression of painful mediations, ravenous for unmediated relations with his neighbor or his God, reaches unknowingly for forms of discourse that are fixed in tradition, for a deep-rooted symbolic. And this is also where we get the compulsion toward repetition and constant parody. And this is also where we get the attempt to appropriate inveterate forms of discourse through parody and the attempt to create—after the "death of God"—other interhuman relations. And this is also where we get the wound that constantly appears in the "I" who is thinking about God.[16]

In this formulation, the thinking subject's quest—for definition, on the one hand, or contact, on the other—is always doomed. The only means the thinking subject has at his disposal is a *received* language: *means* as *mediation*, which the thinking subject finds oppressive. In the search for contact with the Other, that Other is sometimes an ethically independent thinking subject (the "neighbor"), sometimes an ideal of absolute self-identity (God). In any event, Gombrowicz's characters are incapable of an escape from Self, and the shame of this failure makes them all the more dependent on the Other. Gombrowicz, in fact, raises this bonding power of shame to the level of abject addiction, claiming that "man is deeply dependent on his reflection in the soul of another person, though it may be the soul of a moron."[17] The fact that the individual is dependent (*uzależniony*, "addicted") on the Other's concept of him guarantees that he can never be alone, though the shame that remains an essential condition of that scrutiny simultaneously drives him to panic and flight. The result is a constantly alternating movement toward and away from the individual's Being—his memory, his immaturity and maturity—as reflected "in the soul of another person." This vacillation is made manifest in the appearance of the double.

Giorgio Agamben, in his description of Lévinas's "uncovering of oneself" as "expropriation and desubjectivization," renders this link between shame and doubling even more explicit:

> It is as if our consciousness collapsed and, seeking to flee in all directions, were simultaneously summoned by an irrefutable order to be present at its own defacement, at the expropriation of what is most its own. In shame, the subject thus has no other content than its own desubjectification; it becomes witness to its own disorder, its own oblivion as a subject. . . . W]hoever experiences shame is overcome by his own being subject to vision; he must respond to what deprives him of speech. . . . [Shame] is nothing less than the fundamental sentiment of being *a subject*, in the two apparently opposed senses of this phrase: to be subjected and to be sovereign.[18]

This is a wonderfully compact précis of the dynamics of shame in *Ferdydurke*. Afraid to look up, Józio's cowering double is "overcome by his own being subject to vision," and Józio, pressured by his "being *a subject*," attempts throughout the novel to escape into both senses of that word, into the security of a sovereign self-identity, and the illusory freedom of nondefinition. Being a subject means having only enough definition to recognize oneself as a Self, one who overlaps with other selves and is *subject* to them. Józio cannot stand his own identity—his self-singularity, which the appearance of his double paradoxically serves to emphasize—and in this sense is complicit in his own abduction, the process by which he is *subjected* once again to all the humiliations of adolescence. At the same time, he finds the trials to which he is repeatedly subjected equally unbearable, and this compels him to escape back into his self-singularity, his "sovereignty."

In a sense, the entire text of *Ferdydurke* constitutes Józio's response "to what deprives him of speech." We recall that Józio's first reaction to the appearance of his double is a desperate attempt to write, to reconstitute his identity through language. Appropriately, the novel opens with Józio's reflections on how his book, Gombrowicz's own *Memoir from a Time of Immaturity*, was viciously attacked by critics, and the repetitive adventures recounted in the text are themselves responses to, and manifestations of the shameful immaturity inherent in the mature thinking subject.[19] Gombrowicz revisits this link between shame and silence several times throughout *Ferdydurke*, perhaps most notably in the chapter entitled "Preface to Philidor Lined with Child" ("Przedmowa do Filidora dzieckiem podszytego"), where he writes about the poet-prophet so secure in his selfhood that accusations of immaturity can no longer stifle him, for he is beyond shame: "the poet-prophet of sound philosophy is fixed so firmly in himself that not even stupidity and immaturity are able to frighten or harm him—with head raised high, he can express himself and make himself manifest in his own indolence, whereas you are now barely in a state to express anything, for terror has taken away your voice."[20]

Józio, however, is not a "poet-prophet of sound philosophy," "fixed in himself." Instead, he is open and exposed to the world, which constantly threatens him with its shameful gaze. Gombrowicz incorporates this enforced silence pleasantly into the novel's closing passages, when we find Józio and Zosia sitting together, unsure what to do now that the captive has performed his own kidnapping. Each character is entirely incapable of articulating these shameful circumstances to the other. And it is the presence of an Other that, for each of these characters, both necessitates and forecloses the possibility of such an explanation: "I didn't know what to do. I couldn't explain and voice [*wyjęzyczyć*] to Zosia what had happened on the estate, for I was ashamed [*wstydziłem się*], and anyway, I didn't find the words. Whereas she probably figured it out more or less, for she was ashamed [wstydziła się], too, and she really couldn't voice it [*wyjęzyczyć*]."[21] Gombrowicz assembles an analogically repetitive chain: the captive becomes the captor, but unable to voice his experience (*wyjęzyczyć*, literally, "to express in language"), he feels only shame. This shame is itself infectious, and Zosia, the captive's captive, feels it as well. But she is also incapable of expressing it in language.

It would perhaps be overreaching to suggest that Zosia is herself a double of the protagonist, but here she clearly reflects aspects of his interiority, and the prototype for this mirroring is the instance of doubling in the novel's opening chapter. The various instances of emotional infection and interpersonal entanglement that we find in ample evidence in *Ferdydurke* ultimately stem from and reflect that initial moment, in which the protagonist is entangled with no Other but his Self. Typically for Gombrowicz, this doubling of the synthetic whole echoes the symmetry of analytic parts. Józio says of his encounter with the double, "Furtively, from under the blanket, I looked as though not at myself, and I saw that face, which was mine and not-mine. . . . That's my nose . . . that's my mouth . . . those are my ears, my home."[22] The element that seems not to belong is "my home," but this shift in attention from body parts to environment is in fact highly productive. Through this shift, Gombrowicz in effect emphasizes that Józio's double is domestic rather than alien: they share the same singular space, since they are the same, nonsingular subject.

Decades later, Gombrowicz would recycle this scene in the second volume of his *Diary* (*Dziennik 1957–1961*). Gombrowicz's friend Simon pays an unexpected visit, and he remarks that his daughter has just been horribly scalded. She is still in the hospital; Simon does not know what to do with himself. Gombrowicz and Simon sit facing each other, unable to say anything, and Gombrowicz tells us:

> Yet I went silent, he went silent, and we sat, so to speak, nose-to-nose. One-on-one. Hand-to-hand. Leg-to-leg. Knee-to-knee. One-on-one. Until this stupid identity in this, my room, started to bug me, and I think, how is it that he repeats me, I repeat him, one-on-one—suddenly the scalding of the child scalded me until I hissed—and then, I see, though so similar, we can't go on sitting here, and in general it's better not to sit but get out, get out, get out, a way out, any, an expulsion, a distancing, became pressing, burning![23]

In this passage, we are drawn again to the signature inventory of body parts, the arms and legs of Gombrowicz finding their necessary counterparts in those of Simon. But we should be especially intrigued by Gombrowicz's annoyance at "this stupid identity in this, my room." Gombrowicz uses the word "identity" (*tożsamość*) in a metaphysical, rather than a conventional, sense: he is referring to their equivalence, not to their status as individuals. This draws the two distinct individuals, Gombrowicz and Simon, into an uncomfortable, "stupid" congruence. "Stupid," because the two individuals should not be identical, especially in Gombrowicz's own domestic space. In a similar way, Józio emphasizes that the unbearable expropriation of Self—the appearance of the double—occurs in his own home. This is what makes such an identity "stupid," since it underscores the intrusion of the Other into the ontological zone of the Self. That is, it should not be possible for one to be equivalent to another in the same way as one is equivalent to oneself. Or so the thinking subject, pained by the encroachment of the Other, would like to think.

In fact, this intrusion of the Other is a basic function of Being, and Gombrowicz does not oppose it so much as he points out—repeatedly, in one colorful example after another—that it compels the individual to escape. It does not matter whether such a flight is from the Self or from the Other in whom the Self is mirrored, since both escapes are ultimately impossible. The urgent need to flee, to break out of this unwholesome identity—with oneself, with the Other—remains real: "get out, get out, a way out, any, an expulsion, a distancing, became pressing, burning!" But Gombrowicz's phrasing already forecloses the possibility of any such escape, since he describes the need to flee as *palące*, literally "burning," though also a conventional word for "urgent," as it is in English. This picks up the connotative cue of the child's scalding, which Gombrowicz already feels through his symmetry with Simon. Thus the author's need to escape inscribes within itself the very same association from which escape becomes necessary.

In both the *Diary* and *Ferdydurke*, the consequence of identity is predictably the same: the subject must try to escape, to break free of this shameful self-equivalence, even though such an escape is ultimately impossible, since there can be no escape from Being. There is a basic difference between these two scenarios, however, insofar as the double in the novel appears as the literal desubjectification of the subject, the *ex*-propriation of his Self from himself, whereas in the *Diary* we find the reverse movement, the *ap*-propriation of the Other into the Self, if only momentarily. But I would suggest that for Gombrowicz, an author who assigns vital importance to all things "interhuman" (*międzyludzkie*), the difference is one of polarity, rather than of quality. The splitting of the Self is merely the obverse of ontological intercourse with the Other, and both movements create a shameful intimacy.

Gombrowicz explores this intimacy with particular élan in the novel's fifth chapter, "Philidor Lined with Child" ("Filidor dzieckiem podszyty," written in 1935), an intermezzo in which we witness a duel between Philidor, a proponent of synthesis, and Anti-Philidor, the paragon of analysis. But Gombrowicz addresses our inability to escape from ourselves as early as the story "Adventures" ("Przygody") first published as "Five Minutes before Falling Asleep" ("Na 5 minut przed zaśnięciem") in *Memoir from a Time of Immaturity*. In "Adventures," the narrator-protagonist is tormented by a double, manifested as a white man who is black on the inside, who—as the narrator acknowledges—may not even exist. And appropriately, the double comes up with tortures that, despite the indelible connection between narrator and tormentor, underscore the narrator's isolation in himself, as well as the equally terrifying prospect of self-splitting. He tells us, "Oh, I simply don't know how to say how horrifying our 'I' is when transferred into an alien domain."[24] The notion that "our 'I'" *can be* "transferred into an alien domain" is indeed terrifying, but it is also so shameful that it resists articulation, as the narrator informs us in reference to his fiancée, to whom he can say nothing of the trials he has endured with his black double: "But despite the fact that women ostensibly love the romantic, with her I kept quiet about the black man and about my other adventures—in light of the incomprehensible and burning shame, which cautioned me—not to say too much."[25] The narrator's adventures with his double, which form a tale of simultaneous subjectification and desubjectification, are too shameful to tell, though this hero has somewhat less difficulty relaying the adventures to the reader. Gombrowicz characterizes this shame as "burning" (*palący*), the same word he will use in his *Diary* to describe the need to flee his "stupid identity" with Simon. Indeed, the situations are conceptually linked: it is intimacy that is shameful, whether it reveals our vulnerability to the Other or, to reiterate Lévinas's original point, our "presence to ourselves," an ontological condition from which there is no escape. The double emerges in these texts as the literalization of this intimacy, and the countless instances of interpersonal entanglement that we witness in Gombrowicz radiate from this primal, *intra*-personal dynamic of subjectification and desubjectification.

Gombrowicz explains this dynamic in unusually direct language in a 1951 letter to Martin Buber. Responding to Buber's suggestion that Gombrowicz's play *The Wedding* (*Ślub*, 1953) is not really dramatic, since his characters are not "separate and self-contained," Gombrowicz asks: "Can there not exist a drama that is not—between people, but in a person himself? If someone suffers from an incurable disease—isn't the drama realized between himself and his disease? If someone is confronted with his fate, with his destiny—must that necessarily play out through the mediation of people?"[26] These are, of course, rhetorical questions. For Gombrowicz, it is not only conceivable, but necessary that such internal conflicts play themselves out within the individual thinking subject, and yet Gombrowicz's own tendency is to externalize these conflicts through a double, the "'I' in an alien domain." That is, what occurs within the individual echoes outward into interpersonal action, wherein the subject not only casts himself outward, as we see at the beginning of *Ferdydurke*, but also creates and resists the identification of himself with others, as we see in the *Diary*. Along these lines, in his letter to Buber Gombrowicz moves quickly from asserting a drama within the subject to rejecting the possibility of "separate and self-contained" people altogether: "[I] cannot provide a conflict between people who exist 'on their own,' as you say, because my vision, my intuition rests precisely on the fact that there are no people 'on their own.' My hero's drama is not—a confrontation with other people, but merely with the forces that arise *from people, between* people."[27] For Gombrowicz, the subject oscillates continuously between his own subjectification and desubjectification. He is always singular—or sovereign—because he cannot escape his own Being. But at the same time, he is always plural—or subjected to others—because others bombard him in turn with their Being. The sudden impulse to escape, as constant a motif in *Ferdydurke* as it is in much of Gombrowicz's oeuvre, represents both a fundamental need, and an inevitable failure.

When we reexamine the thematic substructure of the double in its relation to shame, speechlessness, and the gaze of the Other, we find that Central European literature between the world wars is rife with instantiations of the same basic mechanism. In the Polish context, one might turn to Bruno Schulz's compact narrative "Solitude," which was included as the penultimate story in *Sanatorium under the Sign of the Hourglass*, though Schulz most likely wrote the earliest version of the story, originally entitled "About Myself" ("O sobie"), in the late 1920s.[28] In "Solitude," Schulz constructs an imaginary space without doors or windows, where the subject has no choice but to face himself:

> Sometimes I see myself in the mirror. What a strange, amusing, and painful thing! A shame to admit it. I never see myself *en face*, face-to-face. But a little deeper, I stand there a little further in the depths of the mirror, a bit to the side, a bit in profile, I stand there lost in thought and look to the side. I stand there motionlessly, looking to the side, a bit behind myself. Our gazes have stopped meeting.[29]

For a very brief, essentially plotless text, "Solitude" has it all: the mirror image treated as the Other, the expropriation of the Self, the confession of shame, the gazes that form the foundation of that shame, but that by failing to meet one another refuse to connect the subject with himself. As we might expect under these circumstances, the rest of Schulz's narrative addresses the possibility of escape.

The interlinked themes of identity and escape were of equal concern to Richard Weiner, whose work offers many avenues of fruitful comparison to Gombrowicz and Schulz. Weiner, a Paris correspondent for the Czech daily *Lidové noviny*, was experiencing a rebirth of literary ambitions at the time Gombrowicz, fleeing the paternalistic pressures of family and cultural life in Poland, arrived in France. We have already seen, however, that there is no escape. As Janusz Margański points out, Gombrowicz's flight to Paris was itself culturally prescribed.[30] And according to Margański, Gombrowicz, who has come to represent the strongest strains of Polish modernist literature, was ambivalent about the forms of cultural production he encountered in Paris: "Gombrowicz did not chase after modernism; admittedly, he observed and analyzed it, but he also fled from it."[31]

Unlike Gombrowicz, Weiner had already established himself as a poet and prose author by the time he relocated to Paris in 1919, where he became a full-time journalist. Jindřich Chalupecký, Weiner's best postwar critic, describes this move as a "double escape": "An escape from his Czech surroundings, and just as much an escape from his own calling as a writer."[32] While living in Paris in the 1920s, Weiner wrote hundreds of Czech-language feuilletons, addressing issues that ranged from surrealist aesthetics to the cultural significance of Marcel Proust. At the same time, he participated directly in the international artists' group Le Grand Jeu, which included the French poets René Daumal (1908–44) and Roger Gilbert-Lecomte (1907–43), and the Czech painter Josef Šíma (1891–1971). In late 1925, Šíma began experimenting with the use of prisms in painting, and he explained his method of capturing "the unity of the world" to Weiner, who shared his ideas at the time: "Regardless of how diverse the material, it is 'one.' This monism lends unpredictable dimensions to reality. In this reality memory is reflected in the mirror of the present moment, from the perspective of the future."[33] For Šíma, monism consists not only in the ultimate unity of all things, but also in the fusion of past, present, and future. Present experience becomes an extension of past memory. At the same time, the present is tied inextricably to the future, which it anticipates. Weiner's second phase of literary production, which lasted from 1927 to 1933, demonstrates both the influence of Le Grand Jeu and Weiner's increasingly problematic relationship to this perspective on space-time and matter.[34]

The most important product of this last wave of activity is *A Game for Real* (*Hra doopravdy*, published in 1933). Weiner's last work, and one of his most challenging, is a masterful illustration of the themes of doubling, interpersonal infection, and entrapment. Consisting of two thematically intertwined novellas, *A Game for Real* opens in much the same way as *Ferdydurke*, with the unbearable doubling of the protagonist. Yet a significant difference in the first novella, entitled *The Game of Quartering* (*Hra na čtvrcení*, 1929–31) is that it opens with the hero not at home, but on his way home. On the metro, he encounters a strange double, though not of himself; this man is the spitting image of Vicente Escudero, the Spanish flamenco dancer who was a Paris sensation in the 1920s, and he starts to follow the narrator, who then has difficulty returning home. In fact, as new doubles appear, they foreclose a definitive return to the protagonist's domestic space.

What the hero does not understand is how the Other(s) can get into his house when only he has the key. But then he realizes that the Other has no difficulty being attached to the hero, since the two are one:

> And who exactly is this stranger behind my door, whom I was supposed to dread and did not; who took my dread *on himself* and behind whose corporeal self—for he was

> corporeal—I tread, with so obdurate an ennui, as though behind my own shadow? Who is this unexpected disturber of the rhythm of my bachelor life, and who, in spite of everything, does not ruin it? Under whose gaze, attentive but remote, today as any other day (when I am undoubtedly alone) do I set out on an apathetic inspection of my ground-floor apartment, my abode, where it is so easy for a stranger to barge in? My God, who is this, he who is paradoxically present, who exists so rarely and, for just that reason, seems not to exist, and under whose eerie, fearful surveillance I am executing a series of stereotypical, authenticating passes, after which I will lie down *with a calm awareness* that I can calmly go to sleep, that I am alone, that I am alone again despite the fact that he is with me! I'm not bothered, I'm not bothered by this someone I see and do not remark.[35]

The scene is at first comic: it is late at night, and the narrator cannot open his own door because there is an equal and opposite force pushing against it from the other side. Once the hero manages to get inside, however, Weiner concentrates on the sense of displacement that is a necessary consequence of the double's appearance. For the double, as we have seen in Gombrowicz and Schulz, is the Self *and* the Other, the expropriation of the Self *as* Other. The double is, to borrow Julia Kristeva's productive term, the *abject*, the unfinished Being of this individual thinking subject set outside the subject.[36] This is why the hero feels he should be afraid, and yet he is not afraid. He senses that this Other is "corporeal," and yet he can follow him around the apartment "as though behind my own shadow." The narrator characterizes the double as a "disturber of the rhythm of my bachelor life," and yet the Other "does not ruin it."

These paradoxes, which the protagonist recognizes as such when he calls the Other "paradoxically present," go on and on. The Other's gaze is "attentive but remote," and this is entirely appropriate, since the Other is both here and not-here: "I am alone again despite the fact that he is with me." Weiner develops the paradox further by switching fluidly between proximal and distal demonstrative adjectives, referring to the Other by turns as "this" (*ten, tento*) and "that" (*onen*). As an expropriation of the Self, the double confronts the thinking subject with entanglement with the Other and, at the same time, with the isolation of his own identity. Where Gombrowicz represents the incommensurability of these two selves through immaturity—the unfinished "I" longing for contact versus the adult "I" longing for self-enclosure—Weiner calls it a "bachelor life" (*staromládenecký život*, literally "the life of an old-young man"), a life that this narrator implies should be solitary, though he is at pains to emphasize how much the "paradoxical presence" of another does not upset him.

Both Gombrowicz and Weiner assure their readers that the appearance of the double is no dream, though it is in some way associated with the dream life. When the double appears to Józio at the beginning of *Ferdydurke*, the latter has just awoken from a troubling dream. When the double appears in *The Game of Quartering*, the narrator is about to go to bed, an act that will require him simply to accept the double's presence, *"with a calm awareness,"* as a necessary condition of Being.

Yet for Weiner, as for Gombrowicz and Schulz, the gaze of the thinking subject does not meet that of his double or, more generally, of the Other who would seem to double him. In the first chapter of *Ferdydurke*, Józio's double cowers in the corner, refusing to return his gaze. In Schulz's "Solitude," the speaker's mirror image also refuses to look him in the eye, so that it is possible for one to view the Other "a bit in profile." In *The Game of Quartering*, the speaker is likewise unable to see any of several potential doubles except in profile, as when he observes his dubious friends Mutig and Fuld: "And I realized that if I am seeing them both in profile, then they must therefore be facing each other. And it occurred to me (as though for the first time) that each time I endeavored to overpower his supposed virtue, Fuld always and without exception stood in such a way that I couldn't see him except in profile."[37] Mutig and Fuld mirror each other, but they also mirror the narrator in an inescapable associative chain. Indeed, the protagonist of Weiner's text sees himself mirrored in several other characters, and he sees them mirrored in each other as well.

The reader may continue to wonder why the thinking subject cannot catch the gaze of his double. One reason—and this speaks to the ontological structure of the double—is that to do so would imply the completion of an exchange, or the closing of the circuit, between the Self and the Self-as-Other. We can imagine how, hypothetically, this would constitute the reintegration of the Self, since the distance between the Self and the Other would collapse in the meeting of their gaze.[38] A more interesting reason for our purposes, however, addresses the role of shame in the splitting of the Self. As Gombrowicz demonstrates in *Memoir from a Time of Immaturity*, *Ferdydurke*, the *Diary*, and elsewhere, when the thinking subject is mirrored in another—whether that Other is truly an independent thinking subject or simply a double of the Self—shame holds open the circuit of intersubjective exchange. That is, shame expresses both the subject's need for, and failure to attain Lévinas's "excendence," to escape from his own Being. The double manifests that failure by being one with the subject and, at the same time, outside the subject. The double, as an intermediate state situated between identity and alterity, cannot be recovered by an immediate gaze or verbal communication. Faced with his own reflection in another, the thinking subject cannot catch the Other's gaze, because this would be tantamount to catching *his own* gaze; he cannot speak, because his shame prevents him from communicating with himself.[39]

Weiner takes this problematic to new heights. In *The Game of Quartering*, the narrator eventually finds that the presence of the double eliminates all possibility for solipsism. The hero can see himself outside himself, but he can no longer see himself in a mirror:

> But the fact that I was face-to-face *with myself* was not the eeriest thing; eerier still was the ardor with which my thought was trying to persuade my hesitating senses that this was no delusion; eerier still was the certainty that my senses, at just this moment

> my sight, had begun to live outside of my thought. . . . I was on my feet, a step before the tall mirror over the fireplace—I say before the tall mirror over the fireplace, knowing with sunlike clarity that I'm in front of the mirror—which, however, did not answer me. And again: eerier than this betrayal of me, who despite an unspoken but age-old pact did not issue forth from those depths, was my ardent, gloomily high-spirited thought, trying to persuade my startled senses not to be afraid, not to run away, that there was nothing to worry about, that this empty mirror was a correct mirror, *that this was how it had to be*.[40]

"*This was how it had to be*": Weiner recognizes that the expropriation of the Self in the form of a double expresses a necessary and inescapable condition of Being. (Indeed, what would it say about the ontological structure of the double if the hero *could* see himself simultaneously in the room and in the mirror?) In this passage, the speaker's difficulty is not in reconciling his psyche with the fact that the mirror "did not answer" him, but in suppressing the visceral reaction of his "startled senses" against what seems an unnatural phenomenon. Yet the narrator realizes the paradox of being "face-to-face" with himself: he tells us that the way in which his thought (*myšlenka*, also "idea," "concept") attempted to convince his senses not to rebel against this necessary condition of Being was *eerier* than the appearance of the double. Weiner underscores the paradox adjectivally, describing his thought as "gloomily high-spirited." And just as the speaker's senses "had begun to live outside of my thought," his thought seems to live outside his Being, at least insofar as the thought is strange enough for the thinker to be surprised by it.

Faced with his double, Weiner's hero recognizes in a purely Gombrowiczean manner the extent to which he is both sovereign and subject. Then, in a wonderful demonstration of the dynamics of shame and defacement, the narrator calmly states, "He's stolen my face; he's stolen my face." To which one of his interlocutors asks, "Which one?"[41] Here we might recall Agamben's formulation about shame: "It is as if our consciousness collapsed and, seeking to flee in all directions, were simultaneously summoned by an irrefutable order to be present at its own defacement, at the expropriation of what is most its own." The protagonist of *The Game of Quartering* constantly wants to escape from his own existence, but at the same time he has no choice but to bear witness to his own defacement, a process that is reiterated with every Other he encounters.

The second part of *A Game for Real*, *The Game for the Honour of Payback* (*Hra na čest za oplatku*, 1930–31), repeats the doubling motif of the first novella, but also elaborates the role of shame in manifesting the double. The protagonist is known only as "Hanba" (shame, dishonor), and the story follows his psychological torment in having missed the opportunity to slap a man named Mr. Steel, who has offended him (One is reminded of Philidor's inability to slap Anti-Philidor in the fifth chapter of *Ferdydurke*.). Like the protagonist of *The Game of Quartering*, however, this hero feeds off his own shame: "he was ashamed . . . and relished his shame."[42] He also spends a great deal of time in front of the mirror, but unlike the narrator of The Game of Quartering, Hanba sees himself in the mirror, which is consistent with his early confession to Zinaida, the servant to whom he tries—and fails—to relate: "I don't know how to exteriorize."[43] Thus the hero finds his double in his own mirror image, which is both his Self and *not himself*:

> He is immersed in affectionate and deferential self-regard, so that he has betrayed the community of the street; he has become solitary; but then what is solitude to someone whose plethoricity is such that he is a community unto himself? Has the street cast him out? Rather, he has wiped *it* out. He and his image have fallen in love, mutually alluring, invincible, they were in control; he was in control. . . . And now he passes by the mirror, a snoop; he cast a momentary sidelong glance . . . whom does he see? An elderly child. And that ruinous kitchen boy of moral petitions says: "That one there's fussy about his looks; when we're fussy about our looks, we become cocky. Fussy about our looks!"[44]

In this passage, Weiner is a little tongue-in-cheek in his treatment of his hero's solitude, which is more generally a source of torment. The man and his mirror image are in love with each other to the exclusion of the outside world. But this does not matter, since this hero is a Whitmanesque universe unto himself: he contains multitudes. Weiner coins a neologism, "plethoricity" (*pletoričnost*), to illustrate the inherent multiplicity of the self, the sense that the individual thinking subject is "a community unto himself." While Gombrowicz constructs the notion of immaturity as an expansive cosmos within the individual, Weiner reaches here for the remarkably similar notion of the "aged" or "elderly child" (*obstárlé dítě*). It is almost as a wicked afterthought that he has this child—the unfinalized core of the hero—speak back to the hero, warning him that "when we're fussy about our looks, we become cocky." Weiner uses the word *sebevědomí*, "self-assured" or "self-confident," though etymologically the word suggests self-awareness, and one senses that this meaning might apply as well. When one looks at himself too much in the mirror he is in danger of becoming self-aware. This self-awareness can lead the thinking subject only to the unhappy conclusion that he is neither a self-contained whole, nor an integral part of a larger community, but something in between: a "community unto himself." Zdeněk Vašíček refers to this condition ironically as Weiner's "impersonality" (*neosobnost*), noting that "this is not the life problem of man as an individual; it is a question of humanity's very existence."[45] Gombrowicz would most likely agree.

In the quasi-interviews of his *A Kind of Testament*, Gombrowicz describes the composition of *Ferdydurke* as an attempt to defend his own individuality.[46] There are many well-documented reasons for why Gombrowicz might have felt a literal need to defend his personhood against his family background: the painful last gasps of Polish aristocratic culture, his own literary and artistic ambitions, and even against the critics who had attacked his first book. Weiner, whose *A Game for Real* turned out to be his last and most lasting contribution to Czech letters, appears to have conceptualized the novel in similar ways. For while *Ferdydurke* and *A Game for Real* both present their authors' struggles against literary conventions and cultural conditioning, there is a more pressing metaphysical dimension to how Gombrowicz and Weiner approach individuality in these texts. This approach concerns the spatial distribution of the thinking subject's existence, which is not limited to his own body but rather extends to others and, in the extreme case, is fully expropriated into the body of the double. An examination of shame and doubling in Gombrowicz and Weiner reveals the degree to which that defense of individuality is doomed to failure, to the "impersonality" of personhood. For these authors, the impossibility of escape is a foregone conclusion even before the story of that escape begins. And yet the thinking subject must try to escape nonetheless, simply because this is a fundamental rule of the game of being.

Notes

1. Gombrowicz was not averse to the fruits of intellectual culture—far from it—but he demonstrated an almost theatrical aversion to public displays of intellectual refinement. For example, Janusz Margański notes that during Gombrowicz's residence in Paris, Henri Bergson was "at the peak of his fame," and that Gombrowicz "certainly knew a bit about him, but also programmatically ignored him." Margański, *Gombrowicz wieczny debiutant*, 142. All translations are my own.
2. For a brief consideration of how Bakhtin's notion of laughter may apply to Gombrowicz, see Jarzębski, *Gra w Gombrowicza*, 299–301.
3. Gombrowicz, *Dzieła*, 2:5.
4. Ibid., 6.
5. Ibid., 21.
6. Among the most recent contributions to this discussion are Cataluccio, 141–53; and Jaszewska.
7. Lévinas, 55.
8. Gombrowicz, *Dzieła*, 2:49–66.
9. Ibid., 15.
10. Ibid., 11.
11. Ibid., 17.
12. Lévinas, 63–65. Writing twenty years later, Jean-Paul Sartre makes the opposite claim about shame: because shame arises from the gaze of the Other, whose freedom the "I" wishes to claim for himself, it has the effect of reifying identity: "Shame reveals to me that I *am* this being, not in the mode of 'was' or of 'having to be,' but *in-itself*" (262; author's emphasis). But these models of shame are not mutually exclusive for Gombrowicz. On the contrary, his construction of shame requires the endless repetition of movement in both directions: the thinking subject attempts to flee his own identity, but he also

flees the Other. These flights are both necessary and impossible. The thinking subject can never be completely coterminous with himself in the way Lévinas describes, and he can never assent to "being-with," to borrow Jean-Luc Nancy's productive term. Instead, Gombrowicz constructs an uncomfortable middle ground between these ideals, an intermediacy that is at once comic and horrifying. This is why Józio wakes up "in laughter and horror."

13. Williams, 81–84.

14. I am grateful to Joanna Niżyńska for calling this to my attention.

15. Margański, *Gombrowicz wieczny debiutant*, 190.

16. Ibid., 193.

17. Gombrowicz, *Dzieła*, 2:17.

18. Agamben, *Remnants of Auschwitz*, 105–6; author's emphasis.

19. In the most thorough Lacanian treatment of Gombrowicz's prose, Hanjo Berressem provides a savvy reading of this inferiority complex. For Berressem, the thinking subject's shame stems from his inferiority in relation to the symbolic order that has been imposed on him. No matter how well he succeeds in defining himself, there is always a more fully realized set of definitions just out of his grasp. At the same time, the thinking subject recognizes that the definitions culture has provided are inadequate in relation to his own sense of Self: "Gombrowicz is caught in the double bind that, on the one hand, the subject is ashamed of its libidinal inferiority in the light of the ideal symbolic order (the reality principle and the superego) and that, additionally, this shame is heightened by the inferiority of this specific symbolic order in relation to other, better symbolic orders. Gombrowicz's shame, then, is the result of both a personal and a cultural inferiority. On the other hand, however, the ego is ashamed of its submission under any, and especially under an inferior, cultural law. Gombrowicz is once more caught in this split between ego and subject. While the imaginary ego is ashamed of the symbolic, Oedipal subject, the subject is ashamed of its libidinous, immature ego. Ultimately, the pleasure principle is ashamed of the reality principle, and vice versa" (*Lines of Desire*, 113). His reading adds a structuralist psychological nuance to our considerathion of Gombrowicz's ontology.

20. Gombrowicz, *Dzieła*, 2:80.

21. Ibid., 248.

22. Ibid., 14.

23. Gombrowicz, 8:284.

24. Gombrowicz, 1:103.

25. Ibid., 106.

26. Gombrowicz, Letter to Martin Buber.

27. Ibid.

28. Schulz, "Samotność," in *Sanatorium pod klepsydrą,* 1938. See Schulz, *Opowiadania*. For the story's dating, see Ficowski, 58.

29. Schulz, *Opowiadania*, 311.

30. Margański, *Geografia pragnień*, 52–54.

31. Ibid., 62.
32. Chalupecký, 27.
33. Random, 34.
34. For a compact summary of Weiner's influence on Le Grand Jeu, and vice-versa, see also Linhartová, 34–36.
35. Weiner, 220–21.
36. Kristeva's notion of the abject has been used effectively to treat several topics in Gombrowicz's work, especially his construction of identity. See, for example, Longinović; and Jerzak.
37. Weiner, 240.
38. In the most extensive study of Weiner's prose to date, Steffi Widera suggests that, particularly in Weiner's early work, the motif of the double occurs in a syncretic Judeo-Christian framework, in which shame splits the Self, which is then reintegrated in a moment of redemption (*Erlösung*), itself consummate with death's reintegration of the Self into the Absolute. See Widera, 246–62. What complicates this model for the later work, and especially for *A Game for Real*, is how Weiner generally refuses to reintegrate the thinking subject and his double. When such redemption seems possible, it is then frustrated by repetition.
39. Leonard Neuger notes that in Gombrowicz's work this tends generally toward incommunicability or, as he puts it, "auto-incommunicability," nonsyntagmatic and nonnarrative language. See Neuger, 108.
40. Weiner, 282–83.
41. Ibid., 283.
42. Ibid., 302.
43. Ibid.
44. Ibid., 388–89.
45. Vašíček, 115.
46. Gombrowicz and Roux, 31–32.

WHAT KIND OF A HERO AM I? POLISHNESS AS AN EXISTENTIAL SITUATION

The Case of Sławomir Mrożek

Artur Grabowski

The subject of this essay is the whole, mostly dramatic, oeuvre of Sławomir Mrożek. However, the material I have focused on is the recently published correspondence between him and his longtime friend, the outstanding literary critic Jan Błoński.[1] I have chosen their letters as my main point of reference for I am convinced that the analysis of the playwright's more intimate writings will shed some new light on his works and on the circumstances in which they have been created. From the very beginning, the letters, exchanged mostly in the 1960s and 1970s, were meant as a "testimony in progress" and as evidence of a consciously undertaken artistic and existential self-analysis.

The correspondence was made possible by Mrożek's emigration and Błoński's contract at a French university, which freed both writers from the restrictions of censorship, but the letters were also provoked by the loneliness and isolation that such a situation generates. It is apparent that while writing his letters Mrożek was aware of their importance. He focuses mainly on literary matters, mostly his own literary output, and conducts a detailed self-analysis. Occasionally, however, he constructs his literary persona for the benefit of the critic who admires him and understands him very well. From the very first letter, written after his escape to the West, Mrożek is composing a sort of a "confessional treatise," as if he found in his exile an opportunity to search for a more authentic self. "I don't know what it is worth," he writes in October 1963, starting his long journey, which is soon to initiate his metamorphosis, "[b]ut even if it turned out to be worth nothing or very little, I would still find my stay here important. It allowed me, as it would a man pulled out of the closet, to look at my life more carefully."[2] As the correspondence progresses, the topic of spiritual and intellectual autobiography strengthens and develops, until it finally dominates the exchange. In fact, Mrożek writes not only an artistic but also a life manifesto. Already in the second letter his plan is made clear in the diagnosis of his past situation: "the inauthenticity, the unseriousness, of everything perhaps wore me out more than my present situation."[3]

The letters testify to a long and complicated process of coming to terms with emigration, which Mrożek sees as both a metaphor and a subject matter. Emigration is for the writer not only a state of mind but also a moral and philosophical challenge. Sometimes he is both serious and unwillingly comic when summarizing the consequences of his spiritual adventure. When, in the third letter, he says: "I have caught a cold in Venice," the unimportant event serves as an opportunity for what he calls a "retreat" and for a critical "reading" of his spiritual condition.[4] In one of his last letters such semireligious conclusions return in Mrożek's definition of literature as a "philosophical-religious imperative."[5] When making the decision to live abroad, the writer initially expects to free himself from Polishness, which he clearly finds oppressive. Quite soon, however, he begins to realize that life away from his homeland entails strengthening the ties with it. Apparently, and understandably, he first wants to rid himself of the burden of Polishness, to spit out, so to speak, its toxins. Yet this subject does not disappear in the course of his correspondence. What changes is his emotional attitude toward it. The writer realizes that Polishness has become an integral part of his imagination and sensitivity. Therefore, rather than reject it, he tries to reformulate his attitude toward it. To this effect, he changes the language of Polishness and introduces new contexts into his examination of it. Instead of detaching himself from Polishness, he proclaims himself its heir and makes it a part of his spiritual biography. This process lasts no longer than five years, between the fall of 1963, when the young artist decides to begin a new life, and the end of 1968, when the Russians invade Czechoslovakia and History makes him take a decisive step.

Apparently, Mrożek needs a new self-definition, but creating a "new Pole in himself" is not only difficult but also painful as he finds some "sins" in Polishness that awake in him the sense of guilt. Thus, his endeavor requires courage to examine the dark side of the national character in himself personally. This method of personalizing national problems becomes a tool for creating philosophical discourse out of a particular historical situation.

Years later, he says about himself, "I dared to correct my fate."[6] Usually a decision to live away from one's country, even though emotionally wrenching, is determined to some degree by external circumstances. It is often the political situation and a threat of persecution that make it impossible for an artist to create and have his works published in his own country. This was not the case with Mrożek. At the time of his departure from Poland in 1963, Mrożek the writer was not only accepted but also celebrated. He was young, satiated with fame, and rewarded with money. The authorities did not pressure him to support the official propaganda. Quite the contrary, when after an initial period of youthful flirtation with socialist ideology, he openly derided and unequivocally criticized his socialist homeland, he became, paradoxically, useful to, recognized by, and even promoted by the communist authorities. Their revenge reached him much later, when he started publishing openly political remarks. However, until 1968 he was the most often staged author in Poland, managing to live in Italy on Polish royalties!

Right from the start of his adventure abroad, Mrożek seems to defy the fate of a typical Polish intellectual. What makes him different? Instead of running away from persecution, he is running away from financial, social, but above all, as it becomes clear later, moral comfort. In the Polish context at the time, it is truly an unusual decision to make. Its motive is personal, not political; its cause is moral, not social. His decision comes from a sense of guilt, from a sense of personal responsibility, rather than from the conviction of his innocence as a victim. It is aimed at future growth, not at permanent suspense. Why? "Simply because it's too easy for me. . . . And what I am still concerned with is how to grow."[7] Mrożek departs because he wants to change himself, to change what was created in him by his homeland.

II

What could one see living in Poland in the 1950s? Here it is: the People's Republic of Poland, the land of the mediocre people who are neither particularly good nor particularly bad but who have a grotesquely high opinion of themselves. Not surprisingly, Mrożek's "broken and brutal" characters seem to be transplanted straight from Bolesław Leśmian's ballads, from folk songs and the simplest village tales to the industrial city of Nowa Huta and to the artistic cafés of Cracow. They create a composite portrait of a "primitive" creature of brutal stupidity and simplistic moral reactions. They epitomize a typical Polish complex ingrained as deeply in national history as in prehistoric sources of the nation's characteristics. In his early plays and short stories, the author diagnoses the pervasive state of "ill fitting" as the most common experience in a communist system whose ruthless forms destroy human sensitivity and open the door to the eruption of primitive instincts. Communist rules and principles, which Western intellectuals equate with modernity, were nothing but a symptom of barbarity for Poles. However, in Poland, in "the funniest barrack in the camp,"[8] they produced conformism—a soft version of nihilism.

Mediocrity was truly the greatest crime committed by the People's Poland, the omnipresent humiliation and belittling smallness of everything, including emotions, thoughts, faith, and even crime. Mrożek, the future author of historiosophical treatises in dialogues, meanwhile writes what is safely called "satire." These traditional comedies of manners with their schematic, grotesque representations became the chronicles of that era. Almost all the comedies of the author of *Tango* can be described as follows:. The hero, a man of weak physical and mental constitution and lacking support from the other members of society, comes face-to-face with those ideals that shaped him in the past and now demand realization. From the very beginning, the hero defines himself with the help of a myth, rather than by his life experience. In *Turkey*, one of Mrożek's early plays, the subject of the writer's critical approach is still the Romantic Pole, the one who later, in *Tango*, transforms into Arthur, a post-Romantic European. Whoever he is, the character is more allegorical than real, not because of the author's decision but because of his own self-image. He sees himself as a hero from a legend rather than as a member of a concrete society. Consequently, he sets superhuman goals for himself, goals of implausible proportions. On the other hand, he feels coerced rather than destined to reach them. While trying to realize these ideals, he quickly comes into conflict with his own innate weakness. As a consequence, in practice his actions turn into the opposites of the principles that he theoretically embraces.

In the short comedy *Out at Sea*, two men use ideological arguments to persuade their fellow shipwreck survivor to commit suicide. They are not cynical aggressors who follow their wild instincts in the guise of a civilized discourse. Instead, they use "moral" rules, which they admittedly never internalized, but which they treat as a privilege, as if the rules were "technical" tools. So, what turns these characters into criminals? Is the sophisticated system to blame for its mismatch with these crippled creatures and their biological primitivism? It is also not certain whether the characters are too immature to enjoy "civil rights" or whether the civil forms of coexistence were forced upon them setting off their defensive mechanisms. The inflated rubber elephant in Mrożek's famous short story "The Elephant" could be read as a satire from the "funniest barrack," but it also serves as a proof (not a symbol!) of a common human desire to believe in the unreal rather than in nothing at all. The characters produced by the soft version of socialist realism, and by its softly controlled literature, were soft indeed, as the soft lines of Mrożek's cartoons attest. They believe themselves to be like figures from an uncritically accepted legend. Not surprisingly, they do not even notice when their national hero, as a person, turns into the antithesis of his role, and when the world in which he would like to act turns into a degraded version of the mythical space.

The hero is motivated not only by a longing for a different world but also by an imperative to escape from the world in which he is caught and which, for some reason, he finds uncomfortable. True, the hero's cage is historically specific, but the atmosphere in it evokes, in a grotesque way, a globally valid existential problem. This problem is not just the hero's, as he is usually a victim of his own blindness, but becomes the audience's problem. They, his countrymen, who take seats in the national theatre, come face-to-face with the allegory of the outside reality. Such transfer of responsibility perfectly inscribes Mrożek's dramatic form in the tradition of Polish political theatre. The heroic character (a Pole is necessarily born heroic) feels that everyday circumstances do not support his self-development; they are not only morally and materially unsatisfying but also, what is even worse, degrading.

In *The Emigrants*, written years later, the protagonist, divided into two antagonistic characters, brings his "underground" manners to a windowless basement (which is both his grave and his shelter) in the western dreamland. Does this trip come too late for him? Is his direct confrontation with the "open society" so shocking that it necessarily robs the erstwhile slave of his internal freedom? Or maybe the mythical hero can never fit into the egalitarian reality? Both affirmative and negative answers to these questions are possible. The conditions of his life before his great escape were clearly humiliating, but what is being destroyed onstage is not his national character but his national self-image. Out of the confrontation of his unrealistic expectations with the inevitable arises a caricature, a grotesque, and finally pure nonsense.

This does not mean that Polish tragedy is destined to be a comedy of national "manners and characters." Such determinism does not work in an archaic society of noble and peasant origin that is trapped in the modern bureaucratic machinery. The scenario must always remain mythical, even though it is now parodied with bitter irony. It seems clear that the existential problem arising from Polishness is caused neither by the oppressive other nor by the catastrophe of being bored. It is essentially mythical and only formally political. Its mythical sources remove the Polish playwright from the vicinity of Sartre's existentialism and Beckett's metaphysics and place him near Ionesco's religiously marked psychoanalysis of our civilization. Pathetic seriousness and no-less-pathetic pure nonsense characterize a personality that, while inclined toward maximalist challenges, has no tools and opportunities to achieve them. By confronting pathos with primitivism, Mrożek discovers that quintessentially Polish tone, the grotesque, or if we were to go farther, a distinctly Slavic spirituality. From Gogol's and Hašek's insignificant man living in his imperial (and therefore too-large) homeland to Ivo Brešan's peasant Hamlet and Václav Havel's lost leaders: all are characters embodying the drama of spirit (and usually in search of a bottle).

Mrożek's hero loses his battle while being fully aware of his situation. He is not an unconscious puppet in the hands of fate but someone suffering because of his own impotence. This is the reason for his aggression, which is usually turned against himself. Its psychological cause is obvious. The failure of a grandiose project brings about depression, which stems from the sense of unfulfillment. Its symptoms are the loss of trust in one's own abilities and, in consequence, loss of faith in the future. Is, then, Polishness a variant of nihilism? Yes, but a very particular one. A Central European antihero (Mrożek alludes to other Slavs in *Vaclav* and *Contract*, for example) is not like a Frenchman, a German, or a Russian, a nihilist by choice, who bravely rejects faith as an illusion. A Pole seems condemned to nothingness, which he cannot overcome. Isn't such an "essential Slav" a kind of a barbarian from the "heart of Europe"? Indeed, this "cultural complex" is as painful as it is funny. When a character like Arthur from *Tango* searches for an idea, he finds only ideology; when he, like Alpha from a play with the same title, searches for an object of faith, he finds only hypotheses. Yet what he always discovers is not a *horror vacui* of ideas and reality but a frustrated person, a black hole of emotional implosion. He knows vaguely, but feels painfully, that it is his own identity, his own identification with the mythical figure that lurks unrecognized in the shadows. His "nothingness" unravels like a personal essence—an unfulfilled, ambitious challenge that weakens his self-reliance.

What transpires from this constant whining and complaining, which the author of this tragicomedy presents in a new light, as metaphysical anxiety and unsatisfied hunger for values? While an idea in Arthur's project is sanctioned by the absolute, ideology becomes only a temporary compromise in the name of human imperfection. "Therefore, there is no political system in the world that I would accept as progressive even at this moment, not to mention years into the future. Each of them is, in my view, damned."[9] The reason for such condemnation is not the collapse of the project but its incompleteness, which makes the participants suffer. Works of compromise are condemned to a short-lived existence and are therefore not worth launching. Life itself, then, in its daily labors is not sufficiently worth living. As a consequence, our hero instinctively chooses to sacrifice his real self in order to save human perfection—even though such perfection might be just a phantom.

Mrożek's hero, just like most of the Polish romantic heroes, is apparently in despair and on his way to suicide. However, as befits a cowardly buffoon, he usually attempts to commit it indirectly, most often by somebody else's hand. Adam Mickiewicz's Konrad from *Forefathers' Eve*, Juliusz Słowacki's Kordian, and Count Henry from Zygmunt Krasiński's *Undivine Comedy* are not the only characters fitting this bill. Stanisław Ignacy Witkiewicz's drugged artists and the protagonist of Witold Gombrowicz's *Marriage* also belong to this category.[10] In each case, their suicide is both a punishment and an offering. In each case, the protagonist puts his neck under the guillotine of principles which he does not want to betray. In one of his early letters from the "Mediterranean shore," Mrożek, crossing the line of the shadow, confesses: "I do not need to add what is clear—I long for 'really' and 'it's worthwhile,' but the tragedy lies in the fact that every 'worthwhile' and every 'really' becomes stale at the moment of capturing and realization, of giving shape to them. . . . The question is: what to do with it all in order to present that pursuit, and then its impossibility, in a less vulgar form."[11]

Mrożek's adventures of a "Polack" are grotesquely tragic. Their real protagonist is a human being facing his failure to fulfill his humanity. The cause of his tragedy is not only innate impotence but also some self-destructive hypocrisy. Mrożek paints a portrait of a man who hides his fundamental fear of life and deep doubts about the value of everyday life behind a mask of honest belief in the highest moral values. The author shares this experience, and even his lucky exile/escape cannot change him completely. Now, during his midlife crisis, he seems to know that what he calls his "system" (which is "more a trick than an art") comes from a sense of incompatibility. This system, "generally speaking, consists perhaps in detecting the gap between forms and their content, and the awkward inconsistencies in this respect, in pulling out the embarrassed, naked, trembling and shameful meaning from the armour of form."[12] Is it a description of a creative method or of an ethical system? Living in a make-believe place (both literary and political) corresponds to writing. From a distance, Polishness loses its unbearable concreteness and appears as a stage figure.

Although the self-made "outsider" hates his former Polishness, his identification with it still does not allow him to reject it without a feeling of losing something life-giving. Mrożek's new comedies, written from a Western perspective, change their rhetorical patterns from satirical to persuasive and become more "tragic" in the process, as if the author were trying to defend something that he unconsciously deems worthy of acceptance. On the other hand, this typical Polish hypocrisy is also the source of his rebellion against easy acceptance of moral compromises. It is the source of that special "something" which, according to the Polish people, differentiates them from those societies that do not take the ideals of moral perfection too seriously and—maybe because of that—achieve success. On the one hand, the feelings of guilt and shame turn the Polish man, once a proud knight, into a little opportunist. On the other hand, they are the signs that faith in moral purity has not entirely dried up. However, even such radiant faith has its dark side. Its fruit is a belief in the inherent innocence of human beings, which seems to free them from the obligation of self-perfection. Inertia, or a lack of the will to exist, shows its face here again.

The subject of Mrożek's comedies and satirical short stories is in fact bondage—a standard theme in Polish literature. Mrożek's take on it, however, is original. Rather than describing the lack of freedom in terms of repression and presenting it from the point of view of the suffering victim, the author describes enslavement as internal proclivity, as a fall into bondage due to a spiritual weakness. Mrożek is interested in the internal mechanism of assenting to slavery, which results from fear of freedom. His literary hero is in fact a mediocre everyman whose heroic self-recognition happens only in a mythical space and whose existence, even if only imaginary, should be continued. Is it the same curse that has befallen Stanisław Wyspiański's Konrad? The purpose of existence is to deliberate, and thus deliberation must be morally supported and maintained in artistic creation. It is safe to say that the plots of all Polish comedies are always the same—they are deliberations. In exile, Mrożek discovers not only his own, but a national (or essential), form of social and existential game.

The reasoning one could extrapolate from these plots follows: bondage begins with mistrust in the possibility of freedom. Such doubt, however, is a defensive mechanism against the fear of self-determination. For freedom changes a group into particular individuals and deprives an individual of the support of the group. In its absolute form (and only that form is really worthwhile) it condemns people to existential loneliness and puts them in a position of permanent moral tension by requiring constant revisions of their value systems. As a consequence, true freedom demands a deeply morally grounded person, an independent individual. But if freedom is not fully realized, it produces a depersonalized individual, one missing the source of his moral decisions, a hollow man. That is precisely what the Polish man fears the most, according to Mrożek. He fears becoming a self-reliant human being. And why is self-reliance so terrifying? Because to be a true individual means to see oneself as the sole subject of one's own action, to create oneself as the character of one's own story. Such an independent, morally responsible individual (someone never beyond good and evil) has always been at the core of the Polish dream—from the *liberum veto* and Mickiewicz's "Great Improvisation" to Karol Wojtyła's teaching and Jerzy Grotowski's "performer."

The fear of freedom in Mrożek's hero is also born of cultural shortcomings, as heroism in Polish culture is much more an ideal and a challenge than an accessible way of behaving. Among Polish cultural paradigms, one is missing: the model of working on one's personal development. A separate, strong individual is simply viewed negatively and often stands accused of betraying partisan loyalty. The welfare of the community dominates Polish culture, which is only seemingly altruistic. In reality, this subjugation to community welfare incapacitates an individual, making it impossible for him or her to become a strong pillar of the community. The individual accuses communal values of causing his weakness, but by the same token he feels guilty of not being strong enough to serve the community, to perform his civil or tribal vocation. Existentially trapped and psychologically confused, the Pole is looking for an easy escape. An analysis of Mrożek's characters suggests that Polish culture encourages dreaming about freedom rather than striving toward it. Such a culture promotes a life of illusion, which offers moral comfort. Loyalty becomes a dominant virtue in such a cultural model, which is based on a cooperative falsification of reality. Hence, every expression of individuality threatens cultural order because it discredits it. Fear of freedom creates weak individuals who are unable to accept the challenge of action for the benefit of the community. Nevertheless, this challenge is still imposed on them. This mechanism explains how a feeling of moral discomfort becomes a source of self-defending hypocrisy or aggression.

III

That is how Mrożek used to describe his countrymen—in plays and stories allegorically, in letters openly. But is the subject of this portrait necessarily Polish? In one of the letters the playwright writes to his friend, he says: "I am not an enthusiast of such things as universalism, eternal matters, the world of the universal spirit, humanity and all-encompassing humanism, man as such and the like, because for me these are concepts that must arise, like everything else, from some form, from something particular, which, in our case, has to be Poland."[13] These assumptions still testify to the restrictions imposed on Mrożek by Polishness. However, already in this sentence lies a seed of a creative method that unexpectedly transforms his weaknesses into strengths and helps him find nothing less than an archetype in the particular deficiency of being a Pole. Polishness serves as an archetype of a weakness innate in all humans, a depiction of an existential failure of all humanity, which is called to greatness but suffers from permanent dissatisfaction. Starting with an honest analysis of his own cultural formation, or the Polish complex of which he was one of the victims, Mrożek was able to create a universal portrait of a modern man. It is usually a man of refined moral sensitivity who has to live in a world devoid of values. This man's religious feelings have not atrophied, but the opportunity of his communion with the Absolute has been taken away from him.

Is this universalized Pole a victim of modernity or a witness to its disaster? In the case of Mrożek's work, the farther he moves away from his homeland, the more Poland becomes his point of reference, a model of a certain existential situation that reflects the particular, and at the same time universal, qualities of the human condition. The experience of this condition is both tragic and painful. However, Mrożek divorces it from national martyrdom and instead relates it to the private suffering of an individual who has been shaped by Polish culture.

Following the success of *Tango*, Mrożek has a good chance of becoming a global commentator on the moral and the metaphysical condition of abstract man, like his fellow writers from Martin Esslin's groundbreaking book *The Theatre of the Absurd.*[14] Indeed, he focuses on himself and deepens the self-analysis, but the results of these choices are surprising. He often makes a sharp U-turn, switching from the analysis of his own personality to the analysis of national mentality. In opposition to Gombrowicz or Czesław Miłosz, both of whom he feels compelled to confront, he does not "free himself" from Poland but turns his home country into a point of resistance and also of reliance. The other two writers, Mrożek believes, in some way rejected Polishness. Gombrowicz did it by escaping into abstract cosmopolitism, Milosz by escaping into the mythical Lithuania of his childhood. Mrożek is convinced that such escapes are symptomatic of Polish mental cowardice, which avoids moral discomforts.[15] Such avoidance restricts the individual and makes the development of an unexpected and potentially original Polishness impossible. A Pole, deceived by one kind of Polishness, does not allow some other kind to come to the surface. Where, meanwhile, can one search for it?

The playwright's "self-analysis in letters," which has the classical form of an internal dialogue (a model play, in fact), bears all the traits of professional playwriting and penetrates both his psyche and his creative methods. April 1964 (right after Easter?) brings a meaningful confession in one of his longest monologues:

> Anyway, I'm returning to my assumption that the total expression of one's personality—including both its particularities and all that such personality inherits from what is general and historical—makes its use more just and, in spite of appearances, more difficult; more difficult because it demands taking greater responsibility and risk, if one fails or succeeds partially. In such a case we risk ridicule and shame, even if only in our own eyes, for as it is well known in our own conscience, we will never be sure, or in our own conscience we will rather never have a feeling of complete victory.[16]

What matters most in this quotation is the proclamation of intimacy together with the mystery of an individuality that is shaped by an absolute, although hidden, authority. The individual no longer struggles with the social—they both meet in the spiritual.

As the correspondence progresses, Mrożek's metamorphosis accelerates. His dramas soon become more personal and by the same token more universal. Mrożek's method is not to introduce cosmopolitan themes but to internalize those problems that he saw at one time as objectively social. Now he tracks the mechanisms of collective reactions and probes the psychology of tribal existence first in himself (as he probably does not believe in a civil society). He searches for signs, traces, and common scars inherited from his ancestors in his own mentality, whether they are desired or not. It suffices that they are true. He uses psychoanalysis (but never in its popular, eroticized version) to describe political phenomena; he presents social issues as if they were his private, personal problems. His psychological experiences and philosophical convictions seem to parallel his creative process. In the end, a certain anthropology of history emerges from the writer's analytical introspection, which is carried over from letter to letter.

According to Mrożek, human beings, organizing themselves into groups, act like an individual organism. Therefore, the playwright conducts seemingly social interhuman games as if they were internal (psychological, in fact) contests played in the mental space of an individual human being. Political forces appear here merely as predispositions and limitations of an individual. A singular and universal Somebody (like a modern Everyman who naïvely sees himself as an irreplaceable subject) becomes the arena for all humanity. In him, the internally antagonized human condition gambles with itself by betting its self-created and unattainable ideal. A group accepts such a blind gamble because it is unable to understand itself fully. Every now and then it tries, but like every analyst who analyzes himself, it veils the truth about itself with self-created ideological "revelations," which it takes for a real diagnosis of its condition.

Unlike Gombrowicz, who sees a gap in the very center of man left by a metaphysically rooted person, Mrożek believes in the psychologically rooted modern subject, in a Persona, in the permanently hidden human essence, which is no longer necessarily "created" but still remains mysterious enough never to reveal itself entirely. This understanding of man differs from Gombrowicz's notion of people being created by other people in their interactions. Mrożek's idea is that an individual man always generates new interactions from the depths of his own nature. People form groups because individually they are somehow incomplete and need to be complemented by others. This incompleteness gives a clownish but pompous quality of permanent almost-heroism to Mrożek's characters. In it, the universal human debility is easily recognizable at every angle. Therefore, their creator extends his mercy to his characters and makes his readers feel some sympathy toward those dwarfs. Both Gombrowicz and Mrożek seem to look for hope against nothingness, although each sees it coming from a different direction. Both are afraid of the "too simple" answer provided by Christian personalism, which would have been automatic to anyone brought up in prewar Poland.

At this point it may come as a surprise that the model for these universal reflections is still the People's Republic of Poland. It functions now as a rhetorical "figure" and a practical "object" of emotional figuration useful in the self-disciplining process. "Actually, by the word 'Poland' I do not mean anything concrete, but my own special patchwork, a phantom for intellectual and emotional exercises, a handy mannequin for boxing my own head."[17] At first sight, the degraded reality of the socialist state seems to be the result of the "economy of permanent shortage." From the metaphysical perspective, though, the "socialist economy" is a corrupt version of *aeconomia divina*, which of course has been ruined by people, by their human imperfection. Crippled humans always want something simple and small. In order to secure an abundance of it, they congregate, and form and support parties that build empires. People enter into alliances in the name of some interest whose sources lie in the darkness of their desires. "I'm writing that from experience," says a former supporter of the ruling party, and he adds: "These things are deep inside, which doesn't mean they are less important than the conscious ones."[18]

When writing about Poland, Mrożek unexpectedly recalls Nazi Germany: "But it could have happened anywhere," he claims, "because it can happen in a person, and Germans are people, too."[19] People need to "belong" because they want to "possess" the world. They need to feel safe in the midst of togetherness. "What peacefulness you are rewarded with," Mrożek says ironically, "you walk around, look around, and everything is yours, the militiaman is yours, Nowa Huta is yours—comrade militiaman, comrade Nowa Huta."[20] This is Mrożek's diagnosis of how man's smallness creates political systems or extemporaneously formed orders of coexistence. In turn, these systems, with theatrical obviousness and in unexpected forms, demonstrate their imperfection to belittled men. The time comes, then, for a newer and more perfect order. After a short break, act 2 repeats act 1. In this respect *The Tailor*, Mrożek's allegorical apocrypha of the great History of Civilization, brings to mind Gombrowicz's *Operetta*, but the two plays differ significantly. Gombrowicz proposes an alternative, even though unrealistic, form of coexistence; Mrożek leaves no hope. Both individual rebellion and universal revolution are intrinsic to the situations and characters in Mrożek's plays, and both end invariably in defeat. Gombrowicz may be naïve; Mrożek must be cruel. The former can afford to be irresponsible, as he is a socially oriented "civil citizen." The latter always feels guilty, as a believer who dares to doubt the validity of the inherited symbols. The reason for Mrożek's feelings of guilt and doubt is his conviction that no matter what kind of economy man creates, it will always be a worldly compromise with a transcendent project, and that means a travesty at the outset. The compromise results from the very incompleteness that constitutes the human element in man and that remains the very essence of humanity. What we end up with is a medieval *Civitas Dei*. The prospect of the Perfect Republic of Peoples is within us and at the same time out of our reach! Just like a communist paradise.

Mrożek's characters are unrealized ideas for human freedom. Man has an innate predisposition to metaphysical opportunism and finds slavery tempting. The playwright reveals that the abandonment of spiritual effort is man's most cardinal sin. Is this sin specifically Polish, or is it just simply human? The best way to see it is as the Polish version of European decadence, which manifests itself as idealism aligned with nihilism. Could not all Polish suicidal uprisings, failed from their inception, come to mind at this juncture? The eternal immaturity of Polish youths taking part in these uprisings may be irritating indeed, but it is also difficult not to feel sympathy for the young idealists. What would Poles be like without their faith born of literature, this "naïve perversion," as Mrożek would say? Mediocre citizens? The fear of mediocrity, the quintessential Polish anxiety that human destiny might indeed be limited to "citizenship" within some obediently accommodating social deal, gives birth to herd fanaticism and the Sarmatian caricature of individualism, but also to a dream of an individual capable of rising to the highest call to live in moral purity. This is also a dream of a perfect, therefore absolute, form of human bond.

Such "absolute" form is not political at all. It is religious. A man has to call it into being as God does—out of nothingness. Unfortunately, he cannot bring it to fruition because he is just a man—that is, a metaphysical cripple. What is at play here is not so much some ordinary powerlessness, but rather the desire for security. Is not such a Perfect Republic, some earthly and political organization in which one law fulfills the needs of each citizen and of the whole community, a semireligious idol? Is not the idea of such a kingdom too ambitious an expectation? Maybe, then, it is nothing more than safe hypocrisy, the desire for an ideal moral order in which everyday life acquires moral sanctions and is comfortable at the same time? Maybe convenience and comfortable ease of conscience are really at stake here? If so, one has to run away from such comfort because it is not easy to resist! However, out in the wilderness, other temptations await.

IV

The most terrible of them all is despair. After acute depression come peaceful reflection and deeper insight, and then ascetic revelation. The closer Mrożek gets to the absolute, the more familiar he becomes with the dark side of discomfort. As if his Polish fondness for nihilism reflected the not-less-Polish desire for the uncompromised achievement. Thus, Mrożek concludes his treatise in letters: "So, I'm beginning to suspect that somehow the point of it all is not the changes but a fundamental *depouillement*."[21] Who is speaking now? Isn't it the dwarf from *Striptease* or a grotesque hero of *Out at Sea*, or, finally, the emotionally vulnerable intellectual from *Love in the Crimea*? The protagonist of Mrożek's epopee did not have to change, but he had to take off his theatrical costume in order to uncover—who?—much to his surprise, either the "eternal Slav," looking stubbornly for the unearthly treasure, or the eternal Pole on his eternal battlefield. Such a hero, shaped by Romantic ideals (even if he is critical of them), lacks a sense of moral irony. In societies that have been formed by the ideals of the Enlightenment, it is moral irony that protects the abated will to life by permitting discreet hypocrisy. The ethical idealism (or the naïveté of the Slavs, if you will) presents a particular challenge that in practical life results in an unconscious escape from everyday activity. Such activity seems simultaneously unworthy of any effort (for it requires compromises) and incapable of subordinating life to goals that in fact surpass human abilities. Mrożek, the protagonist of such narratives about Polishness, experiences this aporia as his disappointment with life, intellectual barreness, and spiritual weakening. Over the years, his letters to his friend are filled with various complaints about his feelings of inner emptiness. He does not react to his condition like a typical Pole, however. Instead of withdrawing into resignation and celebrating his resentment (an attitude he often caricatures in his plays and short stories), Mrożek begins a process of self-improvement. This atypical reaction to the weakening effect of Polishness is not an escape from Polish nihilistic idealism. Quite the contrary, it is an alternative, and so far rarely traveled, road to spiritual growth.

The virtue Mrożek probably values most is personal responsibility resulting from individual freedom. His personal journey is not about historical revisionism. He plays the game with himself because he wants to "accept himself entirely," and that means to accept blame: blame for everything that is his, for what becomes of him and what he inherited. Mrożek deeply believes that the recognition of defeat under the scrutiny of conscience, or to put it differently, the expression of morality in a desire for purity so real that it leads to painful self-purification, is the only way to return dignity to a degraded mankind and to restore the meaning of life to an individual.

Isolated on the Italian Riviera and encouraged by his friend, Mrożek admits to his Polish proclivities, but goes against the inherited impotence. While his confession is a lengthy one, it does end with final purification. He admits that he, too, was beginning to suck up to the authorities—and not out of fear but for profit; he, too, almost became one of the boys, and supported the system in the name of loyalty. Finally, he, too, was later in the noble opposition, but as he explains: "jeering, deriding Stalin, I was taking it out on the world and people."[22] When assessing his reactions, Mrożek turns to the universal meaning of his personal choices: "It also has to be said that this is not a particularly laudable reaction, that is, not a reaction typical of a strong man, but rather of a weak, a hysterical one, who runs away, hides, removes himself from the field as much as he can."[23] His deep identification with being a "Polack" reveals to himself a Polish archetype of weakness.

Mrożek becomes aware of this weakness thanks to his fear. "Generally speaking, my break into my own consciousness," he says, "happened through fear."[24] He does not fully understand this fear but associates it with Polishness. He even stresses the difference between this fear and its Western counterpart, which takes the form of survival anxiety. After further scrutiny, he identifies it as moral anxiety, a feeling of shame produced by conscience. Finally, the playwright treats his isolation as a personal test of strength. With time, his adventure, his unending vacation turns into a decision: "Maybe, because I am not coming back"—that is, I am going forward in an unforeseeable direction—"I am also moved by yearning for the impossible, for something more that is beyond the foreseen."[25]

In Mrożek's efforts to overcome himself, in his perseverance, one can clearly see traces of Polish idealism, the disinterested determination to maximize the moral value of life. Paradoxically, even though life is not worth living without such an absolute goal, it is practically impossible to live with it. Equally paradoxically, the need to endow life with the highest moral value turns out to be an offshoot of Polish skepticism. Only a strong individual, a powerful personality, a metaphysically rooted person can attempt such a life. Mrożek's "Polack" is made of those two attitudes: idealism and skepticism, and while they are in constant battle with each other, he marches to a steady beat. The writer seems to follow his own creation. He wants to shape his own destiny, to take full responsibility for himself, rather than shift it onto existing political systems. He believes and doubts, and then doubts the reality of his doubt. To put it differently, Mrożek intentionally deconstructs convenient notions about the world and wants his consciousness to keep up with their fragmentary character. In his view, such a "wasteland" is preferable to a "dreamland." Call it reactionary, but this is what Mrożek really thinks. The new Pole in him is disciplined to maintain a well-balanced, "upright position" in an unbalanced world deprived of clear points of reference. Not surprisingly, the Polish playwright turns his personal project into a universal endeavor. His attitude is composed of conservative political philosophy, one that looks for absolute sanction, and of postmodern anarchy, which does not believe in the universal, only in "the other." Yes, the foundation of privacy is soft. That is why man has to engage in projects that get him to the surface. There is, above all, faithfulness (and those are his friend's words) to "what we value, even if it is not victorious."[26] One would like to say: what does not perish as long as we live.

Somewhere deep down, Mrożek's disillusion again has Polish origins, although it leads the writer into the purest asceticism. At this stage of his journey, he describes emptiness, bareness, and destitution. The subject matter of his work written at this time becomes decidedly more profound—from *The Slaughterhouse*, a dramatic dissertation about art, through the philosophical *Hunchback*, *The Tailor*, and *On Foot*, all historiosophical treatises, to the psychoanalytical *Amor*. At this time, too, he creates an excellent, mysterious, and symbolic short story about a young farmhand at a mill who finds his own corpse in the river. What does it mean to find oneself dead? It means to make the first, indispensable step toward resurrection. Mrożek does not dare to admit it, but his friend has no such qualms. He clearly suggests the direction of his search to the writer: "you are looking for emptiness and truth, which you might (who knows?) extract from that very emptiness. But what does such emptiness mean? It is You, a dialogue with yourself, exploiting, torturing yourself, squeezing somebody else out of yourself."[27] The writer already expects to find a different self, but he is still afraid of it. This self is a stranger, after all. Who knows what the devil . . . ? The critic dares to go deeper: "since one looks for values in oneself, in the dialogue with oneself, it means that one wants to see a third person in oneself, some hitherto hidden witness, or some kind of essence."[28] Mrożek, however, still does not believe that there is a name for it in the Polish language, hence his concern with "an essential experience of humanity," with "a dimension . . . you will not see in the tradition of Polish thinking."[29] Why not, one may ask? A positive model, a remote ideal for both friends, is a frequently quoted Polish poet, Cyprian Kamil Norwid, and, closer in time, theatre reformer Jerzy Grotowski[30]—two artists consistently faithful to their calling. And where did they come from?

In the discussion of the correspondence between Mrożek and Błoński, it is important not to underestimate the less active, but not less important, of the two partners. Jan Błoński, an inquisitive reader and the playwright's contemporary, played the role of psychoanalyst (when deciphering the subtexts of his friend's letters) and confessor (when accepting Mrożek's self-blaming without judgment). On the one hand, he helps the writer when his decisive confession is too harsh to verbalize. On the other hand, he serves the playwright as a "soft liberal" counterimage—for though Błoński is similar to Mrożek in sensitivity, he differs from the writer in his reactions. The critic, too, was abroad at the time, but his escape from "the funniest barrack in the camp" was from the very beginning partial and temporary. He was rather an "internal emigrant," a typical (in a positive sense) Polish intellectual of the "old school." Błoński belongs to this school and therefore consciously makes dramatic choices. A nobleman from a semi-French family, he accepts with more ease all that for Mrożek is a punch in the nose.

Their relationship is both impressive and moving. The artist relies on his critic, and the braver one encourages the one who is more restrained. It works in both directions. The six-hundred-page story of spiritual development testifies to how productive their relationship has become. "This is a dialogue and a mutual stimulation, a process, not an exchange of information," says the playwright.[31] If Mrożek's letters create his bildungsroman, his friend was no doubt an integral part of it. Together they seem to create two sides of in independent-minded Pole, one with no complexes, no fears. Who is such a creature? "Is such an assumption possible: a European of Polish language?"[32] Błoński knows his friend well, and the writer does not disappoint him. Seven years later, in 1971, the critic's question turns into an assertion: "Many gestures that have moral, metaphysical, religious meaning everywhere else—or have no meaning at all . . . —are being marked here by a totally useless national and political function."[33] He is sure by then that Mrożek is already a liberated and reborn writer.

Mrożek's creative writing turns out to be his best support. He describes it in terms of a religious vocation from which he sometimes tries to escape, as befits a true prophet. Ultimately, a new approach to literature emerges out of all this self- and soul-searching: "All that I care about anymore is reaching some kind of truth, my explicitness for myself and for others, a sense that an ever-increasing purification of oneself and of the world—which I create, by living, out of non-necessity, out of twists and turns and trifles—is possible, and that it has to be done and is worth doing."[34] At this moment, he asks his friend a question, as if he were asking a mirror: "what kind of a hero am I?"[35] Now, it seems, he understands that literature is not self-sufficient, that he would like to use it for a higher purpose. His view on writing has little to do with the anecdotes of a popular satirist, and much more with the ideas of Polish Romanticism. He feels "some kind of a religious-philosophical imperative . . . which would allow practicing literature not for its own sake, but which would place the entire motivation beyond it."[36]

Sławomir Mrożek's letters are more than just letters. They seem to have been endowed with an intentionally literary character. This does not mean that the writer's private writings were shaped to become a "creative" self-portrait. It is not self-creation but rather self-analysis that serves as a tool for a long confession. From this point of view, Mrożek's correspondence with Błoński is a crossover between an intellectual autobiography and a personal essay and places the whole collection in the vicinity of semireligious practice. From the very beginning, the playwright is not recording his thoughts about himself but working on them in the process of writing, which turns into a spiritual exercise (Grotowski comes to mind). He probably counted on some kind of therapy at the beginning, but he created, in the process, both a work of art and a literary figure of himself. This figure is made of Polishness—equally mythical and private. It is composed as much of Polish official culture as of the intimate nature of the writer's Polishness. But in both cases it is the same innate space, a national cultural paradigm, rooted in the private self. What is at stake here is a myth that is not a convenient illusion for the benefit of the collective hallucination but instead becomes a source of authentic identity and life force for all Poles—each and every one individually. What Mrożek created during those few years was a new Polish writer and a new Polish literary hero.

Reading Mrożek's letters together with his plays and stories provides a new perspective on his whole oeuvre. The hero of the letters reveals the consistency of his fictional characters, who can be seen as essentially one person—an allegory of Polish and Slavic spirituality confronting cultural patterns of modern Western societies. It is essentially a European subject created from a particular perspective. This literary figure is also deeply rooted in the personal biography of its creator, which makes it convincing and understandable not only in literature but also in everyday life. It is now clear what makes Mrożek's plays so overtly dialogical. It is not his favorite couple consisting of an idealistic intellectual and primitive boor, but the inner life of a mind in constant disagreement with itself. The new hero—the writer himself—is certainly Polish in origin and universal in his existential suffering.

NOTES

1. Mrożek's and Błoński's correspondence was published in 2004 and comprises their letters exchanged in the years 1963–96.
2. Błoński and Mrożek, 39. All translations are my own.
3. Ibid., 40.
4. Ibid., 42.
5. Ibid., 198.
6. Ibid., 493.
7. Ibid., 63.
8. Stanisław Barańczak's popular phrase.
9. Błoński and Mrożek, 149.
10. Konrad, the protagonist of Adam Mickiewicz's *Forefathers' Eve,* transforms into Konrad from Stanisław Wyspiański's *Deliverance,* where he is an actor playing the role of Konrad from Mickiewicz's drama; but previously the same Konrad finds his "alternative" antagonist in Juliusz Słowacki's drama about a certain Kordian, a typical Polish noble and poet, who will pass quickly to the protagonist of Zygmunt Krasiński's *Undivine Comedy* about Count Henry, a poet and political leader who believes in nothing but to whom Christ himself comes at the moment of his suicide to convince him of His victory over earthly nothingness. Then, the nobles' loss of their position and the artists' loss of their creative potential will visit Stanisław Ignacy Witkiewicz's plays, where characters are trying to face romantic challenges but only theatrically. And chronologically the last of them (before Mrożek's play) comes Witold Gombrowicz's drama *The Marriage*, whose protagonist, Henry, an intellectual and an officer, will provoke murder instead of committing suicide in order to provoke God (like Count Henry and the poet Konrad) to convince him that he is not dreaming. In Sławomir Mrożek's *Tango* (a mixture of Wyspiański's *Wedding* and Gombrowicz's *Marriage*), the protagonist, with the Anglo-German name Arthur, will try to take the thread of History in his own hands. The harsh awakening from a dream about himself as an Achilles on a riot is waiting for him at the hardworking hands of Eddy, a worker and a leader of the bright future.
11. Błoński and Mrożek, 85.
12. Ibid., 83.
13. Ibid., 52.
14. See Esslin. The tag "East European absurdist" clung to Mrożek for the rest of his Western career.

15. Błoński and Mrożek, 77.
16. Ibid., 100.
17. Ibid., 351.
18. Ibid., 160.
19. Ibid., 161.
20. Ibid., 160.
21. Ibid., 493–94.
22. Ibid., 319.
23. Ibid., 319.
24. Ibid., 337.
25. Ibid., 343.
26. Ibid., 260.
27. Ibid., 221.
28. Ibid., 221.
29. Ibid., 224.
30. Ibid., 353. The playwright met the director several times and always expressed his admiration for Grotowski's independence.
31. Ibid., 544.
32. Ibid., 134.
33. Ibid., 498.
34. Ibid., 463.
35. Ibid., 463.
36. Ibid., 198.

The Something More of "almost nothing"

Miron Białoszewski's Kairotic Everyday

Joanna Niżyńska

In an episode from Miron Białoszewski's *Hums, Lumps, Threads* (1976) entitled "Going Out," the narrator is filled with wonder during an evening walk through a city:

> I go home along Próżna Street. On one side, there are still three houses connected by a strange system of gates and courtyards. On the other side the houses are bigger. Two of them old. The Secession building in particular concerns me. Five floors. With a tiny courtyard, and balconies hung skyward from the corners. When it gets a bit warmer, this is where they snore. And how. Even the walls bounce around. Afterwards I stand at the bottom of the courtyard, spellbound, and look up. I listen. I checked today. The windows were unopened. From inside I could hear nothing but breathing. Lu. told me recently, because I'd reminded him of something from his walks along the street. And that they didn't have a punch line. He:
>
> yes – he says to me – I love it best when almost nothing is happening . . .[1]

Nothing in particular happens during the walk, but the incident occupies a particularly meaningful place in the narrator's ritualistic revisitation of the city. "The snoring courtyard" exemplifies Białoszewski's approach to the representation of the everyday.[2] This episode, like so many in the "small narrations," borders on the trivial in the near absence of eventfulness. However, this non-eventfulness—the snoring of Próżna's inhabitants—is exactly what enchants the narrator. The signification of the emphatic closing line of the episode, which privileges the "almost nothing," goes beyond this particular episode; Białoszewski creates an everyday that overflows with its own surplus, that does not cease being the everyday but at the same time becomes "something more."[3]

This "something more" challenges the commonsense understanding of what is meant by the everyday, and it may well be the secret of Białoszewski's popularity as a writer. In this commonsense understanding, the everyday lacks events amid the endless repetition of mundane tasks and activities. When events do happen, they are bracketed as "holidays," which, often nostalgically, are contrasted with the everyday's inertia. The everyday's open-ended, transparent flow—its repeatability—is never considered worthy of a story since it is never seen for the first time.

Indeed, the everyday has been theorized as that which resists signification and defies the possibility of eventfulness. It has been viewed as intrinsically deficient, always in need of being filled, never sufficient unto itself. Thus, for Maurice Blanchot, the everyday's essential trait is its imperceptibility; it is a stagnant and tedious realm with only the *potential* to be a site of signification. Within the discourse of existentialism, for example, the everyday is a repetitive, "instrumental" realm that prevents access to the authenticity of the subject (of the Heideggerian *Dasein*, for instance). In Marxist and post-Marxist discourses (broadly understood), such theorists as Michel de Certeau and Michael Bernstein, who exalt the everyday, view it either as the inherently oppositional sphere of praxis or, like Michel Foucault, as a sphere of total control emanating from the power structure. Certeau and Henri Lefebvre juxtapose the everyday with a repressive public life and view it as a realm that has been commodified and manipulated by the structures of capitalism, but that has at the same time the inherent potential of becoming the realm of authenticity, if it can be revolutionized and transformed (i.e., freed from the all-pervasive system of control). These views of the everyday draw on such binary oppositions as everyday versus non-everyday, authentic versus inauthentic, and oppressive versus free. All such binaries grow out of the belief that the everyday must be transformed in order to retrieve a hidden existential or political potential.

In Białoszewski's writing, the everyday is neither the oppositional nor the inert, but an all-encompassing sphere meaningful in itself, beyond which there is nothing. Białoszewski creates this everyday via many intertwined aesthetic strategies (e.g., the reenactment of orality, the avoidance of "high" style, and careful thematic choices). One of the most important of Białoszewski's strategies is his idiosyncratic treatment of temporality, which can be better understood through a distinction between the juxtaposition of two types of temporality, *chronos* and *kairos*, and Blanchot's view of the everyday's imperceptibility.

Chronos, as Frank Kermode understands it, is a passing or waiting time, whereas kairos is "the season": a point in time "filled with significance, charged with a meaning derived from its relation to the end."[4] Chronos is what we usually associate with the experience of the everyday; it is just a succession, an empty duration during which nothing happens. Kairos represents a point of concentrated time, of transtemporal significance, in which (usually a posteriori) the pattern of meaningfulness becomes immanent. "The divine plot," as Kermode says, "is the pattern of kairoi in relation to the End."[5]

Kermode sees the seeds of this distinction between types of time in the theology of the New Testament: in "the coming of God's time (kairos), the fulfilling of the time (kairos—Mark 1:15), the signs of the times (Matt. 16:2–3) as against passing time, chronos."[6] By introducing the distinction between chronos (time) and kairos (the fulfillment of time), Christian theology established anchoring points in history by which the past (that of the Hebrew Bible, for instance) was validated and the future always already imbued with teleological meaning.

In opposition to Kermode's binary view of time, Blanchot perceives the everyday as a chronos that leaves no room for a "holiday" (that which would cancel and suppress the ordinary). Time for Blanchot is a pure chronos whose nature is quantitative and successive; it neither awaits, nor permits splendid moments.[7] The everyday is not what is inserted between the non-everyday but what is, in a sense, cancelled and unapproachable by language and representation. Thus, he claims, "the everyday designates for us the region of speech where the determinations true or false, yes or no, do not apply—it being always before what affirms it and yet incessantly reconstituting itself beyond all that negates it."[8]

The Blanchotian view of the "escaping" everyday, and the theological distinction between kairos and chronos provide reference points for exploring Białoszewski's construction of the everyday. This everyday possesses kairotic qualities, but these qualities do not belong to a distinct realm of significance that transcends temporality. Rather, the kairos of Białoszewski's everyday emerges from the very amorphous substance of chronos. Not belonging to an order outside of chronos, Białoszewski's kairos seems to involve the radical experience of temporality through everyday events (or, perhaps one should say, nonevents). In other words, even though Białoszewski does not distinguish between two distinct orders of time, not all moments of time are experienced in the same way.

Białoszewski's everyday involves a chronos whose flow becomes visible in its own kairotic moments. Thus, the kairotic moment can be identified with the moment when chronos discloses itself in the repeatability of everyday events. The pattern of this disclosure resembles the Heideggerian understanding of aletheia, "truth," which refers to the "unconcealment" of being unmediated by concepts or propositions (in its Greek etymology, *aletheia* is formed by joining the word *letho*, "to conceal," with *a*, a prefix that negates this concealment). Similarly, in Białoszewski's writing, kairos and chronos do not belong to mutually exclusive orders of time; kairos does not exist outside of chromos, but rather constitutes its disclosure, its "non-hiding." We might say, then, that Białoszewski's kairos is the *aletheia* of the chronos. Moreover, just as for Heidegger such a disclosure happens not in everyday praxis, but in art, so does the everyday become a work of art in Białoszewski's writing. Clearly, on a metalevel, Białoszewski's writing imposes an aesthetic form and, thus, visibility and transmittability on the sphere of human life whose repetitiveness and boundlessness are both particularly challenging for representation, and resistant to abstract thought and analytical propositions. Thematically, too, Białoszewski performs his claim that "reality is an artist" with the caveat that in his ontology there is no reality other than the everyday.[9] In the episode from Próżna Street, for instance, all of reality participates in an act of artistic creation. To the snoring of the Próżna inhabitants, the walls of the house respond by "bouncing around" (literally: "so that the walls are playing," in the idiomatic Polish expression *aż mury grają*). With the walls orchestrating the snoring of people, the whole of reality performs for the enchanted narrator.

To further explore Białoszewski's treatment of kairotic moments as chronotic, it might be useful to look at his representation of death, traditionally understood as a radical kairotic moment or, as Lefebvre calls it, "the distinctly non-everyday."[10] In Białoszewski's writing, death appears as *to już*, a phrase he uses both in his "small narrations" and in his earlier poetry.[11] Although colloquially *to już* can be translated as "it's over," or "this is it," its literal meaning is closer to "it was" or, to convey its sense of completed action more precisely, "it already was." Interestingly, this literal meaning points to a larger issue in Białoszewski's treatment of temporality, namely, his insistent return to changes that go unnoticed because they happen in—or rather between—infinitesimal units of time. This fascination with the microtemporal reduces the traditionally privileged status of death to an always already belated recognition of its occurrence. Thus, in one of the small narrations, Lusia describes with the words *to już* her a posteriori recognition that her sister Baśka, the narrator's close friend, has died:

> Lusia rushed up and stood in my doorway.
> "It's over [*to już*], Miron."
> Basia died at four, a little after four. Lusia, together with Mira, her other sister, rushed immediately to the hospital because they'd been sleeping in their coats by the telephone. Baśka was sitting up, her head swaying. Lusia started to cry. Baśka said to her.
> "Dummy."
> She pointed to the tiny radio borrowed from her tiny neighbor
> "Remember the radio . . ."
> Then she lost consciousness. Lusia ran to fetch a priest.
> "Don't tell mother he didn't make it."
> Mira held Baśka's hand.
> At one point I couldn't tell if it was her pulse or just mine. And imagine—me, who's so frightened of the dead.[12]

Baśka's death is granted no visibility. Rather than constituting a kairotic rupture in the chronotic everyday, it is always already embedded in the fabric of chronos. Although Lusia and Mira witness Baśka's death, it actually goes unnoticed, its precise moment unrecorded: "at four, after four." Even Baśka's body does not signal a moment of clear passing from life, but almost in a symbolic act of transmitting life, her fading pulse merges with her sister's. Baśka never becomes the Other, and her place never becomes "the place where I am not."[13] On the contrary, when her pulse merges with Mira's, Baśka's place becomes the place "where I am," not because death renders itself a means for experiencing existential authenticity, but because the invisibility of the border between life and death is rendered as familiar. Mira's astonishment at the experience ("And imagine—me . . . ") only deepens the familiarity and ordinariness of death. The very manner in which Baśka's death is related brings it from the sphere of potential ontological inquiry to the sphere of an animated conversation between friends.

The narration of the death firmly embeds Baśka's last moments in the realm of the profane through her sense of mundane responsibilities (her concern for the borrowed radio), and Lusia's worry lest her mother discover that the priest did not arrive in time to administer the last rites. Baśka's death is also domesticated because the narration is focalized by her sisters; there is no psychologizing, or pointing toward the otherness of death. It is as if positioning Baśka's death outside the everyday's open-ended flow, as a kairotic rupture, would have rendered it abstract, less individual.

In Białoszewski's world, the (potentially) eventful moments of rupture are short-circuited, the event of death always already incorporated into the open-ended flow of the quotidian, and distinguished from the quotidian only a posteriori. Thus, there is nothing "authentic" to be learned in moments of crisis (the very word *crisis* proves inadequate here). This lack of illumination does not signify that human life is inauthentic, however; rather, in Białoszewski's all-embracing quotidian, the category of authenticity proves useless as it presupposes a distinction between the inauthentic (traditionally associated with the quotidian and noneventful) and the authentic (the nonquotidian and eventful). Białoszewski's treatment of death shows that even the most extreme events do not anchor his everyday, as if the very idea of anchoring negated the open-ended flow of the everyday. The elusiveness of this flow is manifested by a repetitive belatedness, by an endless repetition of *to już*, to which even something as radical as death cannot grant the visibility of "now." On the contrary, if we adopt Blanchot's view that the essence of the everyday is its invisibility, then in Białoszewski's works death, being imperceptible, represents the quintessential everyday. In the absence of any "panoramic" vision, death becomes a vanishing point where change is infinitesimal, hardly palpable, and always already disappearing between one heartbeat and the next. And yet, between these beats, the status quo is irrevocably changed, and that which is invisible is not made visible, but made part of the everyday. Death's presence is as subtle as life's, but it is a presence that is present *in* life, not as the boundary of life.

While Białoszewski passes over significant changes such as death with a deficiency of eventfulness and a nonclimactic tone, ordinary, even banal events generate an excess of eventfulness. Thus, in *Hums, Lumps, Threads* the sudden experience of a spring day elicits epiphanic exaltation. Sandwiched between the narrator's memory of his youthful days as a journalist in "Dispach from the Countryside" ("Wiejski reportaż") and an episode about a Swedish hotel in Warsaw in "Looks Like It's Not Just the Swedes' Fault" ("Podobno to nie tylko Szwedzi winni"), the episode "When Will We Say So Again?" ("Kiedy znów tak powiemy?") is written in the form of a diary entry. Its title does not signal the subject matter, and it carries no connection with the episodes preceding and following it.

Sunday, March 31, 1974

After that non-winter the world opened up gently, unhurriedly. Birds began to sing. The sun struck. So that we knew. We watched.

And suddenly, today—the weather brought warmth to the shade, people came out . . . bit by bit; Sunday. I'm standing at the window: the trees burst forth here, and

> here, and my saved maple has budded, and my poplar has furry buds today. I lean out the window . . . and three willows are hanging green, all in leaves.
>
> So it's already happened. Just like that. And it's only March 31. Like in a dream. I can't believe it.
>
> —What a moment! what a moment!
>
> All is still before us—the dream is fulfilled.[14]

The episode is permeated by the elation, ecstasy, intensity, and mysteriousness that typify literary epiphanies. The ordinary world "opens up" to reveal—if only for a moment—its hidden potential in the miraculous force of spring. Although the narrator recognizes the moment as cyclical, and thus anticipated ("So that we knew. We watched"), he nonetheless configures it as kairotic. With his emotional exhilaration, the narrator imbues this cyclical transformation with the significance of an unexpected event overflowing with its own surplus.

What is striking, however, is that the narrator's amazement at this bursting vitality manifests itself in a language similar to that of the description of Baśka's death, as if both fall into the same category of temporality. While Baśka's death is marked as *to już* ("it already was"), spring's epiphany is "Więc już. Już! Stało się. Jest"—literally, "So it already was. Already! It happened. It is." It is as if the coming of spring, like that of death, has occurred between heartbeats. In his belated recognition of the change, the narrator can only repeat in amazement, "What a moment! What a moment."

As in the teleological view of kairos, the special position of the moment in the flow of time is viewed a posteriori in this exclamation, after the moment has passed. Białoszewski's kairoi, however, do not contribute to the future's meaningfulness, and thus they differ from the apocalyptic kairoi of Christian theology. The concluding sentence of the episode—"all is still before us, and the dream has been fulfilled"—presents the fulfillment of time in which the future still lies ahead unchanged, and not organized and prefigured by the kairotic "moment." Belatedness, epiphany, kairotic time, and the totality of future—in this one episode, contradictory conceptions of time emerge in a description of a topic that can so easily slip into a literary cliché.

The use of the same language to express infinitesimal units of time in the scene of Baśka's death and in the epiphanic moment of spring's arrival demonstrates that, regardless of their character, the specific moments of transformation—life into death, winter into spring—always pass unnoticed and unrecorded. However, only the spring day generates an epiphanic tone; the discreet scene of Baśka's death is marked neither by this intensity, nor even by the narrator's presence.[15] In a reversal of hierarchy, Baśka's scene is marked by a deficiency of eventfulness, whereas a spring day on which nothing remarkable happens overflows with it. In Białoszewski's writing, the known and the repeatable acquire the attributes of the revelatory, while the unique and extreme acquire those of the familiar. It is in the ordinary that Białoszewski's narrator exercises the emotionally engaged, exalted "I" that sees the pattern of time.

This springtime epiphany, however, is not just the literary translation of a cognitive event. That would reduce the scene to a rhetorical, and rather conventional, topos. Epiphanies punctuate Białoszewski's narrative based on a chronotic sequence ("one damn thing after another," to use Kermode's expression) that in itself possesses a kairotic value. Indeed, there is no extraordinary in the everyday. Its temporal structure is based on the repeatability of kairotic moments within ordinary experience. Interestingly, by specifying the date at the beginning of this passage, Białoszewski suggests his desire to indicate not only the repeatability of his kairos, but also its cyclical nature (which, per se, excludes an apocalyptic view of time). This cyclicality, however, only adds to the narrator's always fresh and always repeatable amazement. The response to the title of the episode—"When Will We Say So Again?"—could well be "Next spring."[16]

Through his treatment of temporality and linguistic patterns, Białoszewski creates an idiosyncratic model for the everyday that reverses our expectations regarding what it is and is not. On the one hand, he fuses ordinary and cyclical sensory experience (of, for instance, the arrival of spring) with the emotional intensity of epiphany; on the other, he frames unique situations (such as death) with mundane preoccupations and emotionally restrained tones. The language employed for both types of temporality performs the distinction between epiphany and everydayness, elation and restraint. The language used both by Baśka's sister and the narrator of the spring day experience conveys their surprise at this reversal (finding the kairotic in the cliché and the chronotic in the unique). These reversals notwithstanding, the change in the status quo always occurs in the infinitesimal, and is recognized only belatedly.

What is the critical value of this "decod[ing] of the world according to the everyday," to use Henri Lefebvre's words?[17] Perhaps the word *decoding* is somewhat misleading. Białoszewski, after all, decodes nothing. His everyday is an all-encompassing, fully exposed realm that conceals neither secrets nor deeper structures. No event, as *A Memoir of the Warsaw Uprising* most radically attests, can change the everyday into the non-everyday for Białoszewski. In a parallel to his treatment of genres, in which he obliterates the temporal gap between the time of the event and the time of writing (and thus anything that would create distance between the narrator and the everyday), Białoszewski erases from his everyday anything that could create the impression of a "panoramic vision," which would deprive the everyday of its transparency and repeatability. The cumulative effect of its representation is not knowledge of it as a "Great Pleonasm";[18] it is an understanding of it in the Heideggerian sense of knowing what it means to stand in its presence, rather than grasping it as an object of knowledge. Such an understanding presupposes a subject far removed from a Cartesian ego, or a transcendental subject, and posits a subject characterized in terms of its situatedness, finitude, and temporality, briefly, by its "belonging" to the world (rather than being an agent in, or master over the world).

"Whatever its other aspects," writes Blanchot, "the everyday . . . allows no hold. It escapes. It belongs to insignificance; the insignificance being what is without truth, without reality, but also perhaps the site of all possible signification. The everyday escapes."[19] Białoszewski creates an everyday that is "the site of all possible signification" not only by making it visible (which every narrative does), but also by showing its invisibility in his treatment of time. This treatment performs the escape of the everyday. Such a representation of the everyday resists conceptualization, with the open-ended repetitions that constitute Białoszewski's small narrations producing no theory of the everyday.[20] The significance of the everyday in Białoszewski's post-*Memoir* writing manifests itself not in kairotic moments of meaning, but in the narrator's permanent state of alertness to the ever-present possibility that chronos will imperceptibly slip into kairos. This insistence on domesticating life into the all-embracing everyday points not only to the affirmation of life, but also to a refusal to face the traumatic as traumatic, as the radically non-everyday. The everyday, like spring, is permeated by *entelechia*—the force of life. To be astonished by the everyday requires a special type of attentiveness to the "almost nothing"—to the nonevents, the subtle presences, the barely perceptible voices.

"Almost nothing," in Białoszewski's writing, "is always something monotonously different."[21] The "almost" and the "is" are important because it is not that nothing is happening in the everyday, but that "almost nothing" happens and continues to happen. This "almost" is the foundation on which Białoszewski builds his everyday. Changes in the everyday happen, as in Baśka's death, in infinitesimal spaces between one heartbeat and another. In this sense, life itself is the everyday; as Lefebvre would say, "The days follow one after another and resemble one another, and yet—here lies the contradiction at the heart of everydayness—everything changes."[22] In this stationary movement, the everyday is never seen for the first time but is always already there.

Yet, in spite of never being seen for the first time, Białoszewski's everyday is far from a repetitive, stagnant realm that, as Blanchot puts it, opens itself into history only in moments of effervescence.[23] Białoszewski's everyday is constituted by side-gazing at and decentering the very events, things, and phenomena that literature tends to position centrally and endow with kairotic value. One aspect of this decentering tendency is the focus, without distinctions or hierarchies, on barely traceable signs of life, like the animated blob of marmalade in the volume *The Heart Attack* (*Zawał*, 1977), or the merging of Baśka's pulse with her sister's, or the sounds of snores coming through courtyard windows.

This consistent incorporation of everything into the narrative flow makes it familiar and domesticated without depriving it of the power to astonish. Instead of noticing moments in time—the *Augenblick* of presence and meaning—Białoszewski wants us to notice the interstices between moments and their all-encompassing flow. Both enchantment with the snoring on Prózna

Street and fear of falling bombs during the uprising are in these interstices and in this flow. To live in time means refusing to allow this flow to escape our attention. For a writer who spent a good portion of his career on minimal things, this is quite a maximalist postulate. "The aspects of things that are most important to us are hidden because of their simplicity and familiarity. (One is unable to notice something—because it is always before one's eyes)," observed Wittgenstein. "And this means: we fail to be struck by what, once seen, is most striking and powerful."[24]

Without central events amidst the proliferation of nonevents, Białoszewski's "life-writing" actualizes the everyday as the only realm of life. It is precisely the banality of the everyday that leads Białoszewski to affirm life everywhere. It is this astonishment permeating many of Białoszewski's narrations that often masks their unrealistic settings. How easily the reader passes over the narrator's claim that he could hear the breathing of the sleeping inhabitants of Próżna Street through their closed windows ("The windows were unopened. From inside I could hear nothing but breathing."). But the question of whether this is a realistic or unrealistic situation is irrelevant simply because, throughout several volumes of small narrations, Białoszewski's narrator has accustomed his reader to the extraordinary receptivity of his ear.[25] His receptive ear catches not only language, but also random sounds and the residual noises of life—like the snoring on Próżna Street—as a frequency of life. To Blanchot's claim "Nothing happens; this is the everyday,"[26] Białoszewski emphatically responds, "I love it best when *almost nothing* is happening."

Notes

A modified version of this paper, translated into Macedonian, was published by the Institute of Macedonian Literature, Skopje.

1. Białoszewski, "Wyjście," in *Szumy, zlepy, ciągi. Utwory zebrane* 5:179–80. All translations by Joanna Niżyńska and Philip Redko.

2. From the publication of *A Memoir of the Warsaw Uprising* in 1970 until his death in 1983, Białoszewski's writing focuses on describing the ordinary, the mundane, and the prosaic—the everyday life of undramatic times—usually from an autobiographical perspective. Michał Głowiński, in searching for a term that would accommodate the obliteration of genre distinctions in Białoszewski's prose of this period, introduced the phrase "małe narracje" (*Gry powieściowe,* 319), which later some critics (e.g., Stanisław Barańczak) extended to encompass Białoszewski's late poems and dramatic pieces. Thematically, these pieces revolve around such things as a passerby whom the narrator observes from his window, daily events in the life of the narrator, a hospital stay, and flashes of memories from his childhood and wartime youth.

These post-*Memoir* works also include travel diaries of the writer's trips to Egypt and the United States, as well as his boat trip along the coast of Europe. Those who look for exoticism in these diaries will be disappointed; for the narrator, an outing to Garwolin in the suburbs of Warsaw is as stimulating as a journey to the Big Apple. In this period, Białoszewski also wrote *transy i transiki* ("Trances and Little Trances"), meditative reveries arising from observing such everyday objects as the poplar tree in front of his window.

3. Cf. Michał Głowiński's striking description of Białoszewski's everyday: "But such is the paradox of Białoszewski—in his work this everyday doesn't stop being the everyday, but it simultaneously becomes something more. He plays out life in this everyday." "Niezwykłe zwykłe," 6; my translation.

4. Kermode, 47.

5. Ibid.

6. Ibid., 48. Kermode was influenced in his understanding of chronos and kairos by the theologians Oscar Cullman (*Christ and Time*) and John Marsh (*The Fullness of Time*). As Kermode emphasizes, neither Greek nor Hebrew carries the antithesis between chronos and kairos; Hebrew has no word for chronos, and thus does not provide the distinction between the plain duration of chronos, and the concentrated time of kairos (47–48). It is interesting to note, however, that although it was never juxtaposed with chronos, for the Greeks kairos was an important concept. It meant "opportunity" and was often used in rhetoric to designate the right moment of speech (see, for instance, Gorgias, who speaks of *kairou chronou techne* [the art of knowing the right time]; fr. B-13).

7. Blanchot, *Infinite Conversation*, 242. Thus, for Blanchot the everyday is radically atheist, and the Lord's Prayer "secretly impious: give us our daily bread, give us to live accordingly to the daily existence that leaves no place for a relation between Creator and creature." Ibid., 245.

8. Ibid., 242.

9. Kirchner, 215; my translation.

10. Lefebvre, "Everyday and Everydayness," 11.

11. The phrase *a to już* serves to convey the same pattern of temporality in the description of the death of Janek, another friend of the narrator, in the volume of poetry *Misdirected Sentiments* (*Mylne wzruszenia*, 1961). Its use as the title of the poem emphasizes the phrase's role:

> "this is it" ["and it already was"]
> I'm looking at Janek with the oxygen tube
> he's falling asleep
> what'll happen?
> I'm thinking
> when will it happen
> I arrive
> I'm looking with an oxygen tube

he's falling asleep
when will it happen
not yet not yet
I'm leaving for a moment
I'll come back soon
I'm asking over the phone
—how is Janek?
and it already was (*Utwory zebrane*, 1:309)

In the *Memoir*, the phrase appears while the narrator describes a "communion out of hunger" (i.e., a holy communion performed in extreme situations when no wafer can be provided). In the poem, *to już* has a function similar to that in Baśka's story; the same sense of belatedness (and invisibility) is conveyed in the *Memoir* vis-à-vis the sacred moment.

12. Białoszewski, *Utwory zebrane*, 9:11.

13. Certeau, 194.

14. Białoszewski, *Utwory zebrane*, 5:172–73.

15. By "discreet" I understand the quiet presence of the narrator within the narration as a voice relating the story without conveying emotional engagement.

16. As Adam Zagajewski points out in his review of *Hums, Lumps, Threads*, "W Warszawie jak na wsi" (In Warsaw as in the countryside), Białoszewski's narrator lives according to seasonal changes.

17. Lefebvre, "Everyday and Everydayness," 9.

18. As Lefebvre calls the everyday in Blanchot, *Infinite Conversation*, 240.

19. Blanchot, *Infinite Conversation*, 239.

20. The most straightforward form of these repetitions is the "doubling" in Białoszewski's post-*Memoir* writings, i.e., the same motifs and events are represented in prose, poetry, and drama.

21. This is what the narrator catches in the headlights of a bus travelling a country road in *Konstancin, Utwory zebrine*, 9:162.

22. Lefebvre, "Everyday and Everydayness," 10.

23. Blanchot, *Infinite Conversation*, 238.

24. Wittgenstein, par. 129.

25. Aural receptiveness minimizes the intervention into the world; in the post-*Memoir* works, Białoszewski's narrator tends to favor it over other forms of receptiveness. Although his overtly colloquial accounts of the daily conversations of and with his friends provide rich material for the exploration of Białoszewski's sense of sociology and theatricality of language, such episodes as Próżna Street highlight a different aspect of Białoszewski's auratic leitmotifs: namely, that listening to the "snoring courtyard" connotes no understanding. Many sounds represented in the small narrations present different levels of inarticulatibility and trigger different emotional responses (from enchantment to, in other episodes, horror). The snores of Próżna enchant the narrator,

but they are not meant as requests for mutual understanding between the narrator and the snorers. Neither are they meant as communication; rather they function as a pure expression that cannot be translated into any other form of expression, thus signifing the limit of symbolic substitution.

26. Blanchot, *Infinite Conversation*, 241.

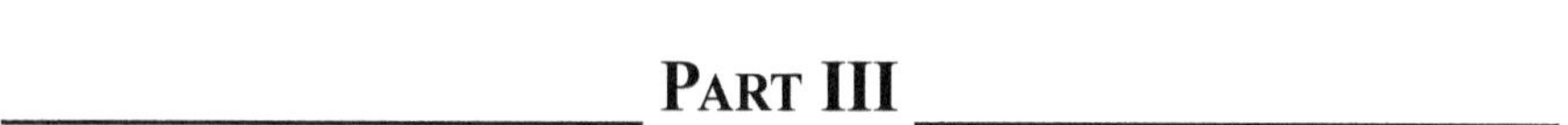

Part III

New Dynamics

Freedom and Community

The Experience of Solidarity in Polish Literature from 1980 to 2005

Przemysław Czapliński

In the history of Polish society, the 1990s are a period of de-solidarization, with the previous, radically simplified division into "the establishment" and "the rest of us" giving way to a—radically diversified—collective. Up until the nineties, as everyone was perfectly aware, the two camps encompassed a number of social classes: a pauperized intelligentsia, numerous members of the proletariat, and peasants. Following 1989, these classes quickly attained social distinctiveness, significance, and political representation. Quicker still—they lost it all. Old divisions yielded to new ones, determined by access (to money, power, prestige, information, knowledge, protection, education), while earlier criteria of differentiation turned out to be anachronistic. The middle class—its existence now as much a fact as a postulate—began to play a decisive role in this new reality.[1] It is not a bourgeois ethos that distinguishes this class, but rather its aspirations and social mobility, in other words the willingness to constantly change one's qualifications, as well as place of residence and employment, in pursuit of a "sense of stability." To this one should add the homogenizing role of mass media, which—in dissolving the differences between individual members of society—delineates a new, global mentality of the "media bourgeoisie." Thus, in late modernity, we either want to belong to the middle class, or we are characterized in reference to it.[2] There are, apparently, no distinct identities anymore, only strata of the dominant class: the upper middle, the middle middle, the lower middle, and so forth. Despite this general movement toward homogeneity, it is difficult to find in the history of Polish society a period during which we would have been equally conflicted, at odds with one another, and wary of both each other and the institutions we have created. The new world manufactures uniformity, but uniformity, paradoxically, produces conflicts.

The Great Narration of Solidarity—a myth as beautiful as a dream and as real as history—constitutes collective memory's answer to contemporary times. It consists only of great assets: the years of 1980 and 1981. In the history of Poland and probably also that of Europe and America, these years mark a period when the collective became a unity, when the state was daily revealed to be less and less necessary, when society itself created, through democratic elections, institutions essential for its life, when informal ties dominated over institutionalized ones, when no one had to worry that they would be left on their own, and—simultaneously—no one had to fear being denied the right to personal space. It is therefore not surprising that after 1989, when the collapse of cordial relations became a fact, the experience of those two years is invoked in public discourse with great frequency. This experience carries within it a lesson in communitarianism that every society, especially one undergoing capitalist stratification, needs. It carries within it a lesson in embarrassment that every society, especially a postcommunist one, most certainly deserves.

Is simple recollection of past history enough, then, to transform contemporary society and restore that communal bond? Unfortunately, no—it is not. The process of representing the Solidarity period encounters numerous problems (indeed, problematization is the point of literary representation of anything). In order to understand these problems, as well as to speak about Polish literature's encounter with Solidarity—understood not only as a labor union, but also as a historical event, a social movement, a type of association, and a new method for participation in history—it is necessary to begin in the 1970s.

The Literature of Communal Anxiety, 1975–80

Starting in the mid-seventies, a literary current began to emerge in Polish culture, which—bearing in mind the achievements of "the cinema of moral anxiety"—can be given the name of "the literature of communal anxiety." Works that were part of this burgeoning current asked whether there was still something that unites Polish people: whether there are any existent values in Polish life capable of transforming a collective into a community—a society that could actively stand up for its own subjectivity.

There are numerous differences between a collective and a community. A collective produces functional ties, resulting from needs and mutual interests, whereas a community—a community of faith, custom, background, or beliefs—exists because of suprafunctional ties that are formed out of a common respect for the same values in all of us. As members of a collective we expect primarily cooperation from another person, while in a community we are prepared to lend a disinterested hand to someone who cannot offer us anything. In a collective we can define ourselves only as "we," and any attempt at underscoring one's "I" automatically places us on the group's margins, while in a community a "we" demands an active "I." A collective is created and disbanded every day—at work, on the street, during a soccer match, at a church, at a party, in the cinema; a community outlasts generations. A collective provides a feeling of momentary identity; a community equips everyone with values that persist beyond time spent with the group. A collective exists only as a mass; a community can survive due to a single individual.

The search for common values, like a fever that sends shivers through an entire organism, was perceptible basically everywhere; in the cinema of moral anxiety (including the films of Andrzej Wajda, Krzysztof Kieślowski's *Camera Buff*, and Krzysztof Zanussi's *Contract*), in painting (for instance, in the works of Jerzy Duda-Gracz), and in alternative theatre, to recall the unsettling—for their audiences—productions of the Theatre of the Eighth Day, such as *Oh, How Nobly We Lived* (*Ach, jakże godnie żyliśmy*) and *Discounts for All* (*Przecena dla wszystkich*). The portrait of society that emerged from these works was increasingly disturbing.

The Pulp

The title of Jerzy Andrzejewski's great novel *The Pulp* (*Miazga*, completed 1970, published 1979) is characteristic of the type of societal descriptions that were appearing in Polish literature throughout almost the entire 1970s decade: descriptions catastrophic in nature.

In text after text readers saw a collective that was dividing into groups and cliques, plunging into a moral swamp, and destroying its traditions. Andrzejewski named this state of society "pulp";[3] Tadeusz Konwicki elaborated it as "sloppiness" in two key books of the period, *The Polish Complex* (*Kompleks polski*, 1977) and *A Minor Apocalypse* (*Mała apokalipsa*, 1979); Kazimierz Brandys diagnosed it as "unreality" in a novel thus entitled (*Nierzeczywistość*, 1975; first published in samizdat edition in 1977).[4] Equally succinct, if much more blunt was the verdict of one of the heroes of Marek Nowakowski's short story "The Wedding Once Again" ("Wesele raz jeszcze," 1973; first published in samizdat edition in 1981), who claimed that "Everyone is rotten, everyone allowed themselves to rot."[5] It is precisely this combination of rotting and acquiescence that aptly expresses the most important themes of Polish prose. From the pages of novels and stories emerged a collective that was cunningly sentimental, phony, and bastardized; capable of sacrifice in the name of transitory values, and entirely indifferent to the higher good; willing to collaborate with real socialism in the public sphere while nursing pro-independence gestures in the quietude of the domestic one. Some novels, especially those belonging to the "artistic revolution," declared that authentic life is not possible in a collective, others that an authentic community is impossible in Poland.[6]

In effect, readers saw in literature a society that—precisely as a community—allowed itself to be dismantled by communism; a society that was broken, either estranged from, or antagonistic toward itself, aggressively divided in the struggle for everyday goods, tormented in queues, celebratory of small triumphs, and blind to a creeping defeat.[7] The corrosion of the most important values organizing collective existence—such as freedom, independence, patriotism, faith—meant that neither the individual nor the masses were able to resist the corrupting influence of communism. And so, with the passive consent of all, alongside staged spectacles of resistance, the Polish people stopped noticing, as Konwicki wrote in *A Minor Apocalypse*, that they are part of "a nation that is evaporating into nothingness."[8]

"Until they saw their own numbers . . . "[9]

There was another aspect to these years, however. It was a time when the Workers' Defense Committee (KOR) was first established, a time of the first papal visit to the country, of the first strikes in Pomeranian port cities, of negotiations in Gdańsk, and of the struggle for Solidarity. Everything that we had earlier read in novels started to seem untrue, or—in the worst case scenario—like a warning uttered in order to prevent, rather than eradicate, evil.

What this means is that, starting in 1979, the probing of the collective mentality, the posing of problematic questions and the giving of drastic answers, the depictions of a society stripping itself of a common language and heading toward a life beyond the principle of responsibility were to some extent—or perhaps even in their entirety—shown to be erroneous. As such, these depictions had to surrender themselves to critical self-analysis. History joined in the action, and community turned out to be its subject. Within the perimeter of this community, the impossible became possible; not only did strong communal ties not exclude individual subjectivity, they were conditioned by it; collective values supported the articulation of individual desires and needs, while individuality added dynamics and authenticity to the collective structure, thus preventing organizational inertia. It became apparent that the experience of a positive community was of the greatest importance and absolutely fundamental; here was a collective that agreed that the care for a higher "common good"—the ability to live with dignity—was the foundation of its existence. Thanks to the acceptance of this "common good," collective freedom became conditional on sharing in the care for the dignity of individuals (no community can build a dignified life by stripping individual people of their dignity), while individuals recognized that their freedom would be incomplete without participation in collective actions (no person can live in dignity if they do not feel a sense of responsibility for others).

The events from the birth of the Workers' Defense Committee until the introduction of Martial Law, therefore, realized scenarios that were the exact opposite of those put forth by literature; contrary to diagnoses of decay, pulverization, and rottenness, society proved itself capable of restoring communal myths. These myths consolidated collective identity while simultaneously adding meaning to individual existence. This should be reiterated one more time: it thus transpired that a "positive community"—one that does not appropriate anyone's subjectivity, is supportive of individual pursuits, and allows for active participation in the shaping of a collective life—is possible.

A Trial of Greatness, 1981–89

The birth of Solidarity and everything that preceded it belied the "black" descriptions provided by our literature. Leszek Szaruga was correct, after all, when he wrote: "[N]either Konwicki in *A Minor Apocalypse*, nor Orłoś in *The Third Lie* managed to capture the social changes that were taking place in Poland—the events of 1980 surprised prose: the heroes of August did not exist in it before August, nonexistent were the powers ripening in society."[10] As a result of this "blindness" our literature had, as it were, some sociology homework to do: it had to narrate how it came to be that a community was born inside the dead heart of socialist realism.

Had history continued upon a peaceful track, perhaps it would have been possible for our prose to complete this task without entirely letting go of criticism, doubt, and caution. Perhaps it would have been able to undertake "a critique of solidaristic reason" and expose, as Sergiusz Kowalski has done in his first-class book, its numerous traps and seeming unities, the strength of the weak and the weakness of every strength;[11] perhaps in this way literature would have supported the always necessary movement of self-criticism. In the meantime, however, the introduction of Martial Law dramatically complicated, and perhaps even made it impossible for literature "to render the highest kind of justice to the visible universe." Writers found themselves in a very uncomfortable situation: speaking critically of Solidarity would mean supporting official propaganda, while speaking of it with praise meant entering into the anticommunist pact, a pact that for a few years united even the most diversified groups, and suspended all thought against the obvious. A common enemy unified people who, without regard for divisive differences in their worldviews, acted together in the underground structures of Solidarity.[12]

Writers took on a similar approach after December 1981: in representing the conflict between "society" and "the authorities," they fashioned society into an undifferentiated collective, identical both morally and in terms of its worldview. And it was on the side of this collective that, in solidarity, they took their place. Since they perceived Polish society as a simple collective, however, and in addition as weak, disadvantaged, humiliated, and beaten, the spiritual support provided by their prose led, in practice, to reproduction of collective stereotypes. The great novels of the seventies were full of doubt as to whether the community could be revived, even if they were simultaneously overflowing with civic and democratic longings. After these novels, which spoke of loneliness chosen out of despair, there appeared in our prose a current of antisocialist realism. The books that belonged to it obstinately repeated a few simple sentences: that we are neatly divided into "us" and "them," that "they" are completely evil while "we" are righteous and good, that Solidarity could be destroyed but not defeated, that a society beaten on the ground was elevated to spiritual heights, and that—as soon as socialism disappears—a Pole would finally be a human being to another Pole.[13]

In this manner our literature—calling forth diverse clichés for support—was helping August 1980 pass its trial of greatness. This impression of greatness was imposing at the time: everyday speech was filled with analogies of national uprisings, occupations, and resistance movements. Public discourses placed Solidarity in the pantheon of Polish history, reserving for August a place right beside the Warsaw Uprising, and locating the experience of Martial Law somewhere in Siberia. It is astounding how conflicted, or at the very least inconsistent were the metaphors that proliferated throughout the months preceding December 13, 1981. Among them were some obvious figures of genesis (the beginning of a civil society),[14] metaphors of national emancipation (August 1980 as the fulfillment of revolts against communist rule), images of divine intervention[15] and of the restoration of common sense in economy (the potential of economic development as bound up in the absurdities of socialism and set free by the August agreements), lexicons of identities both narrow (Pole-Catholic-Solidarity activist) and diffuse (democracy, freedom). To assess these discourses—to grasp them, to break them down into their component parts, to establish their changing meanings and common usages, their poles of semantic strength and their "blind spots"—was not possible at that time.[16] For the mission of literature at the time consisted not only in identifying past experiences, but also in integrating its descriptions of reality with public discourse—in repeating the words of mass euphoria. And when the role assigned to literature is to repeat social experience, its style becomes limited to the reiteration of clichés of mass expression. This was the very source from which socialist realism sprang.

Its basic design transformed novelistic plots into proofs meant to accomplish an important task: present everyday Polish life in such a way as to ensure that communism, placed in its context, would appear like a system of evil (of crime, corruption, wastefulness, immorality). Of course, the enigma of the birth of Solidarity disappeared in a plot that denounced communism. Instead, the emergence of a community from the rock bottom of an economic and moral collapse became a matter of course, a given, a basic sociological fact that, requiring no explanation, explained everything all by itself. The literature of the Martial Law period thus reproduced a fragment of the earlier narrative about the destruction of social bonds, while weaving the threads of the conquest of communal apathy and of the creation of Solidarity into a motif of the miraculous. In this way, literature was able to complete its outstanding homework in sociology with the aid of sacral language. Janusz Głowacki's novel *Power Trembles* (*Moc truchleje*, 1981) seems a fitting example of how this concept was realized. It presents the birth of Solidarity as an incomprehensible—and for this reason inexplicable—miracle, in confrontation with which "power trembles."[17] Thus we see a shipyard worker (and more precisely a "prole") undergoing a metamorphosis: from a pauper who sees himself as an object, an informer manipulated by the obtuse functionaries of Polish People's Republic (PRL), a slave whose consciousness was carved out by socialist newspeak, to a human being who begins to think of himself as part of a community. It has to be acknowledged that Głowacki's novelistic "method," which consisted of constructing blind devotees of bad causes, worked very well as a means of critiquing the system. No one humiliated the Polish People's Republic of the 1970s more completely than the "prole" who defended the "socialist cause" using the idiom of inefficient dim-wittedness.[18] It also has to be added, however, that the same method could not account for what came afterward, namely the birth of a community. For this reason Głowacki's novel entrusted this secret to its conclusion—the scene of the signing of the August agreements and of the commencement of a new society. It could be said that if half the shipyard workers were like Głowacki's hero, the PRL would have never been defeated. And vice-versa: if such a community could be born of such blockheads, Solidarity would have been created by the members of the Motorized Reserves of the Citizens' Militia (ZOMO).

The homogeneous discourse of "solidaristic" praise that coalesced in the first months of Martial Law, and (bound up with it) the critique of communism that was reduced to the level of truisms constituted a trap for literature. This trap was only partially avoided by those authors who attempted to put this discourse into some kind of quotation marks. It was possible to maintain control over pathos, or at the very least to dilute this loftiness with ambiguity, through the use of an everyday perspective, the avoidance of battle scenes, or through the mediation of martyrdom analogies. Thus, in *Underground River, Underground Birds* (*Rzeka podziemna, podziemne ptaki*, 1984) Konwicki used irony to simultaneously de-heroize the resurrectionist connotations of his characters, and to confirm—at the moment of the main protagonist's death—their legitimacy; Jacek Bocheński exposed the devastation of social communication—attributed to communism, but manifesting itself, as it were, beyond the political sphere—by placing his heroes in a hospital, and allowing them to enter into prolonged conversations with one another (*State after Collapse* [*Stan po zapaści*], 1987); Nowakowski related dozens of monologues of common people in his well-known *The Canary and Other Tales of Martial Law* (*Raport o stanie wojennym*, 1982; 1983), which enabled him to show their/our everyday life as the last line of defense against communism, and to thereby boost the value of ordinariness (as opposed to that of heroic battles, strikes, and manifestations); Jarosław Marek Rymkiewicz allowed his heroes to indulge in grandiose deliberations about the obliterated nations of the past, and—based on this analogy—to construct a putative definition of the moral greatness of Polish society (*Polish Summer Talks of the Year 1983* [*Rozmowy polskie latem roku 1983*], 1984); and Gustaw Herling-Grudziński referenced Martial Law in Poland through a parabolic tale of the plague in a seventeenth-century Italian city in his short story "The Plague in Naples" ("Dżuma w Neapolu," 1990).

All of these works were read "hot off the press," enthusiastically received, and quickly forgotten. Still, it is difficult to resist the impression that writers at that time did not have any other choice than to walk into the trap of stating the obvious. Firstly, because literature was then faced with the option of being either engaged, or not read at all. Only engaged literature had a chance at participation in the collective life and a guarantee of social approval.[19] There was also something much more valuable at stake than this, namely, greatness: the first unadulterated, authentic, all-encompassing experience of greatness. During the first papal visit to Poland in 1979, and then even more strongly and evidently in August 1980 and throughout the entire sixteen months that followed, we felt that we could be better—individually and all together. It was "an experience of an incredible 'upward suction,' some kind of a calling urging us to transcend our own selves."[20]

It could be said that in the first months of Martial Law, already after the internment of Solidarity activists, the real war was fought over precisely this greatness; declared by the government and carried out with the use of despicable means, it had as its aim the degradation of recent experiences. The authorities of the time were unable to go as far as the Orwellian idea of erasing the past. Nevertheless, they decided to diminish it, reduce it, strip it of its aura. The "spinning" of concepts, falsification of truth, and attribution of base motivations to Solidarity activists were the means by which official channels of mass communication, the educational system, and government spokesmen worked toward this aim. A social community was a lethal threat for the government of the Martial Law period; in order to survive, the ruling class of the Polish People's Republic had to infect the collective space with a plague, in other words—as Herling-Grudziński expressed it—it had to kill "in the survivors, in their children, grandchildren, and great-grandchildren, . . . any taste for, appreciation of, and enjoyment of community life."[21] And since this goal was being accomplished by using a language of slander, libel, and baseness—a petty and mean language—only a language of greatness could serve as its countermeasure. The battle was being fought over the form of history—not over the question of whether Solidarity existed, but rather over the question of its nature. Literature could not abstain from this fight. Lending its voice to a society forced into muteness, it chose to call greatness by its first name. It could be said that literature saw the salvation of communal greatness in the surrender of its own claims to it. For this reason, it left behind testimonies instead of masterpieces.

A Trial of Purity, 1989–95

There was another trial—a much more difficult one—awaiting literature of the post-Solidarity period, as well as Solidarity itself and every member of that community. It was the trial of purity—of fidelity to the idea. To put it differently, it was a trial of resistance to the temptations of power, greed, corruption, and pettiness, and also to the lure of an easy condemnation of other human beings.[22]

The earlier struggle for greatness was in some ways simple, if painful: it required heroism. After December 1981, those who wanted to equal the emotional force of reminiscence had to either fight or speak of the common cause with grandeur.[23] The time for the test of the idea was yet to come. It arrived after 1989, namely at a time when government started to use the language of Solidarity. It was a dangerous moment of the appropriation of the social revolution, and of its integration into the legitimatizing processes of the new order. If the new rulers—not only "solidaristic" after all—were able to append the idiom of a successful revolution to their own discourse, then the participants of the transformation after 1989 would have been stripped of the language of protest. Authorities that use the rhetoric of revolt—especially, as was the case in Poland, of a revolt that overturned an old regime and elevated its own leaders to the top—cut off society's tongue. For this reason, very shortly after the turning point of 1989, literature diametrically changed its method of presenting past experiences: a tone of virulent critique appeared in the place of praise of the conquered. Its excessiveness made it seem as if writers were trying to clear a backlog of work. It could be interpreted differently, however: since the discourse of a past community found itself dangerously close to the authorities—moreover, to sanctioned and increasingly dispersed authorities—literature had to resort to satire in order to show how an idea is transformed, in the hands of politicians, into pure rhetoric. The method chosen by the majority of writers consisted of putting the alliance between Solidarity and authorities to the test of purity; in other words, on making sure that the authorities would not be able to appropriate, and use as rationale for the "marketization" of reality, everything that had been noble throughout the entire decade, and became powerful toward its end.

It should be added here that Polish prose entered onto this path for the second time. The path had been initially explored, almost immediately after the introduction of Martial Law, by writers of the official circulation. Their understanding of the "test of an idea" was consistent at the time with the demands of propaganda—it relied on the search for the sordid in someone else's greatness. In this regard the highest degree of zealousness was shown by Roman Bratny, who—in his novel *A Year in a Coffin* (*Rok w trumnie*, 1984)—was the first to occupy himself with the disgrace of Solidarity by presenting August 1980 as a time of social savagery, a return to a typically Polish bedlam, self-seeking aggrandizement, and self-interest. A little more imaginative was Józef Łoziński's version presented in *Hunting Scenes from Lower Silesia* (*Sceny myśliwskie z Dolnego Śląska*, 1985), in which he—admittedly—exposed to ridicule the rule of the police baton, but where he simultaneously represented the "solidaristic" revolution as proletarian revenge underpinned by (here the writer took his inspiration from Freud) sexual rivalry over a woman. There were also no shortage of critical accents in Tadeusz Siejak's *The Desert* (*Pustynia*, 1987), which characterized trade unionists as people ruled by resentment, or quite simply careerists who—having seized power—cannot see how easily they are being manipulated by the party. Siejak was attacking the myth of "clean hands," suggesting that construction (understood literally, from an engineering standpoint) was more valuable at the time than interference in politics. Viewed from some perspective, these texts appear to prove something obvious: that it was impossible to undertake a critique of the solidaristic legacy as long as the critiqued were stripped of the right to speak. When a radical change took place in 1989, literature began the process of de-mythologization.

Perhaps the most risky attempt at "diminishment" was undertaken by Jacek Kaczmarski, who settled accounts with his own biography in the vitriolic novel *Self-Portrait with a Scoundrel* (*Autoportret z kanalią*, 1994). Pointing the sword of sarcasm toward oneself was an extremely difficult, but honest gesture; it is unfortunate that Kaczmarski, in wishing to authenticate his criticism, did not spare anyone. The Workers' Defense Committee circles, the leaders of Solidarity, the post-December emigrants—all of these people, argued the author, were "stage performers," meaning people constantly seeking approval rather than social change, who were desirous of public attention rather than the truth. It is possible that Kaczmarski wrote his novel in order to write himself out of the heroic legend of Solidarity, by proving how little his hero deserved to be a part of it. The problem here is that, in denouncing the title scoundrel, the author could not resist the temptation to attribute the same motivations to everyone else. Meanwhile, the phenomenon of collective—mass, crowd, and thus precisely not solo—participation in Solidarity totally escaped this mode of thinking.

The real "test of the idea," "the trial of purity," required something else: not the desecration of the Solidarity experience, but the realization that greatness is never the product of someone else's smallness. All too frequently after 1989 the participants of past events seemed to forget that the despicable nature of the opponents (and, as Herbert wrote in his poem "To Ryszard Krynicki—a Letter," "we had opponents despicably small")[24] does not make us great. The warning that was being transmitted by literature was thus meant to prevent a "descent into saintliness," as well as to ensure that the greatness of collective achievements was not treated as an individual success. It would appear that such was Janusz Anderman's aim in his novel *Prison Illness* (*Choroba więzienna*, 1992), the best of the de-mythologizing texts. For the author set its action at the beginning of the Third Polish Commonwealth, thereby confronting its hero, a former internee, with a practical problem: how to convert experiences from the struggle for freedom into a concept for a life in freedom. As a result, the defeat of its hero, who in wishing to make a film about Solidarity allows himself to lie and misrepresent matters, does not turn into a demystification of August, but rather becomes an exposé of an issue that touched us all. For we were all asking ourselves how to saturate everyday life with the moral message of the community, how to stay true to Tischner's dictum that "the deepest form of solidarity is the solidarity of consciences" during times of particularistic consciences.[25] In this sense, Anderman's hero was being defeated in part on our behalf, and in part in order to spare us from a similar fate.

Pragmatism threatens every idea. Yet the test of an idea is passed not by the individual who concedes that maintaining it in a pure state is impossible, but by those who, knowing that temptations of power are inevitable, nevertheless attempt to confront them. A person matures by expecting to find him- or herself compliant, and becomes cynical by expecting others to be so. In this sense, the test of the idea—an idea that had at its disposal big words and social support—took place at the time when Solidarity came into power. Anticipated by Anderman, it is of this that works that attempt to "settle accounts" with the past speak: Andrzej Horubała's *The Drenched* (*Umoczeni*, 2004), Bronisław Wildstein's *Future with Limited Responsibility* (*Przyszłość z ograniczoną odpowiedzialnością*, 2003), or Piotr Siemion's *Finimondo* (2004).[26] They portray the confrontation of past dreams about politics grounded in an ethical code with the unavoidable pettiness of everyday pragmatics. They speak, therefore, of the defeat of a political movement that was built on the illusory belief that great ideas will, on their own, translate themselves into the practice of gaining and maintaining power. The unquestionable merit of these books lies in their harsh, merciless exposure of the demoralization of the power elites in the new Poland—of corruption caused by the inability to transform the ethos of struggle into a civic ethos. Simultaneously, their great shortcoming lies in suggesting that the best solution for average people is to isolate themselves from the (demoralizing, dirty, petty, and despicable) political sphere, where the only things that matter now are money, influence, and status. These works thus fall into a contradiction. They reach for the legacy of Solidarity in order to accuse present-time politicians of failing to pass the test of small temptations, of falling into dwarfism in their governance of the everyday today, when before—faced with great issues—they too were great. At the same time, the authors do not have any ideas for our everyday reality other than suggesting we surround it with a hermetic wall, thus separating ourselves from the debris of politics. We see therefore, on the one side, politicians who have not matured enough for the greatness of the legacy of the past, who have not remained loyal to the rule of the primacy of ethics over politics; yet their alternative is not a civil society, or even a neighborly one, but the "small everyday" proposed by our writers, which they perceive as a sphere of petty bourgeoisie civilities. Of course, these literary texts are a reaction of engaged and frustrated people, frustrated because powerless, but it is nevertheless difficult not to notice that their failure is rooted not in the moralizing addressed to the ruling class, but rather in their lack of ideas for a worthwhile everyday, governed by "solidaristic" precepts. Were these precepts to retain their significance, they would have to do so not only among the authorities, but also in our everyday life. The fact that the people in power have not passed this test does not mean that we have succeeded in the task. After all, the test of pettiness is a trial we go through every day.

A Trial of Difference, 1995–2005[27]

In January 1982, the second month of Martial Law, a slogan appeared on the wall of an apartment building that I walked by every day. It read: "Winter is yours, spring is ours." The sense of the slogan was clear: what the foe by force seized in December, sword in hand we will gain in March. March and April went by, and once May came around a continuation of the slogan appeared on the same wall. In its entirety it now said: "Winter is yours, spring is ours, summer belongs to the Moomins."[28] Nonsense added to sense? Not necessarily. It seems that someone was thereby signaling a number of issues. First, that not all of the content of a social contract can be expressed within the parameters of a "yours-ours" code. Second, that the wall of an apartment building is not only a political blackboard, but also simply a means of social communication. Third, that some "Other" is joining this communication, someone outside of the dichotomous system, someone without access to a language of his/her own, who signals the desire to make his/her presence known, and to join in the communication with a parody of dominant discourses. This simple if amusing slogan was, therefore, indicating something worrisome—the dominance in social discourse of collective and political issues over the vocabularies of other groups and individuals. In this manner difference was invading social life.

A few years later, in 1986, Adam Zagajewski published a memorable book of essays entitled *Solidarity and Solitude* (*Solidarność i samotność*), in which he argued for the artist's right to seclusion—a right not to preoccupy oneself with noble issues of the collective, to abandon the social duty that writers willingly and en masse took up after the introduction of Martial Law, to wave goodbye to engaged and anticommunist literature, and to choose that which is individual, separate, and idiomatic instead. Zagajewski was thus trying to achieve in literature what social communication was going to experience only a few years after the 1989 breakthrough, namely the pluralization of opinions and vocabularies. Yet, despite this interesting anticipation, the book was anachronistic and excessively simplified. The author expressed in it ideas that were almost the same as those of Stefan Chwin and Stanisław Rosiek, who six years earlier, in the manifesto *Without Authority* (*Bez autorytetu*, 1980), wrote—more convincingly, with better justification—that an individual should never state individual truths using the discourse of a collective. Chwin and Rosiek's words could not have come at a worse time, however: by the time their book reached the bookstores, Solidarity already existed, and ten million people had found in its homogeneous dictionary the deepest truths of their lives. Six years later, after a period of successive ritualization in all levels of social discourse, Zagajewski's book appeared both important and innovative (not to say courageous). Meanwhile, however, despite its grandiloquence and rhetorical and narrative ornamentation, *Solidarity and Solitude* had only the appearance of an escape from a discursive stalemate: after all, the author was saying that the opposition of "totalitarian–anti-totalitarian" should be countered with the opposition "collective–individual." The place of literature oriented toward fighting with totalitarianism was to be taken by literature "of the singular." Engaged works out of necessity treated the individual like an exemplar of a repressed society; the type of narration projected by Zagajewski would undertake "more difficult spiritual tasks."[29] Earlier—a predominance of collective and political issues, now—the search for metaphysics and individualism. Combating one dichotomy with another is always rhetorically successful, but it only has the appearance of a reform. For if past literature was suffering from a metaphysical deficiency, books still to come—in accordance with Zagajewski's ideas—would have all collective matters removed from them. The author was thus making a simple error: he considered the overestimation of collective bonds and the undervaluing of private worlds to be the root cause of the crisis in literature, while at the same time everything he proposed boiled down to a reversal of these proportions. Moreover, in all honesty, even individualism did not stand much of a chance in his book. Swallowed up by "the common cause" before, it was now to disappear in metaphysical vapors. This said, the sheer fact of the book's publication, as well as its lively reception proved that a new outlook on the issue of the collective was necessary.

After 1989, the problem formulated by Zagajewski (of the excess of collective, and shortage of private content in literature) returned. Its significance becomes more apparent the more centralized Polish social life becomes, and the fewer social differences find their representations in a symbolic forum; this movement "toward the center" becomes marked approximately from the mid-nineties onward. In order to understand this trial better it is necessary to return for a moment to Nowakowski's *The Canary and Other Tales of Martial Law*. Among its numerous scenes a few stood apart from the rest, ill-fitted to the whole. These were the marginal stories, which portrayed either an average alcoholic who translates the acronym KPN (which stands for the Confederation of Independent Poland) to mean "cognac distilled at night" (*koniak pędzony nocą*), or Amalia Bessarabo, a mysterious Gypsy obsessed with the accumulation of food reserves. The appearance of such characters—from beyond the Grand Narrative of Solidarity, disengaged from collective history—made it obvious that society is never uniform.

In the meantime, the majority of novels written after 1989, at least during the first few years, focused on the lost unity. Narrative after narrative dramatically revealed the coming apart of all bonds (not only of solidaristic ones, but also those of custom, class, or family) under the pressure of capitalist market forces. Telling in this context is a scene out of Nowakowski's *Homo Polonicus* (1992), perhaps the first literary characterization of the "modern-day hero." Its main character, Stasio Bombiak, is getting rich in the New Poland courtesy of the black market; among other things he smuggles Russian spirits, which he then routes into legalized trade. One of his (Russian, obviously) "mules" cheats him on a transport, in response to which Bombiak hires a "bodyguard" (an ex-militia man, obviously) to punish the Russian. To this punishment Bombiak adds a warning: "Among us, trade solidarity is obligatory." The beaten up Russian answers: "Yes, yes! Solidarity conquered Communism," upon which Stasio Bombiak reflectively comments: "There is no talking to someone like that. He's confused one thing with the other."[30]

Of course: according to the Bombiaks of this world, the Solidarity that deposed communism should not be confused with "trade solidarity." From now on, politics and economy should walk a separate path, as should the past and the present, the rich and the poor, the resourceful and the "suckers." Nowakowski was thus giving notice of an imminent new threat to the legacy of August 1980—a peculiar "depravation" of the concept "solidarity." In keeping with the pragmatic attitudes of the "new class," the term should be synonymous with nothing more than a deal. In this way Nowakowski was showing the breakdown of society into groups increasingly indifferent, even conflicted toward one another. It must be noted, however, that the author located the reason for this in a distorted and easy subject—the small "grey zone" capitalists interested in an unstable country, threadbare laws, and a market unable to cope with social demands. This "new class," mobile, made up of members of all social spheres, was clearly not the middle class, but rather its barbaric vanguard. Its birth came courtesy of the market, which in the new Poland was always a step ahead of economists and lawyers. Nevertheless, the literary response to the existence of this "class," expressed in the reactivation of musings about social unity, was anachronistic and frustrating. For the revival of a memory wherein solidarity stood for a homogenous society was equivalent then, at the beginning of the nineties, to the calling forth of a ghost that never did have a body. Solidarity was a movement that united—as opposed to eliminated—differences. The literary focus on "barbaric capitalists," who were, moreover, displayed against a background of the solidaristic legacy, was akin to taking the easy way out; thus the writers—beside Nowakowski, also Piotr Wojciechowski in *The School of Charm and Survival* (*Szkoła wdzięku i przetrwania*, 1995)—identified the new class as the main perpetrator of social conflicts, the most dangerous force wearing down the solidaristic capital. Our literature thereby made the new class into a scapegoat that allowed us to save remnants of the illusion of a communal legacy.

Not all prose writers reacted to the new reality by arousing nostalgia for unity. More significant appear those books that tried to show such a unity as never having existed in the first place. It is only fitting to begin by pointing out narratives about social groups that, already during the Martial Law period, did not fit the dichotomous divide into Solidarity versus communism: Andrzej Stasiuk's *The White Raven* (*Biały kruk*, 1995), Jan Sobczak's *Drift* (*Dryf*, 1999), Piotr Siemion's *Low Meadows* (*Niskie łąki*, 2000). Each one spoke about experiences from the Solidarity period and, simultaneously, accented the fact that the biographies of its protagonists occupied a place on the margins of political history. A dialogue between the main characters of Stasiuk's novel sounds demonstrative in this respect:

> "Tell me, what were we doing during 1980?
> "The usual stuff. Nothing."
> "And '81?"
> "Same shit."
> "Eighty-two?"
> "Again."[31]

This ostentatiously expressed "nothing" should be understood in reference to the Great Anticommunist Cause. Doing nothing meant not engaging in the battle with the regime. Doing nothing was thus "simply life," "the everyday," "the average," "the other." Consequently, the everyday stood in dangerous proximity to "nothingness," meaning the lack of the right to act in the Main

Narration, which groups together the most important participants of collective history. It is possible to likewise characterize the life of the hero of *Drift*—Leszek Wałęsik, a drug addict who, at the beginning of the eighties, was wandering the streets of Warsaw in search of marijuana.[32] The biographies of the heroes of *Low Meadows* appear equally disconnected from the "common cause." Siemion depicts people who, admittedly, paint antigovernment slogans on walls ("Solidarity will win!"), but do so as a prank, to stir up trouble, rather than for ideological reasons (which is why they add: "Solidarity will win—No fucking around!").[33] It should be understood here that these are not only individual biographies, but representations of numerous "othernesses." With the help of these books the phantasm of a homogenous society began to crack, as did the Great Narration that gathered everyone in one "us–them" dichotomy.

A straightforward path leads from these books to the understanding that the present-day challenge of solidarity is much more difficult, for it requires the consideration of a multiplicity of differences. What is worse, a multiplicity once discovered demands a return to the Solidarity period with an eye for events, positions, and even groups that might have been marginalized from the onset. These groups were perceived as minor not because they were less important, but because in the context of the Great Narration their "citizenship" was weaker, and they were from the beginning displaced from communal history. In this way we had erased from memory the participation of women in Solidarity,[34] as well as the experience of "street democracy"[35] that has been neutralized in the new Poland.[36]

The books that reconstruct these "lost chain links," like the already mentioned *Critique of Solidaristic Reason* by Kowalski, allow us to understand the role that contemporary literature dealing with Solidarity must assume. It is the role of a guardian of social differences. Only this approach can prevent the dangerous shift that sometimes takes place in Polish political life. In the rhetoric of various parties today, the former positive community (created "in the name of" rather than "against" something), open and tolerant, becomes exploited as an emblem of actions that are patriarchal, Polish-centered, pro-Catholic, or self-entitled in nature. This kind of appropriation is possible only through insisting that everyone belonged to Solidarity, and that everyone who belonged to it was identical. This is why literature is undertaking a double excursion into the past. The first—described in *The White Raven*, *Drift*, and *Low Meadows*—reveals that not everyone wanted to fit into a "solidaristic" movement. The other, transmitted by means of critical reflection by scholars such as Agnieszka Graff or Shana Penn, reminds us that not everyone was wanted by Solidarity. The conclusions both routes lead to are plain: insisting at the present time on the—untruthful—image of Solidarity as either an all-encompassing and monolithic movement, or an open and diverse one, means that we have become an exact negation of that community. The more we try to deceive the past, the more visible become our troubles with social communication. It is a communication increasingly narrow, increasingly resistant to the very thought of the possibility of an "Other." At stake here is not only tolerance toward other religions, ethnicities, or sexualities; of primary importance is the possibility of another society. After all, it germinated in the "solidaristic" distance from both communism and capitalism. What had lacked concreteness in that program actually appears to indicate now the most difficult, but at the same time the truly valuable legacy of August: the chance to preserve common ties under free market conditions.[37]

When literature written and published toward the end of the 1990s and at the beginning of the twenty-first century speaks about the community of August, it should be understood that it speaks as much about times past as—and to a greater degree —about the possibility of a community in Poland of the transformative years, about solidarity in the new society. For whatever Solidarity might have been, today it remains a communal challenge, which for literature means the examination of common discourses: of the language that we use to establish understanding and in our descriptions of a "shared" reality. Literature shows us, therefore, the discourses we use in the building of a community. In stating what Solidarity once was, it asks what solidarity can be today. It is for this reason that literature, as if impulsively or intuitively, introduces into communication a double problem: it broadens the community by including groups hitherto unnoticed, and it breaks with unity. The broadening of community is expressed through representation of others: those that do not wish to submit to any communal operations, as well as those that—and this is much more dangerous—are perceived as foreign. The very existence of these others signifies that the vision of a homogeneous society is a utopia that will, sooner or later, lead to symbolic violence. Solidarity of a democratic society is expressed in a constant (never end-oriented) renewal of interhuman bonds that are not dependent on group affiliations, bonds numerous, if slight. It is precisely this kind of change in attitudes, in other words the renewal of the idea of solidarity and its confrontation with social differences, that literature is advocating.

The second method of breaking with unities is governed by the same purpose. It relies on the tearing of associations that were formed in public discourse, and especially in the language of new politics, between the fight for democracy and the power attained thereby. At stake here is ensuring that the politics of a new government and the governance of new politicians, the media and the parliamentary discourse, and the fusion of a free market economy with the Church's blessing, do not cover up existing differences, that they do not absorb the past as a monolithic mass to be used as a unanimous vote of support for themselves, and as an argument allowing for the exclusion of some groups from public debate.

Literature does not help to resolve any of these problems. Exposing differences, it reminds us that they exist.

Solidarity, Literature

The sentiments expressed by the historian Jerzy Holzer in his 1984 book *"Solidarność" 1980–1981: Geneza i historia*, regarding the lasting impact of the experiences of the Solidarity epoch on Polish society, can be answered today, more than twenty years after those events, with the words of a sociologist: "the impressive manifestation of a civil society rebelling against a regime did not lead to a pluralistic, tolerant and responsible civil society, which would be capable of dealing with conflicts and changes, and which could rouse the trust of its citizens toward each other and their government. In all of the post-communist countries, the desire for personal gain, mafia networks, and widespread cynicism appear to be stronger than respect for law and political engagement."[38]

To put it differently: past experiences do not seem like a long-lasting legacy. If they have lasted, it is as a source of successive misunderstandings and uncertainties. Literature, trapped in the pincers of revolutionary longings and conservative presentiments (we dream of change, and suppose that everything will remain as of old), every once in a while, though very faintly, calls out for a revolt, and much more frequently, and quite distinctly, brings social frustrations to a boil. Unable to distance itself from discourses of collective confrontations, it replicates idioms of conflict. It is easier, therefore, to count it among political party programs, than it is to take from it a lesson in difference, which would allow us to view our lives from a different perspective. Yet, despite the miserable state of our literature, which reflects the miserable state of public debates, it is possible to see within it precisely what happened to the Polish evaluation of Solidarity.

For our thinking about August falls under the changing rule of three complexes. The first is a complex of greatness. We fall prey to it when we believe that Solidarity was such a significant innovation that nothing could actually fulfill it, and that—faced with such a magnificent past—the most we can do is humbly preserve it in a nostalgic memory. The second complex is related to purity. It reigns over us whenever we think that behind every great cause is hidden some kind of baseness; that every revolution, every noble event in a collective history must be tainted, or perhaps even orchestrated, by traitors and informants; that behind every Solidarity stands Public Security agents; behind the Round Table, negotiations in Magdalenka;[39] and behind every reform, low political ambitions. Whenever we think in this way, we perceive the public sphere as a domain of dirt, reserving the notion of nobility for the private sphere only. The third complex concerns identity; we are under its spell when we suppose that everything of historical importance is created by people who are identical to one another, and that Others—ethnic, religious, or sexual "misfits"—constitute an obstacle on the road toward a good society. The first complex causes us to see the past as too great to be repeated, according to the second we look at history with too great a revulsion to treat it as an example, while the third complex makes us notice only that which is similar to ourselves throughout history, rather than that which is different. Here is the sum total of the paradoxes. If we translate them into the present, it will transpire that these complexes, not so much revealed as reproduced in literature, paralyze social communication. They command our understanding of the way in which reality is shaped, or rather, they create a paradoxical tension between radical disapproval of contemporaneity, and civic idleness; between calling for the creation of a "Fourth Commonwealth," and being satisfied with spectacles of moral condemnation. For contemporaneity, much like Solidarity, is perceived as too distant to reach, too foul to participate in, and too diverse to act in (history is created by people who are like one another);[40] we either meekly wait, or look upon it with disgust, or concentrate on the elimination of social differences.

Thus our literature reveals (reveals rather than problematizes) a society that dreams of a revolution without solidarity. We fantasize about self-instigating change, one that will take place without our participation, or without the necessity of making plans with our neighbor. We do not trust our neighbors if they are like us, and we do not accept them if they are different. Today's motto states: "Revolution—yes, Kowalski—no!"[41] Nevertheless, it is obvious that without a "neighborly society," a change of social structure will always be limited to the exchange of ruling parties.

Having revealed the three complexes mentioned above, literature appears to be enticing us to mature at long last, to part—in other words—with the fantasy of a community so great, so pure, and so homogenous as to be superhuman. This kind of Solidarity never existed, the novels argue, and so its return is impossible. For this reason, if prose today—in a devastated public space and a de-solidarized society—wants to query the relationship between freedom and community once again, it has to do so against the legendary Solidarity, and in the name of a possible solidarity. This prompts us to think about ideals that are worthy of our participation in political life, about politics that can take into consideration small matters and fend off the temptations of small-mindedness, and about a society that enjoys its diversity. Still, though advocating departure from nostalgic fantasies, our prose is unable to present a vision of a better society. Its weakness does have some merit, however: desperately helpless when faced with contemporary life, and helplessly despairing of the loss of an ideal, there is only one thing left for literature to do—represent ever more social differences. It is precisely then—when we encounter descriptions of that period that are controversially different from our own beliefs, when we read novels about a highly diversified society—that we will be able to understand that Solidarity began when very different people decided to talk to one another. Herein lies the germ of the most revolutionary idea of our time.

—Translated by Agnieszka Polakowska

Notes

A modified and extended version of this paper has been published in Polish in *Polska do wymiany: Późna nowoczesność i nasze wielkie narracje* (Warsaw: WAB, 2009).

1. In this context, see Domański's pioneering book, *Polska klasa średnia*.

2. According to Domański, at the beginning of the nineties, "from 45 to 50% of adult Poles suddenly started to identify themselves with the middle class" (5).

3. Unlike its English equivalent "pulp," the Polish word *miazga* does not have a secondary connotation of cheap, sensational literature—Trans.

4. The English translation is entitled *A Question of Reality*, which does not fully convey the meaning of "nierzeczywistość"—the absence, lack of reality—or unreality—Trans.

5. Nowakowski, 139.

6. The corrosion of communal ties was evident in other books as well: Kazimierz Orłoś wrote about self-poisoning with lies in *The Third Lie* (*Trzecie kłamstwo*, 1980); Bogdan Madej about the slow descent of Polish life into petty wheeling and dealing in *Rat Ointment* (*Maść na szczury*, 1977); and Jan Komolka about the totalitarian impulse—based on repression of the "Other"—being a form of integration in small societies in *An Escape to Heaven* (*Ucieczka do nieba*, completed 1975, published 1980).

7. As Jean Baudrillard succinctly put it, "this symbolic disobligation is accompanied by a general deregulation." *The Intelligence of Evil*, 50.

8. Konwicki, *Mała apokalipsa*, 8.

9. This phrase is taken from the lyrics of Jacek Kaczmarski's song "Walls" ("Mury," 1978), which quickly became the unofficial "anthem" of Solidarity—Trans.

10. Szaruga, 28.

11. Sergiusz Kowalski, *Krytyka solidarnościowego rozumu* (Warsaw: PEN, 1989).

12. See Friszke's article "Głos solidarności" in *Rzeczpospolita* (July 9/10, 2005), where he speaks about the creation of the *Tygodnik Solidarność*, and thus the period of 1980–81. The author mentions, among other things, the conflicted circles of experts from the Society for Educational Courses (TKN) and the Committee for Social Self-Defence of the Worker's Defense Committee (KSS KOR), the opinions about the candidacy of Andrzej Micewski for chief editor (Friszke claims that "the editors of pre-August underground press had the worst opinion about the chief editor"), and the departure from the editorial board of Kazimierz Dziewanowski (who decided that, since his opinions could not appear in the *Tygodnik Solidarność*, "the representation of diverse beliefs

and stances that were part of the widespread Solidarity movement" became impossible in the paper).

13. Adam Zagajewski named this transference mechanism in 1986: "The disturbing facet of antitotalitarianism is that one of its greatest sources of strength, its splendid spiritual tension, depends on placing all the world's evil in one place: totalitarianism. One then gets a schematic image of the cosmos, where the evil of totalitarianism is opposed to the good of antitotalitarianism. Lo and behold, the miraculous and angelic cure, we become better than we really are, for all evil has been sucked out by the totalitarian beast. We become a little like angels. I read Polish poetry, of which a great part now expresses an antitotalitarian spirituality. I read these poems, my own sometimes as well, and I think that they were written by morally flawless beings. Angels write poems, angels read poems. At such times I think maliciously that life in slavery is not deprived of certain pleasures, for one has the Great Alibi. They, the totalitarians, are evil. We are good and innocent. Order reigns in the world, even though it is extremely unjust: they keep us enslaved, we oppose them." *Solidarity and Solitude*, 68–69.

14. The figure of "genesis" already functioned during the years when Solidarity was born, but it was given a name later. "The legend of August 1980 constitutes, in the collective imagination of Poles, a kind of conception myth. This peculiar moment of the past, like the times of innocent childhood, simultaneously charms and affronts us with its naivety" Gawin, 68; "Solidarity is a myth, but a myth in the true sense of the word—a story about the beginning, about the source from which spring constitutive norms and ideals." Krasnodębski, *Rzeczpospolita*, June 2, 2001.

15. "The miracle of solidarity really did take place, and there are, fortunately, still some people who can remember it, and who are ready to testify to it," Stawrowski, "O zapomnianej solidarności," 62; "It was almost a miracle," Szczepański, 100; "It was a miracle," Gowin, *Rzeczpospolita*, June 16, 2001; "It was an experience of a peculiar 'time of grace,' of a saintly 'time,' of a challenge to transcend our own selves," Stawrowski, "Solidarność znaczy więź," 17; "I still believe that Solidarity was a gift from God, and that such will be her place in history," Rymkiewicz, *Tygodnik Solidarność* 44 (1993): 11–12; "From the point of view of our present experience, Solidarity becomes so unreal that I can only interpret it with the language of miracles." Śpiewak, "'Cała polityka sprowadza się do boksu.' Z socjologiem P.Ś. rozmawia Małgorzata Subotić," *Rzeczpospolita*, June 24, 2000.

16. A peculiar position is occupied by Czesław Dziekanowski's book *Frutti di mare*. It is a record of the "linguistic state of consciousness" of all of August's participants in Gdańsk: the laborers, Solidarity" activists, and members of the Polish People's Republic. The author decided to give this chaos a single trajectory, however: that of an evolution of individuals and the entire collective from the state of disintegration (and purely self-entitled attitudes), through an increasing identification with those killed in December 1970, to a

community whose cohesion is noticed (as well as valued and respected) by the party-affiliated shipyard director.

17. The expression "power trembles" ("moc truchleje") originates in a poem by Franciszek Karpiński "God is born, power trembles" ("Bóg się rodzi, moc truchleje," 1792), now a popular Polish Christmas carol—Trans.

18. Here is the beginning of the prole's—admittedly daring—monologue: "I cannot complain. I am built coarsely to a large extent, as a tool of labor I am efficient and widely applicable. As a truthsayer, I add right away that after the accident, with which bad fate punished me during my first days of work as a rust remover at the shipyard known by the name of V. Lenin, my right side is more efficient than the other. This is laughable in comparison with the workers who were reduced to ashes in the same accident. True, it makes itself known by panging or stiffening, and sometime even by the swelling up of the injured left leg, to such an extent that I have to give it a break, but this happens only after some 20 to 26 hours of incessant, deadline-driven work. When, by means of action, we pose a merciless challenge to the entire world." Głowacki, 6.

19. The termination of this "contract," or the breaking of the "anti-socialist agreement," actually took place only toward the end of the 1980s. In the fourth issue of *Brulion* (1987/1988) there appeared a review of two poetry volumes: Gwido Zlatkes' *Song about Treason and Other Poems (Piosenka o zdradzie i inne wiersze*, 1987) and Helena Komorowska's *A Steel Spiderweb (Żelazna pajęczyna*, 1987). Entitled "J'Accuse" and written by MET, the text de-mystified the mechanism of a literary system in which a suitable biography was sufficient for becoming a poet: "What is the harm in the printing of poems by Gwido Zlatkes, who with an unquestionable passion worked in the Solidarity Press Agency (Agencja Solidarności AS). What is the harm of it: we have the paper and the machines, and the author does not have any objections! Gwido Zlatkes, Helena Violetta Komorowska, Leszek Szaruga, Tomasz Jastrun, Lothar Herbst. What will happen when it becomes clear that poems and (may God prevent it) novels are also being written by other activists of the opposition?" MET's diatribe was aimed at the identification of political merit with literary abilities, at the application of ethics as a substitute for aesthetic criteria, at the use of biography and politics as measures of poetic value. The contributors of *Brulion* thus hit upon a weak point of oppositional culture: its conviction that an anticommunist, anti-totalitarian, and pro-democratic attitude automatically engenders good literature. The unveiling of this weakness immediately led to the exposure of another—the mechanisms of concealment and discussion restrictions that were created by the oppositional culture ("one does not speak of the weaknesses of an endangered culture," "one does not question the value of independent writing"). Within the framework of communication thus ritualized, the "backing up of arguments" replaced true exchange of opinions. This is precisely what *Brulion* did not want to agree to. With its critical texts, which were, after all, very modest at the beginning, it provoked its elders to expound their arguments, to "stick out their tongue": it

then transpired that, within the parameters of this tongue, past justifications were losing their significance and were being replaced with authoritarian impulses, which made it possible to publically demand someone's silence. In the process of the debate begun by *Brulion* it was possible to see that hierarchical language is incomplete, inefficient, and ineffective, and simultaneously still in possession of claims to representing "that which is most important."

20. Stawrowski, "Doświadczenie 'Solidarności,'" 115.

21. Herling-Grudziński, *Volcano and Miracle*, 237.

22. In this sense, the case files, the vetting, and "Wildstein's list"—as a spectacle of morality, rather than a pragmatic solution to a problem of public life—represent the defeat of solidaristic legacy in its encounter with that which is petty. For all of these things lead not to the delineation of regulations (i.e., an order against the holding of public office), but to ostracism, the exclusion of "suspicious" people, and also (perhaps most importantly) to the attainment of a better position in the power struggle. It is difficult to overlook the fact that literature, especially drama, quite quickly merged into this current of public life (i.e., *Miś Kolabo*), reproducing the basic gestures of politicians who "help" society build a new community: this time a community of the angry, the unblemished, the uncompromising, those who will banish the "besmirched" beyond the margins of life.

23. Gustav, the hero of *The List of Adultresses* (*Spis cudzołożnic*), tries to escape from this very trap. He has a choice of either the heroism of battle, elevated by association with "collective history," or the insignificance of private existence. His method consists of appropriating a high style to speak about private matters. The heroic-comical effect delivers a blow to both sides of this tightly bound arrangement: laughable is the hero who speaks of his erotic and alcoholic exploits in a high style, and "inhuman" appears the tradition that makes it possible for an individual to find his place in it only if he is willing to become "a fragment of something written long ago," "an excerpt from a bitter allegory"—only if the blood in his veins transforms into "cellulose." Pilch, 122.

24. Herbert, 113.

25. Tischner, 11–12.

26. I consider these novels in the section devoted to the years of 1989–95 because I believe that they represent a belated reaction to the corruption and demoralization of Solidarity circles. This is because their authors use a phantasm of unity (the idea of Solidarity as an internally undifferentiated movement) to criticise Polish political life. It is from this perspective that they describe the disintegration of the myth, which occurred in the first half of the nineties rather than the first years of the twenty-first century.

27. This date of commencement, like the previous ones, is to a large extent provisional. If there is something that speaks for the year of 1995, it is the publication of Andrzej Stasiuk's *The White Raven* (*Biały kruk*) and Izabela Filipiak's *Absolute Amnesia* (*Absolutna amnezja*), which introduce into public

discourse a clear difference in attitude—the ostentatious distancing of self vis-à-vis the history of mass resistance—and even signal (if Filipiak's novel is taken into consideration) that history creates its own hierarchy, which devalues private life.

28. Moomins are troll-like, extremely good-natured characters from a book series by Tove Jansson. The series has inspired a number of TV, radio, and comic strip adaptations, enjoying considerable popularity in Poland—Trans.

29. Zagajewski, *Solidarity and Solitude*, 62.

30. Nowakowski, *Homo Polonicus*, 34.

31. Stasiuk, *White Raven*, 200.

32. The name of *Drift's* hero clearly echoes that of Lech Wałęsa, the hero of Solidarity and Poland's president from 1990 to 1995. What is less obvious is the connotation of aimless wandering in the name (from *wałęsać się*, "to wander about")—Trans.

33. Siemion, *Niskie łąki*, 49.

34. See Penn; Graff.

35. See one of the most important, and most effectively forgotten books devoted to this subject: Świderski's *Gdańsk and Athens* (*Gdańsk i Ateny*). In its third chapter ("On Democratic Organizations") the author writes: "During the eighties, two models of unmediated democracy were tried in Poland: beside strikes—street demonstrations. Both forms were characterized by the fact that 1) everyone, men as well as women, was able to participate in them, and 2) that everyone could speak (*isegoria*) about any subject they deemed significant. Simultaneously, both strikes and street demonstrations were characterized by 3) organization, structural cohesion, and institutionalization, as well as 4) mobility: their models could be transported to other places, other cities. It seems that the first, symbolic reactions of Solidarity were simultaneously *brave and dialogic*, and thus democratic in the Greek understanding of the word." Świderski, 141–43.

36. In fact, Cezary Michalski's *Force of Repellence* (*Siła odpychania*) speaks of this, for the novel shows liberal democracy to be a force that deconstructs *demos*, and leads to a "democracy without the people." See also an inspiring article by Agata Bielik-Robson, where she writes about a surprising turn in the history of Polish intelligentsia after 1989: not wishing to abandon their function as instructors of "symbolic codes," and simultaneously without having access to power, the intelligentsia begins to "break democracy," meaning it starts to proclaim the necessity of separating the private sphere from the public one. The rarefied rhetoric of contempt for the "mass" quality of contemporary culture is turned against past bonds of loyalty (engendered already by romanticism), which ameliorated individual alienation, and reminded people of the responsibility of "solidarity with the people." The author writes: "Is then . . . the experience of street Solidarity, the positive experience of community in action, not that missing lesson reminding intelligentsia of the role

that it has abandoned? Does it not suggest experience, in which a language must set its roots in order not to sound false? To the usual accusation that this role is anachronistic I respond right away—not at all. For if we define it as first and foremost a role of articulation, and thus of providing the community with clear languages in which it would be able to express its goals, there is nothing anachronistic about it. In the meantime, the Polish intelligentsia after 1989 not only does not favor the principle of articulation, and along with it the ordering of the public sphere, but quite to the contrary: having lost contact with local experience, and choosing for itself confusing linguistic hybrids, it brought about an almost complete paralysis of social communication." Bielik-Robson, 140–41.

37. See Żiżek's statement: "It would be interesting to read once again the initial program of 'Solidarity'—there is nothing there about capitalism. Much is said, however, on the subject of social dreams. I think that we should fight for this legacy; it is a fundamental matter, otherwise—if this dream about communal solidarity disappears—we will live in a terrifying society, where market rivalry will co-exist with a new type of tribalism. It will be horrific to live in such a society. We, post-communist countries, to put it in a marxi-messianic style, have a mission of discovering a new form—I'm not kidding!—well, I am kidding, but I am thinking about it in all seriousness—of discovering a new form of social life, which would be able to avoid old snares. Perhaps we are capable of saving humanity." Żiżek, 13.

38. Hassner, 59–60.

39. Magdalenka was the site of numerous talks between representatives of the PRL, Solidarity, and the Catholic Church, which took place both prior and during the Round Table negotiations, and aimed at establishing a common platform for said negotiations—Trans.

40. We wait, therefore, for the attainment of a similar state of social homogeny in contemporary times as that which we project upon the "solidaristic" past, and which had never actually existed.

41. The surname "Kowalski" is equivalent to the ubiquitous "Smith."

Contested Modernity

New Drama in Poland

Tamara Trojanowska

Dramatic Fever

Polish critics have quite recently proclaimed a spectacular renaissance of Polish theatre and drama, after almost a decade of showing little interest in the genre despite the intense and varied activities of its practitioners. This revival cannot be attributed to any one factor. It is partly generational, for it coincides with the appearance on Polish stages of over eighty young theatre directors, and almost as many playwrights over the last few years. However, defining it in this way is possible only by narrowing the traditional understanding of a generational gap from twenty to just a few years.[1] The revival is also aesthetic in nature, as the young theatre and drama practitioners proceed to transform theatre language, redefine the relationship between stage and audience, and rethink their own role in society. It is the last of these three aspects of the recent changes that I wish to address in this essay. Even though Polish contemporary drama certainly did not come into existence in the twenty-first century, as some critics would like us to believe,[2] what has changed in the last few years, and what makes young playwriting unique, is its keen interest in the social function of the genre. I will take a look at some aspects of this interest, and particularly at the place of the new plays in public discourse.

The much-discussed renewal of Polish drama and theatre is the result of many favorable circumstances. One of them is the conclusion, by the end of the 1990s, of a lengthy and turbulent restructuring of theatre as an institution, and the subsequent stabilization of its new structural framework. Another is the new crop of young, talented, and dynamic playwrights and theatre directors, whose interests in the promotion of contemporary drama happily coincide with the rapid proliferation of new dramatic texts. The very active involvement of theatre critics in the promotion of the young playwrights and the appearance of alternative venues for theatre marketing also play an important (in many cases a decisive) role in the revitalization of the genre. A special credit is due to theatre managers and directors who are now in their forties for promoting their younger colleagues and peers: Anna Augustynowicz (b. 1959) in Szczecin, Jacek Głomb (b. 1964) in Legnica, Piotr Kruszczyński (b. 1967) in Wałbrzych until 2008, Paweł Miśkiewicz (b. 1964) first in Wrocław and then in Warsaw, Maciej Nowak (b. 1964) in Gdańsk (now a director of the Theatre Institute in Warsaw), Adam Sroka (b. 1959) in Radom, and Bartosz Szydłowski (b. 1968) in Cracow. Numerous new festivals, workshops, and stage readings, which are often organized in provincial towns and smaller cities, complete the helpful network of venues for young dramaturgy, and confirm an important new characteristic of Polish theatre life—its decisive decentralization. Even the best of the young directors work outside of the once established theatre centers of Warsaw, Cracow, or Wrocław, and many of the best theatres are now located in the provinces, though some of these provincial cultural centers have been fading lately.[3]

It is not surprising, therefore, that in the last few years, unlike the preceding decade, Polish criticism has been afflicted with a high dramatic fever. It is worth remembering here that, in the 1990s, drama attracted the attention of only a few specialists in the field, and did not even begin to receive recognition comparable to new poetry or prose.[4] As I have argued elsewhere, "the generational approach, privileged in the criticism of the so-called 'new' prose and poetry, was fruitless when applied to the dramatic output. The distinct sense of 'otherness,' the rejection of immediate predecessors, and the initial refusal to compromise its aesthetic and intellectual programs, were all missing."[5] In recent years, however, what had once been missing appeared by storm. The young debutants have speedily produced a hefty crop of texts, by now running in the hundreds. They have created their own distinct artistic profiles, defining themselves as different from their not-so-much-older forerunners, and—being media savvy—they almost immediately attract widespread and heated press coverage and critical attention.[6] New names are entering this hot market in quick succession on the heels of those who are not much older.

Most of the presently popular playwrights have had their debuts in the new millennium, thus avoiding the thorny road through systemic reforms of the arts that was commonly encountered by writers just a few years older. Some of these artists managed to join in the momentum of the new situation, as is the case with Marek Pruchniewski (b. 1962), the prolific screenwriter Cezary Harasimowicz (b. 1955), or the late debutant Anna Burzyńska (b. 1957). New texts that would have until quite recently waited in a long line-up to be published in the respected monthly *Dialog*,[7] and then (maybe and cautiously) tried out in one or two theatres, are now cramming periodicals, competing anthologies, the internet, and most of all, the stages.[8] Since the playwrights' peers, over eighty in total, have become theatre managers and directors, the fate of contemporary Polish drama has been sealed: theatre debut has become easier than ever before, theatre initiatives promoting new dramaturgy have multiplied, and critical wars have made theatre a rather zesty topic.

Polish Culture Wars

Indeed, in the most popular dailies and periodicals, theatre critics have been fighting over the new phenomenon with unprecedented fervor. The core of this struggle seems ideological, even though aesthetics is an important argument for both the supporters and the challengers of young playwriting. However, this sharp split, parallel to the one in Polish post-1990 identity politics, is more value than ideology oriented, and thus fits the description by James Hunter of a "culture war."[9] For the main issue at stake in much of the public discourse in Poland is, without a doubt, the broadly understood cultural identity of Polish society, with national self-knowledge, self-image, and memory serving as its main battlefields. This increasingly vicious polemic is part of the now more than a hundred-years-old Polish discourse of modernity, with its twenty-year history in post-1990 Poland marking a new chapter. Although new, this chapter already has an impressive bibliography: from countless articles by such influential figures of Polish political and intellectual life as Adam Michnik and his team at *Gazeta Wyborcza*, as well as the main challengers of *Wyborcza*'s decade-long dominance on the media market: *Rzeczpospolita* (with such journalists as Rafał Ziemkiewicz and Bronisław Wildstein) and *Dziennik*, to compelling historical, sociological, and cultural studies by such scholars as Marek Cichocki, Antoni Dudek, Maria Janion, Zdzisław Krasnodębski, Marcin Król, Ryszard Legutko, Andrzej Mencwel, Jadwiga Staniszkis, Paweł Śpiewak, and Andrzej Walicki, to name just a few. It is impossible to summarize the ebbs and flows of this explosive discourse here, but some of its arguments may shed a useful light on the public offensive of drama and theatre in the last decade.

In his excellent book *Power and Memory* (*Władza i pamięć*), Cichocki, a philosopher and political scientist, analyzes the century-old hostility between the Polish radical intelligentsia and the dominant Polish paradigms of gentry and Romantic culture, including their links to Catholicism. The main thrust of his argument is that the radical thinkers in Poland have always perceived an inherent incompatibility between modernity and these cultural traditions. Hence the fight for modernity, both on the left and on the right (as exemplified, respectively, by the works of Stanisław Brzozowski and Roman Dmowski), has been imagined as a necessary negation, and in some cases as a destruction of these traditions. In short, Cichocki's diagnosis is that:

> Modernity comes to us as a rapid wave of modernization. . . . The change that modernity brings with it is thus not a result of the work of many generations, nor does it emerge from civilizational processes, but each time constitutes a violence that history inflicts upon people. It thus becomes a fatalistic necessity. The wave of modernization is very rapid, and its impulse derived from the outside, therefore only very rarely do Poles manage to give modernity their own character, and to use its dynamics for the growth of civilizational tissue in Poland. Hence, Polish attitudes to modernity usually take extreme forms—Poles either reject modernity, or they lose their heads in it.[10]

Undoubtedly, for the last two decades the main battle between the promoters and challengers of Poland's new project of modernization after the collapse of communism has been fought in and by the media. Almost from its first issue, the chief Polish daily *Gazeta Wyborcza* (now second in circulation to the tabloid *Fakt*) fashioned itself as a source of uncontested influence on the opinion- and identity-forming market.[11] Its personal, financial, and finally political connections made it part of a very effective oligarchy that kept command over intellectual life in Poland, affecting also the interpretation of Polish affairs abroad since it became the primary source of information for foreign journalists, who trusted the liberal self-definition of their source. This self-definition is not entirely misleading, but its understanding of liberalism does differ from the meaning given to it by western intellectuals who, as Śpiewak reminds us, see liberalism as Richard Rorty once saw it: "self-ironic, self-critical, constantly self-doubting. It refuses itself—and here lies its strength—the right to arbitrary demands. It rebuffs not only dogmatism, but also paternalism. It is a culture that avoids 'head-on collisions,' and sometimes even sides with a gracious silencing of fundamental, perhaps even non-erasable differences."[12] Any reader of *Wyborcza* knows how far its rhetoric is removed from this model. It is ironic, critical, and doubting all right, but completely misses the "self" part of the equation. The daily has been nothing short of paternalistic for most of the 1990s, and it still espouses such a voice. Finally, like most other media, it thrives on—rather than avoids—head-on collisions.

In countless battles over modernization, the sharpest conflicts have developed around a few key issues. One is the evaluation of dominant cultural traditions and their role in the creation of a modern Polish nation. The two extreme views follow Cichocki's diagnosis, and either decidedly condemn these cultural paradigms as incompatible with modern society, and therefore disposable, or—conversely—deem them sacred but mortally endangered, and therefore in need of unconditional preservation. They either see the gentry, the Romantic, and the Catholic paradigms as main sites of backwardness, obscurantism, xenophobia, anti-Semitism, and unwarranted worship of national martyrdom, thus presenting them as self-evident targets for apparently well-deserved attacks, or they categorically equate them with national identity and sovereignty, and see them as a bulwark against all modern evils. Another set of conflict-ridden issues centers around the evaluation of Poland's more recent communist past, and its modernizing aspirations. *Wyborcza's* attitude toward such critical political issues as de-communization and lustration of public officials, for example, has been unequivocally negative, to the point of absolving the system's implementers of all wrongdoings.[13] In turn, the opposite view holds that we should evaluate the communist past with unequivocal moral measures. Polish collective memory has been a subject of similarly dualistic, and in the long run harmful assessments, seen as a site of either dangerous national phantasmagorias in need of quick and decisive eradication, or—on the contrary—of incontestable truths in need of unreserved protection.[14] The heated debates over such controversial, but also narrower, issues as abortion, gay marriage, in vitro fertilization, and religion in schools, not to mention the shape of the national literary canon, have quickly followed suit with similarly ferocious divisiveness, where both extremes hold each other in a grip of mutual and perpetual dependency.

The clash of the extremes that dominated the political and ideological fronts in the 1990s had to finally face a more open and sophisticated debate about the most important question of "how to preserve some elements of tradition, while modernizing Poland, or in other words, how to balance Polishness and its place in Europe."[15] The relentless crusade for modernization against tradition, and the obsessive defense of Polish national traditions against all signs of modernity, had to give way to more viable civilizational alternatives that try to transcend the fundamental cultural antagonisms imbedded in a Polish discourse of modernity. Already in the mid-1990s, something new was brewing on the identity market within a circle of young, bright, well-read liberal-conservative intellectuals, who tried to create an alternative, modern counterbalance to the influence of both demagogic modernizers, and equally demagogic traditionalists. Some of them resurfaced in the first decade of the new millennium when Michnik's *Gazeta Wyborcza* lost its hegemony over the intellectual market with the launching of *Europa-Tygodnik Idei*, initially a supplement of the tabloid *Fakt*, then of the new daily *Dziennik*, and now of *Newsweek*, and with Paweł Lisicki—a conservative journalist—taking up the post of editor-in-chief of *Rzeczpospolita* in September 2006.[16] The discussion about Poland's past and present, about its traditions and current modernization entered a different and more interesting phase with this long-overdue diversification of the media market. The debates in *Europa* that concentrate on the global context of Polish problems and present the views of acclaimed international intellectuals on the most pertinent concerns facing the world have opened new a discursive space. The already-mentioned scholars and their in-depth analyses of Poland's historical experiences and current options have also shaped this space.[17]

In the context of the periodic resurfacing of the main conflicts over modernity, it is not a coincidence that theatre acquired such extraordinary importance in the very late 1990s and the first few years of the new millennium. Granted, as I have already mentioned, there were compelling reasons why it could start playing a much more significant role then, rather than a few years earlier. Yet I suspect that the vigorous battle for its shape and public function that has lately unraveled in the press has a lot to do with these persistent questions of modernization, even if most theatre critics prefer to see it as part of a primarily ideological struggle.[18] The first sign of this connection is the strong divisive line between the two camps of, on the one side, unconditional enthusiasts of young theatre and, on the other, its uncompromising rejecters. Roman Pawłowski, Joanna Derkaczew, and Joanna Targoń (of *Gazeta Wyborcza*), Piotr Gruszczyński (once of *Tygodnik Powszechny*), Łukasz Drewniak (once the editor-in-chief of *Didaskalia*), and Paweł Mościcki (of *Krytyka Polityczna*) play the leading role in the first camp.[19] They have invested much of their careers and growing prestige in the promotion of young theatre and drama. Others, like Grzegorz Niziołek (b. 1962), Tadeusz Słobodzianek (b. 1955), and Maciej Nowak have joined their ranks in very practical ways, for all three have effective outlets for such concrete promotion.[20] Some of their allies come from ideologically akin, but professionally unrelated quarters, as is the case with Sławomir Sierakowski (b. 1979), the already risen star of the Polish new left, its main activist, and the editor of its key forum, the quarterly *Krytyka Polityczna*. Their most engaged (and enraged) opponents are Elżbieta Baniewicz of *Twórczość*; Paweł Głowacki (b. 1965, the main theatre critic in *Dzien-nik Polski* in Cracow; Elżbieta Morawiec; Tomasz Mościcki (b. 1965), a photographer and theatre critic of *Dziennik*; Janusz R. Kowalczyk of *Rzeczpospolita*; or Rafał Węgrzyniak, a theatre scholar. Such "centrists" as Jacek Kopciński, the editor-in-chief of *Teatr*;[21] Jacek Sieradzki, an editor-in-chief of *Dialog*; or Jacek Wakar, a reviewer in *Dziennik*, can do little to mediate the antagonisms.

The critical debate swells daily with new and usually increasingly infuriated voices. Its careful study, including its fairly recent self-assessments,[22] leaves the reader with a gnawing question about whether such an exercise is worth the effort. After all, theatre life in Poland and the new drama on its stages are not limited to the subject of this debate, namely the collision between, on the one side, socially and politically engaged, leftist theatre and, on the other, universal, philosophical, and artistic theatre. Are the promoters of socially and politically engaged theatre agents of a leftist takeover of Polish culture, and of the ideological conspiracy against its most valuable traditions, as some of their adversaries claim?[23] Or are they simply defenders of the underdog, lovers of tolerance, equality, and progress, and the only ideological option that treats the arts seriously, as they would like to be perceived?[24] Are the opponents of such theatre old-fashioned and nostalgic admirers of the modernist idea of art's autonomy, or are they just reasonable champions of quality acting, directing, and playwriting working against intellectual and artistic kitsch? Do they have legitimate concerns with the new cultural and identity politics in leftist theatre of the young, or have they simply carried over the worn-out association of engaged art with socialist realism, propaganda, and totalitarianism into a new situation in the new millennium? Is the project of Polish political theatre dangerous or necessary for Polish culture? Does its shape matter? Will this debate be lost, and if so how soon, in the yellowing pages of daily newspapers and periodicals, or in the still more transient webpages?

Having more than once lost patience with this debate, I still believe that it is an important part of a much bigger issue, indeed a decisive one in the shaping of the public examination of Polish identity, for it poses the question of how to effectively discuss the richly diversified and rapidly changing cultural phenomena, or—to put it another way—how to truly debate values. The question of whether such a discussion will continue as an antagonistic battle of two irreconcilable extremes, or whether it will manage to negotiate between the opposed positions, remains as intriguing as the question of whether Polish politics can transcend similar hostilities for the benefit of public good. Both questions are rooted, as Andrzej Rychard suggests, not so much in the different interests of the fighting sides, but rather in their different values.[25]

So far, the discussion has been developing alongside the division identified by Cichocki, and has created two—both equally fictitious—images of critics and theatre artists. One image, created by the "modernizers," separates them into two groups: the first is composed of the young, progressive, engaged, courageous, tolerant, and transgressive—in short, modern and preferably leftist people—the "Enlightened"; the other consists of the old-fashioned, dissatisfied, conservative, preservationist worshipers of autonomous art—in short, the traditionalist, and preferably rightist "Sarmatians."[26] Another way of framing this opposition is to present it as a conflict between those who understand the unavoidably political dimension of human existence, and the need for an artistically revolutionary politics of art, and those who understand politics too narrowly, do not grasp the codependence of engagement and autonomy, and dismiss political theatre on this basis (as goes Paweł Mościcki's argument).[27]

The alternative image reverses this rationale and evaluation of the stances, placing on the one side the cynical, leftist appropriators of theatre as a public forum (see Węgrzyniak), the manipulative creators of cultural facts (e.g., in Tomasz Mościcki's articles), the promoters of obsessive vulgarity, interventionist, journalistic or socialist-realist poetics, and mediocrity (in Baniewicz's texts), and—on the other side—genuine creators of valuable, lasting art that stands the test of universal aesthetic and intellectual criteria. Never mind that the old often belong to the same generation as the young; that the progressives have some very traditional leanings and nostalgias; that the preservationists often rightfully demand originality and basic quality; that the "Enlightened" often replicate uncritically the latest craze, while the "Sarmatians" complain about the mutilation of the classics as if there had been no Romantics, no Wyspiański, no Grotowski or Swinarski in the past, as if they forgot that, after all, the now enshrined Romantics were once the *enfants terribles* of the nineteenth century.

The fallout of this critical war is at least twofold. On the one hand, the rivalry of ideological worldviews and aesthetic inclinations has brought theatre into the center of public debate, and revived a very important and overdue discussion about the role and place of theatre in cultural and political life. Theatre has once again become important for the young generation which has its cult stages and directors. On the other hand, as Wakar has noticed, the intensification of the opposite positions to the point of demagogy has paradoxically led to the disappearance of public debate.[28] What started as an exciting battle for the new theatre, for its new function and aesthetics, has turned into—even for the devoted reader from afar—an intellectually tedious squabble among individual critics, whose personal attacks and ironies are easily predictable, and whose opinions about other critics, artists, and productions are often unreliable. A potential debate has thus turned into professions of faith, and only very recently has regained its initial seriousness. This has had a number of negative, damaging effects on artists as well. Instead of critics to accompany, but also assess their growth, they have had to deal with either uncritical acolytes or bitter enemies.

YOUNG DRAMA

What is the actual material that the warring factions throw into this battle? On the one hand, they speak of the new playwriting and its impact on audience sensitivities, theatre language, and public communication. On the other, they refer to the young, controversial, and "hot" theatre directors whose frantic activity has been transforming the theatre scene. The trajectories of new drama and new theatre do not always coincide. To some of the star directors, Polish drama, contemporary or otherwise, has had no appeal. What for decades has been the foundation of Polish theatre repertoires and a director's career is of little interest to, for example, Grzegorz Jarzyna, Maja Kleczewska, or Krzysztof Warlikowski.[29] They transform the aesthetics of Polish theatre by reinterpreting classics other than Polish (from Sophocles, Shakespeare, and Racine to Dostoyevsky, Bűchner, and Brecht), and the work of their other-than-Polish contemporaries (including David Harrower, Brad Fraser, Sarah Kane, Bernard Koltes, Tony Kushner, and George Walker).

Conversely, the new texts find an enthusiastic following particularly when their playwrights are also active theatre directors, as is the case with Tomasz Man (b. 1968), the author and director of such plays as *Katarantka* (2001) and *History of a Certain Love* (*Historia pewnej miłości*, 2001). Man also directs the works of the best among his peers: Krzysztof Bizio's *Showcases* (*Gabloty*, 2006), *Trash* (*Śmieci*, 2005), *Let's Talk About Life and Death* (*Porozmawiajmy o życiu i śmierci*, 2001 and 2004), and *Lament* (2003);[30] Michał Walczak's *Sandbox* (*Piaskownica*, 2004) and *A Trip inside the Room* (*Podróż do wnętrza pokoju*, 2005); and *Day of the Wacko* (*Dzień świra*, 2006), a play of the much older Marek Koterski (b. 1942). Przemysław Wojcieszek (b. 1974), a recognized film director, directs primarily his own texts.[31] Jan Klata (1973) has become more notorious as a director than as a playwright. His own *Graperuit's Smile* (misspelling intended, *Uśmiech grejpruta*, 2003) and *Stop it, Will You?* (*Weź przestań*, 2006) were certainly well received, but his contested reputation came with his staging of Nikolai Gogol, Andre Gide, William Shakespeare, Stanisław Ignacy Witkiewicz (pen name Witkacy), and Juliusz Słowacki, which stormed Warsaw en masse in 2005 during his individual festival "Klatafest."

What distinctive characteristics of the young drama can account for some of the recent excitement? The playwrights Michał Bajer (1981), Krzysztof Bizio (1970), Paweł Demirski (1979), Magdalena Fertacz (1975), Cezary Harasimowicz, Paweł Jurek (1966), Tomasz Kaczmarek (1970), Maciej Kowalewski (1969), Dana Łukasińska (1972), Tomasz Man, Marek

Modzelewski (1972), Monika Powalisz (1973), Marek Pruchniewski, Paweł Sala (1968), Andrzej Saramonowicz (1965), Maria Spiss (1977), Michał Walczak (1979), or Przemysław Wojcieszek, to name just a few, already have easily recognizable profiles, and are increasingly difficult to put together into an all-embracing portrait. However, it is still safe to summarize most of their works as socially engaged, sensitive to social ills and injustices, open to the most immediate social and economic realities of capitalist Poland, and critical towards social pathologies. Their unabashed involvement in the public domain of social discourse is crucial to the self-definition of these young artists. So is their sensitivity towards psychological dynamics, personal conflicts, bodily and sexual experiences, and emotional traumas. All have a particularly keen ear for the collisions and interpenetrations of various discourses—public and private, official and colloquial, natural and fake, spontaneous and scripted.

These young playwrights have learned theatre language primarily from expressionism, Brecht, British documentary drama (as practiced at the Court Theatre), Russian "theatre.doc," and from the so-called "brutalists,"[32] whose cruelty, pathology, and hysteria—a "psychodrama of tormented helplessness and despair"[33]—they have not copied, however. Rather, the "brutalists" have sensitized young Polish writers to individual pain, human violence, corporeality and sexuality, and to their possible links with transcendence. They are a generation brought up on mass media, computers, and advertising, the means and techniques of which affect their craft. Many have close relationships with film as screenwriters (for example Sala, Saramonowicz, Wojcieszek). Some have other masters, for instance, old-fashioned modernists like Henrik Ibsen, August Strindberg, and Anton Chekhov. It is obvious that they have also studied the Polish modernist canon of Witkacy, Witold Gombrowicz, Tadeusz Różewicz, and Sławomir Mrożek.[34] In all of these sources the young writers have discovered the strength, necessity, and means of transgression, engagement, and doubt, which they have turned into the most important methods of relating to both reality and theatre.

As I have already discussed elsewhere, thematically their plays oscillate between the dire and the banal in individual experiences of everyday social and economic reality, which has become the primary focus, and also the main source of the tension between the weighty and the weightless, the stable and the fluid, in the process of modernization.[35] The playwrights understand these tensions historically when they consider the participation of their own generation in the crucial historical moment on the one hand, and observe its insignificance to the outcome of the modernizing processes on the other. In that sense, the present modernization is indeed a fatal necessity to be either embraced or rejected. Each attitude, however, produces equally toxic results. At other times, when the relationship between man and reality appears in its extremes—either as traumatic or as tiring, repetitive, and trivial—they understand these tensions socially and existentially. The young playwrights' assumption that the everyday has a toxic or traumatic nature comes from people's anguished inability to negotiate modernizing processes with the meaning of individual existence, and from the anxiety and insecurity that dominates one's relationship with an increasingly unstable and paradoxical reality. The sensation of the tiring, trivial, and repetitive is induced by the rapid rise in consumerism, kitschy aestheticization of the everyday, and mindlessness of pop culture.

The tensions between the extreme and the banal are all pervasive in the new plays. The extremes range from the tragic consequences of unemployment (Sala's *Mortal Combine*, 2004; Bizio's *Lament*, 2003; Łukasińska's *Agata Looks for Work*, 2004) to the equally tragic problems of workaholism (Burzyńska's *Most Suicides Happen on a Sunday*, 2003; Spiss's *A Child*, 2004); from the extreme poverty and deprivation that destroy human relationships (Klata's *Stop It, Will You*, 2005; Pruchniewski's *Lucia and Her Children*, 2003) to aggressive and socially degenerative consumption (Jurek's *Porno Generation*, 2000; Klata's *The Grejprut's Smile*, 2002); from a petrifying internal emptiness afflicting all generations to their difficulties with taming a chaotic and complex reality (Modzelewski's *Coronation*, 2003; Wojcieszek's *Personal Jesus*; Jurek's *Delusions*); from hurtful loneliness to toxic relationships (Man's *Katarantka*, 1998 and *111*, 2004; Harasimowicz's *Ten Floors*, 2000; Bizio's *Trash*, 2004; Pruchniewski's *Lucia and Her Children*; Kaczmarek's *The Suffering Mother*, 2004; Fertacz's *Absynt*, 2005; Bajer's *The War Zone*, 2006); from all kinds of addictions (Bizio's *Toxins*, 2002) to all kinds of transgressive liberations (Wojcieszek's *Whatever Happens, I Love You*, 2005); from depression, illness, handicap, and otherness (Walczak's *Sandbox* and *Trip*, Sala's plays, Mroczkowska's *Justyna, a Sister of My*..., Bizio's *Trash*, Man's *Katarantka*, Bajer's *Verklärte nacht*, and Modzelewski's *Touch*) to artificial propriety; from self-destruction to excessive aggression towards others (Sala's *Gang Bang*, 2002 and *Starting Today, We Will Be Good*, 2002). On the other hand, the new texts also probe the encroaching banality and triviality of the everyday, of mass culture, consumerism, and the postindustrial, capitalist society.[36]

Probing the tensions between the weighty and the weightless allows the playwrights to scrutinize different kinds of pathologies of public and private Polish realms. Not surprisingly, they most often visit their perplexing intersections. Those include the dominant models of social practices (e.g.. Polish religiosity in Kaczmarek's *The Suffering Mother* and Pruchniewski's *The Pilgrims*) and collective culture (the controlling nature of mass culture in Maciej Kowalewski's *Miss HIV*, or the devastating hierarchies among subcultures of Sala's *Mortal Combine*). They may revisit the ethos of the collective experience (Wojcieszek's *Kill Them All*), or the collision of cultural stereotypes with gender and sexual self-definitions (Modzelewski's *Coronation* and *Touch*, Wojtyszko's *Uterus* and *Whatever Happens, I Love You*.) They drag out the skeletons from abusive and dysfunctional familial closets (Pruchniewski's *Lucia and Her Children*, Man's *Mother and a Leopard*, Walczak's *Trip inside the*

Room, Mariusz Bieliński's *Over* and *Quiet*, the plays of Bizio and Sala), and delve into the tormented bodies and psyches of their characters.

Thus, it is not difficult to imagine where the new drama searches for its heroes. It goes in two diametrically opposed directions: either to the economic ghettoes of big cities (the so-called *blokowiska*) and the impoverished provinces, to closed institutions and criminal environments, or to the elite enclaves of rat racers and media workers, and finally to the internet's' computers—the ultimate location of illusory intimacy that is, in fact, a public domain. In all places it finds a mix of extreme experiences and trivial existences of lost, lonely, disappointed young people, who are helpless in the face of an incomprehensible reality, but also aggressive and rebellious toward it, at once longing for a dignified life, and thrashing their last chances to live it. It also finds frustrated mid-lifers who either can no longer keep up with the race or have been barred from it at its very start. The radicalization of stage language and aesthetics results from a similar tension between the extreme and the trite. The vulgar is extreme for beyond it language changes into gibberish. At the same time it embodies the essence of banality.

Paradoxically, the plays of the new millennium are often stylistically, aesthetically, and most of all linguistically transgressive, while in their diagnoses of the new economic, social, and cultural realities they remain both critical and nostalgic, and in many cases overly moralistic, as most leftist diagnoses are. Granted, the young do not advocate a simplistic return to seemingly lost values. They are too realistic to believe in ideal times in the past, and they are too critical toward it. However, unlike many devotees of progress and social utopias, these playwrights are more than cautious with their enthusiasm for modernization, carefully calculating its possible costs: the demise of social relations, the atrophy of a belief in the common good, the rising aggression, egotism, and materialism of Polish elites, abusive social structures—whether corporate, religious, or familial, and the growing indifference to human suffering, to name only a few. They do maintain that, with such aggressive re- and de-valuations, we live brutal and painful lives deprived of dignity. Human dignity, then, becomes one of the unrecognized subjects of the new Polish theatre. The inherent tension between banality and evil that made Hannah Arendt's phrase describing twentieth-century genocide so effective seems at the core of everyday life in a democratic system, undoing the appearances of its stability, security, and justice.

It seems that what Matei Calinescu calls the century-old "split . . . between modernity as a stage in the history of Western civilization . . . and modernity as an aesthetic concept,"[37] in other words the encounter with two modernities—one brought about by capitalism, the other by the rejection of it—could be of help in the conceptualization of observed tensions, for it also captures the dichotomy embodied by Polish critical discourse. However, although highly critical of civilizational modernity, recent dramatic literature can hardly be described as militantly modernist in aesthetic terms. The complaints of some critics about its aesthetic simplicity and moralizing socialist-realism leanings often have their merits. These plays neither follow Cichocki's dichotomy of modernity and tradition, nor their forceful politicization by "progressive" critics. Rather, they reveal the ambivalent attitude of Polish playwrights to both the present and the past. Despite their criticism of Polish cultural traditions, including the traditions of Polish modern theatre, these writers do not unconditionally support the present modernizing project, focusing instead on its inherent dangers to both public, social existence and individual, private lives. Their critical attitude to the past is also far away from categorical condemnation. Finally, there is little faith in their works in some kind of a glorious future toward which we can all aspire and strive. Nonetheless, it is apparent that these plays situate themselves close to the cultural battlefield. They emerge from it, however, with unexpected twists.

The sources of these twists rest, in my view, in a different understanding of the civilizational moment that the playwrights are compelled to dramatize, and which their critics miss. In so doing they resemble Zygmunt Bauman's theorists who "insist on fighting old battles in which they acquired expertise and prefer this to the change from a familiar and trustworthy battleground to a new, as yet not fully explored territory."[38] Unlike their critics, the Polish playwrights experience firsthand what Bauman diagnoses as a new, liquid phase of modernity. In other words, instead of the conflict between capitalism and aesthetic modernity known from Calinescu's description, and between modernity and tradition from Cichocki's diagnosis, the young playwrights deal with a fundamental process of liquefaction of modernity, which is, indeed, "in many ways a *terra incognita*"[39] not only to their critics, but also to the writers themselves.

Their sense of bewilderment, be it about social, economic, or interpersonal relations, comes from the disappearance of the stable ground in which solid modernity once took root, and from a recognition of a decisive civilizational shift that shapes our lives now, as Bauman shows in a series of recent books.[40] To go back to the framework that I have mapped out for the new plays, the traumatic in them originates in this civilizational shift, with the banal being its most oppressive characteristic, since there is little space for the extraordinary or the heroic in the liquid. Young plays speak primarily to the experiences of this unexpected face of modernity—not the one desired and fought for by older generations, which still imagined modernity as a solid structure, though clearly different from its debauched communist project. They speak from a place very close to Bauman's arguments about the overwhelming sense of uncertainty, insecurity, and anxiety characteristic of present human relationships with the world.

This sensation derives from "the decline of early modern illusion: of the belief that there is . . . an attainable *telos* of historical change . . . some sort of good society, just society and conflict-free society" and from "the deregulation and privatization of most of modernizing tasks and duties."[41] The stories they tell about the jobless and the workaholics, the affluent and the impoverished, the mainstream and the marginalized, testify to this loss of the belief in our mastery over the future, and to the growing burden put on the individual to assume responsibility for all choices in life. The playwrights speak from the place in which relationships between individuality, community, and freedom have become increasingly problematic, where "individualization is a fate, not a choice," but also where "the gap is growing between individuality as fate and individuality as the practical and realistic capacity for self-assertion."[42] In such a place "the most common troubles of individuals-by-fate are these days *non-additive*. They are not amenable to 'summing up' into a 'common cause,'"[43] and lead to "the corrosion and slow disintegration of citizenship,"[44] as well as to the privatization of the public sphere. Hence the fragmentation, exasperation, and loneliness that all of their characters experience when faced with an abundance of choice, and the limitations of circumstance. Finally, they relate the experiences to "the seductive lightness of being,"[45] to borrow along with Bauman this well-known phrase from Milan Kundera's book, to the newly valorized instantaneity and "the state of unfinishedness, incompleteness and underdetermination,"[46] to new nomadism and consumerism that seriously erode their heroes' ability to choose, their sense of responsibility, and their means of building an individual identity as well as social bonds.

It is paradoxical that the first generation that could have fully benefited from the redrawing of modernity's project in Poland after 1989 was immediately thrown into its problematic aftermath—its liquid form that promises much, but whose delivery is as unpredictable as its characteristics. This is not to say that the young playwrights feel completely out of their element in such a reality. Quite the contrary, many capitalize on the opportunities that liquidity offers, and embrace its most seductive promise of the power that comes with speed. However, they still feel uneasy about its fallouts: the disappearing past and the unforeseeable future, the vanishing collectivity and civility of coexistence, or the serious damage to human bonds and relationships. The importance of their plays does not lie in the degree of their political engagement, which evaporates under closer scrutiny of its projected effectiveness and the playwrights' own position within the shifting paradigms. Neither does it come from their aesthetic discoveries or intellectual depth. It rests in the intuitive, rather than conceptual discovery of how dangerous to individual and social life the consequences of the liquid form of the new reality can become.

Neither unbridled enthusiasm nor unconditional condemnation does these texts justice. Both attitudes hinder the writers' opportunities now to problematize, rather than just dramatize the human encounter with liquidity, an encounter that raises many disquieting questions regarding the relationships among individuals, society, politics, public discourse, and identity, not to mention the relationship between liquid modernity and its traditional, solid form, which lingers—unrecognized—in the new plays, and still waits for its interpretation. The other, even more important task that also awaits dramatic and critical attention is the recognition of the ambiguous positions that both drama and criticism occupy within the flow of modernity. Both are the children of their time—and this time is, after all, a liquid time.

Notes

1. Even though much has been said about the generational profile of the young, such a criterion has to be redefined, since the twenty years that traditionally divide one generation from the next have now shrunk to just a few years. The difference between those who were forty or thirty-something in the 2000s—like Andrzej Saramonowicz, Paweł Jurek, Krzysztof Bizio, Tomasz Kaczmarek, Marek Kochan (1969), Maciej Kowalewski, Tomasz Man, Jacek Papis (1969), or Paweł Sala—and those born in the1970s—Robert Bolesto (1977), Paweł Demirski, Magdalena Fertacz, Jan Klata, Dana Łukasińska, Marek Modzelewski, Joanna Owsianko (1974), Monika Powalisz, Maria Spiss, Michał Walczak, or Przemysław Wojcieszek—is in their memory of the past, and their experience of the new, capitalist Poland (with all its gains and losses) as adults. The twenty-somethings—such as Michał Bajer, Szymon Wróblewski (1983), or Dorota Masłowska (1983)—have little recollection of the communist Poland.

2. Much of what was written during the 1990s, and once critically acclaimed, has disappeared from the critical radar (and theatre stages) since then, but the drama of that decade was as diverse, and in many cases more innovative—thematically and formally—than the plays of the new millennium. The plays of Lidia Amejko (b. 1955), Artur Grabowski (b. 1958), Ewa Lachnit (b. 1957), Jerzy Łukosz (b. 1958), or Paweł Mossakowski (b. 1957) are just a few examples of once prolific and acclaimed playwrights.

3. See Pawłowski, "Wraca centrala."

4. In comparison to literary criticism that accompanied new poetry and prose, theatre criticism lagged seriously behind. Before Baniewicz's book of 2000, in which she discusses primarily theatre productions, no other book tackled the new plays of the 1990s, in contrast to the many valuable publications about poetry and prose by authors such as Jerzy Jarzębski, Przemysław Czapliński, Marian Kisiel, Karol Maliszewski, and Marian Stala, to give just a few examples.

5. Trojanowska, "New Discourses in Drama," 111.

6. Among the new books about the new theatre and drama are Gruszczyński's, Plata's, and Kopciński's. See also Pawłowski's introductions to the anthologies: *Pokolenie porno i inne niesmaczne utwory sceniczne* and *Made in Poland: Dziewięć sztuk teatralnych z Polski*. Finally, see the new dictionary of Polish theatre since 1997: *Wątroba: Słownik polskiego teatru po 1997 roku.*

7. *Dialog* is still the main periodical devoted to the publication of new plays, but it no longer provides most of the dramatic material for Polish stages, which often turn now to other venues.

8. In addition to the already mentioned anthologies (see note 6), there are a few other ones on the market: *Echa-repliki-fantazmaty: Antologia nowego dramatu polskiego*, ed. Sugiera and Wierzchowska-Woźniak; *Gang bang, Komponenty, Nocny autobus*, ed. Gańczarczyk and Niziołek; *TR/PL: Antologia nowego dramatu polskiego*; *Radom Odważny: Festiwal nowej dramaturgii*, ed. Korłub. The best webpage regarding all things theatrical in Poland is www.e-teatr.pl.

9. See Hunter, *Is There a Culture War?*

10. Cichocki, 71.

11. The first issue of *Gazeta Wyborcza* was published on May 8, 1989; *Fakt* first appeared on the Polish market in October 2003.

12. Śpiewak, "Zgubny brak autoironii." Krasnodębski brands the modernizers "Polish Liberals," and defines their position as follows: "Polish Liberals represent the views of some postmodern Western intellectuals. Their idea of open society is a society that is not only culturally diverse but also culturally unfocused, one that does not possess a common unifying political culture. This is an interesting position, and it is often brilliantly articulated; but it plays only a marginal role in Western European political practice. Strictly speaking, it is not a Liberal but a radically leftist position. It is a product of a marriage between Liberalism and leftist thought, a kind of postmodern Liberalism." ("Democracy on the Periphery," 1036). He further explains: "While Western European Liberalism was nurtured by a distrust toward those in power, the post-1989 Polish Liberalism shaped itself under the influence of a deep distrust of the elite toward a society deemed immature" (1037).

13. Śpiewak's *Memory after Communism* (*Pamięć po komuniźmie*) analyzes Michnik's Manichean stance towards Poland's communist past in interesting, well-balanced, and sophisticated terms.

14. Indeed, since Polish historical trauma has never been properly mourned, it turned, as Sigmund Freud had predicted in such cases, into melancholia. See Freud's "Mourning and Melancholia," 14:243–58. See also Ewa Thompson's "Ways of Remembering: The Case of Poland" in this volume.

15. Rychard.

16. *Dziennik* was introduced on April 18, 2006. In April 2008, discussions about the most pertinent political and ideological issues published in *Europa* appeared in book format, under the title *Firsthand Ideas* (*Idee z pierwszej ręki*). *Gazeta Wyborcza* also became a subject of book-length studies and public debate. See Remuszko; Ziemkiewicz.

17. The list includes such intellectual authorities (from both the left and the right of the political spectrum) as Alain Besançon, Noam Chomsky, Richard Dawkins, Niall Ferguson, Alain Finkielkraut, Francis Fukuyama, René Girard, André Glucksmann, John Gray, Jürgen Habermas, Paul Johnson, Robert Kagan, Slavoj Žižek, Jacques Le Goff, Tariq Ramadan, Richard Rorty, Guy Sorman, Amartya Sen, Peter Sloterdijk, and Michael Walzer.

18. The articles engaged in the ideological discussion about the theatre can be found at: http://www.e-teatr.pl/pl/artykuly/80,watek.html.

19. Roman Pawłowski (b. 1965) is also the editor of two already-mentioned anthologies of the new plays: *Pokolenie porno* and *Made in Poland*; Piotr Gruszczyński (b. 1965) has initiated many battles with his texts published in *Tygodnik Powszechny*, *Dialog*, *Didaskalia*, and *Notatnik Teatralny*, which he later collected in his controversial book *Patricides: The Younger and More Talented in Polish Theatre* (*Ojcobójcy: Młodsi zdolniejsi w teatrze polskim*.)

20. Grzegorz Niziołek is a dramaturg in the Old Theatre in Kraków, a professor in the Theatre School there, and an organizer of the new drama festival baz@rt. Tadeusz Słobodzianek, one of the best playwrights of the 1990s, recently became a director of the Drama Laboratory—a vibrant theatre workshop in Warsaw featured prominently in the dossiers of many young playwrights. Also quite recently, Maciej Nowak finished his six-year tenure as the controversial manager of Teatr Wybrzeże in Gdańsk (2000–6) to administer the new and prestigious Zbigniew Raszewski Theatre Institute in Warsaw.

21. Jacek Kopciński is also a professor of the Institute of Literary Research in the Polish Academy of Science, and an author of books on the playwriting of Miron Białoszewski (*Gramatyka i mistyka: wprowadzenie w teatralną osobność Mirona Białoszewskiego*) and Zbigniew Herbert (*Nasłuchiwanie: Sztuki na głosy Zbigniewa Herberta*) and on contemporary theatre (*Którędy do wyjścia: szkice i rozmowy teatralne*).

22. For further discussion about the state of theatre criticism in Poland, consult Sieradzki, "Krytyka kreatywna"; Baltyn; and the fervent discussion in the daily *Dziennik* initiated by Tomasz Mościcki ("Jaka jest kondycja polskiej krytyki teatralnej"), and continued by Łukasz Drewniak (no. 154), Elżbieta Baniewicz (no. 153), Jacek Wakar (no. 156), Tomasz Stawiszyński, Janusz Majcherek, and Elżbieta Morawiec. See http://www.e-teatr.pl/pl/artykuly/121,watek.html, or *Dziennik online* (July 2007).

23. See Węgrzyniak.

24. See Duniec and Krakowska; and texts by Paweł Mościcki

25. See Rychard.

26. This last identification refers to the mythical origins of the Polish gentry, particularly popular in the sixteenth and seventeenth centuries, that later became synonymous with traditionalism, republicanism, and often with xenophobia and cultural backwardness. For an in-depth analysis of this gentry paradigm see Bogucka; Porębski, *Polskość jako sytuacja*; Ulewicz; Waśko.

27. See P. Mościcki, "Zaangażowanie i autonomia teatru."

28. Wakar.

29. The most renowned Polish theatre directors staged both the Romantics and their contemporaries. Some, like Jerzy Jarocki, have had no interest in the Romantics, but are the best interpreters of their own contemporaries—in Jarocki's case, of Tadeusz Różewicz and Sławomir Mrożek.

30. Other plays by Bizio: *Tocsins* (*Toksyny*, 2002), *Celebrations* (*Celebracje*, 2006), *Rains* (*Deszcze*, 2005, together with Tomasz Man), *Autoreverse* (2005), *Fotoplastikon* (2005).

31. So far these include *Made in Poland* (2004), *Whatever Happens, I Love You . . .* (*Cokolwiek się zdarzy, kocham cię*, 2005), *Personal Jesus* (*Osobisty Jezus*, 2006), *Fall Asleep Now in the Fire* (*Zaśnij teraz w ogniu*, 2007), *Love Will Forgive You Everything* (*Miłość ci wszystko wybaczy*, 2008), *There Was Such Love Once but There Is No Certainty That It Was Ours* (*Była już taka miłość ale nie ma pewności że to była nasza*, 2008). Wojcieszek's film credits, as a writer and a director, include *To Kill Them All* (1999), *Louder than Bombs* (*Głośniej od bomb*, 2002), *Down the Colorful Hill* (*W dół kolorowym wzgórzem*, 2004), and *A Perfect Afternoon* (*Doskonałe popołudnie*, 2005).

32. This popular label has been attached to the dramaturgy of Sarah Kane, Mark Ravenhill, Marius von Mayenburg, Teresa Walser, and the Canadian born Brad Fraser. Poland's most popular young directors have directed Kane's plays: Grzegorz Jarzyna (*4.48 Psychosis* in Poznań, 2002) and Krzysztof Warlikowski (*Cleansed* in Wrocław, 2001). Jarzyna also took an interest in Fraser's *Unidentified Human Remains*. Anna Augustynowicz directed Ravenhill's *Polaroids* and Mayenburg's *Parasites*, Piotr Kruszczyński and Adam Sroka presented two productions of Mayenburg's *Fire in the Head*.

33. Burska.

34. For an analysis of Różewicz's impact on the young theatre, see Trojanowska, "Różewicz i teatr lat ostatnich," and "Kto młodym przewodzi"; Walczak; Sala.

35. See Trojanowska, "Kto młodym przewodzi."

36. The original titles of these plays (in the order in which they appear in this paragraph) are: *Mortal kombajn, Gang Bang, Od dzisiaj będziemy dobrzy; Lament*; *Agata szuka pracy*; *Większość samobójstw zdarza się w niedzielę*; *Dziecko*; *Łucja i jej dzieci, Pielgrzymi*; *Pokolenie Porno, Urojenia*; *Koronacja*; *Zabić ich wszystkich*; *Katarantka, 111, Matka i lampart*; *Dziesięć pięter*; *Śmieci, Toksyny*; *Matka cierpiąca*; *Absynt*; *Strefa wojenna*; *Justyna, siostra mojej*; *Verklärte nacht*; *Dotyk*; *Miss HIV*; *Nad, Cicho*.

37. Calinescu, 41.

38. Bauman, *Liquid Modernity*, 48.

39. Ibid.

40. In addition to Bauman's *Liquid Modernity*, see also his *Community*; *Liquid Love*; and *Consuming Life*.

41. Bauman, *Liquid Modernity*, 29.

42. Ibid., 34.

43. Ibid., 35.

44. Ibid., 36.

45. Ibid., 118.

46. Ibid., 62.

Conflicts around the Canon

Jerzy Jarzębski

A few years back, in an article on the difficulties surrounding our contemporary understanding of the canon, I identified three main approaches to this notion.[1] The canon can be seen, first, as a set of seemingly timeless Exquisite Works that constitute the scaffolding for the edifice of a universal culture; second, as a collection of literary works most popular within a given culture at a specific point in time; and finally, as those works that are placed on school and university reading lists and used for educational purposes.

Literary works from the first group enjoy an enduring presence, their "canonical" existence endorsed by tradition and by numerous critical and literary bodies and institutions. They play a role in shaping what we usually call cultural heritage: of a nation, continent, transnational culture (defined by shared qualities, as is the case with the Mediterranean culture), or the whole world. Here we need to take into consideration the fact that global culture itself has undergone a process of integration over the last few centuries. The endorsement of this set takes place through continual negotiations. Whereas the membership of some of the texts (such as Homer's epics; dramas by Aeschylus, Sophocles, Euripides, Shakespeare, or Molière; Dante's *Divine Comedy*; *Don Quixote* by Cervantes) is obvious and can no longer be questioned, relatively new works are a different matter. At the beginning, the ship of literature takes on board too many canonical texts, many of which are thrown overboard with the passage of time. The deletion from the canon of the works that have not stood the test of time is as interesting as the acquisition of new titles.

Works from the second group are constantly verified by the readers' market, by questionnaires or ranking lists, or by their own contribution to local and worldwide exchanges of thought. Advocates of the first approach to the canon usually look scornfully on the temporary fluctuations in the careers and popularity of canonical texts. I don't think they are right: we should care which part of the canon of the first type is being read at any given historical moment. Such texts become indispensable to the intellectual equipment of those who actively participate in culture; conversely, if a text is present in encyclopedias and literary compendia but absent from present-day reading lists, it remains to a large extent culturally dormant.

As for the third group, it is assembled in the most arbitrary way, being the product of a conscious endeavor to meet the demands of the present moment on the part of a whole range of educational institutions from the Ministry of Education to the literature teachers who select some titles from those already placed on optional reading lists. This last set of texts changes often, especially during periods of fundamental state transformation, since subsequent regimes frequently treat it instrumentally in their attempt to introduce a desirable literary picture of the past as a means of educating the young according to the preferred ideology. The Poland of the last few decades has been a particularly symptomatic example of a state in which the educational canon is constantly adjusted to meet the changing requirements formulated by politicians.

Does there exist, then, something like an "objective canon," a point of reference for the "unobjective" educational canons? Harold Bloom, the author of the best-known book on the canon in recent years,[2] constantly claims to oppose all relativism, preferring a canon based on objective aesthetic criteria. When it comes to presenting a world canon of the twentieth century, however, he enumerates dozens and dozens of relatively unknown English-language writers, particularly Americans, but hardly ever mentions authors from the Balkans (not a single Bulgarian or Romanian, and merely three representatives of Serbian and Croatian literatures, figure in his book), ushering into the canon only a couple of writers for each of the Central European literatures (Polish, Czech, or Hungarian). I am writing this not to complain, for the thousandth time, about the underappreciation of our literary accomplishments, but rather to emphasize that the canon is construed not from a cosmic distance but from a specific vantage point on the map of world culture. Harold Bloom's vantage point is situated in such a way that one can see from it some third-rate local stars (if they are placed relatively close to his university and its program of studies), but overlook some truly distinguished authors who happen to be thousands of miles away, entangled in different historical and cultural narratives.[3]

How does the "objective canon" exist, then? It seems that its existence resembles that of a "rigid body" in physics, or the Kantian "thing in itself"; in other words, such a canon is not something independent of the activities of literary historians but rather a postulate revealed in countless and always imperfect approximations. Sometimes its shape is defined by a collective effort to form a consensus among numerous scholars from various countries.[4] This process inevitably brings about compromises, and its end result is always controversial and flawed. As a matter of fact, the canon of the first type is to some extent also a product of various institutions (educational, cultural), although its subjectivity is better hidden, since it is less influenced by particular political purposes, and its persuasive functions are less clear, being the result of multiple agreements and compromises. We might conclude, therefore, that both the "objective" canon and the canon functioning within a particular educational system are interdependent: the "educational" canon exists in relation to the presumed presence of the objective canon, and this relation might range from the postulate of the collapse of the two (as is the case when a school wishes to transmit timeless knowledge, not connected with any given historical moment or place), to the different variants of deliberately instrumental teaching, which brings together canonical titles according to heavily stressed political, social, ideological, and economic objectives. It lies in the hands of teachers, moreover, to extend the canon, to enrich it with new, recently published works, whose significance and virtues are considered sufficient for their inclusion into the school curriculum. And this process of extension has lately experienced a crisis that seems telling in Poland.

Let us recall the time just after World War II, when Poland underwent a particularly drastic cultural experiment that widely affected the educational canon. Stalinism performed an operation that, as is known, cut out all or almost all texts considered "reactionary" or "backward," leaving untouched only those works that ideologues wanted to regard as "progressive." This was evidently meant to bring about a radical change in the reading habits of Poles, who were previously educated mainly by means of patriotic literature with strong religious overtones. This maiming of the canon was accompanied by yet another great experiment: Polish and world classical authors approved by the regime were widely distributed in large print runs of accessibly priced editions. At the same time, literary and cultural life in Poland was being centralized: publishing houses and journals were nationalized, the Polish Writers' Union with its strictly ideological goals was established, and so on. Spreading socialist-realist kitsch, these leaders of cultural life in Poland simultaneously made every effort to eliminate commercial kitsch (lowbrow literature, cheap romance, American-style thrillers, etc.). As a result, the tackiness of ideologically driven literary production became all too obvious when compared with the classics; and the more ambitious literary criticism, except for the Stalinist interlude, set high standards for books, both thematically and aesthetically.

The whole bizarre nature of socialist-realist literature consisted, then, in the fact that its kitsch, although supported by the regime ("militia novels," neo-production novels, literary denunciations and invectives written to political order), was usually spotted and disarmed by critics and readers. The real hierarchies of value were rather obvious to everyone knowledgeable, however superficially; that is, I do not think that an average reader would hesitate when choosing between Zbigniew Herbert, Sławomir Mrożek, Jerzy Andrzejewski, or Wisława Szymborska on the one hand, and Ryszard Liskowacki, Stanisław Ryszard Dobrowolski, Władysław Machejek, or Eugeniusz Kabatc on the other. The canon construed according to the criteria of that time would certainly not include, because of censorship, numerous distinguished authors (emigrant writers first among them), whereas the selection made from the remaining authors would probably be right (Machejek's books were eagerly reprinted by the regime, though they were not yet out of print; nobody was, however, forced to admire him as a distinguished author). Writers obedient to the regime were excluded from serious critical discourse when the samizdat came into being. Though they were awarded scholarships, prizes, and publishing opportunities, they did not gain true recognition, and their books frequently fell victim to exceptionally witty and scornful comments written by leading opposition critics and columnists of the younger generation.[5] Paradoxically, during communism, the canon of contemporary texts was being created and maintained in the consciousness of more educated readers relatively easily, even though many of the books it embraced were officially banned. Problems began, surprisingly, when Poland regained its independence, experiencing both a political overturn and fundamental economic changes in the process.

When describing post-1989 events, it is worth bearing in mind all three types of canon, for they interwove and affected one another. First of all, independence led to the immediate modification of the educational canon that is consciously formed by leaders of cultural life. These changes were meant to fill in the gaps of school and university reading lists with titles that were formerly banned or officially inaccessible. Changes of this type, however, normally require long consideration, as well as consultation among teachers, literary critics, eminent scholars, and writers themselves. They require, in short, some workable form of the "objective canon." After 1989, attempts to complete the canon as quickly as possible led to many mistakes, taking at times rather extreme forms. For example, at one point in time school reading lists were overcrowded with memoirs and nonfiction in order to compensate for the wrongs censorship had inflicted upon Witold Gombrowicz's *Diary* or Gustaw Herling-Grudziński's *A World Apart*, and to do justice to either the patriots imprisoned by the communist regime after the war (such as Kazimierz Moczarski, the author of *Conversations with an Executioner*) or the silent heroes of the ghetto uprising (Hanna Krall's *To Outwit God*). These titles squeezed out some works of fiction, including formerly well-known books that were now associated with the time past, even though they did not contain anything politically incorrect. But after a while reading lists underwent yet another change.

My purpose here is not to relate subsequent metamorphoses of the school canon, even though an analysis of the underlying political reasons behind these changes would be interesting. I am interested in something else, however. The activities of those educators reveal a great uncertainty about the correct shape of the twentieth-century literary canon in its first, "objective" form. They gave rise to an illusory conviction that the canon had become falsified to such a degree that it demanded changes executed by immediate decisions (characteristic more of "educational" canon formation). Some decisions openly insisted on reestablishing the prewar or emigrant canon, as if in communist Poland no excellent, artistically revolutionary books had been published. The publishers joined in, wanting to quickly make up for past losses, and started to joyfully print previously forbidden authors, such as Ferdynand Ossendowski, Eugeniusz Małaczewski, Ferdynand Goetel, or Sergiusz Piasecki, who were not bad or at least, as was the case with Piasecki, not typical, but who were also not necessarily canonical. At the same time, such eminent authors as Wilhelm Mach, Kazimierz Brandys, Adolf Rudnicki, or Andrzej Kuśniewicz were gradually forgotten. Finally, around 1995, all the above-mentioned authors were overshadowed by young writers who had only just entered the literary market. And here another problem with the canon emerged, which lasts to this day.

Everyone who treats canon-related issues seriously must be intrigued by the moment when a new book enters the set of canonical works. What decides on this entry? A consensus of experts? Popularity with readers? The book's usefulness to the processes of education and upbringing? All of the above? We can see how the motives shaping the three types of canon interweave—but which one dominates?

Under communism, a book entered the canon primarily when it had acquired a large number of enthusiastic reviews by reliable critics. Moreover, such a book had to be useful in creating a synthesis of a given literary period, which meant that it had to be both original and typical. Criteria of the third kind were decisive rather seldom, and only during certain periods. For instance, Andrzejewski's *Ashes and Diamond* was included in the canon of school reading lists mainly for its persuasive function: it could be used to convince its readers that communism should be chosen over ideals or faithfulness to the military oath. After the end of the Stalinist era similar motives played a lesser part. It may be tempting to conclude that, in a free Poland, the decision on whether or not a book should enter the canon would be influenced primarily by its "objective" artistic and intellectual value, as agreed upon by independent assemblies of literary critics and scholars, or additionally approved by clear and open criteria of teachers who choose this rather than another model of education through literature. Yet the realization of this ideal has been hindered by commercialization.

All too soon it became obvious that nothing was more profitable than publishing titles from obligatory reading lists, which—in a wider perspective—thereby influenced the shape of the canon in its second, popular, version. One cannot blame Polish publishers for their charge to conquer the market at all costs. Throughout the nineties, Poland did not have financially stable publishing houses. The old and renowned publishers could not manage the new economic situation, while the market success of new publishers might have been ruined by one or two wrong decisions to invest in an unprofitable book. As a result, publishers entered the battle over popular authors and tried to create literary hits by winning over influential critics and the media so that a book could be enthusiastically reviewed, sometimes even before its launch. Such activities decreased financial risks but simultaneously undermined the authority and credibility of literary criticism and its pronouncements. Additional confusion was caused by equally unreliable bestseller lists published by periodicals. In recent years, the opinions of the literary audience (which create the canon of the second type) have become increasingly important, and they translate into the commercial success of a book. Here we have a peculiar vicious circle: the votes of the audience are influenced by the media machine, which in turn acts under the influence of the most powerful publishers. This is true not only of new books but also of classics. Hence wide-ranging public questionnaires that ask participants to select the hundred greatest works of the twentieth century, or "the most important Polish (world) novels," and so on.

In the most famous questionnaire of this kind, conducted at the end of the twentieth century by the weekly *Polityka*, known critics and intellectuals were first asked to name the greatest novels of the twentieth century, and then the readers were asked to rank thus-selected titles according to their own preferences. The ranking was supposed to result in a publishing series. In this way, powerful publishers gather information about those classic texts that can be successfully brought out. The "objective" canon (which should be guarded by critics) looks for confirmation in the judgments of the mass reader. Therefore, following the interference of the first and third types of canon, the rules for creating the first and second types have become dangerously mixed.

What is the conclusion then? Clearly, past classic authors will do well in present times; their position will not be shaken by this or that opinion poll among contemporary readers or this or that decision shaping the current school canon. The real problem is with books aspiring to the canonical sacrum. Kazimierz Wyka used to quote Adam Mickiewicz in such cases, saying that one needs to wait till the "fig is sugared, and tobacco settled." If we wait, however, school and university students will be deprived of any contact with most recent literature. This is not only true of the schools. Every reader of the younger literary press, especially *Lampa* (The Lamp) and *Ha!art*, will notice numerous comments by young writers who abhor the very institution of "media success," or any other success that consists in being published by one of the dominant publishers (Świat Literacki, Znak, Wydawnictwo Literackie, W.A.B.). A book's membership in the "media canon" is beginning to be perceived as a kind of stigma. Equally, the authors who have moved from niche circles to literary salons (such as Dorota Masłowska, Michał Witkowski, or Sławomir Shuty) start to be considered as "traitors" surrendering to the world of commercialization.

This phenomenon could be treated as an eruption of envy, so typical of artistic circles, if it were not for its scale and its connection with opinions about the world created by Polish capitalism, which dominates much of national literature nowadays. More and more books critically examine present-day reality, viewing it as a product of big corporations and media. Dorota Masłowska, Andrzej Stasiuk, Sławomir Shuty, Krzysztof Olszewski, Daniel Odija, Mariusz Sieniewicz, Dawid Bieńkowski, and Tomasz Piątek—to name only the most famous of such authors—scornfully comment on a world ruled by the rat race, a world that has no mercy toward outsiders, the poor, or social exiles, and which is simultaneously infatuated by media stars, a world that repeats the most stupid of slogans as its mantra. When literature as a phenomenon appears in this world, it loses its credibility and esteem. Thus niche writers and critics try to find patrons among those old masters who did not make a media career and opted instead for the status of outsider, such as Stanisław Czycz, Marian Pankowski, or Tymoteusz Karpowicz.[6]

The problem is, however, that the world of media success also devours some of the "poor but honest" niche writers. What then? What should such a

Masłowska do? An author of the best literary debut of recent years, rebellious, sneering at media idioms—what should she do with her own popularity, which is constantly heated up by the media? Relinquish it and return to the niche she has transcended? Even such an act of protest or despair would be immediately swallowed up and taken advantage of by the media. The (almost farcical) drama of the rebels who oppose the system of power, money, and information transfers consists in the fact that this system is the only reality in which one can achieve measurable success, meaning success that translates into growing print runs, income, and popularity. To the extent that it is implicated in this system, therefore, literature contesting this system contests itself also.

What kind of conclusions regarding the processes of completing the canon can be drawn here? Clearly, since it is accused of being implicated in commercialization, the process has lost its "virginity." At the same time, the purity of the division into the three canon types outlined here has been muddied. The absolute and objective nature of the first type of canon is now called into question: there simply is no independent body that would guard its objectivity and noncomplicity in politics or commercialism. It might very well be a situation quite common in the present world, where literature increasingly resembles business. This might well be the source of the nostalgia experienced by those authors who remember the times when, admittedly, censorship was at work and writers challenging the regime had problems, but the word *canon* sounded serious and pure and one could fight with the regime for its integrity and completeness, risking more than money.

NOTES

This essay has been published in Polish as "Konflikty wokół kanonu" in *Przegląd Polityczny* 76 (2006): 15–19.

1. See Jarzębski, "Metamorfozy kanonu."
2. See Bloom.
3. For this reason Bloom's canon, pretending to be a set of objectively great works, actually is in its imperiousness a rather typical example of the "educational canon."
4. An example of such a collective effort may be the manual *Lettres européennes: Histoire de la littérature européenne*. Ouvrage réalisé par une équipe de cent cinquante universitaires de toute l'Europe géographique, sous la direction d'Annick Benoit-Dusausoy et de Guy Fontaine (Paris : Hachette, 1992). It is exactly these one hundred and fifty scholars from different countries who were supposed to secure the desired objectivity for this book.
5. Stanisław Barańczak, author of the underground volume entitled *Książki najgorsze* [The Worst Books], and Jerzy Pilch, columnist of a spoken magazine based in Kraków, *NaGłos* [OutSpoken], were notorious for their extremely sharp pens.

6. The first two authors were the subject of academic studies and panels arranged by *Ha!art* and its circles. Karpowicz is the hero of the recently published *Mówi Karpowicz* [Karpowicz Speaks] by Spychalski and Szoda.

THEORIZING CULTURAL CHANGE IN POSTCOLONIAL POLAND

Magdalena Kay

After the extraordinary efflorescence of postcolonial studies, this is a moment when nonterritorial, transnational literary paradigms, as opposed to rigidly demarcated national or regional models, are finally beginning to seem imperative. Scholars are paying attention to forms of community that are not bound by conventional commonalities. A recent essay by Jahan Ramazani calls for a newly rigorous examination of the transnational nature of literary influence, while the borders—geographical and theoretical—of postcoloniality have been an inexhaustible subject of debate since the late 1990s.[1] Postcolonial studies is a paradigm of knowledge that is exemplary for its *inherently* transnational focus, yet even in this field the borders between north and south, and east and west, are too strictly policed. I do not believe there is much to be gained from policing these borders: establishing a false civilizational dichotomy between "the West and the rest" or "Europe and its 'others'" obscures the extent to which Europe itself is fractured. The east of Europe should be viewed not as a monolithic entity but as an area that is itself cross-cut by vectors of political power and currents of emotional trauma.

In a recent article on world literature, Milan Kundera powerfully emphasizes the difficulty, even the cultural impossibility of naming "Eastern Europe" or "Central Europe." The cohesion of these terms is effected by the shared history of the countries in this region, not by their shared culture. In the previous two centuries, this history has been defined by the rise and fall of multinational empires: "In the twentieth century, after World War I, several independent states rose from the ruins of the Hapsburg Empire, and thirty years later all of them but Austria found themselves under Russian domination. . . . To my mind, there is nothing more admirable in the Europe of the second half of the twentieth century than that golden chain of revolts, which, over forty years, eroded the empire of the East, made it ungovernable, and tolled the death knell of its reign."[2]

Kundera notes that Poland was the most frequent site of these revolts. Poland's fortunes are remarkable in that the entire country was erased from the map of Europe for well over a century after the Third Partition of 1795. Poland makes for a fascinating test case for postcoloniality: its physical borders are almost impossible to delimit, given its shifting boundaries throughout history and the claims of hybrid "borderland" populations, and its nationhood has long been, quite literally, a matter of imagined community.[3] People living on the same land for generations have found that they are not official citizens of their home territories. A number of Poles fiercely opposed membership in the European Union for reasons of national cultural protection, as if it were another empire threatening Polish sovereignty, while others embraced this new membership as a long-deferred birthright, seeing it as a chance for Poland to finally fully inhabit the adjective "European."

Poland's ex-centricity to the "main" part of Europe places the country in an oblique relation to theory today.[4] Neither fish nor fowl, always dominant or always subaltern, Poland is a "stranger" to Europe. As such it stands to benefit from the hospitality that postcolonial theory can and should offer to second-world countries. It may be metaphorized as a stranger-to-be-accommodated, as Edmond Jabès once described this state in *Le livre de l'Hospitalité*: "One day I recognized that what was more important for me than anything else was how I defined myself to the degree that I was a stranger. . . . I then realized that, in his vulnerability, the stranger could only count on the hospitality that others would offer him. Just as words benefit from the hospitality the white page offers them or the bird from the unconditional space of the sky."[5] The idea of hospitality as radical cultural reconceptualization has also been put forward by theorists such as Iain Chambers and Paul Gilroy.[6] The transitional state of post-1989 Poland is not an "unconditional space" to inscribe by a hospitable theoretical outreach, but an already inscribed page that is, nevertheless, ready for a new transnational language to be added to it.[7]

In a groundbreaking article on the post-Soviet as postcolonial, David Chioni Moore notes that "it is difficult to theorize a silence—that is, this lack of dialogue between current postcolonial critique and scholarship on Central and Eastern Europe, the Caucasus, and Central Asia."[8] The three-worlds theory is an obvious cause of this silence, as well as the attendant fact that for many Western European and North American intellectuals the socialism of the second world seemed like the best political alternative to first- and third-world systems. Marxist scholars are hesitant to make the Soviet Union into a French- or British-style villain. Moore additionally points out the difficulty of accommodating the widespread post-Soviet desire to belong to Europe in theoretical terms, since "colonial desire" is thought to focus upon the colonial master state. In the case of Poland, there is certainly very little desire to belong to Russia, and very much desire either to belong in the European Union or to protect the *national*—Polish—cultural inheritance. Even the Russians themselves, as Moore points out, culturally mimicked the French and the British, thereby complicating a theory of colonial desire and influence. One cannot put this situation under the rubric, basic to postcolonialism, of the West colonizing the East and orientalizing its colonies; it is an example of the East pushing westward.

During Poland's long period of subjugation, Romanticism served as a political and artistic nation-building endeavor that linked literature with politics, the prophet with the collective. Poetry was its privileged literary discourse. At first glance this seems like an empowering position for poetry to occupy, especially from an American perspective, yet its long-term effect was the creation of an essentialized construct of the writer. I do not want to disdain all nationalist discourse and overvalorize the hybrid metropolitan intellectual, however; I suspect that a desire to "move beyond the nation" often rests upon a stable understanding of one's own nationality and that it is difficult for those who have been denied a nation to move beyond the idea of nationhood. The desire for a mythopoesis of the nation has placed contemporary Polish literature in a situation where everything is expected from the writer, but nothing is freely given. The post-Romantic activist-poet is no longer given a clear national mission. The mode in which transnationalism is imagined has itself changed: the global aspirations of the Communist International have been frustrated, but the newly global market for literature contains its own structures of dominance, and the former second world is still far behind in the race for economic and cultural power.

I believe that if we reconceptualize the teleological struggle for national culture as one of infinite process, and not as a linear journey toward an endpoint, Polish Romanticism does not need to become an incarcerating prison of overused symbols and rigid postures. The experience of long-deferred nationhood forced Poles to shift attention from "who we are" as a nation to "who we will be" in the future, at the end of our victimization. The somewhat maligned word for this is *messianism*. But this conceptual shift (to "who we will be") may be an instrument of survival, and may even have emancipatory potential in the post-post-Romantic world of clashes of civilizations. Instead of viewing the messianic model of cultural self-definition as irredeemably tainted by religiosity and essentialism of the worst kind, we can reconceptualize the nation as an imaginary system that coheres around a set of ideals. People participate in the idea of the nation as represented by forward-looking expectations. Meanwhile, the social life of post-1989 Eastern Europe is becoming increasingly mediated by the global marketing of images, and culture becomes increasingly detached from specific places, histories, and traditions. I do not think the "global supermarket effect," where any cultural identity can be sampled at will, obtains in Eastern Europe yet. But the fact that an intense tradition of national idealism—in other words, nation as long-range goal, as spiritual value—suddenly combines with full-fledged globalization means that the imaginary dimension of nationhood may receive an enormous amount of new fuel. In this new system, the possible comforts of tradition are challenged by an imperative for cultural translation. Translation also involves positioning. It necessitates the establishment of an identity for the translated content. In a political context, an identity may be formed for a specific time and place. This is a provisional and strategic positioning. Yet it is difficult to position a nation that has thought of itself as a vanishing point in the far future. In the case of Poland, the provisional nature of its discourse of national identity becomes, I believe, one of its promising qualities. The nation is always being translated, not reified into a single static entity.

The ever-withheld subjecthood of a postcolonial country highlights the phantasmic character of any identity—there is always something fantasized about unity. It is a truism at this point to say that identity depends upon the supplement of otherness and that wholeness depends upon lack, but there is truth in it. I have my quarrels with the very word *identity*. I dislike its connotation of perfect similitude, which is simply an inoperable concept when we look at human beings instead of mathematical equations. Identification is usually thought to be "constructed on the back of a recognition of some common origin or shared characteristics," to quote Stuart Hall, a theorist who insisted upon the conjunctural and processual nature of identity.[9] Yet even in Hall's language, the bodily metaphor of the back, and the concomitant metaphor of building ("constructed on"), communicate a solid physicality about identity that bothers me. The identity of a postcolonial country cannot be metaphorized as a structure resting on a solid fundament, because the conditions that brought that national identity into being framed it in terms of an endless deferral. Ties such as shared language are physically strong but are subject to attrition by the imperial ruler, through the imposition of an imperial language for instance, or the use of strict censorship and surveillance systems in educational institutions that effectively attack the native language.

The identity of postcolonial Poland, therefore, should be conceptualized not as a concrete structure built on a solid fundament but as a process of self-imagination. Although the work of cultural theorists associated with the Birmingham school, such as Hall or his student Paul Gilroy, focuses on the fallout of British imperialism, its concept of culture crossing can also help to theorize Eastern Europe. Gilroy's seminal idea that cultural identity is formed as a process of movement and mediation, of "routes" of travel and change as opposed to "roots" of tradition, can be used to clarify how a national self-image is formed as a constant response to political upheavals and to the experience of subjugation, not as a stable point of opposition.[10] Gilroy links the idea of redemption through suffering with a notion of ethnicity as an infinite process. Suffering the ignominy of unachieved nationhood gives the suffering people the ability to view culture as a provisional and changing set of practices. This is not meant to provide an apology for domination or to feed into a reactionary messianism; it is meant to seek out a positive basis for future conceptualization of the nation that comes out of the postcolonial peoples themselves.

The problem with any experience-centered knowledge claim is that it may carry an assumption of a whole, stable subject. If we view Poland in the context of other decolonized countries, then it becomes impossible to universalize suffering as the experience of a singular postcolonial subject. The changing types of subjugation that Poland has experienced—Russian, Prussian, Austrian, the Nazi invasion, and Soviet imperialism—are themselves not unitary. The imagined community of a unified Polish people arose in response to shifting structures of repression. The Polish community needed to constantly reimagine its own subjecthood and piece together its disassembled parts. The process of creating culture is not an unproblematic transmission of one fixed essence—"the soul of the people"—throughout time, but takes place as a series of local reactions, a coming together in particular conjunctures around specific struggles. In a subjugated country, it takes place in the interruptions of official doctrine. It is a series of subversions. Ethnicity is not an organic and unchanging quality emanating from the continued interrelation of people, land, and history but a disruptive process that seeks to perpetuate itself against great odds.

This idea of identity as disruption is a rich means of knitting together the lived necessity of a postcolonial country with the poststructuralist view of identity as a fantasized unity. Identity is always incomplete, arising from a lack of wholeness. This lack is "filled" from outside us, by the ways we imagine ourselves to be seen by "others." The margins of our identities are always inscribed upon by people external to us, and we cannot exercise total control over the construct that we call identity, which will never be completed. In a colonial situation, the areas that others inscribe swallow the self-determining portion of a country's identity, and the "center" of its identity becomes an endangered space. Self-identification is not an automatically given right, something inherently natural, but it is a constant struggle, a push back against an imposed force. It is an act of anti-inscription, writing the self as an active oppositional agent.

If we accept that the cultural subject is formed negatively, as an agent of subversion, as well as positively, then the achievement of independence poses a new crisis for an epistemology of the subject. International recognition of Poland's autonomy suddenly creates a situation in which the cultural subject must learn to shift from a strategy of subversion to a strategy of negotiation with difference. Now that I am recognized as an independent agent, how can I position myself vis-à-vis all the "others"? Paradoxically, this positive event—the achievement of autonomy—is a trauma, because the postcolonial subject must fundamentally change the way in which identity is positioned. The politics and poetics of endless deferral, of suffering and hope, come to an abrupt end. The question is now how to put a new process of identification into place.

I use the phrase "process of identification" rather than "identity" because moments of political transition highlight the processual nature of identity—in other words, identity as identification. The experience of emigration is often allied with a realization of the provisional nature of "home," yet I believe this realization is also (albeit gradually) forced upon the inhabitants of a nation whose existence cannot be taken for granted. One may, at a particular historical juncture, become a foreigner in one's own birthplace. Polish poet Adam Zagajewski was placed in this situation when the city of his birth and his family's history, L'viv (then Lwów), became part of Ukraine instead of Poland. A further estrangement occurred when he visited the city and found it to be a showpiece of Stalinist architecture, rather than the historical gem he had imagined.[11] In the past two decades, similar stories have proliferated among Poles who, it seems, cannot go home. They are forced to conceive of home as an imagined and mobile habitat, a "mode of inhabiting time and space," instead of a simple singular location, sustained across encounters with the "other" here and now.[12]

Let us turn from theory to poetry to see how a brief poem by a contemporary poet, Marcin Świetlicki, can be read in this theoretical context. It is entitled "After the Night":

> Tonight the sky was to go bright
> with the tail end of a dead comet.
> But there was fog, nothing could be seen.
> The night was brightened by the dull supermarket
> lights. That's it. Somehow everything lately
> washes out like that. The end of the world will come,
> sigh and go out.[13]

I am often reluctant to read poetry through politics, because a good poem can never be reduced to a political opinion. And this poem is not an opinion but an evocation in which the social backdrop of long-awaited independence gives texture to the symbolic landscape of the poem. There is no first-person speaker, yet the poem does not sound impersonal—there is a voice animating these lines. This voice fails to inject the opening image with any real expectation. The first line minutely quickens its emotional pace at the end with "go bright," but this sliver of anticipation (of brightness) is resolutely quashed by the deep emotional diminuendo that follows. We cannot feel full anticipation for the comet because it is presented as already dead, a movement that has been long in the making but which has lost its guiding light. We have two planes of knowledge here: the surface-level glamour of the sky going bright and the deeper knowledge of its cause. The poem happens on two psychological levels: the imagination of perceived grandeur and the disillusioned communication of actualities. We may recall the constant duality of the postcolonial subject imagining his/her nation on the one hand and living the daily reality of subjection on the other hand, or the doublespeak of the Soviet subject whose canny formulations disguise a kernel of idealism.[14]

Yet here the ideal image of the comet is unavailable, leaving the observer unsure whether the guiding light of national liberation does indeed exist as a comet behind the disillusioning fog. Is there a transcendent sign that can serve as a pure, bright, heavenly goal for the people? In the original Polish, the *roz* prefix is repeated three times, in the first, fourth, and sixth lines. This prefix denotes extension and thoroughness, and it is used twice in the poem in the compound *rozświetlić*, meaning "to go bright" or "to brighten": the first time by means of the comet, the second time by means of supermarket lights. I quote the poem in full:

> Tej nocy niebo miało się rozświetlić
> resztką ogona umarłej komety.

Ale mgła była, nic nie było widać.
Noc rozświetlały mdłe supermarketu
światła. I tyle. Coś wszystko ostatnio
tak się rozmywa. Koniec świata przyjdzie,
westchnie i wyjdzie.

The third time the *roz* prefix is used, it is in the word *rozmywa*, "washes out," or "washes away." The extent of illumination imagined in the first line devolves in this way into erasure and attrition once idealism has lost its force. Why has it lost its force? Because a merely teleological model of self-definition will not readily adapt for progress beyond the longed-for telos, which, when it comes, will never be as grand a salvation as people hope for.

I am reading this poem as an atmospheric, psychological, and rhythmic dramatization of the process whereby an end-focused hope is forced to give way to a realization of continual process; the messianic hope for eventual resurrection has an apocalyptic element in it, as this poem clarifies in its symmetrical structure. It begins by envisioning the passage of a bright comet and ends by envisioning the passage of the world's end, as if this end were a human figure that comes, watches, sighs, and moves on. The imaginary is a mode of visionary knowledge that spans different national traditions, even while its backdrop retains its cultural uniqueness, and this poem summons two non-Polish predecessors. Świetlicki knows English well, and he has poetically reproduced an echo of Seamus Heaney's "Exposure" in the first two lines of "After the Night":

A comet that was lost
Should be visible at sunset,
Those million tons of light
Like a glimmer of haws and rose-hips.[15]

Świetlicki has also summoned T. S. Eliot's "The Hollow Men" in the last two lines of his poem:

This is the way the world ends
This is the way the world ends
This is the way the world ends
Not with a bang but a whimper.[16]

Heaney's poem begins with a missed comet but ends with an intense evocation of the brilliance he has missed; Eliot's poem begins with hollowness and ends with a rhythmic apocalypse. Świetlicki has chosen not to evoke the aesthetic brilliance of the salvational comet, as does Heaney, or to give full rein to the drama of jagged poetic rhythms, as does Eliot in the full length of his poem. It is rare to find a contemporary Polish poem with such an even syllable count as this: each line in the original has exactly eleven syllables, except for the last, which has five. The authorial control exerted over poetic form does not create an incantatory chant (as Eliot does) but actually puts a check on emotion. The author is post-Romantic and postcatastrophist. One senses that his emotional energy has been spent. He presents the *opportunity* for a Romantic posture when he invokes the comet[17]—and, I would argue, he summons the *possibility* of idealism when he isolates the word "lights" at the beginning of the fifth line—but ultimately rejects it by the deflationary phrase "That's it." Evocative imagery gives way to colloquial disenchantment. The tone is conversational, the scope universal. "Everything" gets washed out, who knows why. We don't even merit a proper "end of the world," which may have the unnoticeable demeanor of a dissatisfied passerby who looks and then moves on.

The uncomfortable position that this poem puts us in is, I believe, a position in between long-deferred expectation and full normalization. This is the position of the so-called second world today. I have chosen not to come down too heavily on the "supermarket lights" as symbolic of the spiritual bankruptcy of capitalism, because it seems a bit too simplistic to move from one villain (the Empire) to another (International Capitalism). The fact remains that the poem inhabits its own posttraumatic landscape, which does not have a ready-made label attached to it. A decade ago, Stuart Hall wrote: "This question of how to 'think,' in a non-reductionist way, the relations between 'the social' and 'the symbolic,' remains the paradigm question in cultural theory—at least in all those cultural theories (and theorists) which have not settled for an elegant but empty formalism."[18] This remains a central issue for all theories that seek to bridge the sociopolitical (postcoloniality as a historical condition) and the literary (postcoloniality as literary perspective). This is why I focus upon the details of one poem: the symbolic cannot be adduced as an illustration or allegorization of the social, but its own complexities and internal dissonances must be examined. Hall mentions that "what is socially peripheral may be symbolically central":[19] one should not assume an easy correspondence between the social and the symbolic, or between theory and art. The self-reflexive formalism of postcolonial theory that causes it to pay scrupulous attention to (first and foremost) itself continues to be one of its pitfalls. The case of Polish literature provides it with an additional challenge, since it represents a kind of Western literary periphery that, nevertheless, makes use of a "central" symbolic constellation.

Perhaps transitional countries such as Poland can indeed be considered central to the interests of postcolonial theory if we consider them as "third spaces," between a history of subjugation and a future of free development, between nationalist aspiration and fully capacitated political agency. Third spaces are between paradigms. They must be conceived in between conformity and absolute difference. There is a danger in hypostasizing difference. In politics, it can lead to violence toward the other; in theory, it can lead to new essentialisms that are built on the back of relativism. Attention to third spaces, liminalities of all different kinds, is necessary to combat dichotomous thinking. The state of the former second world reveals the partiality of first-world concepts such as postnationalism. More than a decade ago Michael Ignatieff argued that "globalism in a post-imperial age only permits a post-nationalist consciousness for those cosmopolitans who are lucky enough to live in the wealthy West . . . cosmopolitanism is the privilege of those who can take a secure nationalism for granted."[20] Since then, cosmopolitanism has been contested and only partially reclaimed as a mode of multiple allegiances instead of a falsely universalizing epistemology (as in James Clifford's famous concept of "discrepant cosmopolitanisms").[21] The question remains of how to conceptually negotiate the uncomfortably liminal space leading up to Ignatieff's so-called postnationalist consciousness. I am not sure that this consciousness ever exists in full, but even if it may be possible, a triumphant vision of global energies is very far from Świetlicki's foggy uncertainty, where "everything" gets washed out instead of becoming vitalized. The spread of a new global culture cannot be equated with an easy transformation in which a country like Poland suddenly leaps from the cultural paradigm of nationalism to a postnationalism that equals postmodernism. We must always remember the disjunctive temporality of the postcolonial state. Cultural development does not follow a straight line but moves in fits and starts; cut off by World War II and the advent of Stalinism, Poland's Modernist period was not allowed to play itself out into postmodernism. Świetlicki's short poem forces Romantic messianism and prewar catastrophism to join forces with Eliot's Modernism and Heaney's post-Romantic contemporaneity. The effect is startling and unclassifiable: in the end, one must take the poem not as a clear statement of alliance but as an extraordinarily ambiguous effort to assess the claims of Romanticism upon the contemporary world.

This sort of comparison—traversing worlds, traversing movements—pushes us toward a broader vision of cultural influence. The substance of world literature—or, as some would prefer, the worlding of literature—is a current focus of theory, yet by definition this subject cannot be conceptualized without attending to the specificities of influence. A break is usually put between Anglo-American Modernism and the contemporary period, yet recent scholars have pointed to the ethnocentricity of this scheme: Modernism (even if we take it as a singular movement) is not "over" in the rest of the world. Wai Chee Dimock has astutely observed that texts assume new forms of legibility each time they cross a national border, changing shape and emerging as fundamentally different texts abroad.[22] Readers must negotiate the difference between texts "over here" and "over there." Eliot's "Hollow Men" becomes a different poem when it reaches the changing second world, where it may function as a poem confronting a deep transition that approaches apocalypse, in which certain lyrical resources of poetry—language as chant, language as performative incantation, word as talismanic artifact—can serve as salvational resources for a poet confronting a crisis. Scholars have noted the danger of first-world readers' appropriating texts from the third world, but one must also recognize that readers in less powerful countries can make their own strategic use of canonical first-world texts. For example, Charles Pollard argues in *New World Modernisms* that Caribbean poets Derek Walcott and Kamau Brathwaite listened to Eliot reading his poems and heard a surprisingly *local* inflection, "the riddims of St. Louis," in his speech. Pollard couches this observation in an argument that Anglo-American postcolonial theory relies too heavily upon a faulty historical parallel: modernism is to postmodernism as colonialism is to postcolonialism.[23] Modernism may be recast in postcolonial contexts, and it may *combine* with postmodernism, as it has in Poland, a country that has traditionally looked to the West for its cultural influences. Świetlicki uses both Eliot and Heaney as his precursors in the search for a source of transcendence in a postapocalyptic landscape, and in so doing stitches together two stages of English poetic development through the experience of Poland's own transition.

What can a postcolonial theoretical paradigm reveal, and what can the experience of Poland give to enrich this paradigm? Can a country such as Poland be thought of as a "third space" between the postcolonial and the fully independent nation, and can it serve as a testing ground for theories of liminality and multiply located belonging? The question of cultural identity is never only a question of locating a people; it is also a matter of displacement and relocation. Contemporary (post-Derridean) theory's attention to difference also makes conceptualization a matter of displacement, dislocation; this is how concepts are challenged, by a constant disruption of what has been established. Postcolonial theory can be revitalized if "the global culture linked with postmodernism" ceases to be its main subject, and if "the traditional association between national spaces and cultural practices" is rethought as a complex relation with multiple liminalities (spaces between practices, between spatial labels).[24] The challenge for scholars is to articulate these aspects of identity instead of transcending them and creating a new tautology based on the subsumption of complexity: Poland = postcolony, or the Polish nation = the former Polish state, such as back in the "good old days" of the Polish-Lithuanian Commonwealth. By using the adjective "postcolonial" we can extend the experience of dislocation into a transnational framework. Stories of de- and reterritorialization (I use Gilles Deleuze and Félix Guattari's terms as usefully broad, textured concepts that encompass many different forms of change) help to cultivate an appreciation for the ineluctable multispatiality of contemporary experience.[25] An experience taking place between different territories, languages, and peoples must involve us in translation, since no single language can be adequate for its telling. Viewing Poland as postcolonial engages us in a critical project of complex translations, as one particular type of postcoloniality (we may call it the post-Soviet type) is translated into theoretical terms. These terms, though, must not overwhelm the specificity of Poland's postcolonial situation (its localness). The local can never be completely contained in a theoretical system.

Eastern Europe has not reached an end of history, as Francis Fukuyama would have it, but it has moved into what I would call an interstitial postcoloniality that is not an endpoint but a transitional stage in a process of self-definition. I would like to motion toward an expansion of the intellectual terrain of postcoloniality to encompass the former second world. This means that postcolonial studies will not be restricted to a first world–third world dichotomy. This dichotomy is showing signs of wear and tear as it ages, and it will not serve forever. I do not want to suggest that Western scholars in the unquestionably first world can hold forth a sophisticated theory as a panacea, or a lifeboat to rescue a victimized populace. This cannot be done by theory. We can, however, relocate the specific disciplinary strategies of postcolonial inquiry without weakening their core insights. Representation is not a completely free act but operates under the pressure of constantly changing currents of power, and a study of postcolonial Poland must bear in mind not just the power flowing from the Soviet imperial center but also the one stemming from the strong tradition of Romantic resistance and the energies of globally circulating cultural forms. A nation is not just a political entity: it is a system of cultural representations that registers, in subtle ways, the changes it undergoes. Reading postcoloniality through the dense formal medium of poetry reveals patterns of symbols that usefully complicate a purely political understanding of this term. By appending the adjective "postcolonial" to Poland, I hope to gesture toward a large-scale comparative framework.

Notes

1. Ramazani, 332–59. For a slightly older, yet extremely incisive discussion of the borders of postcoloniality, see Moore-Gilbert.
2. Kundera, "Die Weltliteratur," 28–35.
3. This term was first coined by Anderson.
4. All one needs to do to convince oneself of this state is to peruse the foreign travel section of a bookstore. "Europe"—meaning Western Europe—is granted several shelves or an entire bookcase, whereas "Eastern Europe" is often allotted one paltry half shelf.
5. Edmond Jabès, translated and cited in Chambers, 1.
6. The Gilroy work that I refer to is *After Empire*.
7. This is a terribly literal gloss on the concept of colonial desire, but I must refer the reader to Bill Johnston's work on Poland's eager adoption of the English language as an empowering and international second language for the country. Most Poles are very willing to learn new methods of communication. See Johnston, 126–45.
8. See Moore, 522.
9. See Hall; Hall and du Gay. The opposition of "routes" to "roots" is established powerfully in the work of anthropologist James Clifford. The 1990s were a fertile time for theories of constructed identity. The focus on movement, on mobile and mediated identities, has continued into the twenty-first century.

10. I am referring to Paul Gilroy's *The Black Atlantic*.

11. See the author's musings on whether one should visit the "mythic places" that one idealizes in Zagajewski, *Obrona żarliwości*, 160–69.

12. See Chambers, 2–4.

13. The original title is "Po nocy"; my translation.

14. For a clear discussion of doublespeak in the Soviet bloc, see the chapter entitled "Ketman" in Miłosz, *The Captive Mind*, 54–81.

15. Heaney, 143.

16. Eliot, 82.

17. It is interesting to note that in "Exposure," Heaney does develop a historical context for his rumination about "drops and let-downs," and fills his poem with delicate political gestures, though not heavy-handed political attitudes. Heaney summons a Romantic poetic persona even as he sinks him down into his disillusionments.

18. Morley and Chen, 286, 303.

19. Hall in Morley and Chen, 303.

20. *Blood and Belonging* (BBC documentary series, 1993–94). Ignatieff in Morley and Chen, 10–11.

21. The phrase appears in Clifford's essay "Traveling Cultures." The concept is expanded in Clifford's *Routes*.

22. This argument is contained in Dimock, 173–88. See also Damrosch.

23. See Pollard.

24. I take these phrases from Gikandi, 617.

25. For a differently sited defence of these experiences, see Seyhan.

The Empire Writes Back

Paweł Huelle's *Castorp* through a Postcolonial Lens

Dariusz Skórczewski

Castorp by Paweł Huelle, one of Poland's most accomplished contemporary writers,[1] has usually been interpreted vis-à-vis Thomas Mann's *The Magic Mountain.* A meticulous reader of Mann's masterwork may remember that before his arrival at Davos, Hans Castorp spent four terms studying at the Danzig Polytechnic Institute. It is around this digression that Paweł Huelle builds the plot of his novel, inserting into the biography of Mann's protagonist an extensive Gdańsk-based episode. Both Polish and German critics almost unanimously agree in praising Huelle for his skillful exploitation of literary tradition,[2] and at the same time for reviving the myth of Gdańsk, together with the distinctive atmosphere of this Baltic town and its vicinity.[3] They tend to focus on recognizing the germs of Mann's novel in Huelle's *Castorp*, looking for shared aspects of their treatment of time, narrator, philosophy, and so on. Although not intending to deflect the attention of the cognoscenti from these by-no-means-erroneous interpretations, this essay constitutes a move in quite a different direction, one aimed at exploring the postcolonial overtones present in *Castorp* and thus pinpointing the key differences between Huelle's and Mann's texts. It is my belief that reading Huelle's novel in the light of postcolonial theory reveals aspects of this work, primarily on its narrative as opposed to its aesthetic level, that allow *Castorp* to be viewed as a powerful counternarrative to the Grand Narrative of Western colonialism.

The situation of Paweł Huelle's *Castorp* is reminiscent to a certain extent of that of Jean Rhys's *Wide Sargasso Sea*. In this celebrated novel, Rhys challenges the canonical imperial narrative of Charlotte Brontë's *Jane Eyre*. By lending a voice to Brontë's animal-like and repulsive Bertha Rochester, whose name she changes to Antoinette Cosway, Rhys invites her readers into a contrapuntal rereading of Antoinette-Bertha's traumatic life-story from a clearly non-British perspective. As a result, in *Wide Sargasso Sea* we see a polemic response by a former British colony to the image of the periphery presented in the master narratives of the metropolitan center.[4]

This is how Rhys "writes back" to Brontë and the colonial discourse encapsulated in *Jane Eyre*.[5] It is my conviction that Huelle's novel should be viewed from a similar position. When interpreted alongside a standard colonial narrative, *Castorp* reveals itself as a novel that "writes back" to the tradition of European imperial writing. This essay briefly covers the four aspects of the novel that transgress the colonial paradigm—spatial arrangement, language, identity, and genre—and their implications for a postcolonial reading.

Writing about the specific qualities of colonized spaces, Frantz Fanon asserts:

> The zone where the natives live is not complementary to the zone inhabited by the settlers. The two zones are opposed, but not in the service of a higher unity. Obedient to the rule of Aristotelian logic, they both follow the principle of reciprocal exclusivity. No conciliation is possible, for of the two terms, one is superfluous. The town belonging to the colonized people, or at least the native town, . . . is a place of ill fame, peopled by men of evil repute. . . . The colonized man is an envious man. And this the settler knows very well; when their glances meet he ascertains bitterly, always on the defensive, "They want to take our place."[6]

Indeed, Gdańsk in *Castorp* is more than just a provincial melting pot bearing some marks of a splendid Hanseatic past. It is a town where the German population believes itself to be threatened by "uncivilized" and unpredictable savages, as remarked by an unnamed German character: "In this town we are in a completely different situation. You give them a finger and they jump up to your throat."[7] Viewed through the protagonist's eyes, Gdańsk seems to comply perfectly with Fanon's criteria of literary representation of colonized spaces. Dominated by Germans, it has Prussian barracks with Prussian soldiers, a newly established German university with German and Prussian students, and its every street and building resonates with the German language. The indigenous Polish and Kashubian people constitute an enclave driven to the margins of the world and its spatial representation. They occupy an array of impervious zones and do not mix with the dominating German population:

> Both Kashubians and Poles alike, indistinguishable to him by their language, were like a gray layer of dust: covered long ago with cobblestones, only at times to unveil its existence in places assigned to it throughout centuries: a suburban tavern, port warehouses, construction site, poor hut on a lowland, here and there a store in a district where no water supply system, tram communication, or gas lighting was installed.[8]

Besides the city of Gdańsk, Hans Castorp also gives himself to the exploration of the nearby woods and countryside, where he finds delight in contemplating the alien (Polish) landscape. In the descriptions of these landscapes, Huelle employs many tropes and figures that are well established in Polish literary discourse and familiar to Polish audiences, such as weeping willows, storks in the meadow, and birch groves. However, these elements are configured in a way that breaks with their two standard functions: emotional and identifying. They are no longer emblems of "Polishness," since Castorp is unable to recognize them as such. Rather, they are mere objects of his enchantment, thus underscoring Castorp's dominant position and their own vulnerability; they seem to exist only to give pleasure to the representative of the metropolitan center. In *Castorp*, Gdańsk's vicinity provides Germans with landscapes that bear features of "otherness" forceful enough to be tantamount to the exoticism of East and South-West Africa under German colonial rule.[9]

The protagonist and his German peers from the patrol of "Wandering Birds" are mystified and excited by the vast and uncivilized tracts of Kashubia they traverse. These landscapes are empty, depopulated, and virgin, calling for ownership, inheritance, patrimony—a commonplace trope in colonial literatures.[10] This appropriation transpires in *Castorp* on the symbolic plane. The protagonist admires these foreign landscapes from a perspective that, following Edward Said's definition, can be described as "oriental."[11] The subject's fascination with the observed objects is that of a conqueror who symbolically appropriates the exotic and stimulating territory through an epistemological act. Franz Schubert's song "Das Wandern," which Castorp sings during one of his excursions, seals this act of appropriation. The invocation of this song in the narrative is more than a mere sign of the cross-cultural association between nature and art transpiring in Castorp's sensitive soul; it becomes the most adequate instrument to reflect the enthusiasm aroused in Castorp by his encounter with Polish nature. Interestingly, a corresponding act is performed by Castorp's German peers, who in a similar context sing the words of Joseph von Eichendorff's "Wer hat dich, du schöner Wald" ("Who built you up so high, beautiful forest?") to a composition by Felix Mendelssohn-Bartholdy.[12] Both Castorp and his peers find themselves unable to describe the contemplated alien landscape in its own terms. Instead, by referring to the two aforementioned works of the German Romantic era, they all impose a colonial discourse onto this landscape. This discourse appropriates the territory at the same time as it "appropriates the means by which such acts of appropriation are to be understood."[13] Such means of appropriation here are the two "innocent" cultural texts of German Romanticism.

The importance of spatial arrangement for the postcolonial overtones present in Huelle's novel becomes apparent very early. Already in the opening interaction between Hans Castorp and his uncle Tiennaple, the uncle reveals views on the "East" that are characteristic of any Western imperial discourse. In this scene, Huelle revives the classically orientalist image of the East presented by Mann in *The Magic Mountain*.[14] In *Castorp*, the East is a formidable territory where unpredictable events may occur, a realm in which "forms that have been worked out with much difficulty may plunge into chaos."[15] By warning his nephew, Uncle Tiennaple actually duplicates the myths concerning the Orient's lurking temptations and the dangers that await an unwitting newcomer. These myths proliferate in a great many imperial literatures. "Please, consider how easy it is to deviate from a once-taken road. An insignificant word, an instant of weakness, a moment of oblivion may all ruin the efforts of many years. In the East these things simply happen more often, although one cannot rationally prove it."[16] Interestingly enough, the prophecy encapsulated in this warning is fulfilled in the novel. Castorp eventually does succumb to the East in a way that imitates the widely exploited literary representation of the Orient. The East is embodied in a tempting woman with a sensual scent of musk and "delicately protruding cheekbones that, together with the peculiar, slightly whimsical expression of her mouth, gave an *exotic* allure to her face, an ambiguous and attracting *strangeness*."[17]

We are frequently reminded by the novel's characters that the era of colonization left its mark on their reality. Pastor Gropius, "having spent twenty years in the midst of the blackest tribes of Bantustan,"[18] is offered a parish near Gdańsk that is in close proximity to the metropolitan center. Another character, the Dutch merchant Kiekernix who reaps profits from trading with overseas colonies, in informing his copassengers about the peripheral status of Gdańsk calls it a "provincial shit hole with no theatre worthy of the name."[19] The dialogue that takes place between these two characters is quite revealing. The pastor gives a speech in defense of German imperialism, justifying it as a "civilizing mission," a universal argument of every spokesman of a colonial enterprise. The rhetoric of *mission civilisatrice* reproduces figures of speech widely employed by British and French writers and politicians of the nineteenth and early twentieth centuries:

> We came late to Asia and Africa, that's true. But how about Eastern Europe? For centuries we have been the carriers of law, order, and harmony of art and technique. Without us the Slavs would long ago have fallen into anarchy. It is thanks to our benevolence that they find their place in the family named civilization and culture.[20]

Kiekernix offers an immediate riposte to the pastor's claims, one that seems to imitate some of the arguments offered by the more aggressive postcolonial critics. Let me quote it *in extenso*, for it lays out the direction in which the author develops his narrative:

> Ladies and gents, please imagine that one day an armada of foreign, Indian or Chinese vessels calls at Amsterdam. . . . They force us to worship their God, they kill our king, rape our women, and drive our men to coalmines or plantations. Syphilis, smallpox, quinsy, cheap vodka, and opium do the rest. Then their preacher tells us to thank them for their care through which we found ourselves in the family of civilization and culture. . . . That's exactly how Indians, Asians, and blacks feel today.[21]

And we may add: so do Kashubians and Poles. In this remarkable passage, the postcolonial problematic is powerfully brought into the very core of the novel. Kiekernix's voice fixes the plot of *Castorp* in the sociopolitical reality of the early twentieth century according to the established patterns of literary representation in British, French, or German writings of the time. Such patterns were thoroughly examined by Said. This is where Huelle's respect for the principles of spatial organization in colonial discourse ends, however. From this point on in *Castorp*, we encounter examples of the transgression of those orientalizing clichés.

For the eponymous hero the Prussian presence in Gdańsk is an unpleasant burden. Castorp's attempt at crossing the boundary of urban space during one of his outings ends with only a qualified success because of his accidental and undesired encounter with his German peers. That encounter highlights Castorp's stance as an outsider vis-à-vis other Germans in the novel. Clearly playing the role of an "understanding link" between the two separated zones, the protagonist distances himself from his compatriots, especially those who represent the chauvinist Prussian mentality. This distance is powerfully manifested through the binary structure of the novel's scenery.

Huelle's Castorp strolls along the streets of Gdańsk and Sopot performing typical acts of perception. Despite his young age and a certain philosophical immaturity (it is still before he meets Naphta and Settembrini, the two advocates of the opposing discourses of dictatorship and liberalism in *The Magic Mountain* who inspire him to seek answers to life's most vital questions), his encounter with the culture of an oppressed nation makes him richer than his Mann-invented predecessor. Castorp matures through his discovery of his own identity as a member of a nation that exercises authority over the population of Poles and Kashubians, both of which are viewed to be inferior. This bildungsroman thread is very subtly intertwined into the very tissue of Huelle's plot.

Although certain areas of the novel's space, such as hotels and ships, are marked by German names, most places bear Polish names. Instead of Soppot and Danzig we have Sopot and Gdańsk. In a similar vein, "ulica Kasztanowa" (Chestnut Street) is not replaced with "Kastanienstrasse." To a newcomer from a colonial center, this space continually demonstrates its inherent strangeness, mysteriousness, and impenetrability. This space extends itself into other areas of the nonexistent Poland. As Castorp becomes directly involved in the novel's intrigue, we see his finger traversing a map of Russia, searching for Lublin.

Leaving behind the novel's scenery, we now move on to the issue of language. The sentence "Only German is spoken here!" points to the symbolic role played by this language in the novel. [22] German in *Castorp* is an instrument of hegemony that incorporates the famous dictum by Fanon: "A man who has a language consequently possesses the world expressed and implied by that language."[23] It is the official language in German-ruled Pomerania, as well as the language of communication between characters, despite its various regional dialects so assiduously identified by the protagonist's ear. First and foremost, however, it is the language of power. When contaminated, it must be unmercifully rejected not only for the sake of purity but also to maintain power. The accent of the university's clerk, for instance, a most unfortunate person ridiculed by his environment, drives him to suicide. On the other hand, Dr. Ankewitz, a Polish exile from the Russian partition, can start his psychiatric practice in the German empire owing to his perfect command of German.

The hegemony of the German language, however, is powerfully challenged by Huelle. The first instance of transgression occurs when Castorp meets a poor Kashubian boy. The boy is at first depicted in full conformity to the well-established pattern of imperial narratives: his clothes are ragged and his "bare feet shod with flimsy sandals."[24] He is a typical representative of the indigenous people of Gdańsk, looked down upon by the colonizers. Similar to the Arabs in the work of Albert Camus,[25] he remains anonymous, with no certain identity. Despite his subalternity, however, the boy bests Castorp with his language competence, which the latter painfully realizes at the end of their flawed conversation. In an imperial novel,[26] for example Gustav Freytag's 1855 *Soll und Haben* (Debit and Credit), the protagonist would most likely dismiss this confrontation with some denigrating comments on the Poles' undeveloped civilization, the barbarism of the obscure and rustling Polish speech, or the supremacy of the Prussian educational system and its civilizing mission.[27] Huelle's Castorp, however, does none of these things. He refrains from striking a triumphant note, giving himself up to the strange feeling of "not having access to something that for others is as clear as air" instead.[28] This agonizing epistemological difference realized by Castorp through his failed interaction with the boy stigmatizes his perception and contributes to his maturation, which involves the questioning of and emancipation from German cultural hegemony. In Freytag's *Soll und Haben* we are offered "a racialized account of Polish subjects in which the Eastern borderlands [of the Prussian empire] are portrayed as a primitive, chaotic, wild space begging for colonial incursion."[29] In *Castorp*, however, the imperial dismissal of Poles for their alleged cultural inferiority and backwardness is powerfully challenged through the protagonist's encounter with the anonymous boy.

The second break with language domination is in the relationship between the widowed Mrs. Hildegarda Wybe and her Kashubian housekeeper, Kaszibke. Although a member of the subjugated ethnicity, Kaszibke reveals herself to be a very vivid, strong, and outspoken character in the novel. Huelle does away with the stereotype that is so commonplace in imperial literatures, in which the subaltern servant is invisible and silent, without the right to his or her own opinions.[30] Kashibke, in contrast, can be considered a graphic illustration of a recovered voice of the subaltern.[31] Kaszibke seems to be introduced into the narrative for one purpose: to reverse the traditional order and divulge the dependence of the colonizer on the colonized. Although she is given piano lessons by her mistress, the Kashubian girl actually dominates Mrs. Wybe through her simple yet forceful language. It is Kaszibke, and not Mrs. Wybe, who actually holds power in the home where Castorp rents his room. She is not subject to the patriarchal order, as demonstrated by her disrespectful attitude to Castorp, whose authority as a male representative of the metropolis is thus jeopardized. She speaks out against Mrs. Wybe, even allowing herself to raise her voice with impunity in her mistress's presence—behavior unheard of in imperial narratives. Her coarse speech along with her self-assured gestures displays the power she exerts over Mrs. Wybe: "For reasons that were completely inconceivable for Castorp, it was the girl who appeared to rule over Mrs. Wybe, and not the other way round. It seemed as if the employer was afraid to offend the servant in any way."[32]

Mrs. Wybe excuses herself in Castorp's presence for her subservience to Kaszibke by blaming her disconnection from the imperial center: "You see, in Berlin everything was different."[33] In this way the metropolitan hegemony over peripheries is questioned yet again. Kaszibke seems to display the ambivalent effect of colonization. She performs as if she were a replica of the colonizer, imitating the colonizer's speech and gestures; she is the colonizer's mirror image, yet this image is distorted and caricatural, in accordance with what Homi Bhabha described as "mimicry."[34] The colonizer's behavior is copied by the colonized population, yet this imitation is deeply subversive, bearing traces of mockery and menace. A symbolic act of this subversion is Kaszibke's mediocre performance of a classical piece by an Austrian composer: "The composition, which seventeen years earlier was entrusted by Strauss to an orchestra and the admirable soprano of Bianchi, resonated miserably and forlornly in the apartment on Kasztanowa Street, like a denial of the Viennese nimbleness from which it was born."[35] Consequently, the authority of colonial discourse as epitomized by Mrs. Wybe is threatened, and the colonial domination is destabilized. It is worth noticing that these repeated acts of destabilization are performed by a female rather than a male character, another example of the way in which Huelle subverts principles of imperial narratives in his novel.

A third instance of the transgression of the colonial narrative with respect to language is related to the mysterious Wanda Pilecka, who is the epitome of otherness in both appearance and behavior. Although Polish by ethnicity, her position in the novel is that of Castorp's outspoken partner rather than of a silent representative of a subjugated nation, as exemplified by her free multilingual conversations at the table. Captivated by Pilecka's charm, the protagonist seeks to discover her true identity and is initially led astray by her multilinguistic proficiency to consider her as Russian. This is how we come to the third aspect in which *Castorp* contravenes the colonial script, namely, the issue of identity.

Castorp is astonished by the discovery of Wanda's true nationality, and his bewilderment grows even larger when he finds out that her lover is a Russian officer. This finding destroys the stereotypical image of Polish-Russian relations suggested by Castorp's all-too-rudimentary knowledge of Poland's history. This knowledge, as a matter of fact, only reiterates the clichés of German imperial education of the time: "In the history class at the gymnasium he only had one lesson about Poland: the anarchy and alcoholism of the noblemen led to the partitions, because this ulcer in the very midst of Europe had to be cut out quickly for hygienic reasons."[36] In the novel, knowledge of subjugated ethnic groups such as Poles and Kashubians is an element of the discourse of power. It encompasses historiography, anthropology, and ethnology and resembles the writings on conquered peoples produced by British, French, or German scientists, writers, and travelers. As Said points out in *Orientalism*,[37] such knowledge is never a neutral and disinterested description. On the contrary, its purpose is to solidify power over the object of study. Huelle's plot follows this pattern. To paraphrase Said, in *Castorp* Germans do know Poles, and Poles are that which is known by Germans and exist only insofar as they are narrated.[38] This is how we come to realize the importance of the evolution of the protagonist's awareness for the postcolonial overtone of the novel. Castorp's deeper acquaintance with Poles extracts them from the condition of virtual nonexistence, giving them a more subjective and autonomous status in the novel, one unattainable in imperial narratives such as Freytag's *Debit and Credit* or Nataly von Eschstruth's *Polish Blood: A Romance*.

This is how Wanda Pilecka, a representative of the nation whose colonization seemed legitimate and even advantageous in light of Castorp's education, is elevated to the position of his partner and even his would-be lover. Throughout the novel, she constantly appears as a relaxed person, which is an unusual characteristic for a member of a colonized nation to have. Although she initiates Castorp into some parts of her biography, and even thanks him for providing her with an alibi, Wanda never loses her dignity, nor does she develop any kind of dependence on him. Instead, she gains authority over him, first by destabilizing his burgher lifestyle by becoming a hidden object of his desire, and then by halting their acquaintance with an elegant yet firm gesture. The subtle erotic passage between Wanda and Castorp has an equivocal ending: on the one hand, it violates the stereotypes that the two nations have of each other, while on the other it lends support to one of the foundational Polish myths—that of Queen Wanda who refused to marry a German prince.[39]

Castorp's unfulfilled desire to become Wanda's lover and his emasculation by her add yet another connotation to the postcolonial overtone of the novel. By arranging for his protagonist to cede his dominant position to Wanda, Huelle executes a reversal of the German imperial narrative:

> In the post-1890 *Ostmarkenromane*, marriage would not serve as a viable option to solve political/colonial tensions in the Eastern borderlands. . . . Most of these novels tended in fact to use the topic of marriage, normally to a Polish woman, to underline the threat against German cultural values. German men were portrayed as victims of the Polish national cause, which used Polish women to emasculate them. These novels coincided with an emergent discourse in the sciences of racial degeneration— addressed particularly by the then recently established *Rassenhygiene*—that was common at the turn of the century, and that would especially target women in the experts' quest to culturally and biologically lift up Germany. In this context, the "horrors" of mixed marriages, so universal in the overseas colonies, were being echoed in the descriptions of German-Polish national struggles.[40]

Given this tendency in German prose at the turn of the twentieth century, that is, shortly before Castorp enrolled in Gdańsk Polytechnic Institute, an intimate relationship with a Polish woman should not have been considered an option by Castorp. As conscientious as he is about the historical precision of his narratives, Huelle must have been aware of this context. The fact that it is Wanda, and not Castorp, who takes the initiative to part in Huelle's novel, however, shows this aspect of the German colonial narrative from a different, subversive perspective. Castorp, a male member of the colonizing population, is thus emasculated. Besides his being unable to control his own emotions, he loses authority over his own narrative and is subjected to the more powerful narrative, or perspective, of Wanda. As a result of their parting, Wanda's position is solidified, while that of Castorp is diluted. Pilecka's voice is a blatant example of a female discourse in Huelle counterbalancing and challenging the dominant, male discourse of the empire.

To be sure, such a reconfiguration within the novel's narrative is purposeful. The biography of Castorp emphasizes his affiliation with the center of the German empire. Wanda's role in the development of Castorp's awareness of the empire is critical. It is through Theodor Fontane's *Effi Briest*, the novel stolen from Pilecka by the protagonist, that Castorp's memories, along with the imperial myth, are invoked: "His own life, growing in the shade of harbor cranes and ocean ships, of the stock market, worldly interests, and colonial merchandise, in comparison with a rutted sandy road in Pomerania, or the Sunday sermon of a village preacher, suddenly seemed full of light."[41]

Castorp goes from a metropolitan center, where civilization, power, capital, and prosperity coexist in harmony, to the peripheries where those values are challenged by the different values that he has only begun to discover, principally through his fascination with the charming stranger. It is interesting to notice that before Castorp meets Pilecka, Poles are almost absent from the plot of Huelle's novel. The hero and his environment are German, while the exotic peoples of the East appear only to reaffirm the purpose of colonial discourse, namely, "to construe the colonized as a population of degenerate types . . . in order to justify conquest."[42] The scandalous assassination of a German goldsmith by a Polish apprentice and his fiancée that made local headlines flawlessly fits this paradigm, consigning the dominated to the realm of anarchy. It also reinforces the essential imperial stereotype of savage, primitive, and atavistic indigenous peoples who are bereft of human agency and therefore must be civilized by the enlightened empire.

When Wanda and her Russian lover enter the scene, a "Polish-Russian knot" is tied together to broaden Castorp's horizons and shift the narrative onto a postcolonial plane. [43] The protagonist is presented as a newcomer who arrives at the peripheries from a metropolis in order to deconstruct the imperial myth and discover the actual identity of the subjugated peoples, a process that in turn allows him to grow conscious of and become disturbed by his own identity. Significantly, the theme of identity is pervasive throughout the novel. It is constantly rehearsed through the introduction of a host of characters whose key role is to affect Castorp's own outlook and perception. Besides Pilecka, such characters include the captain and crew of the steamship *Mercury*, on which Castorp voyages to Gdańsk; Castorp's travel mates, who define their positions on various issues with reference to their nationality, social rank, religion, and degree of involvement in the colonial enterprise; the Kashubian boy who challenges Castorp's cultural competence; Dr. Ankewitz and the clerk who admit Castorp to the Polytechnic Institute, each of whom initiates him into a world new to the protagonist; and even the ticket inspector of uncertain identity who, despite his lower status, treats Castorp with disdain for his awkwardness in using public transportation. Thus, Castorp is placed into an array of relations to other characters and situations that eventually drives him to question his well-settled canonical image of Germany and imperial Europe derived from his formal education. He comes to the realization that he belongs to a colonizing nation, and this discovery is a source of repulsion rather than pride to him. The process of gaining this awareness constitutes a vital layer of Huelle's narrative. It culminates in the symbolic gesture of his rejection of both German and Russian imperialism in the final pages of the novel. Having encountered these two imperial discourses, woven into the lecture on Goethe and a Russian textbook, respectively, Castorp demystifies them and ostentatiously refuses to participate in the colonial enterprise represented by them.

At this point it becomes patent that Huelle breaks with the traditional scheme of the Western European bildungsroman, thus transgressing the fourth aspect of colonial narrative listed at the beginning of this essay. In a formative novel, the theme of the relationship between the metropolis and the periphery is interwoven with the topic of maturation and initiation into adult society. As Estonian critic Piret Peiker explains, the traditional Western bildungsroman fits the following scheme:

> Typically, a young individual leaves home, frequently after a conflict between generations; he goes into the wide world, often traveling from province to metropolis, where he experiences and learns, develops and matures as an individual. Having become reconciled with society, or at least having consolidated his attitude towards it, he returns home, where he is recognized as an adult member of society with legitimate agency.[44]

Bypassing Castorp's further vita as presented in Thomas Mann's narrative, the Polish prequel to *The Magic Mountain* only partly follows the above scheme and does so only to ultimately undermine it. The dilemmas that Huelle's protagonist is exposed to, and the way he thinks, acts, and behaves, are atypical of those in a bildungsroman. Castorp does leave his home in Hamburg after a conflict with his elderly uncle, and he does learn, develop, and mature as a result of his travels, but he travels in the opposite direction—from center to periphery—and his education is consummated in a way that questions the formative dimension of a typical bildungsroman journey. He evolves from an unaware representative of the German colonial enterprise into its fierce opponent. His initiation into adulthood leads Castorp to distance himself from his compatriots and to take sides with the subaltern instead, another unprecedented deviation from such standard colonial narratives as Dickens's *Great Expectations* and Brontë's *Jane Eyre*. Instead of reconciliation with society and recognition as its adult member, Castorp experiences alienation that leads to his powerful rebuttal of the German and Russian colonial projects. This alienation and rebuttal are grounded in the fact that Castorp's encounter with the periphery becomes for him a thought-provoking lesson on the dubious nature of the colonial enterprise and the subject status of the colonized people. Maturity thus achieved contradicts and subverts the imperial social pattern reinforced by the Western formative novel. From the conclusion of the novel readers may assume that Castorp's world is never going to be as stable and consistent as it should be according to the requirements of the bildungsroman. Such a modification of the genre is evidently telling. The Enlightenment's grand topos of ongoing progress in the world fueled by the unhampered activity of an individual, inscribed into the Grand Narrative of colonialism, is thus demystified in *Castorp*.

All these ingredients of Paweł Huelle's novel demonstrate that although it is in many ways indebted to Thomas Mann's *Magic Mountain*, as rightly maintained by critics, *Castorp* is a product of the literary consciousness of the postcolonial era. Although writing from the shadow of the European Grand Narrative, Huelle does not confine himself to reiterating its modes of representation. Instead, he finds his own path of "writing back" from the periphery to the center. The author of *Castorp* uses a postcolonial perspective to dexterously exploit the narrative strategies of colonial discourse. He deploys these strategies with the intent to enter into a polemic with the discourse itself and to propose a different approach to the Grand Narrative of the Western European novel. *Castorp*'s brief final *Nachgeschichte*, consisting of some snapshots of Gdańsk's complex history throughout the twentieth century, leads to the following conclusion: the Gdańsk-based episode in Castorp's biography is narrated from a perspective accessible only to a writer of our time, a perspective brought into existence as late as after the demise of the German and Soviet empires and the dismantling of their colonies. One can only hope that German critics and scholars, so enthusiastic about Huelle's perfect imitation of Mann's style and his skillful reconstruction of Gdańsk's and Sopot's ambience at the turn of the century, will also spot this dimension of the novel and thereby break the silence surrounding German "white colonialism."[45]

NOTES

A modified and extended version of this paper has been published in Polish as "Dlaczego Paweł Huelle napisał Castorpa?" in *Teksty Drugie* 3 (2006): 148–57.

1. Paweł Huelle's first novel *Weiser Dawidek* (1987) was unanimously hailed by Polish critics as the preeminent book of the 1980s. Huelle was awarded numerous prizes and awards, including the Kościelski Foundation Prize (1988); the Andreas Gryphius Prize (1992), a German award in recognition of efforts to reconcile European nations; the Polish PEN Club Award (1995); and the Alfred Jurzykowski Foundation Prize (1996).

2. See, for examples, Döbler; Drewnowski; Głowiński, "Nad *Castorpem*"; Jung; Kurzke; Madejski; Scharffenberg; and Zaleski.

3. *Castorp* is not the first Polish narrative to revive the myth of Gdańsk as a multicultural town with a glorious Hanseatic past in which three traditions (Polish, Kashubian, and German) merge and leave their imprints as in a palimpsest. It was preceded by Huelle's *Who Was David Weiser?* and his collection of short stories *Opowiadania na czas przeprowadzki* (1991, English title *Moving House: Stories*), as well as Stefan Chwin's *Hanemann* (1995; English title *Death in Danzig*). On the reading of Gdańsk as a palimpsest, see Bagłajewski, Halikowska-Smith, Quinkenstein, Schmidgall, and Ubertowska.

4. Ciolkowski, 351.

5. I am referring here to the notorious statement first voiced in an article by Salman Rushdie (8), and subsequently repeated by Ashcroft, Griffiths, and Tiffin in the title of their collaborative book *The Empire Writes Back*.

6. Fanon, *Wretched of the Earth*, 39.

7. Huelle, *Castorp*, 98.

8. Ibid., 160.

9. For a discussion of German-colonized Africa as a source of inspiration for German art, see N'guessan.

10. McClintock, 30.

11. Said, *Orientalism*, 3.

12. Huelle, *Castorp*, 163.

13. Spurr, 28.

14. This image of the "Orient" in Mann is encarnalized in the enigmatic and exotic Russian lady Claudia Chauchat.

15. Huelle, *Castorp*, 8.

16. Ibid., 10.

17. Ibid., 95, italics mine.

18. Ibid.,14.

19. Ibid.,15.

20. Ibid., 23.

21. Ibid., 23.

22. Ibid., 108.

23. Fanon, *Black Skin*, 18.

24. Huelle, *Castorp*, 50.

25. Said, *Culture and Imperialism*, 175–76.

26. Kopp, *Ich stehe*, 225.

27. Cf. Macaulay.

28. Huelle, *Castorp*, 51.

29. Ureña, 5.

30. McClintock, 163–66.

31. Spivak, "Can the Subaltern Speak?," 271.

32. Huelle, *Castorp*, 57.

33. Ibid., 58.

34. Bhabha, *Location of Culture*, 86.

35. Huelle, *Castorp*, 111.

36. Ibid., 184. The views held by Castorp concerning Polish lands and Poles are reflective of Bismarck's *Kulturkampf* policies, among them the decided sharpening of the German government's already stern anti-Polish offensive during the 1880s (cf. Berghahn, 27; Blanke, 55–91; Davies, *God's Playground*, 2:92–93). These views also replicate some points of the program outlined by the German philosopher Eduard Hartmann in his 1885 article "Rückgang des Deutschtums" ("Retreat of Germandom"). Hartmann promulgated arguments for "strengthening the cohesiveness of Germany and germanizing the minorities. He demanded that alien and inimical elements be eliminated [*ausrotten*]" (see Wandycz, *Lands of Partitioned Poland*, 236; cf. Blanke, 45–46.)

37. Said, *Orientalism*, 15.

38. Huelle, *Castorp*, 34.

39. According to the pre-Christian folk myth first recorded by Master Wincenty Kadłubek in *Chronica Polonorum* in the early thirteenth century (Kadłubek, 17–18) and repeated by subsequent chroniclers such as Jan Długosz, the mythical Queen Wanda, beautiful daughter of King Krak, chose to commit suicide by throwing herself into the Vistula River instead of marrying a German prince, who would have thus become a ruler of the Polish lands. See also Davies, *God's Playground*, 1:52.

40. Ureña, 6. Ureña's inference is based upon Kopp, "Contesting Borders." See also Lieskounig.

41. Huelle, *Castorp*, 113.

42. Bhabha, *Location of Culture*, 70.

43. Huelle, *Castorp*, 185.

44. Peiker, 4.

45. Reviews of *Castorp* by German critics have generally passed over its postcolonial overtones in silence. One potential reason for this is that thus far, postcolonial methodology in the area of German studies has been noticeably confined to analyses of German imperial discourse during the "scramble for Africa" and thus focused on only one pattern of colonization (overseas colonialism). Consequently, German colonization of contiguous territories, i.e., the German *Drang nach Osten*, has been almost entirely excluded from German postcolonial critique (cf. Berman, 237), and the problems of German "white colonialism" in East Central Europe (primarily Poland) have been substantially neglected (a rare exception being Lieskounig's analysis of *Soll und Haben*).

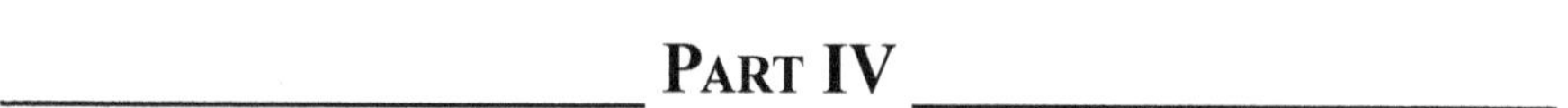

Part IV

Memory, Trauma, Mourning

Ways of Remembering

The Case of Poland

Ewa M. Thompson

Of the ten countries admitted to the European Union on May 1, 2004, Poland is the largest. While Poles like to think that the admission signaled Europe's welcoming of its stepchildren back into the European fold, their presence in that fold is precarious. One missing element is *acknowledged* history; each European country has managed to export such history abroad as part of the body of remembered events that, taken together, form the canon of European identity. Polish history, and the history of other countries collectively called "Eastern Europe," remains unacknowledged in European (and American) memory. Therefore, in my essay I shall appeal not to that presumed knowledge but rather to another and more universal kind of knowledge: an awareness of the fact that exclusion from the standard texts celebrating memory has momentous consequences for an ethnic or cultural group. It makes the group appear dumb and unable to articulate itself, and it leaves it open to being defined by others.[1] As Paul Ricoeur suggests, history "overly remembers" some events at the expense of others.[2]

While it is impossible, in the short run, to remedy the absence of Polish history in the standard histories of Europe (Norman Davies being an admirable exception), it may be possible to enter the historical edifice through a side door, as it were, by reflecting on the ways of remembering common in Poland and in other non-Germanic countries of Central Europe. I am using a crutch here, and the crutch is the interest in memory that surfaced in scholarship some decades ago. I have in mind the work of such scholars as Jan Assmann and Aleida Assmann, Paul Ricoeur, Pierre Nora, Jay Winters, Hayden White, and Ron Robin, as well as the various conferences that have been organized in the nineties relating to memory, such as the Bivigliano conference in 1998, or the 2001 Princeton workshop on memory in which I participated.[3] These works and these scholars combine an interest in history with an interest in individual and group identity, and trace the interaction of the two. They show that history "wie es eigentlich gewesen," as German scholars used to put it, is problematic, because "how it really happened" requires continuous updating. History is related to memory, and what is remembered and what is forgotten constitute an interesting object of study.

Why is it worthwhile to study memories? One reason is that the memories of a given ethnic group are a key to the understanding of that group. The collective memories of a national group—for it is mainly within nation-states that memories are catalogued and conserved—provide a key to the self-understanding of a national group, and for those who do not belong to it, they provide clues to the way its politicians and people react to events or generate them. A study of the ways of remembering also enables us to see more clearly what is being forgotten or suppressed.

Another question that could be posed is, Why should Poles or anyone else remember anything at all? Even before Francis Fukuyama erroneously proclaimed the end of history, some thinkers noted that humanity might be much better off if history were entirely forgotten, if we all became a people without memory.[4] Such postulates are, of course, utopian. The freedom to remember and to preserve the memory of the past is a condition necessary for a civilized society to exist.[5] Without the freedom to remember we lose our ability to put events in perspective and to understand the present state of the world. As Karol Wojtyła put it in his last book, "[m]emory is the faculty which models the identity of human beings at both a personal and a collective level."[6] Therefore, memory is important not only for nationalistic reasons but also, and primarily, because it helps to make us into civilized beings and enables us to solve problems.

The terms used in this essay—memory, communal memory, collective memory, traumas, closure—should be addressed first. Let us start with *memory*.[7] Memory is what we remember. Memory and commemoration are meant to prevent the disappearance of individuals and communities into the "memory hole."[8] There are *personal memories*, there are *family memories*, and there are *communal memories*. The first two are self-explanatory, and they should be treated with caution as ingredients of historical memory: false memories and memories into which interpretation has been injected are commonly proffered in the courts of law.[9] *Communal memory* is the memory of a group of people who live in a certain neighborhood and who remember what happened in their particular area because they witnessed it themselves and while witnessing it experienced no outside pressure aimed at altering their memories. Under normal circumstances, communal memories are trustworthy, and they enjoy legal, historical, and moral acceptance. One of the wounds inflicted on colonized nations by their occupiers is the *delegitimization of communal memory*: the memories of those who lived in a particular area for generations are dismissed; instead, the colonialist's version of events is ushered in. This is true with regard to Polish memories of World War II, as opposed to Russian memories, which have generally been accepted in the West as legitimate. This is also true of Ukrainian memories over the last several centuries: here not only Russia but also Poland contributed to the delegitimization of communal memory.[10]

One should make a distinction between communal memory and *collective memory*.[11] Unlike communal memory, collective memory is acquired not by direct participation in events but by reading or hearing about them, that is, indirectly. Collective memory is the property of cultural groups and nations. It is shared by communities that do not necessarily live in the same neighborhood but have the same group loyalties. Collective memory reworks, compresses, and ideologizes communal memories. It sometimes mythologizes events and incorporates them into the already congealed categories of *national mythology*. It is sometimes identified with *historical memory*, although the latter term is also used for cultural memory, which is a happier and healthier sort of memory. What is the difference? Collective memory is transformed into cultural memory when all the traumas have reached closure and there is little bitterness in remembering one's history. Cultural memory is a civilized memory, a memory that is not a signal for vengeance or an invitation to bitterness. It rearranges events of the past into categories that become part of one's cultural identity; it enriches a person instead of embittering him or her. Needless to say, such embitterment easily arises if a cultural community feels slighted or not properly recognized. However, with the passing of time and the creation of written texts and other artifacts, the *collective traumas* that a cultural community (nation) has experienced reach a sense of closure, and its members consign them to the past. The traumas become part and parcel of the cultural memory of a nation, rather than a means of inflaming imagination. Some group traumas become part of the world's cultural memory.

But the key distinction between collective memory and cultural memory is the lack of bitterness and of a desire to "get even." The history of the United States provides many examples of this kind of healthy development. It is true, of course, that in the United States cultural memory developed in extremely propitious circumstances, the most important being a lack of external diplomatic, economic, or military pressure. As they progress and mature, both collective and cultural memories begin to include conceptual knowledge and develop their own canon of texts, musical works, paintings and sculptures, movies and stage plays, and folk art. The two blend and diverge from each other, and fortunate is the nation-state whose cultural memory prevails over the collective one. Thus one can speak of a *hierarchy of memories*: from individual and family memory to communal memory to collective memory, and then to a sense of closure and consignment of past traumas to cultural memory.[12]

With these distinctions in mind, it must be said that Poles have faced difficulties in partaking of the process of transformation of memories. This process was thwarted by the colonial occupation of Poland after World War II and earlier, in the period of the so-called partitions of Poland.[13] Such obstacles can hardly be appreciated in the United States, which has, since winning its independence from Britain, never been occupied by a foreign power. The most important cultural aspect of colonial occupation is that writing and publishing historical books (which are the reservoirs of memory) and distributing historical information are severely curtailed. Between 1939 and 1989, there was no freedom to remember in Poland. Of course, Poles did remember even under the Soviets, but these memories were weakened and distorted by the lack of free discussion. The denial of access to memory, which was a prime feature of communism, was therefore destructive to Polish political culture and to the political culture of other Soviet-occupied nations as well.

Here is an example of such damage. In a book entitled *Sites of Memory, Sites of Mourning*, historian Jay Winter writes about the collective remembrance of World War I in European cultural history.[14] He speaks of communities in mourning, of war memorials, war poetry, and the grieving process. But Winter's Europe ends at the Oder River; it does not include Poland or other countries of non-Germanic Central Europe. Here you have one of the many consequences of a denial of access to memory in Poland after World War II, when memories of World War I congealed through hundreds and thousands of books written about that war in the first-world countries. Under the Soviet occupation the Poles could not insert their presence into European discourse because they could not publish freely. The same could be said about the period of partitions when the word "Poland" was deliberately erased from discourse.[15] Similar things happened to other Central and Eastern European nations. Since the relevant books remained unwritten, there was no transfer of communal, collective, or cultural memory beyond the borders of the ethnic community. The colonizer's interests reinforced the dropping of non-Germanic Central Europe into the memory hole. Thus the common cultural mistake of excluding Poland from such books as Winter's became standard, and few recognize it as a mistake. The culture of commemoration that Poland shares with Western Europe was obliterated from Western Europe's cultural memory.

The Western European nations entered the Great War and came out of it with their identities bruised but essentially intact: France remained France, Germany remained Germany, and England remained England. They read one another's books. They recognized one another and honored one another's memories. The memories of the Great War in Western Europe included traumas, but under these circumstances they also included closures. In contrast, the traumas experienced by the countries of Central and Eastern Europe received no recognition outside their respective ethnic communities. Therefore, the sense of closure that the Western European nations shared and enjoyed escaped non-Germanic Central Europe. The traumas remained vivid and active. The books that would outline these traumas had not been written. The cultural memories of the Western Europeans developed without taking their Eastern neighbors into account, a fact that then translated into not only cultural but also economic, political, and military developments. Western Europeans then accused their Eastern neighbors of chauvinism, nationalism, and assorted xenophobias without realizing or indeed caring about the impossibility of achieving closure without outside recognition of one's communal and collective memories. After 1945, when Western Europe began to enjoy peace, liberty, and the Marshall Plan, Poland and other Central European countries were subjected to Soviet occupation, colonial dependency, and the manipulation or destruction of communal memories owing to the forcible dislocation of populations from the east to the west. Books discussing these events were not allowed to appear.

Parallel to these developments, throughout the period of Soviet occupation there was no significant accumulation of capital in Poland, and the ensuing lack of economic stability further prevented the orderly archiving of memories. While in West Germany memories were freely sorted out and spoken about, in the East parts of history were suppressed, with disobedience resulting in punishments extending all the way to imprisonment, torture, and death. In these conditions, the custom of excluding non-Germanic Central Europe from books about Europe solidified. The Poles experienced all the traumas Winter's book describes, and then some, yet their traumas remained outside the field of vision of those in the perception-setting countries who wrote about World War I, the interwar period, and World War II and its wake.

Thus, on the one hand, books could not appear in Poland that would allow the memories to be sorted out and discussed in conditions of peace and stability; and on the other, an image of Europe was created in books written in English, French, and German that excluded Poland and other non-Germanic nations of Central and Eastern Europe from participation in Europe. This non-image was caused, and further solidified, by a lack of recognition of collective memories in non-Germanic Central Europe—and, as Nancy Fraser noted, recognition is a major value in the postmodern world.[16]

Have Poles lost their collective memory because of these developments? Obviously not. While the books on Polish history that should have been written did not appear, and while Western European writers ignored the geographical area whose memories had not been brought to their attention by recognized books or official celebrations, Poles did remember by various means that bypassed the orderly archiving of memories taking place in free countries. In conditions of colonial occupation on the one hand, and a lack of material means to preserve and archive artifacts of the past on the other, Poles relied on other ways of remembering that may seem inefficient to the inhabitants of free countries. Closure was difficult to achieve for reasons already mentioned, and therefore Polish memories are mostly collective rather than cultural.

Memories start with the place where the event giving rise to memory happened. As the poet Tadeusz Gajcy said in "Specters" ("Widma"), Poland has countless places of memory, mainly the specters of harm done to the people, localities where traumas were experienced—but also places of glorious victories. The lost battles, the executions of random passersby on Warsaw streets by the Nazis, the hangings of leaders of Polish uprisings by the Russians, the defense of cities, places of torture, places of suffering, but also victories over invaders at Grunwald and, in 1920, on the Vistula River—all of these remain in Poland's collective memory not so much by having been archived in "definitive" books but by osmosis, as it were, by committing to memory messages about such places.

A great many of the Polish places of memory may not have been celebrated in books or at official functions in Soviet-occupied Poland, much less in the memories of Poland's neighbors who made a contribution to their appearance, but they were preserved by individual visits to them, by word of mouth, by teaching about them to children at home, by adult discussions in private spaces, by commemoration in theatres, cemeteries, and churches. Illegal *samizdat* literature also played a role.

Among the foremost ways of remembering places of memory was the invention of a substitute location for commemorating the traumas and glories of the nation. In these locations, the rituals of memory were enacted by dissident citizens in defiance of the government. Foremost among these substitute localities were the country's theatres, with their intelligentsia audiences and a slew of patriotic actors.

In Soviet-occupied Poland, and also in Russian-occupied Poland before World War I, producers staged plays that dealt with the country's collective memories. The viewers treated these performances as national celebrations, and they treated theatres as substitute places of memory. They reacted by applauding scenes meant to pillory the invading evildoer and extol the native hero. In this way a substitute and temporary closure was achieved. While the authorities usually caught up with these defiant commemorations, hundreds and thousands of theatergoers managed to see the performances before they were closed down. In 1955, Adam Mickiewicz's *Forefathers' Eve* (1823–32) was staged in Warsaw. The play presents Russians in an unfavorable light, and at that time the Russians were perceived as the chief perpetrators of communist mischief. *Forefathers' Eve* played to a full and enthusiastic house until the authorities shut it down. In 1956, during the Hungarian Revolution, theatres in Warsaw and Cracow staged *November Night* by Stanisław Wyspiański, another drama of anti-Russian resistance dating back to the early twentieth century.[17] In 1958, when the period of the so-called thaw was drawing to a close, Sławomir Mrożek's play *The Police* was staged in Warsaw's Dramatic Theatre. It was closed down by the real police. The Polish theatre played a cat-and-mouse game with the communist authorities, as historical plays about Polish resistance were successfully staged and then banned, and then staged again. (Mickiewicz's *Forefathers' Eve* was also banned in 1967, but shortly afterward six different theatres simultaneously staged it.) Polish theatre specialist Kazimierz Braun remarked that in the 1950s and 1960s, "[t]heater developed a cryptic stage language, comprised of allusions, symbols, allegories, and metaphors through which it communicated with the public."[18]

A similar situation was repeated under martial law in the 1980s. The satirical plays of Mrożek, then several decades old, were wildly applauded and seen as metaphors of past and present situations. Adam Mickiewicz's *Forefathers' Eve*, performed again in theatres in Warsaw and Cracow, became an occasion for symbolic articulation of moral superiority over the Russians, perceived as executioners of Poland in the nineteenth century and also in the twentieth. Juliusz Słowacki's *Salomé's Silver Dream*, magnificently staged in the Wielki Theatre in Warsaw in the 1980s, became an occasion for a melancholy recounting of past mistakes of policy toward Ukraine. Both contemporary and historical plays were interpreted as symbolic of workers who fell during the periodic risings in factories in 1956, 1970, 1976, and 1980. The plays were interpreted as containing hints about the unresolved murders of Catholic priests, the imprisonment of Cardinal Stefan Wyszyński, and the execution in prison of several thousand Polish patriots in the 1940s and early 1950s. The allusions to tsarist brutality in the 1830s were seen as emblems of contemporary brutality emanating from Moscow. These theatrical performances placed contemporary events in historical perspective; they enhanced collective memory in a peaceful way and thus prepared the audience for closure and relegation of past events to cultural memory. Each such replay of past events in the theatre, each rehearsal of collective memory, brought Poles closer to the archiving of traumas, because these performances were symbolic vindications of the catastrophes they presented. They reinforced the language of right and wrong in terms of which Poles saw their history, and they prepared audiences for a symbolic retribution by honoring heroes and victims. In the absence of free publishing the Polish theatre provided Poles with opportunities to rehearse closure, if only in a tentative fashion.

The Polish map of memory was also rehearsed and confirmed by the numerous films made of those works of Polish literature that contributed to the foundational myth of Poland as a nation. Here the Achilles' heel of subjugated nations, their excessive concentration on their delegitimized communal memories and wounds, turned out to be an advantage. Over the last two centuries Polish writers obsessively narrated Polish political tragedies by writing novels, poems, and plays about them. These words of fiction were then transformed into movies. One such successful transformation was *Pan Tadeusz* by Andrzej Wajda, which broke all records of first-night attendance in Poland. There were films made of Henryk Sienkiewicz's *Trilogy* and *Quo Vadis*. *The Promised Land* by Wajda (originally a novel by the Nobel-winning Władysław Reymont) portrayed the sufferings of industrialization, while *The Man of Iron* mythologized Solidarity.

Not all people went to theatres, of course. But both those who did and those who did not went to Polish cemeteries on All Souls' Day, celebrated in Poland on November 2 each year. As the place where primarily religious ceremonies are usually performed, the cemetery was beyond the reach of the communist authorities and could be used as a gathering place for those who wanted to commemorate an event. All Souls' Day is a uniquely Polish celebration that combines paying honor to one's own relatives with honoring the heroes of the nation. On that day the entire country proceeds to cemeteries to light candles on the graves and monuments not only of relatives but also of people who are perceived as worthy of remembering—those who died during the various Polish insurrections, those who perished during demonstrations against tyranny, and soldiers who fell on the battlefield.

At the Powązki Cemetery in Warsaw (the Polish equivalent of Arlington National Cemetery), the graves and monuments commemorating the uprisings of 1831, 1863, and 1944 receive much attention on All Souls' Day. The monuments to these uprisings are covered with burning candles and flowers, and spontaneous group prayers are not unusual. It is a sight to behold, as people who have no personal relation whatever to, for example, Romuald Traugutt gather at his monument and place flowers on the plinth. Neither the state nor the local authorities supervise these gatherings; they were frowned upon but not forbidden under communism, and they persisted even in Stalinist times. Another place at Powązki that is covered with lighted candles and flowers on November 2 is the plot where the heroes of the Polish Resistance in World War II lie buried, young men aged 16–24 who are still remembered by their military aliases: Zośka, Rudy, and Alek. These are people Zbigniew Herbert wrote about in his poetry, while Aleksander Kamiński described them in his fictionalized account of Nazi-occupied Warsaw titled *Kamienie na szaniec* ([Stones for the Barricades], 1943). The graves of these young idealists are sixty years old, yet the remembrance is still vivid. Such scenes are recorded not only in Warsaw but also in other Polish cities and towns. Like their theatre counterparts, these November commemorations help bring people to closure with regard to the war traumas. The repetition of these ceremonies year after year has taken the sting out of the initial bitterness, and it has shrouded in dignity the otherwise sordid defeat Poland experienced at the hands of the Soviets and the Nazis.

Catholic churches have also served as places of memory. There is hardly a church in Warsaw that does not have some kind of war memorial inside or outside. In St. John's Cathedral (rebuilt after destruction by German air attacks in September 1939), there are bits and pieces of the old cathedral displayed on the walls. They are cemented to the wall and make a powerful impression. A visitor to the cathedral is reminded of the fact that at this very spot there once stood another structure, another cathedral hit by bombs and artillery shells, and that massive numbers died at that very place. The cathedral thus serves as a museum, as a place of religious worship, and as a place of mourning. It offers opportunities for commemoration, for grieving, and for spiritual engagement. Another church in Warsaw's Old City—that of the Sisters of the Holy Eucharist (*Sakramentki*)—was likewise leveled by German bombing, burying in its ruins the entire convent of nuns who were at that time on their knees adoring the Eucharist. This is the stuff of legends, and the remarkable deaths of these nuns are duly remembered in commemorative plaques displayed in the rebuilt church.

The erection of monuments has been central to Polish ways of remembering. The monuments dedicated to the heroes of World War II in particular are part of the Polish landscape. The communists allowed these monuments to be erected because they commemorated the struggle against the Nazis; Soviet crimes in Poland remained a taboo subject until the relegalization of the Solidarity Labor Union in 1989. After the demise of communism Soviet crimes began to be commemorated as well. Most of these monuments are located where the people they honor died, but some of them are placed in substitute locations. Among the latter, the most remarkable is the series of monuments dedicated to the victims of Katyń. Not only Poles in Poland but also the Polish diaspora took great interest in this matter. Cities as diverse as Toronto, Canada, and Johannesburg, South Africa, have Katyń monuments today. Nothing mobilizes the Polish diaspora more effectively than an announcement that a Katyń monument is being built: money flows easily for that purpose. This indicates that the Katyń trauma has sunk deeply into the collective memory. Of all the murders of Poles by the Soviets this one is best remembered.[19] Until recently it was difficult to archive it because the Russian government was reluctant to admit guilt, let alone make symbolic amendments. The Russians have finally admitted their complicity in the murders, but no symbolic apology followed. During President Putin's visit to Poland in January 2002, he dismissed the matter of apology out of hand. Shortly before that visit Gennady Zyuganov stated that no apology for Katyń should ever be given, because the Soviets lost half a million people while "liberating" Poland. Of course, this liberation is perceived by many Poles as fifty years of further colonial dependency. When the collective memories of neighboring countries differ so dramatically, it is virtually impossible to achieve closure.

More recent traumas have also brought a large number of monuments into being. A workers' demonstration took place in Gdańsk in 1970 during which the police killed a number of participants. In response, shortly after the Solidarity Labor Union was legalized, a monument to the slain workers was erected in December 1980. Directly at the entrance to the Gdańsk shipyards the workers built three crosses mounted on very tall steel beams. The inscription underneath reads: "The Lord giveth his people strength / the Lord giveth his people the blessing of peace" (Psalm 29). One hundred and fifty thousand people showed up for the unveiling of this monument in December 1980.[20] Two hundred thousand people attended the unveiling of a similar monument in Poznań honoring workers killed during a peaceful demonstration in 1956. A monument was also erected at the entrance to the Wujek coal mine where a number of miners were killed by the police during the struggle for the legalization of Solidarity in 1981. All these tragedies have not yet reached closure owing to the fact that for various legal reasons, those responsible for the killings have not been brought to justice.

As stated before, the observance of many anniversaries was not possible in Poland while the country was not sovereign. But Poles developed substitute ways to commemorate these as well. After the 1863 uprising, it became fashionable in Poland to wear jewelry made of black enamel. The symbolism of these ornaments was clear: they featured crosses, crowns of thorns, irons and chains, Polish eagles, and the Lithuanian Chase. The tsarist authorities forbade public display of Polish and Lithuanian symbols, but they could not prevent people from replicating them in their jewelry.[21] A similar way of defying the authorities was resurrected after the suppression of Solidarity in 1981, when people began to wear Solidarity badges even though such badges were illegal.

The singing of a certain religious hymn was a favorite act of defiance of churchgoers on Sundays. The hymn had two endings, one expressing thanks to God for free Poland (this was the obligatory version under communism), and the other asking God to restore freedom (the subversive version). The singing of the forbidden version was not entirely risk-free because churches had spies assigned to them; these spies would observe people's mouths to see what words they were singing. The culprits might then be interrogated by the secret police or beaten up by police-sponsored assailants.

After 1989 all anniversaries began to be celebrated. The battle of Warsaw in August 1920 became one of the favorite commemorations, as well as the Soviet aggression against Poland on September 17, 1939—a recently legitimized memory—and, of course, the Constitution of the Third of May 1791. This last commemoration was discouraged under communism for reasons having to do with Russian nationalism: alarmed by Poland's reforms in 1791, Catherine the Great attacked Poland and shortly afterward engineered the second partition.

These celebrations of defeats have been absorbed into the nation's memory as a means of strengthening rather than weakening its sense of identity. Polish novelist Eliza Orzeszkowa's novels include one entitled *Gloria Victis*, glory to the defeated. The Polish collective memory has internalized this expression. Józef Piłsudski is credited with a similar maxim, "To be defeated and not to surrender—this is victory" (Być pobitym, ale się nie poddać—to zwycięstwo). In such contexts, defeats are not considered shameful but rather are treated as the fall of a just man pitted against unjust enemies. This interpretation is, of course, common among ethnic groups that suffer many defeats: victims usually perceive themselves as just and view their oppressors as unjust. However, the foreign engineers of these defeats refuse to remember them and incorporate them into their historical memories.

Museums also serve as tools of remembering. They play a lesser role in Poland than in Western Europe where a museum is an archive for the numerous works of art accumulated by a country. Under conditions of colonialism, such accumulation did not take place in Poland. Thus the most important museum in Poland is the Auschwitz Museum in Oświęcim. Like so many other places of memory, Auschwitz commemorates a defeat—in particular, the Shoah. Virtually all Polish children take a trip to that museum sometime during their schooldays, and the sight of the ovens, roomfuls of eyeglasses, hair, and shoes remains seared in their memory forever. But under communism, the Jewish Holocaust was polluted by mendacity. First, the communists misinformed the public about the number of people killed in Auschwitz, claiming it was four million. Recent research has scaled that down to one million. Second, the communists did not tell the Polish public that it was primarily Jews who were slaughtered in Auschwitz-Birkenau. The Polish children who visited—and I was among them—were told that the Nazis killed such and such number of people, and the subtext was that these people were mostly Polish.

In their eagerness to erase nationalistic differences, the communists actually multiplied them. The downplaying of the Jewish tragedy brought anger from Jewish survivors abroad, which in turn caused a defensive counterreaction from Polish Christians. But the departure of the Russian army in 1993 brought significant changes to the remembrance of the Shoah in Poland, and the trauma of Auschwitz is beginning to achieve its proper closure.

All these celebrations have to do with collective memory rather than with communal memory. As I mentioned before, Polish communal memory has been delegitimized by hostile foreign interventions. Those who sided with the Soviets in order to survive have one set of memories, those who fought against the Soviets have another. In such conditions the creation of a common communal memory has become an unattainable luxury. The shrinking or delegitimization of communal memory is one of the major traumas of the last sixty years, a trauma that is hardly recognized or articulated outside the borders of Poland. It has had fatal implications for the self-image of many communities, as well as for Poland's international image. This in turn has further delayed the achievement of closure, and it has made Polish cultural elites rely on collective rather than communal memories in seeking legitimization.

The ceremonies of remembering that I have described do not reignite conflicts; instead, they contribute to the healing of wounds. They are not to be compared to the German cries for revenge before Hitler's ascendancy to power, or to the behavior of Dostoevsky's Underground Man, who merely replays old hurts and is unable to achieve closure. In fact, certain traumas have already reached the point of closure in Poland, including that of Polish-German relations. The Germans have acknowledged their guilt concerning the Jews. There is a consensus in Poland as to what happened to Christian Poles under Nazi occupation. The trauma of the Warsaw Rising in August–September 1944 has achieved a point of closure with the building of a commemorative museum.[22] The issue was also symbolically closed by the erection in Warsaw of several monuments dedicated to the Warsaw insurgents, including one to "The Child Insurgent" on Podwale Street, showing a child whose head is barely visible under a big helmet and whose little legs are too short for his soldier's boots. These monuments are fitting symbols of closure for this major trauma suffered by the city and the nation. Another element that helped to archive this tragedy was the rebuilding of the Old City in Warsaw and the symbolic reparations paid to Polish slave laborers by the German companies that profited from their labor during the war.

Things are different with regard to the much longer period of Soviet occupation. Here there is still a great deal of bitterness. There is a sense of loss because of the unjustified disappearance of memory on the Russian side. There is a widespread perception in Poland that one of the unwritten conditions of the relinquishing of power by the communists in 1989 was that there be no punishment of the individuals who illegitimately wielded power for half a century in Poland. Except for a few notorious cases, former communist functionaries were allowed to keep their jobs and even run for office. The lack of apology from these individuals, not to mention proper punishment, creates bitterness and cynicism in Polish society and delays the achievement of closure.

The unwillingness of the Russians to face up to their colonial past is also a major hurdle for all the peoples of Central and Eastern Europe who came under Soviet Russian domination. The Russian government has refused to apologize for the crimes committed by the Soviets, even though Russia has declared itself to be the successor state of the Soviet Union. It appears that the Russians are opposed to a reexamination of their history during their imperial period between Peter the Great and the fall of communism. They are also unwilling to revisit the problem of the Russian-Soviet advantage during the communist period. Unexamined versions of Russian history continue to be taught in schools in Russia, and they have made their way into American textbooks of Russian history, for example, the books of George Vernadsky and Nicholas Riasanovsky. In my book *Imperial Knowledge*, I analyzed textbooks written in free Russia in the 1990s, and I noted that postcommunist textbooks continue to serve a basically unchanged menu of interpretations of Russian imperial expansion.[23] Obviously the Russians have greater access to world attention and recognition than the Poles, Czechs, Slovaks, or Romanians. Their unwillingness to look at their own history from a postcolonial perspective makes it hard for Poles and others to achieve closure and to correct the version of history of Central and Eastern Europe still present in the American academy, among others.

In order to provide a systematic access to memory, the Institute of National Remembrance (Instytut Pamięci Narodowej) was created in Poland in 1998. Its goal is to help Poles come to terms with the cataclysms of the past and to memorialize moments of intense collective suffering. The institute resembles a similar organization in Russia called Memorial, except that Poland finances its own institute whereas Memorial is financed primarily by the Soros Foundation. The Institute of National Remembrance is also charged with the investigation of Nazi and Soviet crimes. The institute administers the archives of the communist Ministries of Internal Affairs, Defense, and Education. It also collects documents related to crimes committed against the Polish nation by the Soviets and by the Nazis. It publishes books and organizes conferences and exhibits.

The discourse on national memory that the institute tries to generate is not based on finger-pointing. With varying results, the institute attempts to be nonpolitical and nonpartisan. One of its directors, Roman Kiereś, said in an interview with Polish daily *Rzeczpospolita* that his goal is to collect data rather than to judge. Among other things, the institute has made friendly moves toward Poland's minorities, particularly Jews and Ukrainians, and it has investigated controversial issues concerning minority relations. The institute also tries to provide Polish citizens, usually descendants of victims, with access to documents that detail the victimization of their parents and grandparents. That so basic a task still has to be performed in Poland sixty years after World War II ended testifies to the depth of the traumas inflicted by half a century of occupation by the Soviets. The institute maintains contact with Memorial in Russia and with similar institutions throughout the region of Central and Eastern Europe. By emplotting Polish history in such a way as not to exclude the Other and by accepting the Other's story as well, the institute helps to relegitimize the narrative of Polish history. This will eventually result in the creation of texts that will transform the connection between past and present into one in which the past becomes a source of identity rather than of pain, anger, and impotent frustration. In other words, the institute tries to speed up the transformation of collective memory into cultural memory. There are naturally many pressures put on the institute, and given its limited financial means the investigations are not always satisfactory.

All these attempts to access and archive Polish memory have had little impact so far on how the Polish past is perceived outside Poland. The fact that Polish memories often differ dramatically from the memories of Western Europeans (and therefore of the world) is a serious problem, a problem that delays the closure of war wounds in Poland. As soon as the Soviets loosened their colonial grip on Poland, thousands of historical books appeared commemorating the nation's traumas and setting the record straight. But such an outburst cannot make up for the decades of neglect. It will take time for these books to penetrate the Western intellectual establishment. As mentioned earlier, one of the reasons that Poland is out of step with Western perceptions of European history is that for fifty years (and also during the entire nineteenth century) Poland was forced to remain silent in the international arena.[24]

Israeli scholar Ron Robin has recently described Israel as a "tense" (as opposed to a "relaxed") nation.[25] Similarly, Poland is also a tense nation. Poland's collective memory is still replete with remembrances of events that call for acknowledgment. Poland is often jolted by periodic reminders that Polish traumas have not been recognized in the standard narratives of European history, in books such as Jay Winter's *Sites of Memory*, in commemorations of the events of World War II, in the failure to acknowledge the decisive Polish contribution to the defeat of the Turks in 1683, to mention just a few random events. To paraphrase Alasdair MacIntyre, scholars who work in the Polish area have to rise to the importance of the task of continually trying to devise new ways to allow Polish memories to be incorporated into world history.[26] It remains to be seen whether the Polish educated classes will rise to the task. When memories are articulated, sorted out, compartmentalized, explained, and commemorated, the traumas of the past will finally become the past. It is to be hoped that this process will proceed apace in Poland until a point is reached when Polish culture transforms itself from a culture of traumas to a culture of acknowledged memories.

NOTES

1. This issue was eloquently articulated in Said's *Orientalism*. On the importance of recognition in international relations see Fraser, 107–20.

2. See Ricoeur, *Memory, History, Forgetting*, 80–92. This monumental work is both a history of memory and a classification of it; it surpasses the objective of the present essay, which intends to sketch out the Polish ways of remembering as strategies of communal survival.

3. The Bivigliano conferences produced a volume edited by Strath, which contains papers by Hayden White and Ron Robin, among others. The Princeton Workshop on Memory (organized by Aleida Assmann) took place on May 4, 2001. The volume edited by Nora is also seminal to many works on collective memory: it analyzes the bifurcation of France's memory into republican and nationalist. Like Ricoeur's work, it is tangential to my purposes because it deals with a nation-state whose memories have generally been acknowledged without hostile interference.

4. See Fukuyama.

5. See Assmann and Hölscher.

6. John Paul II, 144.

7. In my identification of the various kinds of memory I am indebted to Aleida Assmann's guest seminars at Rice University's Center for the Study of Cultures in fall 2000. See also Assmann's introduction to her *Erinnerungsraume*.

8. This term was first used in George Orwell's *1984*.

9. False childhood memories are a notorious example. Pezdek et al., 437–41.

10. This process took place in Soviet-occupied Poland after World War II as the history of western Ukraine and western Belarus (formerly under Polish rule) was rewritten by the occupiers and their collaborators, and it became standard history afterward. See Hnatiuk.

11. See Assmann and Frevert.

12. The concept of cultural memory is developed in J. Assmann.

13. The difference between a colonial conquest and other land grabs is the presence in the conquered territory of an awareness of a history separate from that of the occupiers, and of a group consciousness that has converged, or is about to converge, into the consciousness of a separate nationhood. Thus Charlemagne's empire was not a colonial empire, whereas the empire of the Austrians or Russians in the nineteenth century was. Thompson, "Nationalism, Imperialism, Identity," 250–61.

14. See Winter. Likewise, in Aleida Assmann and Jan Assmann's work the Polish experience is fully deleted.

15. Alexander I demanded of Napoleon that he not revive Poland. Accordingly, the Treaty of Tilsit (1807) between Alexander and Napoleon created a duchy of Warsaw out of Prussian-occupied Poland, whereas Russian-occu-

pied Poland was ceded to Russia in perpetuity. Article IX of the treaty reads as follows: "[The area of Białystok, recently conquered from Prussia] shall be united in perpetuity to the Russian empire, in order to establish the natural limits between Russia and the duchy of Warsaw."

16. Fraser.
17. See Braun.
18. Ibid., 277.
19. See Allen.
20. Ash, *The Polish Revolution*, 102.
21. Marcinek, 61; Edwards, 1:11.
22. See Cienski.
23. See Thompson, *Imperial Knowledge*.
24. But things are slowly changing in that sphere as well. I would like to mention a recent project to commemorate the world's traumas through works of art, a project undertaken in the United States. The name of the project is the Legacy Foundation; it was initiated by Clifford Chanin. The Legacy Foundation has its own Web site, www.legacy.org. Legacy is a foundation whose self-imposed task is to gather works of art dedicated to the commemoration of events during which people died in large numbers, not by accident but by the design of others. The Legacy Project describes itself as a gathering place for persons interested in the enduring legacies of the many violent traumas of the twentieth century. It explores issues of remembrance in different cultures and tries to understand the contemporary significance of historical tragedies. So far it has displayed on its Web site dozens of paintings and other artworks symbolizing world traumas. It seeks out artists who portray the consequences of cataclysms and build enclosures for remembrance. The site displays the trauma of the Jewish Holocaust, the slaughters accompanying the split between India and Pakistan, and other mass slaughters in Southeast Asia and Africa. One of the exhibits consists of two abstract paintings commemorating the annihilation of Lidice, a Czech village, after the assassination of Reinhard Heydrich during World War II. Among the items representing Polish traumas are poems by Zbigniew Herbert and an autobiography of a prisoner of the communists, Włodzimierz Kołaczkiewicz.
25. Robin, 315–20.
26. MacIntyre, 236.

The Trains of Memory and Commemoration

Private and Public Archiving of the Past in Tadeusz Różewicz's *The Professor's Knife*

Olga Ponichtera

The real voyage of discovery . . .
Consists not in seeking new landscapes,
But in having new eyes,
In seeing the universe with the eyes of another,
Of a hundred others,
In seeing the hundred universes that each of them sees.[1]

To dwell means to leave traces.[2]

Tadeusz Różewicz's *The Professor's Knife* (2001) is a poetic text framed by photographs on the volume's covers. The front cover depicts the object in question—the knife—while the back folio shows a photograph of a train wagon that is part of a memorial to the victims of the Holocaust at Yad Vashem. The volume consists of the cycle "The Professor's Knife," composed of six individually titled parts, as well as four other poems that follow the cycle and are not included as an integral part of it. In this paper, which is a part of my larger dissertation project, I limit my analysis primarily to the above-mentioned titular cycle. As such, I conceive of Różewicz's text as constructed on the interplay of collective historical and cultural memory and private reminiscence, which deals with the problem of remembering and commemorating the victims of the Holocaust. As Kazimierz Nowosielski notes, Różewicz is a poet belonging to a group of writers whose oeuvre has been defined throughout the years by their sense of loyalty to those who perished.[3] In a present labeled by critics as a time of "entropy of historical memory" caused by new media technologies promoting amnesia,[4] the poet reexamines the well-known, and depleted, if not clichéd, tropes and symbols of Holocaust memory to disclose how prosthetic memory is constructed, how its functioning changes within different historical, political and cultural contexts, and finally how our individual archives of memory, which are dependent on institutionally shaped and sustained cultural memory, are susceptible to becoming naïve and unreflective constructs of palimpsests.[5] For Różewicz's poetic volume, the defining sites of memory (*lieux de mémoire*) are the main iconographic tropes (the professor's knife, trains, and the image of the victims' bodies), which the writer presents both in the narrated text and in their photographic form. I examine these tropes to argue that through maintaining the tension of personal memory with iconographic tropes that have become the core of Holocaust representations both in scholarly and popular media discourses, Różewicz alludes to tropes within the textual memory of his own oeuvre that, through decades of overuse, have become similar to Holocaust cliché images. Thus reflecting on the workings of personal memory within the historical and cultural memory archive, the poet also confronts the memory of his own texts, and through these, frequently sardonic intertextual links, he remembers, rereads, reinterprets, and rewrites his own authorial self. He stresses that both the individual (human/existential) and cultural, textual memory are filtered through the individual subject (the poet) and the inevitable engulfing chronos. The aging poet becomes a prism through which his individual biographical and textual history as well as cultural memory seeps in in the form of textual and iconic tropes.

Różewicz's understanding of the functioning of memory in history echoes that of the French historian Pierre Nora, who proposes that the real, inviolate, social memory embodied by primitive archaic societies has perished with them, while modern societies motivated by change organize their past as an archival historical memory.[6] In Nora's conception, archival memory relies on a trace: its materiality, particularity, and the visibility of the recording or image.[7] Public historical memory in modern societies is shaped by public sites of memory such as museums, memorials, and monuments.[8] Moreover, this memory consists of a certain shared "canon" of cultural literacy or *sociolect*, which comprises common allusions, references (i.e., books and nonverbal artworks, such as paintings and monuments), and norms that provide shared cultural reference points.[9] Nora's conception of historical memory has been criticized as a postmodern approach to history, which "reduces the memory of the past to the history of images."[10] I consider this criticism too simplistic and would like to suggest that Różewicz's text, which shows a similar approach to historical memory, does not simply compare memory to an archival data bank, but rather stresses its dependence on the recorded material and converses with this canon of cultural literacy, critically showing that such a canon does not exist in a vacuum but is institutionally, and thus politically and culturally, fashioned.[11]

In his conception of memory, Nora alludes to key ideas found in Maurice Halbwachs's theory of collective memory. Halbwachs's understanding of memory is sociological and opposed to the idea of memory as a purely subjective phenomenon, a conception voiced, for example, by the nineteenth-century philosopher Henri Bergson. Halbwachs links the act of remembering to the repository of images which comprise the social relations in which individuals partake.[12] Nora presents a similar view, yet his notion of memory is broad. For him, geographical places, historical figures, architecture and monuments, artistic objects, and symbols can embody the historical consciousness of a particular social group or a nation.[13] He defines the expression *lieu de mémoire* as "any significant entity, whether material or nonmaterial in nature, which by dint of human will or the work of time has become a symbolic element of the memorial heritage of any community."[14] He also extends the concept of an archive to include all objects of material representation that sustain contemporary memory.

Różewicz in *The Professor's Knife* concentrates on comparable elements of memory (both material and immaterial objects, as well as tropes and symbols) that carry the memorial heritage of individuals and/or communities. He shows that cultural memory is unavoidably an institutionally constructed archive dependent on the visibility of a trace. Like Nora, the poet believes in and converses with this canon of shared cultural literacy. However, while at the core of Nora's memory project lies the question of national memory, Różewicz is far from employing a national perspective. He emphasizes that prosthetic memory is frequently a product of memories collected in an ad hoc fashion through the consumption of both history books and a popular media culture that transcends national boundaries embracing a global or cosmopolitan form. Moreover, Różewicz does not necessarily himself embrace this form of prosthetic memory, but by acknowledging its mode of operation, he emphasizes that individual memory inevitably exists within it and is influenced by it.

While cultural memory in Różewicz's view is based on the archive and relies on a visibility of traces, in *The Professor's Knife* the poet alludes to Freud's famous metaphor of the railway system as a conceptual model for interpretation of the past in memory. Thus, Różewicz's overall structure of the volume may be conceptualized as centered on two main ideas: one is the idea of memory as a material trace utilized within history and commemoration, and the other is the metaphor of the railway as a figure for the mobility, open-endedness, and connectivity of memory (and conversely as an open and vastly branching structure inevitably amenable to misremembering, forgetting, and silencing). For Różewicz, as for Freud, particularly in his essay on "Screen Memories" from the *Interpretation of Dreams* (1900), the mobility of the railway epitomizes the process of mnemonic narration and interpretation, which is a complex and open network of associations and connections.[15] Since there is no "master memory narrative," memory, like history, is not a reproduction of the past but a "mobile interpretation of what remains in the space of the present."[16] In Różewicz's text the personal archive of memory is contingent on a cultural archive which is read through a series of extended networks, a succession of associations that do not come together into a coherent nodal point but remain perpetually incomplete.

Moreover, the railway in *The Professor's Knife* stands as a commentary on the stock images of cultural memory that came to represent the Holocaust. Although memory may be a system of open railway networks with an infinite possibility of associations, the Holocaust settled in cultural memory as a repetition of the same few iconic images, which by now have become decontextualized clichéd tropes. Despite the Holocaust's extensive documentation, as the historian Sybil Milton noted, "although more than two million photos exist in the public archives of more than twenty nations, the quality, scope and content of the images reproduced in scholarly and popular literature has been very repetitive."[17] The few stock images which have recurred as illustrations in textbooks and been reproduced on book covers and in films are these: 1) the massive iron gate entrance to Auschwitz I with the *"Arbeit mach frei"* sign; 2) the train tracks leading into the main guard house at Auschwitz II Birkanau; 3) the camp watchtowers with barbed wire fences; 4) corpses in enormous mass graves.[18] Różewicz confronts these clichéd tropes that in their endless repetition in effect distance and anesthetize us to the event. As Dan Stone observed, since the first photos of Auschwitz appeared, the meaning assigned to it has been conveyed through the symbolic framework of the barbed wire, the ramp, and the famous entrance gate—images which are important elements of the camp, yet they are "not the camp but how only we wish to keep seeing it."[19]

The Professor's Knife: Written Testimonies and the Mysteries of an Object

The main image of Różewicz's poetic volume—the knife—appears simultaneously in the volume's title and as a photograph on its cover; however, the lyrical subject begins to speak about the object only in section 4 of the poetic cycle. The poet does not hide his continued fascination with this object, yet its delayed introduction also suggests a dose of uneasiness or reluctance of the poet as he approaches this topic. As the text suggests, Różewicz has been examining and speaking with his friend Mieczysław Porębski (the knife's owner) about it for over half a century, though crucial aspects of the past have also been avoided or silenced in this lifelong friendship. It is also noteworthy that although Różewicz thought about writing the knife's story for many years, only now, at the end of his existential and poetic journey, he decided to confront this topic. The poet takes the iconographic image and the object itself from the sphere of private/personal archive. Paradoxically, by representing the authentic, material object via a photograph, Różewicz mediates the testimony of the object, and by inserting it into his own private archive (his poetic text), now intended for public consumption, he strips the knife of its existence within the realm of physical objects, yet by reducing it to a photograph, he simultaneously ensures its wider and lasting existence in the cultural archive. I propose that the treatment of this object-symbol in *The Professor's Knife* is characterized by a prominent aesthetic choice that Różewicz repeatedly makes in his poetics, that is, a focus on the image/object rather than a description of emotions.[20] Throughout the poet's long career, many critics have commented on this feature of Różewicz's style. Already Jan Błoński in his book *Poets and Others* (*Poeci i inni*, 1956) remarked that the poet "utilizes 'atoms of speech' [and] instead of naming emotions, . . . uses 'words-objects,' as if his attention were a beam of light which illuminates the objects from darkness."[21] Kazimierz Wyka described this slightly differently. He claimed that "the iconographic material resulting from Różewicz's imagination is reminiscent of an old childish play with picture blocks."[22]

In *The Professor's Knife*, this building block of images, which will continuously accumulate around the image of the knife, fulfills important functions. It serves as a documented trace of the past; it converses with the reader's iconographic and textual cultural memories and highlights the palimpsest nature of remembering. The image of the knife is a trace of the past and itself an object of testimony, which holds the memories of past events. To the uninitiated observer, the photograph of the knife remains a mystery just like the object itself was a mystery and remained a "Columbus's egg" for the poet for many years. Now parts of its testimony are revealed and turned into a text. As a trace, it highlights the performative nature of remembering by not only triggering the lyrical subject's recalling of the past whenever he comes into contact with the object, but also by suggesting that our psychology frequently, like a knife, cuts certain memories to either repress, forget and silence them, or conversely in attempt to unearth, confront, assemble, and bring into order memories of the past. The knife as a tool that cuts off and frees and an object that potentially wounds yet may also bring one's salvation in a struggle is a symbol of conscious memory work in an effort to order and deal with a fragmented past as well as a figure of traumatic memory which we consciously or unconsciously wish to cut off from our present.

The particular knife of Różewicz's volume was made in secret in a concentration camp, and as an object, it maintained its secrets for many years. As the poet confesses, he has been meaning to write about this knife for over half a century. Perhaps the metamorphosis of the object itself has prompted him to finally commit its story to paper. The poet observes that, like everything else, including personal memory, objects also are threatened by the destructive forces of time and by forgetting: "Robigus coats the short knife / with rust / and slowly consumes it."[23] Robigus, whom the poet terms the "demon of rust" and of the passing of time and forgetting, first takes away and later devours the details from memories of those who are closest to us. Różewicz indeed does not reveal emotions about death and dying, yet conveys them through images. "Mieczysław [the owner of the knife] was left on his own" since "Hania [his wife] passed away five years ago."[24] When the two friends visit her grave at a cemetery, this most private of conversations about the professor's deceased wife does not appear in Różewicz's text. However its essence, which conveys the utmost fear of departing memory, is present in the text as a series of images: "Robigus the rust demon / covers the past with rust / covers words and eyes / the smiles / of the dead / the pen."[25] Perhaps the existential fear of the liminal time of aging and mortality, both in the sense of physical mortality and also in terms of failing memory, as well as the ending of one's creativity (hence "pen"), is what prompts the poet to finally undertake this mnemonic journey.

Apart from the object itself, which enters the poet's textual archive in the form of a photograph, Różewicz also cites Porębski's words from a letter in which he referred to the history of his knife: "MIECZYSŁAW: I thought some more / about that knife of mine / made from the hoop of a barrel. / It was kept in the hem / of your striped prison uniform, / because they confiscated things / and it could cost you dearly . . . / And so its function / was not only practical / but much more complex / (we should talk about it some more)."[26] Regardless of whether this is an actual citation from a letter written by Porębski that exists in the poet's personal archive or it is just a mystification, such an approach to the presentation of the knife's history is reminiscent of the quasi-documentary approach that we have seen for instance in *Matka Odchodzi* (1999). However, the paradox is that the reader never learns much more of the history of the knife than what is given in the aforementioned lines. The reader of Różewicz's volume never learns what was "much more complex" as opposed to the practical function of the knife to which Porębski alludes. Porębski says that they should return to this issue at some point, but they never do. One might only assume that its unnamed function may have had something to do with the knife's symbolism as an object of power and defiance. As a symbol in the public cultural archive, a knife is one of the oldest domestic tools and weapons used by man, and also a symbol of power and law.[27] Confronting the iconographic image of the knife as it is shown in the photograph with the symbolic existence of this trope in Western culture, Różewicz highlights the absurdity of its traditional practical and symbolic functions within the context of its historical existence. The knife may represent the law and may be both a domestic tool and a weapon; all of these notions, as they exist within the public cultural archive, testify to the preposterous existence of the professor's knife within its historical context. With the Holocaust, the poet claims, as a society, we have returned morally to the iron epoch of primitive handmade tools. As a weapon, the little knife could possibly function only in a personal one-on-one encounter. As a symbol, however, it conveys the situation of a defenseless individual who undoubtedly has the law of ethics on his side, yet is faced with the structured efficiency of Nazi murder that disqualifies him as an opponent. Possession of a knife, however, in the circumstances of concentration camp reality gave the individual the greatest power and defiance one could have within that reality. This little object defied the subordination of one's life to another's power—although these functions are never named, it is obvious that the knife could be used as a means of self-annihilation, thus placing the most important aspect of one's existential choice, the one of one's own life or death, in its owner's hands.

The further the reader gets into *The Professor's Knife*, the more one is convinced that the actual story of the object is missing from the text. We learn that the professor "with the knife in the camp / [was] cutting bread dividing it up."[28] However, this trope in Różewicz's text opens up a wide area of intertexts for the poet, alluding both to personal and textual memory, as well as the cultural memory of the Holocaust, which he builds around the motif of the knife. In section 6 of the poem, titled "The Last Age," Różewicz cites from Ovid's *Metamorphosis*: "The iron age was last / truth shame and honor vanished / in their place were / fraud deceit trickery violence / and pernicious desires / . . . Now harmful iron appeared / and gold more harmful than iron."[29] Różewicz prompts his reader to assume that his creative method in *The Professor's Knife* is similar to Ovid's: in a mock-epic style, he builds a mythical history of the world shown through the metamorphosis of images, where the event of the Holocaust is the defining experience of memory. The knife seems to be just a pretext or a reoccurring motif that Różewicz uses to connect the memories of his own existential, intellectual, and creative life experiences. Some of these contexts become apparent when the lyrical subject comments on his fascination with the knife at various times during his long acquaintance with the professor:

> "strange knife" I thought— // . . . it lay between Matejko and Rodakowski / between Kantor Jaremianka and Stern / between sheets of paper / between Alina Szapocznikow //. . . "strange knife" I thought / I took it in hand / laid it down again // "strange knife" I thought / it lay between a book on cubism / and the end of criticism // . . . Mietek was in the hospital on Szaserów Street // the knife lay on some newspapers // at the airport I read the slogans / writers stick to writing Zionists go home.[30]

Of course, this is a "strange knife" in more than only the aesthetic sense. The primitive knife "from the iron age / . . . from a death camp"[31] is presented among prominent names of wide cultural significance. Placed among historical and critical books on art on the professor's desk, this artifact of Holocaust trauma is inserted into the realm of high culture. It is a paradoxical trace of the past, because by its physical aesthetics, it fits among the unwritten testimonies, such as the urns, tools, coins, painted or sculpted images, or funerary objects that are the usual targets of archaeology.[32] However, despite its unusual primitive appearance, no one had to excavate this knife from ancient times. It was created in the mid-twentieth century and in terms of temporal sequence, it paradoxically belongs among the cultural traces that surround it. Różewicz implicitly may be alluding to Theodor Adorno and Max Horkheimer's 1944 book *Dialectic of the Enlightenment*, in which the Frankfurt school theorists argue for the failure of the Enlightenment, most traumatically shown in the events of the Holocaust. Różewicz alludes to a wide range of cultural memory: from nineteenth-century painters, the artistic movements of the avant-garde, to the Cracow Group of painters who became the poet's colleagues once he began his studies at the Jagiellonian University. Here the poet refers to an artistic and intellectual formation that had a great impact on his youth and his first contacts with the world of art.

Through the personal memory of Porębski's table (be it real or imagined), Różewicz might be constructing the context for the knife out of his own memory of meetings with the group of people that included Porębski. In creating such an image of the professor's table, Różewicz alludes also to Porębski's professional interests as an art historian and to the texts that comprise his oeuvre. Although he does not name titles but rather recalls imprecisely "a book on cubism" or "the end of criticism," it does not escape the reader's attention that Porębski is an author of a book on Matejko's paintings, as well as the titles to which Różewicz's lyrical subject alludes, such as: *Cubism: An Introduction to Twentieth-Century Art* (1966) or *A Farewell to Criticism* (1966). The lifelong friendship between Różewicz and Porębski had its beginnings with Różewicz's enrolling to study art history at the Jagiellonian University after the war. The biographies of the poet and the art critic share many points, including the fact that the two men are of the same age (Porębski, like Różewicz, was born in 1921). The critic, however, is a survivor of Auschwitz, whereas the poet, who was an AK soldier, does not share this traumatic experience. The knife seems to be a mediating object that allows Różewicz to partially enter the memories of his friend's traumatic experience, yet it is simultaneously an object which retains its mysteries. Neither Porębski nor Różewicz fully exposes the story of the knife. The knife is an object of prosthesis: for its owner, for Różewicz, and for the reader. Positioned on the desk, seemingly useless (the lyrical subject hypothesizes that Porębski may be using it to open envelopes, or as a paperweight), the knife becomes a gadget of prosthetic memory, in Baudrillard's sense of an object-gadget, where the object of consumption loses "its objective function (as a tool) to the benefit of its function as a sign . . . characterized by a kind of functional uselessness (since what is consumed is precisely something other than the 'useful')."[33] It is the knife as a sign of another's experience of trauma that is consumed and functions as prosthesis in Różewicz's volume. Yet the details of Porębski's camp experience and the particularities of the knife's context are absent.

Finally, the knife is a trope that links Różewicz's present everyday existence, including its banal aspects such as eating breakfast with a lifelong friend (Porębski), to the memory of his earlier textual existence in well-known and repeatedly cited lines of his early poetry. In a section entitled "Columbus's Egg" ("Jajko Kolumba") which includes the breakfast scenario, a knife, although not directly named, is present: "years later Mieczysław and I / are sitting at breakfast / the twentieth century is ending // I cut bread on a board / spread butter / add a pinch of salt."[34] Różewicz's readers remember that in 1956 in "In the Midst of Life" from *Open Poem* the poet wrote: "knife serves to cut bread / people are nourished by bread."[35] The motif of a knife used to cut bread—one of the uses of Porębski's knife while he was a prisoner in a concentration camp—is found in the same context in Różewicz's earlier poetry. In "In the Midst of Life," Różewicz's lyrical subject was attempting to reclaim ordinary reality and ethics by relearning and affirming the most basic and banal functions. At the end of the twentieth century in *The Professor's Knife*, these functions no longer have to be reclaimed or asserted. To the old poet, slicing bread is no longer marked with ethical and existential doubts—

it is a banal activity. Ordinary life in post-Holocaust reality, even to those who lived through it or witnessed it and carry its traumas, is possible. Różewicz fully accepts and embraces this possibility, yet rejects the tolerance of a notion that historical memory and the tools for its reading are disappearing in the postmodern world. Hence, in this text in which his private archive turns into cultural memory, he struggles against the "Robigus / who in antiquity / ate metals / —though he never touched gold—- / consumes keys / and locks / swords plowshares knives / guillotine blades axes / rails."[36] Robigus here is a destructive force of chronos that adds countless screens of images and nets of cultural references to our memory of the past. Różewicz, who states that he has been promising himself to write about his friend's knife for many years, yet not fulfilling his promise until now, might be in fact prompted by the destructive force of Robigus and chronos, knowing that the story of the individual experience will undoubtedly disappear along with the inevitable passing of its owner.

Linking the knife (a symbol of Porębski's individual experience) with tropes of his own earlier textual archive, Różewicz may be mourning in advance the passing of a lifelong friendship. As Baudrillard contends, one should cast aside the myth that "man prolongs himself in his objects."[37] However, "the object is that by which we mourn ourselves [and others]—in the sense that it represents our own death, but transcended (symbolically) because we possess it."[38] The knife, as an object present in the title of a poetic cycle and as a photo on the cover of the volume, becomes an individual "monument" to a friend that is meant as much to mourn in advance as it is to commemorate. For Porębski as well, the knife on his work table, positioned among other ordinary objects, may be helping him to mourn the victims who shared his experience but did not survive. The mourning process, then, would be an act of ordinary, everyday, and daily experience. As for Różewicz, his poem is figuratively captured, positioned in between two photographs—the knife on the front cover and the Yad Vashem memorial to Holocaust victims that closes the volume. It is thus positioned between the trace of an individual experience and the musealized trace of the experience of millions who perished. This "in between" position connects the knife with the image of the train wagons: an important association to which I will now turn my attention.

Train Wagons: Public Monument versus Personal Memory

Various metal objects such as keys, locks, swords, knives, and train tracks are subjected to the same fate of destruction by "the demon of rust" and forgetting. With this list, Różewicz connects not only the tools that were the weapons of history, but also well-known Freudian metaphors and symbols of memory, traumatic memory, and memory repressed in the unconscious (keys, locks, and train tracks). In *The Professor's Knife* the poet uses the images of train tracks and trains as metaphors for mnemonic recall. Track and train images are also the most famous iconographic representations of the Holocaust and Różewicz picks up on this in order to show that his own private memory archive inevitably interweaves with these stock images prevalent in places that document and commemorate the Holocaust. Sites of memory, such as the museum, the memorial, and the monument, shape public memory.[39] Andreas Huyssen posits that the power of the museum or the monument arises from its material quality, which the television screen, internet or reminiscence cannot provide.[40] In contemporary culture, subject to the overbearing presence of the fleeting screen image, its simulacrum, and immaterial communication, the presence of a physical object carries cultural significance. In focusing on the image of the train, Różewicz enters a field of imagery from various geographical, temporal, and cultural contexts that come to life in his mind. He writes: "Freight trains / cattle cars / the color of liver and blood / long strings / crammed with banal Evil / . . . they end their flight / in a fiery oven / . . . the train ends / its journey / turns into / a monument."[41] The poet at once refers to the image of the train present in his personal memory, the stock images of trains and railways used in the representation of the Holocaust, and the actual monument in the form of a train wagon dedicated to the memory of Holocaust victims in Yad Vashem. Simultaneously he directs his readers to the photograph of this monument on the back cover of his volume of poetry.

The Holocaust monument is in fact a counter-monument.[42] It does not belong to the tradition of the monument erected as a mark of heroic celebration and a figure of triumph. Rather it is a memorial of suffering that stands as a denunciation of crimes against humanity. In the poet's verse, the image of the train from the past, arising in his memory, has the color of blood and animal organs. The verse "long strings" pertains both to the length of the train itself (the number of its wagons) and the deposit of the bodies that are packed inside its walls. This association is evident in the Polish original because the poet uses the word *składy*, which translates as "accumulation" or "deposits." The cattle wagons are "crammed with banal evil." Those transported are victims of the "banal evil" of the perpetrators of the Final Solution. Różewicz makes an intertextual reference to a phrase coined by Hannah Arendt in her book *Eichmann in Jerusalem: A Report on the Banality of Evil* (1963). Arendt discredits the idea that Nazi criminals were psychopathic and that common people were incapable of unimaginable cruelty against other human beings when it came to the question of obeying orders. In Różewicz's memory, the train wagons fly by in a hurry to end up in the crematoria ("they end their flight / in a fiery oven"). The process of the transformation of the actual cattle wagons into a Holocaust monument is equally fast ("the train ends / its journey / turns into / a monument.") The historical time of the transport and the temporal distance between the occurrence of the Holocaust and its commemoration as a monument is treated in Różewicz's text as a split-second association within one's memory. However, this split-second association does not eliminate the durée of chronos which loads the poet's psyche with a net of images and cultural texts.

The Holocaust monument from Yad Vashem shown on the back cover of the volume leads the poet to consider trains with various origins and destination points, housed in different historical times, and different cultural texts. There is "the stone train / . . . over the abyss," the gold train that "toward the end of the war / . . . left Hungary," as well as "the Inter Regnum—a train / to Berlin." The trip on the "Inter Regnum" to Berlin is probably closest in temporality to the poet's present. Traveling on that train, Różewicz reads one of his favorite poets, Norwid: "I open my book / a poem by Norwid / I am building / a bridge / to link the past / with the future / *The past is today, / but a little further on*." [43] He cites a verse from Norwid, which instantly directs his reader to the poem from *Vade Mecum* titled "The Past." Its first stanza illuminates Różewicz's take on the past, memory, and responsibility as follows:

> Death, pain, the *past*, are not God's,
> But his who breaks the laws;
> So—he can't bear the days;
> And sensing evil, wants *remembrance* spurned![44]

In Norwid's view, pushing away memories implies a fault and a sign of breaking the laws of ethics. The responsibility for the past weighs on the present and, in light of Norwid's poem, Różewicz's lyrical subject counts himself among those responsible for the past, and thus also responsible for preserving memory. However, in contemporary reality when memory is permeated with another banal evil, that of gullible mass media simulacra, the subject is constantly faced with breaking the law of memory ethics. There are those, of course, who similarly to the perpetrators of historical crimes would like to forget certain aspects of historical collective memory. Such is the case with the gold train which "toward the end of the war / . . . left Hungary." Those who may hold the secret of its story are unwilling to testify: "American officers / mixed up in the Affair / they knew nothing / had heard nothing / besides they're dying off."[45] With the lack of traces, this train adopts a mythical aura. Here a factual historical crime is catalogued in the collective memory archive among the mythical, unreal, or hearsay stories: "gold trains amber rooms / sunken continents / Noah's ark / maybe my Hungarian friends / know something about the train / maybe its *Kursbuch* survived / its last schedule / from besieged Budapest."[46] Naturally, Różewicz ironically scrutinizes the "mythical mysteries" of this train, yet in this instance the poet is not an archivist-investigator. His reader never learns whether a document of the train's schedule exists.

Thus, there are two antagonistic trains (one being the commemorative monument from Yad Vashem, the other the "mythical" gold train of unknown or unclear traces). It is highly unsettling that still within the history of the most radical "wilful, systematic, industrially organized, largely successful attempt to exterminate an entire human group within twentieth-century Western society" there is such an even deliberate, muddling of memory. Różewicz also questions our contemporary culture of commemoration. The Yad Vashem monument is volatile, as it can be "brought to life by cries / of hatred / from racists nationalists / fundamentalists / [and it may] . . . crush like an avalanche / onto humanity / not onto 'humanity'! // onto people." [47] Undoubtedly, this reflection points to the catastrophic vein in Różewicz's worldview. If the stone train comes crushing down, Różewicz states, the catastrophe will fall on humanity, yet most importantly on the individual person. The verse "like an avalanche / onto humanity / not onto 'humanity'! // onto people," in the original Polish reads: *"jak lawina / na ludzkość / nie na 'ludzkość'! // na człowieka."* While Bill Johnston translated the Polish *"na człowieka"* in the plural as "onto people," it is possible to translate it as "onto men" or "onto a man," thus playing on the ambiguity of the Polish singular *człowiek*. I would argue that Różewicz's priority in *The Professor's Knife* is first and foremost the responsibility and self-reflexivity of individual memory as it exists in the interregnum—the in-between space—of individual and collective spheres.

Here the focus on individual memory and subjectivity standing in opposition to the collective once again links the images of Holocaust trains of collective cultural memory to the individual perception of these images, and also individual memories of train travel. Once again, this time when discussing the different trains, Różewicz makes a covert reference to his friend Porębski. Różewicz's poetic text and real or imaginary individual experience of travel on the Inter Regnum train to Berlin connects semantically to Porębski's experience (here his textual output as a critic). It might be a pure coincidence or a link imposed on the text by Różewicz's overzealous reader, that Professor Mieczysław Porębski is the author of a book entitled *Interregnum: Studies on the History of Polish Nineteenth- and Twentieth-Century Art* (*Interregnum: Studia z historii sztuki polskiej XIX i XX wieku*, 1975). The individual biographical experience of the two friends, the art historian and the poet, meets on the semantic level of language. According to the *Oxford English Dictionary*, which defines "interregnum" as "a period when normal government is suspended, especially between successive reigns or regimes," the meaning of the interregnum puts the emphasis on the idea of connectivity (of what comes before and its relationship to what follows) in a sequence. This path of interpretation again brings to the fore Nora's conception of the value of materiality of a trace in historical memory and Freud's view of memory as an interconnected network of railways. In Porębski's title, the "Interregnum" is the study of the history of Polish iconography, in Różewicz it is both, a real train and a memory train that leads the lyrical subject into an exploration of the in- between space of the real and the imagined, the present and the past of palimpsests and memory traces that appear in our memory as iconographic images.

Różewicz's reader questions whether this hidden connection of semantics between the lyrical subject's individual experience and the title of Porębski's (historical) art scholarship can be evidence for what Ryszard Nycz calls the poetics of "mutually exclusive alternatives"[48] that according to the critic characterize

Różewicz's late poetics. Such a parataxic structure of the whole of the poetic text, Nycz argues, "hides the connections between parts, or rather transfers the responsibility of its deciphering onto the reader."[49] Nycz goes on to claim that Różewicz's late poetics have gone back in some aspects to their point of origin, where the classic modernist motif of the unwritten (uncreated) work (*"dzieło nienapisane"*) again gains importance. However, the critic asserts, this is not a creative incapacity, but rather an experience of indecision in the sphere of aesthetic and worldview options between, as we read in the poem entitled "Poem" ("Wiersz"), "I wanted to describe it" and "I don't want to write it" (*"Chciałem opisać"* and *"nie chcę go pisać"*). In Różewicz's late oeuvre, the semantics of the multiplicity of meanings bring the antinomy of comprehensive hypothesis.[50] Różewicz leaves the multiplicity of meanings of the "interregnum" to be deciphered by the reader. Similarly, the relationship between the individual trace of traumatic memory (the knife) and the trace associated with its collective nature (the train) is left in silence. Undoubtedly, Różewicz is aware that the professor's knife is a "keepsake" from Porębski's work on the train tracks as a prisoner of a concentration camp, yet this information is never given by the lyrical subject in the poem. In a dialogue with Tomasz Fiałkowski, Porębski says about the knife:

> My little knife—a keepsake from prisoner's work on the train tracks—is only a piece of a much larger whole to which first and foremost the vision of the train as a transport through time belongs. This poem has for me an epic dimension because everyone, together with Master Przyboś and our deceased loved ones, appears in it. It is baffling how large a world was captured in it and how each detail has meaning. This is truly the summa of our lives and the time that was given to us.[51]

The reader never learns what the nature of Porębski's forced labor on the train tracks was. One can only hypothesize that he might have been maintaining the railway tracks. In this hypothesis, however, the reader's interpretation is biased by the most common iconographic portrayals of prisoners' work on train tracks. Here, the reader becomes caught up in the clichéd imaginarium of the Holocaust. The question of what the role was of the professor's knife in this forced labor remains unanswered. Różewicz leaves this trace of a personal history and trauma as a trace left in silence. This is a tactic that shields the whole story of the knife. Perhaps it also shields the most intimate, emotionally charged details of his friend's trauma that Różewicz does not wish to expose. This silence appears whenever Różewicz touches on the deeply personal and emotional aspects of someone's memory, as in the instance when the two friends visit the cemetery and the grave of Porębski's wife, yet they do not speak directly about her. The story of this object, then, is in itself an example of what Nycz calls the aesthetic and worldview indecision where the poet's intention of "I wanted to describe it" ("Chciałem opisać") is coupled with unwillingness, "I don't want to write it" ("nie chcę go pisać").[52]

In *The Professor's Knife*, the materiality and visibility of a trace is central for memory and commemorative processes. Freud's metaphor of memory as a complex network of railway tracks illustrates Różewicz's ventures into numerous memory avenues of the cultural and textual sphere, in which the poet revisits popular images of collective trauma representation. He examines the in-between position—the space where the individual and collective memory touch is more problematic for him. Exposing the details of collective cultural memory (i.e., the scandal of the gold train) comes easily to the poet, who is a voracious reader of mass media culture. Różewicz easily draws on the palimpsests of clichéd images that repeatedly serve to represent the Holocaust, yet when dealing with a personal memory trace (e.g., the knife), both the mnemonic and creative processes become filled with silences and restrained discourse. The knife as a memory trace is a difficult mnemonic prosthesis for Różewicz for it touches on a private relationship and a very individual experience and account of traumatic memory, one which Różewicz did not share with Porębski. Memory dealing with the collective sphere, although the vastness of its trauma is incomprehensible, is easier to approach as it has been repeatedly mediated through mass media technologies. Such prosthetic memory, for Różewicz, is much more open to many trails of mnemonic associations. Its secrets, scandals, or inconsistencies are exposed with verve and are rarely surrounded by creative reluctance or silence.

Notes

1. Proust, 360.
2. Benjamin, *The Arcades Project*, 9.
3. Nowosielski, 52.
4. Huyssen, 249.
5. "Prosthetic memory" is a term used by Landsberg, who argues that modernity made a new form of cultural memory, which she terms prosthetic memory, both possible and necessary. Such memory surfaces when an individual encounters a historical narrative at an experiential site, be it the cinema or a museum. Landsberg argues that mass culture technologies and cinema facilitate common social frameworks and structure "imagined communities" that are not necessarily geographically or nationally bounded, yet share prosthetic memory as a sensuous phenomenon that attains much of its power through affect.
6. Nora, "General Introduction," 2 and 8.
7. Ibid., 8.
8. See Huyssen, 249–61.
9. Hartman, 239.
10. Hutton. quoted in Carrier, 37.
11. Carrier, 47.
12. Kritzman, x–xi. Please note that Halbwachs's conception of collective memory, as fully dependent on "the frameworks of social memory," namely

family, religion, and social class, is an outdated concept in memory theory. For example, Landsberg argues that Halbwachs's culturally specific concept of collective memory, "tied to a culturally and historically specific group of people," is no longer adequate, as mass culture technologies have created shared social frameworks for people who inhabit different sociocultural spaces. Landsberg proposes that modernity brings about a new form of public cultural memory, termed *prosthetic memory*, which emerges at the "interface between a person and a historical narrative about the past." Landsberg, 2 and 8. See also note 5.

13. Ibid., x.
14. Nora, "General Introduction," 17.
15. Presner, 29 and 239.
16. Ibid., 29.
17. Milton, quoted in Hirsch, 217.
18. Hirsch, 225–26.
19. Stone, 27.
20. Błoński, "Szkic portretu," 230.
21. Ibid., 274.
22. Wyka, 324.
23. Różewicz, *New poems*, 17.
24. Ibid., 14.
25. Ibid., 14.
26. Ibid., 16–17.
27. Kopaliński, 766.
28. Różewicz, *New poems*, 26.
29. Ibid., 25–26.
30. Ibid., 18–20.
31. Ibid., 25.
32. Kuhn, 170.
33. Baudrillard, *Revenge of the Crystal*, 77. One should note, however, a key distinction, for in Baudrillard the gadget is defined by its ludic function, which the knife in Różewicz's text does not possess.
34. Różewicz, *New poems*, 8.
35. Różewicz, *Selected poems*, 54.
36. Różewicz, *New poems*, 4.
37. Baudrillard, *Revenge of the Crystal*, 51.
38. Ibid.
39. Huyssen, 249.
40. Ibid., 255.
41. Różewicz, *New poems*, 3–7.
42. Huyssen, 258.
43. Różewicz, *New poems*, 5–6.
44. Norwid, *Selected Poems*, 58
45. Różewicz, *New poems*, 5.

46. Ibid.
47. Ibid., 7–8.
48. Nycz, "Tajemnica okaleczonej poezji," 103.
49. Ibid.
50. Ibid., 103–4.
51. Porębski, *Krytycy i sztuka*, 167.
52. Nycz, "Tajemnica okaleczonej poezji," 103.

Marked by Loss

Mourning and Melancholia in Tadeusz Kantor's *I Shall Never Return*

Milija Gluhovic

I would visit it frequently,
an unusual place.
Its imprint is also deeply engraved on me.
I would believe in what I was told,
that is, that people live there u n d e r g r o u n d.
Now they live in p e a c e.
I remember that I liked to
go there.
While there, I would be in the grip of a
mood. . . . Only much later
would I have a name for it;
m e l a n c h o l y,
Pensiveness.
—Tadeusz Kantor, *A Journey through Other Spaces*

Memory as mourning and melancholy is central to Tadeusz Kantor's cycle of performances entitled "The Theatre of Death" (1975–90). One can argue that each of the performances from this cycle, from *The Dead Class* (*Umarła klasa*, 1975) to *Today Is My Birthday* (*Dziś są moje urodziny*, 1990), moves through the mortuary zones of grief and mourning. Positioned within the Polish discourse of national remembrance in which they intervene, these performances draw their effectiveness from the irreparable wounds of trauma to which they appeal. In this sense, they aim precisely to summon up the presentness of memory, to insist on unfinished business: guilt and reparation remain the dominant themes. Embracing not only the past but also the future, they open spaces for cultural convalescence to be achieved through the performance of mourning.

In his *Wielopole, Wielopole* (1980), for instance, Kantor brought on stage the forgotten past and people of his birthplace, Wielopole—whose Jewish population was wiped out in the Holocaust—forcing his audience to reexperience the traumatic explosion of an irreparable past in a way that impedes emotional indifference. With his *Let the Artist Die* (*Niech sczezną artyści*, 1986), he continued his project of cultural witnessing by invoking onstage the tragic life stories of many thousands of Poles who perished at the hands of the NKVD at Katyń and other secret locations in the spring of 1940, which the Polish communist regime, subordinated to the Soviet Union, occluded for so many years. The performance thus acted as a site of resistance in an instance of officially instituted melancholia, a socially instituted foreclosure of mourning, showing that the survival of memory—our susceptibility to being reminded of what the official culture would prefer us to forget—depends on an art of witness.

In this essay, I will discuss *I Shall Never Return* (*Nigdy tu już nie powrócę*, 1988), the penultimate production of Kantor's "Theatre of Death," which commemorates the death of his father, who perished in Auschwitz.[1] Engaging recent conceptualizations of mourning and melancholia articulated by Nicolas Abraham and Maria Torok, Jacques Derrida, and Judith Butler, I argue that, for most of his lifetime, Kantor was unable to mourn the loss of his father, not only because the loss was painful and traumatic, but also because of the ambivalence he felt toward him. I suggest that Kantor incorporated and encrypted this loss inside himself until late in his life, beginning the process of mourning only after a discovery he made about his father in 1984. While I argue that it is precisely this process of coming to terms with the loss of his father that Kantor stages in *I Shall Never Return*, I also show that this performance should be understood not as expressing a singular subjective account of loss but as reaching outward toward the collective sites of memory, history, and trauma.

Tadeusz Kantor was the second child of Helena Kantor, née Berger (1880–1962), and Marian Kantor-Mirski (1884–1942). Kantor's father never returned home to his family after his departure with the Second Division of the Polish Legion to fight in World War I. Upon leaving the army on December 15, 1921, he first settled in Silesia and then in Zagłębie Dąbrowskiego, before finally returning to Tarnów, his hometown, in 1938. On September 8, 1940, he was arrested and put in prison in Tarnów, from which he was deported to the Auschwitz concentration camp on February 20, 1942. He was executed there on April 1, 1942.[2] In *I Shall Never Return*, Kantor quotes the telegram that was sent to his mother by German authorities, in which she was notified that her husband died of a "heart attack."

As Marie-Thérèse Vido-Rzewuska has suggested, "The fact that his father never returned is one of the major ambiguities of Kantor's work."[3] She has also argued that Kantor's attitude toward his father changed after he attended a conference dedicated to the memory of Marian Kantor-Mirski. Organized by the Zagłębie Museum in Będzin in June 1984, the conference celebrated Kantor-Mirski's accomplishments as a soldier (he was decorated with the Cross of Merit and the French Order of Victory) and as an ethnologist who wrote a number of papers about the history of Silesia—the accomplishments that played a part in his arrest and confinement in Auschwitz. Participating in this event allowed Kantor to see his father in a new light. As Vido-Rzewuska describes, Kantor emerged from the conference "quite shattered, saying, 'Why did I only get evil reports of him?'"[4] The blurred image of Kantor's father—the result of first his absence and then his untimely death—introduces a degree of uncertainty and indirectness into the considerations of his influence on the author, which nevertheless testify to the strength of this influence. Some kind of disguise, metamorphosis, or recontextualization accompanies the continuing influence of the dead. In this essay, I propose that this influence is most intelligible in *I Shall Never Return*, where Kantor stages the return of his dead father as the return of the mythical figure of Odysseus.

Significantly, this was not the first time that the figure of Odysseus appeared in Kantor's theatre. On June 21, 1944, in Cracow, Kantor and his Underground Theatre troupe illegally staged *The Return of Odysseus* (*Powrót Odysa*), a play written by Stanisław Wyspiański (1869–1907), the creator of the "Polish Theatre of Death."[5] Wyspiański's play, written in 1904 and published shortly before his death in 1907, belongs to the last stage of his work in which the theme of death is predominant. In this text, the playwright closely followed Dante's bold reappropriation of Homer in the Ulysses canto (canto 26) of Purgatorio. While in The Divine Comedy Odysseus is sent to hell in punishment for destroying Troy, Wyspiański's protagonist suffers from traumatic memories related to the siege of Troy and his long voyage home. The fact that Odysseus in this performance was presented as a German soldier returning from Stalingrad suggests that Kantor's decision to stage this play in Cracow in 1944 was influenced by its topicality at the time.[6]

The sense of estrangement between the son and the father, thematized in Wyspiański's play, may also have had strong bearings on the young Kantor. In a comment written in the margins of his stage script (*partytura*) of *The Return of Odysseus* from 1944, Kantor underlined this feeling: "Father is back after years of war. They have little in common now, father and son, and little to say to each other. All their attempts to come close to each other remain futile and ludicrous."[7] Furthermore, after Odysseus kills a herdsman in act 1 of Wyspiański's play, Telemachus kills another servant with an identical gesture and is overwhelmed by a feeling of joy and euphoria. In this way, Wyspiański illustrates not only a violent legacy bequeathed from one generation to another but also a strong urge on the part of the son to identify with his ego ideal (father). Considering the ambivalent feelings that Kantor had for his father, I believe that this motif may have provided the subterranean motivation for his decision to stage the play both in 1944 and in 1988.[8]

However, it is only with his performance of *I Shall Never Return* that Kantor makes an ingenious use of Wyspiański's play as a figural vehicle for his act of bearing witness to Auschwitz and the death of his father. The artist may have drawn his inspiration here from the first act of Wyspiański's drama, where the protagonist's ontological status is put in doubt by the author, when Odysseus says in his address to the herdsman: "You know, old man, maybe I'm a ghost and frighten people."[9] The precedent was already established by Dante, whose Ulysses and his men are swallowed up in the open sea beyond the Pillars of Hercules, in sight of Mount Paradise, and at the pleasure of the Christian God. Analogous to Ulysses and his companion Diomedes, who return only as a speaking flame encountered by Dante and Virgil in purgatory in order to tell their story of passing the limit and consequent submersion, Kantor's father returns to Ithaca (Cracow) only as a specter on his son's stage.[10] Thus, in the aftermath of Auschwitz, Kantor rewrites Wyspiański so as to replace Odysseus's return to Ithaca with a very different story, in which return is resignified once again.

The trope of return is crucial for Kantor's theatre practice. Commenting on his wartime staging of Wyspiański, in a 1980 prose piece entitled "The Infamous Transition from the World of the Dead into the World of the Living (Fiction and Reality)," Kantor wrote:

> It is not merely the war and Troy that Odysseus returned from. More importantly, he returned from "out of the grave," from the realm of the dead, from the "other world" into the sphere of life, into the realm of the living, he appeared among us. *The Return of Odysseus* established a precedent and a prototype for all later characters of my theatre.[11]

On another occasion, Kantor offered a similar definition of his theatre:

> I hold that theatre is a ford across the river. It is a place through which the dead figures from that shore, from that world, cross over into our world and now into our lives. . . . And what happens next? The answer might be given by the Dybbuk . . . the spirits of the dead who enter into the bodies of others and speak through them.[12]

The idea of the dybbuk, "the soul of a dead person who has not come to complete rest" but inhabits the body of a living person and speaks through the mouth of the host, is a potent metaphor for Kantor's theatre, which could be thought of essentially as a raising of the dead.[13] As we shall also see later, the old Jewish scenarios of dybbuk possession and exorcism bear some striking similarities to the psychoanalytic process of incorporative melancholia, which I will employ here in order to illuminate the work of mourning performed in Kantor's *I Shall Never Return*.

In his writings, as well as in his theatre practice, Kantor refuses the idea of textual "integrity." Instead, he sees each work as both text and pretext for further texts and performances. This intertextual approach renders his oeuvre a coextensive and simultaneous rather than a chronological—time-bound—creation. Moreover, it is an approach impregnated by a view of memory as coexistent with the present, a view that his collage texts and performances further encourage. According to Denis Bablet, with his 1988 production of *The Return of Odysseus* Kantor wanted to create a retrospective of his theatrical career, from the war times to the present moment. While he initially considered restaging *Balladyna* by Juliusz Słowacki, the first performance he staged in his underground theatre in 1942, he finally opted for Wyspiański's piece. In Bablet's estimate, the text "held an evident advantage over *Balladyna* (hardly known abroad). It came from the very heart of European mythology."[14]

Kantor's *I Shall Never Return* is a palimpsest composed not only of Kantor's texts, performance sequences, and characters from his earlier productions but also of parts and particles from such diverse cultural artifacts as myth, autobiography, dreams, literary paraphrase, quotation, and self-citation. The story of the return of Odysseus is presented in the form of recycled images and sequences from Kantor's earlier performances: *Wielopole, Wielopole*, *Dainty Shapes and Hairy Apes*, and *The Dead Class*, "building up a structure of interlocking memories as audiences experience each new element of the work as haunted by the experience of previous works."[15] Toward the middle of the performance, after a wedding ceremony between a Dead Bride and a Young-Kantor-Mannequin, a knock at the door is heard. A Cleaning Woman rushes and opens the door. We can see the Ghost of Odysseus standing in the doorframe. In his guide for the performance, Kantor writes:

> He comes from the depths of time. / Wartime, 1944. / But it's only his *REMAINS*. / As if they had been pulled out of the grave. / A Military Uniform, / Stretched out, like on a cross. / . . . And, from somewhere above we hear a voice saying: ". . . I am Odysseus, / Lord of Ithaca." / The Cleaning Woman cries: / "On the night of January 24 / 1944 / Odysseus returned to Cracow, / his Ithaca."[16]

A repeated knocking is heard. There is a new guest in the doorframe—the specter of Kantor's father. It is a mannequin bound to a pillory with a rope, like Odysseus to the mast of his ship. A machine gun is fastened to the pillory and points at the back of the father's head. We hear the song "Ani maamin" and then a voice from a loudspeaker, "I died on 24 January, / 1944. / That same date."[17] The voice that we hear, however, belongs not to the specter of Kantor's father but to his son, Tadeusz. The phrase ("That same date") refers to the explanatory lines of the Cleaning Woman from the previous sequence when she announced the date of Odysseus's return to Cracow. While Kantor's first staging of Wyspiański's *The Return of Odysseus* took place in occupied Cracow on June 21, 1944, in *I Shall Never Return* the artist has Odysseus return to the same war-torn city for the first time on January 24, 1944, the same day that he remembers receiving the news of his father's death in Auschwitz.[18]

To mourn effectively is to dispense with the dead; to mourn unsuccessfully is to remain permeable to the dead. As David Savran suggests:

> virtually every ghost in the contemporary theatre signals a crisis in the constitution of the subject, for whom the ghost represents an other who has been lost and yet is imagined to inhere both inside and outside the self. For these bereaved subjects, the ghost functions as a symptom of a melancholic process whereby the subject attempts to incorporate that which he or she has lost.[19]

To refuse or to be unable either to mourn or to stop mourning is to encourage the admission of a foreign body into oneself that will play havoc with all manner of fortifications and defense, in an exemplary disruption of understanding. Such may be the painful consequences of the death of a father and of the preservation of the dead father.

Kantor's *I Shall Never Return* marks such unresolved, deeply personal loss. However, as Freud observed, finding in archaeological excavation a metaphor for the psychoanalytic recovery of the past, that which is shoved "underground" into the unconscious and sealed up may simply be better preserved. "There is, in fact, no better analogy for repression, by which something in the mind is at once made inaccessible and preserved," wrote Freud, "than burial of the sort to which Pompeii fell victim and from which it could emerge once more through the work of spades."[20] As we shall see, in *I Shall Never Return*, that which is buried also comes up to the surface, and if there is something sealed up or forced under, it does not disappear, but instead festers until the moment when it can erupt into consciousness once again. Following Vido-Rzewuska, I suggest that, for Kantor, this moment came in 1984, when he attended the exhibition that honored the memory of his father, and after which he was able to begin the process of grieving and "decorporation" of the cryptic object.

Let us remember here that, for Freud, melancholia is characterized by the inability of the subject to separate itself from the object and thus recognize what has been lost, while a successful work of mourning constitutes an articulated reaction to loss. Julia Kristeva, too, saw the "cure" for melancholy in interpretation and representation in addition to cathartic exercises such as art, religion, and literature, which discharge drive and affect associated with the repressed.[21] In line with this thinking, one could argue that Kantor's act of calling up the theatrical ghost of his father, allowing him to tell his story in *I Shall Never Return*, could be seen as signifying the process of transforming melancholia into mourning, unconscious into conscious.

Writing after Freud, Nicolas Abraham and Maria Torok make a distinction between "introjection," a mechanism of so-called normal mourning where the object of loss is acknowledged as lost, and "incorporation," which characterizes mourning in which the object of loss cannot be dispensed with. The latter mechanism belongs more properly, therefore, to melancholy—the state of disavowed or suspended grief in which the object is magically sustained "in the body" in some way.[22] For Maria Torok, "incorporation" intervenes when introjection, for any reason, fails. According to Derrida, "cryptic incorporation always marks an effect of impossible or refused mourning."[23] Mourning that is impossible, refused, or unaccomplished represents the failure or unwillingness to settle debts with the past, to abandon a loved one—the father, say—to the past, to a dead memory. But to stay in touch in this way, to perpetuate identification by incorporating a loved object, involves never being able to come to terms with the death of the loved one. In Abraham and Torok's words, "incorporation is the refusal to acknowledge the full import of the loss, a loss that, if recognised as such, would effectively transform us."[24]

But how can the dead live inside someone? Where would they find "lodging"? Abraham and Torok use the concept of the crypt to designate a unique intrapsychic topography that inexpressible mourning erects inside the subject as a secret tomb that houses the dead "other" as "living." They see the crypt as a formation constituted through the fantasy of incorporation, which simulates introjection. In "Mourning or Melancholia," Abraham and Torok describe the crypt's structure as follows:

> Reconstituted from the memory of words, scenes, and affects, the objectal correlative of the loss is buried alive in the crypt as a full-fledged person, complete with its own topography. The crypt also includes the actual or supposed traumas that made introjection impracticable. A whole world of unconscious fantasy is created, one that leads its own separate and concealed existence. Sometimes in the dead of night, when libidinal fulfilments have their way, the ghost of the crypt comes back to haunt the cemetery guard.[25]

Thus, mourning that operates—or fails to operate—by incorporation can never be reconciled to the lost object that it is able to preserve. Incorporative mourning keeps the loved object at bay by including it within the ego. In other words, the loved object can be included within the ego only if it is at the same time withheld, held in. According to Derrida:

> Incorporation is a kind of theft to reappropriate the pleasure object. But that reappropriation is simultaneously rejected: which leads to a paradox of a foreign body preserved as foreign but by the same token excluded from a self that henceforth deals not with the other, but only with itself. The more the self keeps the foreign element as a foreigner inside itself, the more it excludes it. The self *mimes* introjection. But this mimicry with its redoubtable logic depends on clandestinity. Incorporation negotiates clandestinely with a prohibition it neither accepts nor transgresses.[26]

Such incorporation insures that what is perpetually disavowed will always return, even if what perpetually returns continues to be disavowed. Cryptogenic incorporation is, among other things, the means by which a loved one is neither "digested" in the mind nor vomited out. Derrida describes incorporation as "an act of vomiting to the inside"; cryptic incorporation involves a process—neither purely a fantasy, nor the consequence of a "real" event—of "eating the object (through the mouth or otherwise) . . . in order to vomit it, in a way, into the inside, into the pocket of a cyst."[27] A door is silently sealed off like a condemned passageway inside the self.

Discussing the phenomenon of melancholic incorporation, Abraham and Torok further assert that the "shadow of the object . . . comes back to haunt by being *reincarnated in the person of the subject*."[28] The moment of uncanniness is brought about through the shadow-effect of the other that, in Abraham and Torok's terms, "*carries the ego* [or some other façade] *as its mask*."[29] Where the phantom (i.e., an incorporated object) indicates a rift in the ego, it returns to haunt its host through a mechanism that, according to these authors, "consists of exchanging one's own identity for a fantasmatic identification with the 'life'—beyond the grave—of an object of love."[30] Although it takes many forms in endocryptic identification, "the 'I' is understood as the lost object's fantasised ego" that haunts the subject through a kind of ventriloquism.[31] As Judith Butler further explains, "The experience of loss compels the subject to incorporate that other into the very structure of the ego, taking on attributes of the other and 'sustaining' the other through magical acts of imitation."[32] I propose that it is precisely this act of melancholic sustenance that is dramatized in *I Shall Never Return*.

Several scenes in the performance in which Kantor identifies with his father suggest such an act. During a wedding ceremony, for example, a Priest recites the marriage service to a couple addressing a Young Tadeusz Kantor Mannequin as Marian Kantor, and a Dead Bride as Helena Berger, Kantor's mother. Even without this explicit address, the intertextual reference to Kantor's parents' wedding ceremony from *Wielopole, Wielopole* in this scene establishes a certain parallelism and suggests Kantor's identification with his father. Moreover, as already mentioned, after the appearance of Marian Kantor's mannequin in the midst of the performance, it is Tadeusz Kantor's voice that comes from the loudspeaker and says: "I died on 24 January 1944." This too, I believe, implies that the oscillation between the "self" (Kantor) and the "other" (his father) is precarious. Finally, in the description of one of the last scenes provided in the performance guide, Kantor makes his identification with the father figure/Odysseus quite explicit when he writes: "Odysseus (mannequin) departs for ever. I remain. I—Odysseus."[33]

Because the melancholic (unlike the mourner) refuses to relinquish the love object, "internalisation becomes a strategy of magically resuscitating the lost object, not only because the loss is painful, but because the ambivalence felt toward the object requires that the object be retained until the differences are settled."[34] Discovering a positive image of his father during the conference in Będzin enabled Kantor to start the process of mourning, namely, "introjection" and "decorporation" of the cryptic object, with respect to his father. The false "I" was reconverted into the third person, as Kantor then understood that it was possible to evoke the prodigal love of his father, the love of forgiveness and acceptance—without subjecting him to shame or losing him morally. The entombed experience was acknowledged and the crypt unlocked, its contents laid out in the open and recognized as the unalienable property of the subject. However, no totalizing answer seems possible to the question of whether this change means "letting an object go," whether mourning can be successful or not.

That mourning is and remains cryptic is suggested near the end of the performance, in the scene of an encounter between Kantor and the stage figure of his father (Odysseus), which follows the play-within-a-play representing the return of Odysseus. Here, Kantor takes his stage script from the 1944 production of Wyspiański's *The Return of Odysseus* and sits down at the center table at which Odysseus sits as well. He adjusts Odysseus's scarf and lightly touches his hand. "But Odysseus, sitting stiffly / in his Wartime Uniform / gives one the impression / of a MANNEQUIN," writes Kantor in his notes.[35] What does this silent encounter tell us? Does this (im)possible return of the father ensure that, if there is something outstanding between generations, it continues to be unresolved? It seems that the ambivalence between the son and the father is renewed rather than dissipated. But if this suggests, in whatever way, a facility of transgenerational communion, this communion is shrouded in an overdetermined unintelligibility. The return of the father, the extraordinarily enduring influence of the dead, is achieved at the price of expository fluency, of the ability to act or communicate intelligibly. Kantor can renew contact with the dead, but this contact, it seems, tends not to the efficiency of understanding between generations but to irresolution, to an uncertain communication that does not exhaust itself in a definitive reconciliation of the parties involved. The return of the dead, it could be said, coincides with certain interruptions of communication, which nevertheless indicate an uncanny communicative power.

As Kantor begins to read the lines from the third act of Wyspiański's *Return of Odysseus*,[36] he and Odysseus are joined by the Cleaning Woman, who sits by the table and starts translating the Polish text into Italian from the line "The Shores of my fatherland":

> I found a Hell in my own Fatherland,
> Entering a graveyard. . . .
> I slaughtered everything, pushed all away;
> And all deceptive happiness fled from me.
> Nothing, nothing behind me, or in front . . .
> . . . .
> these shores of my fatherland, Ithaca . . .
> I raced along these paths in my boyhood,
> Chasing the birds—hey! Gulls fly over the seas:
> The birds of my youth . . .
> There! There! There is Ithaca!
> . . . There—is my fatherland . . .
> there is the song of my life consummate!
> No one—alive—finds out his childhood home . . .
> My fatherland—I've carried it in my heart,
> And now I carry it in my desire,
> Today I only long for it, a shade . . .
> A shade myself, I long after a shade . . .
> I hear a crowd . . .
> A boat full of people!
> They look at me—they call to me!
> . . . .
> I cannot make them out. Who may they be?
> They call out—they complain—or, they rejoice?
> The waves divide me from their voices, waves,
> Dividing us—The boat of the dead![37]

The story being read by Kantor reflects the stage picture we see: to the sounds of *Salve Regina*, the stage figures follow Charon's boat in a stylistic representation of the crossing of the Styx. They all exit. After Kantor has finished his reading, Odysseus gets off the table and starts leaving the stage. Then, suddenly, he turns and glances at Kantor. For the first time in the performance they look at each other. The two men enter each other's eyes, and thus a sense of communion, of repair or healing, of recognition might be felt. Then, as Kantor writes in his notes for the performance, "Odysseus (mannequin) departs for ever. / I remain. I—Odysseus."[38]

Early on in this essay, I pointed out that the phenomenon of incorporative melancholia, which I engaged in order to illuminate the act of mourning enacted in Kantor's performance, could be seen as analogous to the process of dybbuk possession expressed in Jewish folklore. In the final part of this essay, I would like to pursue this argument a bit further in order to tease out a broader relevance of this claim for my analysis here. Dybbuk possession involved spirits of the dead as possessing agents, and as in other cultural variants of possession-as-disease, the exorcism of the dybbuk was construed as a patterned sequence of steps through which the spirit's identity and posthumous vicissitudes were disclosed and the conditions for its departure negotiated. The mystical doctrine of transmigration of souls (*gilgul*), which provided the ideational basis in which the dybbuk phenomenon germinated, was formulated as early as the twelfth century.[39] While most of the early cases of dybbuk possession were recorded in Italian and Middle Eastern Sephardic communities in the sixteenth and seventeenth centuries, "during the eighteenth and nineteenth centuries East European Hasidic communities, mainly in Russia and Poland, supplied most of the reports."[40] According to Yoram Bilu, "the general disintegration of the Jewish traditional centers in Europe and the Middle East in our time has eliminated them altogether. As a result, no contemporary cases of dybbuk possession have been available since the 1930s."[41] S. Anski, the pseudonym for Shlomo Zanvil Rappoport, who conducted ethnographic expeditions to study Jewish communities in Volhynia and Podolia from 1912 through 1914, revitalized these beliefs with his enormously successful play *The Dybbuk*, performed in Yiddish by the Vilna troupe in 1920.[42]

In the play, a young woman, Leah, is possessed by the soul of her late beloved on the day of her wedding to another man. The dybbuk speaks from within Leah, refusing to leave her body until painful exorcism is performed and certain secrets from the past are revealed. From a psychoanalytic point of view, one could argue that the reason behind Leah's insanity is unfulfilled mourning, and that possession here could be seen as "a cultural device through which an intrapsychic conflict is assigned an 'interpersonal' dimension."[43] The similarities of the psyche's play between internal and external objects, between processes of identification and separation, at work in *The Dybbuk* and *I Shall Never Return* are, I believe, overt. In both, the living cannot forget the dead, and the dead refuse to be forgotten by the living. However, the cultural haunting enacted through Kantor's performance cannot be confined to the perception of an individual, but is historical and collective in its nature.[44] As Avery Gordon reminds us, "Haunting is a constituent element of social life. It is neither premodern superstition nor individual psychosis; it is a generalisable social phenomenon of great import. . . . The ghost is not simply a dead or missing person, but a social figure, and investigating it can lead to that dense site where history and subjectivity make social life."[45]

I Shall Never Return shows that the survival of memory (here, the memory of the Holocaust), the ability of the culture's obscenities to return, and to return in a striking guise that haunts the mind, depends on the art of witness, capable of keeping fresh, or of presencing and of representing, what more conventional representations consign to an (unpresenced) past. In *I Shall Never Return*, as well as in his other "Theatre of Death" performances, Kantor reactivates historical scenarios of dybbuk possession (what Richard Schechner calls "strips of behavior");[46] he makes use of these historical antecedents for his theatrical practice in order to dramatize the scarce boundary between the living and the dead, the interpenetration of the dead with the world of the living. While Pierre Nora has famously argued that in modern society textual memory (*lieux de mémoire*) has essentially replaced embodied memory (*milieux de mémoire*), Kantor's theatre shows the ways in which embodied memory operates in conjunction with the archive (here Anski's text comes to mind) to create and sustain cultural memory.[47]

This becomes explicit in the last section of *I Shall Never Return*, which overtly transforms the subjectivity of grief into a broader historical and collective context, or, in Krzysztof Pleśniarowicz's words, in which "[t]he end of the biography is identified with the end of the epoch."[48] In this scene, titled "The Great Emballage of the End of the XXth century," a group of "Those Serious Gentlemen," the masters of power, spread black shrouds of oblivion over the figures and objects on the stage, thereby constructing a mountainous graveyard for a lifetime of Kantor's memories. The tune of the "Rakoczi March" from Berlioz's oratorio accompanies this act of annihilation. From this mass-grave emballage, the priest's cross sticks out for a moment only to disappear a few seconds later into the sea of black shrouds. Then, singing the old Hasidic chant "Ani maamin," replete with suffering, the Cleaning Woman/Songstress of the Promised Land slowly exhumes the corpses buried under this immense mourning veil—the memories will not be completely obliterated.[49] As she leads them away from the stage, the doors close behind them for the last time.

As the finale of the performance strongly suggests, Kantor's Kaddish for his father—his most personal work, and his most heartfelt—is also his requiem for the twentieth century. Pleśniarowicz calls it Kantor's "most legible invocation of the Holocaust so far."[50] As I attempted to demonstrate in this essay, with this performance Kantor provides an example of a work of mourning in which the ghosts and phantoms of culture are to be entertained rather than exorcised. Like the most significant artworks of contemporary culture, this performance of Kantor's is not a work of mourning in the Freudian sense. It does not enforce the gradual detachment of libido or desire from the object. Instead, it reframes the question of mourning in ethical terms, thus functioning as a resonant text, a complicated web of temporality in which memory is not only taken in, introjected, or accrued, but reworked, projected, and given back to a collective subject, thus allowing the past to find a "place" within the identity of the remembering community.

Notes

1. *I Shall Never Return* premiered on April 23, 1988, at Piccolo Teatro Studio in Milan. My analysis here is based on my viewings of a video recording of the performance played at Piccolo Teatro Studio the following night (April 24), as well as a version filmed by Polish Television for their Teatr Telewizji series (March/April 1990, director Andrzej Sapija), both housed at the Cricoteka, the Center for the Documentation of the Art of Tadeusz Kantor, in Kraków. I also refer to the Polish and English versions of the programs for the performance, and Charles Kraszewski's unpublished translation of the program in Polish, supplemented by his translation of the verbal parts of the text taken from two video recordings of the performance—from the theatre Albeniz in Madrid (February/March 1989) and the Polish Television version—as well as his description of the scenic action (from the Madrid stage production). Finally, in the Cricoteka, I consulted numerous video recordings of the rehearsals of this performance conducted in 1987 in Kraków and in 1988 in Milan.

2. The date of Tadeusz Kantor's father's death noted above comes from a recent monograph on Marian Kantor-Mirski, written by Zdzisław Kantor. The author bases this information on the entry in Archiwum Państwowego Muzeum Oświęcim-Brzezinka, Księga Stanów Dziennych w K.L. Auschwitz B-AU-I-3/1/2, nr inw. 31534, T. 2, s. 209 (26-27). See also Rzewiczok and Gliwa, 9.

3. Vido-Rzewuska, 233. In a piece of poetic prose entitled "Father," Tadeusz Kantor writes: "His imprint / My eyes could not look high enough, / so there are only his / *boots*, / which are knee high. / My sensitive ear would catch / incomprehensible / curses of the father and / his strange walking pattern: / one two, one two. . . . / Nobody else walked like this. / Then I learned words to describe it: / To march, marching." Tadeusz Kantor, *Journey through Other Spaces*, 183. Vido-Rzewuska refers to this fragment as the only memory Kantor as a child had of his father (see Vido-Rzewuska, 233). Based on an interview with Tadeusz Kantor, Guy Scarpetta records a much later encounter between Kantor and his father: "Suddenly, one day in the 1930s in Cracow, a certain very elegant man, with a platinum plate visible in his skull (a war wound? a trepanation?) addresses him: 'You are my son' . . . He offers young Tadeusz Kantor a coffee and, in front of his fascinated son, begins to play all instruments in the band, surrounded by young women." Scarpetta, 192.

4. Vido-Rzewuska, 235.

5. On Tadeusz Kantor and the Polish "theatre of death," see, for instance, Pleśniarowicz, "Polski Teatr Śmierci"; and Morawiec, "Wyspiański a 'Teatr Śmierci.'"

6. Pleśniarowicz makes an attempt at reconstructing this production and finds that it evolved through three conceptions. According to him, "Perhaps, due to these numerous versions and transfers (for safety reasons), it is impossible to establish the exact dates." He further observes that Tadeusz "Kantor himself referred to the date of June 21 . . . but it is not possible today to state whether the date was precise and which version of *The Return of Odysseus* is concerned." "Odysseus Must Really Return," 57–59.

7. Tadeusz Kantor, *Return of Odys*. "*Partytura*," 5.

8. I am aware that, in the light of Wyspiański's and his critics' interpretations of the figure of Odysseus as "a destitute man morally equal to the degenerate suitors" (Sugiera, 86), "a compulsive killer" (Terlecky, 123), "a criminal" (Howard Clarke in Wyspiański, *The Return of Odysseus*, xiv), and "a war criminal" (Tadeusz Kantor, *Return of Odys. "Partytura,"* 1), the analogy I establish between Tadeusz Kantor's father and Odysseus might appear troublesome. Furthermore, as already noted, Odysseus in Kantor's performance from 1944 was presented as a German soldier returning from Stalingrad. My intention is not to conflate the positions of victim and perpetrator, or to blur the distinction between inflicting and receiving a wound. However, I believe that Tadeusz Kantor's choice of conflating the date of his father's death with the date of the return of Odysseus to Kraków in this performance allows for this kind of interpretation.

9. Wyspiański, *The Return of Odysseus*, 12.

10. In this regard Tadeusz Kantor's performance could be compared to Primo Levi's text *If This Is a Man* (*Se questo è un uomo*), in which Levi makes use of Dante's Ulysses canto, that is, Dante's revision of Homer, in an act of bearing witness to Auschwitz.

11. Tadeusz Kantor, *Journey through Other Spaces*, 145. In 1905, Wyspiański wrote an essay on *Hamlet* that might have influenced his shaping of this and subsequent scenes in act 1. The ghost returning from the world of the dead is also a common figure of the Polish Romantic drama, to which both Wyspiański and Tadeusz Kantor are indebted.

12. Pleśniarowicz, *The Dead Memory Machine*, 189.

13. Rokem, 54.

14. Bablet, 153.

15. Carlson, *The Haunted Stage*, 104. Carlson employs terms such as "recycling" and "ghosting" to describe this kind of intertextual approach to theatre and mentions Tadeusz Kantor as one of its major exponents (104–5 and 107).

16. Tadeusz Kantor, *I'll Never Come Back*, 319–20.

17. Ibid., 321.

18. Lawson, 433.

19. Savran, 121.

20. Freud, 9: 40.

21. Kristeva, *Black Sun*, 24.

22. In this essay, I am referring primarily to a compilation of Nicolas Abraham and Maria Torok's essays in *The Shell and the Kernel* (1994). They also write on related issues in their earlier book *The Wolf Man's Magic Word: A Cryptonimy* (1986).

23. Derrida, "Foreword," xxi.

24. Abraham and Torok, *Shell and the Kernel*, 127.

25. Ibid.,130.

26. Derrida, "Foreword," xvii.

27. Ibid., xxxviii.

28. Abraham and Torok, *Shell and the Kernel*, 141.

29. Ibid.

30. Ibid., 142.

31. Ibid., 148.

32. Butler, 57.

33. Tadeusz Kantor, *I'll Never Come Back*, 331.

34. Butler, 61–62.

35. Tadeusz Kantor, *I'll Never Come Back*, 330.

36. In the performance, Tadeusz Kantor read the lines from the copy of the play he used when staging it in 1944. Wyspiański's text shows Odysseus on an empty shore reliving his chaotic memories that bear an indelible mark of trauma: the burning of Troy, the nymph Calypso, a Harpy, repetitive callings of singing Sirens, and a boat of the dead.

37. From Stanisław Wyspiański's *The Return of Odysseus*, quoted in Tadeusz Kantor, *I'll Never Come Back*, 330–31.

38. Ibid., 331.

39. See Scholem, Chajes.

40. Bilu, 165.

41. Ibid., 163.

42. Tadeusz Kantor saw the famous Evgeny Vakhtangov's production of *The Dybbuk* performed by the legendary Yiddish Habima troupe at the Bagatela Theatre in Kraków in 1938, which made a deep impression on him (Pleśniarowicz, *Dead Memory Machine*, 19).

43. Bilu, 168.

44. In retrospect, this could be argued for Anski's play as well (see note 16 above).

45. Gordon, 7–8.

46. Schechner, 35.

47. Freddie Rokem, in his book *Performing History*, refers to Anski's *The Dybbuk* as a "central intertext of the Israeli [theatre] productions" and explains why the play continues to have a strong grip on Israeli audiences: "After the war, however, with six million Jewish souls who had not been properly buried, and who had thus not reached complete rest, the Israeli cultural discourses gradually developed an unconscious obsession with becoming possessed by these Dybbuks" (55). In Tadeusz Kantor's performance, as well as

in a more recent production of *The Dybbuk* by Krzysztof Warlikowski, and a 1996 short story by Hannah Krall about the Holocaust dybbuk, the legend of a spirit who possesses a living person could be also seen as a figure for Poland's relationship to its missing Jews. These works suggest that the past lives in the present and that to exorcise it may be misguided—may, in fact, not be possible.

48. Pleśniarowicz, *Dead Memory Machine*, 267.

49. In his Kraków rehearsals Tadeusz Kantor used the song "Lily Marlen" for this sequence. However, as he revealed in an interview with Denis Bablet, while rehearsing the performance in Milan, he "met a Jewish singer . . . who sang [for him] a song once sung by the Jews entering gas chambers, the religious song 'We Trust the Messiah Will Come' (Bablet, 158), and ultimately he decided to include it in the performance.

50. Pleśniarowicz, *Dead Memory Machine*, 242.

THAT UNCANNY SOAP

Zofia Nałkowska and the Economy of the Holocaust

Bożena Shallcross

I did not make up anything.
—Zofia Nałkowska on *Medallions*

In Nałkowska everything is a construction.
—Michał Głowiński (not on *Medallions*)

Soap, Ladies and Gentlemen, die Seife, die Seifenkugel, *you know, certainly,* what *it is*.
—Francis Ponge

Soap's telos is to purify, to clean and disappear completely. Hence soap's semantics should be in conflict with its impure origins, in the same manner in which its cleansing effect clashes with dirty hands. Contrary to Francis Ponge's assessment, as consumers, we have only a vague idea of its contents (including the main ingredient, animal fat) and of the chemical process it takes to transform that coarse material into a pleasantly scented, neatly molded and packaged cosmetic.[1] Our consumption of soap is one of the least complex, and thus most overlooked, objectual interrelationships, being much like any other everyday occurrence. The narrative of soap's consumption is brief and takes place entirely on the body's surface, between the skin and the pleasantly disappearing product.[2] The gist of this narrative can be told in one sentence: the soap made of the animal body washes another body—in other words, the body washes the body. But what, ladies and gentlemen, if the human body is washed by soap manufactured from another human body?

The implications of a human subject's producing and using a cosmetic made from bodily matter retrieved from other human subjects draws us into the sphere of ethics. In this case, however, the ethical proves to be entangled with less-than-sublime questions of economics and the welfare of a society at war. Both aspects of the question are conveniently intertwined with the promotion of economico-ethical happiness under the banner of utilitarianism. Since Jeremy Bentham published his *An Introduction to the Principles of Morals and Legislation*, utilitarian philosophy has evolved into several distinct strands, including codifying utilitarianism into a normative theory of ethics. The British philosopher's promotion of an ethics calling for overall happiness for both the agent of action and everybody affected by the action privileges results over methods. Utilitarianism's teleological character, neatly opposed to deontological ethical theories concerned with moral duties and obligations and not with goals and ends, has eventually evolved into the present-day consequentialism. We can trace utilitarian principles in a variety of twentieth-century developments in economics, mathematics, social sciences, and yes, politics. The idea of universal happiness, promoted by politicians, sounds dangerously familiar to many East Europeans made unhappy, to say the least, by totalitarian systems. The utilitarian doctrine of motivation, privileging ends above means, would vindicate many dictators and their followers, including such Nazi scientists as Rudolf Spanner.

Dr. Spanner's research and his use of corpses for the production of soap represent one of the most notorious cases of the reification of the human body for utilitarian purposes. What is for the Polish reader a well-known fact remained more controversial elsewhere in the world.[3] Zofia Nałkowska's "Professor Spanner," the opening story of *Medallions*, is framed by historical facts: Rudolf Spanner, together with a crew of lab helpers and prep workers in the forensic laboratory of the Danzig medical school, recycled human fat into soap.[4] As the Soviet Army was advancing, Dr. Spanner, avoiding his (scientific? moral? technical?) responsibility, fled to the western part of Germany. After the war, only two members of the laboratory staff, already compromised as collaborators, were arrested and interrogated by the Committee for Researching Hitlerite Crimes.[5] A German prosecutor who interrogated Spanner in 1948 dropped the case against him. During the investigation, Spanner denied making the soap; the denial was consistent with his wartime treatment of his experiments with soap as a secret operation. The Polish prosecutor, who in 2005 opened the case against the late Spanner, also found him not guilty of any crime.[6] Thus, Spanner's *numéro savon*[7] turned out to be a classic case of the divide between juridical and ethical law, a divide that effectively helped him to avoid punishment. A simple bar of soap can, therefore, reflect in miniature what occurred across the board during World War II, when an ethics of motivation replaced deontological theories of morals.

Among the better-known aspects of Holocaust phenomenology is the obliteration of the ontological distinction between objects and people, an obliteration sanctioned precisely by the teleological ethics of utilitarianism and of totalitarian power.[8] The transformational paradigm to which human corpses were subjugated in order to be entirely changed and disposed of has been understudied, with the notable exception of historical studies, where archival materials, oral history, and statistics are analyzed to answer the question how the Nazis dealt with "human waste." These studies offer gruesome data about somatic fragments of human bodies, about skin, bones, and hair accumulated and sorted only to be recycled for a wide variety of utilitarian purposes. This vulgarized recycling of "human waste" structured a new objectual interrelationship among the three parties involved in production: Nazi scientists, workers (usually slave laborers), and "the raw human matter." In this essay, the transformational model addresses such issues as the durability of and changes in the (in)animate matter and its vestiges constructed within the narratives of the Holocaust as well as on its contextual fringes.

The Holocaust subjugated both material objects and dead bodies to the recycling process, whose first stage was to make them ontologically equal. Manufacturing soap from human fat represents an extreme example of the transformational model, according to which both the surface and the core of the individual body are metamorphosed and processed beyond recognition.[9] Human, human-made, and organic matter, vulnerable as never before, was deemed to be completely recycled, without any remainder left. In the trajectory of the permanence and impermanence of matter, which was a defining path for the Holocaust transformational paradigm, the intent to erase traces of the raw material became paramount. In order to achieve this goal, recycling of various degrees occurred, during which even such an illusive residue as smell was targeted. Objects and corpses were subjected to the change whose first stage made them ontologically equal.

From the historical distance of over half a century, we see that one of the Holocaust's projects was to transform or negate the presence of cultural traces, archival materials, material remainders of massacres, vestiges of crematoria—in sum, traces of life, traces of death, and even traces of traces. Texts of the Holocaust, themselves testimonial traces, contain descriptions of transformational processes that questioned the durability of bodily matter and material objects, their core's resistance to recycling.

Hence, the question that comes to mind is: How long does a man remain a man and his body a vessel of this human content? Nałkowska represented the stages of transformation as a scientific spectacle, juxtaposing the anonymity of fat with forms still bearing the vestiges of human shapes. Because of this process, the dehumanization of ideologized medicine was mediated through the discourse of traces. Julia Kristeva would consider the inscription of vestiges on cadavers as an argument for her concept of the abject corpse, which is neither the subject nor the object. In the reality of the Holocaust, a corpse was only an object.[10]

Toward the end of the war, the racial and ethnic diversity of the corpses utilized by Spanner became quite broad. However, during the earlier stages of his operation, the corpses were Jewish. In general, the processing of corpses speaks of both a perverted utilitarianism and of an ideological shift in the Nazi approach to the Jewish body. The Nazi vision of the perfect society targeted the (supposedly) dangerous, effeminate, and diseased Jewish body, drawing on a mixture of medieval conceptions and modern philosophy (supported by a deviant science). The Jewish body had to be eliminated from society. But once the project of eliminating the revolting body was moved from the level of ideology to the stage of its practical realization, in particular after the Wannsee conference, another shift took place. This shift endowed the Jewish corpse with a set of new, yet opposite, qualities. When death removed the threat and disgust that the body represented, new traits were inscribed on corpses through their treatment. On the one hand, being a mere husk inside which Jewish gold (a commodity par excellence) was hidden, the body was useless. On the other, it became a locus of diverse resources, even a commodity in itself. In this radical change—characteristic of the transformational paradigm to which the dead body (and material object) was subjugated—its previously pronounced and targeted racial, cultural, and ethnic essence was completely erased. Usefulness, therefore, replaced the assumed uselessness of corpses, which were perceived only as objects. Such a permissive resourcefulness, a part of Nazi utilitarianism, could be facilitated only by overarching totalitarian power.

Upon closer scrutiny, the story of Spanner's production (and first attempts at circulation) of the soap demonstrates a syndrome of denial and repression, supported by any number of ideological rationalizations. According to the explanations given to the committee by two other medical professors—a dull expression of their false consciousness—his readiness was justified by the Reich's economic demands and by his loyalty to the NSDAP.[11] The testimonies, delivered in front of the committee, have a certain Conradian effect, for the witnesses spoke of the antagonist Spanner in his absence. One articulated his utilitarian principle of improving the quality of life in the Third Reich, while the other defined him as a totalitarian subject. What is so extraordinary about the comment concerning his obedience to the party is the fact that it escaped the eye of another totalitarian subject—the Polish censor who accepted Nałkowska's *Medallions* for publication at a time when the press in Poland was under communist control.[12] Thus, censorship, understood as a part of a larger discourse of traces and obfuscation, appears at the fringes of *Medallions*.

Utilitarian morals were fused with the ideological semantics of the Nazis by the incorporation of a much older tradition of dehumanization, which resulted in treating the body as reified "meat." Spanner's lab serves as a case in point, for it was a part of a smoothly functioning war machine whose executioners were eager to improve the mechanization of death: after the installment of a guillotine in the Danzig prison, Spanner dealt with an abundance of "raw material" for his covert research. The recycling in Spanner's lab demonstrated this mechanized treatment each step of the way: the cadavers were first "halved, quartered, and skinned"; then the bones were removed, and the so-called saponification concluded the process. The writer described its end result as "a whitish, rough soap" formed in metal molds.[13] A process that can be considered as both a parallel and a precedent for this commodification of the body is the fragmentation of the animal body that occurs in slaughterhouses. The animals in a slaughterhouse are killed, skinned, disemboweled, cut into pieces, boiled, smoked, packed, and so on, all in the name of producing food for humans.[14] For Daniel Pick, a slaughterhouse is a metaphor for war, emphasizing the division of labor and the speed of processing carcasses.[15] Each worker's duty is to process a specific morsel of each carcass, so that the animal never appears as a physical whole but only in parts multiplied by similar parts from other animals. The division of labor determines the slaughterhouse's *apposition* to an assembly line, where each worker plays a small role in a precisely outlined production process; instead of assembling and piecing together, a slaughterhouse system disconnects and undoes an original bodily unity. Likewise, division of labor determined the manufacture of soap in the Danzig institution. Excepting Spanner and two of his lab helpers, nobody involved in manufacturing the soap observed or participated in the entire cycle, a cycle that involved leading the prisoners to the guillotine, executing them, and collecting and transporting their bodies to the lab, where the "production" resulted in the creepy final artifact.

Vagaries of the Scientific Self

The uncanny connection between the war and meat production did not escape Nałkowska, who ruminated in her *Diary, 1939–1944* about the link between the war machinery and those people who were caught in it as if in a "meat grinder."[16] While there was nothing particularly new in making this association (after all, the cynical expression *mięso armatnie*, "cannon fodder," functions in many languages), for this writer it resonated differently, because she connected the concept of the self, as anchored in the soma, directly with the meat that constituted her own diet.[17]

> It's strange that this, which makes me happen, through which I participate in the world, through which I feel myself—is *meat* (the meat brought from "town" for dinner). For thinking about man in chemical categories can be borne easily. The fact that life "borrows" free elements of the dead world does not cause resistance; there is a quiet acceptance and understanding of it. But when viewed with the eye of "naïve realism," meat as an organ of life and consciousness, as the site where the sweetness and horror of life occur—what an arbitrariness, what a perfunctory concept.[18]

Dialectical materialism, which she embraced in her youth, although not in any orthodox manner, eventually took in her writing a form of monism. She was convinced that in a strictly biological sense there was no ontological difference between nature and humanity. As she claimed in an interview in the 1930s: "Man is made more or less of the same material as the world; he is con-generic with it."[19] In her later response, the writer modified somewhat her biological monism by including another ideological element from her formative period: the belief in science. The fusion of dialectical materialism with a scientific approach to reality made her proclaim, with what would seem now an inflated optimism, a radical faith in the "Soviet experiment" and its limitless scientific progress.

> Considered from this angle the future and durability of the Soviet experiment seems to me to depend on whether "matter," as a gnoseological category, will prove—so to speak—its developmental capacity, its capacity to adapt to the ever more stunning discoveries within hard science, blowing up the essence and quality of matter as the subject of physics.[20]

As if intoxicated by the prospect of future technological advancement prompted by scientific research in its Soviet variation, she had no forebodings of its deployment against mankind. This ideology of materialist cognition with no ethical safeguards would return like a boomerang in her *Medallions*.

Curiously though, in defining material unity, this follower of Marxism never engaged dialectical materialism in her own fiction and overlooked the idea of her characters' material/somatic foundation, focusing instead on their psychological dimension and their interactions with the world.[21] *Medallions*, in which the stories of cannibalism, torture, starvation, horrible wounds, and beatings made the suffering bodily matter come to the narrative foreground, is the obvious exception. In the collection, Nałkowska not only revised the bio-ontological position of the human subject; she also modified the world, which framed the subject in terms of a radical corpo-reality.

Nałkowska's carefully measured reportage from Spanner's lab was preceded, by several years, by her voicing of a futuristic trust in physics and its transformation of matter, and it almost overlapped in time with the monistic claims articulated in her wartime diary. As such, these claims marked an important direction in her thinking about the limitations of our cognition. However, the writer did not interconnect them, as if the ethical consequences of Spanner's activities made them incomparable to anything else that was a part of human cognition and scientific knowledge. In examining these convictions, the author engaged in no critical thinking and did not even entertain a simple suspicion in regard to her concept of materiality and matter. Her contemplation—on three different occasions—of this problem remained strictly ideological-scientific. That's why her "Professor Spanner" lacks a more complex discursive ethical dimension, besides the strong moral judgment already present in the volume's inscription: "This fate people dealt to people" ("Ludzie ludziom zgotowali ten los").

Had she consistently revised the concept of the homogeneity of matter, would she then have adopted utilitarianism and—in its name—vindicated Professor Spanner, who obviously chose not to distinguish the human and animal *soma*? Or would her position be irresolvable because of the apparent split in ethical, juridical, and scientific reasoning? Had she ever connected her prewar vision of "blown-up matter" with the wartime construction and usage of the atomic bomb, would she have condemned one or the other? As far as we know, the writer never reached the realization that she should rethink her own scientific fetishes, including her concept of somatic homogeneity, which troubled her so much during the war. The Nazi experimentation in recycling was a direct challenge to Nałkowska's scientific ideology, in which the separation of the somatic and the individual (human) became obsolete, but she did not see its implications for her own thought; yet one cannot blame her for this.[22]

At the same time, Nałkowska was not alone in overlooking the question of the body outside theologies of embodiment. Her approach merely illustrates a larger gap that exists between the humanities, on the one hand, and technology, including the philosophy of the hard sciences (such as physics), on the other.[23] Chris Shilling, examining the gulf between the scientific and the humanistic poles of knowledge, points out the impact that Husserlian phenomenology had on the polarization of the past century's intellectual landscape. More important for the Polish writer, deliberations on complex issues of the body, its materiality, and its relationship to the thinking self were equally overlooked by the Marxist thinking that was so close to her own.[24]

"Meat in the Pot"

Despite the emphasis on the historical referent in "Professor Spanner," both the text and the referent, fortified by diverse intertexts and contexts, do not produce the expected "reality effect" in the sense theorized by Roland Barthes. Instead, they generate in Nałkowska's narrative that effect of uncanny "corpso-reality" which is crucial for the transformations of the Holocaust's objectual world. This effect has to do with the human dimension of the *soma*.

The description of the soap factory that opens the story "Professor Spanner" is conceived in somber tones of grief and understatement. The manner in which the narrative unveils the lab as a chamber of horrors—and, in doing so, relies on intertextual links—indicates to what extent the distinction between fiction and truth in this short piece of reportage became obsolete. As the narrator, along with the whole group of other visitors/investigators, moves through a chain of rooms belonging to the medical lab and depicts their contents, she conveys the overall sensation that something is fundamentally wrong with this place. This feeling coincides with the construction of the passage, from the ground level to the basement, as an archetypal descent into the underworld (*katabasis*). It is a passage from the solemn to the abject, from the highest to the vulgarized, from the whole to the fragmented, from the aporia of the place to the recognition of its function. The site ultimately discloses its dead corporeal reality—its corpso-reality.

Although Nałkowska's description of this site integrates several textual and visual traditions, the parallel to a slaughterhouse/meat-processing factory as a workplace ruled by the mechanized neutralization of ethics is particularly pronounced. It is not the evident speed of these mechanized, serialized executions that stuns the writer, although this factor is also implied in the narrative's focus on the bodily marking left by the death machine. Each cadaver has a clean cut on the neck signifying the separation of the head from the body (read: the separation of life from death). For Nałkowska this line is too perfect, too precise—to such an extent that she perceives the preserved corpses as made of stone. Only later will the cause of that neatness become clear: it was a guillotine blade that made such a disquietingly neat cut.[25]

Elias Canetti made a gruesome remark that seeing a heap of corpses is an ancient spectacle; it empowered the victorious and satisfied the powerful. However, that ancient sight is not what Nałkowska reports from Danzig. Not quite. Her experience there modifies Canetti's observation by emphasizing the difference between any dead bodies and dead bodies that have been quartered and boiled. She conveys the difference by engaging her narration's performative means. During the walk through the lab, the actual utilitarian purpose of the spectacle of dehumanization beheld by the visitors becomes obvious to them only when they come across the cauldron filled with the dismembered human torso.[26] Everything in this episode is concerned with showing corpsoreality: the lifting of the lid, the color of the liquid, the pulling out of the dismembered and flayed body.[27] Almost indiscernibly, Nałkowska changes the status of that which was collected to that which is displayed, thus transmogrifying the space of the forensic lab/soap manufactory into a chamber of horrors. For the dead, the gesture of showing, and thus "museuming" their cadavers is beyond their knowledge. As they lie extended, they resemble the dead Psyche from Freud's last written note: "Psyche is extended, knows nothing about it."[28] Like her, they are unaware of the ongoing panoptic spectacle. Being museumed and shown, they are subsequently subjected to an aestheticizing performative strategy by which Nałkowska elevates their immobile bodies to the status of works of art, to stone sculptures.[29] Ultimately, the discreetly aestheticized description of corpses is overshadowed by images of a drastically chopped up and deformed human *soma*. The description of one heap of shaved heads lying chaotically one on top of another as looking "like potatoes poured onto the ground"[30] turns the spectacle into something grotesque and almost unreal, despite the comparison taken from a naturalist vocabulary.

Nałkowska's polarized representation of the human *soma* (portrayed either as sculpted stones or as potatoes) might appear unwarranted to a critic seeking consistency in her narrative. This conflicting construction subjects the fragmented *soma* to two contradictory systems—modernist aestheticism and naturalist authenticity—stemming from the author's previous unresolved and intrinsically incoherent philosophy.[31] However, from my critical perspective, which does not privilege consistency, the rupture caused by her engaging two different imageries, meant to produce the most effective means of representation, affects precisely the representational dimension and contributes to a greater dramatic tension within the narrative.

The fact that Nałkowska's reportage is dominated by the uneven, oscillating pull of contradictory values and perspectives is best documented in the imagery of collective and individual deaths. For the writer, this must have been a formidable challenge, as she strove to find an adequate strategy of representing the morbid spectacle of recycling human *soma*. The need to communicate mass death called for the representation of a total distortion of unique bodily forms. Therefore, Nałkowska suspends the spectacle of erasing individual bodily forms, of turning them into anonymous piles of meat and cauldrons of fat, in order to expose two bodily fragments to the visitors' and readers' voyeuristic gaze.[32] One of them is the able-bodied and tattooed torso of a sailor.

Despite its defacement, the headless torso still bears traces of its previous individuality. Beholders can follow the chain of signification that retains his personhood; the ship indicates his line of work, the build of the body speaks of his strength, and the tattoo "God is with us" is a confession of his Christian faith.[33] This personalizing marker is quickly subjected to the narrator's questioning of the effectiveness of the sailor's belief.[34] This verdict denies any agency to the sailor, rendering him entirely powerless. If the soul cannot be redeemed, how can the body? From an eschatological perspective and a soteriological promise, the parallel between the body of Christ and the fallen sailor should be critical. Both corpses lie extended, vulnerable, and are given to the gaze of indifferent onlookers. The sailor's body is decapitated, exposed, and denigrated by the intended consumption in the form of soap, while Christ's body was sacrificed, exposed, consecrated for a highly significant religious consumption, and eventually resurrected. Therefore, from the narrator's point of view, the gap between them is irretrievable. Christ's *Hoc est enim corpus meum* is an article of faith for which there is no room in the narrative and which has no power to redeem the sailor's defaced and powerless cadaver. Through this and similar narrative interventions present in her collection, Nałkowska negates any soteriological possibility, a maneuver that was in sync with her pronounced atheism, and creates one of her volume's most complete and coherent projects.

In yet another glimpse, the writer creates a descriptive tool in the form of a death mask. This image of a singular death reverses the meaning and the form of the sailor's corpse: all that remains of the body is the head severed from the torso.[35] In approaching this death mask, the writer focuses on detailing its facial features and seeking the meaning of the lasting expression registered on its surface at the moment of death. In this instance, her mimetic precision demands an unusual degree of insight, getting literally under the skin at the risk of destabilizing her usual nonintrusiveness. Although throughout *Medallions* the authorial position is defined by a nonintrusive approach to the victims' lives and narratives, in these two brief glimpses of individualized death, the author deemed intervention necessary, for these were particularly disturbing images. The writer's usual gesture of self-decentering would have proven ineffective in conveying the disturbing moment of facing the dismembered youth.[36] Therefore, she creates space for a rather discreet valuation in the otherwise factual description—the victim's age, his smile, his raised eyebrows—as if to prevent the mere mechanical listing of the "parts among parts." By retreating to her old vocabulary (and interpretative habit) connoting the feeling of strangeness, oddity, and disbelief, she enables an evaluative mechanism that refers as far back as Ezekiel's vision of the bodies of deportees from Jerusalem in a foreign city, described rather bluntly as "the meat in the pot."[37] While the prophet's better-known intimations of his people's rebirth are hardly relevant to Nałkowska's nonredemptive and nonsoteriological conception, his rhetoric combined with the pictorial concreteness characteristic of his first vision preempts not just the accumulation of chopped-up corpses in Spanner's lab but, to a certain extent, twentieth-century artistic practices of dissolving the body as well.

Ewa Frąckowiak-Wiegandtowa remarked that the adjective *dziwny* (odd, strange) had belonged to Nałkowska's entrenched lexical repertoire since her debut; the writer's predilection for an adjective that blurred everything did not meet the critic's acceptance.[38] The word, particularly popular in the literature of Young Poland, can indeed easily obfuscate the meaning of its context and even sound naïve. In the case of her Holocaust narration, though, we deal with a different, quite subtle, and relevant meaning of "most odd, perplexing" as a qualifier for the encounter with the dead youth. Balancing this difficult act between the tender and the dispassionate, Nałkowska conveys the individual death in terms of an extreme experience with which she empathizes *against all odds*, especially against the overwhelming sense of loss and dehumanization. This impossible gesture comes with a price: the crisis of *Einfühlung* is enhanced by the rather universal awareness that someone else's experience of dying cannot be reconstructed. The boy's death mask suggests the extent to which one can, or rather cannot, go in an attempt to reconstruct someone else's passage to death. There is no easy way out of this cognitive conundrum even though the necessity of distinguishing the passage to death from death's finality is critical to the entire Holocaust experience, an experience that goes beyond the demands of representation.

Nałkowska ends her attempt at invoking individual death with a nod toward the inaccessible. Was it the victim's young age or the brutality of his execution that he himself could not conceive? Since it would be preposterous to use a prosopopeic voice and speak in his name, the unreachable/unspeakable is negotiated through the spectator's contradictory rhetoric of oddity and *Einfühlung*. The writer's reading of the skin scripts on the sailor's headless body along with the mortuary traces left on the youth's facial features points to the insurmountable distinction between the living spectators and them, the dead.[39] This has to do with the dynamics of (un)knowing throughout the narrative, in which both the dead and the living have access to different aspects of knowledge and its lack. The visitors' final realization of the fact of recycling the corpses into soap constitutes their knowing (and the victims' unknowing), and reflects the path from the single body to the recycled cosmetic.

In her wartime diary, Nałkowska pondered over the eerie repetitious nature of the war experience, of its uncanny resemblance to other wars, of how all that always-already was, *wszystko już było*. Her contemplation of the war pointed to the repetitious nature of its universal cruelty, as well as its mimetic representation. If we follow the author's premise that *wszystko to już było*, several new cognitive possibilities are open for interpretation, shifting the narrative from the historical referent to the author's artistic construal.

Besides and beyond the accuracy of the parallel with the slaughterhouse, Nałkowska's narrative also engages other contextual, religious, literary, and pictorial traditions. Under her pen, the modernist order of the slaughterhouse is intertwined with another form of imagery—the Shakespearean imagery of horror. The eerie witches, Macbeth's helpers, brew a potion out of morsels of animal bodies mixed with pieces of human corpses: "a liver of a blaspheming Jew," / "Nose of Turk; and Tartar's lips / Finger of birth-strangl'd babe."[40] This concoction of anatomical fragments is based on a simple recipe; it consists of everything that in Shakespeare's time represented the Other and therefore could be sacrificed. Likewise, Spanner's vats contained a diversified human *soma*, diverse in terms of its ethnic and racial origin, for they contained bodies of Jewish men and women sent from the Stutthoff death camp, some from the Danzig prison, among them executed German officers, possibly victims of the escalating purge of the anti-Hitlerite opposition.[41] One can surmise that some of the bodies, sent from the entire Pomerania region, were Polish.

Smell of the Truth and Two Digressions

Both the medical and the chemical processes taking place discreetly in the Danzig forensic lab were grounded on the fundamental claim that the body could be completely transformed into a new and utilitarian product devoid of any human traces. The soap was the outcome of a long cycle that began in execution rooms and ended in a chemical puzzle that shaped the pseudoscience's ultimate objective. Narrowing down the recycling meant an elimination of the last remaining human trace—the soap's peculiar odor. Nonetheless, the interrogated lab worker confesses that "It didn't smell very good. Professor Spanner tried hard to get rid of the smell. He wrote away to chemical factories for oils. But *you could always tell the soap was different.*"[42] The disgusting soap could not erase the abject vestiges of the utilized bodies, thus emphasizing the tension, inherent in every type of soap, between its sanitary use and abjection. If the body in the Nazi project were to be transformed totally (into soap), it was presumed that its new utilitarian ontology would retain no vestiges of its previous status, nothing human.

In order to avoid Roland Barthes's "epochal" mistake of entirely overlooking nonsemiological reality in his essay "Soap-Powders and Detergents,"[43] I shall add that the trace of human smell could have been easily removed with the progress of science, but that was the case neither for Spanner's work of the 1940s, nor for its symbolic representation in Nałkowska's reportage. Instead, his product revealed the limits of scientific progress and, subsequently, of the transformational method that he used: even in its radically altered form the soap continued to be abject—exuding, in one of the unwilling consumers' own words, an "unpleasant" human odor.

In the lab's utilitarian microcosm, where "everything was permitted," reaching a solution was only a matter of time. Yet the divide between the utilitarian approach toward the body and the principle of absolute permissiveness did not necessarily lead to a clash between them. In fact, Hannah Arendt pointed out that the claim of absolute permissiveness was already a part of the nineteenth-century utilitarian understanding of common sense.[44] If we follow her analysis of permissive utilitarianism within totalitarianism, one thing becomes quite clear. The enclosed realm of a concentration camp and a zone such as the one under Spanner's rule share one characteristic: the totalitarian power that allows the cruelest, craziest, and "most odd" (many of them nonutilitarian) concepts to be materialized. And it was permissiveness in its totalitarian version that facilitated Spanner's "inventiveness."[45] Everything else, therefore, including the prospect of an industrial production of the soap, seemed to be certain.

The excursion into wartime conditions in France seems to be only a bit out of place here, for along with the war's grandiose projects of social hygiene and greatly simplified personal hygiene came a shortage of cosmetic supplies. A product such as soap, usually taken for granted, became scarce in France during the war. The provincial town of Roanne in central France, and later the village of Coligny, north of Lyon, served as the wartime refuge of Francis Ponge and his family, who experienced war through "restrictions of all kinds, and soap, real soap, was particularly missed. We had only the worst ersätze—which did not froth at all."[46] A shortage of soap motivated the poet to focus his postphenomenological gaze on "a sort of stone,"[47] "Magic stone!"[48] "Slobbering stone,"[49] in short, on construing the naturalness of soap as stone.

Even during the postwar years, Ponge perceived the improved quality of soap as illusory. Whenever he tried to touch its pebblelike form, the soap would foam and slide easily from his hands. Thus, gazing at its absence, he reflected on its slippery, almost deceitful, yet tangible concreteness. For him too, soap's teleology was to disappear—either in water or in the war. Like a stone, Ponge's soap had its weight, but its flowery aroma was beyond his olfactory expectations, for "it was a little more strongly scented."[50] I do not suggest that he became a bit blind to the odor of history; rather, the stench of decomposing corpses, that horrible stench mentioned by Tadeusz Borowski, Janet Flanner, and W. G. Sebald, never reached Roanne and Coligny.

Arguably, no analysis of the sense of smell can match Patrick Süskind's novel *Perfume*, which made a compelling equation between the soul and the individual's essence as constituted in a bodily smell. Thus, this odor, if captured and retained (and this is his protagonist-alchemist's highest objective), would preserve the core of an individual soul. But, the perfumer had to kill a virgin in order to extract her unique essence. Is the German writer speculating about the immortality of the soul in the manner that I struggle to dispel on these pages? Hardly. Rather, he is mapping the innermost sphere of personhood; the most intimate and little-known bond between the physiological and the spiritual. Nonetheless, for both writers the intimate and somatic demonstrated something that can be qualified as an irreducible phenomenon, indivisible and invisible, a remainder that addresses our senses despite the annihilation of its human form.

In a sense, the process of manufacturing soap brings to mind sublimation. The parallel does not get one too far because the trajectory of soap consumption from its unrefined origin to its end as dirt- and sweat-removing cosmetic consists of several hurdles. Spanner's *savon* did not yield itself to pleasant consumption, for it was abject from beginning to end. Acting like a grotesque reverse of Patrick Süskind's alchemist attempting to find a formula for an essence, the German doctor with dirty hands furtively searched for an effective recipe to manufacture a good-quality soap (that could have been used in every German bathroom) by dispelling its essence. Süskind's alchemist's goal was to discover and preserve, perhaps even respect, the uniquely individual bodily essence, while Spanner intended to obliterate entirely the bodily core in his final product. The symbolic concept of (un)recyclability did not exist in his mortuary science prior to recycling.

Having said that, I wish to conclude that this odor—the invisible remainder/reminder of the soap's true origin—signaled a particular glitch of recycling. The trace of the human agent, if you will, worked against the total reduction of the reified body into nothing, that is, into matter. Thus, the human agent destabilized, albeit temporarily, the unvoiced ideological assumption about the utilitarian and biopolitical status of human subjects. The undesirable smell of the extract spoke of the trace, of the illusive core that kept reminding its consumers of their own bio-ontology. Only a complete obfuscation of the human agent could make the process successful. Instead, the somatic object of scientific desire, which was sought in order to be destroyed and not to be desired again, resisted the transformation and turned out to be a remainder/reminder of the seemingly neutralized truth. Of all types of Holocaust recycling, this one failed the most miserably.

Notes

An earlier version of the paper appeared in Polish (trans. Kinga Maciejewska) as "Dziwne mydło: Zofia Nałkowska i gospodarka Zagłady" in *Teksty Drugie* 5 (2007): 62–73. A self-translated version of the paper also appeared in *Rzeczy i Zagłada* (Cracow: Universitas, 2010).

1. Although I am interested in the phenomenology of soap as an object, its chemical processing deserves to be addressed briefly: "A cleansing and emulsifying agent that is made usually either from fats or oils by saponification with alkali in a boiling process or the cold process or from fatty acids by neutralization with alkali, that consists essentially of a mixture of water-soluble sodium or potassium salts of fatty acids, and that may contain other ingredients such as . . . perfume, coloring agents, fluorescent dyes, disinfectants or abrasive material." *Webster's Third New International Dictionary*, s.v. "soap."

2. Although soap was known in ancient civilizations (Pliny thought it was invented by Gauls), its modern production, defined above, harks back only to the nineteenth century.

3. Aside from Spanner himself, numerous Holocaust revisionists denied that the production of soap from human fat ever took place. The Israeli scholar Yehuda Bauer, however, found enough documents to substantiate the opposite claim, mainly based on the book *Noc a mlha* by Ota Kraus and Erich Kulka. More documentary evidence exists in testimonies provided by the British prisoners of war John Henry Witton and William Neely. As far as I know, Nałkowska's text was never a point of reference in this discussion. For more details, see the exchange in *Jerusalem Post* (April–May 1990) between Bill Hutman ("Nazis Never Made Human-Fat Soap"), Neil Kuchinsky ("Human Fat Soap"), and Yehuda Bauer ("Human Fat Soap").

4. For more on pseudo-medical research, see Shelley.

5. However, Nałkowska mentioned only one laborer. For a thorough research account of the Spanner case, see Jolanta Davis's unpublished manuscript.

6. The only direct result of the revised case was the fact that the plaque was mounted on the lab's façade to commemorate the unwilling subjects of this ethically dubious scientific research.

7. "Numer z mydłem" (Number with a soap), as Nałkowska referred to it in her *Dzienniki* 6:150. All translations, unless indicated otherwise, are mine.

8. See, for example, Werner's engagement of the reification discourse in *Zwyczajna apokalipsa*.

9. A comprehensive discussion of these methods will be offered in my forthcoming book *The Holocaust Object: Proximity and Vestiges*.

10. See Kristeva, *Powers of Horror*. I approach the cadaver in a radically different manner, namely, as an object that only discreetly reflects its previous ontology.

11. Lifton's magisterial monograph *The Nazi Doctors: Medical Killing and the Psychology of the Genocide* and Kater's *Doctors under Hitler* are still the most comprehensive studies on the subject.

12. I owe this observation to Samuel Sandler.

13. Nałkowska, *Medallions*, 9

14. Sinclair's novel *The Jungle* sharply criticized the meat processing in infamous Chicago slaughterhouses and could serve as a useful point of comparison to the processing of human flesh organized by Spanner.

15. "The individual must accomplish his or her specific action at a frenzied pace, often amidst a pool of blood." Pick, 184.

16. Nałkowska, *Dzienniki*, 5:305.

17. Even prior to the war, Nałkowska observed that a fish farm was a sort of a concentration camp.

18. Nałkowska, *Dzienniki*, 5: 490; emphasis in original.

19. Essmanowski, 3.

20. This is a passage from Nałkowska's contribution to the 1933 survey entitled "Polish Writers and Soviet Russia" conducted by *Wiadomości Literackie*; quoted in Frąckowiak-Wiegandtowa, 53.

21. As observed by Frąckowiak-Wiegandtowa.

22. This connection did not escape Miłosz's attention. In "The Lesson of Biology," the poet observes that science polluted the mind and, for example, "'the survival of the fittest' in its vulgarized form prompted naturalism in literature but also created the climate for exterminating millions of human beings in the name of a presumed social hygiene" (*The Witness of Poetry*, 50).

23. See Shilling, for example.

24. See James, 249–50. The critic claims that the current discussion of the bodily sense in cultural studies has been conditioned by the strong pull of symbolization/abstraction and has seldom gone beyond these limits. I have to add that the present examination of the cluster of problems by the feminist branch of cultural studies inspired by Marxism also leaves much to be desired.

25. The cut linked Mr. Guillotin's technological improvement of the older incarnation of the machine to its much better Nazi version: the Enlightenment's rationalization of death machine fused with a public visualization of execution was replaced in a truly Foucauldian shift by its modernist, secretive enactment.

26. "There, on the cooled hearth, stood a huge cauldron brimming with a dark liquid. Someone familiar with the premises poked under the lid and retrieved a boiled human torso, skinned and dripping with the liquid." Nałkowska, *Medallions*, 4.

27. In 1300, Pope Boniface VIII issued a peculiar document that may be linked to Spanner's practices. In his bull entitled *De sepulturis*, he issued a proclamation to excommunicate everyone engaged in boiling the bodies of crusaders who perished in distant lands. Boiling the bodies to the bones facilitated transportation of the remains home for burial. Only later was the bull misunderstood as a prohibition of dissection.

28. Freud, 23:300. He wrote this last note on August 22, 1938, a year before his death.

29. Nota bene, the jacket design representing a sculpture of a human head for the cover of the first Polish edition of *Medallions* refers to this aestheticized fragmentation of the body in Nałkowska's narrative.

30. Nałkowska, *Medallions*, 4.

31. As Frąckowiak-Wiegandtowa diagnoses the writer's thinking in her monograph.

32. "In one sarcophagus, the so-called headless 'sailor' lay prostrate on a heap of cadavers. He was an impressive youth, as big as a gladiator. The silhouette of a ship was tattooed on his broad chest. Across the contour of the masts hung the sign of vain faith: God is with us." Nałkowska, *Medallions*, 4. Tattooing is known to have been used to mark distant travels, seafaring, and religious (Christian) devotion since early Christianity; what makes the passage

depicting the tattooed torso remarkable is Nałkowska's intermingling of the above aspects.

33. Apparently, the skin script was in Polish, which adds more weight to the argument against connecting this phrase with the World War I and World War II "Gott mit uns" calling; furthermore, its iconography, as recorded by Nałkowska, differs from its better-known German counterpart. The phrase inserted on belt buckles of the German imperial army was intended as part of a design, which included a laurel wreath and, as its most prominent sign, the imperial crown. The Wehrmacht soldiers' belt buckle consisted of yet a more complicated design: the very same religious expression, the Hakenkreuz, a laurel leaf wreath, and an eagle. In each case we deal with an ancient tradition of invoking God's help.

34. It is poignant that the sailor's cadaver has also lost its ability to radiate its original wholeness, the quality that Rainer Maria Rilke imagined in his poem "Archaische Torso Apollo."

35. "A small, cream-colored head of a boy, who couldn't have been more than eighteen years old when he died, lies in the corner of one vat. His dark, somewhat slanted eyes weren't closed, the eyelids were only slightly lowered. The full mouth, of the same color as the face, bore a patient, sad smile. The strong, straight brow was raised as though in disbelief. In this most odd and inconceivable position, he awaited the world's final verdict." Nałkowska, *Medallions*, 4.

36. In "Professor Spanner" the writer uses the plural "we."

37. See Ezekiel 11:1–13.

38. Frąckowiak-Wiegandtowa, 36. The critic, however, does not speak of Nałkowska's *Medallions*.

39. Derrida in his book about the French philosopher Jean-Luc Nancy, and Nancy's *The Touch of the World* in particular, keeps retreating to the quotation from Freud concerning the dead Psyche as unknowing, simply because it was very inspirational to Nancy, thus as a gesture of respect and homage; see Derrida, *On Touching*, 12–13. In contrast to the representation of dead corporeality by the Polish author, Freud defines Psyche's dead body as unknowing by retreating to more universal limitations of not knowing, while Nancy sexualizes her extended and half-exposed corpse that yields itself to the scopic inquiry of living spectators, most notably, Eros.

40. Shakespeare, *Macbeth*, act 4, scene 1.

41. Poignantly, Nałkowska reported the utilization of ethnically diverse bodies, which defies the popular perception that the soap was made of "pure Jewish fat." Each bar was marked with the sign "R.I.F," which was mistranslated and misspelled as *Rein Idische Seif* (pure Jewish soap), while it stood for *Reichstelle fur Industrielle Fettversorgung* (State Center for Supply of Fats). The tension between essentialism and utilitarianism reaches its peak here through the appropriation of the uncanny soap for a "purist" and essentialist objective.

42. Nałkowska, *Medallions*, 9; emphasis mine.

43. Jackson, 138. Jackson chastised Barthes for his obliviousness to soap's and similar products' reality.

44. Arendt, 440.

45. For example, there were 350 corpses in the morgue, in contrast to the anatomy institute's standard requirement of approximately 14, the number necessary to teach local medical students the craft of dissection. The abundance of corpses forced Spanner, anticipating their usefulness, to store some of them in case of future shortages or an expansion of his manufactory. This excess illustrates well the permissive aspect of totalitarianism.

46. Ponge, 11.

47. Ibid., 14.

48. Ibid., 21.

49. Ibid., 28.

50. Ibid., 63. The reader should not be mystified by this arguably frivolous statement, since during World War II Ponge was also a soldier, an insurance worker, and a Resistance organizer.

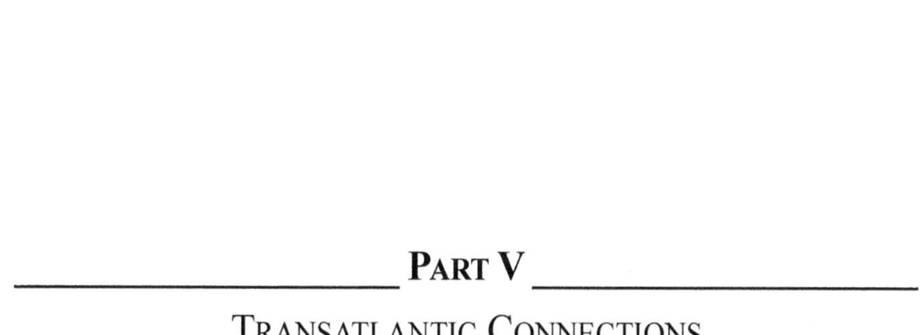

Part V

Transatlantic Connections

Polish Émigré Writers in New York in the Files of the FBI

Jan Lechoń, Kazimierz Wierzyński, and Józef Wittlin in New York

Halina Stephan

Within the conventional narrative of Polish émigré literature, there are numerous potential microhistories that do not fit into the macronarrative. As microhistories tend to do, they challenge and even subvert the established history and force a revision of historical memory. In the usual narrative of the émigré experience, images of the writers and the memory of their activities are embedded in a Polish context. Although in real life the host setting of the emigrant activities determined the parameters of cultural and literary life, that setting is usually treated as a background to the exile narrative. The microhistory of the Polish exile documented here has not even been preserved in historical memory; rather, it is found within the bureaucratic files of government institutions.

The interaction of leading cultural émigré figures with American politics in the late forties and early fifties as shown in select FBI files compiled for Jan Lechoń, Kazimierz Wierzyński, and Józef Wittlin illustrates the importance of the host context, its political climate, and its institutions for the functioning of Polish culture abroad. The files originate at a time when the United States began to conduct a cultural offensive in Europe that was supposed to link European intellectuals with American culture. The reasons for the well-known nonengagement of Polish émigrés in the cultural initiatives of the U.S. government and the resulting marginalization of leading Polish writers within American cultural politics can be deduced from select FBI files that also show how the American distrust of the émigrés manifested itself in a careful surveillance of their political and private lives, which almost precluded any possibility of participation in state-sponsored activities.

The FBI files provide a look at the underside of immigrant existence in the United States. Jan Lechoń's leap from the fourteenth floor of the Henry Hudson Hotel in New York City in 1956 may be etched as an iconic moment in the history of Polish exile literature, but it becomes very deflated in the FBI files, which show a rather sordid subtext of immigrant existence. The documents compiled by the FBI about Jan Lechoń, Kazimierz Wierzyński, and Józef Wittlin show another image of the exiled poets and indicate possible reasons for their marginalization in postwar U.S. cultural politics.

It is important to remember that the postwar immigrants entered a country that was involved in various cold war initiatives aimed at developing European cultural unity under American patronage. The first institution to promote this agenda was the American Committee on United Europe, run by the Office of Strategic Services, the forerunner of the CIA. In 1949, alongside this organization, Allen Dulles, later the head of the CIA, set up the National Committee for Free Europe with the purpose of supporting anticommunist forces in Europe and with the intention of using "the many and varied skills of exiled East Europeans in the development of programs which would actively combat Soviet domination."[1] A section of the National Committee for Free Europe known as the Mid-European Center acted as a fact-gathering institution and produced printed materials about Eastern Europe. Radio Free Europe was another offspring of this CIA-funded initiative.

Poles abroad were not unaware of the importance of the National Committee for Free Europe, later known as the Free Europe Committee. A representative of the London-based Polish government in exile reported:

> NCFE functions almost as a first resort, where people are sorted out into the usual bores and interesting individuals who need to be taken seriously from a political point of view, and there is the same sorting of issues. . . . It is absolutely obvious that NCFE wants to establish a relationship of dependence with as many emigrants of a better quality as possible.[2]

Indeed, the Free Europe Committee sponsored the formation of what some called "the cultural equivalent of NATO," namely, the Congress for Cultural Freedom. From 1950 until 1967, with the covert support of the CIA and under the official leadership of Nicholas Nabokov, a cousin of the famous novelist Vladimir, the Congress for Cultural Freedom developed a series of projects supporting liberal noncommunist trends in European culture. Among the participants of its inaugural congress in Berlin in 1950 were the editors of the Parisian Polish émigré journal *Kultura*, Józef Czapski (who was a member of the steering committee) and Jerzy Gedroyć, who eventually managed to put Konstanty Jeleński in change of the East European section of the secretariat of the congress.[3] Jeleński then "administered the Congress's Central European Program, with its aim of strengthening Western values behind the Iron Curtain."[4] Czesław Miłosz and Andrzej Panufnik, who defected from socialist Poland in the early fifties, were considered important figures with an impact on the work of the Congress for Cultural Freedom.[5]

Unlike the politically far more astute *Kultura* group and Miłosz, whose defection marked a triumphant moment for the congress, the New York emigration, represented most prominently by Lechoń, Wittlin, and Wierzyński, did not participate in any of these initiatives. Their vehemently anti-Soviet stance meant that they could find favor in the United States, which was suspicious both of pro-Soviet and pro-Nazi moods among the immigrants. But in reality their contacts with American institutions turned out to be only episodic. Lechoń was recruited into and briefly received a stipend from the National Committee for Free Europe. Józef Wittlin was temporarily employed by a section of this organization, the Mid-European Center, which produced research materials about Eastern Europe.[6] Eventually, however, their only activity sponsored by the U.S. government was occasional participation in cultural programs produced by Radio Free Europe. Some reasons for their nonengagement can be deduced from their FBI files.

It is well known that the United States provided a refuge for a large number of intellectuals who fled Hitler-dominated Europe or, like the Poles living in New York, were afraid to return to Soviet-controlled Poland. However, distrust of the exiled intellectuals meant that, to a varying degree and despite their anti-Soviet orientation, Lechoń, Wittlin, and Wierzyński remained under the surveillance of the FBI and the Immigration and Naturalization Service. By the time they settled into a life in the States, the country had developed a specific anticommunist agenda and interior bureaucratic structures that protected that agenda. Offices such as the FBI, the Office of Strategic Services, the Immigration and Naturalization Service, and the Office of Censorship kept track of the immigrant intelligentsia by filing appropriate documents and conducting interviews with informants. In more extreme cases, surveillance, such as was also conducted especially among exiles from Nazi Germany, included opening mail and tapping telephones, following individuals, burglarizing homes, searching luggage and garbage, and installing listening devices.[7]

Nowadays in the United States, the right of access to government files is guaranteed by the Freedom of Information Act of 1966 and the Privacy Act of 1974. Concerning the reliability of released materials, it must be said that agencies have a right to withhold information. Deletions in the text are coded according to numbers of exemptions under the Freedom of Information Act. The identity of confidential sources is never disclosed. The FBI also blacks out the names of people who are still living or whose death cannot be easily confirmed, data on staff and methods of surveillance, and data about the informants, as well as anything that can be interpreted as related to national security. In effect, the security agencies have various ways of circumventing the Freedom of Information Act, so a researcher can never be sure that the files are complete or even approximately so.

The FBI files that were compiled about Lechoń, Wittlin, and Wierzyński, do supplement already available biographic information but also clearly show that beyond the Potemkin village of "Warsaw in New York"[8] usually described in exile studies, there existed a solid political apparatus that in invisible ways could affect the lives of the exiles.

Lechoń may have assumed the mantle of the Polish exile poet, but in reality he had already resided abroad (in Paris) since 1930. He left Europe on July 21, 1940, going from Lisbon to Rio de Janeiro. He arrived in New York on August 11, 1941, having waited for his U.S. visa longer than his colleagues Józef Wittlin and Kazimierz Wierzyński, who arrived from Brazil a few months before him. Lechoń immediately began to work for the *Tygodniowy Przegląd Literacki* (Weekly Literary Review) and in the years 1943–47 edited and published an illustrated *Tygodnik Polski* (Polish Weekly).[9]

The FBI documented three events in Lechoń's American existence: his entry to the United States in 1941, his efforts to get a job with the Voice of America in the early fifties, and his death in 1956. At least such are the three files that I was able to obtain. The official notification enclosed with those files stated:

> This is in response to your Freedom of Information Act (FOIA) request to our New York Field office for records concerning Mr. Jan Lechoń (deceased). A search of the indices in our New York Field Office has located one main file (New York file number 105-1417) which is responsive to your request. The corresponding FBIHQ files numbers (40-4328 and 123-5047) were also processed.[10]

Lechoń's first entry in the FBI file is a memorandum dated July 14, 1941, prepared upon his application for a U.S. visa. He is listed as a "well-known Polish writer and intellectual, formerly Press Attaché at Polish Embassy in Paris."[11] We also find out that already on January 24, two months after his arrival in Brazil, he was in possession of a visa to Canada, possibly for transit to the United States. His visa application was supported by a warm recommendation from an unnamed source, who saw him as "a favorable person."[12] Furthermore, it is said that "Polish Embassy is interested. Serafinowicz is assigned to Polish Information Bureau in New York."[13] The background check summarized on July 17 resulted in heavily censored information: "one (blacked out)—assumed to act as (blacked out) of the Haitian Legation in Rome, and in such assumed capacity issued (blacked out) including himself and one Jan Lechoń, who is possibly identical with the applicant."[14]

Lechoń's major and most complete FBI file was compiled upon his attempt to obtain employment with the Voice of America. On May 24, 1950, an official memo from J. Edgar Hoover requested an investigation of "Jan Lechoń Serafinowicz: Special Inquiry—State Department: Public Law 402, 80th Congress (Voice of America)."[15] The memo states that the central files of the FBI so far contained "no information of a derogatory nature concerning loyalty," but the request is made to check the files of the State Department, HCUA (House Committee on Un-American Activities), and INS (Immigration and Naturalization Services), instructing that "through records, interviews, etc. will [be] obtain[ed] information concerning applicant's residence, education, and employment listed as being outside the United States."[16] In response, three reports were filed by special agents as follows: a report from Washington dated June 27, a report from New York dated June 14, and a report from San Francisco dated June 5.

The key piece of the file is a form "Request for Investigation," which was apparently a document required from all applicants for jobs with the State Department, signed by Lechoń himself. It contains information about his education and his literary activities in Poland, as well as his professional engagements in the United States. Since 1949 he lists himself as performing "literary work for the National Committee for Free Europe, Inc." We also find there a list of seven of his home addresses, starting with Paris and Rio de Janeiro and ending with five places in New York City. Among five references he provides are two professors, a member of the House of Representatives Judiciary Committee, and a businessman, all of whose names have been blacked out on the form.[17]

In a report filed from San Francisco an agent informs us that one of Lechoń's references, a person from the Department of Slavic Languages at the University of California, describes him as "a man of excellent character, reputation and associates as well as an internationally known poet. [He] states that applicant is strongly anti-Communist and patriotic citizen of the US." This person recommends him for "a position of trust."[18] However, relatively quickly information surfaces that will eventually prevent Lechoń from obtaining a job with the Voice of America. An FBI agent lets it be known that one of the references "has been advised that Lechoń is a homosexual, but has no proof. He did not reveal source of this information [but] feels he could not recommend Lechoń for any position with the govt, although Lechoń is extremely capable."[19] As a result, the FBI requested that "all offices attempt discreetly to prove or disprove above allegations."[20] Someone (unnamed) is to be interviewed with regard to Lechoń's activities at the Paris Embassy, and a search will be conducted in New York for "other close associates" in order to "prove or disprove allegation that Lechoń is a homosexual."[21]

Soon enough, an interview with one of Lechoń's acquaintances produces the following information: "Applicant [is] well known in the Polish circles as a homosexual, and when applicant came to US from Brazil in forty one, he brought another homosexual who was an English actor, last name [blacked out]." Further, while working for *Tygodnik Polski* "applicant misappropriated funds" and should be considered "morally corrupt and completely dishonest."[22]

On June 14 an official form summarizes in sixteen pages the results of the investigation, which inform that Lechoń indeed entered the United States on August 12, 1941, on the SS *Uruguay* from Brazil on a Polish passport. He filed papers for citizenship on November 23, 1945, and between 1942 and 1947 served as co-editor of *Tygodnik Polski*, "dedicated to fight Communism and Fascism."[23] We also find out that "[s]ince 1947, [he] has worked as free lance writer. Literary output described as very meager.[24]" Furthermore, "one reference states that Lechoń is known as a homosexual in Polish circles. States, however, that he has no proof to verify this allegation. Other reference, social and acquaintances, fellow workers and neighbors state Lechoń possesses good moral character, is dependable, reliable, capable and honest. No credit or criminal record [is] located NYC or Nassau County, NY."[25]

From the National Committee for Free Europe, Inc., comes the information that Lechoń filed an application with the committee around June 1949 and was placed on the so-called Stipendiary List for a term of one year. It is explained that this list "contains the names of writers and broadcasters whom the committee feels have a potential value as propaganda agents in their respective fields."[26] It further states that Lechoń came to the committee highly recommended as "Poland's greatest living poet," but "his literary output for the past eight or ten years has amounted to nothing."[27] A person from the National Committee further informed that "it had been the Committee's intention to hold Lechoń for radio operations in the coming months, but, at the moment, he feels that he would recommend that Lechoń's services will be dispensed with after July, 1950." Of concern seemed to be the information that Lechoń was "given to emotional outbursts against the more liberal minded elements among the émigrés. Since 1945 has had no support from the Polish London Government."[28] Further in the report the information again surfaces that Lechoń "possesses a poor reputation and is morally corrupt" or may be a "a poor security risk if employed by the United States Government."[29] One acquaintance complains that Serafinowicz was "once upon a time brilliant" but has become "used to living off subsidies and borrowing money from his friends" and is not to be recommended because "if anyone would give him a position as a porter at a railroad station, he could steal a customer's suitcase."[30]

By December 15, 1950, we find out that Lechoń had failed to get a job with the Voice of America and had been given to understand that "the reason for his being unsuccessful in securing employment had been Serafinowicz's moral conduct in the past."[31]

In his lifetime, Lechoń had no more dealings with the FBI, at least none that have been made available to me. The final record comes from June 8, 1956, and was initiated a day after Lechoń's suicide. Apparently, the New York police, the State Department, and the FBI shared the following notes: "The subject who has been residing at 505 East 82nd street, New York City, has been missing for the last day or two and (blacked out) just learned that the subject jumped out of a window of the Hotel Henry Hudson, New York City, at 4:00 p.m. June 8, 1956, and killed himself. (Blacked out) stated that Lechoń is a poet and is a Polish immigrant who has not yet been naturalized. (Blacked out) inquired whether there was anything that FBI could do to look over subject's papers before the Polish officials got to them. (Blacked out) stated there was no intelligence interest in the matter as far as he knew."[32]

However, the FBI inquiry produced information that some of Lechoń's acquaintances indicated that he had been "under pressure to return to Poland," giving his death a political tinge. Seemingly, "Radio Poland had during past six months broadcast invitations from Polish Government to Lechoń and two other Polish writers, inviting them to return to Poland and that the door was open for their return."[33] The person quoted in the file said that "Lechoń has been furnished transcripts of these invitations by Radio Free Europe, which monitored Radio Poland."[34] The possibility of a political subtext initially attracted the FBI to the case, but it apparently could not be substantiated. Interviews gathered in the FBI file confirm instead that Lechoń had been very depressed for several days, had feared that he would take his own life, and had even gone to confession and received the sacrament. On the day of his death he had lunch with one Zygmunt Sulistrowski, a rather colorful adventurer and director of a semipornographic film titled *Naked Amazon*, and followed it with the aforementioned suicidal leap. Additional information obtained by the FBI was as follows:

I. It had been thought already two weeks earlier that Lechoń would take his own life;
II. It was believed that he was taking narcotics;
III. At the time of his death he literally had no money;
IV. He wrote a letter to his doctor before his death (the contents were not disclosed);
V. Financially, he was well off, earning $400 a month with Radio Free Europe and receiving financial help from several (named, blacked out) people of Polish descent.
VI. He had a homosexual relations with an Englishman, around thirty-five years old, who was the reason for his difficulties and to whom he paid $300 a month;
VII. He was a devout Catholic and had no physical ailments.[35]

Does this bureaucratic summary in any way enhance our image of the poet or our view of the Polish exile community in the United States? It either provides or reconfirms basic facts about a writer whom some considered the leading poet of his generation but who almost fifty years after his death still lacks a biography. Beata Dorosz of the Institute of Literary Research (IBL) of the Polish Academy of Sciences (PAN) is preparing Lechoń's calendarium but acknowledges that his life abounds in blank spots.[36] These blank spots largely relate to Lechoń's private existence as a homosexual, an identity that in turn had an impact on the public role he could play in his new country. But from the beginning Lechoń did his best to ignore the American context of his life. Instead he maintained for himself a phantasmagoric "Warsaw in New York," according to Wojciech Wyskiel, who analyzed Lechoń's construction of self and society in emigration. For this reason, Lechoń's three-volume diary provides little information on the broader context of his New York existence.

While it appears that Lechoń's homosexuality was the factor that prevented him from participating in American cultural institutions, it is also likely that his lack of political consciousness and his provincial nationalism were equally influential. What is striking in the entire FBI account is the marginality of Lechoń's position in New York. Lechoń was ignored or bypassed by the important cultural developments occurring in the States. In his journalistic writing he styled himself as a spokesman for the cultural mission of Poland, which in his imagination was to lay the moral, intellectual, and political foundations of a new order of Central and Eastern European nations. In reality, however, he did not manage to obtain employment with the Voice of America, did only sporadic programs for Radio Free Europe, and only very briefly held a stipend from the Committee for Free Europe, which found him unproductive and too dogmatic. At no time was he involved in the Mid-European Studies Center, and he generally remained outside all interesting dialogues of power conducted in the United States in the early fifties.

The two other leading poets who shared the limelight with Lechoń among the Polish émigrés in the late 1940s and early 1950s were Józef Wittlin and

Kazimierz Wierzyński. Both of them have FBI dossiers too, but they are considerably thinner and much less complete than Lechoń's. Both played the role of public figure among American Polonia but failed to make a mark outside that setting. A memo from J. Edgar Hoover of May 23, 1946, to the director of the Strategic Services Unit of the War Department reports that Kazimierz Wierzyński "was President of the Association of Writers from Poland" and adds that "this association published 'Tygodnik Polski,' a newspaper subsidized by the Polish Government Information Center of New York City."[37] The only other entry dates from November 23, 1962, and summarizes the interaction that Wierzyński may have had with the FBI throughout the years. According to an informant from 1943, Wierzyński was believed to be a member of the "Pilsudski Group" and "its various organizations . . . described as 'most dangerous to the United States and the Allies.'" The same informant described Wierzyński as "an 'expressive poet' and an admirer of the Fascist rule."[38]

In 1944 a source of "unknown reliability" described Wierzyński as "a semi-fascist who had been financed by the pre-1939 Polish Regime" and stated, ominously but not incorrectly, that "he was of German descent and his present name was not his real name."[39] There is also an indication that Wierzyński was interviewed by the FBI in 1950, probably about Lechoń's job application to Voice of America, and an appropriate report (which was not made available to me) was filed. In general, it appears that Wierzyński was the subject of a background check performed in 1962, but the reasons for this are unclear and the released materials amount to only four pages.

Unlike Wierzyński, who was accused of "semi-fascist" sympathies, Wittlin was a subject of inquiry because of his apparent leftist leanings. Wittlin's FBI file consists of some forty-eight pages, but it is indicated that nineteen additional pages were withheld "to protect information."[40] The first inquiry about Wittlin is connected with his visa application and dates from November 5, 1941. It appears that "a confidential informant" produced the information that Wittlin was a member of the Council of the European P.E.N. Club in America, which "is said to be Communist in character."[41] We also find out that Wittlin and Heinrich Mann agreed with Ludwig Renn on writing an anti-Nazi book, which was to be published by the El Libero Libre publisher in Mexico City. Renn, a German exile, was then chairman of the Board of Directors of El Libre, where "many individuals are said to be Communists" and where agents of the Soviet secret police were reported to be among the staff.[42] From a priest who was a curator of the Polish Roman Catholic Union Archives and Museum in Chicago comes a similar bit of information that "(Manfred) Kridl, (Władysław) Malinowski, and (Józef) Wittlin were all 'leftists,' and ... that Wittlin was definitely pro-Lublin in his sympathies. It is to be noted that the provisional Government setup up in Poland by the USSR in 1945 was known as the Lublin Government."[43]

On March 15, 1956, on the basis of some secret information (withheld), the FBI launched a "full background investigation," including Wittlin's current employment and residence as well as current activities and associates.[44] We find out that in 1950 Wittlin worked in the Department of State as a Polish translator of documentary movies. From 1951 until 1954 he was employed by the Mid-European Study Center as a writer and researcher, and at the time of the inquiry he was a freelance writer for Radio Free Europe, where he appeared on "panel type programs for the Polish section of Radio Free Europe."[45]

Other documents provide an extensive biography with minute details on Wittlin's schooling and employment, including a request to interview him in person in 1956. Two attempts were made during which apparently "the subject was unavailable for the interview." Finally the interview took place at Wittlin's apartment in New York on September 24, 1956.[46] Considerable parts of the interview summary are blacked out, but it is said—probably as a response to an inquiry about the invitations issued to the émigré writers by the Polish government—that Wittlin stated that "he had no desire to return to Poland and that he and his wife desired to spend the rest of their lives in the United States as United States citizens. He did state, however, that some day he would possibly like to return to Poland only for a visit."[47] We are also provided with a nice physical description of Wittlin, his weight, height, and the state of his hair. In conclusion, the FBI agent reports that "Joseph Wittlin was friendly and cooperative with the interviewing agents throughout the course of the interview. He appeared sincere and truthful in his statements and noted that he desired to cooperate with this Bureau in any manner possible."[48]

Clearly Wittlin, more than Wierzyński, was thought to merit the attention of the FBI. Wierzyński's alleged "fascist" leanings proved of no interest to FBI machinery set up to pursue an intensive anticommunist line. On the other hand, Wittlin's leftist leanings and wide international connections made him suspect, although he generally presented no danger and was clearly not involved in any activity that could have affected the political climate in the United States.

Characteristically, the New York Polish émigré community did not play any significant role in American cultural organizations. The reason for this, most likely, was its alienation from Realpolitik, its excessive Polish nationalism, and its unabashedly conservative attitude—all of which elements are very visible in Lechoń's profile. These traits, it seems, made them useless from the perspective of the new international politics. Furthermore, they remained sidelined by the *Kultura* group, which was clearly more cosmopolitan and which better understood the American position. The surveillance by the FBI may have limited Lechoń, Wittlin, and Wierzyński in their ability to obtain regular jobs, but it also showed that they had little potential for finding a place within the new power structures. Lechoń's longtime experience of working at the Polish embassy in Paris did not sensitize him sufficiently to politics. And while he and other exiles were busy recreating "Warsaw in New York," the new superpower ignored them in all of its extensive cultural activities directed to postwar Europe.

Notes

An earlier version of this paper was published under the same title in *The Polish Review* 51, no. 1 (2006): 41–54.

1. Saunders, 30.
2. Tarka, 123.
3. James Burnham, the major consultant of the Office of Policy Coordination, a part of CIA covert operations, was "the organization's main point of contact with the group of Polish exiles associated with the Paris-based journal Kultura, a tendency which he considered representative of what 'the liberal movement as a whole ought to be,' 'activist… but also intellectually sophisticated' and, 'finally, willing to accept 'American leadership.'" Wilford, 90
4. Coleman, 212
5. Inspired by the defection of Czesław Miłosz, the Congress of Cultural Freedom organized in September 1951 in Castle Adlau, near Strasbourg, a meeting for invited participants focused on two questions: "1). How can we reach the mind of the Communist intellectual? 2). The Diamat (Dialectical Materialism) is a persistent challenge of the free world. What are the ways and means to respond to this challenge and what common anti-Diamat action can be devised for the intellectuals of the Free World?" Scott-Smith, 139. Nicholas Nabokov, commenting on Andrzej Panufnik, wrote: "He is entirely ready to cooperate with us for he is totally sold on the ideas of the Congress for Cultural Freedom. . . . I am sure that if we can extend this man a helping hand we would win an extremely useful permanent friend for the Congress who might be as important to us as has been in the first year of our existence the Polish escaped writer Czesław Miłosz." Ibid., 163
6. However, the *Report of the Mid-European Studies Center: Publications and Projects* does not list Wittlin among the authors of any of its publications.
7. On the observation of the German exiles, see Stephan.
8. I am referring here to a term used in a seminal study of the literary culture in emigration by Wyskiel.
9. For Jan Lechoń's publishing activities, see Stanisław Kowalski.
10. Letter signed by J. Kevin O'Brien from the U.S. Department of Justice Federal Bureau of Investigation, dated August 21, 1998.
11. Memorandum for Departmental Committee of July 14, 1941. FBI file no. 40-4328.
12. Ibid.
13. Ibid.
14. Ibid.
15. Memorandum by J. Edgar Hoover, May 24, 1950. FBI file no. 123-5074.
16. Ibid.

17. Request for investigation data, April 14, 1950. FBI File Number 123-5074.

18. Report from San Francisco, June 5, 1950. FBI file no. 123-804.

19. Report from New York, June 6, 1950. FBI file no. 123-5074-3.

20. Ibid.

21. Ibid.

22. Report from Washington, June 7, 1950. FBI file no. 123-5074-5.

23. Report from New York, June 14, 1950. FBI file no. 123-3385.

24. Ibid., 1.

25. Ibid.

26. Ibid., 5.

27. Ibid., 6.

28. Ibid.

29. Ibid., 7.

30. Report from Washington, DC, June 27, 1950. FBI file no. 123-4716, p. 6.

31. Memorandum to Director, FBI, December 15, 1950. FBI file no. 123-5074-13.

32. Memorandum to A. H. Belmont, June 8, 1955. FBI file no. 123-5074-15.

33. Ibid., 4.

34. Ibid.

35. Teletype from New York, June 13, 1956. FBI file no. 40-4328.

36. Dorosz, 767–90.

37. Memorandum from J. Edgar Hoover, May 23, 1946. FBI file no. 97-2204-3PI.

38. Memorandum, November 23, 1962. FBI file no. 62-5-13754.

39. Ibid. Before it was changed, Wierzyński's last name was Wirstlein.

40. Letter signed by J. Kevin O'Brien from the U.S. Department of Justice Federal Bureau of Investigation dated September 14, 1998.

41. Memorandum from J. Edgar Hoover to the Visa Division, Department of State, November 5, 1941. FBI file no. 40-4698-2.

42. Memorandum from J. Edgar Hoover to the Visa Division, Department of State, February 22, 1943 (date unclear).

43. Memorandum, December 1, 1954. FBI file no. 40-4698-6.

44. Memorandum from Director, FBI, March 15, 1956. FBI file no. 105-45464.

45. Report from New York, June 22, 1956. FBI file no. 105-45464.

46. Report from New York, October 9, 1956. FBI file no. 105-45464-7. It is also recorded that Halina Wittlin was earlier interviewed by the FBI, immediately after the termination of her job at the Polish Research and Information Service. Prior to the interview, in a letter to the director, a comment is made with regard to Wittlin: "it is felt that the subject has potential as double agent or informant." FBI file no. 105-45464.

47. Ibid.

48. Ibid.

POLISH LITERARY THEORY IN THE ANGLOPHONE WORLD

The Case of Roman Ingarden

Andrzej Karcz

Twentieth-century Polish literary theory, like all Polish literary study, has enjoyed the status of a particularly strong discipline. As such it has also caught the attention of foreign literary scholars and has resonated, for example, with literary scholarship in the English language. As a consequence, some of the main ideas, trends, schools, and figures of Polish literary theory have been, even if in a limited way, present in the Anglophone world. In an attempt to describe this phenomenon I will consider specific English-language books and essays on literary theory, regardless of their place of publication, and examine in them the signs of Polish literary theory. Since no comprehensive study of the subject has been conducted either in Poland or elsewhere, I will concentrate on just one particular representative of Polish literary theory, the phenomenologist Roman Ingarden (1893–1970).[1] Even preliminary observations about the presence of Polish literary theory in the Anglophone world—observations based on the reception of one theoretician's work—shed light on some vital qualities and preoccupations of Polish theory and also indicate the interests, influences, and findings of certain Anglophone critics and scholars of literature.

Outside Poland, Polish literary theory is usually considered to be an integral part of East and Central European criticism and Slavic literary theory. And while many unique features and specific qualities of Polish literary theory may be overlooked when seen collectively through the lens of Slavic theory and criticism, a "distinctively Slavic tradition in literary study" helps to account for Polish theory's prominent standing outside Poland.[2] Made up of many diverse phenomena, the Slavic tradition embraces both nineteenth-century trends in literary study that cross over to other disciplines as well as areas of social and political life, and prominent twentieth-century schools of Russian, Czech, and Polish literary scholarship, such as formalism, structuralism, semiotics, and phenomenology. The more specific indicators of this tradition include Roman Jakobson's study of language and literature, Mikhail Bakhtin's philosophy of culture, the Prague Linguistic Circle, the Polish integral or formalist approach to literature, the Tartu-Moscow school of semiotics, and Roman Ingarden's philosophy of literature.

Nineteenth-century trends in Slavic literary study were marked by critics' and scholars' heavy involvement in the social and political issues of the day and their purely ideological approaches to literature (a phenomenon that brings to mind the attitudes and practices of poststructuralist critics of the last three decades of the twentieth century in Western Europe and America).[3] But under the leadership of first the formalist and then the structuralist schools, twentieth-century Slavic literary theory broke away from nineteenth-century trends and proclaimed and practiced, quite successfully, autonomous approaches to literature, which placed a literary work and its internal structure at the center of analysis. The new methods were put to use with varying effectiveness from country to country, as imposed Marxist criticism after World War II (and in the Soviet Union after 1917) left little room for other schools of literary criticism.

In the mid-twentieth century Slavic autonomous approaches to literature attracted the attention of literary scholars and critics in Western Europe and America. In particular, two Slavic schools were found especially appealing: Russian formalism and Czech structuralism. Their reverberation in the West was to a large degree caused by the international scholarly activity of such well-known figures as Roman Jakobson and René Wellek, as well as a few others.[4] It also coincided with some analogous developments in literary theory in France (French structuralism) and the Anglophone world (the New Criticism).[5] In Germany, too, the work of the Russian formalists and the Czech structuralists found receptive ground, especially in the 1960s, at the time of the formation and expansion of German hermeneutics and the aesthetics of reception. This process was facilitated by the fact that it was German philosophical thought that, at the beginning of the twentieth century, had often served Slavic literary scholars as their source of inspiration. The work of the Polish phenomenologist Roman Ingarden, a pupil of Edmund Husserl, is a good example of this inspiration. But it was his own original contribution to aesthetics and literary theory, and not his dependence on Husserl, that attracted the attention of West European and American scholars. Some of them found Ingarden's phenomenological theory of literature as appealing as Russian formalism and Czech structuralism.

But Polish formalism and Polish structuralism, the two schools that significantly contributed to the Slavic tradition in literary study and that unequivocally played the most important role in Polish literary scholarship of the twentieth century, have not been as well known in Western Europe and America as their Russian and Czech counterparts. Admittedly, the close cooperation of the Polish formalist school with Russian formalism and the Prague Linguistic Circle in the 1930s, and the affinity of Polish and Czech structuralism, facilitated some attempts to disseminate the ideas of the two Polish schools outside Poland.[6] The phenomenological aesthetics of Ingarden was also helpful in this process, as some of his ideas, like those referring to the mode of existence and the structure of the literary work, correspond to several basic formalist and structuralist pronouncements. And yet, despite all such affinities and correspondences, Polish formalism and Polish structuralism have remained little known outside Poland in contrast with Roman Ingarden's theory.[7]

II

The chief disseminator of Ingarden's literary theory in the Anglophone world was René Wellek, a Czech-American scholar who before the war was a member of the Prague Linguistic Circle. Even though Ingarden's German and Polish works on literary theory were not translated into English until the 1960s and '70s, Wellek, clearly intrigued by Ingarden, very early on held in his English critical studies a dialogue with the Polish philosopher.[8] "I was, I believe, the first person to refer in English to Roman Ingarden," he wrote.[9] Indeed, as early as 1936, five years after Ingarden had published his first book devoted to literary theory, *Das literarische Kunstwerk*, Wellek wrote a paper in English titled "The Theory of Literary History" in which he briefly praised Ingarden's analysis of the strata in the structure of a work of art and its "metaphysical qualities."[10] In his paper Wellek also criticized Ingarden for his supposed "error" of analyzing the work of art "without reference to values." Wellek touched upon the same problems and applauded the "ingenious book" *Das literarische Kunstwerk* in his 1941 essay "Literary History," and again in a 1942 paper, "The Mode of Existence of a Literary Work of Art," which was later included in two anthologies of literary theory in 1948 and 1953.[11] In addition, the 1942 paper was included in the first edition of *Theory of Literature* (1949). This influential book, coauthored with Austin Warren, had three editions (1949, 1956, 1966), was reprinted several times in England and America, and constitutes the first major work in English that discusses Ingarden's fundamental ideas of the strata of a work of literature, its aesthetic structure, form, and mode of existence.[12] While embracing and speaking approvingly of these ideas, Wellek also, as in his 1936 article, briefly repeated his reservation about Ingarden's understanding of values, which Wellek saw as being superimposed on literature by phenomenology.

Wellek's dialogue with Ingarden continued in his later publications, too, including above all the major essay "Roman Ingarden (1893–1970)," which he first published in his 1981 book *Four Critics: Croce, Valéry, Lukács, and Ingarden* and later in volume 7 of his monumental *A History of Modern Criticism: 1750–1950*.[13] In this essay Wellek presents his assessment of the Polish philosopher's overall significance for literary study and discusses the main notions and problems of literary theory that Ingarden addressed, especially the mode of existence of a literary work understood as an "intentional object," its four layers, its sentences termed quasi-judgments, the nature of meaning and truth in literature, indeterminacy, concretization, metaphysical qualities, the process of reading, and the aesthetic value in a work of art. From among these problems, Wellek chooses the mode of existence of a literary work, the analysis of its layers, and the concepts of concretization and indeterminacy and declares them Ingarden's major contributions to literary theory. The concept of concretization, Wellek writes, has given a stimulus to studies of readers' reactions or *Rezeptionsaesthetik* and the concept of "spots of indeterminacy" has been used creatively by the German representative of reception theory, Wolfgang Iser.

In his assessment Wellek also points to the weaknesses he sees in Ingarden's theory. They include the technicality of the philosopher's language, the features distinguishing the "literariness" of a work of literature, the problem of value, and the separation of the layer of schematized aspects from the layer of represented objects. In the closing remarks of his essay Wellek refers to the critique of him that Ingarden expressed in a 1966 article and in the preface to the third German edition of *Das Kunstwerk* (1965). Ingarden, after reading a German translation of Wellek's *Theory of Literature* (1959), complained that Wellek had made insufficient acknowledgment of his indebtedness to him and misread some of his key notions, such as the metaphysical qualities, the problem of value and structure, and the concept of norms. In his response, Wellek explained that Ingarden's critique had resulted from some misunderstandings and indicated that the German translation of *Theory of Literature* available to Ingarden had been imprecise and that he had been unaware of Ingarden's later writings in which the problem of value was further addressed. In the end, while defending the distinctive attributes of his own position, Wellek did acknowledge his deep indebtedness to Ingarden.

Wellek's dialogue with Ingarden vividly illustrates the presence—more: the resonance—of the Polish philosopher's literary theory in the Anglophone world. Ingarden's critique of Wellek in the preface to the German edition of his book was made available to the English-language audience when *Das Kunstwerk* was for the first time translated into English and published in 1973 by Northwestern University Press as *The Literary Work of Art*. This English edition was introduced by its translator, George G. Grabowicz, who in a very elaborative, sixty-page essay expertly presented Ingarden's basic views on literature from the layers in the structure of the literary work, through the spots of indeterminacy and the act of concretization, to the metaphysical qualities emerging from the work. In the same year, Ingarden's second book on literary theory, *The Cognition of the Literary Work of Art*, was made available in English by the same publisher.[14] Thus, with Ingarden's several earlier essays published in journals and anthologies during the 1960s and '70s, with his *Selected Papers in Aesthetics* published in 1985, and with his essay "Phenomenological Aesthetics: An Attempt at Defining Its Range" published in 1986 in the anthology *Critical Theory since 1965*, Ingarden's most important works on literary theory and literary aesthetics have become accessible in the English language.[15] True, thirty or more years passed between the publications of Ingarden's first works, whether German or Polish, and their appearance in English translation. Their dissemination in the Anglophone world was indeed a slow process, which may reflect the overall difficult penetration of Ingarden's oeuvre abroad caused by both political and other factors. Wellek, for example, lists such factors as the "technicality of Ingarden's language" and the "circumstances of the time," that is, the Nazis coming to power in 1930s Germany, the war, and the postwar communist regime in Poland.[16] Important for sustaining Ingarden's presence in the English language was, therefore, the interest in his ideas not only of Wellek but also of many other, sometimes very diverse, literary scholars and critics eager to present comprehensively and discuss at length the complex issues of Ingarden's phenomenology of literature.

We first need to mention those scholars who devoted full attention to Ingarden in their monographs, edited volumes, and other major studies published as book chapters, articles, and essays. In 1975, two Polish editors, Piotr Graff and Sław Krzemień-Ojak, prepared an impressive volume of articles translated into English, *Roman Ingarden and Contemporary Polish Aesthetics: Essays*.[17] The volume presents a "panorama" of different views on Ingarden's aesthetics by Polish philosophers, aestheticians, and literary and art critics. The three essays on Ingarden's key literary issues are authored by leading Polish literary scholars: Michał Głowiński writes "On Concretization,"[18] Henryk Markiewicz contributes "Places of Indeterminacy in a Literary Work," and Katarzyna Rosner, in the essay "Ingarden's Philosophy of Literature and the Analysis of Artistic Communication," considers the similarities and differences between Ingarden's theory and the semiotic approach to literary work. While Graff's English volume shows responses of Polish aestheticians to Ingarden's ideas, the 1981 monograph *The Poetics of Roman Ingarden* aims at providing a "comprehensive exposition" of his literary theory by the American scholar Eugene H. Falk. Taking a creative approach, Falk offers simplified definitions of Ingarden's terms and traces the layered structure of the literary work, its sequential order, metaphysical qualities, and mode of existence.

Comparable to Graff's and Falk's works, other edited volumes and monographs include more studies with a focus on Ingarden's aesthetics and ontology. Among them are two edited collections of articles published in English in the Netherlands: *On the Aesthetics of Roman Ingarden: Interpretations and Assessments* (1989), edited by Bohdan Dziemidok and Peter McCormick, and *Ingardeniana III: Roman Ingarden's Aesthetics in a New Key and the Independent Approaches of Others* (1991), as well as a monograph published in Canada, *Roman Ingarden's Ontology and Aesthetics* (1996), by Jeffrey Anthony Mitscherling.[19] Like dozens of other volumes in the series "Analecta Husserliana," *Ingardeniana III* was edited by Ingarden's former student Anna-Teresa Tymieniecka, who has inspired many other studies devoted to this Polish philosopher's thought. Two such studies contain important contributions: the article "Roman Ingarden's Literary Theory" by Hans Rudnick and the essay "The Ontology of Objects in Ingarden's Aesthetics" by Kazimierz Bartoszyński. Hans Rudnick also edited *Ingardeniana II*, a volume containing several other important essays on Ingarden's aesthetics and literary theory, including Josef Strelka's article on the points of indeterminacy and Zhang Jin-Yan's comparative study of Ingarden's theory and the New Criticism.

From among the remaining major studies of Ingarden's theory, one needs to list the general chapter in Robert Magliola's book *Phenomenology and Lit-*

erature: An Introduction (1977) and the eight-page chapter included in volume 8 of *The Cambridge History of Literary Criticism* (1995). The author of the latter chapter, Robert Holub, discusses Ingarden's key ideas including the structure of the literary work, especially its strata, harmony, and spots of indeterminacy, and the way readers experience the work in the acts of concretization and cognition. The last ideas contribute to reception theory, and the editor of *The Cambridge History* also takes note of that in another chapter by mentioning Ingarden's influence on Iser. The remaining major studies—for example, Victor Michael Hamm's article "The Ontology of the Literary Work of Art: Roman Ingarden's *Das Kunstwerk*" (1961) and Peter M. Simons's essay "Strata in Ingarden's Ontology" (1994)—are more specialized and address specifically Ingarden's ideas of the ontology and structure of the literary work. In pointing to these studies, one should not overlook works addressing one of the most important problems in Ingarden's literary theory—the nature of sentences in literature and the subsequent issue of literary fiction. In English, the problem of sentences in literature was newly discussed by Jan Woleński in "Sentences, Propositions and Quasi-Propositions" and by Josef Seifert in "Ingarden's Theory of the Quasi-Judgments." Seifert also coauthored, with B. Smith, an essay, "The Truth about Fiction," devoted to a subject rather neglected in studies of Ingarden's ideas.[20] However, Ingarden's contribution to the theory of fiction is invaluable and deserves to be studied, for example, comparatively, as in the article "Three Models of Fiction: The Logical, the Phenomenological, and the Anthropological (Searle, Ingarden, Gans)" (1998) by Richard Van Oort.

Crucial for sustaining Ingarden's presence in English, all the monographs, edited volumes, book chapters, and essays indicated above show which ideas formulated by Ingarden have attracted the strongest interest. Half of those studies deal with general problems of phenomenological aesthetics and ontology, particularly the ontology of the work of art; the other half are linked to the issues of literature and literary theory more directly, as they address the structure of the literary work, its mode of existence, the notions of fiction, concretization, and cognition, as well as the theory of reception. These few issues subsume (one might also recall Wellek's choices) all of the interest in Ingarden's theory of literature. Other English-language studies, not mentioned here yet, and the major dictionaries, guides, and encyclopedias of literary theory and criticism confirm this observation.[21]

Judging by the frequency and systematicness with which Ingarden's ideas have been addressed, it appears that the mode of existence and the structure of the literary work dominate the discussions in a number of studies by Anglophone critics. Already in 1954 Victor Erlich pointed to these two ideas in his remarks on Russian formalism. He observed that Ingarden "sought to apply the Husserlian categories to one of the most difficult problems of literary theory—that of the mode of existence of [a] literary work."[22] He also saw close connections between formalist-structuralist formulations and Ingarden's remarks on such issues concerning the structure of the literary work as the special status of its sentences and the related problems of fiction and truth.

Like Erlich's monograph, other English-language studies on Russian formalist theory also refer to Ingarden and his key notions of the special status of sentences in the literary work and its layered structure. Krystyna Pomorska mentions these notions, as well as Ingarden's understanding of fiction and truth, in her book *Russian Formalist Theory and Its Poetic Ambiance* (1968). Ewa M. Thompson, in turn, in *Russian Formalism and Anglo-American New Criticism: A Comparative Study* (1971) quotes *Das Kunstwerk* when she speaks of the ontology, structure, and metaphysical qualities of a work of literature. She also applies Ingarden's layers, especially the sound layer, to her analysis of the ways in which the Russian formalists and the American New Critics studied poetry. References to Ingarden are also made in my own study *The Polish Formalist School and Russian Formalism* (2002). At times Polish formalist scholars found themselves in agreement with Ingarden, and I point to those of his ideas that the formalists considered analogous to their own. They included especially the examination of the structure of the literary work, the treatment of it in terms of layers, and the description of the work's sentences as "quasi-judgments" or statements not claiming to be true. The same or similar ideas were also embraced by Czech scholars, the representatives of the Prague School, and in his study *Literary Structure, Evolution, and Value: Russian Formalism and Czech Structuralism Reconsidered* (1989) Jurij Striedter examines, among many other things, the Czech "debate" with Roman Ingarden's theory. The debate included connections and disputes between the Czech structuralists and the Polish phenomenologist. Striedter indicates, for example, that the Czechs disagreed with Ingarden's idea of what constitutes the structure of the literary work and where its objective aesthetic value is located. On the other hand, the Czechs "borrowed," most notably through the theoretical pronouncements of Felix Vodička, Ingarden's other notions like the idea of the literary work as a system of related layers or the concepts of indeterminacy and concretization. The borrowing was not uncritical: Vodička insisted on analyzing the lower layers and thus disputed with Ingarden who, as Striedter tries to explain, often passed over lyric poetry and dealt chiefly with prose literature in which lower layers of sound formations do not matter as much as in poetry. As will be shown below, Striedter also discusses the notion of indeterminacy as shared by the Czech structuralists and Iser.

The mode of existence and the structure of the literary work are the subject of discussion also in other critical studies. Endre Bojtár's Hungarian book translated into English, *Slavic Structuralism* (1985), describing the Slavic tradition of literary theory, examines the subject in two sections of a forty-page chapter devoted to Ingarden. Other books, like *Introduction to the Analysis of the Literary Text* (1988) by the Italian scholar Cesare Segre and *Twentieth-Century Literary Theory: A Reader* (1988) edited by K. M. Newton, touch upon the subject only briefly, but they find it especially helpful in explaining more universal issues of contemporary theory. While providing basic information about Ingarden's theory, Newton, for example, in his chapter "Phenomenological Criticism," which contains a five-page excerpt from Ingarden's *The Cognition of the Literary Work of Art*, comments on his ideas of the existence and the structure of the literary work, and their dependence upon the reader's consciousness. The layers of the literary work constitute its schematized structure that must be completed by the reader during the process that Ingarden terms concretization. In other words, the work must be concretized by the reader in order to exist. Accordingly, Newton indicates the important connection between Ingarden's notions of the existence and the structure of the literary work, and the whole set of problems associated with the reception of literary works.

As has been shown, the mode of existence and the structure of the literary work dominate discussions in a number of critical studies. But among Ingarden's ideas that have attracted the strongest interest of Anglophone critics are also those of concretization and indeterminacy—notions related to the reader and his reception of literary works. Many theoreticians and critics, especially the proponents of German aesthetics of reception, have found these notions extremely fruitful. Wolfgang Iser, the leading German figure among these proponents who is based in Constance and California, even built substantial parts of his reception theory on the basis of notions devised by Ingarden.[23] Iser's works translated into English, especially *Der implizite Leser* (1972) and *Der Akt des Lesens* (1976),[24] have shaped Ingarden's reputation in the Anglophone world to such an extent that this Polish philosopher's name appears in various textbooks, readers, and dictionaries of literary theory more often under the rubric "aesthetics of reception" and "reader-response theory" than "phenomenology." This is the result of Iser's frequent reference to and regular use, especially in his early works, of Ingarden's particular ideas.

Iser's forty-page essay "Indeterminacy and the Reader's Response in Prose Fiction" was first published in English in 1971 in a volume edited by J. Hillis Miller.[25] Five years later, Iser included a modified version of this essay in his book *The Act of Reading*, and in 1988 and 1997 short excerpts from the essay were reprinted in the two editions of Newton's anthology mentioned above, *Twentieth-Century Literary Theory: A Reader*.[26] This essay addressing the idea of indeterminacy, like the whole book *The Act of Reading*, shows how heavily Iser relies on Ingarden's theory. *The Act of Reading* contains a dozen references to Ingarden in the form of quotations from his works and discussions of the ideas of indeterminacy, concretization, "schematized views," and functions of gaps or quasi-judgments. They are all useful terms for Iser's reception theory.

Iser's other major essay widely available in English, "The Reading Process: A Phenomenological Approach," also describes, analyzes, and gives additional meanings to Ingarden's theories. It was first published in 1972 in the journal *New Literary History* and in his book *The Implied Reader*. Later, between the years 1974 and 2001, it was reprinted in several American and English anthologies.[27] Many critics agree that in this essay, while writing about the process of reading, Iser draws extensively on the work of Ingarden. With references to *Das literarische Kunstwerk* and quotations from *Vom Erkennen des literarischen Kunstwerks*, Iser unfolds his theory of the interaction between the literary text and its reader. Ingarden's notions are very helpful here: the layered structure of the text, its "schematized aspects," its various concretizations or realizations, "intentional sentence correlatives" that construct the world presented by the literary text. As the text offers only "schematized views" of its world, all its indeterminacies and gaps are filled by the reader who links up the sentences and parts of the text during the process of its concretization. In his analysis of the reading process, Iser also goes beyond Ingarden's notions, but they remain at the bottom of many of his further considerations.

It is not surprising, then, that Ingarden's name is present in Iser's other works. There are references to his ideas, especially to "schematized aspects," in Iser's essay "Interaction between Text and Reader" (1980), published in two major American anthologies, and in his book *Prospecting: From Reader Response to Literary Anthropology* (1989).[28] In recent years, however, Iser has shifted his interests from the theory of reception to literary anthropology, and with this change Ingarden's name no longer appears in his works.[29]

The presence and resonance of Ingarden's ideas on reception theory and reader-response criticism can be detected not only in Iser's work but also in the English-language works written by critics who either comment specifically on Iser or address reception theory in general. The Polish structuralist theoretician Michał Głowiński, for example, published two essays in English in the 1970s on the subject of Ingarden's idea of concretization and considered it in terms of its contribution to literary study and the theory of reception in particular. In "On Concretization," the essay already listed above, Głowiński analyzes this fundamental concept carefully and shows its broad consequences for literary study. In the other essay, "Reading, Interpretation, Reception," concretization, in turn, serves Głowiński as a point of departure for his own further remarks on reading and interpretation. Another theoretician, the American critic Frank Lentricchia, in his well-known book *After the New Criticism* (1980), lists the phenomenological approach as one of the three approaches to the theory of reading. The approach, he says, "via Husserl and Ingarden, is represented by Iser's 'The Reading Process.'"[30] Lentricchia analyzes the issue by quoting Iser, who quotes Ingarden. The notions of concretization, schematized views, and indeterminacy are at the center of Lentricchia's analysis of Iser's understanding of the reading process. Similarly, this process is considered by the British theorist Terry Eagleton in his *Literary Theory: An Introduction* (1983). He recalls Ingarden's notions of "schemata" or "schematized views" and concretization and, by referring to Iser's *The Act of Reading*, describes in detail the process in which the reader constructs and organizes the elements of the text into a coherent whole. Eagleton also contrasts Ingarden with Iser and speaks very critically of their theories. To him, Ingarden is dogmatic and limiting in his claim that literary works are organic wholes whose indeterminacies the reader must fill correctly. Iser, in turn, is liberal by allowing the reader to actualize the work in different ways, with no single correct method to do so, except that the work should be made into a harmonious whole and its indeterminacies replaced with a stable meaning. In his critique, Eagleton also sees an epistemological problem with Iser's and Ingarden's reception theories. He doubts whether it is at all possible to discuss the text's schemata without one's own concretization of them.

The notions of indeterminacy and concretization, and the use of them by Iser, are also a subject of discussion in Jurij Striedter's study, mentioned earlier, *Literary Structure, Evolution, and Value*. While analyzing Czech structuralism, Striedter observes that both the Czech structuralists and Iser share Ingarden's notion of indeterminacy. But he also contrasts the Czech scholars, notably Jan Mukařovský and Vodička, with Iser by saying that the Czechs were more interested in the notion of concretization than indeterminacy, while the German theorist applied, above all, the spots of indeterminacy to his theory of reception and his approach to literary fictionality.

Editors of Anglophone anthologies, guides, readers, and dictionaries of literary criticism also comment, usually briefly, on Ingarden and his influence on reader-response criticism and the aesthetics of reception.[31] Hazard Adams and Leroy Searle, the editors of the anthology mentioned earlier, *Critical Theory since 1965*, serve as a good example. Their anthology includes two chapters, one on Ingarden and one on Iser, and in the brief introductory comments preceding the reprinted essays by the two theoreticians, the editors indicate the main points of Ingarden's phenomenology of literature and Iser's reception theory. They aptly comment on Ingarden's insistence on the role and activity of the viewer or reader in the aesthetic process and on his emphasis on the reader's act of reception. The editors also point to the special mode of being of works of art, which Ingarden stresses when speaking of the reader's need to concretize the work. The notion of concretization, they conclude, influenced Iser's reception theory.

III

All the studies, essays, introductions, and entries listed or discussed above have played a pivotal role in maintaining the presence and contributing to the resonance of Roman Ingarden's ideas in the Anglophone world. The catalogue of the publications devoted to the Polish theoretician, or the publications in which there are references to his ideas, is vast and impressive. Thus a conclusion might be drawn that Ingarden's ideas, and with them a substantial part of Polish literary theory, are strongly present in English-language books and journals. However, the presence of Ingarden's theory in the Anglophone world is a more complex phenomenon than the catalogue suggests. Despite the large number of publications, and even despite such scholarly activities as Wellek's close dialogue with Ingarden and Iser's continual use of Ingarden's key ideas, his theories have been slow to reach the English-language audience. The technicality of the Polish philosopher's language and the "circumstances of the time" have already been indicated as causes. Another important cause is the fact that a number of publications in which Ingarden's name appears mention it only in passing or use it to introduce additional information. Such is usually the case in Iser's works and in those by his commentators. Ingarden's presence there is usually indirect. Iser relies on a few of Ingarden's basic ideas and acknowledges his indebtedness, but he uses them for his own purposes while building a different theory. And Iser's commentators seem to treat Ingarden's ideas as only an imperfect basis for the more mature theory formulated by Iser.[32] The result is that in recent literary criticism Ingarden's phenomenological ideas have become better known as notions in reception theory. They play an important role there, but one should not think that they have become in any way more visible. For the fact is that Iser's work (and Ingarden's ideas in it) has not had a great deal of influence on the larger debates in contemporary literary theory, and that reception theory in general has had a marginal impact, limited mostly to Germany and Western Europe.[33]

In contemporary literary theory the importance of Ingarden's phenomenology of literature is unquestionable, and one would expect Ingarden's name to appear in all the major anthologies of contemporary literary theory and criticism. It is therefore very baffling (and appalling) that one of the most important English-language collections of historical and contemporary literary criticism, *The Norton Anthology of Theory and Criticism*, does not even include a modest chapter devoted to Ingarden, while it generously incorporates long chapters dedicated to some obscure second-rate theorists. *The Norton Anthology* thus confirms foreign, especially Anglophone, critics' weakening interest in Ingarden's theory. Danuta Ulicka, an Ingarden specialist, recently gave an extensive account of this tendency in her long essay "What Has Remained of Phenomenology for Us?" ("Co nam zostało z fenomenologii?") and found that the Polish phenomenologist has in the last twenty years been removed from the list of the most important world authorities on literary theory. While the rich assortment of publications discussed above may not entirely correspond to Ulicka's finding, a steady decline in interest among foreign critics in Ingarden's theory can certainly be observed, giving reason to think that most of Ingarden's critical ideas may before long disappear from the Anglophone world.

This situation with regard to Ingarden's phenomenology of literature needs to be seen against the background of the main developments in recent literary theory in America. Dominated by deconstruction, cultural and feminist studies, the New Historicism, and other poststructuralist trends, recent literary theory in America has little room for different, universal, hierarchical, and more "conventional" theoretical systems like Ingarden's phenomenology of literature. The deconstructionist theorists have not been indifferent to some selected models of phenomenology but unfortunately Ingarden's thought has not found itself among them.[34] The gap between his phenomenological aesthetics and poststructuralist theories has been very wide indeed and a lack of communication between them has clearly prevented Ingarden's ideas from being more effective not only in America but in the entire English-speaking world.

Nevertheless, all the listed studies, essays, introductions, and entries show Ingarden's profound impact on world literary study and portray him justly as one of the most important literary theoreticians of the twentieth century. Because of him, Polish literary theory can, even if only through one critical trend set and shaped by one theorist, enjoy the status of a strong "international" discipline in the Anglophone world and beyond.

NOTES

1. Ingarden took the ideas of his teacher, Edmund Husserl, further and extended the range of phenomenology by entering the fields of aesthetics and literary study. In those disciplines he addressed many fundamental problems of the nature, ontology, and structure of works of art and literature. He tackled them as part of his broader philosophical deliberations, but his specific contribution to literary study includes, among other things, an analysis of the structural components of the literary work, a description of the nature of its language, and an indication of the relation of the work to the real world.

2. Cf. how this tradition is related in such studies as, for example, Holquist and Tihanov. Also, see in this context the notions of "Slavic formalism" and "Slavic structuralism" used in Erlich, Harkins, and Bojtár.

3. In nineteenth-century Poland these approaches were a result of the political situation. In the partitioned country, literary study, like every intellectual activity, was subject to such needs as upholding national identity and cultural continuity, and revealing the national spirit and psyche.

4. Among them were Manfred Kridl, William E. Harkins, and Victor Erlich, who in their English language works published in the United States in the 1940s and '50s wrote on the subject of the Slavic schools. See Kridl, "Russian Formalism"; Harkins; Erlich.

5. With regard to the former, see some of the remarks in Merquior. On the New Criticism in this context, see the remarks in Erlich, and Thompson, *Russian Formalism*.

6. The contacts of the Polish formalists with their Russian counterparts and the Prague Linguistic Circle are partly documented in Kridl, *Prace ofiarowane Kazimierzowi Wóycickiemu*, and in the Czech journal *Slovo a Slovesnost* (see, for example, no. 3, 1937).

7. The fact that Ingarden formulated many of his basic ideas first in German has made his phenomenology of literature more accessible to foreign literary scholars. Not without significance was also the fact that Ingarden's first work, *Das literarische Kunstwerk*, has had four editions in Germany: in 1931, 1960, 1965, and 1972.

8. Wellek retrospectively comments on his indebtedness and early references to Ingarden in the essay "Roman Ingarden (1893–1970)," in his *A History of Modern Criticism*: "I find myself in wide agreement with his views and acknowledge learning from him, on many of these questions [of literary theory], more than from anybody else," 379.

9. Ibid., 392.

10. Ibid., 393.

11. Wellek points to the essay "Literary History", and the next one, in his *A History of Modern Criticism*, 393; his "The Mode of Existence of a Literary Work of Art" was also published in two anthologies: one edited by Stallman and the other by Vivas and Krieger. (I learned that they include Wellek's essay from Markiewicz's article "Twórczość Romana Ingardena").

12. Wellek and Warren, 142–57 and 241.

13. As to the dialogue with Ingarden, see also Wellek's references in his *Concepts of Criticism* and *The Attack on Literature and Other Essays*.

14. A translation of Ingarden's *Vom Erkennen des literarischen Kunstwerks* (1968). This German edition was an enlarged version of the Polish edition of *O poznawaniu dzieła literackiego*, which Ingarden published in 1937.

15. Ingarden, "The General Question of the Essence of Form and Content," (excerpt from Ingarden's *Studia z estetyki*, vol. 2); "Artistic and Aesthetic Values," "The Physicalistic Theory of Language and the World of Literature," "On So-called 'Truth' in Literature," "Psychologism and Psychology in Literary Scholarship," *Selected Papers in Aesthetics*, "Phenomenological Aesthetics: An Attempt at Defining Its Range" (the essay is a "slightly abridged translation" and is reprinted from *Journal of Aesthetics and Art Criticism* 3 (1975): 257–69; originally published in Polish in Ingarden, *Studia z estetyki*, vol. 3). To this list of English translations of Ingarden's works (or their excerpts) devoted to literary theory and literary aesthetics one should also add, for example, Ingarden, "Lectures on Aesthetics," "On the Cognition of the Literary Work of Art," "Some Epistemological Problems in the Cognition of the Aesthetic Concretization of the Literary Work of Art."

16. Cf. Wellek's beginning remarks in "Roman Ingarden," 379–80.

17. One should emphasize the general importance of English-language publications by Polish scholars informing foreign audiences of Ingarden's work and Polish literary study. See, for example, the informative essay by Mayenowa.

18. Głowiński's essay was reprinted four years later in Odmark's *Language, Literature and Meaning: Problems of Literary Theory*.

19. Dziemidok and McCormick's volume reprints, among others,

Markiewicz's important article "Twórczość Romana Ingardena," translated into English as "Roman Ingarden and the Development of Literary Studies."

20. The extent of this neglect has been indicated by Ulicka. While describing Ingarden's presence in literary studies, she comments on, among other things, the notions of fiction associated with the theories of speech acts and of possible worlds. Some critics and theorists of fiction applied Ingarden's ideas to studies of the two theories, but their efforts have been ineffective and the results, Ulicka writes, have a limited validity and seem outdated today.

21. It would obviously be difficult to list and review here all such reference books, but a look at the major dictionaries and encyclopedias of literary terms and criticism published during the 1990s confirms that the indicated issues of Ingarden's theory have indeed been the critics' main interests. See Baldick, Harris, Hawthorn, Makaryk, Groden and Kreiswirth, Lentricchia and McLaughlin, Preminger and Brogan, Childers and Hentzi, Payne, Bouissac.

22. Erlich, 166.

23. Another proponent of the German aesthetics of reception, Hans Robert Jauss, was also influenced by Ingarden, but he rarely mentions his name and speaks of the Polish philosopher's ideas in very critical terms.

24. *Der implizite Leser: Kommunikationsformen des Romans von Bunyan bis Beckett* was translated into English as *The Implied Reader: Patterns of Communication in Prose Fiction from Bunyan to Beckett*; *Der Akt des Lesens: Theorie ästhetischer Wirkung* was translated into English as *The Act of Reading: A Theory of Aesthetic Response*.

25. Miller, 2–45.

26. Newton, 226–30. Also, it is worth indicating at this point that chapter 3 of *The Act of Reading*, containing references to Ingarden's notion of quasi-judgments and his view of the nature of literary language, was reprinted as an essay titled "The Repertoire" in Adams and Searle, 360–80.

27. For example in Cohen, Tompkins, Barry, Lodge, Latimer, Rice and Waugh.

28. Iser's "Interaction between Text and Reader" was also published in Leitch.

29. See, for example, Iser, *The Fictive and the Imaginery: Charting Literary Anthropology and The Range of Interpretation*.

30. Lentricchia, 146.

31. See, for example: Selden, *The Theory of Criticism*; Rice and Waugh; Lodge; Groden and Kreiswirth, s.v. "Phenomenology," "Reader-Response Theory and Criticism," "Reception Theory," "German Theory and Criticism"; Childs and Fowler, s.v. "Reader".

32. Cf. the observations in Ulicka, 47.

33. Cf. Leitch, 1672; Groden and Kreiswirth, 611.

34. Cf. Ulicka's pertinent remarks, 52–54.

Of Wives and Mothers

Women Writers Telling Their Own Stories in Postwar Polish Emigré Fiction

Bożena Karwowska

For Asia and Jason

Recent years have brought not only a critical awareness that the vast majority of migrants and exiles are women and children, whose point of view is underrepresented in literature, but also an understanding that the picture of exile projected by women in their literary works varies significantly from the image of exile created by male authors.[1] The dissimilarities undoubtedly arise from differences in social and cultural views of gender roles. The works of many male writers (including such significant authors in Polish émigré literature as Czesław Miłosz and Witold Gombrowicz) promoted an intellectually oriented myth of exile and were interested primarily in the process of exceptionally creative individuals seeking their identity in the cosmopolitan tradition of "the exile."[2] These writers "concentrate primarily on themselves, since they value above all their own development."[3] They are unique by their very nature, capricious, and—by assumption, as exiles—lacking natural successors. In contrast, since female gender constructs are shaped around the function of motherhood (giving birth to and raising children), and thus of ensuring generational continuity, women writers frequently based their literary texts on personal experiences associated primarily with family life and children. As a result, the majority of female exilic authors depicted the "domestic" problems that confronted Poles, both women and men, in their everyday life after the war had dispersed them all over the globe.

The "domestic" character of Polish women's émigré prose can be explained, at least partly, by the fact that in Poland, especially during the period of its statelessness (1793–1918), the public and private spheres acquired a different character than they did in the West. As Małgorzata Fidelis notes, the place of the Polish Mother (*Matka-Polka*) was defined principally in terms of her national function (that is, socially), while the ideas of gender differentiation characteristic of the Western middle class did not have much of an influence on Polish society.[4] Whereas the Victorian model assumed that a woman in the house exerted influence on men by means of "loving care" and "moral example," and in this way also affected the social sphere reserved for men, in Poland both of the spheres were closely connected by a common commitment to the national cause:

> Patriotic goals significantly shaped private and public spheres in nineteenth-century Poland. Independent statehood was identified with family life, and political activity often was conducted at home and included women. In Western Europe, the spheres

> were distinct but mutually supportive: state protection of the private sphere served to maintain bourgeois social and economic order. In contrast, in Poland, the public realm, controlled by a hostile state, was perceived as alien, while the private sphere was a source of freedom and independence in need of defense against state-imposed laws. When Konopnicka (a popular woman poet) wrote "our homes will be our fortresses," she expressed the widespread perception that a Polish household was a state unto itself, a bastion of resistance against political and cultural domination by the partitioning powers. Elevation of the roles of women as mothers and ladies of the house had implications beyond literary meanings; although Poland was not an independent state, women presided over the spiritual Poland at home.[5]

Similarly, for Polish women abroad and perhaps particularly for them, "home" meant a space that combined both private and social spheres.

Getting married was thus of special importance for the women of the generation of postwar émigrés. In her novel *Pogranicze*, Janina Kowalska classifies the women living in Crowley (and other British hostels and camps for Poles) according to their marital status: there are married women (and mothers), four eligible misses, and an old maid. A relationship between a Pole and an English woman is regarded negatively by the "Crowleyan" Polish women. Polish men are attractive to English women, but English women are not what a "wife" should be. As Kowalska writes, the young Polish men from military camps for foreign troops

> were raring to get married and quickly seized whatever came to hand, while it is well known that a good product seldom pushes itself on you on its own. They clicked their heels and kissed hands, which was a novelty and enchanted the women. . . . No wonder that local girls fell for them. . . . But after a general reckoning, which the end of the war brought about, among the newlywed men there was no lack of those who said of each other, where the hell did he dig her out like a dog with its paws. Everybody knows that a woman should know how to make beet-root soup and pierogi, how to launder and houseclean and raise children.[6]

The matrimonial talents of Polish men abroad are a separate and quite an interesting topic but one that lies outside the scope of this essay. As for Polish women, they seemed to prefer and put a higher value on the patriarchal traditions of domestic roles that the English women had just begun to shed for a more public space. In Kowalska's narrative this "public" space is far from being understood in the feminist sense and embraces—almost in an ironic way—mainly shops, pubs, and streets.

Similar in tone are the comments on the "Scottish wife" made in Danuta Mostwin's "'Lanczeneta' przy Alei Północnej." While there is no doubt that cultural differences (or, more precisely, differences in the gender constructions of womanhood) stood in the way of Polish women's acceptance of "foreign" women as suitable wives for Polish men, one cannot exclude factors of rivalry or jealousy, since local British women deprived Polish émigré women of potential husbands. This could also explain why Polish women writers and their protagonists tend not to carry this attitude toward their "American" daughters-in-law,[7] and—what is interesting—that Polish mothers seem to tolerate the English marriages of their sons more easily than those of their daughters, especially in the absence of grandchildren:

> The son of the general's wife married a girl from the upper middle class. She called her mother and tried to learn Polish, though nobody really expected it of her. Whenever she appeared in the room the conversation immediately switched into English. . . . I like her, the general's wife thought, but I feel weary. I like her, she told her acquaintances, she is very gentle and yet boyish. She strides with long steps unaware of the need for flirtatiousness, and in her eyes she has such caring sweetness. When she was lonely she cried. Why can't I love her more?[8]

In the literature of postwar émigré women the role of wife is directly related to the role of mother, responsible for making a home and maintaining the Polishness of the next generation. The theme of raising children "in exile," which as far as one can see is present in women's narratives only, is perhaps the most interesting aspect of Polish émigré women's fiction. The pressure of the patriotic tradition was so strong that it led to the definition of home as the "space of Polishness" irrespective of the nationality of the spouse. Naturally, non-Polish wives could not fulfill the hopes placed in a mother who was Polish. A "good" husband was one who made it possible to establish a Polish home, as is the case with Jose in Janina Surynowa-Wyczółkowska's *Gringa*:

> [Jose] believes . . . that his children owe to their mother not only their light hair and white skin, but also European mentality, as well as the heritage of Polish independence. Jose is building the house in the center of the city and indulges in the illusion that it is a Polish home. So the house has a sharply sloping and red roof. An attic. Window panes have openings in the shape of a heart. . . .
>
> Close to our Polish house thujas imitate spruce trees. The patio imitates a porch. The hall imitates the Polish hall. Swimming pool imitates a pond. And the garage—a coach house and a stable.[9]

The protagonists of *Gringa*, and the characters in other émigré narratives written by women, realize that Polishness is not a matter of language alone, but it is nevertheless the problem of language that is mainly described in relation to children. This may be due to the fact that language is often a distinguishing feature of national identity, a "sign" that clearly differentiates Poles from other nationalities. Before the protagonists of the novels and short stories face the language issue in relation to their children, however, they note it in themselves or other adults. Teresa, the narrator of *Gringa*, notices that she unconsciously inserts Spanish words when speaking Polish when she is still a young, unmarried woman:

> And suddenly I realized that I am attached to that city near the Cordelier Mountains and that I call in my thoughts its scent *perfume*, and its freshness *frescura*. For these

words come handily and easily (and not Polish words).

You are losing your Polish identity, Teresa, I think to myself on my way to the bus.[10]

The problem of language is neither new nor exclusively émigré, which Teresa, the daughter of a Czech father and a Polish mother, realizes when talking to her father:

So I begin shouting that you cannot take into account in this case any *negocio*, *asunto*, or *comercio*, because I am *muy feliz. Dichosa.*

"You say *szczęśliwa* [happy]," he corrected me. "Teresa, make up your mind in which language do you want us to talk. I used to get flogged as a boy when I mixed German and Czech."

To which I respond: "For two years now I have been speaking only in Castellano, and sometimes in English, and I am not even aware that I am forgetting Polish words. He interrupted me: "Yes," he said. "One loses one's nationality surreptitiously, gradually."[11]

How the language situation affects different generations is yet another subject that would be worth a separate study but that falls outside of the scope of this essay. Purity of speech was required of children in Poland (e.g., during the partitions), or of national minorities to maintain national identity, independence, and cultural continuity. But Teresa thinks of Buenos Aires as "the future capital of my Argentinian children" and is aware of the inevitability of assimilation, of the difference in nationality between herself and her children.[12]

The children who appear in émigré women's writings are usually raised to be Polish; they attend a Polish kindergarten, are taught Polish songs and nursery rhymes, and are dressed in national costumes. But above everything else they are taught the Polish language, usually as a result of a conscious decision made by their parents. This process is excellently described in Zofia Romanowiczowa's *Baśka i Barbara*, a novel about bringing up a daughter in a French-language milieu.

Today I made Basia a present of *księżyc* [moon], though I could have given her *la lune*. To tell the truth it was others who pointed out the problem to us. We ourselves thought that there was no problem.

What? You are teaching your child Polish? You are cutting her off from society. . . . You are foreclosing opportunities for her. . . . You will give her complexes. . . .

For we are in the position of parents who, apparently, have a choice. Should we pass on to her what we have inherited, or should we disinherit her? Which of these would make her happier?[13]

Romanowiczowa also provides a rationale for using Polish at home:

It's an alien world around us. Our house is like a tiny boat on an ocean. Are we ourselves to hollow the bottom of the boat so that it would sink, so that there would be no home? So that, when coming back in a few years from school, or an excursion, our daughter would slow her steps at the thought that there, behind the doors, she is awaited by a pair of strangers?

And that supposedly would be for her good? She will learn that other language anyway from the children in the square, from passersby in the street, from the salesgirl in the shop, from air itself. We won't hamper her, we will not close her ears, on the contrary. This city, which for us is merely hospitable, is her city, is the city of her childhood.

But first she must have a home. And in this house we all have to be at home, both—us and her.[14]

Since *Baśka i Barbara* describes the first years of a girl's childhood, we do not know what will happen when Baśka's peers, and French culture in general, start exerting an influence on her, for instance by pronouncing her name with the stress on the last syllable instead of the first syllable. But some questions may arise even before émigré children are submitted to that test, such as those raised by Marek in Mostwin's "'Lanczeneta' przy Alei Północnej":

"Dear God, keep mum, dad, grandma, and grandpa in good health and let us return to Poland . . . "

"Mum"—Marek turns around— "what does it mean, 'let us return'?"

"To return," Boga explains, "is when you and Paul come back home from kindergarten."

"But I cannot return!"

"Why can't you?"

"But, mum, I was never there, I was never in that Poland."[15]

When answering the question of his already grown-up children about the choice of language for their own children, Jose Maria, Gringa's husband, says:

In that respect the parents cannot have any certainty, there is no guarantee. Children do what they want. First they wanted a colorful ball. Then a plastic swan in the swimming pool. At some point you have to open a bank account for them, buy a car. They demand. They require. They ask. . . .They refuse to be persuaded about anything, to have anything imposed on them. So if they speak one or another language, then it won't be because we will teach them that language, but because Bibi will graciously consent to speak Spanish, Antek to speak English, and Barbarita Polish.[16]

Let us note that none of the works under discussion here offer a clear and consistent answer to the question why preserving the Polish language should be important to émigré children. Is it because they were supposed to go back to Poland, or because speaking Polish would make their relations with their parents closer, or because a shared language would allow them to share in the culture of their parents? Perhaps teaching children to speak Polish enabled their mothers to inscribe themselves in the tradition of the Polish Mother engaged in the struggle for the preservation of the nation, despite the many doubts they had about taking on such a role? Żuławska, one of the characters in "'Lanczeneta' przy Alei Północnej," is hardly an exception in thinking to herself:

> Oh, that desperate struggle to preserve the language! That struggle, tragic, going down to defeat like the tenacious flame of a resistance detachment melting away. What instruments, what tools to use? Who will help? She reflects: Mother taught him: dzień dobry, kiełbasa, mam cię w d... [good morning, sausage, lick my a...]. Oh, I have it all you know where.[17]

Without giving a clear answer regarding the advantages of teaching their children their mother tongue, the works of the émigré women writers show the conflicts that can arise from this struggle, especially at the age when children form their personalities, often through opposition to their parents.

These conflicts between émigré children and their parents are described principally in the case of the daughters. The protagonists and narrators are as yet unaware that the problems they are experiencing are also the result of what feminist critics call mother-daughter issues.[18] The women writers are convinced that the source of the conflicts lies in the struggle to maintain Polishness. In the works of women, exile means a rift not only between themselves and the country of origin, but also between their own cultural identity and the culture of their children. This means that children in mixed marriages learn their culture principally from the parents of their father (as is the case with Barbarita, Gringa's daughter) or from their peers, often regarding their mother's culture with dislike:

> "Oh!" shouts Barbarita. "Gringa, you are awful!"
> We are now facing each other, so much alike. We both have light hair and wear dresses in gay, colorful stripes. We both move the tips of our noses the same way.
> "You too are Gringa," I say harshly, "because you are my daughter."
> I get a nasty look from under her disheveled bangs. And she shouts: "I am ashamed to be the daughter of Gringa. The daughter of *una Polaca*."
> I look horrified at my child, the way my mother must have once looked at me. "It's your own children that wrong you most" passes through my mind. "You suffer at the hands of bitten nails and dirty fingers."
> "I would prefer," Baśka shouts, "to be an Argentinian like my father. *Una pura cepa* [a pure offspring]."[19]

Finding a common language with mothers—and more precisely, noticing that conflicts between generations are the norm—comes only after the children have their own children. The prefeminist consciousness of the émigré women writers prevented them from recognizing the "supranational" character of the problem.

Conflicts between daughters and mothers need not involve (at least on the surface) the question of Polishness; they may instead involve the daughters' need to be independent, which often results in their marriages to Americans. According to the parents, such marriages must lead to the loss of Polish identity as manifested both in language and in the gender construction of femininity, though the language aspect seems to be easier to describe. In her story "Córki," Mostwin writes:

> Our daughter left us first. She married a pal from college, an American. It's not that she simply walked out on us, no, it was rather a departure through a series of gateways, doors, gates. Not a farewell, not a parting, not at one stroke, one turning of the key in the lock—but a constant distancing, a continuous grating of the key. With every meeting she seemed more remote, her Polish acquiring an American accent. With increasing frequency she would stop in the middle of a sentence looking for the appropriate word. The general's wife listened to the English chattering of her grandchildren with some effort.[20]

In the same story, the troubles that the parents have with their daughters concern mainly how to make them marry Poles. Leaving Germany for the United States becomes a necessity when "Oleńka graduated from high school, [and] she started being interested in boys," which forces her parents to ask, "What if she marries some German guy?"[21] The move does not alleviate their worries, however; once they are in the United States, they are concerned because "Oleńka says she will marry an American, a Jew, a Protestant, she'll just leave."[22]

The two daughters mentioned here—Oleńka and Grażyna—belong to a group that Ruben G. Rumbaut calls "generation one-and-a-half," comprising children of émigrés who, in moving to a new country, are old enough to remember the culture they left behind and young enough to become part of peer groups in their new country and to base their whole social identity on them.[23] As a result, these children can move between two cultures with some ease, although the émigré women writers also show them as having problems with finding a place in either. According to Rumbaut, those who belong to this group are free "of the impulse of self-justification" that motivates the exilic outlook of their parents.[24] In the situations described in the narratives under consideration here, children born outside of Poland (or those too young to remember much at the time of leaving their home country) share a number of features with generation one-and-a-half. Instead of actual memories of Poland, they have a remembered/imagined notion of Polishness, related primarily to their childhood and home, and constructed by the patriotic émigré narrative. For this generation, the Polishness of the public sphere is created only by the émigrés, Polonian diasporas that are often governed by their own rules and have their own dynamics. The image of these diasporas in the women's prose is not very flattering, to mention only Kowalska's *Pogranicze*, or Mostwin's "Córki."

Interestingly enough, the marriage of a daughter to a Pole, which theoretically should guarantee the preservation of Polishness, does not feature in the prose of émigré women as a happy-end scenario. Even the children whose parents are both Polish, and who can understand the Polish language, address their parents in English, occasionally causing indignation among the older generations, such as that expressed by the grandmother in one of Mostwin's stories: "the son of a man who sacrificed so much for Poland talks to his father in his own home in English!"[25] The subsequent generations of émigrés from

Poland differ from the postwar wave; their history is different from the history of those who did not experience life in the Polish People's Republic on a daily basis. Thus, when Gringa's daughter Barbarita informs her of her engagement to a Pole who was forced to emigrate in 1968, during the official anti-Semitic campaign, the situation is far from straightforward:

> And suddenly Barbarita decided to show her hand. "So then? If there is no anti-Semitism in Poland, then why are you, Ricardo, afraid that *mamita*, despite all the *amistad* [friendliness] that she feels toward you, may not be too happy about our *matrimonio*?"
>
> The worst has come into the open. The perversity of this situation hit me on the head. The bitterness of these Polish words mixed in exasperation with Spanish ones made me choke. "To hell," I curse under my breath in my old way.[26]

The worlds and problems of different generations of émigrés are different not only from one another but also from those of Poles living in Poland, and many of the émigré works (especially the "American" narratives of Mostwin) testify to the lack of understanding between Polish émigrés and Poles from Poland. One is immediately reminded of Marc Robinson's observation that it is impossible for an exile to return to his or her country.[27] The women's writings and their "domestic" character deal with a similar though not directly identified problem: the creation of a distinct immigrant identity, different from the identity created in Poland or by the émigrés of other generations.

It seems that women accept émigré reality more easily than men. The latter are often unable—at least in the pages of the émigré women's writings—to give up their titles and ranks of "president," "colonel," "general," and "major" or their functions of soldiers, insurrectionists, and patriots, none of which have anything to do with their new reality. Moreover, they can perform these roles only in the "domestic" sphere or in the various émigré associations and groupings. In this way they cocoon themselves in the diasporas that let them preserve their pre-exilic gender identity. Émigré life is characterized by the narrowing of the public sphere and the rise of groupings based on direct bonds. The social life of the émigrés is conducted in actual, local time, as if they were living in a traditional society. However, their lives are deeply affected by both individual and collective, identity-forming experiences of war and occupation. Members of Polish diasporas found themselves on the margins of the social sphere in their new countries; it is therefore not surprising that such a model was not attractive to the next generation, which tended to adopt the culture of the new country as its own. Gringa's son Niato, for example, in a conversation with his "uncle," a veteran of the battle of Monte Cassino, tells him:

> You would want, uncle, to imprison me in a Polish ghetto, but I cannot be a foreigner in the country of my father. Do understand. I am proud of the origin of my mother . . . but I cannot listen over and over again to how Aunt Fafa was beaten by the Gestapo . . . or

> how you fought at Monte Cassino. Do try to understand, *Dios mio*, that I have responsibilities toward the country in which I was born.[28]

Grażyna, in Mostwin's story "Córki," takes an equally critical view of émigré social spaces. She does not share in her father's raptures over an émigré ball:

> "A ball!" she laughed, "a ball! And what a ball! A Dance of Skeletons! You think that I am having fun here? That that's where I want to belong? You think that I will let some general's wife find me a husband, that I am interested in this or that general? I want to lead a normal life."[29]

In both of the above cases, the determined rejection by the young generation of the social role that is being imposed on them occurs in a conversation with men who find their own identity in this social sphere. And although female characters are almost exclusively shown in their domestic sphere, and in the related functions of wives and mothers, it is precisely the women who more easily accept what Josef Skvorecky has aptly called "the double landscape."[30] Recalling once again Robinson's observations, one can surmise that women are more capable of feeling loyalty toward both their own culture and their host culture—the culture of their children. One should add, however, that in the émigré experience the gendering of private and public spheres becomes more complicated. Men can enact their social identity only in the private sphere, while women are linked with the social sphere of the new country through their children.

It is loneliness that the female characters of émigré narratives discussed here experience most painfully. According to Said, exile is characterized, above everything else, by loneliness, lack of belonging, and alienation; it is a constant sense of one's own otherness, of not being quite congruent with the surrounding culture and mores. Emigration deprives people of the dignity that is related to the sense of belonging, of the kind of assurance that comes from being rooted in a place and a time.[31] Robinson, too, says that all émigré writers go through a period of doubt and loneliness, and that—although with time they become accustomed to the new reality—the feeling of alienation never leaves them. In the case of women, exilic loneliness is experienced also within the family. It is keenly felt even by such protagonists as Teresa in *Gringa*, or Boga in "Lanczeneta," though both women are surrounded by large, multigenerational families. Because of the cultural differences between parents and children, the exilic domestic space ceases to be a place in which women can fulfill themselves by enacting the role created for them by the patriotically oriented Polish patriarchal tradition. In émigré conditions, home is often the only available space for women, just as the family roles of a wife and a mother are their only identity. Hence, after almost twenty-five years of marriage (and with four grown-up children), Teresa, the heroine of Surynowa-Wyczółkowska's novel, regrets her erstwhile and long-buried scholarly ambitions:

> [T]hey . . . all had "intellectual hopes" for me. And I myself used to devour scholarly books, went to lectures at the Sorbonne, and wanted to study art history.
>
> It almost defies belief that I ended up with cosmetics, pots and pans, cradles and English lessons.
>
> I began uncovering in myself long-buried grievances. On life's balance sheet I am on the side of the vanquished. . . . I consoled myself only with this, that if I went off the rails, then it was not my own fault. . . . It was the war that had derailed thousands of émigrés. But what kind of consolation was that? None whatsoever. It was no more than—a difficult to accept—reality.[32]

Thwarted plans, unfulfilled aspirations, disturbed domestic and social spaces, and an "outdated" identity, but above all else acute loneliness—such is the balance sheet of postwar émigré women's narration. Circumscribed by the consciousness of a prefeminist generation, the writings of Polish émigré women writers reveal the multilayered character of the otherness with which the postwar émigrés/immigrants had to cope. They were different from men, different from the people of their host culture, different from other immigrants, and different from the Poles in their native land, different from blacks, Indians, and Métis. Different from their own parents but also different from their own children, still unaware that they shared many problems with women of other races and nationalities and not really interested in seeking an understanding with them, émigré women writers provide a history of those who have traditionally lacked a "tellable history." Subsequent chapters in this still mostly unknown story have been written by subsequent generations of émigrés and speak of the falling apart of exilic homes, professional problems, addiction to alcohol and drugs. But this is a topic deserving a separate treatment.

Notes

1. See "World of Refugee Women"; and Said, "Reflections on Exile."
2. The formation of post-émigré identity is discussed in my "Tożsamość postemigracyjna." On the evolution of the concept of exile, see my "Kategoria wygnania."
3. See Langer, 15.
4. See Fidelis, 108–25.
5. Ibid., 111.
6. Kowalska, 98.
7. This seems to be one of many possible explanations of this phenomenon. However, a limited interest in this issue among writers makes all of them, at best, speculative.
8. Mostwin, "Córki," 68.
9. Surynowa-Wyczółkowska, *Gringa*, 224.
10. Ibid., 137.
11. Ibid., 141.

12. Ibid., 137.
13. Romanowiczowa, 51.
14. Ibid., 151
15. Mostwin, "'Lanczeneta,'" 60.
16. Surynowa-Wyczółkowska, *Jesień Gringi*, 193.
17. Mostwin, "'Lanczeneta,'" 48.
18. See, for example, Said, "Reflections on Exile."
19. Surynowa-Wyczółkowska, *Gringa*, 215.
20. Mostwin, "Córki," 67.
21. Ibid., 65.
22. Ibid.
23. See Rumbaut and Rumbaut, 331–57.
24. Ibid., 332.
25. Mostwin, "Dwanaście lat," 111.
26. Surynowa-Wyczółkowska, *Jesień Gringi*, 65.
27. See Robinson.
28. Surynowa-Wyczółkowska, *Jesień Gringi*, 193.
29. Mostwin, "Córki," 77.
30. Overland, 7.
31. See Said, *Culture and Imperialism*, 326–36.
32. Surynowa-Wyczółkowska, *Jesień Gringi*, 152.

(Re)Translating the *O'Hariści* into English

Mira Rosenthal

New literary movements often rely on translation to excite change, as writers look outside their native traditions for innovative ideas from other literatures. Examples abound both in recent and distant times: the odd publication history of *One Thousand and One Nights*, a book of unknown origin from ancient storytelling traditions, which was added to and modified based on the uses it served in each language into which it was translated; the galvanizing effect that the ancient Sanskrit drama *Shakuntala* had on late-eighteenth- and early-nineteenth-century literature, in large part because of Goethe's adaptation of the opening prologue in the beginning of *Faust*; and, most important for this study, the use of an attenuated form of French surrealism by poets writing in post–World War II New York as a way to repudiate the popular modes of writing at the time. Certainly, rejecting a native literary tradition by adopting another raises many interesting questions about literary evolution and the presentation of foreign literatures in translation. What kinds of conditions cause writers to look to other literatures? Are foreign canons always simplified in the process of establishment abroad? How do outside traditions lend authority to new modes of writing? And how exactly does aesthetic transfer occur? But even more, what happens when literature that has been heavily influenced by a foreign tradition is then translated into that foreign language? Such a complex gives rise to additional dilemmas and questions, the least of which is how literature in translation is read differently when it draws on the translating language for influence. Twentieth-century American and Polish poetries provide just such a situation of poets responding to, incorporating, and extending the intellectual investigations of other traditions. The way in which American poetry of the 1950s influenced Polish poetry of the 1980s and how American poets in turn read contemporary Polish poetry in translation bear out the nuances at play when a literature reads its own tradition through another.

In the United States, poets first became truly fascinated by Polish poetry in translation in the 1960s, and, in a way, their fascination was also a kind of envy that led to a characterization and canonization of Polish poetry in translation. In 1965, Czesław Miłosz published his anthology *Postwar Polish Poetry*, which quickly garnered wide interest. And a few years later, Miłosz and Peter Dale Scott published a selection of translations of Zbigniew Herbert's poetry. Interest in Polish poetry grew exponentially and gave rise to a kind of envy. Here were writers clearly situated in and drawing from a historical context the likes of which American writers had never experienced and thus could never claim. It was a bittersweet kind of envy, which ultimately led to a heightened interest in and characterization of Polish poetry. Miłosz himself had a lot to do with this characterization. In his introduction to his anthology, he states that postwar Polish poets are preoccupied "less with the ego than with dramas of history" and that their poetry is characterized by "the relish with which it handles and remodels moral maxims."[1] Regarding the historical strife in Poland, Miłosz explains that the poet emerges "better prepared to assume tasks assigned to him by the human condition, than his Western colleague."[2] Authors writing about postwar Polish culture and literature from the viewpoint of the West also began to identify the way in which Western writers longed to situate themselves differently in relation to history, for example, in the ideas Timothy Garton Ash explores in his 1989 book *The Uses of Adversity: Essays on the Fate of Central Europe*. This longing was part and parcel of how American writers read and understood postwar Polish poetry. As Helen Vendler put it, postwar Polish poetry is read in the West first and foremost as "poems of witness to their cultural moment."[3]

What is less known by American poets is that a handful of Polish writers who made their debuts in the 1980s became so interested in the work of the New York school of poets, and of Frank O'Hara in particular, that a group of them were controversially dubbed the "O'Hariści" ("O'Harists"). From the viewpoint of the West, it is perhaps difficult to understand why the younger generation of Polish poets would neglect their own tradition so envied in the West in favor of an imported Western tradition. And why the New York school? In the United States, the critical discussion of the New York school of poets has focused on their position in the artistic atmosphere of post–World War II New York, in particular in relation to the painters of the abstract expressionist movement. Both Frank O'Hara and John Ashbery worked in the art world, O'Hara as an assistant curator at the Museum of Modern Art and Ashbery as a prolific art critic for various publications. Their poetry is characterized less by aesthetic similarities and more by its opposition to the confessional mode popular at the time and to the formal strictures of New Criticism, which emphasized form over content. In as much as it *can* be characterized, the critic Geoff Ward sums up the key elements when he describes the "often invertebrate forms of their poems" as the "structureless structures of endless lists, the pseudo-narrative, the neo-Surrealist."[4]

But when we try to determine which way the vector of influence points, we encounter a bit of a conundrum. The New York school of poets itself was heavily influenced by the European avant-garde and French surrealism in particular, although Frank O'Hara's experiments were quite different from those of John Ashbery, differences that only intensified when the poets "renounced 'straight' Surrealism in the late fifties."[5] The fact that O'Hara wrote on avant-garde writers such as Mayakovsky and Mallarmé and also tried to define the difference between American and non-American art speaks volumes about the creative energy he drew from considering other artistic movements. Likewise, the critical discussion on the difficulty of thinking about poets as diverse as

Frank O'Hara, John Ashbery, Barbara Guest, James Schuyler, and others as a cohesive group under the rubric "New York school" points to the dilemma of their presentation in contexts outside the United States, especially when such a presentation in turn strengthens new movements or schools of poetry in other countries. While the poets can be defined in terms of their historical relationship to abstract expressionist painters, it is perhaps more accurate to think of their association as a "loosely collective practice"[6] rather than a "school." Since the time of their first presentation as a group, when Bernard Myers adopted the term New York school originally coined by Robert Motherwell in relation to painting, most critics have come to the conclusion that there are far more differences than similarities between them.

O'Hara in particular exerted a fascination for young Polish writers in the 1980s that can be traced back to two publications: a special 1986 issue of the Polish periodical *Literatura na Świecie* (Literature in the World) dedicated to the work of the New York school, and the subsequent book of Frank O'Hara's poetry translated by Piotr Sommer, which was published a year later under the programmatic title *Twoja pojedynczość* (Your Singularity).[7] But this fascination wasn't so much a tidal wave of something knew as fuel for preoccupations already manifest in the younger generation. In Cracow, an underground literary journal called *brulion*,[8] founded in 1986, began publishing work by a group of younger poets who wished to define themselves by a new kind of opposition. They called themselves the "New Barbarians." The group was made up of writers born around 1960 or later who had grown up under the influence of the poetry of opposition to communism during the 1970s as well as of the poetic heavyweights who had lived through World War II. These were poets who had persevered against political odds, and to the younger generation their poetry stood for a form of "political correctness" not entirely useful in the 1990s. Such perseverance was a kind of proud resistance striving for the important utterance, a sign of hope in the midst of an experience that had significant historical implications. The younger generation wished to reject all this. Rather than the proud resistance and perseverance of the postwar Polish poets, they wanted a poetry that included playfulness and uncertainty, a poetry that reflected everyday experience rather than that which connected so profoundly to History with a capital H. O'Hara offered this younger generation a vision of such a poetry.[9]

That O'Hara was also against any sort of system and did not subscribe to any particular technique, rejecting the "propagandists" of technique and content,[10] must have added to his appeal for young Polish poets in the 1980s, who were familiar with and still ensconced in the Soviet system. Poland in the 1970s and '80s had seen the workers' rebellion and student protests, during which the generation of '68 gained recognition. Then came the inception of Solidarity and the harsh response of martial law, which led to the jailing of hundreds of intellectuals and Solidarity leaders, and then years of amnesties in a period of increasing but relative and uneasy openness. As Stanisław

Barańczak describes it, during this turbulent time "a strong current of poetry of social protest and ethical concerns emerged and grew alongside new manifestations of existential or metaphysical lyricism."[11] The younger writers gathered around *brulion* were just coming into their own as poets, and the New York school issue of *Literatura na Świecie* helped them to fashion a response to the turbulent times that was very different from that of poets from the generation of '68. First and foremost, they wanted to counteract any preconceived notion of Polishness, be it Polishness as endorsed by the communist government, Polishness understood as organic coexistence with nature put forth by the romantic poets, or Polishness as a search for metaphysical solutions to difficult political experiences as seen in the postwar poets.[12] There is a clear rejection of the grand themes taken up by Miłosz and other poets writing directly after the war and an insistence on individual destiny as modeled in the West.

In the early 1990s, this artistic and ideological phenomenon manifested itself in the pages of *brulion* where a polemical debate ensued between the "New Barbarians" and their opponents, dubbed the "New Classicists," who wished to defend poetic tradition against the encroachment of quotidian life and popular culture. The poet Krzysztof Koehler published a short essay simply titled "O'Harism" in which he attacks the "barbarian" poet Marcin Świetlicki. "Poetry is—and must be, whether it wants to or not—conventionally as well as functionally artificial," Koehler wrote. "That's something anyone who takes up pen and paper should know. After all, we don't speak in poetry on the street. Nor at the university, nor in the army."[13] In the next issue, in a sardonically titled essay "Koehlerism," Świetlicki responded, "I would be very interested to know what that term actually means. True, in a few poems I may have provided pretexts for people to suspect that I had read the poetry of Frank O'Hara, but does that prove anything? Maybe I've actually soaked up more 'Brautiganism,' or even 'Berrymanism.'"[14] The same year that Świetlicki wrote his sardonic reply, an anthology of poetry by the younger generation appeared under the definitive title *The Barbarians Have Arrived* (*Przyszli barbarzyńcy*). This controversial response to O'Hara's poetry on the part of the young Polish poets shows a "thriving poetic culture" generating "rival forms of inventiveness pursued with an extraordinary energy";[15] it can be explained, at least in part, by how well O'Hara's ideas and models spoke to what was already latent in their thinking. That we didn't see a similar growing interest in John Ashbery's work leading to, say, a coinage of the term "Ashberyism" is an involved and interesting subject worth explicating at some future point. But one part of that explication is the way in which the New York school was presented in *Literatura na Świecie* and the emphasis it placed on O'Hara more than any of the other poets. The first 222 pages of the issue were dedicated to O'Hara and drew from seven different sources. The work of and commentaries about John Ashbery (drawn from four different sources) took up 168 pages, and then there were selections of 5–9 poems each from the work of Kenward Elmslie, Kenneth Koch, and James Schuyler. This was the New York school, including also a section of paintings by Willem de Kooning, Fairfield Porter, and Larry Rivers. The omission of Barbara Guest is particularly conspicuous and perhaps points to the predominance of male poets in the pages of *brulion*.

When we read through the poems and commentaries selected for the issue, four distinct O'Haras emerge: (1) the man and his lifestyle, (2) the poet among painters, (3) the urban poet, and (4) the espouser of an antiliterary and anti-system stance (or the writer of spontaneous, process-oriented poems). The first O'Hara—his life and lifestyle as a gay man living in New York City—held the least interest for Polish poets, and they seem to have simply ignored how this aspect of his life might come through in his poetry. There is some mention of his homosexuality in one of the essays included in the issue, but all the other selections focus on his lifestyle almost primarily in terms of the second O'Hara, the poet among painters. This is in contrast to the appeal of O'Hara for American audiences, who seemed to be, in the decades immediately after his death, more intrigued by the life of the man than by the poetry. In 1977 in the preface to her book *Frank O'Hara: Poet among Painters*, Marjorie Perloff wrote, "Because his life was so colorful and his accidental death on Fire Island when he was only forty such a dramatic, indeed a tragic event, interest has centered on the man rather than on the work."[16] Of course, the American interest in O'Hara has changed since then, but in the 1980s in Poland, to the extent that the young Polish poets focused on the man, their interest was primarily in him as a figure among painters rather than as a homosexual in a city of "overt homosexuality," as a *New York Times* headline put it in 1964.[17]

In contrast to the initial American attitude to O'Hara's poems—that they were the quick lunchtime jottings of a charming but nonetheless minor rather than major poet—the *brulion* group focused more on the second two O'Haras. O'Hara was seen as a role model of a poet responding spontaneously to and embodying the energy found in his urban environment, for example in "Poem," which appeared in *Literatura na Świecie*:

> The eager note on my door said "Call me,
> call when you get in!" so I quickly threw
> a few tangerines into my overnight bag,
> straightened my eyelids and shoulders, and
>
> headed straight for the door. It was autumn
> by the time I got around the corner, oh all
> unwilling to be either pertinent or bemused, but
> the leaves were brighter than grass on the sidewalk!
>
> Funny, I thought, that the lights are on this late
> and the hall door open; still up at this hour, a
> champion jai-alai player like himself? Oh fie!
> for shame! What a host, so zealous! And he was
>
> there in the hall, flat on a sheet of blood that

ran down the stairs. I did appreciate it. There are few
hosts who so thoroughly prepare to greet a guest
only casually invited, and that several months ago.[18]

Here the mundane detail of a "few tangerines" and the playful tone of a statement like "[I] straightened my eyelids and shoulders," combined with the ominous reality of the information at the end of the poem, create tension and surprise the reader. O'Hara's poems often touch on the relationship "between a high emotional charge and an art of improvisation."[19] The influence of this combination of a colloquial tone ("Funny, I thought, that the lights are on this late") and energy derived from the accumulation of details can be found in several of the leading poets to emerge from the "New Barbarians."[20]

Marcin Baran's distinct use of the vernacular and his cataloguing of particulars in poems such as "Dreams Sweet as a Fuck" ("Sny słodkie jak chuj") and "Contradictory Fragments of an Act of Filling" ("Sprzeczne fragmenty zapełniania") are reminiscent of O'Hara's manner. The second title alone points back to the kind of contradictory fragments that we are used to encountering in an O'Hara poem, fragments accumulated from an improvisatory moment that add up to more than just an empirical list. In Baran's poems, the settings are urban and filled with particulars, but they are not simply derivative of O'Hara. Baran's particulars are usually a bit more centered on the individual and home as it exists within the city and add up to an individual voice hard-won against this urban reality.[21] His poems often begin at home, "Some unknown flat, a hardwood / floor, a glassed-in veranda, / courtyards strewn with heat."[22] Or as in his poem "Mantras, Hours" ("Mantry, godzinki"), which reads as follows:

When you don't want cigarette
smoke to mix with the air of your flat
at night—go out for a cigarette in the staircase
of an old tenement. Turn on the light. The homeless
haven't sought shelter from cold here.
Inhale, the automatic light
will go off in a minute. Stay
in darkness, deny brightness
its five minutes. The livid shine of night
enters through the high window. The shadow
of the barred elevator shaft encloses you
as if in a cell. No voices bury
the silence. Before the glow reaches the filter—
you are alone. Strive for perfection.[23]

That this poem echoes O'Hara (he focuses on light in a hallway, much as in O'Hara's "Poem") but is not simply derivative is important. It takes certain notions from O'Hara that didn't exist forcefully in Polish poetry up to this point: namely, that a poet can speak in the first person without being too confessional and can talk about the immediate and unpoetic, indeed quotidian, life he experiences while also maintaining a sense of emotional charge.

But Baran's poem shows specifically Polish concerns as well. It is not only positing a new, urban, lived experience but also reacting against the old notion that witnessing is public and necessarily encumbered with national duties.[24] If Baran is echoing O'Hara, he is just as much echoing Zbigniew Herbert's poem "The Envoy of Mr. Cogito," which I think typifies much that American readers love about postwar Polish poetry. The ending of Herbert's poem reads:

> You were saved not in order to live
> you have little time you must give testimony
> . . . .
> only in this way will you be admitted to the company of cold skulls
> to the company of your ancestors: Gilgamesh Hector Roland
> the defenders of the kingdom without limit and the city of ashes
>
> Be faithful Go.[25]

In contrast, the imperative "strive for perfection" that we find at the end of Baran's poem arises from a very personal moment in which the speaker is utterly alone. There aren't even any homeless to keep him company in the stairwell, which will go dark again in a minute when the automatic light switches off. It is not the city that has turned to ash, as in Herbert's poem, but rather simply this cigarette and its glow burning down toward the filter. The poet is not asking to be admitted to the company of ancestors, those "defenders of the kingdom." Here the faith is in the individual.

The example of another Polish poet, Jacek Podsiadło, relates to O'Hara in a slightly different way. Podsiadło is a self-taught mystic who finds himself in confrontation with debased, everyday life. His search for a redefinition of religious life, which he locates in the erotic and the mundane, is reminiscent of O'Hara's facetious renunciation of the metaphysical in poetry—facetious precisely because his poems often signal "the possibility of metaphysical extensions in quizzical and shifting ways."[26] O'Hara in his mock manifesto "Personism," which was included in the New York school issue of *Literatura na Świecie*, says of poetry: "[H]ow can you really care if anybody gets it, or gets what it means, or if it improves them. Improves them for what? For death? Why hurry them along?" As for the apparatus of technique, O'Hara states, "There's nothing metaphysical about it. Unless, of course, you flatter yourself into thinking that what you're experiencing is 'yearning.'"[27] Podsiadło's interests have moved in the direction of employing the catalogue and the antiliterary subject as ways of setting the metaphysical in direct contrast to the mundane, as in his poem "Vanitas; Et Omnia Vanitatis," which reads as follows:

> With my foot dictating the rhythm on the aluminum runner
> of David's cradle, I reach over his head for a ballpoint

to write down death. First there was Murka
under the wheel of a car. Then Mini vanished mysteriously,
as if she'd been kidnapped by the Palestinian counterintelligence. Kosma died
a few days ago, emaciated with diarrhea, the drip and the kisses didn't work,
he miaowed for relief to the very end. Now comes a message saying
that Marylou was killed in a motorcycle crash, chasing the wind. Not long ago
I found her delayed hair in the bathroom. Now the same hair is wasting away
somewhere on French soil. Young flesh perishes. My three-month-old son
makes clever faces and sends off a sly, victorious grin.
He knows something. He may be one of the Palestinian scouts.[28]

The aluminum runner of a cradle, the cat's meow, a stray hair in the bathroom, his son with a victorious little grin all combine, not so much to hurry us along toward death but to fully inhabit our mundane lives in the meantime.

In another poem, Podsiadło states, "I've always wanted to publish a volume of poetry called *No.*"[29] Turning now to the influence of the fourth O'Hara, the espouser of an antiliterary and anti-system stance, we find echoes both in this statement by Podsiadło and also in the poetry of perhaps the most prominent younger poet of the group, Marcin Świetlicki. Not only as a poet but also as a rock musician and, for a short time, as the host of a television program, Świetlicki is known for his obligatory black clothing and constant reversals. His poem entitled "For Jan Polkowski" became such a site of debate in his exchange with Koehler that seven years later he wrote an antipoem entitled "Not for Jan Polkowski," in which he states, "The history of literature devours everything."[30] In the contentious stanza of the original poem "For Jan Polkowski," we can discern the influence of O'Hara's concept of art as a process in which anything can come out. The much-debated stanza reads:

Instead of saying: I have a toothache, I'm
hungry, I'm lonely, both of us, four of
us, our whole street—they say quietly: Wanda
Wasilewska, Cyprian Kamil Norwid,
Józef Piłsudski, the Ukraine, Lithuania,
Thomas Mann, the Bible, and at the end a little something
in Yiddish.[31]

Such a stanza came under attack and was labeled as "O'Harism" not because of a stylistic similarity but because of its polemical assertion of everyday experiences (a toothache, hunger) in opposition to "important" names (such as Wanda Wasilewska, a prime representative of officially sanctioned authors under socialism). Świetlicki stands in true opposition to the tradition represented by Miłosz and, as we can see in his work taken as a whole, in opposition to social bonds in general.[32] Additionally, in contrast to the "company of cold skulls" at the end of Zbigniew Herbert's poem "The Envoy of Mr. Cogito," Świetlicki wishes to reject such important names, such striving to be situated within history.

While it is tempting to draw one-to-one correlations between the work of Frank O'Hara and the Polish poets who, for better or worse, are now historically associated with him, Świetlicki more than anyone proves that such an attempt would be ill informed. Quite in contrast to Świetlicki's circumspect attitude toward social bonds, O'Hara seems to long for a world in which poetry is no longer even necessary in the face of direct relationships. His poems are riddled with references to his friends by name, as in "The Day Lady Died": "in the golden griffin I get a little Verlaine / for Patsy with drawings by Bonnard . . . // and for Mike I just stroll into the park lane / Liquor Store and ask for a bottle of Strega."[33] Or, as in "Why I Am Not a Painter": "Mike Goldberg / is starting a painting. I drop in. / "Sit down and have a drink" he / says. I drink; we drink."[34] The insistence on directly experiencing relationships rather than writing a poem about experience is integral to his mock movement "Personism":

> It was founded by me after lunch with LeRoi Jones on August 27, 1959, a day in which I was in love with someone (not Roi, by the way, a blond). I went back to work and wrote a poem for this person. While I was writing it I was realizing that if I wanted to I could use the telephone instead of writing the poem, and so Personism was born.[35]

Underneath the energy and manic quality with which O'Hara consumed his subjects is his desire for friendship, quite literally "to the point where it was almost impossible for anyone to see him alone—there were so many people whose love demanded attention."[36] The picture of an oft black-hooded Świetlicki withdrawn in a corner produces quite the opposite impression.

The presentation of the younger generation of Polish poets in English translation outside Poland is, at this point, limited to a handful of anthologies, published in both the United States and England. For the most part, the editors of these anthologies historicize the poetry in terms of its connection to the New York school and Frank O'Hara in particular—a tendency, seen also in reviews and criticism in English, that is perhaps inevitable when trying to understand a tradition outside one's own. However, such an emphasis easily leads to the sense that contemporary Polish poets are simply derivative, using O'Hara's manner without substance. And further, why should American readers bother when they can read O'Hara in the original for themselves? First, it behooves American critics to recognize that there are plenty of poets who do not belong to the "O'Harist" moment who are worth translating and reading: Marzanna Bogumiła Kielar, for example, one of the few women often included in such anthologies; or Tomasz Różycki, a poet who clearly draws influence from Miłosz, which certainly sounds different from the rejection of tradition seen in the poets associated with O'Hara. Second, those Polish poets who do share a similar poetic parentage with their Western counterparts provide a parallel and illuminating—not a reductive—understanding of the American tradition; they also can help revise the Western canon of Polish poetry as established in the 1960s. And finally, the Polish poetry of the younger generation exists in and interacts with their own tradition as well, regardless of their supposed rejection of that tradition. What Czesław Miłosz wrote in his introduction to *Postwar Polish Poetry* is also applicable here, that "every poetic current is embedded in local traditions even if it absorbs a great deal from abroad."[37] Precisely through translation, poets are able to reject one tradition by adopting another foreign tradition and transferring the aesthetic value they find there. Assessing such influence can provide a fruitful understanding of how writers define themselves through opposition, through being a foreigner in a foreign land, either literally or through printed words on a piece of paper.

Notes

1. Miłosz, *Postwar Polish Poetry*, xii.
2. Ibid., xi.
3. Vendler, in Barańczak and Cavanagh, xx.
4. Ward, 8.
5. Perloff, 192–94.
6. Ward, 9.
7. In contrast, a book of Ashbery's poetry in Polish translation didn't appear until seven years later.
8. The name can be translated as something like "exercise book" or "rough draft." The periodical started in 1987.
9. Although stylistically very different from O'Hara's, Polish poet Miron Białoszewski's poetry similarly highlighted simple objects and personal events previously outside the scope of poetry. His language is unpolished and colloquial, and he "plays with language, not it would seem, with the positive aim of renewing the poetic medium, but out of an abiding lack of faith in the received literary language." Levine in Białoszewski, *A Memoir of the Warsaw Uprising*, 2.
10. O'Hara, *Standing Still*, 111. He also says that "forced feeding leads to excessive thinness."
11. Barańczak and Cavanagh, 2.
12. Bartczak, 82.
13. Koehler, 280.
14. Świetlicki, "Koehlerism," 284.
15. Mengham, 11.
16. Perloff, xxxi.
17. Gooch, 423.
18. O'Hara, *Collected Poems*, 14.
19. Ward, 40.
20. This aspect is also present in the poetry of Miron Białoszewski, so the possibility of his influence cannot be excluded. See also note 9 above.
21. Bartczak, 88.

22. Baran, 123.
23. Ibid., 125.
24. Bartczak, 88.
25. Herbert, 94, 96.
26. Ward, 60.
27. O'Hara, *Standing Still*.
28. Podsiadło, "Vanitas," 275.
29. Podsiadło, "Nietzsche."
30. "Historia literatury wchłania wszystko." Świetlicki, "Poems," 279.
31. Ibid., 278. Świetlicki, "Dla Jana Polkowskiego."
32. Bartczak, 85.
33. O'Hara, *Collected Poems*, 325.
34. Ibid, 261.
35. O'Hara, *Standing Still*, 111.
36. Ashbery, Introduction, x.
37. Miłosz, *Postwar Polish Poetry*, xiii.

Bibliography

Abraham, Nicolas, and Maria Torok. *The Wolf Man's Magic Word: A Cryptonymy*. Translated by Nicolas Rand. Minneapolis: University of Minnesota Press, 1986.

———. *The Shell and the Kernel*. Edited and translated by Nicolas T. Rand. Chicago: University of Chicago Press, 1994.

Adams, Hazard, and Leroy Searle, eds. *Critical Theory since 1965*. Tallahassee: University Press of Florida, 1986.

Agamben, Giorgio. *Homo Sacer: Sovereign Power and Bare Life*. Trans lated by Daniel Heller-Roazen. Stanford: Stanford University Press, 1998.

———. *Remnants of Auschwitz: The Witness and the Archive*. Translated by Daniel Heller-Roazen. New York: Zone Books, 2002.

Allen, Paul. *Katyn: The Untold Story of Stalin's Polish Massacre*. New York: Macmillan, 1991.

Anderman, Janusz. *Choroba więzienna: Scenariusz filmowy*. Warsaw: Pomost, 1992.

Anderson, Benedict. *Imagined Communities: Reflections on the Origin and Spread of Nationalism*. New York: Verso, 1991.

Andrzejewski, Jerzy. *Miazga*. Warsaw: Nowa, 1979.

Ansky, S. *The Dybbuk and Other Writings*. Translated by Golda Werman. New York: Schocken Books, 1992.

Arendt, Hannah. *The Origins of Totalitarianism*. San Diego: Harcourt, 1985.

Ariès, Philippe. *The Hour of Our Death*. Translated by Helen Weaver. New York: Alfred A. Knopf, 1981.

Ash, Timothy Garton. *The Polish Revolution: Solidarność*. New York: Scribner, 1983.

———. *The Uses of Adversity: Essays on the Fate of Central Europe*. London: Penguin Books, 1989.

Ashbery, John. Introduction to *The Collected Poems of Frank O'Hara*, edited by Donald Allen, vii–xi. Berkeley: University of California Press, 1995.

Ashcroft, Bill, Gareth Griffiths, and Helen Tiffin, eds. *The Empire Writes Back: Theory and Practice in Post-Colonial Literatures*. London: Routledge, 1989.

Assmann, Aleida. Introduction to *Erinnerungsräume: Formen und Wandlungen des Gedächtnisses*. Munich: C. H. Beck, 1999.

Assmann, Aleida, and Ute Frevert. *Geschichtsvergessenheit: Geschichtsversessenheit vom Umgang mit deutschen Vergangenheiten nach 1945*. Stuttgart: Deutsche Verlags-Anstalt, 1999.

Assmann, Jan. *Das kulturelle Gedächtnis: Schrift, Erinnerung und politische Identität in frühen Hochkulturen*. Munich: C. H. Beck, 1992.

Assmann, Jan, and Tonio Hölscher, eds. *Kultur und Gedächtnis*. Frankfurt am Main: Suhrkamp, 1988.

Bablet, Denis. "The Second Return of Ulysses: 'I Shall Never Return.'" In *Theatre Cricot 2: Information Guide, 1987–1988*, edited by Anna Halczak, 151–60. Cracow: Cricoteka, 1989.

BIBLIOGRAPHY

Bagłajewski, Arkadiusz. "Miasto—palimpsest." In *Miejsce rzeczywiste, miejsce wyobrażone: Studia nad kategorią miejsca w przestrzeni kultury*, edited by Małgorzata Kitowska-Łysiak and Elżbieta Wolicka, 317–38. Lublin: TN KUL, 1999.

Bakhtin, Mikhail. *Problems of Dostoevsky's Poetics*. Edited and translated by Caryl Emerson. Minneapolis: University of Minnesota Press, 1984.

———. *Speech Genres and Other Late Essays*. Edited by Caryl Emerson and Michael Holquist. Translated by Vern W. McGee. Austin: University of Texas Press, 1986.

———. *The Dialogic Imagination*. Austin: University of Texas Press, 1987.

Baldick, Chris. *The Concise Oxford Dictionary of Literary Terms*. Oxford: Oxford University Press, 1990.

Baltyn, Hanna. "Siedem grzechów głównych, czyli SALIGIA naszej krytyki." *Teatr*, no. 10 (2006): 69–72.

Baniewicz, Elżbieta. *Lata tłuste czy chude?: szkice o teatrze 1990–2000*. Warsaw: Errata, 2000.

———. "Nie opowiadaj mi swojej historii." *Rzeczpospolita,* no. 284, October 12, 2003, 10.

———. "Republika spłyciarzy." *Dziennik*, no. 153, July 3, 2007: http://www.e-teatr.pl/pl/artykuly/41321.html.

Baran, Marcin. "Mantras, Hours." Translated by Dariusz Trześniowski. In *Carnivorous Boy, Carnivorous Bird: Poetry from Poland*, edited by Anna Skucińska and Elżbieta Wójcik-Leese, 124–25. Brookline, MA: Zephyr Press, 2004.

Barańczak, Stanisław. *Język poetycki Mirona Białoszewskiego*. Wrocław: Ossolineum, 1974.

———. "Rzeczywistość Białoszewskiego." In *Pisanie Białoszewskiego*, edited by Michał Głowiński and Zdzisław Łapiński, 8–22. Warsaw: IBL, 1993.

Barańczak, Stanisław, and Clare Cavanagh, eds. *Spoiling Cannibals' Fun: Polish Poetry of the Last Two Decades of Communist Rule*. Evanston, IL: Northwestern University Press. 1992.

Barrell, John. *The Spirit of Despotism: Invasions of Privacy in the 1790s*. Oxford: Oxford University Press, 2006.

Barry, Peter, ed. *Issues in Contemporary Critical Theory: A Casebook*. Basingstoke: Macmillan, 1987.

Bartczak, Kacper. "The Hazards and Hopes of New Polish Poetry." *Lyric Poetry Review* 8 (2005): 82–95.

Barthes, Roland. *Camera Lucida: Reflections on Photography*. Translated by Richard Howard. New York: Hill and Wang, 1981.

Bartoszyński, Kazimierz. "The Ontology of Objects in Ingarden's Aesthetics." In *Man within His Life-World: Contributions to Phenomenology by Scholars from East-Central Europe*, edited by Anna-Teresa Tymieniecka, 369–93. Dordrecht: Kluwer, 1989.

Baudrillard, Jean. *Revenge of the Crystal: Selected Writings on the Modern Object and its Destiny 1968–1983*. Edited and translated by Paul Foss and Julian Pefanis. London: Pluto Press in association with the Power Institute of Fine Arts, University of Sydney, 1999.

———. *Selected Writings*. Edited by Mark Poster. Stanford: Stanford University Press, 2001.

———. *The Intelligence of Evil or the Lucidity Pact*. Translated by Chris Turner. New York: Berg, 2005.

———. *Pakt jasności: O inteligencji zła*. Translated by Sławomir Królak. Warsaw: Sic!, 2005.

Bauer, Roger. "Comparatistes sans Comparatisme." In *Comparative Literary History as Discourse: In Honour of Anna Balakian*, edited by Mario J. Valdés, Daniel Javitch, and A. Owen Aldridge, 41–47. Bern: Peter Lang, 1992.

Bauer, Yehuda. "Human Fat Soap." *Jerusalem Post*, May 29, 1990, 4.

Bauman, Zygmunt. *Liquid Modernity*. Malden, MA: Polity, 2000.

———. *Community. Seeking Safety in an Insecure World*. Malden, MA: Polity, 2001.

———. *Liquid Love*. Malden, MA: Polity, 2003.

———. *Consuming Life*. Malden, MA: Polity, 2007.

Benjamin, Walter. *The Arcades Project*. Translated by Howard Eiland and Kevin McLaughlin. Cambridge, MA: Belknap Press of Harvard University Press, 2002.

———. *The Writer of Modern Life: Essays on Charles Baudelaire*. Edited by Michael W. Jennings. Translated by Howard Eiland et al. Cambridge, MA: Belknap Press of Harvard University Press, 2006.

Berghahn, Volker R. "Germans and Poles, 1871–1945." In *Germany and Eastern Europe: Cultural Identities and Cultural Differences*, Yearbook of European Studies 13, edited by Keith Bullivant, Geoffrey J. Giles, and Walter Pape, 15–36. Amsterdam: Rodopi, 1999.

Berman, Russell A. *Enlightenment or Empire: Colonial Discourse in German Culture*. Lincoln: University of Nebraska Press, 1998.

Bernheimer, Charles, ed. *Comparative Literature in the Age of Multiculturalism*. Baltimore: Johns Hopkins University Press, 1995.

Bernstein, Michael André. *Foregone Conclusions: Against Apocalyptic History*. Berkeley: University of California Press, 1994.

Berressem, Hanjo. "The Laws of Deviation: Physical and Psychic Aberrations in the Novels of Witold Gombrowicz." In *Gombrowicz's Grimaces: Modernism, Gender, Nationality*, edited by Ewa Płonowska Ziarek, 89–134. Albany: SUNY Press, 1998.

———. *Lines of Desire: Reading Gombrowicz's Fiction with Lacan*. Evanston, IL: Northwestern University Press, 1998.

Bhabha, Homi. "Dissemination: Time, Narrative, and the Origins of the Modern Nation." In *Nation and Narration*, edited by Homi Bhabha, 291–320.

London: Routledge, 1990.
———. *The Location of Culture*. London: Routledge, 1994.
Białoszewski, Miron. *A Memoir of the Warsaw Uprising*. Edited and translated by Madeline Levine. Ann Arbor, MI: Ardis, 1977.
———. *Utwory zebrane*. 10 vols. Warsaw: PIW, 1987–2000.
———. "Listy do Eumenid." *Teksty Drugie*, no. 6 (1991): 83–136.
Bielik-Robson, Agata. "'*Solidarność'* uliczna – elementarz tożsamości" In *Lekcja Sierpnia: Dziedzictwo 'Solidarności' po dwudziestu latach*, edited by Dariusz Gawin, 124–41. Warsaw: IFiS PAN, 2002.
Bieńczyk, Marek. "Do Europy tak, ale razem z naszymi umarłymi [Janion, Maria]." *Gazeta Wyborcza*, February 7, 2001, http://wyborcza.pl/1,75517,130610.html.
Bieńczyk, Marek, and Dorota Siwicka, eds. *Nasze pojedynki o romantyzm*. Warsaw: IBL, 1995.
Bilczewski, Tomasz. "Hermeneutyczny wymiar komparatystyki literackiej." *Ruch Literacki* 6 (2003): 575–87.
Bilu, Yoram. "Dybbuk Possession and Mechanisms of Internalization and Externalization: A Case Study." In *Projection, Identification, Projective Identification*, edited by Joseph Sandler, 163–78. Madison, CT: International Universities Press, 1987.
Blanchot, Maurice. *The Space of Literature*. Translated by Ann Smock. Lincoln: University of Nebraska Press, 1982.
———. *The Infinite Conversation*. Theory and History of Literature 82. Translated and foreword by Susan Hanson. Minneapolis: University of Minnesota Press, 1993.
Blanke, Richard. *Prussian Poland in the German Empire (1871–1900)*. New York: Columbia University Press, 1981.
Bloom, Harold. *The Western Canon: The Books and School of the Ages*. New York: Harcourt Brace, 1994.
Błoński, Jan. "Szkic portretu poety współczesnego." In *Poeci i inni*, 221–64. Cracow: Wydawnictwo Literackie, 1956.
———. *Romans z tekstem*. Cracow: Wydawnictwo Literackie, 1981.
———. *Forma, śmiech i rzeczy ostateczne*. Cracow: Znak, 1994.
———. *Wszystkie sztuki Sławomira Mrożka*. Cracow: Wydawnictwo Literackie, 2002.
Błoński, Jan, and Sławomir Mrożek. *Listy*. Cracow: Wydawnictwo Literackie, 2004.
Bocheński, Jacek. *Stan po zapaści*. Warsaw: Nowa, 1987.
Bogucka, Maria. *The Lost World of the "Sarmatians": Custom as the Regulator of Polish Social Life in Early Modern Times*. Warsaw: Polish Academy of Sciences. Institute of History, 1996.
Bojtár, Endre. *Slavic Structuralism*. Amsterdam: John Benjamins, 1985.
Bouissac, Paul, ed. *Encyclopedia of Semiotics*. Oxford: Oxford University Press, 1998.

Brandys, Kazimierz. *Nierzeczywistość*. Warsaw: Nowa, 1977.
———. *A Question of Reality*. Translated by Isabel Barzun. New York: Charles Scribner's Sons, 1980.
Bratny, Roman. *Rok w trumnie*. Warsaw: Krajowa Agencja Wydawnicza, 1984.
Braun, Kazimierz. *A Concise History of the Polish Theater*. Lewiston, NY: Edwin Mellen Press, 2003.
Brešan, Ivo. "Przedstawienie *Hamleta* we wsi Głucha Dolna." Translated by Stanisław Kaszyński. In *Antologia współczesnego dramatu jugosłowiańskiego*, vol. 1, edited by Ognjen Lakićević, 37–111. Łódź: Wydawnictwo Łódzkie, 1988.
Brill, Susan B. *Wittgenstein and Critical Theory: Beyond Postmodern Criticism and toward Descriptive Investigations*. Athens: Ohio University Press, 1995.
Buczyńska-Garewicz, Hanna. *Miejsca, strony, okolice: Przyczynek do fenomenologii przestrzeni*. Cracow: Universitas, 2006.
Burkot, Stanisław. *Miron Białoszewski*. Warsaw: Wydawnictwa Szkolne i Pedagogiczne, 1992.
Burska, Lidia. "Zrozumieć brutalistów." *Gazeta Wyborcza*, March 1, 2003. http://www.teatry.art.pl/!felietony/zrozumiecb.htm.
Burzyńska, Anna. "Ciało w bibliotece." *Teksty Drugie*, no. 6 (2002): 18–26.
Butler, Judith. *Gender Trouble: Feminism and the Subversion of Identity*. London: Routledge, 1990.
Byron, George Gordon, Lord. *The Poems and Plays*. Vol. 2. Edited by William Peterfield Trent. London: Everyman, 1910.
Calinescu, Matei. *Five Faces of Modernity: Modernism, Avant-Garde, Decademce, Kitsche, Postmodernism*. Durham: Duke University Press, 1987.
Carlson, Marvin. *The Haunted Stage: The Theatre as Memory Machine*. Ann Arbor: University of Michigan Press, 2001.
———. *Performance: A Critical Introduction*. New York: Routledge, 2004.
Carnaham, Heather. "Eye, Head and Hand Coordination during Manual Aiming." In *Vision and Motor Control*, edited by Luc Proteau and Digby Elliott, 179–96. Amsterdam: Elsevier Science, 1992.
Carrier, Peter. "Places, Politics and the Archiving of Contemporary Memory in Pierre Nora's *Les Lieux de mémoire*." In *Memory and Methodology*, edited by Susannah Radstone, 37–58. Oxford: Berg, 2000.
Casanova, Pascal. *The World Republic of Letters*. Translated by Malcolm B. DeBevoise. Cambridge, MA: Harvard University Press, 2004.
Cassam, Quassim. "Introspection and Bodily Self-Ascription." In *The Body and the Self*, edited by Jose Luis Bermudez, Anthony Marcel, and Naomi Eilan, 311–36. Cambridge, MA: MIT Press, 1995.
———. Self and World. Oxford: Clarendon Press, 1997.
———. "Representing Bodies." In *The Philosophy of Body*, edited by Michael Proudfoot, 1–20. Oxford: Blackwell, 2003.

Cataluccio, Francesco M. *Niedojrzałość: choroba naszych czasów*. Translated by Stanisław Kasprzysiak. Cracow: Znak, 2006.

Cavanagh, Claire. "Postkolonialna Polska: Biała plama na mapie współczesnej teorii." *Teksty Drugie*, no. 2/3 (2003): 60–72.

Certeau, Michel de. *The Practice of Everyday Life*. Translated by Steven Rendell. Berkeley: University of California Press, 1988.

Chajes, Jeffrey Howard. *Between Worlds: Dybbuks, Exorcists, and Early Modern Judaism*. Philadelphia: University of Pennsylvania Press, 2003.

Chalupecký, Jindřich. *Expresionisté: Richard Weiner, Jakub Deml, Ladislav Klíma, Podivný Hašek*. Prague: Torst, 1992.

Chambers, Iain. *Migrancy, Culture, Identity*. London: Routledge, 1994.

Chandler, Frank W. "Comparative Literature: Is It Dead?" *Books Abroad: An International Library Quarterly* 10 (1936): 133–36.

Childers, Joseph, and Gary Hentzi, eds. *The Columbia Dictionary of Modern Literary and Cultural Criticism*. New York: Columbia University Press, 1995.

Childs, Peter, and Roger Fowler, eds. *The Routledge Dictionary of Literary Terms*. London: Routledge, 2006.

Chwin, Stefan. *Death in Danzig*. Translated by Philip Boehm. Orlando: Harcourt, 2004.

Chwin, Stefan, and Stanisław Rosiek. *Bez autorytetu*. Gdańsk: Wydawnictwo Morskie, 1981.

Cicero. *On Duties*. Translated and edited by Miriam Griffin and Margaret Atkins. Cambridge: Cambridge University Press, 1991.

Cichocki, Marek. *Władza i pamięć*. Cracow: Ośrodek Myśli Politycznej, Wyższa Szkoła Europejska im. Księdza Józefa Tischnera, 2005.

Ciechowicz, Jan. *Sam na scenie: Teatr jednoosobowy w Polsce. Z dziejów form dramatyczno-teatralnych*. Wrocław: Zakład Narodowy im. Ossolińskich, 1984.

Cienski, Jan. "Modern Poland Carves New Identity." *Financial Times* (London), April 20, 2004.

Cieśla-Korytowska, Maria. *"Dziady" Adama Mickiewicza*. Warsaw: Wydawnictwa Szkolne i Pedagogiczne, 1995.

———. Introduction to *Dziady*, by Adam Mickiewicz, 7–88. Cracow: Universitas, 1998.

———. *O Mickiewiczu i Słowackim*. Cracow: Universitas, 1999.

Ciolkowski, Laura E. "Navigating the Wide Sargasso Sea: Colonial History, English Fiction, and British Empire." *Twentieth Century Literature* 43, no. 3 (Autumn 1997): 339–59.

Clifford, James. "Traveling Cultures." In *Cultural Studies*, edited by Lawrence Grossberg, Cary Nelson, and Paula A. Treichler, 96–111. New York: Routledge, 1992.

———. *Routes: Travel and Translation in the Late Twentieth Century*. Cambridge, MA: Harvard University Press, 1997.

Cohen, Ralph, ed. *New Directions in Literary History*. Baltimore: Johns Hopkins University Press, 1974.

Coleman, Peter. *The Liberal Conspiracy: The Congress of Cultural Freedom and the Struggle for the Mind of Postwar Europe*. New York: Free Press, 1989.

Conrad, Joseph. *Letters of Joseph Conrad to Marguerite Poradowska, 1890–1920*. Translated by John A. Gee and Paul J. Sturm. New Haven: Yale University Press, 1940.

———. *Notes on Life and Letters*. London: Dent, 1949.

———. *A Personal Record*. London: Dent, 1949.

———. *Youth and Gaspar Ruiz*. London: Dent, 1951.

———. "Heart of Darkness." In *Joseph Conrad: Heart of Darkness, An Authoritative Text. Backgrounds and Sources. Criticism*, 2nd ed., edited by Robert Kimbrough, 3–79. New York: Norton, 1971.

———. *The Nigger of the 'Narcissus': A Tale of the Sea*. London: Pan Books, 1976.

Crinson, Mark. "*Urban Memory—An Introduction." In Urban Memory: History and Amnesia in the Modern City*, edited by Mark Crinson, xi–xx. London: Routledge, 2005.

Czapliński, Przemysław. *Ślady przełomu: o prozie polskiej 1976–1996*. Cracow: Wydawnictwo Literackie, 1997.

———. *Literatura polska, 1976–1998: przewodnik po prozie i poezji*. Cracow: Wydawnictwo Literackie, 1999.

———. *Polska do wymiany: późna nowoczesność i nasze wielkie narracje*. Warsaw: W.A.B., 2009.

Cywiński, Bohdan. *Rodowody niepokornych*. Paris: Editions Spotkania, 1985.

Damrosch, David. *What Is World Literature?* Princeton: Princeton University Press, 2003.

Darnton, Robert. *The Great Cat Massacre and Other Episodes in French Cultural History*. New York: Basic Books, 1984.

Davis, Jolanta. "'I did not make up any of this': Nalkowska, Medalions, and the Main Commission for the Investigation of German Crimes in Poland." Unpublished manuscript.

Davies, Norman. *Heart of Europe: A Short History of Poland*. New York: Oxford University Press, 1986.

———. *God's Playground: A History of Poland*. Rev. ed. New York: Columbia University Press, 2005.

Deleuze, Gilles. *Essays Critical and Clinical*. London: Verso, 1998.

———. *Difference and Repetition*. Translated by Paul Patton. London: Continuum, 2001.

———. *Pure Immanence: Essays on A Life*. New York: Zone Books, 2001.

Deleuze, Gilles, and Félix Guattari. *Capitalism and Schizophrenia*. Translated by Robert Hurley, Mark Seem, and Helen R. Lane. New York: Viking Press, 1977–87.

Derrida, Jacques. "Foreword: The Anglish Words of Nicolas Abraham and Maria Torok." In *The Wolf Man's Magic Word: A Cryptonimy*. Theory and History of Literature 37, xi–xlviii. Translated by Barbara Johnson. Minneapolis: University of Minnesota Press, 1986.

———. *On Touching: Jean-Luc Nancy*. Translated by Christine Irizarry. Stanford: Stanford University Press, 2005.

Dilman, Ilham. *Wittgenstein's Copernican Revolution: The Question of Linguistic Idealism*. Houndmills, Basingstoke, Hampshire: Palgrave, 2002.

Dimock, Wai Chee. "Literature for the Planet." *PMLA* 116, no. 1 (Winter 2001): 173–88.

Domański, Henryk. *Polska klasa średnia*. Wrocław: Wydawnictwo Universytetu Wrocławskiego, 2002.

Domański, Henryk, Andrzej Rychard, Paweł Śpiewak, eds. *Polska jedna czy wiele*? Warsaw: TRIO, 2005.

Dopart, Bogusław, ed. *"Dziady" Adama Mickiewicza: Poemat—adaptacje—tradycje*. Cracow: Universitas, 1999.

———. *Romantyzm polski: Pluralizm prądów i synkretyzm dzieła*. Cracow: Ksiegarnia Akademicka, 1999.

———. *Poemat profetyczny: O 'Dziadach' drezdeńskich Adama Mickiewicza*. Cracow: Księgarnia Akademicka, 2002.

Dorosz, Beata. "New York Mysteries of the Life and Death of Jan Lechoń." *Polish Review*, no. 2 (2004): 767–90.

Döbler, Katharina. "Bekannte Romane, alte Gefühle." *Die Zeit*, September 22, 2005.

Drewniak, Łukasz. "To kryzys krytyki, nie teatru." *Dziennik*, no. 154, July 4, 2007. http://www.teatry.art.pl/!felietony/tkkn.htm.

Drewnowski, Tadeusz. "Czarodziejski brzeg." *Europa*, November 10, 2004, 14.

Dudek, Antoni. *Pierwsze lata III Rzeczypospolitej 1989–2001*. Cracow: Arcana, 2002.

———. *Historia polityczna Polski 1989–2005*. Cracow: Arcana, 2007.

Duniec Krystyna, and Joanna Krakowska. "W stronę teatru lewicowo-feministycznego?" *Res Publica Nowa* 2 (February 2006). http://www.e-teatr.pl/pl/artykuly/24329.html.

Dziadek, Adam. "Wiersze, historia i rdza." *Arkusz* 9 (2001): 8-9.

Dziekanowski, Czesław. *Frutti di mare*. Warsaw: Iskry, 1990.

Dziemidok, Bohdan, and Peter McCormick, eds. *On the Aesthetics of Roman Ingarden: Interpretations and Assessments*. Dordrecht: Kluwer, 1989.

Dziewulska, Małgorzata. "Rzeczywistość się buntuje." *Tygodnik Powszechny*, no. 9 (March 2, 2003). http://www.tygodnik.com.pl/ numer/ 279909/ dziewulska.html.

Eagleton, Terry. *Literary Theory: An Introduction*. Minneapolis: University of Minnesota Press, 1996.

Edwards, Henry Sutherland. *The Polish Captivity: An Account of the Present Position of the Poles in the Kingdom of Poland, and in the Polish Provinces of Austria, Prussia, and Russia*. Vol. 1. London: Wm. H. Allen, 1863.
Eliot, T. S. *Collected Poems, 1909–1962*. New York: Harcourt Brace Jovanovich, 1991.
Emerson, Caryl. "Answering for Central and Eastern Europe." In *Comparative Literature in an Age of Globalization*, edited by Haun Saussy, 203–11. Baltimore: Johns Hopkins University Press, 2006.
Erlich, Victor. *Russian Formalism: History—Doctrine*. New Haven: Yale University Press, 1954.
Eschstruth, Nataly, Baroness von. *Polish Blood: A Romance*. Translated by Cora Louise Turner. New York: J. B. Alden, 1889.
Esslin, Martin. *The Theatre of the Absurd*. Garden City, NY: Doubleday, 1961
Essmanowski, Stefan. "Dialogi akademickie: Rozmowa z Zofią Nałkowską." *Pion* 10 (1934): 3.
Etiemble, René. *Comparaison n'est pas raison: La crise de la littérature comparée*. Paris: Gallimard, 1963.
Falk, Eugene H. *The Poetics of Roman Ingarden*. Chapel Hill: University of North Carolina Press, 1981.
Fanon, Frantz. *Black Skin, White Masks*. London: Pluto, 1986.
———. *The Wretched of the Earth*. Translated by Constance Farrington. Harmondsworth: Penguin, 1990.
Féral, Josette. "Performance and Theatricality: The Subject Demystified," translated by Terese Lyons. In *Theory of Drama and Performance*, edited by Féral et al. *Modern Drama* 25, no. 1 (March 1982): 170–81.
Ficowski, Jerzy. *Regiony wielkiej herezji i okolice: Bruno Schulz i jego mitologia*. Sejny: Pogranicze, 2002.
Fidelis, Małgorzata. "'Participation in the Creative Work of the Nation': Polish Women Intellectuals in the Cultural Construction of Female Gender Roles, 1864–1890." *Journal of Women's History* 13, no. 1 (2001): 108–25.
Fieguth, Rolf. *Verzweigungen: Zyklische und assoziative Kompositionsformen bei Adam Mickiewicz (1798–1855)*. Freiburg: Universitätsverlag, 1998.
Filipiak, Izabela. *Absolutna amnezja*. Poznań: Obserwator, 1995.
Fine, Ellen S. "Transmission of Memory: The Post-Holocaust Generation in the Diaspora." In *Breaking Crystal: Writing and Memory after Auschwitz*, edited by Efraim Sicher, 185–200. Urbana: University of Illinois Press, 1998.
Ford, Ford Madox. *Joseph Conrad: A Personal Remembrance*. New York: Ecco Press, 1989.
Foucault, Michel. *The History of Sexuality*. New York: Pantheon Books, 1978.
———. *Discipline and Punish: The Birth of the Prison*. Translated by Alan Sheridan. New York: Vintage, 1979.
———. *The Order of Things: An Archeology of the Human Sciences*. New York: Vintage, 1994.

Fraser, Nancy. "Rethinking Recognition." *New Left Review* 3 (2000): 107–20.
Frąckowiak-Wiegandtowa, Ewa. *Sztuka powieściopisarska Nałkowskiej (lata 1935–1954)*. Wrocław: PAN, 1975.
Freud, Sigmund. *The Standard Edition of the Complete Psychological Works of Sigmund Freud*. 24 vols. Edited and translated by James Strachey. London: Vintage, 2001.
Freytag, Gustav. *Soll und Haben*. Leipzig: Hirzel, 1859.
Friedlander, Saul. Introduction to *Probing the Limits of Representation: Nazism and the "Final Solution,"* edited by Saul Friedlander, 1–21. Cambridge, MA: Harvard University Press, 1992.
Friszke, Andrzej. "Głos solidarności." *Rzeczpospolita*, July 9/10, 2005.
Fukuyama, Francis. *The End of History and the Last Man*. New York: Free Press, 1992.
Galewicz, Włodzimierz, et al., eds. *Kunst und Ontologie: für Roman Ingarden zum 100. Geburtstag*. Amsterdam: Rodopi, 1994.
Gańczarczyk, Iga, and Grzegorz Niziołek, eds. *Gang bang, Komponenty, Nocny autobus*. Cracow: Narodowy Teatr Stary im. Heleny Modrzejewskiej, 2005.
Gawin, Dariusz. "Obecność sierpnia." *Znak* 543, no.8 (2000): 68–82.
Gaynesford, Maximilian de. "Corporeal Objects and the Interdependence of Perception and Action." In *The Philosophy of Body*, edited by Michael Proudfoot, 21–39. Oxford: Blackwell, 2003.
Gikandi, Simon. "Globalization and the Claims of Postcoloniality." *South Atlantic Quarterly* 100, no. 3 (Summer 2001): 627–58.
Gilloch, Graeme, and Jane Kilby. "Trauma and Memory in the City: From Auster to Austerlitz." In *Urban Memory: History and Amnesia in the Modern City*, edited by Mark Crinson, 1–22. London: Routledge, 2005.
Gilroy, Paul. *The Black Atlantic*. London: Verso, 1993.
———. *After Empire: Melancholia or Convivial Culture?* London: Routledge, 2004.
Girard, René. *Violence and the Sacred*. Baltimore: Johns Hopkins University Press, 1977.
Głowacki, Janusz. *Moc truchleje*. Warsaw: Puls, 1981.
Głowacki, Paweł. "Czekając na powrót opowieści." *Dziennik*, no. 170, July 20, 2007. http://www.e-teatr.pl/pl/artykuly/41911.html.
Głowiński, Michał. *Gry powieściowe: szkice z teorii i historii form narracyjnych*. Warsaw: Państwowe Wydawnictwo Naukowe, 1973.
———. "On Concretization." In *Roman Ingarden and Contemporary Polish Aesthetics: Essays*, edited by Piotr Graff and Sław Krzemień-Ojak, 33–45. Warsaw: Polish Scientific Publishers, 1975.
———. "Reading, Interpretation, Reception." *New Literary History* 11 (1979–80): 75–82.
———. "Niezwykłe zwykłe." Interview with Janusz Majcherek. *Teatr*, no. 5 (1993): 5–7.

———. "Nad *Castorpem*." *Przegląd Polityczny* 70 (2005): 65–68.
Gogol, Nikolai. *The Collected Tales of Nikolai Gogol*. Translated and annotated by Richard Pevear and Larissa Volokhonsky. New York: Pantheon Books, 1998.
———. *The Government Inspector*. Translated and adapted by Alistair Beaton. London: Oberon Books, 2005.
Goldberg, Stuart. "Konrad and Jacob: A Hypothetical Kabbalistic Subtext in Adam Mickiewicz's *Forefathers' Eve, Part III*." *Slavic and East European Journal* 45, no. 4 (Winter 2001): 695–715.
Gombrowicz, Rita. *Gombrowicz w Europie: Świadectwa i dokumenty 1963–1969*. Translated by Oskar Hedemann et al. Cracow: Wydawnictwo Literackie, 1993.
Gombrowicz, Witold. Letter to Martin Buber. Buenos Aires, July 25, 1951. Gombrowicz Archive, Beinecke Library, Yale University. Gen. MSS 515, series 1, box 2, item 51.
———. *A Kind of Testament*. Translated by Alastair Hamilton. London: Calder and Boyars, 1973.
———. *Dzieła*, 15 vols. Cracow: Wydawnictwo Literackie, 1986–96.
———. *Diary*. Edited by Jan Kott. Translated by Lillian Vallee. Evanston: Northwestern University Press, 1989.
———. *Trans-Atlantyk*. Translated by Carolyn French and Nina Karsov. Introduction by Stanisław Barańczak. New Haven: Yale University Press, 1994.
———. *Ferdydurke*. Translated by Danuta Borchardt. Foreword by Susan Sontag. New Haven: Yale University Press, 2000.
———. *Polish Memories*. Translated by Bill Johnston. New Haven: Yale University Press, 2004.
Gombrowicz, Witold, and Dominique de Roux, eds. *Rozmowy z Gombrowiczem*. Paris: Instytut Literacki, 1969.
Gooch, Brad. *City Poet: The Life and Times of Frank O'Hara*. New York: Knopf, 1993.
Gordon, Avery. *Ghostly Matters: Haunting and the Sociological Imagination*. Minneapolis: University of Minnesota Press, 1997.
Gosk, Hanna, and Bożena Karwowska, eds. *(Nie)obecność: Pominięcia i przemilczenia w narracjach XX wieku*. Warsaw: Elipsa, 2008.
Gossman, Lionel, and Mihai Spariosu, eds. *Building a Profession: Autobiographical Perspectives on the History of Comparative Literature in the United States*. Albany: SUNY Press, 1994.
Gowin, Jarosław. "Lekcja sierpnia," *Rzeczpospolita*, June 16, 2001.
Górski, Konrad. *Pogląd na świat młodego Mickiewicza (1815–1823)*. Warsaw: Kasa im. K. Mianowskiego, 1925.
Graff, Agnieszka. *Świat bez kobiet: Płeć w polskim życiu publicznym*. Warsaw: WAB, 2001.
Graff, Piotr, and Sław Krzemień-Ojak, eds. *Roman Ingarden and Contemporary Polish Aesthetics: Essays*. Warsaw: Polish Scientific Publishers, 1975.

Grądziel, Joanna. "Miron Białoszewski: Prawo smaku rzeczy nieobecnych." In *Literatura wobec niewyrażalnego*, edited by Włodzimierz Bolecki and Erazm Kuźma, 267–78. Warsaw: IBL, 1998.

Groden, Michael, and Martin Kreiswirth, eds. *The Johns Hopkins Guide to Literary Theory and Criticism*. Baltimore: Johns Hopkins University Press, 1994.

Grudzińska Gross, Irena. "Adam Mickiewicz: A European from Nowogródek." *East European Politics and Societies* 9, no. 2 (Spring 1995): 295–316.

Gruszczyński, Piotr. *Ojcobójcy: Młodsi zdolniejsi w teatrze polskim*. Warsaw: WAB, 2003.

———. "Nowi niezadowoleni." *Tygodnik Powszechny* 24 (January 1, 2006). http://www.e-teatr.pl/pl/artykuly/20192.html.

Grzegorczyk, Marzena. "Formed Lives, Formless Traditions: The Argentinean Legacy of Witold Gombrowicz." In *Gombrowicz's Grimaces: Modernism, Gender, Nationality*, edited by Ewa Płonowska Ziarek, 135–56. Albany: SUNY Press, 1998.

Gutorow, Jacek. "Światło między wersami." *Odra*, nos. 7–8 (2001): 115–16.

Halikowska-Smith, Teresa. "The Past as Palimpsest: The Gdańsk School of Writers in the 1980s and 1990s." *Sarmatian Review* 23, no. 1 (2003): 922–28.

Hall, Stuart. "The Question of Cultural Identity." In *Modernity: An Introduction to Modern Societies*, edited by Stuart Hall, David Held, Don Hubert, and Kenneth Thompson, 595–634. Oxford: Blackwell, 1996.

Hall, Stuart, and Paul du Gay, eds. *Questions of Cultural Identity*. London: Sage, 1996.

Hamm, Victor Michael. "The Ontology of the Literary Work of Art: Roman Ingarden's *Das literarische Kunstwerk*." In *The Critical Matrix*, edited by Paul R. Sullivan, 171–209. Washington, DC: Georgetown University Press, 1961.

Hapgood, Robert. Letter. *PMLA* 114, no. 2 (March 1999): 324–25.

Harkins, William E. "Slavic Formalist Theories in Literary Scholarship." *Word* 7, no. 2 (1951): 177–85.

Harris, Wendell V. *Dictionary of Concepts in Literary Criticism and Theory*. New York: Greenwood Press, 1992.

Hartman, Geoffrey H. "Public Memory and Modern Experience." *Yale Journal of Criticism* 6, no. 2 (Fall 1993): 239–47.

Hassner, Pierre. *Koniec pewników: Eseje o wojnie, pokoju i przemocy*. Translated by Maryna Ochab. Warsaw: Fundacja im. Batorego i Wydawnictwo Sic!, 2002.

Hašek, Jaroslav. *The Good Soldier Svejk and His Fortunes in the World War*. Translated by Cecil Parrott. New York: Penguin Books, 1985.

Havel, Vaclav. *Selected Plays, 1963–1983*. London: Faber and Faber, 1992.

———. *Selected Plays, 1984–1987*. London: Faber and Faber, 1994.

Hawthorn, Jeremy. *A Glossary of Contemporary Literary Theory*. London: Arnold, 1998.

Heaney, Seamus. *Opened Ground: Poems, 1966–1996*. London: Faber and Faber, 1998.

Hegel, Georg Wilhelm Friedrich. *The Philosophy of History*. Translated by John Sibree. New York: Dover, 1956.

Heidegger, Martin. *On the Way to Language*. Translated by Peter Hertz. New York: Harper & Row, 1971.

———. *Poetry, Language, Thought*. Translated by Albert Hofstadter. New York: Harper & Row, 1971.

———. *Being and Time*. Translated by John Macquarrie and Edward Robinson. New York: Harper & Row, 1975.

Herbert, Zbigniew. *Selected Poems*. Translated by John and Bogdana Carpenter, Czeslaw Miłosz, Peter Dale Scott. Cracow: Wydawnictwo Literackie, 2000.

Herling-Grudziński, Gustaw. "Dżuma w Neapolu. Relacja o stanie wyjątkowym." *Kultura*, no. 5 (1990): 22-39.

———. *Volcano and Miracle*. Translated by Ronald Stroan. New York: Viking, 1996.

Hetel, Dominika. "Próba dialogu religijnego—Wielka Improwizacja." In *Pejzaże kultury*, edited by Władysław Dynak and Marian Ursel, 180–89. Wrocław: Wydawnictwo Uniwersytetu Wrocławskiego, 2005.

Hirsch, Marianne. *Family Frames: Photography, Narrative and Postmemory*. Cambridge, MA: Harvard University Press, 1997.

Hnatiuk, Oleksandra. *Pożegnanie z imperium: Ukraińskie dyskusje o tożsamości*. Lublin: Maria Curie-Skłodowska University Press, 2003.

Hodgdon, Barbara. *The End Crowns All: Closure and Contradiction in Shakespeare's History*. Princeton: Princeton University Press, 1991.

Hoesel-Uhlig, Stefan. "Changing Fields: The Directions of Goethe's 'Weltliteratur.'" In *Debating World Literature*, edited by Christopher Prendergast, 26–53. London: Verso, 2004.

Holquist, Michael. "East European Criticism." *Comparative Literature* 43, no. 1 (1991): 60–71.

Holub, Robert. "Phenomenology." In *The Cambridge History of Literary Criticism*, vol. 8, edited by Raman Selden, 289–318. Cambridge: Cambridge University Press, 1995.

Holzer, Jerzy. *"Solidarność" 1980–1981. Geneza i historia*. Warsaw: Krąg, 1984.

Horubała, Andrzej. *Umoczeni*. Warsaw: Prószyński i S-ka, 2004.

Huelle, Paweł. *Who Was David Weiser?* Translated by Michael Kandel. New York: Harcourt Brace, 1992.

———. *Moving House: Stories*. Translated by Michael Kandel. New York: Harcourt Brace, 1995.

———. *Castorp*. Gdańsk: Słowo / obraz terytoria, 2004.

Hunter, James Davison. *Culture Wars: The Struggle to Define America*, New York: Basic Books, 1991.

———. *Before the Shooting Begins: Searching for Democracy in America's Culture War*. New York: Free Press, 1994.

———. *Is There a Culture War?: A Dialogue on Values and American Public Life*. Washington, DC: Brookings Institution Press, 2006.

Hurley, Susan L. *Consciousness in Action*. Cambridge, MA: Harvard University Press, 1998.

Hutman, Bill. "Nazis Never Made Human-Fat Soap." *Jerusalem Post*, April 24, 1990, 2.

Huyssen, Andreas. "Monument and Memory in a Postmodern Age." *Yale Journal of Criticism* 6, no.2 (Fall 1993): 249–61.

Ingarden, Roman. *Das literarische Kunstwerk, eine Untersuchung aus dem Grenzgebiet der Ontologie, Logik und Literaturwissenschaft*. Halle: M. Niemeyer, 1931.

———. *O poznawaniu dzieła literackiego*. Lwów: Ossolineum, 1937.

———. *Studia z estetyki*. 2 vols. Warsaw: PWN, 1957.

———. "The General Question of the Essence of Form and Content." *Journal of Philosophy* 7 (1960): 222–33.

———. "Artistic and Aesthetic Values." *British Journal of Aesthetics* 4 (1964): 198–213.

———. *Vom Erkennen des literarischen Kunstwerks*. Tübingen: Niemeyer, 1968.

———. "The Physicalistic Theory of Language and the World of Literature." *Yearbook of Comparative Criticism* 2 (1969): 80–98.

———. *The Cognition of the Literary Work of Art*. Translated by Ruth Ann Crowley and Kenneth R. Olson. Evanston: Northwestern University Press, 1973.

———. *The Literary Work of Art: An Investigation on the Borderlines of Ontology, Logic, and Theory of Literature. With an Appendix on the Functions of Language in the Theater*. Translated and with an introduction by George G. Grabowicz. Evanston: Northwestern University Press, 1973.

———. "On So-called 'Truth' in Literature." In *Aesthetics in Twentieth-Century Poland: Selected Essays*, edited by Jean G. Harrel and Alina Wierzbiańska, 164–204. Lewisburg, PA: Bucknell University Press, 1973.

———. "Psychologism and Psychology in Literary Scholarship." *New Literary History* 2 (1974): 215–23.

———. "Lectures on Aesthetics." In *Literary Studies in Poland—Roman Ingarden & the Problems of the Theatre*, edited by Hanna Dziechcińska, translated by Bogusław Lewandowski, 11:15–37. Wrocław: Zakład Narodowy im. Ossolińskich, 1983.

———. "On the Cognition of the Literary Work of Art." In *The Hermeneutics Reader: Texts of the German Tradition from the Enlightenment to the Present*, edited by Kurt Mueller-Vollmer, 187–213. New York: Continuum, 1985.

———. *Selected Papers in Aesthetics*. Edited by Peter J. McCormick. Washington, DC: Catholic University of America Press, 1985.

———. "Phenomenological Aesthetics: An Attempt at Defining Its Range." In *Critical Theory since 1965*, edited by Hazard Adams and Leroy Searle, 185–97. Tallahassee: University Press of Florida, 1986.

———. "Some Epistemological Problems in the Cognition of the Aesthetic Concretization of the Literary Work of Art." In *Twentieth-Century Literary Theory: A Reader*, edited by Ken M. Newton, 76–80. New York: St. Martin's Press, 1988.

Iser, Wolfgang. *Der implizite Leser: Kommunikationsformen des Romans von Bunyan bis Beckett*. Munich: W. Fink, 1972.

———. "The Reading Process: A Phenomenological Approach." *New Literary History* 2 (1972): 279–99.

———. *The Implied Reader: Patterns of Communication in Prose Fiction from Bunyan to Beckett*. Translated by Iser with David Henry Wilson. Baltimore: Johns Hopkins University Press, 1974.

———. *Der Akt des Lesens: Theorie ästhetischer Wirkung*. Munich: W. Fink, 1976.

———. *The Act of Reading: A Theory of Aesthetic Response*. Translated by Iser with David Henry Wilson. Baltimore: Johns Hopkins University Press, 1978.

———. "Interaction between Text and Reader." In *The Reader in the Text: Essays on Audience and Interpretation*, edited by Susan R. Suleiman and Inge Crosman, 106–19. Princeton: Princeton University Press, 1980.

———. "The Repertoire." In *Critical Theory since 1965*, edited by Hazard Adams and Leroy Searle, 360–80. Tallahassee: University Press of Florida, 1986.

———. *Prospecting: From Reader Response to Literary Anthropology*. Baltimore: Johns Hopkins University Press, 1989.

———. *The Fictive and the Imaginery: Charting Literary Anthropology*. Translated by David Henry Wilson. Baltimore: Johns Hopkins University Press, 1993.

———. *The Range of Interpretation*. New York: Columbia University Press, 2000.

Jackson, Leonard. *The Poverty of Structuralism: Literature and Structuralist Theory*. London: Longman, 1991.

James, Ian. *The Fragmentary Demand: An Introduction to the Philosophy of Jean-Luc Nancy*. Stanford: Stanford University Press, 2006.

Janion, Maria. *Projekt krytyki fantazmatycznej: szkice o egzystencjach ludzi i duchów*. Warsaw: PEN, 1991.

———. "Zmierzch paradygmatu." In *Czy będziesz wiedział, co przeżyłeś*, 5–24. Warsaw: Sic!, 1996.

———. *Tragizm, historia, prywatność*. Cracow: Universitas, 2000.

Jarzębski, Jerzy. *Gra w Gombrowicza*. Warsaw: PIW, 1982.

———. "Między kreacją a interpretacją." In *Gombrowicz filozof*, edited by Francesco M. Cataluccio and Jerzy Illg, 177–205. Cracow: Znak, 1991.
———. *W Polsce, czyli wszędzie: szkice o polskiej prozie współczesnej*. Warsaw: PEN, 1992.
———. "Metamorfozy kanonu." *Znak* 7, no. 470 (1994): 12–17.
———. *Apetyt na przemianę*. Cracow: Znak, 1997.
———. *Podglądanie Gombrowicza*. Cracow: Wydawnictwo Literackie, 2000.
Jaszewska, Dagmara. *Nasza niedojrzała kultura: Postmodernizm inspirowany Gombrowiczem*. Warsaw: Oficyna naukowa, 2002.
Jauss, Hans Robert. *Toward an Aesthetic of Reception*. Translated by Timothy Bahti. Minneapolis: University of Minnesota Press, 1982.
———. "The Theory of Reception: A Retrospective of Its Unrecognized Prehistory." In *Literary Theory Today*, edited by Peter Collier and Helga Geyer-Ryan, 53–73. Ithaca: Cornell University Press, 1990.
Jerzak, Katarzyna. "Defamation in Exile: Witold Gombrowicz and E. M. Cioran." In *Gombrowicz's Grimaces: Modernism, Gender, Nationality*, edited by Ewa Płonowska Ziarek, 177–209. Albany: SUNY Press, 1998.
Jędrychowski, Zbigniew. "Pastor i Nieznajomy, czyli *Dziady* w Kamieńcu Podolskim (1832)." *Notatnik Teatralny* 16–17 (1998): 251–68.
Jin-Yan, Zhang. "The New Criticism and Ingarden's Phenomenological Theory of Literature." In *Ingardeniana II*, edited by Hans Rudnick, 85–93. Dordrecht: Kluwer, 1990.
John Paul II. *Memory and Identity*. New York: Rizzoli, 2005.
Johnston, Bill. "Heteroglossia and Linguistic Nationalism: English Teaching in Post-1989 Poland." In *Over the Wall / After the Fall: Post-Communist Cultures through an East-West Gaze*, edited by Sibelan Forrester, Magdalena Zaborowska, and Elena Gapova, 126–45. Bloomington: Indiana University Press, 2004.
Jung, Werner. "Der ewige, naive Idealist. Verschmitztes Spiel mit Thomas Mann: Pawel Huelles eleganter Roman *Castorp*." *Frankfurter Rundschau*, August 2, 2005.
Kaczmarski, Jacek. *Autoportret z kanalią*. Warsaw: Wydawnictwo Wodnika, 1994.
Kadłubek, Wincenty, [Mistrz]. *Kronika polska / Magistri Vincentii Chronicon Polonorum*. Translated into Polish from the Latin and edited by Brygida Kürbis. Wrocław: Ossolineum, 1992.
Kallenbach, Józef. *Adam Mickiewicz*. 2 vols. Lwów: Wydawnictwo Zakładu Narodowego im. Ossolińskich, 1926.
Kant, Immanuel. *Perpetual Peace and Other Essays*. Translated and introduction by Ted Humphrey. Indianapolis: Hackett, 1983.
Kantor, Tadeusz. "I'll Never Come Back Here Again." Translated by Charles S. Kraszewski. Cracow: Cricoteka, unpublished manuscript, n.d.
———. "The Return of Odys. Partytura of a Play by Stanisław Wyspiański. Underground Theatre 1944." Translated by Andrzej Branny and Grażyna Branny. Cracow: Cricoteka, unpublished manuscript, n.d.

———. *A Journey through Other Spaces: Essays and Manifestos, 1944–1990.* Edited and translated by Michal Kobialka. Berkeley: University of California Press, 1993.

———. *The Return of Odysseus: The Clandestine Independent Theatre 1944.* Cracow: Cricoteka, 1994.

Kantor, Zdzisław. *Marian Kantor-Mirski (1884–1942).* Cracow: Teatr Mały and Ośrodek Dokumentacji Sztuki Tadeusza Kantora Cricoteka, 2004.

Kaplan, Alice, and Kristin Ross, eds. *Everyday Life.* Yale French Studies 73. New Haven: Yale University Press, 1987.

Karcz, Andrzej. *The Polish Formalist School and Russian Formalism.* Rochester: University of Rochester Press, 2002.

Karwowska, Bożena. "Kategoria wygnania w anglojęzycznych dyskursach krytycznoliterackich." In *Pisarz na emigracji: Mitologie, Style, Strategie Przetrwania,* edited by Hanna Gosk and Andrzej Stanisław Kowalczyk, 79–95. Warsaw: Elipsa, 2005.

———."Tożsamość postemigracyjna—przypadek (między innymi) Czesława Miłosza." *Przegląd Humanistyczny* 49, no. 4 (2005): 1–12.

Kater, Michael H. *Doctors under Hitler.* Chapel Hill: University of North Carolina Press, 1989.

Kermode, Frank. *The Sense of an Ending: Studies in the Theory of Fiction.* Oxford: Oxford University Press, 2000.

Kępiński, Antoni. *Psychopatie.* Cracow: Wydawnictwo Literackie, 2002.

Kirchner, Hanna, ed. *Miron: Wspomnienia o poecie.* Warsaw: Tenten, 1996.

Kisiel, Marian. *Świadectwa, znaki: głosy o poezji najnowszej.* Katowice: Śląsk, 1998.

Kleiner, Juliusz. *Mickiewicz.* 1934–48. 2 vols. Lublin: Towarzystwo Naukowe Katolickiego Uniwersytetu Lubelskiego, 1995.

Kłosiński, Krzysztof. "Imię Róży," *Pamiętnik Literacki* 1 (1999): 5–20.

———. *W stronę inności: Rozbiory i debaty.* Katowice: Silesian University Press, 2006.

Koehler, Krzysztof. "O'Harism." Translated by Bill Martin. *Chicago Review* 46, nos. 3 and 4 (2000): 280–81.

Komolka, Jan. *Ucieczka do nieba.* Warsaw: PIW, 1980.

Konwicki, Tadeusz. *Kompleks polski.* Warsaw: Nowa, 1977.

———. *Mała apokalipsa.* Warsaw: Nowa, 1979.

———. *A Minor Apocalypse.* Translated by Richard Lourie. New York: Farrar, Straus, Giroux, 1983.

———. *Rzeka podziemna, podziemne ptaki.* Warsaw: Krąg, 1984.

Kopaliński, Władysław. *Słownik mitów i tradycji kultury.* Warsaw: PWN, 1988.

Kopciński, Jacek. *Którędy do wyjścia? Szkice i rozmowy teatralne.* Warsaw: Errata, 2002.

———. *Nasłuchiwanie. Sztuki na głosy Zbigniewa Herberta.* Warsaw: Biblioteka "Więzi," 2008.

Kopp, Kristin. "Contesting Borders: German Colonial Discourse and the Polish Eastern Territories." Ph.D. diss., University of California–Berkeley, 2001.

———. "'Ich stehe jetzt hier als einer von den Eroberern': *Soll und Haben* als Kolonialroman." In *150 Jahre* Soll und Haben. *Studien zu Gustav Freytags kontroversem Roman*, edited by Florian Krobb, 225–37. Würzburg: Königshausen & Neumann, 2005.

Korłub. Jolanta. *Radom Odważny: Festiwal nowej dramaturgii*. Radom: Teatr Powszechny im. Jana Kochanowskiego w Radomiu, 2007.

Koropeckyj, Roman. *The Poetics of Revitalization: Adam Mickiewicz between Forefathers' Eve, Part 3 and Pan Tadeusz*. Boulder: East European Monographs, 2001.

Kowalczyk, Janusz R. "Tak zwane przekraczanie granic." *Rzeczpospolita*, October 11, 2003, 10.

Kowalska, Janina. *Pogranicze*. Paris: Instytut Literacki, 1980.

Kowalski, Sergiusz. *Krytyka solidarnościowego rozumu*. Warsaw: PEN, 1989.

Kowalski, Stanisław J. *Jan Lechoń jako redaktor i publicysta w okresie nowojorskim*. Lublin: Redakcja Wydawnictw Katolickiego Uniwersytetu Lubelskiego, 1996.

Krall, Hanna. *The Woman from Hamburg and Other True Stories*. Translated by Madeline G. Levine. New York: Other Press, 2005.

Krasiński, Zygmunt. *Nie-boska komedia*. Introduction by Maria Janion. Edited by Maria Grabowska. Wrocław: Zakład Narodowy im. Ossolińskich, 1965.

Krasnodębski, Zdzisław. "Niedokończony projekt," *Rzeczpospolita*, June 2, 2001.

———. *Demokracja peryferii*. Gdańsk: słowo/obraz terytoria, 2003.

———. "Democracy on the Periphery." *Sarmatian Review* 24, no.2 (April 2004): 1033–45.

———. *Drzemka rozsądnych: zebrane eseje i szkice*. Cracow: Ośrodek Myśli Politycznej, 2006.

Krasowski, Robert, and Maciej Nowicki, eds. *Idee z pierwszej ręki*. Warsaw: Axel Springer Polska, 2008.

Kridl, Manfred. "Russian Formalism." *American Bookman* 1 (1944): 19–30.

Kridl, Manfred, et al., eds. *Prace ofiarowane Kazimierzowi Wóycickiemu*. Wilno: Dom Książki Polskiej, 1937.

Kristeva, Julia. *Powers of Horror: An Essay on Abjection*. Translated by Leon S. Roudiez. New York: Columbia University Press, 1982.

———. *Black Sun: Depression and Melancholia*. Translated by Leon S. Roudiez. New York: Columbia University Press, 1989.

Kritzman, Lawrence D. "In Remembrance of Things French." Forward to *Rethinking the French Past: Realms of Memory*, vol. 1, edited by Pierre Nora, translated by Arthur Goldhammer, ix–xiv. New York: Columbia University Press, 1996.

Król, Marcin. *Liberalizm strachu czy liberalizm odwagi*. Cracow: Znak, 1996.

———. *Romantyzm—piekło i niebo Polaków*. Warsaw: Fundacja Res Publica, 1998.

———. *Patriotyzm przyszłości*. Warsaw: Rosner&Wspólnicy, 2004.

Kruks, Sonia. "Freedoms That Matter: Subjectivity and Situation in the Work of Beauvoir, Sartre, and Merleau-Ponty." In *Retrieving Experience: Subjectivity and Recognition in Feminist Politics*, 27–51. Ithaca: Cornell University Press, 2001.

Krzyżanowski, Julian. *Historia literatury polskiej: Alegoryzm—preromantyzm*. Warsaw: PIW, 1986.

Kuchinsky, Neil. "Human Fat Soap." *Jerusalem Post*, May 20, 1990, 4.

Kuczera-Chachulska, Bernadetta. "Uwagi o kształcie gatunkowym IV części *Dziadów*." *Teksty Drugie* 5 (1998): 5–29.

Kuczera-Chachulska, Bernadetta, and Maria Prussak, eds. *Rozmowy o "Dziadach*." Warsaw: Wydawnictwo Uniwersytetu Kardynała Stefana Wyszyńskiego, 2005.

Kuhn, Annette. "A Journey through Memory." In *Memory and Methodology*, edited by Susannah Radstone, 179–96. Oxford: Berg, 2000.

Kundera, Milan. *Slowness*. Translated by Linda Asher. New York: Harper Perennial, 1997.

———. "Die Weltliteratur." Translated by Linda Asher. *New Yorker*, January 8, 2007, 28–35.

Kurzke, Hermann. "Davos und Danzig: Castorps Jugend: Pawel Huelle ergänzt den *Zauberberg*." *Frankfurter Allgemeine Zeitung*, January 22, 2005.

Laclau, Ernesto. "Inclusion, Exclusion." Paper delivered at the University at Buffalo Humanities Institute Inaugural Conference, SUNY–Buffalo, October 28, 2005.

Lalande, André. *Vocabulaire technique et critique de la philosophie*. Paris: Presses Universitaires de France, 1968.

Lambert, Gregg. *The Non-Philosophy of Gilles Deleuze*. New York: Continuum, 2002.

Landsberg, Alison. *Prosthetic Memory: The Transformation of American Remembrance in the Age of Mass Culture*. New York: Columbia University Press, 2004.

Langer, Jennifer. Introduction to *Crossing the Border. Voices of Refugee and Exiled Women*, 1–20. Nottingham: Five Leaves Publications, 2002.

Latimer, Dan, ed. *Contemporary Critical Theory*. San Diego: Harcourt Brace Jovanovich, 1989.

Lawson, Jeffrey. "Tadeusz Kantor and Teatr Cricot 2: When Theatrical Art Verged on Death." PhD. diss., New York University, 1995.

Leach, Catherine S. Introduction to *Memoirs of the Polish Baroque: The Writings of Jan Chryzostom Pasek, A Squire of the Commonwealth of Poland and Lithuania*, edited and translated by Catherine Leach, xv–lxi. Berkeley: University of California Press, 1976.

Leder, Drew. *The Absent Body*. Chicago: University of Chicago Press, 1990.

Lefebvre, Henri. "The Everyday and Everydayness." In *Everyday Life*, edited by Alice Kaplan and Kristin Ross, 7–12. New Haven: Yale University Press, 1987.

———. *Everyday Life in the Modern World*. Translated by Sacha Rabinovitch. New Brunswick: Transaction, 1999.

———. *Critique of Everyday Life*. Translated by John Moore. London: Verso, 1991.

Legutko, Ryszard. *Esej o duszy polskiej*. Cracow: Ośrodek Myśli Politycznej, 2008.

Leitch, Vincent B., ed. *The Norton Anthology of Theory and Criticism*. New York: W. W. Norton, 2001.

Lentricchia, Frank. *After the New Criticism*. Chicago: University of Chicago Press, 1983.

Lentricchia, Frank, and Thomas McLaughlin, eds. *Critical Terms for Literary Study*. Chicago: University of Chicago Press, 1995.

Leśmian, Bolesław. *Poezje wybrane*. Introduction by Jan Zygmunt Jakubowski. Warsaw: Ludowa Spółdzielnia Wydawnicza, 1967.

Levi, Primo. *If This Is a Man*. Translated by Stuart Woolf. London: Bodley Head, 1966.

Lévinas, Emmanuel. *On Escape*. Translated by Bettina Bergo. Stanford: Stanford University Press, 2003.

Levy, Daniel, Max Pensky, and John Torpey, eds. *Old Europe, New Europe, Core Europe: Transatlantic Relations after the Iraq War*. New York: Verso, 2005.

Lieskounig, Jürgen. "*Branntweintrinkende Wilde*. Beyond Civilization and Outside History: The Depiction of the Poles in Gustav Freytag's *Soll und Haben*." In *Germany and Eastern Europe: Cultural Identities and Cultural Differences*, Yearbook of European Studies 13, edited by Keith Bullivant, Geoffrey Giles, and Walter Pape, 133–47. Amsterdam: Rodopi, 1999.

Lifton, Robert Jay. *The Nazi Doctors: Medical Killing and the Psychology of Genocide*. New York: Basic Books, 1986.

Linhartová, Věra. *Joseph Sima: ses amis, ses contemporains*. Brussels: La Connaissance, 1974.

Lipiński, Jacek, ed. *Recenzje teatralne Towarzystwa Iksów 1815–1819*. Wrocław: Zakład Narodowy im. Ossolińskich, 1956.

Lodge, David, ed. *Modern Criticism and Theory: A Reader*. Harlow, UK: Longman, 2000.

Longinović, Tomislav Z.. "I, Witold Gombrowicz: Formal Abjection and the Power of Writing in *A Kind of Testament*." In *Gombrowicz's Grimaces: Modernism, Gender, Nationality*, edited by Ewa Płonowska Ziarek, 33–50. Albany: SUNY Press, 1998.

Łoziński, Józef. *Sceny myśliwskie z Dolnego Śląska*. Warsaw: PIW, 1985.

Łukaszuk, Małgorzata, and Dariusz Seweryn, eds. *Polska literatura współczesna wobec romantyzmu*. Lublin: Towarzystwo Naukowe KUL, 2007.
Macaulay, Thomas Babington. "Minute on Indian Education." In *Selected Writings*, edited and with an introduction by John Clive and Thomas Pinney, 237–51. Chicago: University of Chicago Press, 1972.
MacIntyre, Alasdair. *Three Rival Versions of Moral Enquiry*. Notre Dame, IN: Notre Dame University Press, 1991.
Madej, Bogdan. *Maść na szczury*. Paris: Instytut Literacki, 1977.
Madejski, Jerzy. "Wytrzymałość materiału." *Nowe Książki* 9 (2004): 53.
Magliola, Robert R. *Phenomenology and Literature: An Introduction*. West Lafayette: Purdue University Press, 1977.
Majcherek, Janusz. "Krytyka teatralna zanika." *Dziennik*, July 9, 2007. http://www.e-teatr.pl/pl/artykuly/41557.html.
Makaryk, Irena R., ed. *Encyclopedia of Contemporary Literary Theory: Approaches, Scholars, Terms*. Toronto: University of Toronto Press, 1993.
Malić, Zdravko. "*Trans-Atlantyk* Witolda Gombrowicza." In *Gombrowicz i krytycy*, edited by Zdzisław Łapiński, 235–56. Cracow: Wydawnictwo Literackie, 1984.
Maliszewski, Karol. *Nasi klasycy, nasi barbarzyńcy: szkice o nowej poezji*. Bydgoszcz: Instytut Wydawniczy "Świadectwo," 1999.
———. "Robigus demon rdzy." *Arkusz* 8 (2001): 8–9.
Mann, Thomas. *The Magic Mountain*. Translated by John E. Woods. New York: Vintage International, 1995.
Marcinek, Roman, ed. *Encyklopedia Polski*. Cracow: Kluszczyński, 1996.
Margański, Janusz. *Gombrowicz wieczny debiutant*. Cracow: Wydawnictwo Literackie, 2001.
———. *Geografia pragnień: Opowieść o Gombrowiczu*. Cracow: Wydawnictwo Literackie, 2005.
Markiewicz, Henryk. "Twórczość Romana Ingardena a rozwój badań literackich." In *Fenomenologia Romana Ingardena*, edited by Zdzisław Augustynek et al., 307–22. Warsaw: PAN, 1972.
———. "Places of Indeterminacy in a Literary Work." In *Roman Ingarden and Contemporary Polish Aesthetics: Essays*, edited by Piotr Graff and Sław Krzemień-Ojak, 159–71. Warsaw: Polish Scientific Publishers, 1975.
Mayenowa, Maria Renata. "Structural Thought in Poland." *Russian Literature* 13 (1983): 313–31.
McClintock, Anne. *Imperial Leather: Race, Gender and Sexuality in the Colonial Context*. New York: Routledge, 1995.
Mencwel, Andrzej. *Przedwiośnie czy potop: Studium postaw polskich w XX wieku*. Warsaw: Czytelnik, 1997.
Mengham, Rod. Introduction to *Altered State: The New Polish Poetry*, edited by Rod Mengham, Tadeusz Pióro, and Piotr Szymor, 11–15. Todmorden, UK: Arc Publications, 2003.

Merleau-Ponty, Maurice. *Phenomenology of Perception*. Translated by Colin Smith. London: Routledge & Kegan Paul, 1962.
Merquior, José Guilherme. *From Prague to Paris: A Critique of Structuralist and Post-structuralist Thought*. London: Verso, 1986.
Mężyński, Kazimierz. "Tragiczne antynomie Gustawa w 'Dziadach' kowieńsko-wileńskich." *Pamiętnik Literacki* 72, no. 3 (1981): 87–105.
Michalski, Cezary. *Siła odpychania*. Warsaw: WAB, 2002.
Mickiewicz, Adam. *Dziady cz. 2, 4 i 1*. Warsaw: Czytelnik, 1973.
———. *Dzieła. Dramaty*. Vol. 3. Edited by Zofia Stefanowska. Warsaw: Czytelnik, 1995.
Miller, J. Hillis, ed. *Aspects of Narrative: Selected Papers from the English Institute*. New York: Columbia University Press, 1971.
Milner, David A. and Melvyn A. Goodale. *The Visual Brain in Action*. Oxford: Oxford University Press, 1995.
Miłosz, Czesław, ed. *Postwar Polish Poetry*. Berkeley: University of California Press, 1965.
———. *The Captive Mind*. New York: Vintage Books, 1981.
———. *The History of Polish Literature*. Berkeley: University of California Press, 1983.
———. *The Witness of Poetry*. Cambridge: Harvard University Press, 1983.
———. *The Land of Ulro*. Translated by Luis Iribarne. New York: Farrar, Straus, & Giroux, 2000.
Mitosek, Zofia. "Obszary porównań (Nowoczesne praktyki komparatystyczne)." *Teksty Drugie* 4 (2002): 98–102.
Mitscherling, Jeffrey Anthony. *Roman Ingarden's Ontology and Aesthetics*. Ottawa: University of Ottawa Press, 1996.
Moi, Toril. *What Is a Woman and Other Essays*. Oxford: Oxford University Press, 1999.
Moore, David Chioni. "Is the Post- in Postcolonial the Post- in Post-Soviet? Toward a Global Postcolonial Critique." In *Postcolonialisms*, edited by Gaurav Desai and Supriya Nair, 514–38. New Brunswick: Rutgers University Press, 2005.
Moore-Gilbert, Bart. *Postcolonial Theory: Contexts, Practices, Politics*. London: Verso, 1997.
Morawiec, Elżbieta. "Wyspiański a 'Teatr Śmierci' Kantora." *Dialog*, no. 2 (1979): 141–48.
———. "Krytycy promują kolesiów." *Dziennik*, July 14, 2007. http://www.e-teatr.pl/pl/artykuly/41747.html.
Morley, David, and Kuan-Hsing Chen, eds. *Stuart Hall: Critical Dialogues in Cultural Studies*. London: Routledge, 1996.
Morson, Gary Saul, and Caryl Emerson. *Mikhail Bakhtin: Creation of a Prosaics*. Stanford: Stanford University Press, 1990.
Mostwin, Danuta. "'Lanczeneta' przy Alei Północnej." *Kultura* (Paris), no. 12 (1959): 36–60.

———. "Dwanaście lat." *Kultura* (Paris), nos. 7–8 (1960): 77–132.
———."Córki." *Kultura* (Paris), nos. 7–8 (1962): 57–78.
Mościcki, Paweł. "Polityka i teatr w Polsce." *e-teatr.pl* (2006). http://www.e-teatr.pl/pl/artykuly/25494.html.
———. "Teatr angażujący." *Gazeta Wyborcza*, March 31, 2006. http://www.e-teatr.pl/pl/artykuly/24708.html.
———. "Przeciw rozumowi cynicznemu w teatrze." *Teatr*, no. 8 (2007). http://www.e-teatr.pl/pl/artykuly/43717.html.
———. "Zaangażowanie i autonomia teatru." *Dialog*, no. 12 (2007). http://www.e-teatr.pl/pl/artykuly/51039.html.
Mościcki, Tomasz. "Krytycy bez zasad." *Dziennik*, July 2, 2007, http://www.e-teatr.pl/pl/artykuly/41200.html.
Mrożek, Sławomir. *Teatr*. 6 vols. Warsaw: Noir sur Blanc, 1992–98.
———. *Opowiadania 1960–1965*. Warsaw: Noir sur Blanc, 1997.
———. *Opowiadania 1974–1979*. Warsaw: Noir sur Blanc, 1997.
———. *Opowiadania 1953–1959*. Warsaw: Noir sur Blanc, 1998.
Nadeau, Robert, and Menas Kafatos. *The Non-local Universe: The New Physics and Matters of the Mind*. Oxford: Oxford University Press, 1999.
Najder, Zdzisław. *Joseph Conrad: A Chronicle*. New Brunswick, NJ: Rutgers University Press, 1983.
Nałkowska, Zofia, *Dzienniki*. Edited by Hanna Kirchner. 6 vols. Warsaw: Czytelnik, 2000.
———. *Medallions*. Translated by Diana Kuprel. Evanston: Northwestern University Press, 2000.
Nancy, Jean-Luc. "Exscription," *On Bataille. Yale French Studies* 78 (1990): 47–65.
———. *The Inoperative Community*. Edited by Peter Connor. Foreword by Christopher Fynsk. Minneapolis: University of Minnesota Press, 1996.
———. *Corpus*. Translated by Małgorzata Kwietniewska. Gdańsk: Słowo/Obraz Terytoria, 2002.
Neuger, Leonard. *Ćwiczenia w wrażliwości: Duże i małe szkice literackie*. Katowice: Wydawnictwo Uniwersytetu Śląskiego, 2006.
Newton, Ken M., ed. *Twentieth-Century Literary Theory*. New York: St. Martin's Press, 1988.
N'guessan, Béchié P. *Primitivismus und Afrikanismus: Kunst und Kultur Afrikas in der deutschen Avantgarde*. Frankfurt am Main: P. Lang, 2002.
Nieukerken, Arent van. *Ironiczny konceptyzm: Nowoczesna polska poezja metafizyczna w kontekście anglosaskiego modernizmu*. Cracow: Universitas, 1998.
Niżyńska, Joanna. "Playing Out Life in the Everyday: Ethical Maximalism in the Works of Miron Białoszewski." Ph.D. diss., UCLA, 2002.
Nora, Pierre, ed. *Les lieux de mémoire*. 7 vols. Paris: Gallimard, 1984–92.
———. "Between History and Memory: Les Lieux de mémoire." *Representations* 26 (1989): 7–25.

———. "General Introduction: Between Memory and History" In *Rethinking the French Past: Realms of Memory*, vol. 1, edited by Pierre Nora, translated by Arthur Goldhammer, 1–20. New York: Columbia University Press, 1996.

———. "Czas pamięci." Translated by Wiktor Dłuski. *Res Publica Nowa* 7 (2001): 37–43.

Nora, Pierre, and L. D. Kritzman, eds. *Realms of Memory: Rethinking the French Past*, vol. 1: *Conflicts and Divisions*. New York: Columbia University Press, 1996.

Norwid, Cyprian Kamil. *Wiersze Wybrane: Vade Mecum*. Edited by Waldemar Smaszcz. Białystok: Łuk, 1993.

———. *Selected Poems*. Translated by Adam Czerniawski. London: Anvil Press Poetry, 2004.

Nowakowski, Marek. *Wesele raz jeszcze*. Warsaw: PIW, 1974.

———. *The Canary and Other Tales of Martial Law*. Translated by Krystyna Bronkowska. London: Harvill Press, 1983.

———. *Raport o Stanie Wojennym*. Białystok: Versus, 1990.

———. *Homo Polonicus*. Warsaw: Pomost, 1992.

Nowosielski, Kazimierz. "Tadeusza Różewicza 'śmierci wielokrotne'" *Kresy* 4 (1997): 49–56.

Nycz, Ryszard. "Tajemnica okaleczonej poezji: Trzy glosy do twórczości Tadeusza Różewicza." In *Zobaczyć poetę: Materiały konferencji "Twórczość Tadeusza Różewicza*," edited by Ewa Guderian-Czaplińska and Elżbieta Kalemba-Kasprzak, 97–107. Poznań: Wydawnictwo WiS, 1993.

———. "'Szare eminencje zachwytu': Miejsce epifanii w poetyce Mirona Białoszewskiego." In *Pisanie Białoszewskiego*, edited by Michał Głowiński and Zdzisław Łapiński, 179–90. Warsaw: IBL, 1993.

Odmark, John, ed. *Language, Literature and Meaning: Problems of Literary Theory*. Amsterdam: John Benjamins, 1979.

O'Hara, Frank. *Standing Still and Walking in New York*. Bolinas, CA: Grey Fox Press, 1975.

———. "Wiersz." Translated by Piotr Sommer. *Literatura na Świecie*, no. 7 (1986): 49.

———. *Twoja pojedynczość*. Translated by Piotr Sommer. Warsaw: PIW, 1987.

———. *The Collected Poems of Frank O'Hara*. Edited by Donald Allen. Berkeley: University of California Press, 1995.

Oort, Richard van. "Three Models of Fiction: The Logical, the Phenomenological, and the Anthropological (Searle, Ingarden, Gans)." *New Literary History* 29, no. 3 (1998): 439–65.

Orłoś, Kazimierz. *Trzecie kłamstwo*. Paris: Instytut Literacki, 1980.

Overland, Orm. "Visions of Home. Exiles and Immigrants." In *The Dispossessed: An Anatomy of Exile*, edited by Peter I. Rose, 7–26. Amherst: University of Massachusetts Press, 2005.

Parker, Andrew, and Eve Kosofsky Sedgwick. "Introduction: *Performativity and Performance.*" In Performativity and Performance, edited by Andrew Parker and Eve Sedgwick, 1–18. New York: Routledge, 1995.

Pavis, Patrice. *Dictionary of the Theatre: Terms, Concepts, and Analysis*. Translated by Christine Shantz. Toronto: University of Toronto Press, 1998.

Pawłowski, Roman, ed. *Pokolenie porno i inne niesmaczne utwory teatralne: antologia najnowszego dramatu polskiego*. Cracow: Zielona Sowa, 2003.

———. "Zadara zrewidował Juliusza Słowackiego." *Gazeta Wyborcza*, November 23, 2005. http://www.e-teatr.pl/pl/artykuly/18726.html.

———, ed. *Made in Poland. Dziewięć sztuk teatralnych z Polski*. Cracow: Ha!art, 2006.

———. "Wraca centrala," *Gazeta Wyborcza*, December 3, 2009. http://wyborcza. pl /1,75475,7324359,Wraca_centrala.html?as=1&startsz=x.

Payne, Michael, ed. *A Dictionary of Cultural and Critical Theory*. Oxford: Blackwell Reference, 1996.

Peiker, Piret. "Post-Communist Literatures: A Postcolonial Perspective." *Eurozine*, March 28, 2006. http://www.eurozine.com/articles/2006-03-28-peiker-en.pdf.

Penn, Shana. *Podziemie kobiet*. Translated by Hanna Jankowska. Warsaw: Rosner i Wspólnicy, 2003.

———. *Solidarity's Secret: The Women Who Defeated Communism in Poland*. Ann Arbor: University of Michigan Press, 2005.

Perloff, Marjorie. *Frank O'Hara: Poet among Painters*. Chicago: University of Chicago Press, 1977.

Pezdek, Kathy, Kimberly Finger, and Dandle Hodge. "Planting False Childhood Memories: The Role of Event Plausibility." *Psychological Science* 8, no. 6 (1997): 437–41.

Pick, Daniel. *War Machine: The Rationalization of Slaughter in the Modern Age*. New Haven: Yale University Press, 1993.

Pięć studiów z dziejów scenicznych dramatów Mickiewicza. Wrocław: Zakład Narodowy im. Ossolińskich, 1968.

Pigoń, Stanisław. *Do źródeł "Dziadów" kowieńsko-wileńskich*. Wilno: Księgarnia św. Wojciecha, 1930.

Pilch, Jerzy. *Spis cudzołożnic*. Cracow: Wydawnictwo Literackie, 2002.

Piwińska, Marta. *Legenda romantyczna i szydercy*. Warsaw: PIW, 1973.

Pizer, John. *The Idea of World Literature: History and Pedagogical Practice*. Baton Rouge: Louisiana State University Press, 2006.

Plata, Tomasz, ed. *Strategie publiczne, strategie prywatne: Teatr polski 1990–2005*. Izabelin: Świat Literacki, 2006.

Pleśniarowicz, Krzysztof. "Polski Teatr Śmierci: Mickiewicz-Wyspiański, Kantor." *Teatr* no. 12 (1993): 17–19.

———. "Odysseus Must Really Return." In *Tadeusz Kantor "The Return of Odysseus": The Clandestine Independent Theatre 1944*, edited by Krzysztof Pleśniarowicz, and translated by Paweł Łopatka, 47–63. Cracow: Cricoteka, 1994.

———. *The Dead Memory Machine: Tadeusz Kantor's Theatre of Death.* Translated by William Brand. Aberysthwith: Black Mountain Press, 2004.
Płonowska Ziarek, Ewa, ed. *Gombrowicz's Grimaces: Modernism, Gender, Nationality.* Albany: SUNY Press, 1998.
Podsiadło, Jacek. "Vanitas; Et Omnia Vanitatis." Translated by Elżbieta Wójcik-Leese and Bill Martin. *Chicago Review* 46, nos. 3–4 (2000): 275.
———. *Wiersze zebrane.* Warsaw: Lampa i Iskra Boża, 2003.
———. "Nietzsche: It Is a Shame to Be Happy!" Translated by Anna Skucińska. *Lyric Poetry Review* 8 (2005): 54.
Pomorska, Krystyna. *Russian Formalist Theory and Its Poetic Ambiance.* The Hague: Mouton, 1968.
Ponge, Francis. *Soap.* Translated by Lane Dunlop. London: Jonathan Cape, 1969.
Pollard, Charles. *New World Modernisms.* Charlottesville: University of Virginia Press, 2004.
Porębski, Mieczysław. *Polskość jako sytuacja.* Cracow: Wydawnictwo Literackie, 2002.
———. *Krytycy i sztuka.* Cracow: Wydawnictwo Literackie, 2004.
Pratt, L. Mary. "Comparative Literature as a Cultural Practice." *Profession* 85 (1985): 33–35.
Prawer, Siegbert. *Comparative Literary Studies: An Introduction.* London: Duckworth, 1973.
Preminger, Alex, and Terry V. F. Brogan, eds. *The New Princeton Encyclopedia of Poetry and Poetics.* Princeton: Princeton University Press, 1996.
Prendergast, Christopher, ed. *Debating World Literature.* London: Verso, 2004.
Presner, Todd S. *Mobile Modernity: Germans, Jews, Trains.* New York: Columbia University Press, 2007.
Proudfoot, Michael, ed. *The Philosophy of Body.* Oxford: Blackwell, 2003.
Proust, Marcel. *A la recherché du temps perdu: La prisonière.* Translated by David Michalski. Paris: Flammarion, 1984.
Przyszli barbarzyńcy. Cracow: Oficyna Literacka, 1991.
Przybylski, Ryszard. *Słowo i milczenie bohatera Polaków: Studium o "Dziadach."* Warsaw: IBL, 1993.
Putnam, Robert D. *Bowling Alone: The Collapse and Revival of American Community.* New York: Simon & Schuster, 2000.
Putnam, Robert D., and Lewis M. Feldstein. *Better Together: Restoring the American Community.* New York : Simon & Schuster, 2003.
Putnam, Samuel. "Comparative Literature: Can It Come Alive?" *Books Abroad: An International Library Quarterly* 10 (1936): 133–36.
Quinkenstein, Lothar. "Danzig/Gdańsk—ein literarischer Spiegel." In *Mythen und Stereotypen auf beiden Seiten der Oder*, edited by Hans Dieter Zimmermann, 221–29. Berlin: Dreieck-Verl. der Guardini-Stiftung, 2000.
Radstone, Susannah. "Working with Memory: An Introduction." In *Memory and Methodology*, edited by Susannah Radstone, 1–20. Oxford: Berg, 2000.

Rajchman, John. *The Deleuze Connections*. Cambridge, MA: MIT Press, 2000.
Ramazani, Jahan. "A Transnational Poetics." *American Literary History* 18, no. 2 (Summer 2006): 332–59.
Random, Michel. *Le grand jeu*. Paris: Denoël, 1970.
Ratajczakowa, Dobrochna. "Sługa dwóch panów: Dwoisty żywot dramatu." *Teksty Drugie* 5–6 (1990): 80–92.
Remuszko, Stanisław. *Gazeta Wyborcza: Początki i okolice*. Warsaw: Oficyna Rękodzieło, 1999.
Report of the Mid-European Studies Center: Publications and Projects. New York: Free Europe Committee, 1955.
Rhys, Jean. *Wide Sargasso Sea*. Edited by Judith L. Raiskin. New York: Norton, 1999.
Rice, Philip, and Patricia Waugh, eds. *Modern Literary Theory: A Reader*. London: Oxford University Press, 2001.
Ricoeur, Paul. *Du texte à l'action. Essais d'herméneutique II*. Paris: Seuil, 1986.
———. *Memory, History, Forgetting*. Translated by David Pellauer and Kathleen Blamey. Chicago: University of Chicago Press, 2004.
Robin, Ron. "Two Cheers for the New Historians: A Critique of Israel's Post-Nationalists." In *Myth and Memory in the Construction of Community: Historical Patterns in Europe and Beyond*, edited by Bo Stråth, 315–20. Brussels: Peter Lang, 2000.
Robinson, Marc, ed. *Altogether Elsewhere: Writers on Exile*. Boston: Faber and Faber, 1994.
Rokem, Freddie. *Performing History: Theatrical Representations of the Past in Contemporary Theatre*. Iowa City: University of Iowa Press, 2000.
Romanowiczowa, Zofia. *Baśka i Barbara*. Paris: Libella, 1956.
Rorty, Richard. *Essays on Heidegger and Others: Philosophical Papers*, vol. 2. Cambridge: Cambridge University Press, 1991.
Rosiek, Stanisław. "Pamiętnik z półgrobu." In *Pisanie Białoszewskiego*, edited by Michał Głowiński and Zdzisław Łapiński, 130–43. Warsaw: IBL, 1993.
Rosner, Katarzyna. "Ingarden's Philosophy of Literature and the Analysis of Artistic Communication." In *Roman Ingarden and Contemporary Polish Aesthetics: Essays*, edited by Piotr Graff and Sław Krzemień-Ojak, 191–221. Warsaw: Polish Scientific Publishers, 1975.
Routh, H. V. "The Future of Comparative Literature." *Modern Language Review* 8 (1913): 1–14.
Różewicz, Tadeusz. *Selected Poems*. Translated by Adam Czerniawski. Harmondsworth: Penquin Books, 1976.
———. *Nożyk profesora*. Wrocław: Wydawnictwo Dolnośląskie, 2001.
———. "Drewniany karabin." *Odra*, nos. 7–8 (2002): 51–55.
———. *Szara Strefa*. Wrocław: Wydawnictwo Dolnośląskie, 2002.

———. "To, co zostało z nienapisanej książki o Norwidzie." *Kwartalnik Artystyczny* 3 (2002): 9–25.

———. *New poems*. Translated by Bill Johnston. New York: Archipelago Books, 2007.

Rudnick, Hans. "Roman Ingarden's Literary Theory." In *Ingardeniana: A Spectrum of Specialised Studies Establishing the Field of Research*, edited by Anna-Teresa Tymieniecka, 105–19. Dordrecht: Riedel, 1976.

———, ed. *Ingardeniana II: New Studies in the Philosophy of Roman Ingarden*. Dordrecht: Kluwer, 1990.

Rumbaut, Rubén D., and Rubén G. Rumbaut. "Self and Circumstance: Journeys and Visions of Exile." In *The Dispossessed: An Anatomy of Exile*, edited by Peter I. Rose, 331–57. Amherst: University of Massachusetts Press, 2005.

Rushdie, Salman. "The Empire Writes Back with a Vengeance." *Times* (London), July 3, 1982, 8.

Rybicka-Nowacka, Helena, ed. *O języku i stylu Jana Chryzostoma Paska*. Warsaw: Warsaw University Press, 1981.

Rychard, Andrzej. "Budująca natura sporów." In "W okopach wojen kulturowych w Polsce," *Europa*, January 26, 2008. http://www.dziennik.pl/dziennik/europa/article114596/W okopach wojen kulturowych w Polsce.html.

Rymkiewicz, Jarosław Marek. *Rozmowy polskie latem roku 1983*. Warsaw: Nowa, 1984.

———. "W dziesięć lat później": Z Jarosławem Markiem Rymkiewiczem rozmawiała Barbara Sułek. *Tygodnik Solidarność*, no. 44 (1993): 12–13.

———. "Hodujmy róże! Rozmowa z Jarosławem Markiem Rymkiewiczem o zdrowych i zatrutych źródłach XX-wiecznej polskiej literatury." *Życie*, January 18, 2001. http://niniwa2.cba.pl/rymkiewicz.htm.

Rytel, Jadwiga. *Pamiętniki Paska na tle pamiętnikarstwa staropolskiego*. Wrocław: Ossolineum, 1962;

Rzewiczok, Urszula, and Katarzyna M. Gliwa. *Drodzy Nieobecni Tadeusza Kantora*: Wspomnienie o Tadeuszu Kantorze, Marianie Kantorze-Mirskim i Józefie Kantor. Katowice: Muzeum Historii Katowic, 2002.

Said, Edward. *The World, the Text, and the Critic*. Cambridge, MA: Harvard University Press, 1983.

———. *Orientalism*. New York: Vintage, 1979.

———. *Culture and Imperialism*. New York: Vintage, 1994.

———."Reflections on Exile." In *Reflections on Exile and Other Essays*, 173–86. Cambridge,MA: Harvard University Press, 2001.

Sala, Paweł. "Różewicz mój osobisty." *Teatr*, no. 2 (2007): 33–34.

Sandel, Michael. *Democracy's Discontent: America in Search of a Public Philosophy*. Cambridge, MA: Belknap Press of Harvard University Press, 1996.

———. *Liberalism and the Limits of Justice*. Cambridge: Cambridge University Press, 1998.

Sartre, Jean-Paul. *Being and Nothingness: An Essay on Phenomenological Ontology*. Translated by Hazel E. Barnes. New York: Philosophical Library, 1956.

Savran, David. "The Haunted Houses of Modernity." *Modern Drama* 43, no. 4 (2000): 117–28.

Saunders, Frances Stonor. *The Cultural Cold War: The CIA and the World of Arts and Letters*. New York: New Press, 2000.

Scarpetta, Guy. "Portrait of the Returning Artist." In *Teatr Cricot 2. Informator 1989-1990*, edited by Anna Halczak, 189–93. Cracow: Cricoteka, 2003.

Scharffenberg, Renate. "Pawel Huelle *Castorp*." *Marburger Forum und Philosophia*. http://www.philosophia-online.de/mafo/heft2005-3/Huelle.htm.

Schechner, Richard. *Between Theatre and Anthropology*. Philadelphia: University of Pennsylvania Press, 1985.

Schmidgall, Renate. "Heimat Danzig als literarisches Thema bei Paweł Huelle." In *Danzig/Gdańsk. Deutsch-polnische Geschichte, Politik und Literatur*, edited by Sophia Kemlein, 175–84. Dillingen: Akad. für Lehrerfortbildung, 1996.

Scholem, Gershom Gerhard. *The Messianic Idea in Judaism, and Other Essays on Jewish Spirituality*. New York: Schocken Books, 1971.

Schulz, Bruno. *Proza*. Cracow: Wydawnictwo Literackie, 1973.

———. *The Complete Fiction of Bruno Schulz*. Translated by Celina Wieniewska. New York: Walker, 1989.

———. *Opowiadania, wybór esejów i listów*. Edited by Jerzy Jarzębski. Wrocław: Ossolineum, 1989.

Scott-Smith, Giles. *The Politics of Apolitical Culture: The Congress for Cultural Freedom, the CIA and Post-war American Hegemony*. London: Routlage, 2002.

Segre, Cesare. *Introduction to the Analysis of the Literary Text*. Translated by John Meddemmen. Bloomington: Indiana University Press, 1988.

Seifert, Josef. "Ingarden's Theory of the Quasi-Judgments." In *Roman Ingarden a filozofia naszego czasu*, edited by Adam Węgrzecki, 13–20. Cracow: Oficyna Cracovia, 1995.

Seifert, Josef, and Barry Smith. "The Truth about Fiction." In *Kunst und Ontologie*, edited by Włodzimierz Galewicz et al., 97–118. Amsterdam: Rodopi, 1994.

Selden, Raman, ed. *The Theory of Criticism from Plato to the Present: A Reader*. London: Longman, 1988.

———. *The Cambridge History of Literary Criticism*, vol. 8. Cambridge: Cambridge University Press, 1995.

Seyhan, Azade. *Writing Outside the Nation*. Princeton: Princeton University Press, 2001.

Shakespeare, William. *The Complete Works*. New York: Avenel, 1975.

Sheets-Johnstone, Maxine. *The Roots of Thinking*. Philadelphia: Temple University Press, 1990.

Shelley, Lore, ed. *Criminal Experiments on Human Beings in Auschwitz and War Research Laboratories: Twenty Women Prisoners' Accounts*. San Francisco: Mellen Research University Press, 1991.

Shilling, Chris. *The Body and Social Theory*. London: Sage, 1993.

Shoemaker, Sydney. "Self-Knowledge and 'Inner Sense.'" In *The First-Person Perspective and Other Essays*, 246–69. Cambridge: Cambridge University Press, 1996.

Sicher, Efraim. "The Holocaust in the Postmodernist Era." In *Breaking Crystal: Writing and Memory after Auschwitz*, edited by Efraim Sicher, 297–28. Urbana: University of Illinois Press, 1998.

Siejak, Tadeusz. *Pustynia*. Warsaw: Iskry, 1987.

Siemion, Piotr. *Niskie łąki*. Warsaw: WAB, 2000.

———. *Finimondo: komedia romatyczna*. Warsaw: WAB, 2004.

Sieradzki, Jacek. "Po co Hamletowi komórka." *Polityka*, May 19, 2005. http://www.e-teatr.pl/pl/artykuly/9091.html.

———. "Krytyka kreatywna, czyli w obronie wujostwa." *Dialog*, no. 3 (2006).

Sim, Stuart. *Jean-Francois Lyotard*. London: Prentice Hall Harvester Wheatsheaf, 1996.

Simons, Peter M. "Strata in Ingarden's Ontology." In *Kunst und Ontologie: für Roman Ingarden zum 100. Geburtstag*, edited by Włodzimierz Galewicz, et al., 119–40. Amsterdam: Rodopi, 1994.

Sinclair, Upton. *The Jungle*. New York: Bantam Books, 1981.

Sivert, Tadeusz, et al., eds. *Mickiewicz na scenie*. Warsaw: PIW, 1957.

Skórczewski, Dariusz. "Dlaczego Paweł Huelle napisał *Castorpa?*" *Teksty Drugie*, no. 99 (March 2006): 148–57.

———."Modern Polish Literature through a Postcolonial Lens: The Case of Pawel Huelle's *Castorp*." *Sarmatian Review* 26, no. 3 (2006): 1229–33.

Sloterdijk, Peter. *Critique of Cynical Reason*. Minneapolis: University of Minnesota Press, 1987.

Sloterdijk, Peter, and Jadwiga Staniszkis. "Czy Polska przetrwa w Europie." *Europa*, November 3, 2007, 2.

Sławek, Tadeusz. "Literatura porównawcza: między literaturą, polityką i społeczeństwem." In *Polonistyka w przebudowie: Literaturoznawstwo–wiedza o języku–wiedza o kulturze–edukacja*, edited by Małgorzata Czermińska et al., 389–401. Cracow: Universitas, 2005.

Słowacki, Juliusz. *Dramaty*. Warsaw: PIW, 1983.

Smith, Anthony D. *National Identity*. London: Penguin Books, 1991.

Sobczak, Jan. *Dryf*. Warsaw: Lampa i Iskra Boża; Czarne: Czarne, 1999.

Sobolewska, Anna. *Maksymalnie udana egzystencja. Szkice o życiu i twórczości Mirona Białoszewskiego*. Warsaw: IBL, 1997.

Śpiewak, Paweł. "'Cała polityka sprowadza się do boksu': Z socjologiem P.Ś. rozmawia Małgorzata Subotić." *Rzeczpospolita*, June 24, 2000.
———, ed. *Spór o Polskę 1989–99: Wybór tekstów prasowych*. Warsaw: PWN, 2000.
———. *Pamięć po komuniźmie*. Gdańsk: Słowo/obraz terytoria, 2005.
———. "Zgubny brak autoironii." In "W okopach wojen kulturowych w Polsce." *Europa*, January 26, 2008. http://www.dziennik.pl/dziennik/europa/article114596/W okopach wojen kulturowych w Polsce.html.
Spivak, Gayatri Chakravorty. "Can the Subaltern Speak?" In *Marxism and the Interpretation of Culture*, edited by Cary Nelson and Lawrence Grossberg, 271–313. London: Macmillan, 1988.
———. *The Post-colonial Critic: Interviews, Strategies, Dialogues*. New York: Routledge, 1990.
———. *Death of a Discipline*. New York: Columbia University Press, 2003.
Spurr, David. *The Rhetoric of Empire: Colonial Discourse in Journalism, Travel Writing, and Imperial Administration*. Durham: Duke University Press, 1993.
Spychalski, Mirosław, and Jarosław Szoda. *Mówi Karpowicz*. Wrocław: Biuro Literackie, 2005.
Stala, Marian. "Czy Białoszewski jest poetą metafizycznym?" In *Pisanie Białoszewskiego*, edited by Michał Głowiński and Zdzisław Łapiński, 96–113. Warsaw: IBL, 1993.
———. *Druga strona: notatki o poezji współczesnej*. Cracow: Znak, 1997.
Stallman, Robert Wooster, ed. *Critiques and Essays in Criticism, 1920–1948: Representing the Achievement of Modern British and American Critics*. New York: Ronald Press, 1948.
Staniszkis, Jadwiga. *The Dynamics of Breakthrough in Eastern Europe*. Berkeley: University of California Press, 1991.
———. *Post-communism: The Emerging Enigma*. Warsaw: Institute of Political Studies, Polish Academy of Sciences, 1999.
———. *Postkomunistyczne państwo: w poszukiwaniu tożsamości*. Warsaw: Institute of Public Affairs, 2000.
———. *Postkomunizm: próba opisu*. Gdańsk: Słowo/obraz terytoria, 2001.
———. *Władza globalizacji*. Warsaw: "Scholar," 2003.
———. *O władzy i bezsilności*. Cracow: Wydawnictwo Literackie, 2006.
Stasiuk, Andrzej. *Biały kruk*. Poznań: Obserwator, 1995.
———. *White Raven*. Translated by Wiesiek Powaga. London: Serpent's Tail, 2000.
Stawiszyński, Tomasz. "Krytycy w sosie własnym." *Dziennik*, July 11, 2007. http://www.e-teatr.pl/pl/artykuly/41655.html.
Stawrowski, Zbigniew. "O zapomnianej solidarności." *Znak* 543, no. 8 (2000): 60–67.

———. "Solidarność znaczy więź." *Tygodnik Powszechny*, June 3, 2001, 8.
———. "Doświadczenie 'Solidarności.'" In *Lekcja Sierpnia: Dziedzictwo "Solidarności" po dwudziestu latach*, edited by Dariusz Gawin, 103–22. Warsaw: IFiS Pan, 2002.
Stephan, Alexander. *"Communazis": FBI Surveillance of German Émigré Writers*. New Haven: Yale University Press, 2000.
Stone, Dan. *Representation of Auschwitz: Fifty Years of Photographs, Paintings and Graphics*. Edited by Yasmin Doorssry. Oswiecim: Auschwitz-Birkanau State Museum, 1995.
Stråth, Bo. *Myth and Memory in the Construction of Community: Historical Patterns in Europe and Beyond*. Brussels: Peter Lang, 2000.
Strelka, Josef P. "Ingarden's 'Points of Indeterminateness': A Consideration of Their Practical Application to Literary Criticism." *In Ingardeniana II*, edited by Hans Rudnick, 157–69. Dordrecht: Kluwer, 1990.
Striedter, Jurij. *Literary Structure, Evolution, and Value: Russian Formalism and Czech Structuralism Reconsidered*. Cambridge, MA: Harvard University Press, 1989.
Styan, John Louis. *The English Stage: A History of Drama and Performance*. Cambridge: Cambridge University Press, 1996.
Sugiera, Małgorzata. "Rewriting Homer: Wyspiański's *Powrót Odysa* and Strauss's *Ithaka*." In *(Dis)Placing Classical Greek Theatre*, edited by Savas Patsalidis and Elizabeth Sakellaridou, 85–96. Thessaloniki: University Studio Press, 1999.
Sugiera, Małgorzata, and Anna Wierzchowska-Woźniak, eds. *Echa-repliki-fantazmaty. Antologia nowego dramatu polskiego*. Cracow: Księgarnia Akademicka, 2005.
Surynowa-Wyczółkowska, Janina. *Gringa*. London: Polska Fundacja Kulturalna, 1968.
———. *Jesień Gringi*. London: Polska Fundacja Kulturalna, 1976.
Süskind, Patrick. *Perfume: The Story of a Murderer*. Translated by John E. Woods. New York: Pocket Books, 1991.
Świderski, Bronisław. *Gdańsk i Ateny*. Warsaw: IFiS PAN, 1996.
Świeściak, Alina. "Taki sam, czyli Inny." *Fa-art* 46, no. 4 (2001): 76–78.
Świetlicki, Marcin. "Dla Jana Polkowskiego." In *Macie swoich poetów: Liryka polska urodzona po 1960 r.*, edited by Paweł Dunin-Wąsowicz, Jarosław Klejnocki, and Krzysztof Varga, 157. Warsaw: Lampa i Iskra Boża, 1996.
———. "Koehlerism." Translated by Bill Martin. *Chicago Review* 46, nos. 3–4, (2000): 282–84
———. "Poems." Translated by Bill Martin and Elżbieta Wójcik-Leese. *Chicago Review* 46, nos. 3–4 (2000): 276–79.
———. *Nieczynny*. Warsaw: Lampa i Iskra Boża, 2003.
Szahaj, Andrzej. *Jednostka czy wspólnota? Spór liberałów z komunitarystami a "sprawa polska."* Warsaw: Aletheia, 2000.

Szaruga, Leszek (pseud. Krzysztof Zawrat). "Polemika z Janiną Katz Hewetson." *Kultura* no. 6 (1982): 26-34.
Szczepański, Jan Józef. "Założenia, które przetrwają." *Znak* 543, no. 8 (2000): 100.
Szmydtowa, Zofia. *Rousseau-Mickiewicz i inne studia.* Warsaw: PIW, 1961.
Szydłowska, Joanna. "Obcowanie z tajemnicą: topos Gdańska w prozie Stefana Chwina i Pawła Huellego jako literacki dyskurs z przeszłością i twórcza refleksja nad przyszłością." In *Literackie strategie lat dziewięćdziesiątych: przełomy, kontynuacje, powroty*, edited by Leokadia Hut and Andrzej Staniszewski, 39–52. Olsztyn: Wydawnictwo Uniwersytetu Warmińsko-Mazurskiego, 2002.
Szymborska, Wisława. *Miracle Fair: Selected Poems of Wisława Szymborska.* Translated by Joanna Trzeciak. New York: W. W. Norton, 2002.
Tai, Hue-Tam Ho. "Remembered Realms: Pierre Nora and French National Memory," *American Historical Review* 106, no. 3 (June 2001): 906–22.
Tarka, Krzysztof. *Emigracja dyplomatyczna: Polityka zagraniczna Rządu RP na uchodźctwie 1945–1990.* Warsaw: Oficyna Wydawnicza RYTM, 2003.
Taylor, Charles. *Sources of the Self: The Making of the Modern Identity.* Boston: Harvard University Press, 1989.
———. *Multiculturalism and the Politics of Recognition: An Essay.* Princeton: Princeton University Press, 1992.
Tazbir, Janusz. *świat Panów Pasków: Eseje i studia.* Łódź: Wydawnictwo Łódzkie, 1986.
Tchórzewski, Andrzej. "Imperatyw 'placu.'" *Poezja* 10 (1984): 43–57.
Terlecki, Tymon. *Stanisław Wyspiański.* Boston: Twayne, 1983.
Thompson, Ewa. *Russian Formalism and Anglo-American New Criticism: A Comparative Study.* The Hague: Mouton, 1971.
———. *Witold Gombrowicz.* Boston: Twayne, 1979.
———. "Nationalism, Imperialism, Identity." *Modern Age* 40, no. 3 (Summer 1998): 250–61.
———. *Imperial Knowledge: Russian Literature and Colonialism.* Westport, CT: Greenwood Press, 2000.
Tihanov, Galin. "Why Did Modern Literary Theory Originate in Central and Eastern Europe? (And Why Is It Now Dead?)." *Common Knowledge* 10, no. 1 (2004): 61–81.
Tischner, Józef. *Myślenie według wartości.* Cracow: Znak, 1982.
———. *Filozofia Dramatu.* Paris: Éd. du Dialogue, 1990.
———. *Etyka solidarności oraz Homo sovieticus.* Cracow: Znak, 1992.
Todes, Samuel. *Body and World.* Cambridge, MA: MIT Press, 2001.
Tompkins, Jane P., ed. *Reader-Response Criticism: From Formalism to Post-structuralism.* Baltimore: Johns Hopkins University Press, 1980.
Trojanowska, Tamara. "New Discourses in Drama." *Contemporary Theatre Review* 15, no. 1 (2005): 109–23.
———. "Kto młodym przewodzi." *Teatr*, no. 6 (2007): 11–15.

———. "Różewicz i teatr lat ostatnich." *Teatr*, no. 2 (2007): 27–31.
TR/PL: Antologia nowego dramatu polskiego. Warsaw: TR Warszawa, 2006.
Tymieniecka, Anna-Teresa, ed. *Ingardeniana III: Roman Ingarden's Aesthetics in a New Key and the Independent Approaches of Others: The Performing Arts, the Fine Arts, and Literature*. Dordrecht: Kluwer, 1991.
Ubertowska, Aleksandra. "Literatura i miasto." *Przegląd Polityczny* 33/34 (1997): 106–10.
Ulewicz, Tadeusz. *Sarmacja: studium z problematyki słowiańskiej XV i XVI w.; Zagadnienie sarmatyzmu w kulturze i literaturze polskiej: (problematyka ogólna i zarys historyczny)*. Retrospective resume by Teresa Bałuk-Ulewiczowa. Cracow: Collegium Columbinum, 2006.
Ulicka, Danuta. "Co nam zostało z fenomenologii? Roman Ingarden a rozwój teorii badań literackich (w Polsce i za granicą w latach 1980–2000)." In *Sporne i bezsporne problemy współczesnej wiedzy o literaturze*, edited by Włodzimierz Bolecki et al., 41–59. Warsaw: Instytut Badań Literackich PAN, 2002.
Ureña, Lenny A. "Mobilizing German Women against 'Cultural Drunkenness': Rassenhygiene and Colonial Discourse in the Prussian-Polish Provinces, 1890–1914." Paper presented at "Gender and Power in the New Europe," 5th European Feminist Research Conference, August 20–24, 2003, Lund University, Sweden. http://www.iiav.nl/epublications/2003/Gender_and_power/5thfeminist/paper_635.pdf.
Ursel, Marian. "Fascynacja—ideologizacja—degradacja? O ewoluowaniu motywu samobójstwa w twórczości Adama Mickiewicza." In *Problemy współczesnej tanatologii: Medycyna—antropologia kultury—humanistyka*, edited by Jacek Kolbuszewski, 447–54. Wrocław: Wrocławskie Towarzystwo Naukowe, 2003.
Varela, Francis J., Evan Thompson, and Eleanor Rosch. *The Embodied Mind: Cognitive Science and Human Experience*. Cambridge, MA: MIT Press, 1991.
Vašíček, Zdeněk. *Přijetí podmínek*. Prague: Torst, 1996.
Vattimo, Gianni. *The End of Modernity*. Baltimore: Johns Hopkins University Press, 1991.
Vido-Rzewuska, Marie-Thérèse. "The Father Figure in Tadeusz Kantor's Work." *Journal of Dramatic Criticism* 10, no. 1 (1995): 233–36.
Virilio, Paul. *Speed and Politics: An Essay on Dromology*. Translated by Mark Polizzotti. New York: Semiotext(e), 1986.
———. *The Aesthetics of Disappearance*. Translated by Philip Beitchman. New York: Semiotext(e), 1991.
Vivas, Eliseo, and Murray Krieger, eds. *The Problems of Aesthetics: A Book of Readings*. New York: Rinehart, 1953.
Wakar, Jacek. "Krytycy modlą się do lustra." *Dziennik*, July 6, 2007. http://www.e-teatr.pl/pl/artykuly/41447.html.

Walas, Teresa. "Zmierzch paradygmatu—i co dalej?" *Dekada Literacka*, no. 5/6 (2001). http://dekadaliteracka.pl/index.php?id=2223.
Walczak, Michał. "Małe baśnie Różewicza." *Teatr*, no. 2 (2007): 32.
Walicki, Andrzej. *Three Traditions of Polish Patriotism and Their Contemporary Relevance*. Bloomington: Polish Studies Center, Indiana University, 1988.
———. *Polskie zmagania z wolnością widziane z boku*. Cracow: Universitas, 2000.
Wandycz, Piotr. *The Lands of Partitioned Poland, 1775–1918*. Seattle: University of Washington Press, 1974.
———. *The Price of Freedom: A History of East Central Europe from the Middle Ages to the Present*. London: Routledge, 1992.
Wantuch, Wiesława. "Miron Białoszewski w poszukiwaniu gatunków lirycznych." In *Pisanie Białoszewskiego*, edited by Michał Głowiński and Zdzisław Łapiński, 152–63. Warsaw: IBL, 1993.
Ward, Geoff. *Statutes of Liberty: The New York School of Poets*. New York: Palgrave, 2001.
Warren, Daniel. "Kant's Dynamics." In *Kant and the Sciences*, edited by Eric Watkins, 93–116. New York: Oxford University Press, 2001.
Waśko, Andrzej. *Romantyczny sarmatyzm: tradycja szlachecka w literaturze polskiej lat 1831–1863*. Cracow: Arcana, 1995.
Wąchocka, Ewa. "Teatr polityczny dzisiaj." *Magazyn Społeczno-Kulturalny Śląsk*, no. 5 (2006). http://www.e-teatr.pl/pl/artykuly/25468.html.
Wątroba: Słownik polskiego teatru po 1997 roku. Warsaw: Wydawnictwo Krytyki Politycznej / Instytut Teatralny, 2010.
Webb, Adam Kempton. *Beyond the Global Culture War*. London: Routledge, 2006.
Weiner, Richard. *Lazebník / Hra doopravdy*. Spisy, vol. 3. Prague: Torst, 1998.
Wellek, René. "The Theory of Literary History." *Travaux du Cercle Linguistique de Prague* 6 (1936): 173–92.
———. "Literary History." In *Literary Scholarship: Its Aims and Methods*, edited by Norman Foerster. Chapel Hill: University of North Carolina Press, 1941.
———. "The Mode of Existence of a Literary Work of Art." *Southern Review* 7 (1942): 735–54.
———. "The Crisis of Comparative Literature." In *Proceedings of the 2nd Congress of the International Comparative Literature Association*, vol. 1, edited by Werner P. Friederich, 149–59. Chapel Hill: University of North Carolina Press, 1959.
———. *Concepts of Criticism*. New Haven: Yale University Press, 1963.
———. *Four Critics: Croce, Valéry, Lukács, and Ingarden*. Seattle: University of Washington Press, 1981.
———. *The Attack on Literature and Other Essays*. Chapel Hill: University of North Carolina Press, 1982.

———. *A History of Modern Criticism: 1750–1950*, vol. 7. New Haven: Yale University Press, 1991.
———. "Roman Ingarden." In *A History of Modern Criticism: 1750–1950*, 7:379–98. New Haven: Yale University Press, 1991.
Wellek, René, and Austin Warren. *Theory of Literature*. New York: Harcourt Brace Jovanovich, 1977.
Werner, Andrzej. *Zwyczajna apokalipsa: Tadeusz Borowski i jego wizja świata obozów*. Warsaw: Czytelnik, 1971.
Węgrzyniak, Rafał. "Nowa lewica w teatrze." *Teatr*, no. 5 (2007): 26–29. http://www.e-teatr.pl/pl/artykuly/40427.html
Widera, Steffi. *Richard Weiner: Identität und Polarität im Prosafrühwerk*. Munich: Otto Sagner, 2001.
Wildstein, Bronisław. *Przyszłość z ograniczoną odpowiedzialnością*. Cracow: Arcana, 2003.
Wilford, Hugh. *The CIA, the British Left, and the Cold War: Calling the Tune?* London: Frank Cass, 2003.
Williams, Bernard. *Shame and Necessity*. Berkeley: University of California Press, 1993.
Winter, Jay M. *Sites of Memory, Sites of Mourning: The Great War in European Cultural History*. Cambridge: Cambridge University Press, 1995.
Witkiewicz, Stanisław Ignacy. *Dramaty*. Warsaw: PIW, 1983.
Witkowski, Michał. *Świat teatralny młodego Mickiewicza*. Warsaw: PIW, 1971.
Wittgenstein, Ludwig. *Philosophical Investigations*. Translated by G. E. M. Anscombe. Oxford: Blackwell, 2001.
Wojciechowski, Piotr. *Szkoła wdzięku i przetrwania*. Warsaw: Agawa, 1995.
Woleński, Jan. "Sentences, Propositions and Quasi-Propositions." In *Kunst und Ontologie: für Roman Ingarden zum 100. Geburtstag*, edited by Włodzimierz Galewicz, et al., 229–35. Amsterdam: Rodopi, 1994.
Wolff, Larry. *Inventing Eastern Europe: The Map of Civilization on the Mind of the Enlightenment*. Stanford: Stanford University Press, 1994.
"The World of Refugee Women. Some Facts." *Women's International Network News* 29, no. 1 (Winter 2003): 84.
Worthen, William B. "Disciplines of the Text / Sites of Performance." *Drama Review* 39, no. 1 (Spring 1995): 13–28.
———. *Shakespeare and the Authority of Performance*. Cambridge: Cambridge University Press, 1997.
———. "Drama, Performativity, and Performance." *PMLA* 113, no. 5 (October 1998): 1093–107.
———. Reply to letter of Robert Hapgood. *PMLA* 114, no. 2 (March 1999): 325–27.
Wyka, Kazimierz. "Zaległe tomy Różewicza." In *Rzecz wyobraźni*, 313–29. Warsaw: PIW, 1977.
Wyrobisz, Adam, ed. *Jan Chryzostom Pasek jako kronikarz XVII wieku*. Rawa Mazowiecka: MOBN, 1987.

Wyskiel, Wojciech. *Jan Lechoń na obczyźnie*. Cracow: Krajowa Agencja Wydawnicza, 1994.
Wyspiański, Stanisław. *The Return of Odysseus*. Translated by Howard Clarke. Bloomington: Indiana University Press, 1966.
———. *Wyzwolenie; Noc listopadowa*. Cracow: Wydawnictwo Literackie, 1987.
Young, James. "The Veneration of the Ruins." *Yale Journal of Criticism* 6, no. 2 (Fall 1993): 275–83.
Zagajewski, Adam. "W Warszawie jak na wsi." *Znak* 11–12 (1977): 1448–57.
———. *Solidarność i samotność*. Paris: Oficyna Wyd. Margines, 1986.
———. *Solidarity and Solitude: Essays*. Translated by Lillian Vallee. New York: Ecco Press, 1990.
———. *Obrona żarliwości*. Cracow: Wydawnictwo a5, 2002.
Zaleski, Marek. "Niedoszła miłość Hansa C." *Tygodnik Powszechny*, June 13, 2004, 11.
Zaworska, Helena. ". . . I obróciłem w żart." *Twórczość*, no. 5 (1985): 48–58.
Zetowski, Stanisław. "Czwarta część 'Dziadów' Mickiewicza monodramatem." *Ruch Literacki* 8, no. 9 (November 1933): 193–97.
Zielińska, Marta. *Opowieść o Gustawie i Maryli, czyli Teatr, życie i literatura*. Warsaw: PIW, 1989.
Ziemkiewicz, Rafał. *Michnikowszczyzna: Zapis choroby*. Lublin: Redhorse, 2006
Zieniewicz, Andrzej. "Narracje z pogranicza zdarzeń." *Miesięcznik Literacki*, no. 1 (1983): 31–39.
Ziołowicz, Agnieszka. *Dramat i romantyczne "Ja": Studium podmiotowości w dramaturgii polskiej doby romantyzmu*. Cracow: Universitas, 2002.
Zweig, Ronald W. *The Gold Train: The Destruction of the Jews and the Second World War's Most Terrible Robbery*. London: Allen Lane, 2002.
Żukowski, Tomasz. "Poezja i peryferie historii." *Res Publica Nowa* 7 (2001): 100–103.
Žižek, Slavoj. "'Nie wierzę w zderzenie cywilizacji': Ze Slavojem Žižkiem rozmawiają Leszek Koczanowicz i Piotr Dehnel." *Odra*, no. 9 (2002): 10–13.
———. "The Ongoing 'Soft Revolution.'" *Critical Inquiry* (Winter 2004): 292–323.

Notes on the Contributors

Tomasz Bilczewski is an assistant professor in the Department of International Polish Studies, and the director of the Center for Advanced Studies in the Humanities at the Jagiellonian University. From 2002 to 2005 he held the post of Secretary to the Chancellor of the Jagiellonian University. He is the author of *Komparatystyka i interpretacja: Nowoczesne badania porównawcze wobec translatologii* (2010), and the editor of *Niewspółmierność: Perspektywy nowoczesnej komparatystyki* (2010). He has received the Prime Minister's Award for best doctoral dissertation in Poland (2009), and is a recipient of the *Polityka* scholarship for outstanding young scholars (2010). His academic interests include comparative literature, literary theory, translation studies, and Polish and English poetry.

Przemysław Czapliński is a professor of Polish Literature at the University of Adam Mickiewicz in Poznań, a cofounder of the UAM Anthropology of Literature unit, and an essayist, translator, and literary critic. He has published more than ten books and served as a coeditor of multiple collections, such as *Zagłada: Współczesne problemy rozumienia i przedstawiania* (2009), *Jaka antropologia literatury jest dzisiaj możliwa* (2009), and *Polska do wymiany: Poźna nowoczesność i nasze wielkie narracie* (2009). He has delivered guest lectures in Berlin, Munich, Tübingen, Leipzig, Dresden, Chicago, Boston, Brussels, and Milan. He is currently coediting *A History of Polish Literature and Culture: New Perspectives on the 20th and 21st Centuries* with Joanna Niżyńska and Tamara Trojanowska.

Halina Filipowicz is a professor in the Department of Slavic Languages and Literature at the University of Wisconsin–Madison. She is the author of *Eugene O'Neill* (1985) and *A Laboratory of Impure Forms: The Plays of Tadeusz Różewicz* (1991; Polish translation, 2000), as well as a coeditor of *The Great Tradition and Its Legacy: The Evolution of Dramatic and Musical Theater in Austria and Central Europe* (2003; with Michael Cherlin and Richard L. Rudolph), and *Polonistyka po amerykańsku: Badania nad literaturą polską w Ameryce Północnej (1990–2005)* (2005; with Andrzej Karcz and Tamara Trojanowska). She has also published numerous articles and book chapters on cultural and intellectual history, cultural comparison and incommensurability, transcultural theory (between postcolonialism and globalization), gender theory, performance studies, and the politics of disciplinary histories.

George Gasyna is an assistant professor in the Department of Slavic Languages and Literatures and the Program in Comparative and World Literature at the University of Illinois. He holds a PhD in Comparative Literature from the University of Toronto, and a BA and MA in Russian and Slavic Studies from McGill University in Montreal. He specializes in modern Polish literature, in particular the twentieth-century novel. He also researches and teaches in the fields of continental modernism and the avant-garde, structuralist and poststructuralist literary theory, the émigré/immigrant experience, and Polish-

Jewish relations. His articles have been published in the *Slavic Review*, *Canadian Slavonic Papers*, *Polish Review*, *Russian Literature*, and *Sarmatian Review*. His book *Polish, Hybrid, and Otherwise: Exilic Discourse in Joseph Conrad and Witold Gombrowicz* was published in 2011.

Milija Gluhovic is an assistant professor of theatre and performance in the School of Theatre, Performance and Cultural Policy Studies at the University of Warwick. His major research interests include twentieth- and twenty-first-century European theatre and performance, memory studies, discourses of European identity, migrations and human rights, and critical theory. He is currently completing a monograph, *Performing European Memories: Trauma, Ethics, Politics*, coediting a book *Performing the 'New' Europe: Identities, Feelings, and Politics in the Eurovision Song Contest* (with Karen Fricker and Royal Holloway), and working on his second book project, in which he explores a wide range of theatrical representations originating from different parts of Europe that address its changing cultures in the post-1989 era.

Artur Grabowski is an associate professor at the Department of Polish at Jagiellonian University in Krakow. His academic interests include modern European comparative literature, drama/theatre theories in philosophical and religious contexts, and the poetics and theory of modern verse. He has published four books of poetry, short stories, and creative nonfiction, four full-length plays as well as several short pieces for theatre, a treatise on modern versification, and two books of literary essays on European Modernism and on visual arts, in addition to numerous articles on both literature and theatre. Over the course of his academic career, he has also worked as a visiting professor at American universities in Chicago, Seattle, and Buffalo, received scholarships from the Kosciuszko Foundation and the Fulbright Foundation, and ran theatre workshops in Poland, Italy, and the USA. He is a PEN Club member and an ongoing contributor to *Teatr*, occasionally directs academic productions, and translates poetry from English and Italian.

Krystyna Lipińska Iłłakowicz holds a PhD in comparative literature, with a specialization in Polish literature and culture, and teaches in the Department of Slavic Languages and Literatures at Yale University. Her interests include cultural exchanges between East and West, identity construction, the significance of small cultures and provincial space in the cultural discourse, as well as the ethos of women in the Polish historical narrative. She has written articles and book chapters on Witold Gombrowicz (most recently in *Witold Gombrowicz nasz współczesny*), Bruno Schulz, Zofia Nalkowska, theatre, film, and contemporary art. Her work has also been published in *Slavic and Eastern European Performance* (*SEEP*).

Jerzy Jarzębski is a professor at the Faculty of International Polish Studies at Jagiellonian University in Krakow, and at the State College for East European Studies in Przemyśl, as well as a board member of the Polish PEN Club. His main research interests include twentieth-century Polish literature, especially the oeuvre of Witold Gombrowicz, Bruno Schulz, and Stanisław Lem, émigré writers, and contemporary Polish prose. Over the course of his career, he has also worked as a visiting professor at Harvard University (1997), and at Hebrew University of Jerusalem (2000–1). He has published fourteen books and more than five hundred articles in eighteen languages. Among his most important publications are: *Gra w Gombrowicza* (1982), *Powieść jako autokreacja* (1984), *W Polsce czyli wszędzie: Szkice o polskiej prozie współczesnej* (1992), *Apetyt na Przemianę: Notatki o prozie współczesnej* (1997), *Pożegnanie z emigracją: O powojennej prozie polskiej* (1998), *Podglądanie Gombrowicza* (2001), *Wszechświat Lema* (2003), *Prowincja Centrum: Przypisy do Schulza* (2005), and *Natura i teatr: 16 tekstów o Gombrowiczu* (2007).

Andrzej Karcz is a scholar in the Department of Historical Poetics at the Institute of Literary Studies of the Polish Academy of Arts and Sciences, and a lecturer at the "Polonicum" Center of Polish Language and Culture for Foreigners in the Department of Polish Philology at the University of Warsaw. From 1999 to 2006 he worked as an assistant professor in the Department of Slavic Languages and Literatures at the University of Kansas. He has also lectured at the Catholic University of Lublin, the University of Chicago, and the University of Pittsburgh. His articles have appeared in Polish and American journals and edited volumes. He is the author of two books, *The Polish Formalist School and Russian Formalism* (2002) and *Teksty z daleka i bliska: Szkice nie tylko o literaturze* (2003), the editor of *Czesław Miłosz: "Mój wileński opiekun": Listy do Manfreda Kridla (1946–1955)* (2005), and the coeditor of *Polonistyka po amerykańsku. Badania nad literaturą polską w Ameryce Północnej* (2005; with Halina Filipowicz and Tamara Trojanowska).

Bożena Karwowska is an associate professor of Polish and Slavic Studies at the University of British Columbia. She teaches courses in Russian, Polish, and Slavic literatures in the Department of Central, Eastern and Northern European Studies. Her fields of interest include reader response criticism, body and sexuality, the literary representation of women in Slavic (especially Russian and Polish) literatures, and the experience of exile and immigration in the eyes of Polish women writers of the postwar period. She has published articles in *Teksty Drugie*, *Canadian Slavonic Papers*, *Przegląd Humanistyczny*, *Fraza*, and *Ruch Literacki*. She has also authored two monographs: *Ciało. Seksualność. Obozy Zagłady* (2009) and *Recepcja krytyczna Czesława Miłosza and Josifa Brodskiego w krajach języka angielskiego* (2000). In 2008 she coedited *(Nie)obecność. Rozważania o zagadnieniach nie wydobytych w narracjach*

XX wieku (with Hanna Gosk). She is currently working on her next book-length project, "Exile in Polish Women's Prose."

Magdalena Kay is an assistant professor of English Literature at the University of Victoria, Canada. She received her PhD in Comparative Literature from University of California–Berkeley in 2007; her doctoral dissertation compared contemporary Irish and Polish poetry while focusing on the theme of spatio-cultural belonging, and culminated in her first monograph, *Knowing One's Place in Contemporary Poetry*. She is currently working on a manuscript detailing the influence of Eastern European poetry on Seamus Heaney, with emphasis on the figures of Zbigniew Herbert and Czesław Miłosz.

Joanna Niżyńska is an associate professor in the Department of Slavic Languages and Literatures at Harvard University, where she teaches Polish studies in comparative contexts. She is interested in the formation of individual and collective identities around traumatic events, a problematics that she explores in her monograph on Miron Białoszewski, *Kingdom of Insignificance: The Traumatic, the Quotidian, and the Queer in the Prose of Miron Białoszewski*, and in a coedited volume on Polish-German post-1989 relations, *German-Polish Post/Memory: The Presence of the Past in Contemporary German and Polish Culture* (with Kristin Kopp). She also works and publishes on the influences of American literature and academic culture on Polish literary and intellectual developments in the post-1989 period. She is currently coediting *A History of Polish Literature and Culture: New Perspectives on the 20th and 21st Centuries* with Przemysław Czapliński and Tamara Trojanowska.

Benjamin Paloff is an assistant professor of Slavic languages and literatures and of comparative literature at the University of Michigan, Ann Arbor, as well as a poetry editor at *Boston Review*. He is the author of *The Politics* (2011), a collection of poems, and has contributed to a wide range of scholarly and popular publications, including the *Nation*, the *New Republic*, the *Paris Review*, and *Slavic and East European Journal*. His most recent translations include Andrzej Sosnowski's *Lodgings: Selected Poems* (2011), Marek Bieńczyk's *Tworki* (2008), and Dorota Masłowska's *Snow White and Russian Red* (2005). In 2009, he was a Literature Fellow of the National Endowment for the Arts.

Artur Płaczkiewicz is a lecturer in the Department of Slavic Languages and Literatures at the University of Toronto. He holds a PhD in Polish literature from the University of Toronto, and specializes in modern Polish literature, in particular twentieth-century poetry. He also teaches courses on Polish culture, film, and language. His articles have appeared in *Kresy* and *Toronto Slavic Quarterly*, and he has published essays, poems, and prose in various journals in Poland and Canada.

NOTES ON THE CONTRIBUTORS

Agnieszka Polakowska is a PhD candidate in the Department of Slavic Languages and Literatures, and a Graduate Fellow at the Centre for Ethics (2010–11) at the University of Toronto. She is currently in the process of writing her doctoral dissertation, which explores the intersections between (North American) theories of literary ethics and historically referential (Polish) literature. Her academic interests are varied, but currently focus on ethics (mainly literary), trauma and memory studies, and "documentary" literature. She holds an MA in English literature and in Slavic languages and literatures, both from the University of Toronto, as well as a BA in English literature from McMaster University, and has been a recipient of the Ontario Graduate Scholarship and the SSHRC's Canadian Graduate Scholarship.

Olga Ponichtera holds an MA in Slavic languages and literatures from the University of Toronto, and is currently completing her doctoral dissertation on the subject of Tadeusz Różewicz's late poetry. She has taught Polish language courses at the University of Toronto as well as McMaster University. She has presented her work at the first and second International Conferences on Polish Studies (Toronto, 2006; Bloomington, 2008), and the 2008 annual conference of the Canadian Association of Slavists. She is the recipient of the Joseph Bazylewicz Fellowship and the Toronto Polish-Canadian Hall Award.

Mira Rosenthal is a poet, translator, and scholar; she earned an MFA from the University of Houston, and is currently a doctoral candidate in comparative literature at Indiana University. She is the author of *The Local World* (2011), which won the 2010 Stan and Tom Wick Poetry Prize, and the translator of *The Forgotten Keys* by Polish poet Tomasz Różycki (2007). She is a recipient of fellowships from the NEA, PEN, the Fulbright Commission, and the ACLS, among others.

Bożena Shallcross is an associate professor of Slavic languages and literatures at the University of Chicago. She has authored numerous articles, translations and books, including *The Holocaust Object in Polish and Polish Russian Culture* (2011), *Rzeczy i Zagłada* (2010), *Through the Poet's Eye: The Travels of Zagajewski, Herbert, and Brodsky* (2002; 2nd edition, 2008), and *Cień i forma: O wyobraźni plastycznej Leopolda Staffa* (1987). She has also edited *The Effect of Palimpsest: Culture, Literature, History* (2011; with Ryszard Nycz), *Polish Encounters / Russian Identity* (2005; with David L. Ransel), *Framing the Polish Home: Postwar Cultural Constructions of Hearth, Nation, and Self* (2002), "The Other Herbert" (special issue of *Indiana Slavic Studies*, 1998), and *Dom romantycznego artysty* (1989).

Dariusz Skórczewski is an adjunct professor at John Paul II Catholic University of Lublin, Poland. In 2001–4 and 2006–7 he lectured as the Kościuszko

Foundation Fellow at Rice University and the University of Illinois–Chicago. He has authored two books, among them *Debates on Literary Criticism in Poland from 1918 to 1939* (2002), and coauthored *The Task of Interpretation: Hermeneutics, Psychoanalysis, and Literary Studies* (2009; with Andrzej Wierciński and Edward Fiała). He has published extensively on postcolonial theory and criticism in the *Sarmatian Review*, *Teksty Drugie*, *Znak*, *Porównania/Comparisons*, *Pamiętnik Literacki*, and the *Polish Foreign Affairs Digest*. He is also a member of the editorial board of *Postcolonial Europe*.

Halina Stephan is a professor emerita of Russian and Polish literature, and former director of the Center for Slavic and East European Studies at Ohio State University. Her publications include *LEF and the Left Front of the Arts* (1981), *Mrozek* (1996), *Transcending the Absurd: Prose and Drama of Sławomir Mrozek* (1997), and the edited volume *Living in Translation: Polish Writers in America* (2003), as well as its Polish version *Życie w przekładzie* (2001). Her articles focus on the Russian avant-garde, Russian science fiction, Polish drama, and émigré literature. She is currently living in Berlin.

Ewa Thompson is a research professor of Slavic Studies, and former chairperson of the Department of German and Slavic Studies at Rice University. Before she came to Rice, she taught at Indiana, Vanderbilt, and the University of Virginia, as well as lectured at Princeton, Witwatersrand, Toronto, and Bremen. She received her undergraduate degree from the University of Warsaw, and her PhD from Vanderbilt University. She is the author of five books, about fifty scholarly articles (in the *Slavic Review, Slavic and East European Journal, Modern Age*, and other periodicals), and hundreds of other articles and reviews. Her books and articles have been translated into Polish, Ukrainian, Belarusian, Russian, Croatian, Czech, Hungarian, and Chinese. She has also done consulting work for government and private institutions and foundations, and is the editor of *Sarmatian Review*, an academic quarterly on non-Germanic Central Europe.

Tamara Trojanowska is an associate professor in the Department of Slavic Languages and Literatures at the University of Toronto. She specializes in the theory of theatre, discourses of identity, and Polish literature of the twentieth and twenty-first centuries. Her most recent publications include: "Polish Theater and Drama at a Turning Point" in *History of the East-Central European Literary Cultures* (Marcel Cornis-Pope and John Neubauer, eds.), "Performing the Urban Palimpsest" in *The Effect of the Palimpsest* (Bożena Shallcross and Ryszard Nycz, eds.) and "Spektakl inności i milczenia: *Iwona, księżniczka Burgunda*" in *Witold Gombrowicz—nasz współczesny* (Jerzy Jarzębski, ed.). She coedited *Polonistyka po amerykańsku. Badania nad literaturą polską w Ameryce Północnej* (2005) with Halina Filipowicz and Andrzej Karcz. She is currently coediting *A History of Polish Literature and Culture: New Perspectives on the 20th and 21st Centuries* with Przemysław Czapliński and Joanna Niżyńska.

Index

INDEX

INDEX

INDEX

www.ingramcontent.com/pod-product-compliance
Lightning Source LLC
LaVergne TN
LVHW010534100826
845148LV00001B/184

* 9 7 8 0 9 4 0 9 6 2 7 3 6 *